The Dominican Republic

written and researched by

Sean Harvey

with additional contributions by
Tom Hutton

ROUGH GUIDES

www.roughguides.com

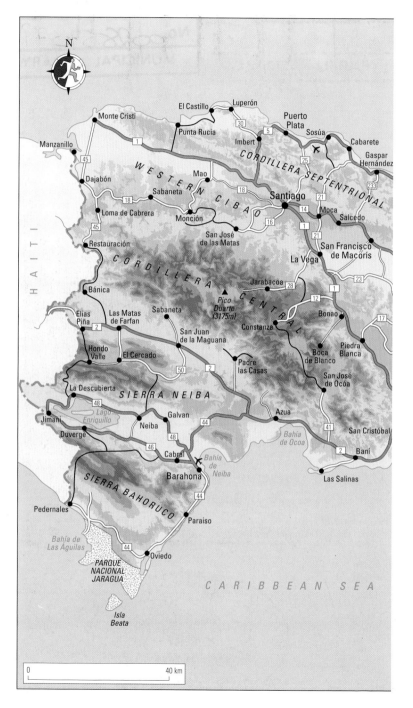

N

El Castillo   Luperón
Monte Cristi   Puerto
         Punta Rucia   Plata   Sosúa
Manzanillo   30   5   Imbert   Cabarete
     1   Gaspar
         Dajabón   CORDILLERA SEPTENTRIONAL   25   Hernández
                   Mao   233
     45   21
         Sabaneta   18   Santiago
     18   WESTERN CIBAO   14   Moca   Salcedo
         Loma de Cabrera   16   1   21
                   Monción   San Francisco
     45   Restauración   San José   La Vega   de Macorís
                   de las Matas
              CORDILLERA   23
                        Jarabacoa   28   1
         Bánica   Pico   12
                        Duarte
     Elías   Sabaneta   (3175m)   Bonao
     Piña   Las Matas   CENTRAL   17
         de Farfán   San Juan   Constanza
     2   de la Maguana   Boca   Piedra
     Hondo   Padre   de Blanco   Blanca
     Valle   El Cercado   50   las Casas   San José
                   2   de Ocóa
         La Descubierta   SIERRA NEIBA   Azua
     48   Lago
     Jimaní   Enriquillo   Galvan   Bahía   San Cristóbal
         Neiba   44   de Ocoa   41
     Duverge   48   2   Baní
         46   Cabral   Bahía
              Barahona   de   Las Salinas
                   Neiba
              44
     SIERRA BAHORUCO
     Pedernales   Paraiso
         44
     Bahía de
     Las Águilas   44   Oviedo
         PARQUE
         NACIONAL
         JARAGUA   CARIBBEAN SEA

     Isla
     Beata

HAITI

0   40 km

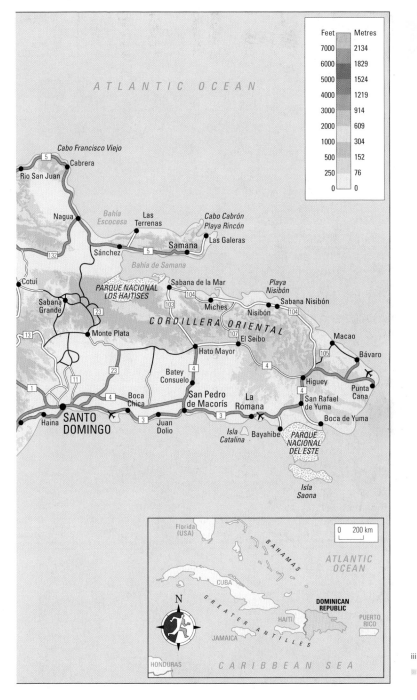

Introduction to

The Dominican Republic

Occupying the eastern half of the island of Hispaniola, the
Dominican Republic (or the DR, as it's often known) is the
most popular tourist destination in the Caribbean,
somewhat of a surprise given its relative poverty and former
instability, not to mention the allure of nearby islands that
perhaps are more wholly given over to holiday-makers. What
traditionally attracts most visitors are the parts of the
country that resemble the image of a Caribbean playland,
the crystal-clear waters and sandy beaches lined with palm
trees, of which the DR has plenty. This vision of leisurely
days spent by the sea and romantic nights filled with
merengue and dark rum is supported by the largest all-
inclusive resort industry in the world; if you're looking to
pay a set rate for airfare, hotel, food and drinks – and have a
carefree Caribbean vacation behind the protection of a
fenced-off compound – you can't do much better than here.

Unfortunately, such a
"perfect" vacation would
mean missing out on
much of what makes the
country so special. Set
on the most geographi-
cally diverse Caribbean
island, the Dominican
Republic boasts virgin
alpine wilderness, tropi-

v

Fact file

• The Dominican Republic shares the island of **Hispaniola** with the Republic of Haiti. The Dominican Republic's 48,734 square kilometres encompass desert savannas, tropical rainforests, alpine mountain ranges, mangrove swamps and several hundred kilometres of Caribbean coast.

• Despite its vast wilderness, the Dominican Republic is a densely **populated** nation, with over 8 million residents. About 90 percent of the people here live below the poverty line, though the nation boasted the highest economic growth in the Americas from 1996 to 2000.

• Twenty years ago, the Dominican **economy** was centred almost exclusively around agriculture, including export crops like sugar and tobacco. Agricultural exports are now dwarfed by tourism and free zone manufacturing, which each bring in approximately $2 billion annually.

• **Ethnically**, the population is of mixed African and European ancestry, as the Tainos who inhabited the island before Columbus were mostly wiped out. The African portion of Dominican ethnicity is the subject of some contention locally, and individuals of mixed African and European descent are typically referred to as Indio, in part to obscure their African heritage.

• Around 90 percent of Dominicans identify themselves as **Roman Catholics**, though the great majority of these do not actively participate in the Catholic church. Of the minority religions, vodú dominicana, which combines Catholicism with African spiritual practices, and strains of evangelical Protestantism are the most widespread.

cal rainforests and mangrove swamps, cultivated savannas, vast desert expanses and everything in between within its relatively small confines – slightly smaller than the US states of New Hampshire and Vermont combined. The opportunities for ecotourism and adventure travelling are staggering: if you were so inclined, in a single week you could scale a 150-metre waterfall on a rope, mountain-bike across remote dirt tracks, ride the best windsurfing waves in the hemisphere, trek to the top of a 3000-metre mountain, and head out in a fishing boat to see dozens of humpback whales crashing about in a scenic bay.

The Dominican Republic also lays claim to some of the more intriguing culture and history in the area, dating back to its early cave-dwelling groups, the Tainos, who recorded much of their activities in the form of rock art – it's quite likely you'll find yourself clambering down a dark cave to view

some of these preserved paintings during your stay. In addition, as Dominicans are often quick to point out, their land was the setting for Christopher Columbus's first colony, La Isabela, and Spain's first New World city, **Santo Domingo**, at the end of the fifteenth century. Though the island quickly lost this foothold, the events that took place during its brief heyday did much to define the Americas as we know them, and examples of period architecture – both preserved and in ruins – remain scattered across the country, most notably in the colonial heart of Santo Domingo, today the nation's capital and centre of industry.

The Zone

The Dominican Republic boasts the hemisphere's oldest and most extensive European ruins from the era of conquistadors. The most impressive relics are contained within Santo Domingo's compact Zona Colonial – known by the growing community of expats who live here as simply "The Zone". Contained within the Zone's old crumbling city walls are the hemisphere's first university, cathedral, monastery, hospital, nunnery and more, including the 500-year-old palace of the Columbus family. Wandering past one jaw-dropping colonial relic after another can certainly transport you back to the time when Santo Domingo was Spain's one tentative toehold in what was known then as the Cannibal Sea, but the thousands of people who live and work in these colonial-era buildings make it more than just an atmospheric outdoor museum. By day old men smoke cigars and argue politics in the park, sharp-dressed business people bustle to bank jobs and vendors sell split coconuts from horse-drawn carts. At night the narrow streets are lined with outdoor cafés and restaurants, local families shoot the breeze (and pass the bottle) from front stoops, and the city's young and wealthy hit the neighbourhood clubs – among the hottest in the city. It would be easy to get lost here for your entire stay, without missing the beach even once. Our comprehensive coverage of the city centre begins on p.71.

Set on the most geographically diverse Caribbean island, the Dominican Republic boasts virgin alpine wilderness, tropical rainforests and mangrove swamps, cultivated savannas, vast desert expanses and everything in between

During the intervening centuries the Dominican people have endured much hardship – interminable civil strife in the nineteenth century, an oppressive dictatorship in the twentieth, intermittent occupation by Haiti, Spain and the United States, and a boom-and-bust economy centred first on tobacco, later on sugar, that never allowed the country to stand on a firm economic footing. Even today, the DR remains a nation in transition. Despite having the highest growth rate of any country in the hemisphere during the second half of the 1990s, thanks in no small part to the all-inclusive tourist industry, many Dominicans still live well below the poverty line. Santo Domingo has grown into a heaving metropolis, five times larger than the next biggest city, and much of the rest of the country is made up of rural tobacco towns or tiny fishing villages often held at the mercy of tropical rainstorms, hurricanes and frequent power outages.

The Dominican people have dealt with these tough circumstances in ever-resourceful ways: extended families maintain close ties and pool their assets, most village homes are built one brick at a time (sometimes taking two generations to complete), and informal shoestring transportation systems connect nearly every city and village in the country. Another coping mechanism has been the extreme pride that residents take in the diverting rhythms of merengue and *bachata* – the national musical forms – and in the exploits of home-grown baseball players who have made good in the North American big leagues. And even if the Latin American "mañana" culture stereotype sometimes holds true, with service that can be less than prompt, any frustrations are more than compensated for by the island's beauty and its surprisingly cheap price: along with its less politically stable neighbour, Haiti, the Dominican Republic is the last true budget destination left in the Caribbean.

Where to go

As stated, many visitors head directly for beachfront resorts, and there's much there to admire, to be sure. The southeastern part of the country probably has the loveliest all-inclusive resort zones, **Bávaro** and **Punta Cana**, both holding more pristine coastline stretching for kilometres on end, broken up by just coconut trees and, of course, hotels. These are slightly outdone, if not in attractiveness then in sheer magnitude, by **Playa Dorada** along the north coast, the largest all-inclusive complex in the world. Fortunately, Playa Dorada is close by **Puerto Plata**, an historic city worth examining for its wealth of Victorian architecture and proximity to developed stations like windsurfing capital **Cabarete**, to the east, and less trammelled villages such as **La Isabela**, home to the remains of Columbus's first colony, to the west.

More great beaches are scattered about the **Samaná Peninsula**, poking out at the country's extreme northeast. Its primary city, **Samaná**, also serves as a base for checking

Whale watching

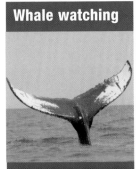

Humpback whales have used the Dominican Republic's Samaná Bay and Silver Bank coral reef sanctuary as a nursery and breeding ground for untold millennia. Taino drawings on the limestone caves of Los Haitises depict breaching whales in the Bahía de Samaná, and Columbus made note of their presence here in 1493. They return each December after spending nine months fanning out across the North Atlantic in search of enormous quantities of food; by late January more than four thousand of them surround the peninsula. They're at their liveliest in Samaná's tepid depths, as males track females, compete for attention and engage in courting displays, while mothers teach their calves basic survival skills. A dozen different whale watching boats depart Samaná harbour daily in season, with strictly enforced regulations in place to protect the safety of the whales. Don't allow yourself to come here during the winter without making an expedition to see them. See pp.160–161 for more details.

out the **humpback whales** that migrate to the Bahía de Samaná in the winter to mate and give birth, and for boat tours to the lush mangrove swamps of the **Parque Nacional Los Haitises**, on the interior of the bay. The sand and surf theme continues in the southwest, mainly straight down the coast from **Barahona**, where you'll find isolated beaches with not many crowds at all on the pebbly waterfront – and, correspondingly, not many facilities either.

On the southern coast the capital city, **Santo Domingo**, offers the most fulfilling urban experience, and should obviously be on anyone's itinerary, not least because it has the country's largest airport; in addition, there are

Guaguas

The Dominican Republic's informal system of guaguas, an unregulated nationwide network of private operators, is a distinctive Dominican experience that you should try at least once. An instant bond of familiarity is formed as passengers – mostly locals – are crammed four- and five-to-a-seat in these half-wrecked vans that often seem held together with little more than packing tape and a strategically placed bit of rope: Amway salesmen pester fellow passengers, Pentecostals proselytize to heathens, a bottle of rum is passed around and – on night runs when the guaguas are less crowded – somebody pulls out a guitar and everyone breaks into song. Aside from the local colour, they're worth using because they're incredibly cheap and cover far more of the country than the bus companies. Guaguas are operated by teams of two, the driver and the *cobrador*, who sticks his head out of the sliding side door (assuming it hasn't been torn off) and drums up business. If you want to catch one, just stand by the side of the road and wave your arms at one as it passes. See p.29 for more details.

the historic forts, churches and homes of the Zona Colonial and, on a more modern note, the nation's top museums, restaurants and nightlife, scattered all about. **Santiago**, tucked away in the interior Cibao Valley, ranks a distant second, though there is no better area to learn about the history of tobacco and see the production of cigars – a major Dominican export – firsthand.

If you're seeking a bit more adventure and outdoor life, you needn't look too hard. The Cordillera Central, the island's largest mountain range, should be a high priority: in addition to choosing between several-day treks through the wilderness to the top of **Pico Duarte** – the tallest peak in the Antilles – you can head to **Jarabacoa**, a resort town blessed with four waterfalls in its immediate vicinity and featuring all manner of mountain sports, or less developed **Constanza**, a circular valley short on tourist development but chock-full of natural grandeur. Few visitors make it out to the rough Haitian border along the DR's western edge, but there are compelling sights here as well – though the singular experience of slowly trawling along desolate roadway, if some of the track can even be called that, straddling two distinct nations is likely the greatest attraction. Chief among the natural highlights, however, is **Lago Enriquillo**, a saltwater lake the size of Manhattan, inhabited by hundreds of iguanas, thousands of tropical birds and even American crocodiles.

When to go

There are two distinct tourist **high seasons** in the Dominican Republic, the summer months of July and August, when travellers from the northern hemisphere have some time off to get away for a couple

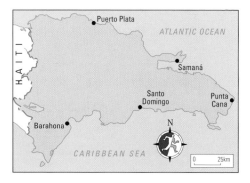

of weeks, and the winter season from December through late February, when the Dominican climate is at its optimum, having cooled down just a bit from summertime. You'll therefore save a bit of money – and have an easier time booking a hotel room on the spot – if you arrive during the spring or the fall, which is just fine, as the **temperature** doesn't really vary all that much from season to season. In the Cordillera Central mountains, you can expect temperatures to be about four degrees cooler on average than in the valleys and along the coast – making those spots prime targets for wealthy Dominicans looking to escape the summer heat.

Keep in mind also that the Dominican Republic is right in the centre of the Caribbean **hurricane** belt, and gets hit with a major one every decade or so; the most recent was 1998's Hurricane Georges, which annihilated

much of the year's harvest and wiped some small villages completely off the map. August and September is prime hurricane season, though smaller ones can occur in the months before and after those, so you may want to play it safe and schedule your trip accordingly. If you are on the island when a hurricane is about to strike, your best bet is to head immediately for the closest high-end tourist hotel, which should have a protected shelter for its guests. Definitely do not wander around outside, and don't be fooled by a brief respite of calm – you may well be in the eye of the hurricane, which means the destruction will start up again soon.

Summer is the traditional **rainy season** in the Dominican Republic, but with weather patterns somewhat disrupted in the past couple of years, you can expect short bursts of rain a few times a week – most of them lasting no more than a couple of minutes, to be quickly followed by sunshine – regardless of the time of year.

Average temperatures and rainfall

	Jan	Feb	Mar	Apr	May	Jun	Jul	Aug	Sep	Oct	Nov	Dec
Barahona												
max. temp. (°C)	29	29	29	30	30	30	31	32	32	30	30	29
min. temp. (°C)	20	20	21	22	22	23	24	24	23	23	22	21
rainfall (mm)	28	33	29	60	189	160	38	82	140	192	64	32
Puerto Plata												
max. temp. (°C)	27	27	28	29	29	31	31	31	31	31	29	28
min. temp. (°C)	19	18	19	20	21	22	23	23	22	22	21	19
rainfall (mm)	191	154	123	151	131	61	72	85	92	132	293	274
Punta Cana												
max. temp. (°C)	27	27	28	28	30	30	30	31	31	30	30	28
min. temp. (°C)	22	22	22	23	24	24	25	25	25	24	24	23
rainfall (mm)	62	46	52	58	108	109	78	97	88	135	117	79
Samaná												
max. temp. (°C)	29	29	30	31	31	32	32	33	33	32	31	30
min. temp. (°C)	19	20	20	20	22	23	24	23	23	23	21	21
rainfall (mm)	147	104	105	135	244	179	207	232	214	227	285	231
Santo Domingo												
max. temp. (°C)	29	29	29	30	30	31	31	31	31	31	30	29
min. temp. (°C)	19	19	20	21	22	23	23	23	23	22	21	20
rainfall (mm)	51	44	44	68	187	152	179	157	165	170	96	70

27

things not to miss

It's not possible to see everything that the Dominican Republic has to offer in one trip – and we don't suggest you try. What follows is a selective and subjective taste of the country's highlights: unspoilt scenery, outdoor activities, colourful festivals and cultural hotspots. They're arranged in five colour-coded categories to help you find the very best things to see, do, eat and experience. All highlights have a page reference to take you straight into the guide, where you can find out more.

01 La Vega Carnival Page **252** ● One of the biggest processions in the country and a massive party with over 70,000 people crowding the tiny streets of the city centre.

ACTIVITIES | CONSUME | EVENTS | NATURE | SIGHTS |

02 **Parque Nacional del Este** Page **133** • Boat tours from Bayahibe lead to the park's idyllic Isla Saona as well to a series of caves chock-full of ancient Taino rock art.

04 **Mercado Hospidaye, Santiago** Page **245** • The mother of all Dominican grocery markets – dark, humid, fragrant and fascinating. You'll see more local culture here in five minutes than you could see in a lifetime of beach resorts.

03 **Pico Duarte** Page **258** • The Caribbean's tallest peak and a challenging but thoroughly rewarding hike. Sunrise from the summit is indescribable.

05 The Zona Colonial Page **71** • The first European city in the New World remains largely intact on the west side of the Río Ozama, with the hemisphere's first cathedral, fortress, university, hospital, monastery and nunnery. Also holds the palace of the Columbus family, and is a major centre for restaurants and bars.

07 The Santo Domingo Malecón Page 82 • A scenic, seven-mile-long outdoor boardwalk and party zone, with discos, bars and outdoor cafés strung out all along it.

06 Museo del Hombre Dominicano, Santo Domingo Page 86 • This museum, one of four in Santo Domingo's impressive Plaza de la Cultura, is home to an outstanding collection of Taino artefacts.

ACTIVITIES | CONSUME | EVENTS | NATURE | SIGHTS |

08 Whitewater rafting near Jarabacoa Page 257 • An adrenaline-fuelled adventure and a great way to see some of the country's finest mountain scenery.

09 Playa Rincón Page **169** • Simply the country's finest and most unspoilt beach. Relax beneath palm trees, swim in crystal-clear waters and enjoy freshly caught fish cooked in a waterside shack.

10 Ron Añejo Page **37** • The delicious dark, aged Dominican rums are superb, and can be had for a few pesos. Though often pictured as part of a tropical fruit cocktail, the best way to order it is as a *cuba libre servicio*: two Cokes, a bottle of rum and a bucket of ice.

11 Baseball fever Pages **45 & 357** • Baseball is the closest thing to a national religion here. See the best young players in the world before they make it big, at Estadio Quisqueya in Santo Domingo, Estadio Tetelo Vargas in San Pedro de Macorís or Campo Las Palmas outside Juan Dolio.

12 **Coffee** Page **36** • Locally grown, strong and aromatic. You should be able to taste the freshness for real.

13 **Snorkelling near La Isabela/Monte Cristi**
Page **225** • The few remaining undamaged reefs in the country offer snorkelling to match that of any Caribbean island.

14 **Constanza** Page **263** • A circular Shangri-la valley set deep in the heart of the Caribbean's tallest mountains, with a multitude of wilderness hikes all around it.

15 **Isabela de Torres cable car, Puerto Plata** Page **199** • If you'd rather not hike, take the easy way up to the north coast's finest viewpoint.

16 **Taino cave art** Pages **133 & 312** • Almost wiped out by Columbus and the conquistadors, the Tainos left a rich heritage of rock art in the hundreds of caves that pock the island, including large troves in the national parks at Del Este and El Pomier.

17 **Lago Enriquillo** Page **288** • A saltwater lake the size of Manhattan, populated by crocodiles, rhino iguanas and tens of thousands of colourful tropical birds.

18 **Amber** Pages **41 & 197** • Unbeatable as an authentic, locally produced souvenir, this semiprecious stone is stunning when set in jewellery. You can also visit the Amber Museum in Puerto Plata to see amber that contains insect life from hundreds of millions of years ago, or the actual amber mines north of Santiago.

19 **The waterfall at El Limón** Page **179** • Hidden deep within the Samaná mountains but accessible by day-trip on horseback, this pristine 150-metre waterfall is one of the prettiest spots on the island, and its base is a great spot for a swim.

20 **Dancing to Merengue** Pages **99 & 348** • The stuttering, fast-paced national music has been around in various forms for the past three hundred years. You can still hear the old-style accordion merengue of the nineteenth century in rural areas, while electronic orchestras with horn sections blast their way into the twenty-first century in the major cities.

21 **La Guacara Taina** Page **96** • Santo Domingo's world-famous disco, set within a five-storey cave complex, where the top live acts in the nation appear nightly.

ACTIVITIES | CONSUME | EVENTS | NATURE | SIGHTS |

23 Mountain biking in the Cordillera Septentrional Page **217** • Choose from all-day downhill rides to full-on epics for experts. The mountain scenery is stunning and the experience of rural Dominican life unforgettable.

24 Tropical fruits
Page **35** • Widely available, cheap and delicious. It's almost possible to live on this alone, or the refreshing *batidas*, which transform the fruit into mouth-watering shakes.

25 Vodú festivals Page **285** • Drums are played for nine straight nights and massive processions celebrate the various syncretic deities of the Dominican Voodoo pantheon in annual festivals at San Juan de la Maguana, Santo Domingo's Villa Mella and across the island.

26 Exploring remote campos Page **223** • Far from the tourist areas along the northeast and southeast coasts, the rural Dominican Republic runs at a pace that seems more suited for a past century, and provides a welcome contrast to the high-energy package resorts.

27 Cabarete windsurfing and kite surfing Page **212** • The world-class conditions, along with a plethora of schools and rental centres, help make Cabarete a top destination for both windsurfing and the burgeoning sport of kite surfing.

Contents

Using the Rough Guide

We've tried to make this Rough Guide a good read and easy to use. The book is divided into six main sections, and you should be able to find whatever you want in one of them.

Colour section

The front colour section offers a quick tour of the Dominican Republic. The **introduction** aims to give you a feel for the place, with suggestions on where to go. We also tell you what the weather is like and include a basic fact file on the region. Next, our author rounds up his favourite aspects of the Dominican Republic in the **things not to miss** section – whether it's an amazing beach, great scenery, or an exceptional outdoor activity. Right after this comes the Rough Guide's full **contents** list.

Basics

The basics section covers all the **pre-departure** practicalities to help you plan your trip. This is where you'll find out which airlines serve the Dominican Republic, what to do about money and insurance, public transport, car rental, food and accommodation. In short, basics contains just about every piece of **general practical information** you might need.

Guide

This is the heart of the Rough Guide, divided into user-friendly chapters, each of which covers a specific region. Every chapter starts with a list of **highlights** and an **introduction** that helps you to decide where to go, depending on your time and budget. Likewise, introductions to the various towns and smaller regions within each chapter should help you plan your itinerary. We

start most town accounts with information on arrival and accommodation, followed by a tour of the sights, and finally reviews of places to eat and drink, and details of nightlife. Longer accounts also have a directory of practical listings. Each chapter concludes with **public transport** details for that region.

Contexts

Read contexts to get a deeper understanding of how the Dominican Republic ticks. We've included a brief **history** and a look at the region's **environment** and **wildlife**, along with articles on **baseball** and the country's vibrant **music** scene. There's also a detailed further reading section that reviews dozens of **books** relating to the area.

Language

The **language** section gives useful guidance for speaking Spanish and pulls together all the vocabulary you might need on your trip, including a comprehensive menu reader.

Index + small print

Apart from a **full index**, which includes maps as well as places, this section covers publishing information, credits and acknowledgements, and also has our contact details in case you want to send in updates and corrections to the book – or suggestions as to how we might improve it.

Map and chapter list

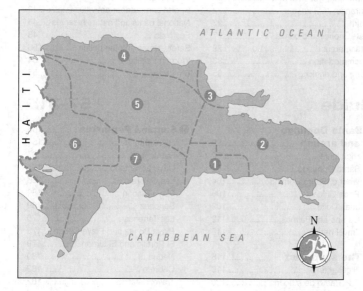

ATLANTIC OCEAN

HAITI

CARIBBEAN SEA

N

Contents

Contexts

317–367

Language

369–379

Index + small print

381–392

Map symbols

maps are listed in the full index using coloured text

═▭═	Highway		⊠	Post office
═18═	Main road		⚲	Church (regional maps)
═══	Secondary road		✿	Synagogue
───	Unpaved road (regional maps)		🏛	Stately home
┄┄┄	Unpaved road (town maps)		🏛	Monument
▓▓▓	Pedestrianised road		⊙	Statue
------	Footpath		♜	Fortress
───	Wall		∴	Ruins
━·━	National boundary		☀	Lighthouse
─ ─ ─	Chapter division boundary		⌂	Cave
───	River		⧫	General point of interest
✈	Major airport		▲	Mountain peak
✗	Municipal airport		⨊	Marshland
★	Public transport stop		⌇	Waterfall
🅿	Parking		▮	Building
◉	Hotel		⊞	Church (town maps)
▣	Restaurant		⊹	Cemetery
⊞	Hospital		▨	Park
🅗	Gas station		▦	Beach
ⓘ	Information centre			

Basics

Basics

✈ Getting there

The recent decline in **air traffic** has not lowered the prices of the large commercial airline companies, which cater largely to expat Dominicans returning home for a family visit, but there are a plethora of other options for getting to the DR from either North America or Europe, many of them quite inexpensive. Most are a result of the huge all-inclusive tourism industry that has been built up along Dominican shores; **package deals** for airfare, hotel and food abound, with astounding rates available to those willing to shop around. But even if you don't want to go all-inclusive, the air **charters** that transfer package tourists to their walled-off destinations regularly offer extra seats to independent travellers for a surprisingly low price. Those headed here from Australia and New Zealand will find fewer bargains, but with a bit of stamina you can make your way to the DR via the major airlines, though you won't be able to avoid an airplane transfer at some point along the way.

Regardless of where you buy your ticket, fares will depend on the **season**, and are highest between mid-June and the end of August; they drop during the "shoulder" season of mid-November to mid-June (excluding Christmas and New Year, when prices and seats are at a premium), and you'll get the best prices during the low season, September to mid-November. Note also that flying on weekends ordinarily adds US$20–40 to the round-trip fare; price ranges quoted below assume midweek travel.

Barring special offers, the cheapest of the airlines' published fares is usually an **Apex** ticket, although this will carry certain restrictions: you have to book – and pay – at least 21 days before departure, spend at least seven days abroad (maximum stay three months), and you tend to get penalized if you change your schedule. Some airlines also issue **Special Apex** tickets to people younger than 24, often extending the maximum stay to a year. Many airlines offer youth or student fares to **under-26s**, though these tickets are subject to availability and can have eccentric booking conditions. It's worth remembering that most cheap return fares involve spending at least one Saturday night away and that many will only give a percentage refund if you need to cancel or alter your journey, so make sure you check the restrictions carefully before paying.

You can normally cut costs further by going through a **specialist flight agent** – either a **consolidator**, who buys up blocks of tickets from the airlines and sells them at a discount, or a **discount agent**, who in addition to dealing with discounted flights may also offer special student and youth fares and a range of other travel-related services such as travel insurance, car rentals, tours and the like. Bear in mind, though, that penalties for changing your plans can be stiff. Remember too that these companies make their money by dealing in bulk – don't expect them to answer lots of questions. Also, don't automatically assume that tickets purchased through a travel specialist will be cheapest – once you get a quote, check with the airlines and you may turn up an even better deal. Be advised also that the pool of travel companies is swimming with sharks – exercise caution and *never* deal with a company that demands cash upfront or refuses to accept payment by credit card.

Some agents specialize in **charter flights**, which are more plentiful and almost always cheaper than a scheduled flight. Again, though, departure dates are fixed and withdrawal penalties are high.

Booking flights online

Many airlines and discount travel websites

offer you the opportunity to book your tickets online, cutting out the costs of agents and middlemen. Good deals can often be found through discount or auction sites, as well as through the airlines' own websites.

Online booking agents and general travel sites

Ⓦ **www.cheapflights.com** Flight deals, travel agents, plus links to other travel sites. UK only.

Ⓦ **www.cheaptickets.com** Discount flight specialists.

Ⓦ **www.etn.nl/discount.htm** A hub of consolidator and discount agent web links, maintained by the nonprofit European Travel Network.

Ⓦ **www.expedia.com** Discount airfares, all-airline search engine and daily deals.

Ⓦ **www.flyaow.com** Online air travel info and reservations site.

Ⓦ **www.gaytravel.com** Gay online travel agent, concentrating mostly on accommodation.

Ⓦ **www.hotwire.com** Bookings from the US only. Last-minute savings of up to forty percent on regular published fares. Travellers must be at least 18 and there are no refunds, transfers or changes allowed. Log-in required.

Ⓦ **www.lastminute.com** Offers good last-minute holiday package and flight-only deals. UK only.

Ⓦ **www.priceline.com** Name-your-own-price website that has deals at around forty percent off standard fares. You cannot specify flight times (although you do specify dates) and the tickets are non-refundable, non-transferable and non-changeable.

Ⓦ **www.princeton.edu/Main/air800.html** Has an extensive list of airline toll-free numbers and websites.

Ⓦ **www.smilinjack.com/airlines.htm** Lists an up-to-date compilation of airline website addresses.

Ⓦ **www.skyauction.com** Bookings from the US only. Auctions tickets and travel packages using a "second bid" scheme. The best strategy is to bid the maximum you're willing to pay, since if you win you'll pay just enough to beat the runner-up regardless of your maximum bid.

Ⓦ **www.travelocity.com** Destination guides, hot web fares and best deals for car rental, accommodation and lodging as well as fares. Provides access to the travel agent system SABRE, the most comprehensive central reservations system in the US.

Ⓦ **www.travelshop.com.au** Australian website

offering discounted flights, packages, insurance, online bookings.

Ⓦ **http://travel.yahoo.com** Incorporates a lot of Rough Guide material in its coverage of destination countries and cities across the world, with information about places to eat, sleep, etc.

From North America

There are plenty of scheduled **flights** to the Dominican Republic from North America, but as they are controlled by just a handful of carriers, most are not especially cheap. American is the main carrier in the United States, Air Canada in Canada, with additional services on Continental, Northwest and US Air. Most flights head into either Santo Domingo or Puerto Plata, though charter flights often use the smaller airstrips at Punta Cana, La Romana and El Portillo. The charters are generally a much cheaper way to go: Boston, Minneapolis, New York, Washington DC and all major Canadian cities have a daily charter service, along with reasonably priced all-inclusive packages. A good number of independent **sailors** make their way to the DR as well, most docking at the north-coast marina at Luperón, and there's also a **ferry** service from Mayagüez, Puerto Rico, into Santo Domingo; aside from this one option, though, getting there by water will be limited to a day-stop on a **cruise ship** itinerary if you don't have your own boat.

By air

There are **flights to the Dominican Republic** from most major Canadian and US cities (some west coast connections require an overnight stay in Miami or New York), but the cheapest and most frequent depart from the "gateway" cities of Miami, New York, Montreal and Toronto. If you've got some flexibility in your schedule, you'll save a lot of money if you wait for special offers, which are fairly frequent to the DR in shoulder and low season (see p.11), and can cut as much as forty percent off the normal ticket price. You can also save a good bit of money if you're travelling from one of US Air's gateway cities (see p.11), as they tend to have the most reasonable fares from North America to the DR. The following sample fares assume midweek travel, and are good for flights to both Santo Domingo and Puerto Plata: Miami US$230–350; Montreal Can$490–610; New York US$450–570; Toronto Can$490–630; Chicago US$560–680; Dallas US$500–630; Detroit US$490–620; Los Angeles US$550–670; San Francisco US$590–700; Seattle US$600–710; Vancouver Can$670–800.

The Dominican Republic is not a stopping point for companies that offer Caribbean air passes, so if you're interested in some **island hopping**, you'll have to cobble together your own itinerary with a Dominican tour operator. A couple of US-based companies run island-hopping tours, too, like Adventures Abroad and Globus & Cosmos (see p.13), both of which hit Santo Domingo and La Romana along with Puerto Rico, St Maarten and Jamaica. Emely Tours (Av Tiradentes/Pastoriza, Edificio Plaza JR, ☎566-4545, ⓦwww.emelytours.com) does flights and packages for three to seven days to Havana and Santiago de Cuba. A lot of Americans also use the Dominican Republic as a setting-off point for **trips to Cuba**. You can accomplish this either by Emely Tours above, or by taking a flight on Cubana Airlines (☎227-2040, ⓦwww.cubana.cu). Keep in mind, though, that the lax enforcement of the Cuban embargo during the Clinton administration has come to an end, and the current US administration is pressuring other Caribbean countries like the Dominican Republic for information on American tourists going to Cuba – so that they can enforce stiff fines for anyone going to Cuba. You should therefore try not to fill out any information forms – and definitely do not let Cuban immigration stamp your passport. If you do have to fill out a form with Dominican immigration, do not list your purpose for visiting Cuba as tourism.

Airlines in the US and Canada

Air Canada ☎1-888/247-2262, ⓦwww.aircanada.ca. Relatively expensive service from all major Canadian cities to Puerto Plata and Santo Domingo – though they all change planes in Miami, where you'll be flying on American Airlines – and charter flights to La Romana and Punta Cana via their Tango subsidiary.

Air Transat ☎1-866/847-1112, ⓦwww.airtransat.com. Direct charter flights to La Romana, Puerto Plata, Punta Cana and Santo Domingo from Calgary, Edmonton, Montreal, Quebec City and Vancouver – Feb–May only. To book a flight, you have to go through Exit Travel at ⓦwww.exitravel.com.

American Airlines ☎1-800/433-7300, ⓦwww.aa.com. Daily non-stop flights to Santo Domingo and Puerto Plata from New York and Miami, with connections from all major North American cities. Their American Eagle branch also has twice-daily non-stops from San Juan, Puerto Rico to Santo Domingo, Santiago and La Romana. You can sign on for "Net Savers" emails alerting you to last-minute cheap fares to the Dominican Republic and other destinations at ⓦwww.info.aa.com.

Continental Airlines ☎1-800/231-0856, ⓦwww.continental.com. Daily non-stop from Newark, NJ, to Puerto Plata, and once-daily from Newark to Santo Domingo.

MLT ☎1-800/437-1787, ⓦwww.mltvacations.com. Charter flights and all-inclusive packages from across the US to Punta Cana and Puerto Plata.

Northwest Airlines ☎1-800/447-4747, ⓦwww.nwa.com. Non-stop from Minneapolis and Newark, NJ, to Puerto Plata (Dec to mid-April only), with connections from Atlanta, Boston, Chicago and Detroit. Non-stop from Detroit and Minneapolis to Punta Cana (Dec to mid-April only), with connections from Chicago.

Pace Airlines ☎1-800/548-1978, ⓔcharter@flypiedmont.com, ⓦwww.paceairline.com. Charter out of Atlanta that runs flights for various tour operators to Puerto Plata, Punta Cana and Santo Domingo, with departures across the southern United States. Sales typically take place via an intermediary travel agent.

Pan Am ☎1-800/359-7262, ⓦwww.flypanam.com. Daily direct flights from Miami with connections from New York and several Florida cities, to Santo Domingo and Santiago.

Sky Service ☎906/677-0233, ⓦwww.skyserviceairlines.com. Daily charter flights to Puerto Plata and Punta Cana from Toronto, with connections available from other major Canadian cities. Reservations are made through one of the five tour companies listed on their website (including phone numbers).

USAir ☎1-800/428-4322, ⓦwww.usair.com. Daily non-stops from New York and Philadelphia to Santo Domingo, with connections from Boston, Baltimore, Chicago, Hartford, Pittsburgh and Washington. These flights are a real bargain, and are typically almost half the cost of a similar flight on other US carriers.

Packages and tours

A number of companies offer good-value **package tours** to Dominican resorts, usually for one or two weeks. Packages are generally only available to the more commercialized destinations, such as Puerto Plata, Sosúa and Cabarete in the north, and Boca Chica, Juan Dolio and Punta Cana/Bávaro in the south. In the US, package tour operators usually operate out of a particular city and can't book connecting flights from elsewhere; one operator, Inter-Island, books flights with American Airlines and so can get you to the DR from any major city in the US, though their prices are a bit higher (see opposite). In Canada, Dominican packages are serviced by a number of giant travel "wholesalers" and charter airlines who don't deal directly with the public; if you want to book one of their packages, you'll have to go through a local travel agent.

All-inclusive package vacations are a surprisingly cheap way to go to the DR, at US$800–1200 per week per person for flight, airport transfer, accommodation and all food and drinks. You should still bring some money along, though, at the very least enough to cover the US$10 tourist card for entry and US$10 departure tax; the occasional all-inclusive traveller has been known to leave for their trip without even enough cash for these. Occasionally charter flights and hotels are under-subscribed and companies are forced to offload all-inclusive packages at a discount – you may get a great price if you're prepared to keep calling a discount travel agent over the course of a couple of months. Another way to cut costs is to book a package that's **not all-inclusive**, which can save you up to a third of the price. Since Dominican resort food is generally mediocre, this is a good idea if your resort is in Puerto Plata or Boca Chica, where you can find plenty of great nearby restaurants, but not so great if you're in Punta Cana/Bávaro or Juan Dolio, where independent restaurants outside the resort

complexes are rare. For more information on the benefits and limits of all-inclusive accommodation, see p.33.

In addition to the massive package-tour wholesalers, several very good **specialist companies** offer tours of the DR based on activities such as windsurfing, whale watching, scuba diving, mountain biking and the like. Prices for these tours vary widely, but they're usually a bit more expensive than the all-inclusive packages; see below for a listing of the very best.

Discount travel agents in the US and Canada

Council Travel 205 E 42nd St, New York, NY 10017 ☎1-888-COUNCIL; ⓦwww.counciltravel.com; and branches in many other US cities. Student/budget travel agency.

Discount Airfares Worldwide On-Line ⓦwww.etn.nl/discount.htm. A hub of consolidator and discount agent web links, maintained by the nonprofit European Travel Network.

Dream Vacations 365 Evans Rd, Suite 201, Toronto M8Z 1K2 ☎1-888/226-3000. Large Canadian travel agency that arranges good-value all-inclusive accommodation and charter flights from all major Canadian airports. Packages start at Can$800–1000; flights run as low as Can$350.

Educational Travel Center 438 N Frances St, Madison, WI 53703 ☎1-800/747-5551 or 608/256-5551, ⓦwww.edtrav.com. Student/youth and consolidator fares.

International Association of Air Travel Couriers 220 S Dixie Hwy, #3, Lake Worth, FL 33460 ☎561/582-8320, ⓦwww.courier.org. Courier flight broker. Membership US$45 per year.

Selloff Vacations ☎1-877/SELL-OFFS, ⓦwww.SellOffVacations.com. Last-second Canadian package vacation retailer that will get you all-inclusive trips with the major carriers, though you have to be willing to go within a week's time of purchase.

Skylink 265 Madison Ave, 5th Floor, New York, NY 10016 ☎1-800/AIR-ONLY or 212/599-0430; branches in Chicago, Los Angeles, Washington DC, Montreal and Toronto. Consolidator.

STA Travel Head Office: 5900 Wiltshire Blvd, Suite 2110, Los Angeles, CA 90036 ☎1-800/777-0112, ⓦwww.sta-travel.com; branches in the New York, San Francisco, Boston, Miami, Chicago, Seattle, Philadelphia and Washington DC areas. Worldwide discount travel firm specializing in student/youth fares; also student IDs, travel insurance, car rental, etc.

Travel CUTS 187 College St, Toronto, ON M5T 1P7 ☎1-800/667-2887 (Canada only) or ☎416/979-2406; ⓦwww.travelcuts.com; branches all over Canada, and an office in San Francisco (☎415/247-1800). Organization specializing in student fares, IDs and other travel services.

Wholesale Travel ⓦwww.wholesaletravel.com. Last-minute all-inclusive packages and charter flights from Canada. Sometimes offers really exceptional deals.

North American tour operators

Adventures Abroad ☎1-800/665-3998, ⓦwww.adventuresabroad.com. Visits Santo Domingo and La Romana as part of a two-week, four-island Caribbean itinerary that costs US$2270 from New York and US$2540 from Los Angeles; you can save US$400 by not going all-inclusive. Other stops on the trip are Montego Bay (Jamaica), St Maarten, and San Juan (Puerto Rico).

Aggressor Fleet ☎1-800/348-2628, ⓦwww.aggressor.com. Week-long US$2000 whale-watching cruises in the Silver Banks Sanctuary, setting off from Grand Turk Island.

American Express Vacations ☎1-800/241-1700, ⓦwww.americanexpress.com/travel. Week-long US$1000 packages to Punta Cana and Bávaro, and a three-night US$680 "Cigar Getaway" based in Puerto Plata, with trips to tobacco plantations and a cigar factory.

Apple Vacations ⓦwww.applevacations.com. Online package vacation company with all-inclusive trips from most of the US to Juan Dolio, Puerto Plata, Punta Cana, La Romana and Luperón.

Aquatic Adventures ☎305/827-0211, ⒻⒻ827-0212, ⓦwww.aquaticadventures.com. Texas-based ecotour outfit that offers US$2200 week-long whale-watching cruises in the Silver Banks Sanctuary, departing from Puerto Plata.

Caribbean Concepts ☎516/333-3200 or 1-888/741-7711. All-inclusive package vacations and charter flights from New York to Puerto Plata, Punta Cana and Santo Domingo.

Conquest Vacations ☎1-800/268-1205, ⓦwww.conquestvacations.com. Canada's largest package tour operator, with reasonably priced all-inclusive trips departing from across Canada to Bayahibe, Boca Chica, Puerto Plata, Punta Cana and Juan Dolio.

Dominican Birding, ☎683-4056, Ⓕ683-4156, ⓦwww.drbirds.com. One-, three- and five-day birding excursions with 4WD into the Dominican wilderness at parques nacionales del Este, Bermúdez, Bahoruco and Jaragua. They guarantee that you'll see at least 21 endemics (they commonly

see 29), and the accommodations they provide are comfortable. Very reasonable at US$80–180, depending on the length of the trip.

Global Exchange ☎1-800/497-1994, ⓦwww.globalexchange.org/tours. A terrific outfit whose small-group tours focus on culture and politics. Several good Haiti tours, plus a US$1400 tour of both Haiti and the DR, concentrating on the history of conflict between the two.

Globus and Cosmos ☎1-800/221-0090, ⓦwww.globusandcosmos.com. Island-hopping packages to Santo Domingo, Puerto Rico, St Maarten and Jamaica. US$3200 from Miami, slightly more from other US cities.

Go Travel Direct ☎416/537-3344, ⓦwww.gotraveldirect.com. All-inclusive packages all along the DR's north coast, including Playa Dorada, Sosúa, Cabarete and Río San Juan. Flights depart from across Canada.

GWV International ☎1-800/225-5498, ⓦwww.gwvtravel.com. Package vacations, all-inclusive or not, and charters from Boston to Puerto Plata, Punta Cana and Santo Domingo. With some prodding it's possible to book directly, but they prefer you go through a Boston-area travel agent.

Horizon Tours ☎1-800/395-0025, ⓦwww.horizontours.com All-inclusive packages and charters from Washington DC to the major resort zones; must be booked through a Washington-area travel agent.

Iguana Mama ☎1-800/849-4720, ⓦwww.iguanamama.com. Full-service adventure tour operator offering good-value packages on flight, accommodation, various water and adventure sports and food. Possible activities include windsurfing, mountain biking, mountain treks and horseback excursions.

Inter-Island Tours ☎1-800/245-3434, ⓦwww.interislandtours.com. All-inclusive package vacations using American Airlines instead of the charter flight operators. Trips are slightly more expensive as a result, averaging around US$1000–1350.

Liberty Travel ☎1-800/216-9776, ⓦwww.libertytravel.com. All-inclusive package deals departing from Minneapolis. Good value at around US$900–1000. They prefer that you book through a Minnesota travel agent.

North Caribbean Adventures ☎1-800/653-7447, ⓦwww.datanet.co.uk/sqs/. Week-long adventure scuba dives run by professional treasure hunters based in Monte Cristi. Join them for high-tech search-and-salvage missions in the bays of Monte Cristi and Manzanillo, where dozens of shipwrecked colonial galleons still lie. US$1200 per week, excluding airfare.

Oceanic Society Expeditions ☎1-800/326-7491, ⊛www.oceanic-society.org. Week-long whale-watching expeditions to Silver Banks Sanctuary via Puerto Plata for US$2000. They give you an opportunity to snorkel and swim with the bottlenose dolphins and humpback whales.
Sunquest ☎1-877/485-6060, ⊛www.sunquest.ca. All-inclusive vacations to Punta Cana, Puerto Plata, Boca Chica and Bayahibe from Toronto and Ottawa, with connections from all major Canadian cities.

By boat

Options for arriving in the Dominican Republic **by boat** are mostly limited to hitting the country as one of the ports of call on a longer **Caribbean cruise**. Celebrity (US and Canada ☎1-800/722-5941, ©info@rccl.com, UK ☎0800/0182525, ©infouk@rccl.com; ⊛www.celebritycruises.com) and Costa (US & Canada ©info@us.costa.it, UK ©info@uk.costa.it, Australia and NZ info@costa.it; ⊛www.costa.it, contact travel agent for phone reservations) both offer routes that stop at Isla Catalina for the day and Casa de Campo the same night. These are both part of week-long trips across the Greater Antilles, with additional stops in other nearby ports such as San Juan, Puerto Rico, Ocho Rios, Jamaica, Labadee, Haiti and Cozumel, Mexico. Prices start at US$600 and go (way) up from there. Other specialist agencies include Cruise Adventures (☎1-800/545-8118, ⊛www.cruiseadventures.com) and Cruise World (☎1-800/994-7447, ⊛www.cruiseworldtours.com).

Otherwise, it is possible to arrive via **ferry** from Mayagüez, Puerto Rico, on *Ferias del Caribe* (DR ☎688-4400, Puerto Rico ☎787/832-4800), but it's a long, uncomfortable trip boarding at 8pm one day and arriving in Santo Domingo at noon the next day. Ferries depart Mayagüez on Mondays, Wednesdays and Fridays; from Santo Domingo the ferry departs on Tuesdays, Thursdays and Sundays at 4pm; the cost is US$144 one-way, plus the US$10 entry tax and US$60 for a private cabin. The food and drink on board are quite expensive, so you're well advised to pack your own dinner; there is, though, a sizeable lounge with live music and dancing until 2am.

From Britain and Ireland

There are no non-stop scheduled flights to the Dominican Republic from the UK and Ireland. You'll have to change planes somewhere along the way, which makes it a long journey at around twelve hours, including the transfer. All scheduled services to the Dominican Republic run daily from both Heathrow and Gatwick.

Many British and Irish visitors to the Dominican Republic arrive on a **charter flight** as part of a package holiday, and even if you plan to travel independently this is still the cheapest way to travel, so long as you can get a flight-only booking. Charters do have limitations, however, notably a fixed return date of one, two or a maximum three weeks. Flights go to both Santo Domingo in the south of the island and Puerto Plata in the north, although the former is better served by scheduled services.

Fares and airlines

Tickets sold by travel agents (see opposite) tend to be much cheaper than those bought direct from the airlines, while the cheapest tickets of all are sold by discount operators; check out the websites listed on p.21 for good holiday deals, or check travel ads in the weekend papers, the holiday pages of ITV's Teletext and, in London, *Time Out* and the *Evening Standard*. Giveaway magazines aimed at young travellers, like *TNT*, are also useful sources.

From both Gatwick and Heathrow, **Iberia Airlines'** early-morning daily departure to Santo Domingo via Madrid is consistently cheap, offering returns from £360 including tax in low season, and for £560 in high season. **Air France** charge slightly more (£400–500) for their daily flights to Santo Domingo, going even earlier in the morning via Paris. It's a longer flight if you go via New York and/or Miami with **American Airlines** and **Continental Airlines** but departures are later in the day, and you do get the option of flying to Puerto Plata, plus a free stopover in the States; prices start at around £450, or £630 in high season. Flying from **regional airports** in the UK, some of the larger carriers have handy offers you can take advantage of: there is a useful tie-up between

British Midland and American Airlines, which allows you to fly into London Heathrow for no extra charge. Iberia, Air France and Continental Airlines, flying via Newark, all offer arrangements.

Charter flights are cheaper, though most are sold as part of a package holiday – you may have to rely on last-minute availability. Thomsons offer a small number of flight-only deals to both main airports, with prices usually around £399 return, but going as low as £299, even in high season. In low season prices are not that much cheaper, ranging from £269 to £299.

There are no direct flights **from Ireland** to the Dominican Republic. Air France offer flights from Dublin via Paris to Santo Domingo at around IL£620 plus tax in high season, and IL£420 in low, and Iberia offer similarly low rates.

Airlines

Air France UK ☎0845/0845 111, Republic of Ireland ☎01/605 0383, ⊛www.airfrance.co.uk.
American Airlines ☎0845/778 9789, ⊛www.aa.com.
Continental UK ☎0800/776 464, Republic of Ireland ☎1890/925 252, ⊛www.flycontinental.com.
Iberia Airlines UK ☎020/7830 0011, Republic of Ireland ☎01/677 9846, ⊛www.iberia.com.

Packages

The package market to the Dominican Republic has been subject to some adverse publicity over recent years and as a consequence fewer companies now offer it as a destination. Amongst those that do, Thomsons offer a week's all-inclusive package in a two-star hotel in the north of the island from a bit over £500 in low season and £700 in high season. Thomas Cook offer two weeks all-inclusive in a three-star hotel from £680 in low season and £770 in high season.

The Dominican Republic isn't usually included in the brochures of most of the specialized Caribbean tour operators, but it is a popular place to get married, and several tour operators offer **wedding packages**: for an extra £350 on top of the cost of the package Thomsons will lay on

licences, ceremony, flowers, cake, etc (see also p.56).

Discount travel agents

Co-op Travel Care Belfast ☎028/9047 1717, ☏9047 1339. Flights and holidays around the world.
Flightbookers ☎020/7757 2444, ⊛www.ebookers.com. Low fares on an extensive selection of scheduled flights.
The London Flight Centre ☎020/7244 6411, ⊛www.topdecktravel.co.uk. Long-established agent dealing in discount flights.
North South Travel ☎ & ☏ 01245/608 291, ⊛www.northsouthtravel.co.uk. Friendly, competitive travel agency, offering discounted fares worldwide – profits are used to support projects in the developing world, especially the promotion of sustainable tourism.
STA Travel ☎0870/160 6070, ⊛www.statravel.co.uk. Worldwide specialists in low-cost flights and tours for students and under-26s, though other customers welcome.
Trailfinders UK ☎020/7628 7628, ⊛www.trailfinders.com; Republic of Ireland ☎01/677 7888, ⊛www.trailfinders.ie. One of the best-informed and most efficient agents for independent travellers; produce a very useful quarterly magazine worth scrutinizing for round-the-world routes.
Travel Cuts ☎020/7255 2082, ⊛www.travelcuts.co.uk. Canadian company specializing in budget, student and youth travel and round-the-world tickets.
Usit Campus ☎0870/240 1010, ⊛www.usitcampus.co.uk. Student/youth travel specialists, offering discount flights. Specialists in North America travel.
USIT Now Belfast ☎028/9032 7111, Dublin ☎01/602 1777 or 677 8117, Cork ☎021/4270 900, Derry ☎028/7137 1888, ⊛www.usitnow.ie. Student and youth specialists for flights and trains.

Tour operators

Airtours ☎0870/241 2567, ⊛www.airtours.co.uk. One of the largest package operators, with a range of holidays.
New Look Travel 111 High St, London NW10 4TR ☎020/8965 8212. Caribbean specialists.
Nilson Sailing 120 St Georges Rd, Brighton, East Sussex BN2 1EA ☎01273/62684, ⊛www.sunworld-sailing.co.uk. Week-long all-inclusive packages to Cabarete for windsurfing, dingy sailing and mountain biking.

Thomas Cook ☎ 0870/566 6222,
🖳 www.thomascook.co.uk. Long-established one-
stop 24-hour travel agency for package holidays or
scheduled flights, with bureau de change issuing
Thomas Cook travellers' cheques, travel insurance
and car rental.

Thomson Holidays Greater London House,
Hampstead Rd, London NW1 7SD ☎ 020/7707
9000. Package holidays, plus some cheap flight-only
deals.

From Australia and New Zealand

The Caribbean is not a bargain destination
from Australia or New Zealand. With no
direct flights to the Dominican Republic,
you'll need to travel first to the US or Europe.
Airlines fly to the DR from Austria (Lauda Air),
Belgium (Sobelair), Germany (Condor, LTU
and Hapag Lloyd), Holland (Martinair
Holland), Hungary (Malev), Italy (Alitalia, Air
Europe), and Spain (Iberia, Spanair), among
others. Pick up onward connections from
there.

Generally, the least expensive and most
straightforward routes are via New York or
Miami, which both have regular flights to
Santo Domingo and Puerto Plata. If you're
planning to see the Dominican Republic as
part of a longer trip, **round-the-world** (RTW)
tickets are worth considering, as they're
usually better value than a simple return
flight. Whatever kind of ticket you're after,
your first move should be to call one of the
specialist agents listed opposite – they can
fill you in on all the latest fares and special
offers. If you're a **student** or under 26, you
may be able to undercut some of the prices
given here; STA Travel is a good place to
start.

Fares and routings

From Australia, the most direct routes you're
likely to find are the Air New Zealand, United
and Qantas regular services to Los Angeles,
with connecting flights on American Airlines,
Continental, TWA or United to New York or
Miami, where you can pick up a flight to the
Dominican Republic. Return fares to New
York or Miami from the eastern states of
Australia on any of these airlines (excluding
taxes) cost from A$2380 in the low season,

and A$2950 in the high season. If you're not
in a hurry, Japan Airlines have cheaper fares
to New York from Sydney via an overnight
stop in Tokyo for A$1800; South African
Airways fly to Miami via Johannesburg for
A$2200 from Perth, A$2300 from Sydney.
Point-to-point return fares from Sydney to
the Dominican Republic (via the US) cost
around A$2500–2950.

From **New Zealand**, Air New Zealand,
United and Qantas fly to Los Angeles with
connections on to Miami or New York;
through fares to Miami start at NZ$2800 in
the low season, and NZ$3800 in the high
season, exclusive of taxes. Flights to the
Dominican Republic from Auckland (via the
US) cost from NZ$4000.

Airlines

Air New Zealand Australia ☎ 13 24 76, New
Zealand ☎ 0800/737 000 or 09/357 3000,
🖳 www.airnz.com.
American Airlines Australia ☎ 1300/650 747,
New Zealand ☎ 09/309 0735 or 0800/887 997,
🖳 www.aa.com.
British Airways Australia ☎ 02/8904 8800, New
Zealand ☎ 09/356 8690,
🖳 www.british-airways.com.
Continental Airlines Australia ☎ 02/9244 2242,
New Zealand ☎ 09/308 3350,
🖳 www.flycontinental.com.
Japan Airlines (JAL) Australia ☎ 02/9272 1111,
New Zealand ☎ 09/379 9906,
🖳 www.japanair.com.
Qantas Australia ☎ 13 13 13, New Zealand
☎ 09/357 8900 or 0800/808 767,
🖳 www.qantas.com.au.
South African Airways Australia ☎ 02/9223
4402 or 1800/221 699, New Zealand ☎ 09/379
3708, 🖳 www.saa-usa.com.
United Airlines Australia ☎ 13 17 77, New
Zealand ☎ 09/379 3800, 🖳 www.ual.com.

RTW tickets

Given the fares and routings listed above,
round-the-world tickets that take in one of
the gateway airports in the United States
are worth considering, especially if you have
the time to make the most of a few
stopovers. Ultimately, your choice of route
will depend on where else you want to visit
besides the Dominican Republic. Various
airlines offer routings including stops in New

York or Miami from A$2000/NZ$2700. The Global Explorer and One World tickets from British Airways, Qantas and American Airlines take in several Caribbean destinations, with routings offered on a mileage basis. A sample itinerary starting in Sydney or Melbourne and flying to Los Angeles, Santo Domingo, San Juan, Barbados, London, Bangkok and back to Sydney or Melbourne starts from around A$2500/NZ$3090. Call any of the agents or airlines for more information.

Packages and cruises

Package holidays to the Dominican Republic from Australia and New Zealand are few and far between, and specialists mostly act as agents for Europe- or US-based operators, simply adding a return flight from Australia onto the cost. **Cruises** account for a small sector of the market: most depart from Miami or Fort Lauderdale or from San Juan in Puerto Rico, and because prices are based on US dollars, they fluctuate with the exchange rate. To give some idea, all-inclusive eleven-day cruises calling at seven islands including the Dominican Republic start at A$900 (A$3000 including airfare from Australia). The luxury end of the market is catered for by Caribbean Destinations and Contours, both of which offer resort- and villa-based holidays as well as cruises, with a choice of accommodation in the Dominican Republic – mostly in self-contained resort complexes. Prices start at around A$4000 for fourteen days, based on low-season airfares from Australia and two people sharing a room.

The two main cruise companies that sometimes call at ports in the Dominican Republic are Celebrity Cruises and Costa Cruise Line (see p.14).

Travel agents

Anywhere Travel Australia ☎02/9663 0411 or 018/401 014, ✉anywhere@ozemail.com.au.
Budget Travel New Zealand ☎09/366 0061 or 0800/808 040, ✇www.budgettravel.co.nz.
Destinations Unlimited New Zealand ☎09/373 4033.
Flight Centres Australia ☎02/9235 3522 or 13 16 00, New Zealand ☎09/358 4310, ✇www.flightcentre.com.au.
Northern Gateway Australia ☎08/8941 1394, ✉oztravel@norgate.com.au.
STA Travel Australia ☎13 17 76 or 1300/360 960, ✇www.statravel.com.au; New Zealand ☎09/309 0458 or 366 6673, ✇www.statravel.co.nz.
Student Uni Travel Australia ☎02/9232 8444, ✉australia@backpackers.net.
Thomas Cook Australia ☎13 17 71 or 1800/801 002, ✇www.thomascook.com.au; New Zealand ☎09/379 3920, ✇www.thomascook.co.nz.
Trailfinders Australia ☎02/9247 7666.
Usit Beyond New Zealand ☎09/379 4224 or 0800/788 336, ✇www.usitbeyond.co.nz.

Specialist agents and tour operators

Caribbean Destinations Australia ☎03/9614 7144, ✇www.caribbeanislands.com.au.
Contours Australia ☎03/9670 6900 or 1300/135 391, ✇www.contours.com.au.
Silke's Travel Australia ☎1800/807 860 or 02/9380 5835, ✇www.silkes.com.au. Gay and lesbian specialist travel agent.
Wiltrans Australia ☎02/9255 0899 or 1800/251 174, ✇www.maupintour.com.

Visas, red tape and extended stays

Citizens and permanent residents of the US, Canada, the UK, Ireland, Australia and all EU countries don't need a visa when visiting the Dominican Republic, but must obtain a ninety-day Dominican Republic tourist card for US$10 (US dollars only) at the airport on arrival; check first with your airline to see if the price of the tourist card is included in your flight. Don't bother trying to get a tourist card before you arrive, as it's far more difficult dealing with the Dominican consulates than simply paying at the airport. New Zealanders must apply to the Dominican consulate in Sydney for an A$80 visa, valid for up to sixty days' stay. Whatever nationality, you'll have to show a return ticket home before boarding your flight, and your passport upon arrival; US and Canadian citizens can substitute a birth certificate and government-issued photo ID for the passport. When you leave the country you'll be required to pay a US$10 departure tax (also US dollars only).

Your **tourist card** is very important; make sure you keep it on you at all times – along with your passport or a photocopy of it – and that you have it with you when you leave the country. If you're asked for it and can't produce it, you may well be detained and fined, though some police officers (but not immigration officers) will ask you instead for a small bribe. A word of warning: foreign passports are a valuable commodity in the Dominican Republic, and **passport thefts** have been known to occur. Make sure you keep a photocopy in a safe place.

If you decide to **extend your stay** beyond ninety days, you can get one automatic ninety-day (US$10) extension of your tourist card from the airport immigration offices. Beyond that you're technically illegal, and can either take the time out to renew the card or simply wait until the day you depart to deal with immigration. If you choose to renew the card in a timely manner, the best bet is to head to the Dirección General de Migración in Santo Domingo (Del Puerto one block north of the Malecón at the passenger port, Mon–Fri 10am–4pm; ☏688-8371). Tourist card renewals here are a bargain at only RD$39 for an additional three months. If you instead choose to wait until departing, arrive at the airport an hour earlier than you normally would for your flight home and either claim you lost your tourist card, which will cost US$10 for a new tourist card plus the US$10 departure tax; or present your expired tourist card and pay an exit fee of RD$12/month beyond the expiration date, plus the US$10 departure tax. Another option is to **cross into Haiti** for an hour (before your tourist card expires) using one of the formal crossings – Dajabón or Jimaní – and then re-enter, fulfilling the same requirements as on your original trip, which will cost a total of US$30 in departure and entry taxes to the Dominican and Haitian border outposts. Finally, if you're planning on returning repeatedly, one way to get around the repeated tourist card charges is to get a multiple-entry **ten-year visa** from a Dominican consulate in your home country. The fee for the visa is nominal, and it will make life easier in the long run if you're going back and forth quite a bit.

Obtaining a **resident permit**, which allows you to work, is very difficult and takes several trips to your Dominican consulate and – between various taxes, levies, possible bribes, etc – costs around US$700; you should only bother if you plan to stay in the country indefinitely. If you want to try, call the Dominican consulate in your home country (see below) and request a residency application. This is only the first step, though, in a nightmarish bureaucratic process that includes police background checks, notarized affidavits from personal references and a variety of other roadblocks. Many foreigners circumvent this by simply working illegally in the country on a tourist card, and avoiding the growing

RD$12/month fees outlined above by claiming that their tourist card was lost. Keep in mind, though, that Dominican authorities traditionally raid one tourist resort (often Sosúa) per year for illegal foreign workers, deporting anyone working without official residency papers.

Dominican Republic embassies and consulates

US

Embassy: 1715 22nd St NW, Washington DC 20008 ☎202/332-6280.
Consulate: 1 Times Square Plaza, 11th Floor, New York, NY 10036 ☎212/768-2480; additional offices in Boston, Chicago, Miami, New Orleans, Philadelphia and San Francisco.

UK

139 Inverness Terrace, London W2 6JF ☎020/7727 6214 (Mon–Fri 10am–1pm;) recorded message on application for tourist cards on ☎0891/600 260.

Canada

2080 rue Crescent, Montreal, Quebec H3G 2B8 ☎514/499-1918.

Australia

343a Edgecliffe Rd, Sydney, NSW 2027 ☎ & ☎ 02/9363 5891.

New Zealand

There is no diplomatic representation in New Zealand.

Living and working in the Dominican Republic

Many foreigners **work** in the tourism industry as adventure sport instructors or reps for all-inclusive resorts; most of these people work illegally on a tourist card, as it's phenomenally expensive and time-consuming to obtain an official work permit (see above). If you're at a North American college, it's worth checking whether your college is one of the many to operate an exchange programme with the Catholic University in Santiago. Especially interesting are the summer study programmes with Indiana University's SCUBA (☎www.indiana.edu/~scuba), the underwater archeology school that discovered La Aleta

(see p.135). Additional study, work and volunteer opportunities are listed below.

Study, work and volunteer programmes

AFS Intercultural Programs 198 Madison Ave, 8th Floor, New York, NY 10016 ☎1-800/876-2377, ☎www.afs.org. One-year exchange for high school students. Students stay with host families, and can choose among several cities and dozens of rural areas.

Bernan Associates 4611-F Assembly Dr, Lanham, MD 20706 ☎1-800/274-4888. Distributes UNESCO's encyclopedic *Study Abroad.*

Council on International Educational Exchange (CIEE) 205 E 42nd St, New York, NY 10017 ☎1-888-COUNCIL, ☎www.counciltravel.co. The nonprofit parent organization of Council Travel, CIEE runs summer, semester and academic-year programmes in the Dominican Republic.

International Education Resource Center 860 E 216th St, Bronx, NY 10467 ☎718/231-8333, ☎547-9210, ☎www.studyabroadierc.com. University student exchange operating from Universidad Nacional Ureña in Santo Domingo. Semesters abroad, summer courses and corporate internships.

North Caribbean Research PO Box 6549, Hollywood, FL 33081 ☎1-800/OLD-SHIP, ☎www.datanet.co.uk/sqs/. Co-ordinates student-volunteer underwater archeological programme excavating DR shipwrecks. Programmes run a week, at US$1200, which includes accommodation, meals, taxes and air tanks, but excludes airfare, insurance, tips and certification fees.

Peace Corps 1990 K St NW, Washington DC 20526 ☎1-800/424-8580, ☎www.drfriends.org. Maintains a large presence in the Dominican Republic, placing people with specialist qualifications or skills in two-year postings. Their operation in the Dominican Republic is considered one of their best.

Studyabroad.com ☎www.studyabroad.com. Web site with listings and links to programmes worldwide.

Transformational Journeys ☎816/361-2111, ☎www.tjourneys.com. Organizes mission trips to the Barahona region, particularly around the sugar-growing regions, in which you'll help build a piece of community infrastructure and stay in the home of a local family.

Worldteach 1 Elliot St, Cambridge, MA 02138-5705 ☎1-800/483-2240, ☎www.worldteach.org. Places experienced teachers in schools worldwide.

Information, websites and maps

The glossy promotional materials handed out by Dominican consuls and tourist agencies are pretty to look at but seriously lacking in hard facts. With the emphasis on the package vacations that have earned the country so much hard currency, they hold little value for independent travellers.

The Dominican government also maintains **tourist offices and toll-free tourist hotlines** throughout the country and in the UK and North America (see below), which are good for hooking you up with tour operators and package travel agents, but be warned that any information they give you on questions beyond this will probably be based on guesswork.

Nor are their **maps** very good, though there are several excellent ones of the country available in the travel bookstores listed opposite. The most detailed and accurate of these is the 1:600,000 Dominican Republic map published by Berndtson & Berndtson; also good are the 1:500,000 map by International Travel Maps and Hildebrand's excellent 1:816,000 map of both the Dominican Republic and Haiti. Less detailed is Mapas Gaar's, El Conde 502, 3rd Floor, Santo Domingo RD (☎688-8004; closed Sun), though it does have a great city map of Santo Domingo on its flipside, and the store where it's sold in the capital has navigational charts and wall-sized, detailed blueprints of most Dominican towns.

Mountain trekkers should look for the outstanding **topographical map** of the Cordillera Central contained in *Caminatas al Pico Duarte*, a booklet published by the Dominican National Parks Department, Av Maximo Gómez just south of the Villa Mella bridge, Santo Domingo (☎472-4204). You're well advised to call them before you hike all the way to their office, as they're frequently out of stock; if so, you can sometimes find a copy in one of the used bookstores that line El Conde in Santo Domingo's Zona Colonial.

Map outlets

In the US and Canada

Adventurous Traveler Bookstore 102 Lake St, Burlington, VT 05401 ☎1-800/282-3963, ⓦwww.adventuroustraveler.com.
Book Passage 51 Tamal Vista Blvd, Corte Madera, CA 94925 ☎1-800/999-7909, ⓦwww.bookpassage.com.
Distant Lands 56 S Raymond Ave, Pasadena, CA 91105 ☎1-800/310-3220, ⓦwww.distantlands.com.
Elliot Bay Book Company 101 S Main St, Seattle, WA 98104 ☎1-800/962-5311, ⓦwww.elliotbaybook.com.
Forsyth Travel Library 226 Westchester Ave, White Plains, NY 10604 ☎1-800/367-7984, ⓦwww.forsyth.com.
Globe Corner Bookstore 28 Church St, Cambridge, MA 02138 ☎1-800/358-6013, ⓦwww.globercorner.com.
GORP Travel ☎1-877/440-4677, ⓦwww.gorp.com/gorp/books/main.htm.
Map Link 30 S La Patera Lane, Unit 5, Santa Barbara, CA 93117 ☎805/692-6777, ⓦwww.maplink.com.
Rand McNally ☎1-800/333-0136, ⓦwww.randmcnally.com. Around thirty stores across the US; dial ext 2111 or check the website for the nearest location.
The Travel Bug Bookstore 2667 W Broadway, Vancouver V6K 2G2 ☎604/737-1122, ⓦwww.swifty.com/tbug.
World of Maps 1235 Wellington St, Ottawa, ON K1Y 3A3 ☎1-800/214-8524, ⓦwww.worldofmaps.com.

In the UK and Ireland

Blackwell's Map and Travel Shop 50 Broad St, Oxford OX1 3BQ ☎01865/793 550, ⓦhttp://maps.blackwell.co.uk/index.html.

Easons Bookshop 40 O'Connell St, Dublin 1
☎01/873 3811, ⓦwww.eason.ie.
Hodges Figgis Bookshop 56–58 Dawson St,
Dublin 2 ☎01/677 4754,
ⓦwww.hodgesfiggis.com.
James Thin Booksellers 53–59 South Bridge
Edinburgh EH1 1YS ☎0131/622 8222,
ⓦwww.jthin.co.uk.
The Map Shop 30a Belvoir St, Leicester LE1 6QH
☎0116/247 1400,
ⓦwww.mapshopleicester.co.uk.
National Map Centre 22–24 Caxton St, London
SW1H 0QU ☎020/7222 2466,
ⓦwww.mapsnmc.co.uk.
ⓔinfo@mapsnmc.co.uk.
Newcastle Map Centre 55 Grey St, Newcastle-
upon-Tyne NE1 6EF ☎0191/261 5622.
Ordnance Survey Ireland Phoenix Park, Dublin 8
☎01/802 5349, ⓦwww.irlgov.ie/osi,
ⓔosni@osni.gov.uk.
Ordnance Survey of Northern Ireland Colby
House, Stranmillis Ct, Belfast BT9 5BJ ☎028/9025
5755, ⓦwww.osni.gov.uk.
Stanfords 12–14 Long Acre, London WC2E 9LP
☎020/7836 1321, ⓦwww.stanfords.co.uk,
ⓔsales@stanfords.co.uk. Maps available by mail,
phone order, or email. Other branches within
British Airways offices at 156 Regent St, London
W1R 5TA ☎020/7434 4744, and 29 Corn St,
Bristol BS1 1HT ☎0117/929 9966.
The Travel Bookshop 13–15 Blenheim Crescent,
London W11 2EE ☎020/7229 5260,
ⓦwww.thetravelbookshop.co.uk.

In Australia and New Zealand

The Map Shop 6–10 Peel St, Adelaide, SA 5000
☎08/8231 2033, ⓦwww.mapshop.net.au.
Mapland 372 Little Bourke St, Melbourne, Vic
3000 ☎03/9670 4383, ⓦwww.mapland.com.au.
MapWorld 173 Gloucester St, Christchurch, New
Zealand ☎0800/627 967 or 03/374 5399,
ⓦwww.mapworld.co.nz.
Perth Map Centre 1/884 Hay St, Perth, WA 6000,
☎08/9322 5733, ⓦwww.perthmap.com.au.
Specialty Maps 46 Albert St, Auckland 1001
☎09/307 2217, ⓦwww.ubdonline.co.nz/maps.

Tourism offices

US

1501 Broadway, Suite 410, New York, NY 10036
☎1-888/374-6361, ⓕ212/575-5448,
ⓦwww.herald.infi.net/~domrep/.

561 W Diversey, Suite 214, Chicago, IL 60614
☎773/529-1336, ⓕ529-1338.
2355 Salzedo St, Suite 307, Coral Gables, FL
33134 ☎305/444-4592, ⓕ444-4845.

UK

Dominican Republic Tourist Board, 18–22 Hands
Court, High Holborn, London WC1 (☎020/7242
7778). Call ☎0900/1600 305 for brochure.

Canada

2980 Crescent St, Montreal, Quebec H3G 2B8
☎514/499-1918, ⓕ499-1393.
35 Church St, Toronto, ON M5E 1T3 ☎416/361-
2126, ⓕ361-2130.

Tourist information hotlines

Canada ☎800/563-1611
Dominican Republic ☎1/200-3500
UK ☎0800/899 805
US ☎1-888/358-9594 or 1-800/752-1151

The Dominican Republic on the web

The Dominican Republic maintains a large
presence on the **web**, though, as ever, fer-
reting out a specific piece of information can
take some time. The following are a few tried
and tested sites.

ⓦwww.aquaticadventures.com Detailed
information (and outstanding photographs) on the
humpback whales of the Bahía de Samaná and
Silver Banks Sanctuary.

ⓦwww.beisboldominicano.com Official website
of the Dominican winter leagues, with full season
schedules, league news and ticket purchasing. You
can also email ⓔinfo@beisboldominicano.com with
specific questions.

ⓦwww.debbiesdominicantravel.com A
dizzying array of links to hundreds of Dominican-
related sites and a deep archive of travellers'
personal accounts of all-inclusive vacations.

ⓦwww.dr1.com The most heavily trafficked
Dominican messages board, and the best place to
get information on the web. Also has a good daily
news bulletin that you can sign up for.

ⓦwww.drbirds.com Great, comprehensive
information on the birds in the Dominican
Republic, plus information on where they are and
what local tours are available.

ⓦwww.drfriends.org Dominican Republic Peace
Corps alumni site, with plenty of information and
links.

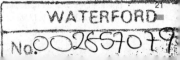

ⓦ www.gaydominicanos.com Website covering local gay life, including events listings and live chat.

ⓦ www.geocities.com/cuyaya/faunae.html A good site covering the most interesting fauna of the DR.

ⓦ www.hispaniola.com A site dedicated to Dominican tourism, with a Dominican Spanish phrasebook, daily weather, a message board and an interactive map of Cabarete.

ⓦ www.iguanamama.com Detailed info and articles on the Cordillera Central and climbing Pico Duarte, along with links to Cabarete businesses.

ⓦ www.indiana.edu/~scuba Comprehensive account of the discovery of La Aleta and surrounding Taino caves in Parque Nacional del Este, including background on the history and culture of the Tainos, and photos of recovered artefacts.

ⓦ www.listindiario.com Online version of the DR's most venerable newspaper, with the best

Dominican news coverage on the internet.

ⓦ www.paginasamarillas.com.do Home page of the Dominican Republic's premier phone company, with a comprehensive yellow pages covering the entire country.

ⓦ www.popreport.com An exhaustive news bulletin and comprehensive roundup of tourist attractions and businesses in the Puerto Plata area.

ⓦ www.presidencia.gov.do/English/welcome .htm Official site of the Dominican President and the National Palace, featuring a good bit of gentle propangada mixed with information about and links to the various government agencies, plus a virtual tour of the Palacio Nacional.

ⓦ www.ticketexpress.com.do Allows you to buy advance tickets for Dominican league baseball games as well as music events across the island.

ⓦ www.wunderground.com/global/DR.html Real-time weather report for ten different regions of the island.

Insurance

It is a sound idea to take out travel insurance coverage before visiting the Dominican Republic unless you're already covered by your current medical plan. In any case, you'd do well to take out an insurance policy before travelling to cover against theft, loss and illness or injury. Before paying for a new policy, however, it's worth checking whether you are already covered: some all-risks home insurance policies may cover your possessions when overseas, and many private medical schemes include cover when abroad. In Canada, provincial health plans usually provide partial cover for medical mishaps overseas, while holders of official student/teacher/youth cards in Canada and the US are entitled to meagre accident coverage and hospital in-patient benefits. Students will often find that their student health coverage extends during the vacations and for one term beyond the date of last enrolment.

After exhausting the possibilities above, you might want to contact a specialist travel insurance company, or consider the travel insurance deal we offer (see box opposite). A typical travel insurance policy usually provides cover for the loss of baggage, tickets and – up to a certain limit – cash or cheques, as well as cancellation or curtailment of your journey. Most of them exclude so-called dangerous sports unless an extra premium is paid: in the Domincan Republic this can mean scuba diving, whitewater rafting, windsurfing and trekking, though probably not kayaking or jeep safaris. Many policies can be chopped and changed to exclude coverage you don't need – for example, sickness and accident benefits can often be excluded or included at will. If you

Rough Guides travel insurance

Rough Guides offers its own travel insurance, customized for our readers by a leading UK broker and backed by a Lloyd's underwriter. It's available for anyone, of any nationality and any age, travelling anywhere in the world.

There are two main Rough Guides insurance plans: **Essential**, for basic, no-frills cover; and **Premier** – with more generous and extensive benefits. Alternatively, you can take out **annual multi-trip insurance**, which covers you for any number of trips throughout the year (with a maximum of 60 days for any one trip). Unlike many policies, the Rough Guides schemes are calculated by the day, so if you're travelling for 27 days rather than a month, that's all you pay for. If you intend to be away for the whole year, the Adventurer policy will cover you for 365 days. Each plan can be supplemented with a "Hazardous Activities Premium" if you plan to indulge in sports considered dangerous, such as skiing, scuba diving or trekking.

For a policy quote, call the Rough Guide Insurance Line on US toll-free ☎1-866/220 5588; UK freefone ☎0800/015 0906; or, if you're calling from elsewhere ☎+44 1243/621 046. Alternatively, get an online quote or buy online at ⓦwww.roughguidesinsurance.com.

do take medical coverage, ascertain whether benefits will be paid as treatment proceeds or only after return home, and whether there is a 24-hour medical emergency number. When securing baggage cover, make sure that the per-article limit – typically under £500 ($800) – will cover your most valuable possession. If you need to make a claim, you should keep receipts for medicines and medical treatment, and in the event that you have anything stolen, you must obtain a signed official statement from the police.

Health

The greatest health dangers posed while travelling in the Dominican Republic come from drinking contaminated water, exposure to the sun and mosquito bites. In addition to taking precautions against these, you should also avoid going barefoot, to minimize the possibility of picking up parasites. If you do get ill, head to one of the many private clinics that you'll find in most Dominican towns, as the public hospitals are notoriously underfunded, with long lines for treatment, unsanitary conditions and minimal equipment. Dominican pharmacies are usually well stocked and prescriptions aren't required, but beware that, unless you ask for a specific drug, you may be given a cheaper alternative carrying more severe side effects.

Inoculations

No specific **inoculations** are required to enter the Dominican Republic, but you should make sure you're up to date with polio and tetanus protection; also strongly recommended are inoculations against **Hepatitis A and B**. **Rabies**, a potentially fatal illness, should also be taken very seriously. There is a vaccine – a course of three injections that has to be started at least a month before departure – but it is expensive, serves only to shorten the course of treatment you need anyway, and is only effective for a maximum of three months. If you don't have a chance or the time to get the shots, stay away from dogs and other potentially biting or scratching mammals. If you get scratched or bitten, wash the wound at once, with alcohol if possible, and seek medical help *immediately*.

Sun and water

The risk of illness from **sunstroke** and **dehydration** should not be underestimated. To guard against sunburn, take at least factor 15 sunscreen and a good hat, and wear both even on overcast days. To avoid dehydration, keep your fluid level up, and take rehydration salts, widely available at Dominican pharmacies. Diarrhoea can also be brought on by too much sun and heat sickness. It's a good idea to bring an over-the-counter remedy from home, though it should only be taken for short periods.

Even Dominicans don't drink the **tap water**, as the local variant on Montezuma's Revenge is horrific. Nor should you drink juice made from concentrate, consume unpurified ice or brush your teeth with tap water. Many travellers even avoid fresh salad. Bottled water is available in every town; in the countryside you can instead purchase plastic packets of purified water (*agua purificada*) for RD$1. For longer stays you can do as the locals do and buy purified water in four-gallon jugs; if you return the bottle for deposit when you're done, it will cost you only RD$40.

If in an emergency you're forced to drink unpurified water, the time-honoured method of **boiling** will effectively sterilize it, though it will not remove unpleasant tastes. A minimum boiling time of five minutes (longer at higher altitudes) is sufficient to kill microorganisms. Boiling water is not always convenient, however, in which case **chemical sterilization** can be carried out, using either chlorine or iodine tablets or a tincture of iodine liquid. When using tablets it is essential to follow the manufacturer's dosage and contact time. Tincture of iodine is better: add a couple of drops per litre of water and leave to stand for twenty minutes. **Pregnant**

women or people with **thyroid problems** should consult their doctor before using iodine sterilizing tablets or iodine-based purifiers. Inexpensive iodine removal filters are recommended if treated water is being used continuously for more than a month or if it is being given to babies.

Swimming in or drinking water from **rivers and streams** has risks as well, particularly the dreaded **giardia**, a bacterium that causes stomach upset, fever and diarrhoea, and **schistosomiasis**, a freshwater flatworm that can penetrate unbroken skin; both are treatable with antibiotics.

Ciguatera

Ciguatera is a nasty toxin transmitted by infected reef fish, and has been on the rise due to growing pollution in the waters of the southern coast. You can avoid most of the risk if you avoid eating parrotfish, pufferfish and barracudas, but the illness also occasionally occurs with more common dishes like red snapper, kingfish and other reef-dwelling sea creatures. Symptoms include numbness and uncontrollable shivers, increasing spastic movements in the lips and tongue, loss of muscular control and severe vomiting. Papaya juice is a popular local remedy, but you should get to a private clinic as soon as possible if you start showing any of these symptoms.

Malaria and dengue fever

Malaria rates are low in the DR, but cases do occur along the Haitian border and around Parque Nacional Los Haitises. The risk to travellers is small, but if you intend to travel in the above areas, you should take a course of prophylactics (usually chloroquine) to be on the safe side. There are slightly higher rates of **dengue fever**, a mosquito-borne haemorrhagic fever characterized by extreme aches and pains in the bones and joints, fever, dizziness and, after four days, a bad rash. There's no cure, other than rest and painkillers, and the only precaution you can take is to **avoid mosquito bites**. The mosquitoes that cause dengue are most often found around stagnant water; wear a generous layer of bug spray during the day, and try to remain in well-screened areas at night; in cheaper hotels use a mosquito net or, in an emergency, wear clothes that cover as much of your body as possible. You should also bring an insect repellent and use it on exposed areas of skin at all times. Some beaches are infected with **sand fleas** at dusk, not generally disease-carrying but possessed of a remarkably painful bite; they ignore most repellents with impunity but can typically be avoided if you use Avon Skin-So-Soft.

Tuberculosis

In the 1990s, a **drug-resistant tuberculosis** strain emerged as a problem in the Dominican Republic, particularly in the crowded, outer barrios of Santo Domingo, though you're not likely to be spending too much time there. The chance of your contracting TB is statistically very low – no more likely than in New York City, for example; if you're worried about exposure, you can cut the risk even further by avoiding public hospital stays, poor urban slums and any contact with prostitutes. Your doctor can give you a simple skin test for TB exposure when you return home; if you're positive, a round of medication can eliminate it from your body before it becomes a problem.

HIV and AIDS

As in most of the world, HIV/AIDS is at epidemic levels in the Dominican Republic; don't allow the current, temporary decline in attention to this growing pandemic to lull you into complacency. The blood supply is monitored for HIV, but you can't rely on Dominican public hospitals using sterilized equipment, so you might want to bring sealed hypodermic syringes as a precaution. With regard to sex, the same common-sense rule applies here as anywhere else: condomless sex is a serious health risk. **Condoms** sold in the Dominican Republic are not of the quality you find at home; best bring them with you.

Dominican law requires all foreigners who seek residence permits to "pass" an HIV test, which should give you some sense of the paranoia with which the disease is viewed here. Some **HIV-positive travellers** feel uncomfortable enough that they pack their medications into aspirin and other innocuously labelled bottles; if your pills require refrigeration, flight attendants and hotel clerks will generally keep them on ice for you if you ask. The main health hazards to watch out for are the tap water and drug-resistant tuberculosis (see above). Consult with your doctor regarding yellow fever immunization; the disease is not currently active in the DR, but the CDC currently recommends asymptomatic HIV-positive individuals travelling in the Caribbean to get immunized for it as a precaution.

Medical resources for travellers

Websites

ⓦhttp://health.yahoo.com Information on specific diseases and conditions, drugs and herbal remedies, as well as advice from health experts.
ⓦwww.fitfortravel.scot.nhs.uk UK NHS website carrying information about travel-related diseases and how to avoid them.
ⓦwww.istm.org The website of the International Society for Travel Medicine, with a full list of clinics specializing in international travel health.
ⓦwww.tripprep.com Travel Health Online provides an online-only comprehensive database of necessary vaccinations for most countries, as well as destination and medical service provider information.

In the US and Canada

Canadian Society for International Health 1 Nicholas St, Suite 1105, Ottawa, ON K1N 7B7 ☎613/241-5785, ⓦwww.csih.org. Distributes a free pamphlet, *Health Information for Canadian Travellers*, containing an extensive list of travel health centres in Canada.
Centers for Disease Control 1600 Clifton Rd NE, Atlanta, GA 30333 ☎1-800/311-3435 or 404/639-3534, ⓕ1-888/232-3299, ⓦwww.cdc.gov. Publishes outbreak warnings, suggested inoculations, precautions and other background information for travellers. Useful website plus International Travelers Hotline on ☎1-877/FYI-TRIP.
International Association for Medical Assistance to Travellers (IAMAT) 417 Center St, Lewiston, NY 14092 ☎716/754-4883, ⓦwww.sentex.net/~iamat; and 40 Regal Rd, Guelph, ON N1K 1B5 ☎519/836-0102. A non-

profit organization supported by donations, it can provide a list of English-speaking doctors in the DR, climate charts and leaflets on various diseases and inoculations.

MEDJET Assistance ☎1-800/863-3538, ⊛www.medjetassistance.com. Annual membership programme for travellers (US$175 for individuals, US$275 for families) that, in the event of illness or injury, will fly members home or to the hospital of their choice in a medically equipped and staffed jet.

Travel Medicine ☎1-800/872-8633, ⊛www.travmed.com. Sells first-aid kits, mosquito netting, water filters, reference books and other health-related travel products.

In the UK and Ireland

British Airways Travel Clinics 28 regional clinics (call ☎01276/685 040 for the nearest, or consult ⊛www.britishairways.com), with two in London (Mon–Fri 9.30am–5.15pm, Sat 10am–4pm): 156 Regent St, London W1 (☎020/7439 9584, no appointment necessary); and 101 Cheapside, London EC2 (☎020/7606 2977, appointment required). All clinics offer vaccinations, tailored advice from an online database and a complete range of travel healthcare products.

Communicable Diseases Unit Brownlee Centre, Glasgow G12 0YN ☎0141/211 1062. Travel vaccinations.

Dun Laoghaire Medical Centre 5 Northumberland Ave, Dun Laoghaire, Co Dublin ☎01/280 4996, ⊕280 5603. Advice on medical matters abroad.

Hospital for Tropical Diseases Travel Clinic 2nd Floor, Mortimer Market Centre, off Capper St, London WC1E 6AU (Mon–Fri 9am–5pm by appointment only; ☎020/7388 9600; a consultation costs £15 which is waived if you have your injections here). A recorded Health Line (☎0906/133 7733; 50p per min) gives hints on hygiene and illness prevention as well as listing appropriate immunizations.

Liverpool School of Tropical Medicine Pembroke Place, Liverpool L3 5QA ☎0151/708 9393. Walk-in clinic Mon–Fri 1–4pm; appointment required for yellow fever, but not for other jabs.

MASTA (Medical Advisory Service for Travellers Abroad) London School of Hygiene

and Tropical Medicine. Operates a prerecorded 24-hour Travellers' Health Line (UK ☎0906/822 4100, 60p per min; Republic of Ireland ☎01560/147 000, 75p per minute), giving written information tailored to your journey by return of post.

Nomad Pharmacy Surgeries 40 Bernard St, London WC1; and 3–4 Wellington Terrace, Turnpike Lane, London N8 (Mon–Fri 9.30am–6pm, ☎020/7833 4114 to book vaccination appointment). They give advice free if you go in person, or their telephone helpline is ☎0906/863 3414 (60p per minute). They can give information tailored to your travel needs.

Trailfinders Immunization clinics (no appointments necessary) at 194 Kensington High St, London (Mon–Fri 9am–5pm except Thurs to 6pm, Sat 9.30am–4pm; ☎020/7938 3999).

Travel Health Centre Department of International Health and Tropical Medicine, Royal College of Surgeons in Ireland, Mercers Medical Centre, Stephen's St Lower, Dublin ☎01/402 2337. Expert pre-trip advice and inoculations.

Travel Medicine Services PO Box 254, 16 College St, Belfast 1 ☎028/9031 5220. Offers medical advice before a trip and help afterwards in the event of a tropical disease.

In Australia and New Zealand

Travellers' Medical and Vaccination Centres 27–29 Gilbert Place, Adelaide, SA 5000 ☎08/8212 7522.
1/170 Queen St, Auckland ☎09/373 3531.
5/247 Adelaide St, Brisbane, Qld 4000 ☎07/3221 9066.
5/8–10 Hobart Place, Canberra, ACT 2600 ☎02/6257 7156.
147 Armagh St, Christchurch ☎03/379 4000.
270 Sandy Bay Rd, Sandy Bay, Hobart, Tas 7005 ☎03/6223 7577.
2/393 Little Bourke St, Melbourne, Vic 3000 ☎03/9602 5788.
45 Stirling Hwy, Nedlands, WA 6009 ☎08/9386 4511.
Level 7, Dymocks Bldg, 428 George St, Sydney, NSW 2000 ☎02/9221 7133.
Shop 15, Grand Arcade, 14–16 Willis St, Wellington ☎04/473 0991.

Costs, money and banks

The Dominican Republic is one of the last true budget destinations in the Caribbean; only neighbouring Haiti is cheaper. As a result, package deals at quality Dominican all-inclusives are relatively low-priced, and in many parts of the country shoestring travellers can spend as little as US$40/£28 per day. The savings are spread unevenly, though, and some things are pricier here than elsewhere: riding from town to town via public transport can cost as little as US$0.35/£0.20, but car rental will set you back at least US$45/£28 a day.

Currency

There are two distinct economies within the Dominican Republic, the **US dollar** economy of the all-inclusive hotels and tour operators and that of the official Dominican currency, the **peso (RD$)**. Throughout most of the country, you will have to change any foreign currency into pesos in order to conduct transactions. At the all-inclusive resorts and other foreign-owned tourism companies, though, all prices will be quoted in US dollars, and Dominican pesos are accepted reluctantly – and at a poor rate.

Pesos come in notes of 5, 10, 20, 50, 100, 500, 1000 and 5000; there are also 0.10, 0.25, 0.50 and 1 peso coins, though only the last sees much use these days. Today the peso floats freely against the dollar, which means that there's some variation in **exchange rate** from day to day. When this book went to press, it had hovered at 16–17 pesos to the US dollar for several years; but keep in mind that devaluation may eat into the peso's value a bit over the lifetime of this edition. Obtaining pesos outside the DR is virtually impossible: wait until you arrive and change some at the airport. If you miss banking hours, you'll do fine for the night with small-denomination dollar bills; it's therefore best for pretty much any foreign traveller to come armed in advance with some US dollars.

Costs

The Dominican Republic can be incredibly cheap if you stick to the smaller hotels and get around using public transport. With the exception of Santo Domingo you'll have no problem finding some sort of modest but decent **accommodation** for US$20 or less (though US$35 will buy you more comfort), and a **meal** at a Dominican *comedor* will set you back no more than US$2.50. Especially cheap are the **buses and guaguas**; the former can get you from one end of the country to the other for US$4 or less, the latter for under US$2.50.

At **resort towns** like Cabarete and Boca Chica, prices are more inflated, but even here a fairly low budget can be kept if you're prepared to put in some effort. **All-inclusive** hotel guests should be sure to bring some cash, as the quality of many hotel restaurants is not outstanding and you'll enjoy your trip more if you get out of your resort complex.

For notes on **tipping** in the DR, see the Directory on p.56.

Changing money

The best places to change money are the **banks**, which offer good exchange rates; keep your receipts, as this allows you to exchange thirty percent of the pesos back into hard currency on departure. In a pinch, smaller **casas de cambio**, which usually offer only slightly worse rates, are fine, though you should avoid the **street money-changers** you'll see in most cities, as counterfeit pesos and sleight-of-hand rip-offs are standard practice. Hotels, especially those in beach areas far from the cities, generally offer unfavourable rates – if possible, change your money when you arrive at the airport if you're going all-inclusive. Before heading out to remote areas like the Haitian border, you'll do well to change your money in a larger town, as many rural businesses won't accept US dollars and the few casas de cambio will offer a lousy rate.

Travellers' cheques, credit and cash cards

Travellers' cheques are undeniably a safe way to keep your money, but to get around the country you'll have to plan on cashing them in only periodically, as aside from large hotels, car rental firms and pricey restaurants, most Dominican businesses don't accept them. Most convenient are travellers' cheques in US dollars, though banks and most hotels will cash cheques in European currencies as well.

The usual fee for travellers' cheque sales is one or two percent, though this fee may be waived if you buy the cheques through a bank where you have an account. It pays to get a selection of denominations. Make sure to keep the purchase agreement and a record of cheque serial numbers safe and separate from the cheques themselves. In the event that cheques are lost or stolen, the issuing company will expect you to report the loss forthwith to their office in Santo Domingo (see p.103); most companies claim to replace lost or stolen cheques within 24 hours. American Express cheques, sold through most banks, are the most widely accepted cheques in the DR.

Credit cards come in handy as a backup source of funds, and are accepted by most mid-range and all expensive hotels, as well as many restaurants – though of course in smaller towns and rural areas they will be slightly less helpful. **Visa** is the most widely accepted brand, usable in ATMs at many banks, while others will give you Visa cash advances over the counter – bring your passport as ID. **MasterCard** and **American**

Express are less useful for cash advances – though American Express has offices in the capital and Cabarete – but are accepted by hotels, high-end restaurants and car rental firms. Your **cash cards** from home will also come in very handy, as almost all sizeable towns and resorts have **ATMs** that allow you to withdraw cash directly from your bank account at home. Take note, though, that there are no ATMs along the Haitian border and in the most rural parts of the country, so stock up before leaving the main towns.

Wiring money

Having **money wired** from home is never convenient or cheap, and should be considered a last resort. Funds can be sent via Western Union (US ☎1-800/325-6000; Canada ☎1-800/235-0000; UK ☎0800/833 833; Australia and NZ ☎0800/270 000), which has branches throughout the country, or MoneyGram (US and Canada ☎1-800/543-4080, UK 0800/8971 8971), which has offices in Santo Domingo and Samaná. Both companies' fees depend on the destination and the amount being transferred, but as an example, wiring US$1000 to the Dominican Republic will cost around US$68 with Western Union, US$60 with MoneyGram. The funds should be available for collection at the local office within minutes of being sent. We have listed the offices in the major towns and cities throughout the guide. It's also possible to have money wired directly from a bank in your home country to a bank in the Dominican Republic, although this is somewhat less reliable because it involves two separate institutions. If you go this route, the person wiring the funds to you will need to know the routing number of the bank the funds are being wired to.

Getting around

The Dominican Republic's bus companies provide an excellent, inexpensive service over much of the country. Lines at the stations move quickly, there's plenty of room for luggage on the vehicles and – aside from the quality of the movies screened on cross-country rides – trips are relatively pleasant and hassle-free. Even more extensive and cheap is the informal network of guaguas – ranging from fairly decent minibuses to battered, overcrowded vans – that cover every inch of the DR; in most cases, you should be prepared for some discomfort – and you'll have a hard time fitting in much luggage, as every square inch of space is packed with passengers.

Car rental is common as well, and affords a freedom you'll greatly appreciate after a few days going from town to town on the guaguas, but the cost is generally high, due to petrol prices, import duties and high accident rates. **Domestic airlines**, on the other hand, are reasonably economical, and can make sense if you're not exploring much beyond the main centres. Finally, a number of **tour operators** in Santo Domingo, Puerto Plata and the all-inclusive resorts organize individual itineraries and packages with transport included.

Buses

Santo Domingo and Santiago are the major hubs for **bus travel**, and some companies do little more than shuttle between the two. **Caribe Tours** (☎221-4422, ⓦwww .caribetours.com.do) boasts by far the most extensive network of bus lines – with connections to the Cibao, the Samaná Peninsula, the Barahona region, the entire Silver Coast and even Port-au-Prince, Haiti – while **Metro** (☎566-7126) can get you from the capital to the Cibao, Puerto Plata and the Samaná Peninsula. Both of these companies have comprehensive brochures available in their stations, listing destinations and departure times. In addition to these two, you'll find several regional bus companies that cover one particular part of the country, though vehicles and drivers tend to vary more in quality; check the travel details at the end of each chapter for a rundown of regional connections. Unless it's a public holiday, you won't need

advance reservations, but you should arrive at least an hour before the bus leaves to be sure of getting a seat.

The bus companies strive to stay in competition with guaguas, and so fares are extremely cheap. Even a cross-country trip from Santo Domingo to Samaná or Monte Cristi will set you back no more than RD$70, while shorter trips fall in the RD$40–50 range. Make sure that the date and time are correct on your **ticket**; even if the mistake isn't yours, you cannot normally change your ticket or get a refund. With the exception of the cheapie Transporte del Cibao, which does an hourly run from Sosúa through Santiago to Santo Domingo, all Dominican buses have toilets in the back. On trips of more than two hours, a rest stop will be taken at a roadside restaurant or service station; during these, Metro drivers offer a complimentary cup of coffee.

Guaguas, públicos and motoconchos

The formal bus companies are great for shuttling back and forth between the major towns, but to head further out into the countryside you're better off trying the informal system of **guaguas** (see box p.x), which acts as the Dominican Republic's circulatory system. Guagua routes interlace the entire country (even the most remote areas) and shuttle hundreds of thousands of people from place to place every day, and they're incredibly cheap; in the southeast and other parts of the country not serviced by Caribe Tours and Metro, they're your best option for public transport. That said, most guaguas are not all that comfortable, and you'll have a much less stressful ride if you speak a little Spanish, as English is not widely spoken by the Dominican masses that use and maintain this informal transport system.

Guaguas are operated by teams of two, the driver and the *cobrador*, who sticks his head out of the sliding side door and drums up business. To catch a guagua, either ask for the location of the local station or simply stand by the side of the road and wave your arms at one as it passes. For longer trips, you'll often have to transfer guaguas at major towns, but even the longest leg of the trip will cost no more than RD$40; more often, you'll be paying RD$5–10. Be aware, though, that attempted **rip-offs** of tourists are not unheard of. You should ask around and find out how much a given guagua ride costs before flagging one down. Don't ask the driver or you may be quoted a rate ten times higher than the norm; instead, clamber into the vehicle and hand over your money immediately without saying a word; if the *cobrador* won't take the money, get out and wait for the next. Keep a careful eye on the road as you go; you'll have to shout for the driver to pull over when you want to get out.

Though the vans are the most prevalent type of guagua, there are other manifestations as well. Routes leading from Santo Domingo to the southeast and the Barahona region are often served by far more comfortable, air-conditioned **minibuses**; along the Silver Coast, the vans are augmented by private cars called **públicos**, which charge RD$5 and only go to the next nearest town and wait to fill up before heading off. *Públicos* also make up part of the **city transport** system in Santo Domingo, and dominate it in Santiago. City routes rarely cost more than RD$2, though you'll have to put up with blaring music and some daredevil driving manoeuvres. In Puerto Plata and other, smaller, towns, city transport is instead in the form of **motoconchos**, inexpensive, small-engined motorbikes that ferry you from place to place; they're faster than the *públicos* but can be dangerous.

Taxis

Taxis are far more comfortable than motoconchos for getting around the cities, and by foreign standards are a relatively cheap way to travel. You'll usually get better rates if you book a taxi in advance, rather than climbing into one at a designated point; reputable operators are listed throughout the guide. It's also possible to hire a taxi for cross-country travel, though this usually costs even more than car rental. At designated pick-up points within airports and towns, there's always a board listing the established rates for travel to various towns across the country.

Driving

Car rental is expensive in the DR, though you can cut your costs a bit – and avoid a lot of hassle – by booking in advance with one of the international operators listed on p.32; Dollar and National are generally the best value, and both offer decent 4WDs. Recognized international firms, along with reputable Dominican agencies Honda and Nelly, are preferable as they're no more expensive and far less likely to rip you off; if you don't have a credit card, though, you'll be stuck with the local companies, who accept passports in lieu of a security deposit. Rates start at around US$45–55 per day, with unlimited mileage but no discount for longer rental periods; you should also get full collision insurance, which will be an extra US$10–12 per day. Even with collision, though, you're contractually responsible for any damage up to RD$25,000. You should therefore take special care to note *all* dents, scratches and missing parts before signing off; nor should you sign the contract if a total price, including all hidden charges, taxes and fees, is not filled out. Anticipate also high **petrol** costs, which float around RD$40 per gallon. Most petrol stations close around 8pm – and there are none whatsoever in the most remote regions – so keep a careful eye on your tank. If all else fails, look for one of the many roadside tables that sell individual litres of petrol for around RD$40.

Rental firms here charge exorbitant rates for **repairs**; if your car is dented you're far better off going to one of the local repair shops, which will charge at most RD$300 (as opposed to as much as RD$25,000). Because of the poor quality of many roads, flat tyres are a common occurrence; fortunately, every town has at least one **gomero**,

Crossing between the Dominican Republic and Haiti

If you're visiting the Dominican Republic and Haiti in a single trip, you'll have to pass through one of two legal border crossings: Ouanaminthe–Dajabón or Malpasse–Jimaní, both of them open daily from 8am to 6pm. Crossing for more than a day at the more informal checkpoints at Belladére–Elias Piña or Anse-a-Pitres–Pedernales will be problematic later when you try to leave the DR, as there are no immigration officials posted to stamp your passport and provide you with a tourist card. Regardless, no one is allowed to bring a **rental car** across the Haitian–Dominican border, so unless you own a car in Haiti, you won't be able to drive into the DR. The least masochistic way to cross is with one of the two Dominican bus companies that make the trip: **Terrabus** (☎531-0383) in Santo Domingo) is a very efficient company with comfortable buses that runs a daily route from Port-au-Prince to Santo Domingo via the border crossing at Jimaní; while **Caribe Tours** (☎221-4422) have recently started offering trips to the Haitian capital that depart Santo Domingo daily at 11am. Otherwise you'll be stuck with the often bizarre Haitian modes of public transport; among the most popular are school buses with their front end chopped off, soldered onto a Mack truck cab – and with the eardrum-pulverizing horn pointed directly at passengers.

independent tyre shops that do great work for as little as RD$20.

Car rental is the most convenient travel option if you're going from town to town across the island, but you can't take rental cars across the border to Haiti. Also, driving a car through the congested, unregulated streets of Dominican cities is often more trouble than it's worth. If you want to explore the beautiful coastal and mountain backroads – which give access to the DR's finest scenery – you're best off renting a good **four-wheel-drive**, which costs from US$70 per day. Rental firms may try to entice you into choosing the cheaper Suzukis, which are the same price as standard cars, but these aren't really intended for rough mountain travel, and after the first bone-wrenching hour along a Dominican dirt road, you'll curse yourself for not spending more. **Motorcycles** can also be rented at many local firms, for around US$25 per day. Be warned, though: motorbike thefts are extremely common, especially in resort areas, so you'll have to keep it locked up at all times. A motorcycle helmet law was enacted several years ago, but it's rarely adhered to and laughable local attempts to comply generally utilize baseball batting helmets or plastic toy American football gear intended for children. That doesn't mean that you should follow suit; insist that a proper helmet comes with your bike.

Dominicans drive on the **right-hand side of the road**, often at a breakneck pace. You'll have to keep a careful eye out along the highways, as large commercial buses and cargo trucks constantly veer into the opposite lane to pass slower vehicles. An array of signals using the car horns and lights are used by local motorists, though most of the time their meaning is obscure; a driver about to pass you will often blink the headlights, while one coming towards you that hits the brights is signalling that he or she is in your lane. You'll also find a bewildering variety of **obstacles** in your path, including turtle-paced ice cream trucks, motoconchos with comically large cargoes of stacked chicken coops or construction equipment (which the driver holds down with one arm), and children running back and forth along the freeway. As you approach towns, watch out for the nasty **speed bumps**, originally intended to prevent accidents but now used by local police to slow passing cars enough that RD$5 **bribes** can be exacted from them. Bribe-taking is the primary concern of law enforcement officers posted along the roads, who don't have enough money for police cars; if they don't actually jump out in front of your car, you should do as the Dominicans do and drive past them without slowing down. Otherwise, pretend to speak no Spanish and keep repeating the word "tourist", and they'll usually let you go.

Car rental agencies

North America

Alamo ☎1-800/GO-ALAMO,
ⓔreservations@goalamo.com,
ⓦwww.goalamo.com.
Avis US ☎1-800/230-4898, Canada ☎1-800/272-5871, ⓦwww.avis.com.
Budget US ☎1-800/472-3325, Canada ☎1-800/268-8900, ⓦwww.budgetrentacar.com.
Dollar ☎1-800/800-4000, ⓦwww.dollar.com.
Hertz US ☎1-800/654-3001, Canada (except Toronto) ☎1-800/263-0600, Toronto ☎416/620-9620, ⓦwww.hertz.com.
National ☎1-800/CAR-RENT,
ⓦwww.nationalcar.com.
Thrifty ☎1-800/847-4389, ⓦwww.thrifty.com.

UK

Avis ☎0870/606 0100, ⓦwww.avisworld.com.
Budget ☎0800/181 181,
ⓦwww.budget.co.uk.
Hertz ☎0870/844 8844, ⓦwww.hertz.co.uk.
Holiday Autos ☎0870/400 00 99,
ⓦwww.holidayautos.co.uk.
National ☎0870/5365 365,
ⓦwww.nationalcar.com.
Thrifty ☎01494/751 600, ⓦwww.thrifty.co.uk.

Ireland

Avis Northern Ireland ☎028/9024 0404, Republic of Ireland ☎01/605 7500, ⓦwww.avis.co.uk.
Budget Republic of Ireland ☎01/9032 7711,
ⓦwww.budgetcarrental.ie or www.budget-ireland.co.uk.
Hertz Republic of Ireland ☎01/676 7476,
ⓦwww.hertz.co.uk.
Holiday Autos Republic of Ireland ☎01/872 9366, ⓦwww.holidayautos.ie.

Australia

Avis ☎13 63 33, ⓦwww.avis.com.

Budget ☎1300/362 848, ⓦwww.budget.com.
Dollar ☎02/9223 1444 or 1800/358 008,
ⓦwww.dollarcar.com.au.
Hertz ☎13 30 39, ⓦwww.hertz.com.
National ☎13 10 45, ⓦwww.nationalcar.com.au.
Thrifty ☎1300/367 227, ⓦwww.thrifty.com.au.

New Zealand

Avis ☎0800/655 111 or 09/526 2847,
ⓦwww.avis.co.nz.
Budget ☎0800/652 227 or 09/976 2222,
ⓦwww.budget.co.nz.
Hertz ☎0800/654 321, ⓦwww.hertz.co.nz.
National ☎0800/800 115 or 03/366 5574,
ⓦwww.nationalcar.co.nz.
Thrifty ☎09/309 0111, ⓦwww.thrifty.co.nz.

Flights

If you're travelling across the country, say from Santo Domingo to Samaná, and aren't especially interested in what lies in between, it's worth considering a **domestic flight**. Air Santo Domingo (☎683-8006, ⒻI381-0080, ⓦwww.airsantodomingo.com) is a good local carrier, affiliated with Air Europa, offering fast, fairly priced connections between Puerto Plata, Punta Cana, El Portillo (near Las Terrenas), Arroyo Barril (near Samaná) and Santo Domingo. They also have flights between Santo Domingo (Aeropuerto Herrera) and San Juan, Puerto Rico. Flights cost RD$500–1000 and last no more than an hour. Another Dominican company, **Caribair** (☎542-6688 or 567-7050, ⓦwww.caribintair.com), has daily flights between Santo Domingo and Barahona, along with connections to Port-au-Prince, Haiti. Caribair also runs **private charters**, as does Uni Charter (☎567-0481 or 0818), both out of Aeropuerto Herrera in Santo Domingo.

Accommodation

The Dominican Republic has become the most popular destination in the Caribbean thanks to its preponderance of all-inclusive hotels, which make package vacations here far cheaper than elsewhere in the region. The all-inclusives do, though, have their downside: the food is usually not that great, and you'll be stuck in a walled-off complex for the whole of your trip, which can get a bit claustrophobic. There are, however, plenty of other options for travellers who want to get out and see the country: luxury high-rise resorts along the capital's Malecón, independently operated beach hotels, rooms for rent in Dominican family homes, and an assortment of bearable budget hotels, many with private bath, hot water and a/c. Away from the main tourist spots you can expect to pay around RD$150–300 for the night; in resort towns prices rise to RD$300–600. If you're willing to haggle, most non-all-inclusive hotels in tourist areas will take RD$25–50 off their price in low season; in the cheap hotels away from the resorts you should be able to knock at least RD$25 off at any time of year. Reservations are essential for the all-inclusives, where you'll get up to 75 percent off the price by booking with a travel agent as part of a package before you arrive. In the major resort towns most independent hotels require reservations for the high season, but in the rest of the country they're not necessary.

Independent hotels and pensiónes

When travelling, most Dominicans stay at the spartan **budget hotels** that you'll find dotted throughout the country. If you do likewise you'll save a lot of money, but beware – you often get what you pay for. That means fairly nondescript, box-like rooms, best avoided except for sleep. Some of them have shared bath, many more cold-water showers. Keep in mind also that when a budget hotel boasts "hot water" showers, this often means a large plastic nozzle on the showerhead that heats the water on the spot – making for a somewhat tepid temperature. Whatever you do, don't touch the nozzles when wet, or you'll risk a painful electric shock. Look to spend between

Accommodation price categories

All accommodation listed in this guide has been graded according to the following **price categories**:

- ❶ Less than US$10
- ❷ US$10–20
- ❸ US$20–30
- ❹ US$30–50
- ❺ US$50–75
- ❻ US$75–100
- ❼ US$100–150
- ❽ US$150 and above

Rates are for the cheapest available double or twin room during the **off-season** – normally April to mid-December. During the **busy season,** rates are liable to rise by up to 25 percent (though this is rare at the cheaper hotels), and proprietors may be less amenable to haggling for a price. Many of the all-inclusive hotels have a minimum-stay requirement, and rates are quoted per person per night based on double occupancy. Payments at most hotels can typically be made in either Dominican pesos or US dollars, though all-inclusives prefer the latter.

RD$100–250 for these establishments, though some, especially in the cities, also offer rooms with a/c and television for around RD$50 extra. It's easy to mistake the many roadside **cabañas turísticas** for budget traveller hotels; in fact these are the type of hotel that charges hourly, and are mainly used by local couples.

There are **no youth hostels** in the DR, but a good way to cut expenses are the traditional **pensiónes** that you'll still find in many towns, though over the past two decades they've begun to die out. These are rooms within a private Dominican home, and so offer an excellent opportunity for contact with local people. Pensiónes vary widely in quality, so you should have a good look at your room before deciding. If you want to shop around, don't feel guilty about seeing the room and then moving on; expect to pay RD$50–200.

Nicer, **mid-range hotels** are available in areas regularly frequented by foreigners. Ranging between RD$300 and RD$650, they feature a/c, strong hot water and more pleasant rooms. Hotels at the lower end of this price range are often especially good value; at the higher end you'll get a few luxuries thrown in, like cable TV or breakfast. If there's one around and you can afford it, you might want to consider the independent **luxury hotels** as well, which usually charge in US dollars (US$80–150). The majority are clustered in Santo Domingo, but you'll also find one in most other major cities and a couple along the rural coast. They range from well-appointed beach hotels and seaside high-rises to full-service, two-storey apartments and renovated colonial stone mansions furnished with sixteenth-century pieces. You can often get better rates (up to 30 percent off) at these hotels on weekends, as they cater mostly to business travellers.

All-inclusives

The Dominican Republic is the archetypal, high-volume **all-inclusive** destination, where a single price covers your room, all meals and drinks, and a variety of activities. If you go all-inclusive, you should do so through a **package** arranged by a travel agent in your home country (see p.12), which will cost you substantially less than arriving at the reception desk and asking for a room.

For couples and families on a tight budget, the all-inclusives can be a wonderful opportunity for a peaceful beach vacation in relative luxury – these places are usually stationed right on the country's prime beachfront. The product offered is usually good, and despite a blanket no-tips policy, the staff are generally pleasant and accommodating. It's remarkable that the hotels – most owned by large foreign chains – can maintain their high level of quality given the dirt-cheap price of their packages. A longstanding issue, though, is the omnipresent **buffet food**, which is often below par; at many resorts you'll have the option of going one or two nights a week to a better restaurant with individual entrees, and a few hotels also reserve a few spaces for room-only deals, which will allow you to spend your money at restaurants in town. Nevertheless, the idea of unlimited access to a resort's facilities at no additional cost is undeniably attractive, and it's possible to counteract the claustrophobia that often comes with several days spent on the grounds by taking an organized tour or a guagua ride into the beautiful countryside beyond.

Camping

There are no **campgrounds** in the Dominican Republic, and few travellers choose to camp here, because of the lack of regulation. If you're determined, your best bet is to ask permission first – from village residents if you're on the beach, from a farmer with a large property if you're in the mountains. Cabin camping is institutionalized, though, along the Pico Duarte trails (see p.258), and a couple of spots are traditionally camped rough by locals, including Parque La Confluencia in Jarabacoa (p.255) and Cayo Levantado on the Samaná Peninsula (p.165); if you do camp rough, make sure to clean up after yourself.

Eating and drinking

If you take all your meals at an all-inclusive hotel, you'll get little sense of how Dominicans eat and drink; the bland "international" buffet fare and watered-down daiquiris on offer at these resorts just can't compete with the delicious, no-nonsense, high-quality cooking at the many mom-and-pop restaurants, or the rum drinks on offer just outside the compound walls.

Dominicans call their cuisine *cómida criolla*, and it's a delicious – if often a bit greasy – blend of Spanish, African and Taino elements, with interesting regional variants across the island. Dishes usually include rice and beans – referred to locally as *la bandera dominicana* (the Dominican flag) – using either *habichuelas* (red beans) or the tiny black peas known as *morros*. Most often the rice is supplemented with chicken, either fried, grilled or served *asopao* (in a rich, soupy sauce). Invariably main courses come with *plátanos* (deep-fried green plantains), which locals often inundate with ketchup, and a small coleslaw salad.

> See p.373 of Contexts for a Spanish/English food and drink glossary.

Local **breakfasts** are traditionally starchy and huge, designed for people who are about to go work the calories off, and typically include *huevos revueltos* (scrambled eggs), sometimes *con jamón* (with bits of ham mixed in); *mangú*, mashed plantains mixed with oil and bits of fried onion; *queso frito*, a deep-fried cheese; *jugo de naranja* (orange juice; also called *jugo de china* in the southwest); and a strong cup of coffee, either *solo* or *con leche*, but always with a healthy dose of sugar.

Dominican **lunches** are quite hearty, and are generally consumed between noon and 2pm. But **dinner** is still the day's main meal, and is almost always a family affair. Aside from the omnipresent chicken, popular main courses include *mondongo*, a tripe stew strictly for the strong of stomach; *mofongo*, a tasty blend of plantains, pork rinds and garlic; and *bistec encebollado*, grilled steak

topped with onions and peppers. **Special occasions**, particularly in rural areas, call for either *chivo* (roast goat) with *cassava*, a crispy, flat bread inherited from the Tainos, made with ground yucca roots; or *sancocho*, considered the national delicacy, a hearty stew with five different kinds of meat, four types of tuber and a bewildering array of vegetables and spices. For the very best in Dominican eating, though, go for the **seafood**, which is traditionally prepared one of five ways: *criolla*, in a flavourful, slightly spicy tomato sauce; *al ajillo*, doused in a rich garlic sauce; *al horno*, roasted with lemon; *al orégano*, in a tangy sauce with fresh oregano and heavy cream; and *con coco*, in a tomato, garlic and coconut milk blend especially prevalent on the Samaná Peninsula. You'll find that the best local fish are the *mero* (sea bass), *chillo* (red snapper) and *carite* (kingfish). Other popular seafoods include *langosta* (clawless lobster), *lambí* (conch), *camarones* (shrimp), *pulpo* (octopus) and *cangrejo* (crab).

Dominican **desserts** are good but extremely sweet; the best of the many types are the *dulces con coco*, made with molasses and coconut shavings. Also popular are *dulces de leche*, usually a bit bland, and *dulces de naranja*, composed of a molasses-orange marmalade that can send you into instant sugar shock. You'll also find a wide variety of cakes, custards and flans on offer, including a distinctive corn custard, *flan de maiz*. A healthier and usually tastier option is to explore the tremendous variety of **tropical fruits**. *Guineos* (bananas), *lechoza* (papaya) and *piña* (pineapple) are the most popular, but you won't regret trying the local *limoncillos*, tiny, delicious lime-like fruits sold in bunches, and *chinola*,

Dominican passion fruit. The DR is especially known, though, for its **mangos**, which look like disfigured grapefruit but hold an out-of-this-world orange-coloured pulp; *fresas* (strawberries) are cultivated in the Constanza region and grow wild in the Sierra Bahoruco, and so are widely available.

Where to eat

Eating out can be extremely cheap in the Dominican Republic, provided you stick to the modest-looking local establishments, many of which serve outstanding food. In the more formal dining rooms, prices are higher but are usually still a bargain by European and North American standards. Either way, with the exception of the *cafeterías* (see below), you'll be charged an eight percent sales tax on your meal and a ten percent "service" charge, though these rarely find their way into the hands of either the government or the waiting staff; it's standard practice to **tip** an additional ten percent. Outside of the major cities **vegetarians** will often have to stick to rice and beans.

The cheapest places to dine are the **cafeterías**, humble establishments with a few tables and a glass case displaying a variety of typical foods like fried fish, chicken stew, rice and beans, *mangú* and *plátanos*. A meal here generally costs RD$15–20, but you're best off frequenting them only at lunch, when the food is fresh; by dinnertime the dishes may have been standing for hours under the heat lamps. Also under glass cases are the fried chicken dishes served at the many Dominican **pica pollos**, popular chain outlets with neon, fast-food decor. Far tastier and less aggressively lit are the **pollo al carbón shacks** that serve heaping portions of grilled chicken, rice and beans, and salad, always a good bet for a cheap meal. Only slightly more expensive, the many Dominican **comedores** are a great resource: unpretentious, family-run restaurants, generally little more than a hole in the wall but often dishing up incredible *cómida criolla*, which will run around RD$40 for a full meal. For a quick snack, check out the greasy goods of the various **street vendors** hawking *empanadas*, flat fried pastries with a ground beef filling; *chicarrones*, crunchy

bits of deep-fried chicken or pork; shredded barbecue pork sandwiches, boiled corn and split coconuts all for around RD$5–7, and peeled oranges for RD$2. From time to time you'll also see small children selling trays of home-made *dulces* for RD$1.

You'll find plenty of **high-end** dining in the major cities and the resort towns, generally featuring a bewildering array of authentic international cuisine including French, Italian, Chinese, Korean, Japanese, Indian and Basque. Count on spending around RD$250–400 at these, and don't expect to be seated if you're wearing shorts, a bikini top or a short skirt. Dress codes are far less formal in the **all-inclusive buffet halls**, but the food is a lot more bland. Even at the best of them, you should expect catering-tray "international" cuisine not much better than what you'd get at a wedding reception; the worst of them serve food that's barely edible and ice-cold.

Shopping for food

Most Dominicans do their shopping at the many small **colmados** that dot the country, little more than shacks packed with various basic food supplies, an ample selection of liquors and some fresh produce. The *colmados* generally extend a line of credit to their local customers, allowing them to purchase a single spoon of tomato paste, for example, for RD$1, which is added to the running tab. These small portions are necessary because most campesinos don't have refrigerators and so only purchase what they need for the day. In the cities and resort centres, you'll find more traditional **grocery stores**, laid out much as they are at home.

Drinking

Dominican **coffee** is among the best in the world. Grown in the heights of the Cordillera Central mountain range, it's a major export earner for the country, sold in the coffee bars and grocery stores of North America and Europe, often misleadingly labelled Costa Rican or Colombian because these nations are more closely associated in the public mind with high-quality coffee production. Most Dominicans take it *solo*, with a great deal of sugar added, which is the way it's sold for RD$1 by omnipresent morning street vendors, and handed out for free in the petrol stations. Dominican *café con leche* is made with steamed milk and is extremely good; the best place to get it is a *comedor*, where you'll pay RD$5–10.

Jugo de naranja, fresh orange juice squeezed as and when you order it, is another omnipresent Dominican morning drink, and makes for a good reason to get up; be sure to ask for it *sin azúcar* (without sugar). Later in the day you should sample the fresh **coconut milk** sold by street vendors and the many Dominican **batidas**, popular fruit shakes made with ice, milk and either papaya, mango, pineapple or banana – freshly made in a *comedor*, they bear no relation to the cartoned stuff bearing the same name. A similar drink that's traditionally served in Dominican homes is the **morir soñando**, a heavenly concoction of orange juice, condensed milk, sugar and crushed ice. Meanwhile, **Coca-Cola** and **Pepsi** have long been popular throughout the country. Once they were drunk as a matter of national pride, because the beverage companies used Dominican sugar to sweeten them. Today, the drinks are laced with American-made corn syrup, but you'll still find them almost everywhere.

There are several Dominican **beer** brands, but by far the best and most popular is **Presidente**, which is served in both normal-sized and surreally large bottles, and compares favourably with beers from across the world. Dominicans are obsessed with getting it as ice-cold as possible – if you don't want it to be a block of ice when you open it, do as they do and rub your hand under the bottom of the bottle before popping the cap. Also popular are the very good, inexpensive local **rums**, Brugal, Barceló and Bermúdez. Of these Bermúdez is the very best, but the dark, aged versions made by all three are quite good. A popular way to drink it is with Coke as a *Cuba libre*. In the discos and bars, ask for a **Cuba libre servi-**cio: a bottle of rum, two Cokes and a bucket of ice.

The Dominican Republic is not a place to drink **wine**: the local variation is less than spectacular and only the finest restaurants import it – and it's quite expensive. Watch out also for a potent local drink called **Mama Juana**, a hard-to-stomach concoction of local wines, rum, honey and leaves and bark from various trees, which locals claim prolongs both sexual potency and life span. After hearing them go on (and on) about its miraculous properties, you may want to try it at least once. Traditionally, it's supposed to be buried underground for at least three months, then laid out in the sun for another three before consumption. You'll find Mama Juana bottles in the souvenir shops that circumvent this extended process, with the appropriate leaves and bark already added, and a recipe for finishing the brew on the label.

Where to drink

The Dominican Republic has a variety of **places to drink**, from surly macho beer halls to elegant outdoor beach bars. In the resort towns, you'll notice a definite split between bars frequented by expats and locals; the former tend to have a broader selection of liquors, whereas the latter stick to the tried and true Presidente, rum and Mama Juana. The only bars you should think twice about visiting are the rowdy, hard-drinking local establishments, which are pretty easy to pick out as they're crammed to the gills with men only, pounding down gallons of booze and occasionally brawling. Most bars typically open around 2pm and don't close until the wee hours of the morning. As you'd expect, weekends are often busiest, Sundays especially, though Santo Domingo turns convention on its head by making Monday the traditional party night. Officially, the **drinking age** in the DR is 18, but anyone who has hit puberty is unlikely to be questioned.

Communications: mail, phones and media

It's easy to keep in touch with home by phone, fax or email while you're in the DR. Storefront phone centres are scattered about the country within almost every single village, though the price can be a bit steep, and internet cafés are a booming business in the major cities and resort areas, though you'll have a hard time finding a connection out in the campos. Mail is slower, less efficient and not guaranteed to arrive.

Phones and fax

The DR has several **private telephone companies**, all of which operate storefront phone centres in Dominican towns and villages, from where you'll be able to call home; branches are noted throughout the guide chapters. The oldest and most dependable is **Codetel**, which charges RD$5 per minute to North America; RD$20 per minute (Mon–Fri 8am–midnight, Sat 8am–6pm) or RD$15 per minute (Mon–Fri midnight–8am, Sat 6pm–Mon 8am) to Europe; and RD$26 per minute to Australia and New Zealand. Another option is to purchase a Codetel **calling card,** sold at Codetel phone centres and most bodegas in denominations of RD$25, 45, 95, 145, 245 and 500. The charge is 7 pesos per minute to North America, RD$15 per minute for Europe. These are especially handy when calling from a hotel room; most long-distance charges from your room are absolutely exorbitant (RD$16–35/minute to North America, twice that to Europe and triple that to Australasia), but if you use a Codetel card they'll simply charge you the price of a local call.

You also have the option of going to one of Codetel's competitors that have sprung up over the past decade, though they're not as omnipresent and the rates are similar. **Tricom**, **Televimenca** and **Turitel** all charge approximately RD$5 per minute to North America; to Europe, Australia and New Zealand either RD$14 or RD$19 (peak hours; see above). The various phone companies have been engaged in price wars of late, so these rates may change slightly over the life of this book. You can also avoid all of the phone companies and call home free via the internet with **Net2Phone** (🌐www.net2phone.com), though the sound quality is not very good and you'll need to bring a headset to plug into the PC. A third option is to **rent a cell phone**, though be warned that the reception is not very good, especially if you're travelling across the island. Codetel is the most reliable and has the best reception of the admittedly limited options. They offer a variety of cellular calling plans, which run around RD$200–300/month, plus RD$16/minute local and RD$22/minute to North America, RD$34 to Europe and RD$41 to Australia/NZ. Phone purchase costs an additional RD$900–1000, or you can either bring your own and have it transferred to Codetel service, or rent one for around RD$300 a month extra (some plans require that you pay for at least three months of service). If you're staying in the country for over a year, it might be worth checking out their long-term plan, which offers you free phone rental provided you pay for 18 months of service. Regardless, you'll need to put an RD$1500 deposit down with any phone rental.

Local calls cost RD$1 per minute, but it's important to note that a telephone call between towns in the DR is considered long-distance, and charged at the same rate as North American calls; all areas of the DR, however, are under one **area code**, ☎809. If at all possible avoid calling collect with any of the local phone companies, as it will set the receiving party back RD$30 per minute.

AT&T, MCI, Sprint, Canada Direct, BT and Cable & Wireless, amongst others, enable their customers to make **phone-card calls** while in the Dominican Republic, though the rates for this service are usually more expensive than using Codetel. If it's not listed below, call your company's customer service line before you leave to find out the toll-free access code in the DR. Calls made from overseas can automatically be billed to your home number.

Codetel offices also provide very useful **fax** facilities. The charge for receiving a fax is generally RD$15, while sending one costs RD$35 per page.

Dialling codes

To call the Dominican Republic from abroad, dial your international access code (see below) + 809 + seven-digit number.

UK ☎ 00
USA ☎ 011
Canada ☎ 011
Australia ☎ 0011
New Zealand ☎ 00

To call abroad from the Dominican Republic, dial 00 + country code (see below) + area code minus first 0 + number

UK ☎ 4
USA ☎ 1
Canada ☎ 1
Australia ☎ 61
New Zealand ☎ 64

Access numbers

North America

AT&T ☎ 1-800/872-2881
Canada Direct ☎ 1-800/333-0111
MCI ☎ 1-800/888-8000
Sprint ☎ 1-800/751-7877

UK

BT Charge Card ☎ 0800/345 144

Useful numbers

Directory enquiries ☎ 411
Emergency ☎ 911
Operator ☎ 0

The internet

As the **internet** connections at Codetel offices are most often slow and unreliable,

you're better off going to one of the hundreds of internet cafés that have sprung up in all of the resort areas and throughout the major cities. Rates vary from establishment to establishment, but are generally around RD$25–50/hr; make sure they have at least a DSL connection, and that they don't require a minimum of one hour's service. In addition, most of the all-inclusive hotels now offer free internet service to their guests, though you're usually limited to twenty minutes or so per visit due to high demand.

Bringing your own laptop, plugging it in and getting local internet service is really not worth it if you're just staying for a few weeks. It is a lengthy process that typically takes at least two weeks to start working, the prices are exorbitant and the speed is not especially good. Also, make sure you use a power strip when plugging your computer into the wall, or fluctuations in the local power supply may well fry your hard drive.

Mail

Dominican **correos**, or post offices, are notoriously slow; even if you use **special delivery** (highly recommended) you'll still have to allow at least three weeks for your postcard or letter to reach North America, and at least a month for it to reach Europe or Australasia. Postage costs RD$3 to North America, RD$4 elsewhere. You can cut these delivery times by as much as a week if you use the central *correos* in Santo Domingo, Puerto Plata or Santiago; these have specific special delivery windows; look for the "*entrega especial*" sign. Sending **packages** is unreliable (damage and theft are frequent) and not recommended unless absolutely necessary; if you must send parcels, bring them unsealed to the post office for inspection. Whatever you do, don't use the postal boxes that you'll see on the streets of many towns – you'll be lucky if the mail is picked up once a month – and don't ever send money or other valuables.

The most convenient way to **receive mail** is to have it sent to your hotel, though most post offices have a reasonably reliable *lista de correos*, where mail is held for you for up to four weeks, for a charge of RD$10 per letter. Bring your passport (or a photocopy) when picking up mail, and make sure that correspondents address letters to you under your name as it appears on your passport.

The media

Century-old *Listin Diario* is the most reputable of the Dominican daily **newspapers**, a broadsheet that has weathered a dozen different repressions of the free press over its history, and still produces the best investigative journalism in the country, along with excellent sports coverage and a decent international roundup. *El Siglo* is a more recent arrival and a bit more plebeian in its outlook, mixing equal opportunity haranguing of the three major political parties with good coverage of local music events and a heavy accent on violent crime. *Hoy* is less enlightening than the other two, with rather perfunctory political coverage, while *Ultima Hora* is the Dominican tabloid, mostly taken up with baseball coverage, Santo Domingo social events and salacious gossip. There's no current **English-language** Dominican paper in print, but you can find the *Miami Herald* at the airports and the *New York Times* in high-end hotel gift shops; the odd copy of *Time* and *Newsweek* is available in bookstores as well.

On **Dominican radio**, you'll find only one American and European pop station in most areas, surrounded by a dozen Latin stations and at least one with 24-hour Pentecostal programming. Flip around a bit and you're likely to come up with a station playing old-style *merengue périco ripao*. In the most rural mountain areas, however, you'll be lucky to tune in to even one station. If you're in the south of the country, flip to *Radio Millon* at 107.9, which features the very best of the golden age of Latin music, a real treat and a nice break from the omnipresent thud of merengue everywhere else. On the Haitian border you can get a Haitian radio station at 103.3 FM that features traditional jazz, bebop and old-style Haitian jazz bands from the 1930s, while around Santiago a good alternative is student radio 89.5, run by the Autonomous University and featuring a lot of African pop music and Latin jazz.

Dominicans have access to cable **television**, which sends out over eighty channels, half in Spanish and half English-language American fare with subtitles, including CNN, various sports channels, the American networks and a number of others that will be familiar to North Americans. Without cable you'll be stuck with at most six local stations; one or two will feature the dregs of American cinema past – some with subtitles, some dubbed – while the rest focus on merengue videos, Venezuelan and Mexican soap operas, local talk shows and baseball games.

Shopping

You'll probably be disappointed with the thin selection of local crafts on offer in the DR. Typical are the tacky "faceless dolls of Higuerito" sold in souvenir shops across the country, glazed clay statuettes of featureless, pale-skinned women in Victorian garb. Your best bet for an ostentatious piece of local folk craft is to buy one of the elaborate papier-mâché Carnival masks, though finding them can take some effort if you're not in Santo Domingo (where you can pick them up in Zona Colonial gift shops). Try in one of the major Carnival towns, preferably La Vega or Cabral, and ask around. They're easier to track down just before or after February; if you come during the festivities and see someone wearing a particularly interesting one, ask and they may well sell it to you at the month's end for around RD$300.

There are, however, other reasonable souvenirs, including wicker furniture and mahogany humidors, though the latter are produced from an endangered tree; here and there you'll also find decent reproductions of Taino statuettes. Much of the stuff on sale, though, is mass-produced tat, like the half-baked imitations of Haitian Naivist art that you'll find for sale along the streets of any town with tourism potential. If you're interested in taking home some **Haitian art**, you'll do far better by going to the reasonably priced Haitian craft galleries in Santo Domingo (see p.102) and Las Terrenas (see p.174).

Another good option is the stores that specialize in jewellery made with **larimar**, a turquoise, semi-precious stone found only in the DR, and **amber**, which is mined in the Cordillera Septentrional. You'll find outlets across the island, but if you go to the locations where these substances are mined, it's possible to get large chunks of the stuff for a few pesos; local miners sometimes even sell bits of amber with insects embedded inside them. Beware, though, that many souvenir stores try to rip off tourists with fake amber or larimar. The museums of larimar and amber in Santo Domingo (see p.102) as well as the amber museum in Puerto Plata (see p.197) will show you how to identify fakes. A good place to go for quality jewellery is **Harrisons**, a high-end Dominican jewellery store with outlets all over the country; you'll find an array of beautiful craftsmanship at these stores for half the price the same piece would cost at home. They're also working hard to preserve the nation's dwindling coral reefs by removing all of their black coral in favour of **black jade**, another indigenous, semi-precious stone.

The most popular souvenirs of all are the local **cigars**, considered by aficionados to be the equal of Cubans. They're easy enough to purchase at souvenir shops across the country, but for a freshly rolled packet that's boxed while you watch, you'll have to go to one of the major cigar towns that surround the city of Santiago (see p.240 for more on Dominican cigars). **Rum** is another major takeaway for visitors, as the local dark, aged rums are among the world's finest. You can find gift packages of Barceló and Brugal's very best *ron añejo* at stores across the country, and in Puerto Plata you can get a decent discount on Brugal's aged rums at their bottling factory tour (see p.199).

It is especially hard to find **books** in the Dominican Republic, and those that you can find are very expensive. The bookstores are generally small and not very good, and buying from Amazon and other online book retailers is difficult because of the poor state of the local postal system.

Sports and outdoor activities

The Dominican Republic's highly lucrative package tourism industry centres on its endless supply of idyllic, palm-fringed beaches and crystal-clear turquoise waters. Opportunities for watersports are naturally tremendous, ranging from swimming, snorkelling and scuba diving, windsurfing and surfing, to deep-sea fishing and whale watching.

Though many beaches are protected from powerful ocean currents by natural barriers, others have dangerous riptides along them, and should be avoided by all but the strongest swimmers (see p.219); meanwhile, the Caribbean waters right off Santo Domingo are shark-infested and should be eschewed by all. Inland, there are plenty of sports available on the island's many rivers and lakes, including white-water rafting, waterfall cascading and lake fishing. The country's five separate mountain ranges provide several options for mountain sports; most popular are mountain biking, horseback riding and several-day mountain treks. In the resorts you'll also find golf courses, tennis courts and, in La Romana's *Casa de Campo*, polo grounds.

Snorkelling and scuba diving

The vast majority of **Dominican reefs** have been damaged beyond repair by careless local fishing practices, notably the daily dropping of anchors by thousands of small vessels. The only place you'll still find a large system of intact reefs is the stretch west of Puerto Plata, between La Isabela and Monte Cristi. By no coincidence, this is also by far the most remote coastal region in the country, and devilishly difficult to access for **scuba diving and snorkelling**. There are, though, a couple of small outfits in La Isabela that can take you out to them (see p.225). A number of tour operators in the resort towns can take you to the more modest reefs around the island; you'll find a decent stretch at the far eastern tip of the Samaná Peninsula, along with a number of interesting **underwater caves**. A dive school called Dive Samaná, in Las Galeras, runs trips to both the reef and caves (p.166). Along the southern coast, the

best snorkelling can be found in the **Bahía de Neiba** just east of Barahona, where you can also sometimes find manatees; at **Isla Catalina**, a small, heavily visited island near La Romana where the fish have been known to eat out of snorkellers' hands; at **Isla Saona**, an enormous mangrove island with decent reefs, just east of Bayahibe; and at **Parque Nacional La Caleta** just east of Santo Domingo, where the National Parks Department sank a retired treasure-hunting ship called the *Hickory* in 1984, which has since been calcified with new reef that is feeding ground for an array of sea creatures. A number of private operators, and most all-inclusive hotels, offer trips to the reefs, wrecks and caves that dot the southeastern coast, along with diving instruction, mostly week-long PADI courses; certification courses and individual dives typically include the price of equipment rental in their rate. These are listed throughout the guide.

Windsurfing, kite-surfing and surfing

The north coast resort of Cabarete is known internationally as the **windsurfing** capital of the Americas and is the venue for the Cabarete Race Week and the Encuentra Classic, both major world competitions. If you don't have any windsurfing experience, learning here will be a challenge due to the strength of the waves and wind. Nevertheless, there are a dozen different windsurfing clubs that offer equipment rental and high-quality tutoring; early morning before the wind builds up is the best time for beginners. Much more appealing for beginners is the burgeoning sport of **kite-surfing**, which takes much less time to learn and is truly exhilarating – even beginners are often shot up in the air by their kites as they skate along the waves. See Cabarete (pp.211–212) for information on prices and operators. Once surfers have mastered Playa Cabarete's waters, many experts often try their hand at Playa Encuentra several kilometres west, where the waves are titanic and conditions are insanely difficult. Along the country's southern coast, scenic beach town Las Salinas has quietly become a centre for windsurfing as well, with milder conditions and a small windsurfing centre that's used mostly by wealthy Dominicans.

Surfing is less organized and done mostly by locals. Though you won't find any schools for surfing, popular venues include Playa Encuentra near Cabarete, Playas Grande and Preciosa just east of Río San Juan and Playa Boba north of Nagua. Be aware, though, that these are challenging spots for the sport, and most have no posted lifeguard; they should only be used by those with a good deal of experience.

Sailing, fishing and whale watching

The DR is a major port of call for Caribbean **sailors**, with especially good marinas in Luperón, Manzanillo and Samaná, where you'll come across a network of dozens of fellow independent sea travellers. Be warned, though, that the Puerto Turístico in Puerto Plata should be avoided at all costs, due to a high frequency of robberies and acts of sabotage. Nautical maps of the surrounding waters are hard to come by; your best bet is to pick one up at the marina in Luperón, though some of them will be a bit out of date. **Day sailors** will find tour operators and independent boats in Puerto Plata, Cabarete, Luperón and Bayahibe that regularly take small groups of passengers on sailing day-trips; prices can run anywhere between RD$300 and RD$800 for the day, depending on the operator.

Many of the all-inclusive resorts feature daily **deep-sea fishing** tours that run around RD$500 for the day – standard catches include sea bass, red snapper and kingfish – though you can get good game fish from tours along the southeast coast, including wahoo, porpoise and marlin. Along the northwest coast between Monte Cristi and Luperón, the remarkable reef makes for some tremendous fishing; expect to catch wahoo,

king mackerel and dorado year-round, with lots of tuna June through August, blue marlin May through September, white marlin August through October and sailfish November through April. Away from the hotels, you'll find good big-game fishing, especially for marlin, in southern coastal towns Boca de Yuma and Palmar de Ocóa. There's little in the way of tourist infrastructure in these towns, so ask around at the hotels for a good boat captain, and make sure he has a working radio and safety equipment. On the south coast, the best months for fishing are June through early September, and you should expect to catch blue and white marlin, dolphin and barracuda. In October through January you can still catch abundant sailfish and wahoo. The best **lake fishing** is near remote inland town Cotuí, where the Lago Hatillo, a pretty reservoir surrounded by rolling hills, holds large quantities of lake bass. The easiest way to fish here is to get a recommendation from the owner of local hotel *Rancho del Lago* (see p.268).

Every winter, over four thousand **humpback whales** from across the Atlantic come to the DR's Bahía de Samaná and Silver Banks Sanctuary to mate, give birth and nurse infants. High season is January and February, with some early arrivals in December and a number of hangers-on in March. Whale-watching boats set out from the city of Samaná every day in high season, and you'll also find three tour operators that feature week-long boat excursions to Silver Banks (see pp.160–161), during which you'll have the opportunity to swim with the whales.

River sports

Mountain resort Jarabacoa, deep in the heart of the Cordillera Central, is the centre for **white-water rafting and kayaking**. Several tour operators with experienced guides run daily trips down the turbulent Río Yaque del Norte. Expect a moderately challenging trip with several tricky twists and turns and a couple of steep drops. You can also spend as long as a week kayaking through the Cordillera Central rivers on excursions from operators Rancho Baiguate and Rafting Franz (see p.257). Jarabacoa, Cabarete and Las Terrenas also have terrific opportunities for **cascading** (descending a rock face on elastic cords) down various waterfalls as high as 75m, which when accompanied by experienced guides is far less dangerous than it sounds, but undeniably exhilarating.

Mountain sports

The DR has five separate mountain ranges, which afford almost infinite opportunities for **mountain biking**. Cabarete's Iguana Mama (see p.215) is the one major mountain-bike tour outfit in the country, offering challenging day-trips into the Cordillera Septentrional and week-long mountain-bike and camping excursions from one side of the country to the other. They're also the best place in the DR to go for **bike rental**, as they rent out several well-serviced Cannondales for US$20/day. You'll find **bike clubs** in Santo Domingo and Santiago that go on major mountain-bike excursions across the island on weekends. Be forewarned, though, that if you can't keep up with their pace, they'll have no qualms about leaving you behind; if you're interested, ask first at Iguana Mama for a personal reference.

The best **mountain hiking** can be found along the five separate trails that lead from disparate parts of the Cordillera Central to Pico Duarte, the highest peak in the Caribbean. Hikes range from three to six days in length; see p.258 for the details of each trail. The truly adventurous will instead want to take the rugged two-day trail from the Haitian border to Nalga del Maco, an enormous system of caverns that's the most revered religious site in the country for devotees of *Vodú* (see p.280). If you're not up for a multi-day excursion, try one of the several great day-trip mountain hiking trails near Puerto Plata, Monte Cristi, Jarabacoa and Constanza, each outlined in the appropriate section of the guide. **Horseback-riding** excursions are also quite popular. In addition to the plethora of outfits that offer day-rides along the country's many beaches, you'll find quality mountain riding operators in Cabarete, Punta Cana, Las Terrenas, Jarabacoa, San José de las Matas and Río San Juan.

Caving

Another tempting outdoor option available is **caving** in one of the many extensive systems throughout the island, many bearing extensive collections of Taino rock art. Among the easiest to see are the coastal caves in Parque Nacional Los Haitises, accessible by boat tour, but the most rewarding of all are the series of Taino caves in Parque Nacional del Este near Bayahibe, where Taino art references to Christopher Columbus and the early Spaniards have recently been discovered. Other prime places for exploration include caves near San Cristóbal, Monción, Cabarete, Las Galeras, Boca de Yuma, Loma de Cabrera, Bánica and Hato Mayor – all of them outlined in the guide. One company, Rancho Jonathan in Higuey (☎551-1015 or 0798), does organized caving excursions, but otherwise you'll have to hook up with a local guide and do them on your own; you'll therefore need to bring your own boots and flashlight.

Golf

Though there are several small, nondescript **golf courses** spread across the island, three of them stand head and shoulders above the pack: the Pete Dye-designed Teeth of the Dog course at *Casa de Campo* in La Romana, and the excellent Robert Trent Jones courses at Playa Dorada and Playa Grande on the Silver Coast. All three have the majority of their holes set on spectacular open oceanfront and are occasionally used as tournament venues. The Jones courses are reasonably priced, setting you back only RD$450 for greens fees, RD$300 for a golf cart and a tip of around RD$200 for a caddy. Teeth of the Dog, though, is far more expensive (and prefers payment in US dollars) at US$125 greens fees, US$20/cart and a standard US$20 caddy tip. You can get a substantially less expensive US$195 three-day greens fees deal if you stay at the *Casa de Campo* resort, but this requires you to spend at least one day on the hotel's second, less appealing course, which is called Links.

Spectator sports

Baseball is the national **spectator sport**; many of the top American major leaguers have come from the DR, including Alex Rodríguez, Sammy Sosa and Pedro Martínez (see p.357 in Contexts for a history of baseball in the DR). A professional winter season is held from mid-November through mid-

February, after which the winner goes on to compete in the Latin American Championship Series, which is sometimes held in the DR. The level of play in these games is quite high; teams include the hottest up-and-coming Dominican kids along with veteran Dominican major leaguers and promising North American prospects sent here by their organization. Cities that boast professional teams are Santo Domingo (which has two teams), Santiago, San Pedro de Macorís, La Romana and Puerto Plata. These teams are often coached by former stars like Tony Peña or Juan Marichal.

Tickets are available at all venues the night of the game (from both the box office and scalpers) for RD$40–150, depending on where you want to sit. Among the distractions in the stands, you'll find live merengue bands blaring music between innings, dancing-concession salespeople and old men in the back of the bleachers making bets on every movement going on in the field. In addition to this professional season, amateur winter seasons take place in San Francisco de Macorís, San Juan de la Maguana, San Cristóbal and a few other towns. In the summer you can alternately check out the workouts and intramural play in the many major league baseball camps, run by teams like the Los Angeles Dodgers, the San Francisco Giants, the Boston Red Sox and even Japan's Hiroshima Toyo Carp.

Surpassing baseball in history, if not popularity, **cockfighting** was brought over from Spain during the colonial era, and is still largely considered the national "sport". Fights are typically held in a two-tiered, circular venue called a **club gallístico**, and more informal events take place in backyards. Throughout the countryside you'll see fighting roosters being carried, groomed and cooed at by starry-eyed owners who see them as a potential meal ticket; gambling is central to the sport. Watching the two birds peck at each other for ten minutes (sometimes killing one another but more often inflicting little damage) is less exciting than observing the rabid crowd. **Fight preparations** are also fascinating: the owners glue translucent brown claws onto the feet, once made of turtle shell but now more often plastic, and then spew mouthfuls of water and oil over the feathers, making them more slippery and harder to claw through. The cocks are displayed to the crowd, bets are barked out in a flurry, the birds are let loose in the ring and the mayhem begins.

National parks and nature reserves

In the 1970s, in an attempt to forestall the complete devastation of Dominican forests and mangrove swamps, President Balaguer set aside ten percent of the Dominican Republic's land as protected parques nacionales (national parks) and reservas científicas (scientific reserves). Over the past twenty years, additional, smaller parks have been added to protect several lagoons and historic sites. The system has worked well, and despite occasional devastation from hurricanes and fires, the protected zones are for the most part ecologically intact.

Especially worth visiting are the craggy mountain pine forests of **Parques Nacionales Bermúdez** and **Ramírez**, which you can explore via the several-day hiking trails to the top of Pico Duarte; the extensive mangrove swamps and coastal Taino caves of **Parque Nacional Los Haitises**, accessible via daily boat tours; the humpback whale sanctuary at **Banco de Plata**, to which several tour operators run week-long cruises; the thousands of flamingos and other tropical birds, crocodiles and rhinoceros iguanas easily accessible at **Parque Nacional Isla Cabritos**; and the extensive system of Taino caves and ceremonial plazas hidden within the inhospitable scrub brush landscape of **Parque Nacional del Este**, which are well worth the effort it takes to get to them.

Park practicalities

Even though the protected lands were not designed specifically with **tourism** in mind, they do usually serve as prime targets for visitors, providing opportunities to visit a broad variety of ecosystems within a fairly small area. Still, facilities are scant, and good maps and guides to each park are somewhat thin on the ground – you can pick up whatever literature there is at any national park office, where you'll also pay a small **entrance fee**, typically something like RD$20–50. The various parks can also be quite difficult to explore on your own, and a **guide** is almost always necessary, if not a fully **organized tour**; check the descriptions and practicalities given throughout the guide for further details.

The proper **gear** is also necessary; we've tried to outline here and in the guide what you'll have to bring, but suffice to say shoes

with the proper traction are necessary for hikes, as is clothing that will keep you warm in the higher peaks. Bring a flashlight if you'll be descending into any **caves** within the parks (or elsewhere, for that matter), and binoculars may well be helpful for all the birdwatching you can do.

Mountain parks

For many visitors, the biggest surprises are the island's five separate mountain ranges, particularly the massive Cordillera Central, which runs through, appropriately, the centre of Hispaniola and which boasts the highest peaks in the Antilles. The majority of the mountain range is divided into **Parque Nacional Bermúdez** and **Parque Nacional Ramírez**. Temperatures get shockingly cold here, especially at night, so you should come prepared with winter clothing and a waterproof coat with a hood. The best way to explore the parks is to take one of the five hiking trails that lead from the mountain range's fringes to **Pico Duarte**, all of them challenging, multi-day treks that involve camping in

NATIONAL PARKS

Laguna Cabral	14
Laguna Estero Hondo	2
Lagunas Redondo y Limòn	9
Parque Nacional Bahoruco	15
Parque Nacional Bermúdez	6
Parque Nacional Cabo Francisco Viejo	4
Parque Nacional del Este	13
Parque Nacional Los Haitises	8
Parque Nacional Isla Cabritos	11
Parque Nacional Jaragua	16
Parque Nacional Monte Cristi	1
Parque Nacional Nalga de Maco	17
Parque Nacional Ramirez	7
Reserva El Pomier	12
Reserva Isabela de Torres	3
Reserva Valle Nuevo	10
La Vega Vieja	5

0   40 km

cabins set up along the trails. South of the national parks in the Cordillera Central is **Reserva Científica Valle Nuevo**, a strip of territory between mountain towns Constanza and San José de Ocóa that you can traverse via an extremely bad but scenic road. It was set up to protect the source of the Nizao and Yuna rivers, which provide much of the hydro-electricity that powers the country.

Far less visited is **Parque Nacional Bahoruco** in the nation's southwest, partially because there are few tourist facilities (though a viewing platform called *Hoyo de Pelempito* has just been constructed for tourists to admire the sky-high views) and it's necessary to have a 4WD to explore most of the crystallized limestone peaks. Even more remote is **Parque Nacional Nalga de Maco** – which protects a section of the Cordillera Central along the Haitian border, and holds a huge series of caves with Taino rock art.

The most easily accessible of the mountain parks is **Reserva Científica Isabela de Torres**, which can be done as a day-trip from Puerto Plata. It encompasses the whole of Mount Isabela de Torres, a flat-topped Cordillera Septentrional mountain that's in the slow process of splitting in two. An excellent hiking trail leads from its southern base to the top, and there's also a **cable car** that – when it's not down for repairs – runs to the peak from Puerto Plata.

Mangrove parks

Another of the invaluable natural resources protected by the Dominican government is the many stretches of **mangrove coastline**, which is one of the world's most delicate and diverse ecosystems, providing a habitat for innumerable underwater species, insects and birds. **Parque Nacional Los Haitises** in the DR's southeast protects 1200 square kilometres of territory, including the country's largest swath of mangrove coast. The park's porous limestone bedrock has hollowed out into hundreds of cave systems, including a number along the Bahía de Samaná that bear evidence of Taino habitation. A series of coastal stops on the **Ruta Litoral** is the only part of the park that you're authorized to visit.

Further east along the north coast is the smaller **Laguna Gri-Gri** in Río San Juan, which doesn't have national park status but is pro-

tected as a government bird sanctuary. This is an extremely dense mangrove swamp with an estuary that's traversed by hourly boat tours; it's thus far easier to visit than Los Haitises.

All the way west along the north coast, **Parque Nacional Monte Cristi** protects another major mangrove ecosystem, this one just off the Haitian border. This park encompasses the many coastal lagoons along the Bahía de Manzanillo; seven desert islands, called Los Siete Hermanos, that are used by endangered sea turtles to lay their eggs; and an enormous desert mesa.

More mangrove terrain can be found on **Isla Saona**, a large island off the DR's southeastern coast which is part of **Parque Nacional del Este**, most of which is a mix of dry forest and desert. Within the park are a number of **cave systems** that hold varying degrees of Taino art.

Desert parks

Two large national parks are composed almost entirely of desert terrain. The largest, **Parque Nacional Jaragua,** encompasses a flint-shaped peninsula in the DR's southwest, and is a critical haven for the fast-dwindling population of migrating songbirds. The mass of it is inaccessible, but at its eastern end you'll find the park office and **Laguna Oviedo**, an enormous lake that's home to hundreds of tropical birds. At the western end, a paved road provides access, ending at a stunning stretch of beach called **Bahía de las Aguilas**. Just off the peninsula's coast are two large islands off limits to visitation.

Easier to visit is **Parque Nacional Isla Cabritos**, due north of Jaragua in the Neiba valley at the lowest altitude in the Caribbean, 40m below sea level. The island referred to in the name is at the centre of **Lago Enriquillo**, an enormous saltwater lake that was once connected to the Bay of Port-au-Prince.

Protected lagoons

In addition to Lago Enriquillo, government protection is extended to several other, smaller Dominican lagoons, all of which offer great birdwatching. The best is **Laguna Rincón** (also called Laguna Cabral), a remarkably peaceful, scenic place, and the largest of the freshwater lagoons. If you're in the southeast, it's more convenient to head to the twin **Lagunas Redondo** and **Limón**, which are just south of fishing village Miches.

Two more, newly protected lagoons lie on the DR's north coast. The **Laguna Cabarete** is surprisingly undeveloped considering its location, abutting resort town Cabarete to the south. Further west along the coast, **Laguna Estero Hondo** has predictably spectacular birdlife as well, and is also home to a number of manatees. One tour operator in the nearby town El Castillo runs manatee-watching boats to the lagoon but requires at least a day's advance notice.

Protected beachfront

Much of the DR's beachfront is becoming increasingly crowded with large, all-inclusive hotels and, in this race for the tourist dollar, not much protection is being offered to the undeveloped stretches that remain. Only one is

specifically set aside by the government, **Parque Nacional Cabo Francisco Viejo** near the town of Cabrera in the northeast of the island, which protects a rocky section of coast backed by rugged bluffs, and a large cape that holds a nineteenth-century lighthouse.

Underwater parks

The **Reserva Científica Banco de Plata**, several kilometres north of the Samaná Peninsula, protects a critical breeding ground of the four thousand humpback whales that make their way to the DR every winter. You won't be able to take a day-trip here, but it can be visited in one of the week-long whale-watching cruises run by a few tour operators (see p.161). Scuba divers will find more of interest at **Parque Nacional La Caleta** just east of Santo Domingo, where three separate shipwrecks (placed there on purpose) serve as artificial reefs.

Festivals

The Dominican Republic has a bewildering barrage of festivals. On every day of the year, there seems to be some kind of celebration somewhere. Even the Haitians, hardly known for their dearth of public holidays, bemoaned the constant cessation of labour due to various fiestas during their occupation and tried to legislate against them. The majority are the regional fiestas patronales, held in honour of the city or town's patron saint, who is often syncretized to an African god.

These traditional fiestas are one of the great pleasures of a trip to the DR; there's at least one in every city, pueblo and campo. The date is dictated by the saint's day as stated in the **Bristol Almanac** (published by pharmaceutical giant Bristol-Myers-Squibb), considered the authoritative source for such matters throughout Latin America. In addition to the actual saint's day, there will often be a nine-night celebration, called a **novena**, leading up to it.

The format of the fiesta follows one of two models. In the more remote parts of the country, the fiestas patronales have retained their original character, and are syncretic reli-

gious ceremonies that feature large **processions** carrying an icon of the saint, religious folk songs accompanied by enormous **palos drums** fashioned from tree trunks, Haitian **gagá** music employing long wooden tubes and keyless metal trumpets that are both blown through and rattled with a stick, and **spirit possession**. Many others in the major towns and tourist areas have shed this religious affiliation, and are today merely flavourful outdoor parties with a lot of drinking and a few traditional **contests** like a race to climb up a greased pole. An intermediate version are the many **cattle festivals** of the southeast, where processions of cattle and

January 1

Santo Cristo de Bayaguana

A festival that has been extant since 1605, featuring a major procession of local bulls to the church in Bayaguana, where some are given to a local priest as a sign of devotion and thanksgiving. A major feast takes place in the evening.

Guloya Festival

The famous mummers of San Pedro de Macorís run a morning procession through the streets of San Pedro's Miramar barrio. A great opportunity to see this unique sub-culture's music, costumes and mini dance dramas.

January 5-6

Three Kings' Day

The major gift-giving day of the Dominican year. In San Pedro de Macorís, hundreds of children crowd around the mansions of the baseball legends who live there, waiting to receive free baseball bats and gloves.

January 21

Virgen de Altagracia

By far the most important religious day on the Dominican calendar, a prayer-of-intercession day to the country's patron. The rural celebrations, in places like Higuey, tend to be the most authentic. *Vodú* celebrations are also held in many campos, including at the Coral de los Indios north of San Juan de la Maguana.

January 26

Duarte Day

Holiday in honour of the Father of the Country, with public fiestas in all major towns, biggest in Santiago and La Vega.

February

Carnival

The pre-eminent celebration of the year, held on every Sunday in February and culminating on February 27. La Vega and Santo Domingo are your best bets. In Monte Cristi the festivities can get more violent, while San Cristóbal holds a populist festival with a definite political edge. See the appropriate sections of the guide for more details.

February 2

Virgen de Candelaria

A religious procession in the capital's barrio San Carlos, in honour of this aspect of the Virgin, who is locally considered the wife of patron San Carlos.

February 14

Valentine's Day

Has become a major Dominican holiday, especially in Santiago. Even the neon *pica pollos* feature live music.

February 16

San Elias

Annual celebration of vodú's Baron of the Cemetery, which takes place in cemeteries across the country. Ironically a celebration of life, with the Baron's "gedes" – unruly spirits known for their bawdy, X-rated humour – possessing celebrants and engaging in constant off-colour hijinks.

February 27

Independence Day

Celebration of independence from Haiti and the culmination of the Dominican Carnival. Battle re-enactments in Santo Domingo, and major parties in other big Carnival towns.

March 19

19 de Marzo

The major fiesta in Azua, in honour of the battle in which the Haitians were defeated here, ensuring Dominican independence.

continued overleaf

March 21
Julito Paniagua
Check this one out if you're in or around Santo Domingo on this day. In the northern suburb of Villa Altagracia, a huge festival featuring music, rituals and food in honor of the anniversary of the death of a famous faith healer who was based at the local Iglesia de las Maravillas.

One week before Semana Santa
Virgen la Dolorita
This saint, syncretized to the Rada spirit Suli Danto, is celebrated on the second Thursday before Easter throughout the campos and in Los Merenos, a small Santo Domingo barrio next to Villa Mella.

Variable, usually early to mid-April
Semana Santa
The Christian Holy Week is also the most important week of Haitian and Dominican *Vodú*. Traditional *gagá* festivals take place in the Haitian *bateyes* and in Haina. Meanwhile, the town of Cabral holds its famous Carnival Cimarrón, in which townspeople adorned with demon masks descend on the city from the lagoon and castigate passers-by with whips.

May 2–3
Santa Cruz
A huge nine-night celebration in El Seibo, with a cattle procession to the sixteenth-century church on the final day, and a very different spring festival in Azua and Baní, where all of the crosses in the area are covered with bright-coloured paper and fiestas carry on throughout the month.

May 3
San Felipe
A huge cultural celebration on Puerto Plata's Malecón, with lots of live music.

Seven weeks after Semana Santa
Espiritu Santo
In honour of the Holy Spirit, syncretized to the Congo region's supreme deity Kalunda. Huge celebrations in the capital's barrio Villa Mella, pueblo Santa María near San Cristóbal, and San Juan de la Maguana.

May 22
Oliborio Mateo
Anniversary of the death of populist faith healer Liborio – at the hands of the occupying American military – is a major festival in his hometown Maguana Arriba, north of San Juan de la Maguana.

May 30
Fernando Rey
Monte Cristi festival in honour of the sixteenth-century Spanish king, celebrated since early colonial times.

June 4
Lupina Cordero
Large festival in Sabana de la Mar in honour of a local faith healer who defied Trujillo.

June 13
San Antonio
This god is linked with Legba, gatekeeper of the spirit world, with major religious festivals in pueblo Guerra east of the capital, Bonao, Haina, Nigua, Miches, Monción and Monte Plata, and a great (if less traditional) party in Sosúa.

June 17–24
San Juan Bautista
A religious festival in San Juan de la Maguana in honour of John the Baptist and his African counterpart Chango, plus a smaller fiesta in Baní, run by a religious brotherhood that dates from the Haitian occupation and performs a distinctive style of music called *sarandunga*.

June 29
San Pedro Apostol
A magnificent Cocolo festival in San Pedro de Macorís, with roving bands of *guloyas* performing dance dramas on the street.

Last two weeks in July
Merengue Festival
An outdoor music festival on the Malecón and at Plaza España in Santo Domingo, with virtually every famous merengue act from the last forty years performing somewhere.

July 24–26
Santiago Apostol
Celebrating Santiago, the warrior patron saint of the Christian armies that conquered Moorish Spain, and appropriated as a symbol of resistance for the *cimmarones*. A large civic festival in Santiago, and a more traditional religious celebration in pueblo Paya, near Baní and at Santa María near the El Pomier caves.

August 1–7
San José
Colourful local festivals in San José de las Matas, when hundreds of townsfolk return from the States for a week-long celebration, highlighted by a candlelit, horseback procession through the centre of the city.

August 14
Festival of the Bulls
Higuey's fiesta patronal, featuring cowboys on horseback, large herds of cattle, and women carrying an icon of the Virgin on their shoulders and singing traditional *rosarios*.

August 16
Restoration Day
Nationwide celebration of independence from Spain, with large parties in Santiago around the Monument and around Plaza España in Santo Domingo.

Every Friday late August to end October
Harvest festivals
African-American Protestant festivals held in a different church on the Samaná Peninsula each week, the biggest in Samaná's La Churcha at the end of October.

August 30
Santa Rosa
Secularized fiesta patronal in La Romana.

September 24
Virgin de las Mercedes
A traditional fiesta patronal in the small Santo Domingo barrio Mata Los Indios, beginning mid-month. Other good spots are Hato Mayor, San Juan de la Maguana and Cueva de Mana, a cave system north of Baní. Everywhere else, Dominicans take advantage of the day off for a long weekend by the beach, so reserve your hotel ahead of time on these dates.

September 29
San Miguel
After the Virgin of Altagracia, San Miguel is the most important Dominican saint, aligned with *Vodú* spirit Belié Belcán, chief of the Rada division of gods, a force for justice and peace, and protector of the Dominican people. Major festivals take place in the capital's Villa Mella and barrio San Miguel, Haina and across the country. Look for the green-and-white frosted cakes consumed by Dominican families on this day, colours associated with Belié Belcán.

October 3
San Francisco
Celebrated mainly in Bánica, where the ceremony is followed by a long procession to the cave where townsfolk believe St Francis of Assisi was born. Also celebrated at Santa María north of San Cristóbal.

continued overleaf

October 14–15
Santa Teresa de Avila

The patron saint of Elias Piña, where you'll see a wonderful syncretic celebration using *palos* drums, *rosario* processions and *gagá*, plus a less traditional merengue party around the parque central.

Third week of October
Merengue Festival

A major music festival in Puerto Plata, with major acts playing all over town; lots of partying on the Malecón. Date varies slightly from year to year.

October 24
San Rafael

An important Dominican saint who's syncretized in Boca Chica with the *Vodú* spirit Damballah. In Samaná you'll see a procession through the town, partying on the Malecón and a traditional Dominican dance called the *bambulá*, which has died out in the rest of the country.

November 1
Todo los Santos

A major *Vodú* festival in the San Juan de la Maguana and southern border region, especially in nearby pueblo Maguana Arriba, where locals proceed to the cemetery to ask for the release of their relatives for the day.

November 4
San Carlos

Syncretized to Rada deity Candelo Sedifé, and honoured with a procession and more secular fiesta in Santo Domingo's barrio San Carlos, and an important *Vodú* procession in Nigua, featuring *palos* drums, *gagá*, traditional songs and spiritual possession.

November 13
Santa Lucía

A major fiesta patronal with religious overtones in Las Matas de Farfán.

November 21
Virgen de Regla

A Cuban *santería* deity adopted as the patron of Baní, honoured with a *novena* culminating in a procession to the church and a citywide party.

November 30
San Andrés

Fiesta patronal of Boca Chica, mostly a block party, but with great *gagá* music.

December 4
Santa Bárbara

Fiesta patronal for the city of Samaná, including a procession that features the music of Doña Bertilia, Queen of the *Bamboulá*, which is a major popular music on the peninsula.

December 25
Christmas

Guloya festivals in San Pedro de Macorís, Haitian Voodoo celebrations in the Haitian *bateyes*, a candlelit procession in San José de las Matas and rural groups of Caribbean-style *Navidad* carollers in the campos.

December 28
Festival of the Bulls

Traditional cattle festival in Bayaguana, featuring unique traditional "cattle songs" that are sung to the bulls in order to bless them and prepare them for the January 1 procession to the local church.

---

cowboys descend on the city from all sides. Regardless, they're invariably lively, and will certainly be one of the highlights of your trip. In the big city festivals, though, **women travellers** should be prepared to deal with unwanted sexual advances, and everyone should take precautions against pickpockets. At the most remote religious festivals like the ones held in San Juan de la Maguana or in the Haitian bateyes, you should also keep in mind that very few tourists make it out this far – and thus you may well be accosted by inebriated participants looking to impress their friends.

The list in the box on pp.49–52 doesn't even come close to being a comprehensive listing of Dominican **fiestas patronales and** **holidays**; even scholars of Dominican folk religion haven't been able to compile one of these. This list, though, covers the very best of the Dominican fiestas, and you'll undoubtedly be in the country for at least one.

Safety, drugs and the police

It's not unknown for all-inclusive tour reps to exaggerate the danger level in the DR, in the hope that you'll buy one of their tours instead of exploring on your own. In fact, aside from the poorest neighbourhoods in Santo Domingo and Santiago, the Dominican Republic is a very safe place: violent crime is rare and you'll feel relatively comfortable wandering through the rural parts of the country, where people are disarmingly open and honest – though women travelling solo need to stay on their guard even here. In cities, you should take the same precautions that you would anywhere else: don't flaunt your wealth with fat rolls of pesos, leave your expensive jewellery at home and avoid walking alone late at night. A more likely scenario is that you'll be the target of a small-time rip-off, but even these can usually be avoided by not changing money on the street and by following the hints regarding guaguas given on p.30.

If you take these few common-sense warnings to heart, you should get through your trip unscathed. It's best to keep a copy of your passport, air ticket and all travellers' cheques at home, and another at your hotel. You will, though, need your tourist card and a photo ID at all times; a photocopy of your passport is acceptable. A couple of additional precautions will keep your belongings more safe: if your room has a lock box, use it, and take a room on an upper floor if you can. Also keep an eye on your things while you're on the beach, and on your luggage at the airport. It's important to have a lock on your bags; if not, look out for the vendors that shrink-wrap luggage at the airports for RD$40.

Drugs

The DR has increasingly become a transshipment point for Colombian **cocaine**, which is usually flown into Haiti, driven across the border in trucks and flown from small rural airstrips to the United States. As a result, cocaine can be found in relative abundance – along with ecstasy and marijuana – at many of the high-end nightclubs and outdoor rave parties frequented by wealthy young locals. Keep in mind, though, that the penalties for drug use and possession are extraordinarily stiff, and Dominican prisons are notorious, consisting of communal cells with a hole in the centre for a toilet; even worse, prisoners aren't fed while waiting for trial, so you'll have to either pay a cop to buy you food or have someone else bring you food every day if you don't want to starve. Drug possession is the one crime you won't be able to bribe your way out of; whatever you do, don't carry it with you into the country.

Prostitution

The **sex industry** is big business in the DR, and for some visitors the sole reason for coming here. There are streetwalkers in

53

specific red-light districts of major cities, along with brothels and a burgeoning trade in the discos of some resort towns. Within the all-inclusives, a growing phenomenon is *sanky panky*, in which underpaid staff members befriend hotel guests for money or gifts. Child prostitution exists as well, though the police are cracking down on it with hard jail time for offenders, and word is slowly getting out that the chance of HIV transmission is tripled when engaging in this activity. HIV is epidemic among sex-industry workers in the DR, though an education campaign has convinced most of them to use condoms.

The police

Corruption is rife throughout the **police force**; many officers do little besides collecting small bribes. Anti-graft campaigns by the past two presidents have yet to make much of a dent in this endemic practice. Nevertheless, you shouldn't give an officer a bribe unless he first asks, albeit rather obliquely; if he does ask, you're probably best off complying, provided he doesn't ask for more than RD$20 or RD$30. To avoid constantly handing out cash, do as the Dominicans do – if you see a police officer at the side of the road waving for you to stop, drive past without slowing down.

The good news for you is that police are routinely instructed not to ask bribes of foreigners, and their only other focus is **crime against tourists**, which they are adamant about quashing; dial ☎911 in case of an emergency. If you report an attack or theft, you can expect dozens of officers and/or soldiers to cordon off a large swath of territory around the place where you were accosted, and line up dozens of likely suspects for you to identify. Beware, though, that they're not always that interested in catching the true perpetrator; as long as some unfortunate is rounded up and made responsible, they're generally happy.

Women travellers

Though violent attacks against female tourists are rare, many women find that the constant barrage of hisses, hoots and comments comes close to spoiling their vacation. Dominican men are quite aggressive, and women travellers should come armed with the knowledge that they will draw incessant attention whether they like it or not. Also, at major festivals and on crowded streets, you may be subjected to a lot of groping hands.

Whatever you do, don't be afraid to seem rude; even the mildest polite response will be considered an indication of serious interest. If someone is unwantedly following you around the street trying to get your attention, the best thing to do is shoo them off disdainfully without even bothering to look at them. Know also that Dominican men often claim that Dominican women "never say yes"; this attitude means that your "no's" to amorous propositions won't be taken at face value. These local sexual mores are all the more aggravated because many poor Dominicans see Western women as a potential ticket out of the country.

Constant attention makes independent travelling a bit less easy-going for women, but many are able to enjoy it regardless. Chances of trouble depend to an extent on where you are. Avoid walking alone on city streets late at night and you'll circumvent much of the risk; it's also a good idea to opt for private taxis over the unregulated motoconchos and guaguas after dark. The stereotype of utopian rural areas where violent crime is unheard of usually holds true, but only to a point; even in the campos, you should trust your instincts and, when in doubt, err on the side of caution.

Directory

DISABLED TRAVELLERS There are unfortunately few facilities that make independent travelling easier for the disabled in the DR, and no rental cars come with hand controls, though certain major monuments do have access ramps. Most of the all-inclusives, though, have wheelchair access to certain rooms and all of their restaurants, casinos, bars and beaches. Call the hotel directly before booking a package and insist on specific details regarding the hotel's infrastructure.

DRESS Dominican society is fairly formal, and a lot of emphasis is placed on personal appearance, with women wearing long skirts and men trousers and shirtsleeves even in August. If you're on the street wearing shorts during the day, you'll simply be regarded as a typical tourist (to which no stigma is attached) but those who are scruffy, unshaven or dressed like backpackers will be looked down upon. To visit many of the sights in Santo Domingo – for example, the Cathedral and the Altar de la Patria – men will have to wear trousers and women long skirts (below the knee); bring along at least one or two such items.

ELECTRICITY The DR's electrical supply, like that in the US and Canada, uses 110 volts AC. Plugs are standard American two-pins, so European visitors should bring suitable adaptors. Intermittent, chronic power outages throughout the country mean that you should make sure your hotel has a generator that they're willing to use 24 hours a day.

GAY AND LESBIAN TRAVELLERS Many resort towns like Boca Chica, Sosúa, Cabarete and Las Terrenas have a small but fairly open gay and lesbian component but, although homosexuality is not technically illegal here, the only part of the country that has a gay club scene is Santo Domingo (see p.97); police raids close even these down from time to time, generally on some cooked-up pretext. Gays and lesbians in the DR are subject to harassment, and bashings have been known to occur as well, so you should be careful as you enter and leave gay nightclubs. Lesbian women dancing together outside the resorts can also expect to be constantly cut in on by Dominican men. A good way to avoid all of this hassle is to book a gay- and lesbian-oriented tour with Amigos Tours (US only ☎1-800/673-5777, ⓦwww.amigostours.com), an excellent company that runs a wide range of trips to the DR (US$500–1500 depending on the tour, airfare not included), using relatively inexpensive, gay-friendly hotels. We've also tried to indicate especially gay-friendly hotels throughout the guide.

LAUNDRY There are laundromats in the major cities of the Dominican Republic, and most hotels will do laundry for you if you wish, though the price for this service has risen dramatically in recent years. These days, you will typically have to pay per item, with the following prices a rough guide to what you should expect: pants RD$10, men's shirt RD$5, blouses RD$8, underwear RD$3, socks RD$5.

SENIOR TRAVELLERS The all-inclusives – particularly *Casa de Campo* – are popular destinations for senior travellers. For discounts on accommodation and vehicle rental, US residents aged 50 or over should consider joining the American Association of Retired Persons, 601 E St NW, Washington DC 20049 (☏202/434-2277 or 1-800/424-3410).

TIME The Dominican Republic is in North America's Eastern Standard Time Zone (same time as New York and Atlanta) and 5hr behind GMT.

TIPPING Most restaurants add a ten percent service charge onto their bills, but this is rarely given to the waiting staff. It's customary to give service staff an additional ten percent.

TOILETS You'll notice a definite lack of public toilets in the DR, and the ones in modest restaurants and petrol stations are often without seats. With the exception of the all-inclusive hotels, you should not put toilet paper down the toilet. The sewage system is not equipped to deal with the paper, and you'll only create a blockage. There's always a receptacle provided for the paper beside the toilet.

TRAVELLING WITH CHILDREN Most families stick to the all-inclusive resorts, which generally have good childcare facilities and plenty of diversions for kids. Regardless, make sure that your children use a heavy sun block (at least SPF25) and brush their teeth with bottled water. Officially, children who are accompanied by only one of their parents may remain in the country for no

more than thirty days. Children travelling without parents must have a notarized permit from their home country's Dominican consulate.

WEDDINGS AND DIVORCES Michael Jackson and Lisa Marie Presley are the most prominent couple to have wed in the DR, and while theirs may not have been the archetype of a successful marriage, a number of visitors do follow in their footsteps. First step is to telephone your nation's consulate in Santo Domingo for an official letter of permission, then go to the Dominican consulate in your country with your letter of permission, passports, birth certificates and documentation of any divorce judgements; they'll give you another letter of permission and set a date and location for a civil ceremony. Shortly after their wedding, Michael and Lisa Marie also took advantage of the DR's fast-track divorces; if you contact a Dominican lawyer ahead of time, you can be in and out of the country in 48 hours. Only one spouse has to be present, provided the other engages a lawyer in the DR and fills out a "Defendant's Special Power of Attorney" document, signs it and has it certified by a notary public. An important word of warning, though: don't believe any lawyer who tells you that neither spouse need be present for the divorce to be finalized; you'll still be legally married unless one of you is there. For a reliable Dominican lawyer and a list of necessary documents, call your consulate in Santo Domingo (see p.19).

Guide

Guide

Santo Domingo
and around

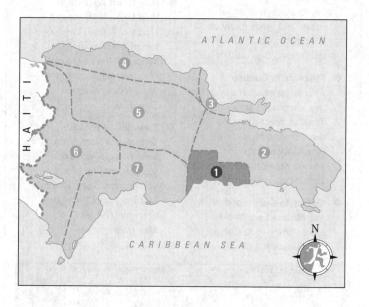

CHAPTER 1 # Highlights

✳ **The Zona Colonial** Pick through the sixteenth-century ruins of the first European city in the Americas, founded and ruled by the Columbus family. See p.71

✳ **The Malecón** Dubbed "The World's Largest Disco" by the *Guinness Book of World Records*, this seaside promenade stretches on and on for miles, and holds many of the city's major discotheques. See p.82

✳ **Plaza de la Cultura** Four large museums and the sumptuous National Theatre. Most memorable are the Museo de Arte Moderno and the Museo del Hombre Dominicano. See p.85

✳ **Old-style Cuban son at the Mauna Loa** Weekly Buena Vista-style Cuban *son* shows in a plush Santo Domingo ballroom torn straight out of the Roaring Twenties. See p.96

✳ **La Guácara Taina** Unique disco set in a massive five-storey cave, with the top names in merengue and *bachata* appearing nightly. See p.96

✳ **Holy Spirit Festival in Villa Mella** Nine straight nights of African Voodoo-based palos music in honour of the Holy Spirit, who is syncretized to the African deity Kalunda. See p.90

✳ **Baseball at Estadio Quisqueya** Dominican winter-league games in the country that brought you Sammy Sosa, Pedro Martínez, Alex Rodríguez and many others. See p.98

Santo Domingo and around

From every approach into the Dominican Republic's bustling capital, **Santo Domingo** gives a bad first impression. Traffic belches fitfully through its streets (which seem eternally under construction), the air pollution is epic, and the monotonous vista of concrete-box construction is alleviated only by the neon signs of strip malls and auto repair shops. Equally jarring is the uneven distribution of wealth in a city of 2.5 million that's dominated by ramshackle slums but has the highest per capita of Mercedes-Benz owners in the hemisphere.

The city certainly isn't the tropical paradise most travellers come to the Caribbean in search of, but once you penetrate the outer sprawl you'll find the old Spanish colonial capital – the first European city of the New World – magically intact along the western bank of the Río Ozama. This was the domain

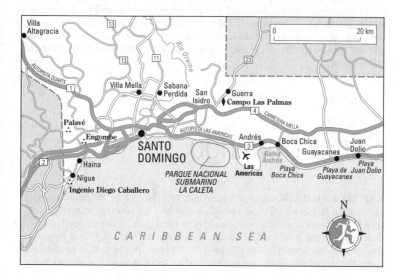

of **Christopher Columbus**: founded by his brother Bartolomé, ruled by him for a time and claimed a decade later by his son Diego. After five centuries, the Columbus palace can still be found alongside the cobblestone streets and monumental architecture of the walled, limestone city the family built, where decisions were made that had major repercussions for the rest of the hemisphere, for better or worse.

Indeed, an extraordinary number of **New World firsts** took place here, including the building of the first cathedral, university, monastery, nunnery and hospital – all a result of the **Catholic Church** sending missionaries to proselytize the natives, and all on display, in various forms of decay, in the Zona Colonial, Santo Domingo's historic district. From the Fortaleza Ozama, one of the structures that remains in that district, **conquistadors** set off to conquer the rest of the Caribbean and the American mainland, ensuring European domination over the hemisphere and the city's continued influence as a power base. Santo Domingo was also where the **Atlantic slave trade** was inaugurated – its newly constructed sugar mills needing forced labour to work the fields, and where Old and New World **diseases** initially exchanged hands, Columbus's men swapping smallpox and tuberculosis for yellow fever and syphilis.

Far more than just history makes Santo Domingo an integral part of any trip to the Dominican Republic; it is, after all, the modern face of the country, and as such has a non-stop liveliness not seen in many other places. Its Latin music scene is the most vibrant in the nation, its baseball stadium jam-packed with fanatics, and it also serves as the main repository of high culture, seen in its number of both small and large museums and venues for more upper-class artistic endeavours, from ballet to opera.

The vitality extends, though in a slightly more disappointing manner, to the very reachable beaches east of the city, at **Boca Chica** and **Juan Dolio**, both fairly built-up with resorts to accommodate visitor traffic; Juan Dolio is by far the better choice of the two, as Boca Chica has become tremendously overdeveloped and unpleasant in recent years. Also in that direction is the Dominican training camp of the Los Angeles Dodgers, **Campo Las Palmas**. Back west, before hitting industrial cities like San Cristóbal and Baní (covered in Chapter Seven, "Barahona and the southwest"), you can scavenge around the ruins at several sugar mills, such as **Palavé manor** and **Engombe**, for another look into the area's past, a perfect complement to Santo Domingo's colonial core.

Santo Domingo

SANTO DOMINGO makes for an understandable start to exploring the Dominican Republic. It's close enough to the beaches and rugged rural countryside, yet dynamic enough that you may not feel such an urgent need to find that desirable patch of sand or slice of adventure straight off. It also helps, of course, that this is the place into which most planes fly and that, at nearly five times the size of its closest city competitor, it's also the nation's transport hub.

Most visitors upon arrival make a beeline for Santo Domingo's **Zona Colonial**, the city's substantial colonial district, with dozens of wonderful old buildings and a dramatic setting right on the Río Ozama. In fact, many never bother to venture outside of this neighbourhood during their stay here, but while it obviously rates the most attention there's plenty more to see and do. As you might expect, the capital also has the country's best restaurants and nightlife, and serves as its cultural centre, with two wonderful museums, the **Museo del Hombre Dominicano** and **Museo Prehispánico**, dedicated to preserving the artefacts of the Taino civilization that thrived here before Columbus; the **Museo de Arte Moderno**'s display of contemporary Dominican visual art; and, perhaps the part that gives you the best look at the city's more populist side, a thriving **music scene** that focuses on the down-and-dirty merengue, *bachata* and *son* played in the clubs.

Santo Domingo's night activity is centred on its **Malecón** – a wide-open, palm-lined boardwalk that straddles the Caribbean Sea, dubbed "The Planet's Largest Disco" by the *Guinness Book of World Records* – and there's plenty more nightlife further inland. Modern Santo Domingo also hides some open spaces that offer relief from the gridlock, including the expansive **botanical gardens**, the wooded sports complex **Centro Olímpico** and a set of tropical cave lagoons called **Los Tres Ojos**. If visiting in the winter, an even higher priority are the spirited professional **baseball games** of Santo Domingo's two teams, Licey and Escogido, at Estadio Quisqueya.

Some history

The Río Haina, which borders Santo Domingo to the west, was once the site of a Taino village discovered by Spaniard Miguel Díaz, who fled Columbus's first settlement, La Isabela, after stabbing a fellow colonist in a drunken brawl. Locals gave him a gold nugget found near the river, which he brought back to the Spanish outpost and Christopher's brother **Bartolomé Columbus**, in charge while his brother was in Spain. The La Isabela outpost had been a complete disaster, and most colonists who hadn't already died from yellow fever had mutinied and abandoned the town. Spurred on, however, by dreams of gold, Bartolomé set sail with his remaining men in 1496 to establish a colony on the eastern bank of the Ozama. When Columbus returned in 1498, he took command of the new town, but had trouble controlling the colonists and was recalled by Spain two years later. His replacement, **Nicolás de Ovando**, moved the city to the western bank and began the monumental stone construction that remains to this day, work that was continued by Columbus's son Diego when he took over in 1509. During their rule the city was a satellite capital of Spanish possessions, from which conquistadors set out to colonize and rule the rest of the Caribbean and the American mainland.

Once new colonies were established, Spain found greater wealth in the silver mines of Mexico and Peru and the city's power and influence quickly eroded. An earthquake in 1562 destroyed much of the town, and in 1586 **Sir Francis Drake** captured Santo Domingo, looted it and burned it down. Though rebuilt, the city failed to regain its strategic relevance, and instead became subject to more attacks over the next century by the British and French until finally, in 1801, Haitian **Touissant L'Ouverture** took it without a fight. A succession of short-lived occupations followed, including the French in 1802, the British in 1803, the French again in 1804, the British again in 1809, and the Spaniards in the same year. By the time this spate of invasions was done, the city was economically devastated.

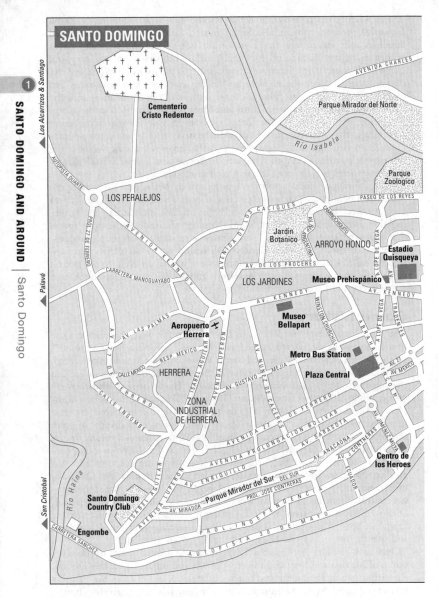

A much longer occupation was to follow – the Haitian domination from 1822 to 1843. They quickly alienated the Dominicans by enacting a land reform programme that robbed the Church and many wealthy white colonists of most of their land. As a result, Spanish merchants in the capital joined with the Catholic hierarchy to form the **Trinitarian movement** – named for its three leaders, the "Trinity" of Duarte, Mella and Sánchez – that led to independence after a long partisan war. But self-determination immediately

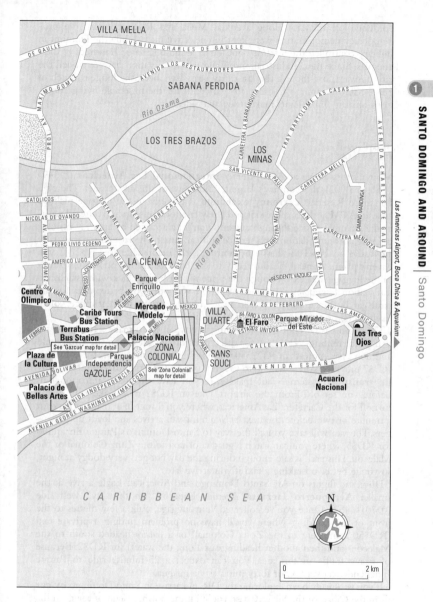

devolved into internal strife as the city was besieged and captured again and again by competing Dominican *caudillos*, a cycle that ended only with the brutal regime of **Rafael Leonidas Trujillo**, who renamed the capital Ciudad Trujillo in 1936 (though it was changed back immediately upon his death in 1961) and transformed it from a mere administrative capital to the national centre of shipping and industry. A military coup and American invasion in 1965 were the last major battles to take place here, during which the Americans cordoned off the city along avenidas Mella and Independencia; the pro-democracy demonstrators were kept in check within it, while the Dominican military controlled the territory outside of it and butchered hundreds of their enemies. Since then, industrialization and urban migration have exploded the city outward, and though the last thirty years have been the longest stretch of peace Santo Domingo has seen in two centuries, the miserable living conditions of many inhabitants make it less than ideal.

Arrival

Most visitors arrive at **Aeropuerto Internacional Las Américas** (☎549-0858 or 0002), the country's largest, 13km east of the city proper. There's a Banco de Reservas **currency exchange** at the exit to the luggage pick-up area, an **ATM** at the airport exit and a few fast-food restaurants scattered within the terminal. Once through customs you'll be accosted by an array of touts offering accommodation, taxi service and car rental. The latter are particularly aggressive, so avoid the hassle by renting a car beforehand (see p.32). If you haven't planned ahead, head directly to the bank of agency booths just south of the luggage area exit. Though the price is a bit higher, stick with established international agencies; a number of people will offer you better rates for the same car, but once they drive you away from the airport to their office, you're likely to be presented with a Yugo or the like.

The airport is far enough away from the city centre to make a **taxi** easiest if you're not renting a car; look for the official brown sticker on the windshield and don't pay more than RD$350. It's possible to get into town for as little as RD$7 provided you're willing to tough it out on the city's **unregulated public transport** system – but make sure you have small-denomination bills before you set off. From the airport, take an RD$2 motorbike ride to the turnoff for the Carretera Las Américas, where you'll wait in a small car park for a minute or two before the next *público* mini-van arrives and loads up passengers. The van will take you all the way to Santo Domingo's Parque Enriquillo for RD$5, where you can catch a guagua or taxi to the Zona Colonial or the Malecón. This park is safe enough during the day, but gets very dodgy at night, so you're better off taking a taxi if you arrive late.

Domestic flights on Air Santo Domingo and American Eagle arrive at the smaller **Aeropuerto Herrera**, Avenida Luperón, on the city's west side (☎701-6457). Once you've collected your luggage, walk a few metres to the front of the building where you'll have no problem finding a private taxi (RD$50 from here to the Zona Colonial) or a *público* headed south to the Malecón (and then another heading east along the water) for RD$2. Because of heavy traffic in this area, you can expect a 25-minute ride to Parque Independencia via taxi or forty minutes via guagua.

If you've already been exploring the DR and arrive in Santo Domingo **by car** from the Cibao or the Silver Coast, you'll hit the northern end of town on the Autopista Duarte, which becomes Avenida Kennedy at Luperón. Arriving **from the east**, follow the signs marked "Centro Ciudad" until you cross the Río Ozama on the Duarte bridge. From here the road becomes Avenida 27 de Febrero; a left on Calle 30 de Marzo will lead you directly to Parque Independencia in the Zona Colonial and – a little further on – the Malecón. Entering **from the west** via the Carretera San Cristóbal – an unlikely event – follow the signs that lead to the Malecón. If you're simply **passing through** the city from one region to another, it's best to take the bypass, which is called Avenida Azar from the west (where it connects from the Autopista Duarte) or Avenida Charles de Gaulle from the east (from Avenida Las Américas).

A fairly sophisticated bus system links Santo Domingo to the rest of the country. If you come **by bus**, you'll have no trouble finding a taxi or public transport from your terminal: Caribe Tours lets passengers off at Avenida 27 de Febrero and Navarro (☎221-4422); Metro at Avenida Winston Churchill and Calle Hatuey, behind the Plaza Central (☎566-7126); and Terrabus at Anacaona 15, across the street from the Centro Olímpico (☎531-0383). Transporte del Cibao (☎685-7210) has slightly more downscale connections from Puerto Plata, Sosúa and Santiago that arrive at Ravelo 92 near Parque Enriquillo, which also happens to be where you'll end up if you're arriving **by guagua** from either the southeast or the Barahona region (trips to Bayahibe, Punta Cana or Barahona run RD$80–120). From here you can catch an RD$2 *público* taxi to Parque Independencia and the Zona Colonial. You can also pick up guaguas headed west at Parque Independencia. Guaguas arriving from the north via Autopista Duarte let their passengers off at Avenida Luperón, where the highway becomes Avenida Kennedy. From there you can take a *público* down Kennedy to the city centre.

Information

The Department of Tourism's main office is on Avenida Mexico and 30 de Marzo (☎221-4660 or 689-3657), but they're not set up to provide information directly to visitors. The **tourist office** in Palacio Borghella, El Conde on the Parque Colón (Mon–Fri 9am–5pm; ☎686-3858), is no better, with a few brochures and a Zona Colonial map but little in the way of hard facts. And though the **National Park Office** does a great job of maintaining the ecosystems under its care, it's not well equipped for public information. Their main office (☎472-4204) is on Máximo Gómez, well north of the city centre and just south of the Villa Mella bridge. **Mapas Gaar**, El Conde 502 and Espaillat, third floor (☎688-8004; closed Sun), is an independent shop that has good road maps, city guides and navigation charts for sailors (though some of the latter are out of date).

There are five daily **newspapers** in Santo Domingo. *Hoy*'s "Revista" section has event listings, as does *Listin Diario*'s "La Vida". *Ultima Hora*, the afternoon daily, and *El Nacional* are good for cinema schedules, and *Diario Libre* is a widely available freebie that does a pretty comprehensive events listing for the city.

City transport

There is no official **public transport** system in Santo Domingo, but the informal network of *públicos* and guaguas is a study in successful anarchy – they manage to cover every inch of the city and its outer districts and can get you pretty much anywhere for under RD$10. Just stand on the corner of a major street and wave your arms at the first car with a taxi sign, provided you don't mind being crammed in with as many other people as can fit. The easiest way to get to the outer barrios of Villa Mella, La Ciénaga and Sabana Perdida is to take an RD$5 *público* bus from Parque Enriquillo.

More comfortable are the **taxis** found at the Parque Independencia, along El Conde and in front of the large Malecón hotels. You can alternately call a taxi from other locations; for a list of reputable operators, see "Listings", p.103.

Driving a car is daunting given the chaotic nature of traffic in the capital, but if you're planning on taking a few day-trips a rental might be worthwhile. If you haven't reserved a car beforehand, or picked one up from the airport, the outlets in the city have a better selection of cars, and you won't be hassled by the freelance touts that crowd the airport; see "Listings", p.103, for a rundown of options. The **best thoroughfares** when travelling from one end of the city to the other are Avenida 27 de Febrero and Avenida JFK – which have recently been transformed into freeways with few traffic lights or intersections.

You'll do plenty of **walking** in Santo Domingo, especially if staying around or in the Zona Colonial. If interested in more out-of-the-ordinary ways of seeing the city, you might try an **aerial tour** with Coturisco, Nunez de Cáceres and Guayacoa, Edificio Centro Coordinador Empresarial, Suite 147-9 (☏683-3660; US$50–150 depending on length), whose helicopters take off from the Herrera Airport. A mellower alternative are **river boat cruises** with Barco Fantástico, which depart nightly between 5.30pm and 6.30pm from the pier at Parque Archaeológica la Ceiba in the Zona Colonial (☏596-9223; RD$100; 2hr).

Accommodation

There's a wide variety of **accommodation** in the city, but budget rooms in decent neighbourhoods are hard to come by. Most expensive are the high-rises along the **Malecón**, which give you great rooms and decent service, though the restaurants attached are generally sub-par; prices here are typically US$50 cheaper on weekends, when there are fewer business travellers. Given the exorbitant rate at these hotels, you should demand a room with an ocean view; initial protestations that they're all booked are best treated with a dose of scepticism. If you've got this kind of money, though, you should really consider one of the smaller luxury pensions tucked away in the **Zona Colonial**, some of them in sixteenth-century mansions.

The Zona Colonial also has a few cheaper, mid-range options, but keep in mind that they're set amid the centre of city activity and thus can get a bit noisy at night. If you want peace and quiet at a more reasonable rate, head to one of the small hotels in residential **Gazcue**, all of which come with hot water, TV and an option for a/c. Make sure to see your bed before paying for it; room quality can vary widely within a single establishment. There are also plenty of less expensive, basic rooms available in the shopping district around Avenida Duarte, but that neighbourhood gets very dicey at night. Wherever you go, make sure that your hotel has a **generator** that provides power during the frequent city blackouts, and that the management is willing to run it 24 hours a day.

Zona Colonial

Aida El Conde 474 and Espaillat ☏685-7692. The only hotel with balcony rooms on El Conde and a good bargain for clean, simple accommodation, though the proprietors can be a bit gruff. No smoking. ❸

Anacaona Calle Isidro Pérez and Hincado at Parque Independencia ☏688-6888. Shabby rooms with private bath and hot water, some of them with a/c, though you'll really only look here if you want to save some money. ❷

Bettye's Guest House Isabela 163 ☏688-7649,

221-4167, © bettyemarshall@hotmail.com. Dormitory beds in rooms with fan and shared hot-water bath, plus a couple of private rooms. If the guest house is full, you're put up in a cot within the owner's Haitian art gallery. Too expensive for what you get, though it's right in the centre of the Zone. ❹

Caribe Colonial Isabela 159 ☎ 688-7799, ⒻⒻ685-8128, ⓦ www.hodelpa.com. A bit of an anomaly within the Zone, a brand spanking new hotel with modern (but somewhat cramped) rooms and eleven suites with balcony and hot tubs. Multilingual staff and 24-hour room service, though the place lacks character or charm. Taxi service provided by a spiffily remodelled 1950s Cadillac. ❺–❽

Conde de Penalba El Conde and Meriño ☎ 688-7121, Ⓕ 688-7375, ⓦ www.condepenalba.com. A fair compromise between comfort and colonial character, this small hotel tucked away on the second floor of a century-old building on Parque Duarte boasts good service, comfortable rooms (a/c, cable TV, phone) and strong hot showers. You pay for the location, though. ❺

Francés Mercedes and Arz Meriño ☎ 685-9331, Ⓕ 685-1289, © H2137@accor-hotels.com. Newly renovated sixteenth-century mansion with nine-teen quality private rooms, decorated with period furnishings, that still retain their original character. Features cable TV, a/c, phone, safe deposit box – but don't use your phone for long-distance calls, as the rate here is even more exorbitant than usual for in-room calls. The attached *Le Patio* restaurant is pretty good but definitely overpriced. The hotel's very best feature is its quiet, starlit courtyard. ❼

Ginette El Conde 505 ☎ 685-7815. Little-known, low-budget pensión with three basic rooms over the Conde and private cold-water baths. ❷

Hostal Hostos Hostos 299 ☎ 688-9192, Ⓕ 682-1245. Relatively new budget hotel set enviably beside the beautiful stone staircase on Hostos off the ruins of the Franciscan monastery. Good for independent travellers, since they have a large kitchen for cooking your own food. If at all possi-ble, call ahead and reserve the suite with balcony that has a great view of the Zone. Discounted rates for stays of five days or more. ❸

Hostal Jerusalem Luperón 4 ☎ 689-4553. A classic Zona Colonial cheapie with twelve basic rooms with fan, private cold-water bath and a public kitchen. A good second option if *Hostal Hostos* is full. ❸

Mercure El Conde and Hostos ☎ 688-5500, Ⓕ 688-5522, © H2974@accor-hotels.com. Not as nice as the converted colonial mansions and a bit

expensive, but the service is friendly, the rooms are nice in a *Holiday Inn* sort of a way, and they have all the expected amenities. The breakfast buffet on the ground floor is excellent value at RD$118 (daily 7–10am) and quite popular with the expats; at other times the restaurant should be avoided. The room prices are the same regardless of single or double occupancy. ❺

Nicolás Nader Luperón 151 and Duarte ☎ 687-6674, Ⓕ 565-6204, © hostal@naders.com. A well-regarded, small luxury hotel with ten spacious, tastefully decorated rooms (a bit nicer than those at the *Palacio*) in a limestone colonial-era man-sion. Within the courtyard are a small art gallery, restaurant and bar. If you can afford it, this should be your first choice in the Zone. ❺

Palacio Duarte 106 and Ureña ☎ 682-4730, Ⓕ 687-5535, ⓦ www.dominican-rep.com/Hotel-Palacio.html. If you can't get into the *Nicolás Nader*, this is almost as good – and unlike its nearby competitor they have free parking. Formerly the residence of infamous *caudillo* Buenaventura Báez, this 1628 mansion has been very well maintained and boasts a dozen large, well-appointed rooms, quality service and all the amenities. It's a pleasure just to walk through the corridors here, with their ageing, massive lime-stone blocks lined with portraits of the island's first Spanish nobles. ❺

El Refugio Arz Meriño 356 ☎ 687-1572, Ⓕ 221-8678. A good Zona Colonial bargain located in the historic Casa de Moneda and close to all of the major historic monuments. The atmosphere isn't as friendly as some of the other local pensiónes, but rooms are perfectly functional and feature a/c, hot water and cable TV. There's also a kitchen area available for guests and a fun, open-air common area that serves as a hangout at night. ❸

Malecón and around

La Casona Dorada Independencia 255 and 0 Báez ☎ 221-3535, Ⓕ 221-3622, © casonadorada @codetel.net.do. Set on quiet grounds away from the road, this refurbished mansion from the nine-teenth century features a restaurant/bar, swim-ming pool, hot tub, terrific laundry service and free parking. Gay-friendly. ❹

Centenario Inter-Continental Malecón 218 ☎ 221-1889, Ⓕ 686-3576, ⓦ www.santo-domingo .interconti.com. Super-expensive, luxurious high-rise not far from the Zona Colonial, with 196 sea-view rooms, four middling restaurants, karaoke bar, swim-ming pool, casino, hot tub and overpriced internet service on the ground floor. The rooms have all the amenities you'd expect and the service is acceptable but – considering the price – not outstanding. ❽

Duque du Wellington Independencia 304 ☎682-4525. Small, quiet hotel a block from the water with friendly service and clean rooms. Reception clerks are very helpful and speak excellent English. Hot water, a/c, phone and cable TV, though you should keep away from the restaurant. Gay-friendly. ❹

El Embajador Sarasota 65 ☎221-2131, ℻532-5306, ⓦwww.occidental-hoteles.com. A grand hotel with a great deal of history (for example, it was where American troops bunkered down during the invasion of 1965). Today it is still far and away the best of the high-end hotels in the capital, set a bit off the Malecón but high enough that many rooms still have ocean views from their terraces. The grounds are also gorgeous and include gardens, tennis courts and a great swimming pool. There's also concierge service on every floor. Many business travellers with money to burn opt for the *Club Miguel Angel* on the top floors, which operates as a top-end hotel-within-a-hotel and features all manner of insane amenities, like private restaurant, breakfast with champagne, secretarial service, in-room internet access and multiple phone lines. ❽

Maison Gatreaux Llúberes 8 ☎687-4856. A great value. The large rooms come with a/c, comfortable beds and especially strong hot showers. Rooms are kept very clean, but the front desk is not especially friendly. US$2 extra for cable TV. ❹

Meliá Santo Domingo Malecón 365 ☎688-0823, ℻687-4274, ⓦwww.solmelia.com. Formerly the *Sheraton*, this luxury establishment boasts a shopping arcade, casino, three restaurants, swimming pool, hot tub and a high-profile disco, but the service has deteriorated somewhat under new management. The rooms, though, are excellent, with cable TV, a/c, coffeemaker and phone. ❽

El Napolitano Malecón 101 ☎687-1131, ℻687-6814, ⓦwww.hotelnapolitano.com. A real bargain given the rates at the other Malecón high-rises. Looks a bit shabbier on the outside but the seventy or so modern rooms are really no worse than at the more expensive seafront hotels. The swimming pool has views of the Caribbean and the casino is open 4pm–4am. The disco here is one of the most popular in the city, but the rooms are insulated from the noise. ❺

Renaissance Jaragua Malecón 367 ☎221-2222, ℻686-0528, ⓔh.jaragua@codetel.net.do. This truly massive complex is by far the finest of the expensive Malecón resorts. The rooms are big and tastefully appointed, the service is excellent and the amenities are what one would expect. On the grounds are a popular disco, four restaurants, a bar, swimming pool/hot tub and a tropical garden. For once, you get your money's worth. ❽

Sea View El Número 2 and Malecón ☎221-4420, ℻688-3207. A nice little mid-range hotel with perfectly acceptable, modern rooms insulated from the city traffic noise. They also have two full-service apartments with kitchens that can sleep larger groups, and a cafeteria next door. ❸–❹

Gazcue

Antillas Independencia and Pichardo (no phone). Very basic rooms close to the Zona Colonial with fan and private cold-water bath, plus two rooms with a/c for only US$2 more. An incredible bargain if comfort is not a top priority, but don't leave valuables in the room. ❶

Coqui Mar Independencia 654 ☎689-9598, ℻221-5214. Certainly nothing special, but an acceptable option for those who don't mind being a bit west of the action. Rooms are clean and unnotable, featuring a/c, cable TV, private hot-water bath and phone. ❹

Felicidad Aristides Cabrar 58 ☎221-6615. Five basic, clean rooms (two with a/c) in a small pensión with fan, private bath and hot water. The interior is not particularly attractive but the residential block is quiet and pretty. ❷

La Grand Mansión Danae 26 ☎689-8758. Unpretentious and functional on a quiet residential street, with private hot-water bath, fan, free coffee and nice rooms. Ask for a second-floor room with a window view of the trees; a/c for US$2.50 extra. All in all, terrific value. ❷

Hospidaje Tu Espacio Cervantes 102 ☎688-4100. Comfy rooms in a local home, with private cold-water bath and fan. Worth a look, if *La Grand Mansión* is booked solid. ❸

La Mansión Dr Báez 1 and Bolivar ☎686-5562, ℻686-2502. Also called *Hostal Primaveral*, this place is pretty basic but popular with backpackers, thus making a convivial spot to meet fellow travellers. Rooms are unremarkable, as is the on-site Italian restaurant. ❷

Plaza Colonial Pellerano and Julio Verne ☎687-9111. Top-notch full-service apartments with large kitchens (though they're not fond of large groups here), just a few blocks from Parque Independencia. Gay-friendly. ❹

Quisqueya Cayetano Rodriguez 201 ☎687-6037. Unremarkable, mid-range private rooms and a dormitory with RD$80 beds – one of the best deals in town and in a safe location. ❶–❸

Raphael Independencia 19, across from Parque El Conde and the cemetery (no phone). 100 peso super-cheapie, but so basic and uncomfortable that

even most budget travellers will want to give it a wide berth. Does feature night security, and is used mostly by Dominicans looking to catch a bit of sleep before boarding a guagua west the next day. ❶
La Residencia Danae 62 ☎412-7568. Clean rooms with private bath, a/c, cable TV and hot water. Nice proprietors make it a pleasant place to stay, though there's little to do in the immediate area and most guests are Dominican travellers. ❸
Venezia Independencia 45 ☎682-5108 ⓕ682-5285, ⓦwww.residence-venezia.com. Quiet little spot just a couple of blocks away from the Parque Independencia, with good security and clean motel rooms. The grounds and facade are quite pretty and security is good. Especially worth trying for the two triple-occupancy rooms with kitchenettes. Amenities include phone, satellite TV and minibar. ❹

Mercado Modelo

Luna del Norte Benito González 89 and Duarte ☎685-3385. The best of the hotels in the area is clean and family-oriented. Rooms come with two beds, private bath with hot water, a/c, 24-hour generator and good security. ❷

The outer barrios

Delta Sarasota 53 ☎535-0800. Best of the several hotels inconveniently located on the west side of town. Good service, modern amenities and a large American clientele, though the restaurant is best avoided. ❺
Gran Lina Máximo Gómez and 27 de Febrero ☎563-5000, ⓕ686-5521, ⓔgranhotellina@barcelo.com. Near the Centro Olímpico and Plaza de la Cultura, and definitely worth consideration despite being so far away from the Zona Colonial. It's a high-end luxury hotel with 217 rooms and eight junior suites catering mostly to business people, famous for its great restaurant (the *Lina*) but also with terrific service and rooms. Also has a casino, swimming pool, hot tub, two bars and children's facilities. ❻
Ruta 66 Av Ruta 66, Las Américas International Airport (no phone). The best option if you have an early-morning flight at Las Américas, which is a mere two-peso motoconcho ride away. The rates are cheap and the rooms are perfectly acceptable, with cable TV, hot water and a/c. ❷

The City

At the beginning of the twentieth century Santo Domingo didn't extend much beyond the Zona Colonial, but a hundred years of heavy rural migration have exploded it outward in three directions. Today no single barrio could be called "downtown" Santo Domingo, as government and corporate headquarters are spread fairly evenly throughout the sprawl. That said, the **Zona Colonial**, **Gazcue** and the **Malecón** – a compact trio of barrios – are the natural home base for visitors. **Parque Independencia** might be the closest thing to ground zero, as it separates the first two and is a mere four blocks from the third; spiking out from the park are avenidas Independencia and Bolivar, major arteries that pass through much of the city beyond this tourist zone.

The Zona Colonial

"Its buildings are as tall and beautiful as those in Italy, and its streets, wide and straight, are far superior to those of Florence."

– Spanish Bishop Geraldini, upon his arrival in 1525.

Though the **Zona Colonial** – a square-shaped district straddling the western mouth of the Río Ozama and encircled by the ruins of the original city walls – is crammed with monumental architecture, it's very much a living neighbourhood, thanks to the trendy cafés, local bars and old clapboard row-houses, where thousands of people live and work. A multimillion-dollar renovation, begun in the 1970s in preparation for the Columbus Centenary, has brought a number of the historic buildings back to their original state, giving you a real sense of how the city looked when first developed. Many of these important

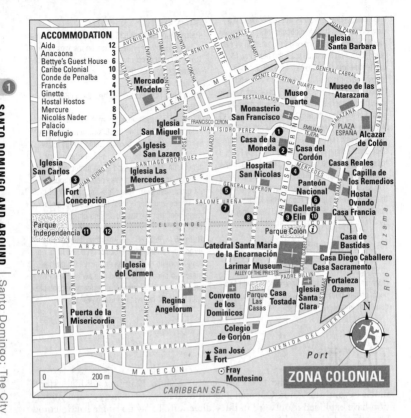

ACCOMMODATION

Aida	12
Anacaona	3
Bettye's Guest House	6
Caribe Colonial	10
Conde de Penalba	9
Francés	4
Ginette	11
Hostal Hostos	1
Mercure	8
Nicolás Nader	5
Palacio	7
El Refugio	2

ZONA COLONIAL

0   200 m

monuments can be seen in a single day if you keep to a brisk pace, though thorough exploration requires at least two or three. Chances are, though, you'll pass through the district nearly every day while in town, since it holds many of the city's best restaurants and bars – not to mention, likely, your hotel. Wandering about you'll no doubt be accosted by freelance guides, who are generally very friendly and sometimes quite knowledgeable; if you tell them you don't want assistance, they'll leave you in peace.

The town gates

A good place to begin exploring the old city is at the massive **Puerta de la Misericordia** (Gate of Mercy), an early sixteenth-century fortified city entrance on the corner of Hincado and Arzobispo Portes, just north of the Malecón. Connected to it from the south are the rubble remains of its watchtower, the San Gil Fort. The gate earned its name during the devastating earthquake of 1842, when local priests erected a tent city beneath it to treat the sick and shelter the homeless. Two years later, on February 27, 1844, freedom fighter Ramón Mella made a dramatic speech here inciting the city to insurrection, and fired off the first shot of the revolution against Haiti. A re-creation of the event is staged every Independence Day.

Follow Mella's torchlit route up Hincado to Calle El Conde and the **Puerta El Conde** (Gate of the Count), an imposing stone structure adorned with a decorative, red-brick belfry, where Mella raised the new national flag for the first time. Named for Count Bernado Bracamonte – whose military tactics saved the city from British invasion in 1655 – the gate leads into beautiful **Parque Independencia**, a popular meeting place encircled by a traffic-choked ring road, with shaded benches and a marker from which all distances in the capital are calculated. Near the park's centre is the honour-guarded **Altar de la Patria** (daily 8.30am–6pm; no shorts or short skirts; free), a marble mausoleum in which Mella is buried beside his compatriots Duarte and Sánchez. At the north end of the park, look for the fenced-off, fortified ramp that leads to the **Fort Concepción** (1678), just beyond the park boundaries, a pentagonal cannon platform with tremendous limestone walls. From here it's just a short diversion four blocks up 16 de Agosto to **Iglesia San Carlos** (16 de Agosto and Trinitaria), a pentagonal church built in 1715 with a pretty white facade. Its thick, fortress-like walls allowed it to double in the early days as a military outpost in times of crisis. Later, in 1838, Trinitarian Juan Pablo Duarte met with Father Gaspar Hernández here, cementing an alliance between the nascent rebellion and the Catholic Church.

Parque Colón and around

Stretching east from Parque Independencia is **Calle El Conde**, once Santo Domingo's main thoroughfare but closed off to motorized traffic in the 1970s and now a broad pedestrian promenade lined with cafés, fast-food restaurants, clothing shops and bookstores. It's an ideal place to people-watch, with hundreds of city-dwellers passing through at all hours and sidewalk vendors selling everything from pirated CDs to split coconuts. Follow the street eight blocks to Calle Arz Meriño, where **Parque Colón**, a pleasant open space surrounded by beautiful colonial and Victorian buildings, holds a statue of Columbus in its centre – heroically staring out towards the horizon with an adoring, topless Taino maiden at his feet. At the west end of the park is the Victorian-style nineteenth-century town hall, no longer the seat of city government but still used for municipal office space, while to the north sits a series of cigar and souvenir shops, including the **Museo de Ámbar**, El Conde 107 (Mon–Sat 9am–5pm; RD$30 museum entry), a high-end jewellery store with a small museum on the second floor featuring ants, termites, wasps and other insects trapped in amber. On the park's east side are **Casa de Abogados**, the old town jail, and **Palacio Borghella**, early nineteenth-century buildings constructed by the Haitians. Borghella was once especially beautiful, but Hurricane Georges destroyed its stunning facade in 1998. Kitty-corner from Borghella – and strictly for enthusiasts – is the **Museo Numismático y Filatélico** on El Conde and Calle Isabela (Mon–Fri 9am–3pm; free), which boasts the largest stamp and coin collection in the Caribbean. More interesting is the top Haitian art on display at the no-frills **Galería Elín**, just off the park and El Conde on Meriño 203 (daily 9am–6pm; T688-7100). The gallery holds an unbelievable collection of the very best Haitian artists (including Ernst Joassaint, Mecene Brunice, Charet Kavanaught and Fritz Cedon) in modest surroundings, many of the works stacked up in rows along the walls. Don't let the presentation fool you – a walk through the shop will give you an encyclopedic survey of the history of Haitian art, and the paintings here cost half what they would in the States or Western Europe.

The Basílica Catedral Santa María de la Encarnación

Most imposing of the buildings along the park is the **Basílica Catedral Santa María de la Encarnación** (daily 8am–4.30pm; no shorts or short skirts, no pants allowed for women; skirts can be rented from nearby souvenir shops for RD$20), intended, when constructed by the Vatican, to be the religious centre of the West Indies, and the base for proselytizing all the indigenous peoples of the Americas. It also played a formative role in the birth of New World Voodoo; in the sixteenth century various Spanish religious brotherhoods called *cofradías* – an Iberian institution since the Middle Ages – used the cathedral for their patron-saint parades. The imported slaves had their own *cofradías* (in which West African god Chango was worshipped under the guise of Christian St John), which would hold religious processions involving traditional drum music, dancing and possession. As the century wore on, the clergy realized that the African *cofradías* were incorporating some distinctly unorthodox practices, and banished them to the churches along the city's northern wall.

Built between 1521 and 1540, the cathedral's exterior actually bears little of the Gothic influence that transformed sacred architecture in Europe – the only hint along the fortified **northern facade** that it's not Romanesque are minimalist stud ornaments around the windows. The **western facade** is instead Plateresque, a style that predominated in Santo Domingo during the reign of Diego Columbus, with an overabundance of friezes and fanciful ornamentation, such as the allegorical frieze above the portals, showing a flight of cherubs making their way past horse-headed sea creatures and impious women – meant to symbolize the ocean journey of the colonists. The original mahogany doors remain intact, and priests still use the same 500-year-old key to lock them at night. The gold Hapsburg seal and statuary that surrounded the portals, though, were stolen by Sir Francis Drake – the current ones are modest reproductions. Look around to the right and you'll see the cathedral's exposed bell tower; the original covering was demolished by Drake (who turned the church into a barracks during his stay) and never replaced.

Inside, under a Gothic ribbed vault, a few items bear noting, including a seventeenth-century marble altar and a sixteenth-century altar, pulpit and pews of mahogany. Beneath the marble floor an underground tunnel, now sealed off, led to the archbishop's palace across the street. Just to the right of the pulpit, one of the thirteen church chapels, **Santa Ana**, bears the tomb of colonial administrator Rodrigo de Bastidas and the only surviving original stained-glass window, an angel hovering over Virgin and Child. Beside it the **Chapel of Life and Death**, where baptism and extreme unction are performed, has a Rincón Mora window – reminiscent of Chagall – showing a decidedly deranged John the Baptist baptizing a clean-shaven Christ. Continuing down the southern wall, the **Chapel of the Apostles** holds an original mural on its 1556 vault, a beautiful mahogany altar with a silver retable and the grave of Royal Secretary Diego Caballero. On the northern wall you'll find the **Chapel of the Virgin of Antigua**, with its gorgeous groined vault and a beautiful 1520 painting of Mary, shipped to Spain by Santana upon annexation and returned in terrible shape in 1892 (it's since been restored); the **Chapel of the Virgin of the Light**, where Columbus was interred for a time; and the **Chapel of Christ in Agony**, where two stone lions stand guard over the grave of Santo Domingo's first bishop, Alejandro Geraldini.

Pass through the cathedral's southern door and you'll enter the enclosed **Plaza of the Priests**; it was once the city cemetery, but Drake burned the cathedral's records and now no one knows who was buried here. Across the plaza, the **Alley of the Priests**, an attractive walkway lined with bougainvillea, leads past the old priests' quarters; note the decorative Islamic brick arches over the doorways.

East of the cathedral

Exiting onto the street from the Alley of the Priests, it's just a half-block east to the largely unadorned **Iglesia Santa Clara** on Billini and Isabela la Católica, the New World's first nunnery and another of the Catholic institutions established here in an attempt to make a regional holy city. Built in 1552, it was severely damaged by Drake and renovated by a blustery local businessman named Rodrigo Pimentel, who was rumoured to have spent most of his nights there. The Catholic primary school that's here now is not technically open to the public, but the nuns will let you wander in to see the chapel on the grounds, its single nave supported by five Gothic arches.

Just south of the nunnery on Calle Isabela and Alfau is another important relic owned by the Church, **Casa Sacramento** (House of the Sacrament), built in 1520 by Diego Caballero and now the residence of the archbishop. Legend ascribes the building's name to an apocryphal sixteenth-century event in which the owner purchased a large orang-utan from a passing merchant. The animal somehow got loose in the courtyard and threatened to hurl an infant off the roof until the baby's mother began repeating the rosary, upon which the primate put the child down and went to sleep. Renovations in the 1930s disguised its colonial bulk in a decorative Victorian wrap. If you like you can walk through the two connecting courtyard gardens, or up to the viewing platforms of the towers, which offer scenic rooftop shots of the neighbourhood.

Across the street from Casa Sacramento at Isabela 54 is the new **Museo Larimar Dominicano** (daily 9am–6pm; free; ☎689-6605, ⓦwww .larimarmuseum.com), a remodelled house from the late 1700s which now holds a variety of exhibits on larimar, a turquoise-coloured stone that exists only in the Dominican Republic. In addition to a number of particularly beautiful examples of raw larimar as it is mined from the Bahoruco Mountains (see p.305), the museum shows how the semiprecious gem was created by local volcanic activity, how it is mined, a number of leaf and wood fossils embedded within it and some pieces of art that incorporate it. You'll also find out how to tell real from fake larimar, and there's of course a very nice jewellery shop on the ground floor. The exhibits have English captions and the staff are helpful and unobtrusive.

More colonial relics lie at the far end of Calle Alfau, including **Casa Diego Caballero**, built by the Royal Secretary in 1523 and rented out as a private residence. You can walk through with the security guard's permission – the stone portal leads to a two-floor, double-arched gallery – but there's little symmetry to the building since the Church gutted half of it and put in a small theatre. The two stone houses now connected to Casa Caballero are linked to a colonial-era ghost story, in which a woman was murdered and dumped in the well between them. A local priest – reputedly the woman's lover – saw her apparition sitting on the front steps of the house every time he passed it; he was finally driven to search the area until he found her body at the bottom of the well, which was thenceforth sealed off.

West of the cathedral

From the entrance to the Alley of the Priests, you can alternately walk a half-block west to **Plaza Padre Billini** at the corner of Billini and Meriño. A small public plaza backed by a row of expensive antique, jewellery and clothing shops, it's named for a seventeenth-century priest who championed the poor; before Padre Billini's time the square was used to stage bullfights. If you're in no mood to shop, cross to **Casa Tostado**, on the plaza's southeast corner, built in 1503 by scrivener Francisco Tostado, whose son was later killed by a Drake cannonball. The exterior's most notable feature is the Gothic double window above the front door, the only one of its kind in this hemisphere. Inside you'll find the **Museum of the Nineteenth-Century Dominican Family** (Mon–Sat 9am–4pm; RD$5), featuring a number of antique furnishings, some Art Nouveau. Check out the geometric *Mudéjar* tiling on the courtyard well, and ask to climb the circular mahogany staircase that leads to the roof. Across the street, the sixteenth-century walls of the old Archbishop's Palace today enclose a car park and **Parque Las Casas**, named for the priest who petitioned the Crown on behalf of the Tainos; a statue of him stands in its centre, only a single clenched fist and a skull-like head protruding from the bulk of his robe.

A block south at the corner of Meriño and García, sixteenth-century **Colegio de Gorjón** served as the New World's second university (after San Tomé de Aquino; see p.80) – check out the stunning courtyard on Calle García, which has a delightful ocean view. Upon the school's opening, the city was – rather optimistically – declared to be "The Athens of the West Indies". Today it houses the Hispanic Cultural Institute and is encased in a beautiful whitewash. Like all early colonial structures its stonework was originally exposed, but in 1712 – under a misconception that the plague was transmitted through bare masonry – Philip V decreed that all buildings in the empire be plastered, and Santo Domingo was whitewashed from end to end.

Calle de las Damas

A block east of the cathedral runs **Calle de las Damas** (Street of the Ladies), the first road laid out by Ovando when he moved the town to this side of the river. The street received its name in 1509, thanks to the retinue of women who would accompany Diego Columbus's wife María de Toledo down it to church every Sunday morning; their proximity to María reflected their standing in the city's social hierarchy. Today it's traversed mostly by tourists who come for a look at the early mansions that line the cobblestone blocks.

On the street's southern end **Fortaleza Ozama** (daily 9am–7pm; RD$10), where Diego and María lived while their palace was under construction, was long Santo Domingo's most strategic site. Built in 1502 and enlarged over the centuries, it's set on a steep bank over the mouth of the Ozama and was the departure point for the Spanish conquests of Cuba, Colombia, Jamaica, Peru and Mexico – finally decommissioned after the American invasion of 1965. Beyond the Neoclassical main gate, the courtyard features a statue (with definite shades of Rodin) of González Oviedo, author of the first *History of the Indies* and commander of the fort from 1533 to 1557. The largest structure is the bulky medieval **Torre de Homenaje** (Tower of Homage), the most impenetrable part of the fortress and used for centuries as a prison. Climb to the top for panoramic views, or head inside where you'll find the hole through which prisoners were dropped to their cell. Also on the grounds are the old arsenal (with a niche bearing an icon of Santa Bárbara, patron of the military), the excavated remains of the provisional fort from 1502 and the intact wall of Fort Santiago, the first line of defence.

Sharing the fort's northern wall is **Casa de Bastidas** (Mon–Fri 9.30am–5pm; free), built around 1510 by Bishop Rodrigo Bastidas, who went on to colonize Colombia. Since then the house has been associated with the fort, often serving as an officers' residence; the seventeenth-century statue of St Bárbara above the main entrance signifies its link with the military. It has a grand courtyard with enormous, ancient *caucho* trees and an impressive arcade with broad arches spanning all four walls.

Across the street you'll pass two more restored colonial buildings, **Sociedad de Bibliofilios** and the **Academía de las Ciencias** – both with lush courtyard gardens behind their thick stone facades – before arriving at **Casa Francia** (Mon–Fri 9am–4.30pm; free), originally the home of conquistador Hernán Cortes. It was here that he plotted his conquest of Mexico; you'll find his family's coat of arms in the second gallery. Note the parallel organization of arches on the first- and second-floor arcades, a departure from Spanish architectural tradition that was copied by later colonial houses. Beneath the ornament, though, these buildings were essentially fortified medieval keeps, reflecting the feudal aspirations of their owners. Across the street, **Hostal Nicolás de Ovando** incorporates the homes of the Ovando and Davila families, both prominent in the early colony. The hotel, which you can explore during the day, is decorated with sixteenth-century furniture and so gives a good sense of colonial private life. Don't miss the double riverfront patio in the back, or the Davila coat of arms flanked by two griffins at the northernmost entrance. Attached to the hotel's north wall is **Capilla de los Remedios**, once the Davilas' private chapel, with an especially pretty triple-arched belfry atop its brick facade.

The hotel looks directly across at **Plaza María Toledo** – a broad walkway with a sixteenth-century fountain – and the **Panteón Nacional** (Mon–Sat 9am–7pm; free), built from 1714 to 1745 as a Jesuit convent. Shortly thereafter, the Jesuits were expelled from Spanish colonies; the building was then successively put to use as a tobacco warehouse, a seminary and a theatre. In 1955 Trujillo renovated it and reinterred most of the major military and political figures from Dominican history. The building's Neoclassical, martial facade seems particularly suited to its sober task, topped with a prominent cupola flanked by statues of Loyola and Jesus. The interior has been completely redone, with Italian marble floors, an enormous central chandelier donated by Spanish dictator Franco and metal crosses rumoured to have been Nazi swastikas – more a measure of local distaste for Trujillo than a verifiable fact. The serenity and patriotic uniformity of the elevated marble caskets around a large eternal flame is at odds with the competing *caudillos'* lives. Nineteenth-century dictator Pedro Santana, for example, is surrounded by his enemies (and successors) Pepillo Salcedo, Gaspar Polanco, Pedro Antonio Pimentel, José María Cabral and Gregorio Luperón, each of whom briefly served as president before being deposed by the next.

Beside the Panteón is **Casa de los Jesuitas**, built in 1508 by Diego Caballero's brother Hernán and taken over by the Jesuits in 1701, who turned it into a renowned school of rhetoric; now it holds the administrative offices of the Museo de las Casas Reales (see overleaf). Check out the beautiful Islamic portal in the courtyard. Another Jesuit property, **Casa de las Gárgolas**, sits adjacent, named for the prominent row of five grimacing gargoyles above the front door. Their state of decay is due in part to the vagaries of time, and in part to a seventeenth-century incident in which they were pelted with stones by a mob, who believed them supernaturally responsible for a series of local murders. One door over **Casa Viloria**, built by the king's chamberlain Juan de Viloria in 1520, continues the supernatural theme, supposedly haunted by Viloria's ghost. Some locals claim that Viloria still appears one night a year and offers to reveal the location of his buried treasure to anyone willing to follow; apparently enough folks took up this offer to dig several holes in the courtyard's tile floor, found when work was begun on the house's restoration.

Plaza España

Calle de las Damas ends at **Plaza España**, an attractive, tiled open space surrounded on all sides by monuments and with terrific views across the river, thus explaining the outdoor cafés that proliferate. This was the centre of colonial power and commerce, with sailors disembarking from the adjoining port, foreign merchants auctioning slaves, and Spain's high officials administering their empire from the Casas Reales. An intact section of the old town wall still skirts the eastern plaza, extending to **Puerta San Diego**, the colonial-era entrance from the port. More decorative than functionally defensive, at night its arcades are a favourite local hangout; on its eastern face you'll find **Parque Archeológico la Ceiba**, holding the excavated foundations of the colony's arrow-shaped, riverfront fort. At the centre a statue of Ovando stands on the previous site of an enormous pillar that was to support an aqueduct from the Río Haina (the Ozama's water being too brackish to drink).

At the southern end of the plaza, **Museo de las Casas Reales** (Tues–Sun 9am–6pm; RD$15), built between 1503 and 1520, was the administrative centre of the West Indies, housing the Royal Court, Treasury and Office of the Governor. The one adornment along its rectangular exterior is the Plateresque window above the main portal, flanked by two miniature pillars and Charles V's coat of arms. Opposite the entrance, an eighteenth-century sundial sits on a pedestal, positioned so bureaucrats could tell the time by simply looking out the window. The museum's first-floor collection is a bit of a hodgepodge, with a few Taino artefacts, Spanish navigational instruments, slave shackles and an example of an old sugar mill. Near the back you'll find a rickshaw in which Spanish judges were carried to court by Tainos, and a sixteenth-century apothecary crammed with colourful glass vials. The second floor is more coherent, holding an armoury donated by Trujillo with examples of weaponry used here since Columbus, plus re-creations of the Royal Court and the Salon of the Governor, where the Crown's emissaries sat in state like petty monarchs, often ignoring edicts direct from Spain.

Opposite the Casas Reales is the **Alcazar de Colón** (daily 9am–5pm; RD$20), the fortified palace of the Columbus family, built by Diego from 1511 to 1515 without the use of a single nail. He chose the site because of its easy proximity to the Casas Reales, where he conducted official business, and so that it would be the first building seen by disembarking sailors and merchants. Also, from its terrace he could look across the Ozama and see the remains of the wooden colony his father Christopher had built. These grounds would also soon decay, hastened by the family's departure for Spain in 1577; a nineteenth-century illustration by American traveller Samuel Hazard depicts it scarred, overgrown with weeds and fronted by two thatch huts. You'd never know it today – the portal's flattened arches, framed by rectangular panels, are pristine. They're also the finest local example of the late Gothic style called **Isabelline**, characterized by plain, linear surfaces adorned only with Islamic portals and delicate vine ornaments. Inside, a **museum** assembles an array of sixteenth-century pieces, few of them owned by Diego but still evocative enough of the life of early Spanish nobility. Reproductions of the stone gargoyles that held up the first-floor ceiling leer down at the collection of mahogany furniture, the religious tapestries and icons that cover the walls, and a display case of period silverware. A narrow, circular stone staircase – with a star-ribbed vault bearing more grimacing Gothic faces at the base of each rib – leads to the second floor, where the private study showcases illuminated manuscripts from Spain and the music salon holds a sixteenth-century harp and clavichord. From here you can walk to the terrace fortifications, the construction of which led Spanish officials to fear Diego intended to barricade his followers inside and declare himself "Emperor of the Americas".

Bordering the Alcazar to the north is a winding row of colonial storefronts known as **Las Atarazanas**. In the old days they held taverns frequented by passing mariners and the city's large public market, where ships stocked up on tropical fruit to combat scurvy. Follow it to the end where the Reales Atarazanas, once the colonial port authority, contains the **Museo de las Atarazanas**, Colón 4 (daily 9am–6pm; RD$15). The museum holds the recovered booty from the wreck of the sixteenth-century Spanish galleon *Concepción*, sunk during a hurricane in the Bahía de Samaná. In addition to a lucid history of the wreck and four centuries' worth of attempts to salvage the considerable treasures it held, its one large room contains coins and bars of silver, pottery, chinaware and a variety of religious items, including dozens of small "poop" dolls that sailors stuffed with straw and the hair of a loved one from home, then hung along the ship's outer deck to stave off bad luck, giving rise to the term "poop deck".

Two blocks north along Avenida del Puerto, the **Centro de Arte y Cultura Popular**, Avenida del Puerto and Parra (Mon–Fri 9am–5pm, Sat 9am–1pm; free; ☎687-8566), consolidates the nation's research into folk religion and art. Run by anthropologist Dagoberto Tejeda, the centre displays a number of contemporary Taino-influenced pieces in its courtyard – most notably the giant, styrofoam *cemi* beside the front door – and has an excellent Carnival exhibit of bull-horned devil costumes. You can also learn about *Vodú Dominicana*: employees of the centre will gladly take you to a mock altar and proceed to explain the religion's practices and beliefs.

West of Plaza España

One block west of the plaza on Tejera and Isabela la Católica sits Isabelline **Casa del Cordón**, built in 1502 as the home of Francisco de Garay (later a founder of Spanish Jamaica). Named for its portal – which has beautiful arabesque ornamentation and a giant, stone monk's belt from the Franciscan order hanging above it in imitation of an *arraba* (an Islamic rectangular portal frame) – it's now used as office space for Banco Popular, but the courtyard with its *Mudéjar*-tiled staircase is open to visitors during the day. A block north on Isabela and Restauración is the musty **Museo Duarte**, Isabela la Católica 306 (Tues–Fri 8.30am–2pm, Sat 8.30am–noon; RD$2), housed in the building where the father of the country was born, with various period furnishings and rather humdrum mementoes related to his life. Just one block west of here, though, is the more appealing **Museo Mundo de Ámbar** at Meriño 452 and Restauración (Mon–Sat 9am–6pm, closed Sun; free; ☎682-3309), which is based on the popular amber museum in Puerto Plata (see p.197). Inside is a nice little exhibit on the origins of amber, a set of Triassic-era insects trapped in the translucent goo and of course the obligatory gift shop with a generous sampling of amber jewellery.

The Art Deco **Banco de Reservas**, on Isabela 201 and Mercedes (Mon–Fri 8am–4pm), is worth a visit for the social-realist mural *Moneda* displayed in its lobby. It's the work of **Vela Zanetti**, an anarchist exile of the Spanish Civil War who lived and worked in the Zona Colonial during the 1940s and 1950s, gleefully tattooing subversive, anti-capitalist statements on the many public commissions he received. Here labourers slaving in factories and fields surround a heroic figure stolidly grasping a gold coin; given the context, the coin is the obvious victor. One block west at Meriño 358, **Casa de la Moneda** sports the city's most beautiful Plateresque portal frieze, on which five faces peer from separate medallions, thought to represent the five ages of a man's life.

The atmospheric ruins of the **Monasterio San Francisco** lie a little further on, where Tejera ends at Calle Hostos. Begun in 1544 when the Catholic Church was transforming Santo Domingo into the religious capital of the hemisphere, the Franciscan monastery weathered an artillery assault from Sir Francis Drake and the brunt of several earthquakes, which levelled the main building and the original chapel adjacent to it. Above the entrance are the curling stone belt of the Franciscan order and a Renaissance bust of Bishop Geraldini, who oversaw its initial construction. The Gothic portal below leads to the **Chapel of the Third Order**, built in 1704 after the original was flattened; the Third Order was an organization of spiritual laymen who followed the Franciscan lifestyle. The coral-pink arcade opens onto the cloisters and the monastery church – a popular spot for local weddings. All that's left of the main building are the foundations and a few mounds of rubble. It was used as an insane asylum through the nineteenth century; at points along the walls you'll see the metal studs that once held inmates' leg chains.

Two blocks south on Hostos, not much remains of the **Hospital San Nicolás**, built in 1503 and mostly torn down in 1911 after being devastated by a hurricane. The most impressive feature left in the pigeon-haunted ruins is the two-storey portal with Renaissance pillars on the ground floor and a tremendous Gothic arch on the top. The Victorian **Iglesia Altagracia** beside it – associated locally with miraculous healing – incorporates the hospital's eighteenth-century chapel. Within it you'll find a life-size statue of **Dr José Gregorio Hernández**, a Venezuelan medical doctor from the 1930s, worshipped throughout Latin America as a saint who performs operations on believers while they sleep. Opposite the hospital, the Italian cultural centre at **Casa Italia** was once the home of nineteenth-century General Pedro Santana, who sold the country back to Spain; when nationalist guerrillas threw the Spaniards out, the general shot himself here to avoid facing trial.

El Convento de los Dominicos and around

Just south of El Conde are three ancient churches worth a detour, the oldest of which, the 1510 **Convento de los Dominicos**, Billini and Hostos (services are Mon–Fri 7–9am, 5.30–7pm, Sun 7.30am–noon, 7–8pm; doors open a half-hour before), held the New World's first university, San Tomé de Aquino, before it moved and became the Catholic University on Bolivar and Núñez de Cáceres, where the city's wealthy send their children. Its striking stone facade is framed by decorative two-dimensional pillars; blue *Mudéjar* tiling runs along the top of the portal, and a profusion of red Isabelline vine ornamentation surrounds the circular window in the centre. Inside, on the vault of the sanctuary's Chapel of the Rosary (the first chapel to the right of the entrance) you'll find an impressive reminder that European Christianity was a syncretic religion long before it came to the New World: an enormous pagan **zodiac wheel** is guarded by Jupiter (spring), Mars (summer), Mercury (autumn) and Saturn (winter), each identified not only with a season but as one of the gospel authors as well. Though there were once many such syncretic church illustrations in Europe, most were destroyed during the Counter-Reformation. The simple but attractive **Chapel of the Third Dominican Order** across the plaza once held the studies of famed Taino apologists Las Casas and Montesino. In colonial times the cobblestone path between them was known as the Street of the Cobblers, home to the city's shoemakers.

A block east on Billini and José Reyes is nunnery **Regina Angelorum** (Queen of the Angels), a monumental piece of architecture with huge external buttressing, decaying gargoyles and a sombre stone facade that took nearly a century to build. Knock on the caretaker's door in the back to have a peek inside, where you'll find a baroque eighteenth-century altar with a stunning silver retable and the marble grave of Padre Francisco Billini at the front of the sanctuary.

Smaller but far prettier is nearby **Iglesia del Carmen**, Arz Nouel and San Tomé, once the secret meeting place of the Trinitarian rebels. Its facade boasts a decorative Isabelline red-brick portal topped by a fanciful Islamic peak and a niche holding a statuette of the Virgin. Erected as a neighbourhood church in the 1590s (after Drake burned down the original), the building manages to retain a cohesive look despite numerous renovations made over the centuries, such as the addition of the **Capilla San Andres** and the philanthropic **Hospital Padre Billini** in the seventeenth. The life-size wooden statue of Christ above the chapel's intricately patterned mahogany altar is brought out every Ash Wednesday and paraded through the streets, a tradition that began in 1630.

Santa Bárbara and the northern wall

The old northern wall that marks the edge of the Zona Colonial holds a number of lovely churches worth a peek, though the run-down barrio alongside is equally interesting. In the sixteenth century this was the city slum, populated by subsistence farmers and stone-cutters who laboured alongside natives in the Santa Bárbara limestone quarry just north of **Iglesia Santa Bárbara**, Isabela la Católica and Puello (daily 8.30am–7pm), a handsome whitewashed church that honours the military's patron saint. Behind it are the remains of the **Santa Bárbara Fort**, to which the church was once attached, and a large chunk of the old city wall, mostly in ruins – what's left has been converted into a neighbourhood park. Ostensibly part of the city's riverfront defences, the garrison was used mostly to keep the Taino (and later African) slaves in line as they laboured in the quarry – which has long since been paved over and is now the city's downscale shopping district (see below).

Walk ten minutes west through a pretty residential area, to the corner of José Reyes and Isidro Pérez, where **Iglesia San Miguel**, a small seventeenth-century chapel, faces a park with an enormous pigeon coop. The old priests' quarters beside the church are used as private apartments; the fort that once stood across the street is in rubble. In the 1650s Spain ordered that San Miguel was to become a hospital for slaves, but local administrators ignored the decree. Further west lies **Iglesia San Lazaro**, Isidro Pérez and San Tomé, which did serve as a hospital for lepers. A bad nineteenth-century plaster job has defaced the red-brick facade, but the Tuscan columns and triple-arched belfry are still intact. More impressive is Gothic **Iglesia Las Mercedes**, a short walk south at José Reyes and Mercedes, its mahogany altar carved in the shape of a serpent. Built in the 1530s, the church was used during Haitian rule to house six thousand African-American immigrants who were eventually shipped off to Puerto Plata and Samaná.

Mercado Modelo

Just across Avenida Mella from San Miguel Fort, the **Mercado Modelo** (Mon–Sat 9am–12.30pm & 2.30–5pm), a sprawling marketplace, heralds the start of Santo Domingo's unofficial shopping district, where historic churches

Dominican syncretism

Syncretic religion – the mixing of European and African religions in South America and the Caribbean – is very much a part of Dominican culture, though Eurocentrism and official disfavour make it an object of shame. Cousin to Haitian Voodoo, it came about during the colonial era, when European Christianity was imposed on African slaves from the Congo and West Africa; the slaves mixed Catholicism, along with elements from a host of other traditions like European paganism, freemasonry and Taino religion, with their own belief system. Over time, various Christian saints came to be linked to deities imported from Africa, allowing the slaves to practise their religion in peace. St Patrick, for example, was the equivalent of Damballa, a powerful *Vodú* deity, because both are associated with snakes; St Elias is identified with Samedi, guardian of the cemetery, while St John the Baptist's association with water has connected him to Chango, Dahomeyan god of the ocean, lightning and tempests.

Practising Dominicans are often unaware (and are offended at the suggestion) of their religion's African roots and the unorthodoxy of some of its rituals. With them a distinction is made between *Santera* and *Vodú Dominicana*, categories that correspond roughly to the Haitian *Rada* and *Petwo* classes of spirit – the *Rada* are benevolent but less powerful, while the *Petwo* are stronger but amoral and mercenary, and require specific sacrifices for their interventions. Known in the DR as the **misterios**, the *Petwo* adherents are a select few who have some sort of transcendent religious experience in which they're forcibly "called" into service by their patron spirit. Rural groups also worship Taino spirits thought to inhabit caves, pools, and streams, leaving offerings of food and flowers at their holy sites. Though popularly attributed to Haitian influence, Dominican *Vodú* was practised in the early sixteenth century and thus actually predates Voodoo.

Vodú practice involves private ceremonies using large altars covered with depictions of saints, offertory candles, plastic cups of rum and numerous crosses honouring the **gedes**, bawdy cemetery spirits known to spout lascivious songs when they possess humans. **Possession** is an integral part of *Vodú* ceremonies, both by saints and the spirits of dead Taino warriors. You'll see *Vodú* paraphernalia, including love potions, spray cans that impart good luck in the lottery and Catholic icons at the many *botánicas* throughout the country. For more intractable problems, fol-

and abandoned forts give way to discount shops and streets jam-packed with foot traffic and guaguas by day – though by night the neighbourhood is abandoned and dangerous. For most visitors, the focal point will undoubtedly be the market itself, a maze of gift shops selling jewellery, Haitian paintings, Dominican and Cuban cigars and various handicrafts, with some outdoor stalls vending produce and the like. At the back entrance is **Super Botánica Gorjón**, the largest shop for syncretic religious items in the city, with icons, potions, crucifixes, candles and cassettes of African-influenced religious music. The barrio beyond is largely a slum, though at its core, **Parque Enriquillo**, Avenida Duarte and Ravelo, is the starting point for guaguas heading across the island's south coast from La Romana to the Haitian border.

The Malecón

The capital's famous oceanfront boardwalk, known as both the **Malecón** and Avenida George Washington, commences within the Zona Colonial at the large industrial port at the mouth of the Río Ozama. An intact section of the old city wall follows it for 100m to the seventeenth-century **San José Fort**, built on a strategic oceanfront promontory after an attempted invasion by the lowers will consult a **brujo**, or spiritual medium, who offers herbal healing remedies and acts as a go-between in barter deals made with the saints; in exchange for good health, for example, you might trade daily prayers for a year, a week-long pilgrimage to Higuey on foot, or a direct cash payment to the *brujo*.

Another manifestation is the many **cofradías** – religious brotherhoods that are an amalgamation of Spanish Catholic fraternities and West African secret societies. Syncretic *cofradías* actually began among black slaves in Spain and Portugal in the fourteenth century, before the discovery of the New World. In Santo Domingo's early days the societies were officially sanctioned by the Church and used the cathedral for their annual processions. Most were then dedicated to San Juan Bautista – who represented the Dahomeyan Chango – but in time slaves came instead from the Congo/Angola region further south, and the societies were taken over by their incorporeal supreme deity Kalunda, who is identified with the Holy Spirit; these *cofradías* are usually named **Hermandad del Congo**. *Cofradías* activities include sponsoring festivals in honour of Espíritu Santo and funeral rites for dead members. After the funeral, a nine-day second wake is held to assist in the passing on of the dead to the spirit world; on the anniversary of the person's death, the brotherhood then holds a ceremony with the family which often involves possession of a family member by the deceased, who parcels out practical advice.

All the aspects of Dominican syncretism are on display at the many public events that honour various saints, namely the **fiestas patronales**. These festivals vary quite a bit in the amount of folk religion they exhibit (some have had most of the religion leeched out of them). In Nigua, 12km west of Santo Domingo, you may also stumble onto a **rosario**, a penitent procession entreating the Virgin of Altagracia in times of drought or distress, with townsfolk marching behind the banner of their patron saint, singing folk songs structured in the manner of the Catholic "Hail Mary" (sung fifty times each in three sessions) and playing tambourines and drums; some devotees carry boulders on their head as an act of penance. Devout individuals and *cofradías* also sponsor private festivals called **velaciones** in their home barrios, though you'll need an invitation to go to one; if invited, etiquette demands that you help defray costs by bringing a bottle of rum and RD$100 to the society's leader.

British in 1655. The cannons that remain appear to point across the street at a fifty-metre-high statue of **Fray Montesino**, a sixteenth-century priest who preached against the Taino genocide, his legendary rage manifested in the flame-like spikes of his hair. This section of the boardwalk is extremely popular at night, with massive crowds and live music on weekends at the commercial port below Puerta San Diego, and a lively crowd at *La Parrillada*, an outdoor restaurant with dancing at night right next to the Montesino statue.

A kilometre further west you'll find **La Obelisca**, a large, two-pronged obelisk that locals equate with two parted legs, placed there by Trujillo in 1941 to honour repayment of a long-outstanding debt to the United States. A kilometre west of that is a second obelisk, **El Obelisco**, built in 1936 to commemorate Santo Domingo's temporary re-christening as Ciudad Trujillo, though now bearing distinctly anti-Trujillo murals depicting the Mirabal sisters, whom he assassinated, as nature goddesses capturing rainbows in a gourd. Beyond here, a line of high-rise hotels, restaurants, discos and festive outdoor parks stretches west for 4km. Dotted all along are a series of **outdoor party zones** (notably at avenidas Sánchez and Máximo Gómez) where you'll see plenty of dancing and activity every evening, though between these bright spots you're likely to be accosted from time to time by local hustlers looking to act as freelance "tour guides".

Past the chain of hotels is the **Centro de los Héroes**, the nation's administrative centre and home of parliament, marked along the promenade by a large pink arch and accompanying globe. At its far western end, the **Teatro de Agua y Luz**, a 1940s outdoor amphitheatre, has more water and light displays: the three large fountains in front come alive with colour on the rare occasions when there's a concert here. From here the waterfront becomes mostly residential, though closer to the Río Haina, a two-kilometre stretch of gaudily lit Vegas-style *cabañas turísticas* marks the longest zone of short-term sex stations in the country.

A quick note for those tempted by the stereotypically Caribbean waters that the Malecón skirts: **swimming** here is a very bad idea. Not only is it polluted, but the food waste being dumped into it from the mouth of the Río Ozama has made it **shark-infested** as well.

Gazcue and around

Well west of the Zona Colonial and north of the Malecón is rambling, tree-shaded **Gazcue**, the city's prettiest residential district, a mostly middle-class

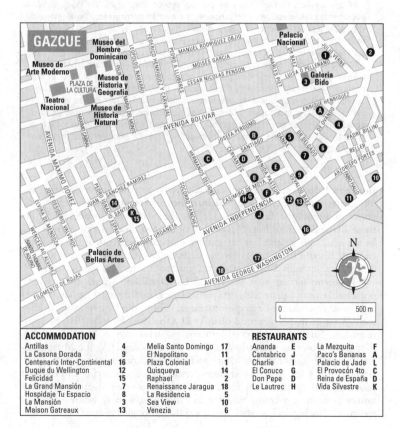

neighbourhood highlighted by the **Plaza de la Cultura**, Máximo Gómez and Ureña, a complex of four museums alongside the National Theatre and Library. While southern Gazcue is in easy walking distance of Parque Independencia and the Zone, the Plaza is far enough away that you'll need a taxi or a guagua to get there.

Museo de Arte Moderno

Of the museums in the Plaza de la Cultura, the first stop should be the **Museo de Arte Moderno** (Tues–Sun 9am–5pm; RD$10), four storeys dedicated to twentieth-century Dominican art, with a magnificent permanent collection on the second and third floors, temporary exhibits on the first and fourth, and installation art in the basement. At times the assemblage can seem a bit random, exacerbated by the frequent rotation of pieces within the museum space, but certain themes, like a reliance on Taino influences, can be spotted. Notable in this regard is Clara Ledesma's *Casetas*, in the **second floor**'s first room, in which Taino-rendered campesinos peek out of a *colmado* and several mud huts at two gringo tourists lying on the beach. In the same room *La Molienda*, by Guillo Pérez, manages to transform a rural train depot into an idyllic pastoral scene, with pastel railroad cars below thin pyres of smoke that drift from serene-looking smokestacks and melt into the sky. The next room holds the arresting *El sacrificio del chivo*, Elegio Pichardo's dark depiction of a family meal that interprets the everyday ritual of dinner as a pagan rite – note the shrunken head in the hand of the child as he waits for the mother to carve the goat. The third room is dominated by another piece incorporating native art, Junior Mendoza's *Ritual de Iniciación*, a mixed-media burlap canvas with a malevolent Taino head – half-painted, half-stitched together with bone and shell fragments – surrounded by nails with a circle of straw dolls tied to them by rope. Equally disturbing is the borrowed Roman Catholic iconography of Rincón Mora's *Rito* in the fourth room, his blood-smeared Christ peering through a glass window with smouldering red eyes.

The most highly regarded proponent of a more pastoral strain in modern Dominican art is **Candido Bidó**, whose stylized idealizations of campesino life have won international acclaim. Bidó's father was a Carnival mask maker in Bonao – the influence is apparent in the faces with hollowed-out eyes, straight noses and exaggerated lips. His serene, distinctive world contains a generous application of indigo blue and almost no green. The museum owns six Bidós, all of them in the second floor's fifth room, including his most famous, *El Paseo a las 10am*, a painting of a Dominican woman in a sunhat with a handful of flowers – the pigeon fluttering by her side is a typical Bidó gesture, as is the use of colour: yellow fields, black mountains, indigo sky, and the sun surrounded by a subduing, dark cyst.

Climb to the **third floor** to get a look at Alberto Bajo's *La Vida del Dominicano en Nueva York*, an enormous triptych in the fourth room depicting a family divided by American immigration. The first panel is of a sleepy Dominican fishing village, the second of the emigrant's cramped Manhattan apartment (with a letter home in the typewriter) and the third of the alien, neon rumble of Times Square. Around the corner in the fifth room are Frank Almayar's *Composición Gráfico de Duarte*, a dot-matrix Warhol rip-off that draws attention to the country's unreflecting obsession with the image of its liberator, and Silvano Lora's *Flor Endemica*, a mixed-media commentary on the bombed-out urban environment that many of the country's children live in. Lora is known locally as an outspoken defender of the oppressed – in 1992, when replicas of Columbus's three ships tried to dock in Santo Domingo in honour of the 500th anniversary of his voyage, Lora dressed up like a Taino, paddled out to the boats in a canoe and fired arrows at them until his vessel was capsized by the Coast Guard.

Museo del Hombre Dominicano

The plaza's other main attraction is the **Museo del Hombre Dominicano** (Tues–Sun 10am–5pm; RD$20), which holds an extraordinary collection of Taino artefacts and a good anthropological exhibit on Dominican fiestas patronales. The ground floor is taken up mostly by the gift shop, but does display a dozen stone obelisks and Taino burial mounds found near Boca Chica in the 1970s. The second floor is closed to visitation; the **third floor** consists of one large room bearing display cases of Taino sculpture, beginning with seated human figures and *cemis* – small stone idols that stood in for the gods during rituals, possessing large, inward-spiralling eyes and flared nostrils. Further down the room is an extensive collection of flints, hatchets and stone spearheads, which can be scanned over before passing to the two cases bearing beautiful animal sculptures and ceremonial daggers. At the far end of the room you'll find jewellery with incredibly intricate carvings made from coral, tooth, stone and conch shell, a case filled with spectacularly nasty-looking death heads and a few examples of the artwork created by the Tainos' ancestors in the Amazon basin. The **fourth floor** moves to Dominican culture after Columbus, with emphasis on the African influence. The first room focuses on the slave trade; the next room is taken up by a comparison of the rural dwellings of African peasants and Dominican campesinos. These are followed by a terrific exhibition on syncretist religious practices in the DR, including photographs of various rural fiestas patronales and a Dominican *Vodú* altar, with Catholic iconography standing in for African gods, votive candles and a sacrifice of cigarettes, a chicken and a bottle of rum. From here walk past the display of local musical instruments that originated in Africa to three large glass cases depicting costumed Carnival celebrations in Monte Cristi, La Vega and Santo Domingo.

Museo de Historia y Geografía

The **Museo de Historia y Geografía** (Tues–Sun 9.30am–5pm; free; ☎686-6668), next to the Museo de Arte Moderno, takes you through an uneven collection of historical memorabilia from the past two centuries. On the first floor is a modest exhibit of a dozen Taino sculptures, but the bulk of the museum is on the second floor, with rooms dedicated to the Haitian occupation of the early nineteenth century, the period of internecine strife that followed it, the American occupation that began in 1916 and the thirty-year reign of Trujillo. Of these the last two hold the most interest. The **American occupation** exhibit features propagandist pamphlets, Marine uniforms and an electric chair in which Dominicans were tortured – above it is a famous photograph of one victim being executed in it, which was used by partisan guerrillas in their efforts to boot the invaders out. The **Trujillo-era** exhibit contains hundreds of artefacts testifying to the dictator's wealth and absolute power, including gold- and ivory-plated personal effects, his military uniform adorned with dozens of medals and purple presidential sash, and the pancake makeup kit he used to hide his Haitian ancestry. You'll also see the Trujillo portraits and signs offering thanks to "El Benefactor" that were posted in every home and above drinking fountains, insane asylums and places of worship, and the *cedulas* (identification cards) that citizens were forced to carry with them at all times, identifying them by number. In the centre of the room sits one of the bullet-riddled cars that was part of the presidential motorcade when he was assassinated. Of the two lesser wings, the **Haitian occupation** exhibit includes some long-winded expositions of the horrors of the time, and is most interesting for the antiquated sabres and muskets used in the War of Independence, and the **late nineteenth century** room's exhaustive display of the accoutrements of presidential pomp – such as *caudillo* Ulises Heureaux's imperial plumed hat – grows tiresome fairly quickly.

Museo de Historia Natural and the Teatro Nacional

Also in the plaza, the **Museo de Historia Natural** (Tues–Sun 10am–5pm; RD$10; ☎689-0106) has a rather ordinary collection of skeletons and other science exhibits, though it does include a model of the Rosario Gold Mine near Cotuí. You're better off turning your attention to the **Teatro Nacional** (☎682-7255), a beautiful white marble palace that serves as venue for the National Symphony, Ballet and Opera. The only way you'll get a view of the sumptuous, baroque interior, however, is to buy a ticket for an upcoming event; at night the faux-Italian Renaissance fountain in front of the building lights up. Less interesting is the **National Library** next door, though it comes in handy if you're doing serious research on Dominican history and culture.

Around the Plaza de la Cultura

Continue north on Máximo Gómez from the Plaza de la Cultura to visit the **Centro Olímpico**, Kennedy and Máximo Gómez, a wooded public park with basketball and tennis courts, Olympic swimming pool, pavilions for gymnastics and volleyball and three baseball fields that are heavily scouted by America's Major Leagues. Only Dominican citizens are supposed to use the facilities, but you're unlikely to be challenged except at the pool; local teenagers hang out at the tennis courts and offer to play travellers for an RD$20 fee.

East of the Plaza de la Cultura, on Avenida Mexico and 30 de Marzo, stands the office of the president, the **Palacio Nacional** (☎686-4771 ext 340, ⓦwww.presidencia.gov.do/English/Palacio Nacional; call two days ahead for tours), an attractive, coral-pink marble edifice that's even better on the inside. It takes some effort to get a tour, but the decked-out glory is impressive: mahogany furnishings, marble floors, gold and silver inlay, monumental murals depicting major historical events and an enormous hall of mirrors with fifty caryatids (pillars sculpted into the shape of women) and six chandeliers. The visitors' entrance is in the back of the palace on Calle Dr Báez, where you'll find two massive bronze lions flanking the portal. South of the plaza on the corner of Independencia and Máximo Gómez is the similarly sumptuous **Palacio de Bellas Artes** (☎682-1325), a rectangular temple to high art that holds regular classical music performances by touring ensembles, and "merenjazz" concerts from top local musicians.

If you were taken with the Cándido Bidó's in the Museo de Arte Moderno (see p.85), it's worth taking a detour to **Galería Bidó** on Calle Dr Báez 5, a half-block north of Independencia (Mon–Fri 9am–1pm; ☎685-5310), a rambling home whose first floor holds one of the city's best private galleries. Sr Bidó has his latest work here, which has undergone some interesting transformations. The doll-like, hollow-eyed faces — which once conveyed pastoral innocence – are now being exploited for their ability to convey existential angst. One piece consists of series of still lifes in which discarded piles of these open-mouthed dolls stare eyeless from a pastel tablecloth. The gallery also features rotating exhibits of other top Dominican artists.

A few blocks west of the Palacio de Bellas Artes begins the seven-kilometre **Parque Mirador del Sur**, a popular walking and cycling area scattered with baseball diamonds, denuded of many of its trees by Hurricane Georges. At the southwest end of the park, a turnoff leads to **Lago Subterraneo** (daily 10am–4pm; RD$3), a small cave lagoon open to the public; the steep limestone cliffs that face it are popular with rock climbers.

Arroyo Hondo

Neither as wealthy as Gazcue below it or as desperate as the barrios beyond it, **Arroyo Hondo** – a bland expanse of residential neighbourhoods that shifts from upper-crust mansions in the south to makeshift shacks in the north – boasts two of the city's best museums, the **Museo Prehispánico** and the **Museo Bellapart**. It's also home to some of the city's most expansive green spaces, the most worthwhile being the **Jardín Botánico**, Avenida Jardín Botánico and Los Próceres (Tues–Sun 9am–5pm; RD$30; ☎565-2860), which has flora from every part of the island, a pavilion with three hundred types of orchid (most endemic), and greenhouses for bromeliads and aquatic plants. Less indigenous but quite striking is the manicured Japanese garden with a maze of shrubs and a pagoda with shaded benches beside a babbling brook. An RD$15 train ride will take you through the length of the park with a stop-off at some of the highlights, but it's far more pleasant to wander about the grounds at your leisure. For an even larger orchid collection go to the nearby **Orchidearia Arroyo Hondo**, at Polanco 28 and Billini (☎567-1351), a private hothouse run by a local botanist, with some for sale.

Further east of the botanical gardens, the **Parque Zoológico**, Paseo de los Reyes Católicos and Ortega y Gasset (Mon–Fri 9am–5pm, Sat & Sun 9am–5.30pm; RD$15; ☎562-3149), has a decent collection of African animals, though some fare better than others. The hyenas and chimps are packed into very cramped quarters, while the rhinos are allotted a large stretch of open field within which to roam. More unusual entries include the endangered solenodons in the reptile pavilion, nocturnal anteaters with comically long snouts and sharp claws. Still, you've likely seen what's on offer here before, and in better surroundings.

Museo Prehispánico

The **Museo Prehispánico**, San Martín 179 and Lopé de Vega (Mon–Fri 9am–5pm; free), is a private collection of Taino artefacts housed in a large room within the Pepsi-Cola corporate building, rivalling the display at the Museo del Hombre Dominicano (see p.86). At the entrance are a few Venezuelan pieces (the Tainos' ancestral home) to provide historical context, a prelude to the fossilized mastodon and armadillo remains, animals the natives hunted to extinction on the island. Further on stand display cases outlining the history of indigenous ceramics, followed by intricate tooth and bone sculptures used in necklaces – one is so small you need a magnifying glass to see the carving. At the far end of the room you'll see jewellery made from conch shells, coral, teeth and clay, before turning left to the opposite end of the room for a view of an intact wooden *duho* – a chair carved with the face of a Taino god, used by *caciques* as a throne during religious ceremonies. Along the wall beside it is a collection of clay animals – which represented various deities – including a dozen frogs, a few turtles, a crocodile and two owls, which were believed to ferry souls to the afterlife. The exhibit turns to more practical items as you double back towards the entrance, but the intricate ornamentation on the pots, cassava grinders and ceremonial axeheads keeps your attention from flagging. Especially arresting is the jet-black monolith of a Taino deity with an ostentatious phallus – originally meant to guard the entrance to a cave.

Museo Bellapart

Also well worth a visit is the **Museo Bellapart**, Avenida Kennedy and Dr Peguero (Mon–Fri 10am–6pm, Sat 9am–noon; free; ☎541-7721), located in a single large room on the second floor of a massive Honda dealership. This small private art museum holds the very best of Dominican art from the first half of the twentieth century. The paintings follow a timeline from the 1890s through the late 1950s. Highlights include social-realist Jaime Colsón's *Merengue* at the entrance, a surreal rendition of a typical Dominican *fandango* which is strongly influenced by Mexican muralist art; the subdued deco aesthetic of Celeste Woss y Gill's *Retrato sin fecha*, a lush portrait of a Latin flapper from the Roaring Twenties gracefully scanning a book; and folk artist Yoryi Morel's ragged depiction of a Dominican campo titled *Dedicado a Mi Madre*. The crowning glory of the collection, though, is Spanish exile **José Vela Zanetti's** *La Vida de los Campesinos* series; his work also graces the walls of the UN Security Council in New York. The painting here marks a stylistic break from the monumental social-realism of his work on public buildings, sketchier and more attuned to the modernism of Van Gogh, with rough-hewn peasants in front of a whorling, almost formless background of barren rolling hills. Especially arresting are *Familia Campesina* and *Retrato Paño Azul*, which offer a poignant human intimacy absent in his more ambitious, sweeping social statements.

East of the Ozama

Though most of Santo Domingo's attractions lie west of the Río Ozama, there are a few scattered points of interest along the eastern bank and beyond. The best-known of these is the controversial **Columbus Lighthouse** (daily 9.30am–5.30pm; RD$15; ☎592-1492), known locally as **El Faro** (simply "the lighthouse"), a monument finally completed, after decades in the making, in 1992 – the 500th anniversary of Columbus's "discovery" of the Americas. The idea for such a tribute dates to the 1850s, when several prominent intellectuals signed an editorial in *Listin Diario* calling for its creation. In 1929 an international competition was held for its design. Given that there were over 450 contestants from 50 countries, it's hard to understand how British architect J.C. Gleave's awful, mammoth cross-shaped entry won out; the edifice resembles nothing so much as an immaculately scrubbed penitentiary. Within this bombastic eyesore stands the baroque **mausoleum of Christopher Columbus**, with dozens of flowery angels hovering above the marble casket alongside a more corporeal 24-hour honour guard. Also on the ground floor, look for a series of galleries with paintings of the Virgin Mary from every country in the Americas; on the third floor is a modest Naval Museum. The lighthouse's most impressive feature is the 250-laser cross of light that it projects onto the city's night sky, though even that is resented by many here – it's said that whenever it turns on, power goes out in villages across the country. Columbus's role in the Taino genocide led to protests in the capital when the lighthouse was opened, and the government's razing of one of the city's poorest neighbourhoods to build it didn't help. Another sticking point was the price tag, estimated to be US$100–150 million.

El Faro towers over the western end of **Parque Mirador del Este**, a pleasant stretch of manicured woodlands spanning the length of the barrios east of the Ozama. At the park's far eastern tip are a series of large caves dotted with freshwater lagoons. Known as **Los Tres Ojos**, or "The Three Eyes" (daily 9am–5pm; RD$10), the caves were used by the Tainos for religious ceremonies; more recently they've been the setting for some half-dozen Tarzan movies. Walkways lead you to three of the lagoons, and a manually powered pulley conducts a ferry to a fourth.

The eastern bank of the Ozama was the first part of the city that was settled, but Christopher Columbus's outpost was constructed from timber, and the lone colonial relic left here is the early sixteenth-century **Capilla del Rosario** (daily 10.30am–4.30pm; free), a pretty, single-nave church with three brick portals supposedly built on the site of Christopher's home. Just north, check out **El Monumento de Azúcar**, on Avenida España, a realist metal sculpture depicting noble campesinos driving oxen and cartloads of sugar cane. Back south, España bends around to the **Acuario Nacional** (Tues–Sun 9am–5.30pm; RD$10; ☎592-1509), which centres on a large Plexiglas tunnel surrounded by a tank full of sharks, manta rays, moray eels and other sea creatures. Also on display are sample underwater ecosystems from around the world, though these aren't quite as arresting. Across the street, **Agua Splash** (Tues–Sun 10.30am–5.30pm; RD$60, children under 12 RD$40; ☎591-5927), a large water park with twelve slides, is best visited during the week – if at all – when the rides are less crowded.

Villa Mella and the outer barrios

The city's **outer barrios** are for the most part extremely poor industrial zones with a mix of concrete-box homes and thatch huts. There are no tourist sights in the traditional sense, and if you want to explore them for a sense of how people here live, you should do so only during the day, as they become dangerous at night. Buses leave Parque Enriquillo every twenty minutes to **Los Alcarrizos**, a concrete suburb buzzing with swarms of motorcycles and with dozens of storefront Pentecostal churches; **La Ciénaga**, a riverside barrio that was hit hard by Hurricane Georges; **Sabana Perdida**, a relatively prosperous, sprawling residential zone northeast of the city; and palm-treed **Villa Mella**, which makes for the most interesting diversion, if only for its frequent syncretic religious festivals.

Villa Mella's population is largely descended from Congolese slaves, and elements of Congo culture are still evident in the local language, religion and music. Indeed, during the festivities of **Espíritu Santo** (seven weeks after Semana Santa), conga drums are played round the clock for nine straight days at both the parque central and Iglesia Espíritu Santo, on Máximo Gómez. The rest of the time you'll have to content yourself with the locally famous chicarrones vendors that line the far northern end of Avenida Máximo Gómez.

Between Villa Mella and the Río Isabela is **Parque Mirador del Norte** (daily 9am–5.30pm; RD$5), the city's largest public park, though it actually sees little use; its six square kilometres are dominated by chinaberry trees, bisected by an enormous artificial lake and a driving route for cars.

Eating

Dining options in the capital range from the small family *comedores* and *pica pollos* present in every neighbourhood to gourmet restaurants with **ethnic cuisines** as diverse as Basque, North African, Korean and Japanese. At the more expensive restaurants, expect to spend about RD$300–400 for a full meal including tax and tip (but not drinks); phone numbers are given in the listings below where reservations may be necessary. **Gazcue** is the city's top restaurant district, but there are plenty of great places within the Zona Colonial and on the Malecón as well. Much cheaper fare can be found in the many informal food shacks and stands that dot the Malecón, where you'll be able to pick up pulled-pork sandwiches, grilled chicken with rice-and-beans or a burger for as little as RD$15. There are plenty of good **grocery stores** spread throughout town, including Nacional, 27 de Febrero and Lopé de Vega; Supermercado Casa Pérez, Arz Nouel and Hincado; and Supermercado Olé, Av Duarte 194. Otherwise, you can get basic food supplies and cooking ingredients at the numerous small *colmados* spread throughout the city.

Zona Colonial

La Briciola Arz Meriño 152 ☎688-5055. Impeccable service and elegant, candlelit ambience in a restored colonial palace that features a menu of fresh home-made pastas and seafood. There's also a very elegant bar called *Doubles* where you can order the same great food in a more casual environment.

La Cafetería El Conde 253. Best of the cafés along El Conde and a hangout for local painters and musicians. Delicious breakfasts with fresh orange juice and *café con leche*. Also sells the best Dominican rums at great prices, along with great cutting-edge Spanish literature. Closed Sun.

Caribbean Blue Hostos just north of El Conde ☎682-1238. Best restaurant in the city hands down, though the relatively high prices (RD$300 or so for a meal) make it a bit of a splurge. The atmosphere manages to be both relaxing and hip, with a high glass ceiling enclosing the colonial courtyard that serves as the main dining room. What brings the crowds is the eclectic menu, all of it cooked in the building's original sixteenth-century wood-burning stove, including tuna sushi, goat meat enchiladas, shrimp risotto and out-of-this-world salads. For dessert try the *trufas mágicas de chocolate*. On weekends the second floor doubles as the Zona Colonial's most popular bar, *Agua Lounge* (see p.95).

Coco's Billini 53, behind the cathedral ☎687-9624. Very formal (and expensive) British expat-run restaurant with superb steaks, seafood and tandoori chicken – a house speciality. Closed Mon.

Comedor Independencia Av Independencia at Parque Independencia. Modest-looking spot, but good for inexpensive Dominican dishes and attentive service.

Dar Valencia Arz Portes 255 and 19 de Marzo ☎686-5213. A Kublai Khan fantasy of the Islamic world at its height, this zany French-Moroccan restaurant is decked out with all manner of mosaics, satins, hookahs and men in fezes swish-

ing through silk curtains amid a plethora of water fountains. Most come for the resultant atmosphere, but the food here is quite good; specialities include escargot, chicken couscous and creole octopus. Closed Sun.

Dulcería Mercedes and José Reyes. Unmarked bakery with heavenly sweets. Don't leave without sampling the super-sweet *coco horneado*.

Harry's Bar Las Atarazanas 29, Plaza España. Not much to look at but actually quite nice, with excellent *cómida criolla* and pleasant proprietors. If you're in search of refreshment, come here for the heavenly *morir soñandos*.

Meson D'Bari Hostos and Ureña. Great food at this terrific local tavern, particularly the *bistec encebollado* – perhaps the best steak in the country. The atmosphere is terrific, the prices are cheap and the service is swift, though it gets noisy on weekend nights when it serves as an extremely popular local bar. The seafood is also exceptionally fresh here, and *cangrejos guisados* is a house speciality.

El Mesón de Luis Hostos and El Conde. Local diner that serves up breakfasts, the best time to come, and typical Dominican dishes for around RD$30; just off the Parque Colón. Closed Mon.

Museo del Jamón Atarazana 17. Tapas bar on the Plaza España featuring enormous hams hanging from the ceiling and close imitations of prosciutto and serrano.

Paco Rabanne Puerta Las Atarazanas, Av Del Puerto. Really fun, moderately priced restaurant in a yacht on the Zona Colonial port, more notable for its location than its nondescript selection of Dominican standards.

Pat'e Palo Atarazana 25 ☎687-8089. Named for the infamous pirate Peg Leg, this somewhat kitschy psuedo-brasserie right on the Plaza España serves solid but pricey seafood, including a yellowfin tuna carpaccio, creole shrimp and lobster fra diavolo. The profiteroles are an excellent dessert choice.

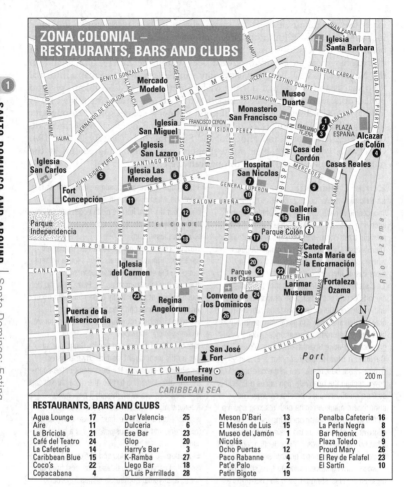

ZONA COLONIAL – RESTAURANTS, BARS AND CLUBS

RESTAURANTS, BARS AND CLUBS

Agua Lounge	17	Dar Valencia	25	Meson D'Bari	13	Penalba Cafeteria	16
Aire	11	Dulceria	6	El Mesón de Luis	15	La Perla Negra	8
La Brícola	21	Ese Bar	23	Museo del Jamón	1	Bar Phoenix	5
Café del Teatro	24	Glop	20	Nicolás	7	Plaza Toledo	9
La Cafetería	14	Harry's Bar	3	Ocho Puertas	12	Proud Mary	26
Caribbean Blue	15	K-Ramba	27	Paco Rabanne	4	El Rey de Falafel	23
Coco's	22	Llego Bar	18	Pat'e Palo	2	El Sartín	10
Copacabana	4	D'Luis Parrillada	28	Patín Bigote	19		

Penalba Cafeteria Parque Colón, El Conde/Meriño. Clean little cafeteria with outdoor tables on the Parque Colón facing out at the cathedral. Food is unremarkable but perfectly acceptable Dominican staples like chicken with rice, and cheeseburgers.

La Perla Negra Mercedes and José Reyes. Excellent and very inexpensive little *comedor* with daily specials – you get what they've cooked up for the day. They often have very good fish specials, and some delicious chicken dishes are thrown into the mix as well.

Plaza Toledo Isabela la Católica and Luperón. Beautiful outdoor courtyard featuring moderately priced dishes like linguini with shrimp or *criolla*

sauce and delicious dessert crepes. Also a good spot for an espresso.

El Rey de Falafel Billini and Sánchez. Definitely worth going out of your way for, this popular food-stand set up next to *Ese Bar* is run by a hip young Israeli-Dominican who makes the freshest, most delicious falafel sandwiches imaginable, cooked while you watch. Make sure to say "no ketchup" or your poor sandwich will pay the consequences.

Malecón

Charlie Llúberes 9 between Malecón and Independencia. Unpretentious à la carte spot specializing in large portions of grilled pork chops, chicken, steak and rabbit.

D'Luis Parrillada Plaza Montesino Malecón and Fiallo. The capital's most popular late-night spot, with outdoor seating along the ocean, cheap food and a hyped-up merengue atmosphere. The speciality here is Argentine-style grilled meat dishes, and the quality of the cooking makes the long waits for service more than worth it. Open 24 hours.

Fogarate Malecón 517. Some of the best Dominican food in the city, doled out in a fun atmosphere full of multicoloured thatched roofs. Try the traditional *asopao* rice with chicken served in a battered tin bowl. Popular with local families.

Palacio de Jade Heredia 6 ☎686-3226. Pricey Chinese, Cantonese and Mongolian cuisine in a fake moated castle with karaoke rooms on the second floor. Specialities include Peking duck, beggar's chicken and shrimp with black bean sauce. Definitely an "experience", but the high quality of the food makes it worth a stop.

Palacio del Mofongo Malecón 517. An open-air terrace from which to admire the ocean and sample quality Dominican food without the campesino kitsch of its competitors.

Vesuvio Malecón 521 ☎221-3333. One of the most renowned restaurants in the city, deservedly so for its vast array of delicious, if expensive, pastas. Particularly recommended are the mostaccioli arrabiata, risotto con frutas del mar, and gnocchi gorgonzola.

Vesuvio Pizzeria Malecón 523. Best pizza in town, with good sandwiches, ham-and-cheese crepes and a few pastas. Run by the same management as next door's *Vesuvio* but more casual and family-oriented.

Gazcue

Ananda Casimiro de Moya 7 ☎682-4465. Popular vegetarian cafeteria and artsy crowd hangout, sometimes showcasing live merengue on Monday nights. Food is good but fairly bland, though the tempuras are quite well done.

Cantabrico Independencia 54. Classy, unpretentious dining room tucked away in Gazcue, with high-priced specialities like Valencian-style paellas and Segovian sucking pig.

El Conuco Casimiro de Moya 152 ☎686-0129. Dominican cuisine glorifying life in the campos – you'll be attended to by singing, dancing waiters. The daily RD$75 buffet is a bargain, and the menu features *sancocho, chivo orégano,* and *guinea aisá.* Set in an oversized *bohío* – a traditional campesino common area inherited from the Tainos.

Don Pepe Pasteur 41 at Santiago ☎686-8481. A good place to go if you've budgeted for one big

splurge. The menu is a display of fresh seafood on ice (try *al horno-*style), including lobster and an assortment of fish. Best of all is the giant crab. Don't miss the dessert tray, with its terrific flans, cheesecakes and crème caramel.

Le Lautrec Casimiro de Moya 144. Discover the best of southern French cuisine in this beautifully apportioned dining room run by an expat painter named Picard. The service is unobtrusive but truly excellent, and the dining room incredibly charming. Menu highlights include confit de pato, cassoulet con habichuelas blancas and nase de gambas. There's also an extensive wine list, and for dessert you can try the flan de coco with passion fruit. The most romantic dinner spot in the city.

La Mezquita Independencia 407. Outstanding little seafood restaurant with a cozy dining room and a loyal local following. Among the many reasonably priced specialities are mero (*criolla* or *al orégano*), octopus, and *lambí.*

Paco's Bananas Santiago and Bolivar ☎682-3535. Large, popular neighbourhood restaurant serving great Dominican food in a casual setting. Recommended are the conch soup, gazpacho, shrimp creole, grilled fish, *pescado con coco* and flan.

El Provocón 4to, Santiago and José Pérez, and with other locations throughout the city. Outdoor patio offering heaping portions of grilled chicken, rice-and-beans and salad. Good for a large, inexpensive lunch. Open 24 hours.

Reina de España Cervantes 103 at Santiago ☎685-2588. Elegant dining room with traditional Spanish cuisine like *mero* Basque-style, hake in green sauce, rabbit in garlic sauce and roast piglet.

Vida Silvestre Rodriguez 153 ☎238-5888. Relaxed, American-style wholefoods cafeteria with organic greens and produce; the only real option for vegans. Open Mon–Thurs for lunch only.

Outer districts

A. Arirang 27 de Febrero 346 ☎565-5611. Surprisingly well-done Korean restaurant with traditional grills at the table and a fine spicy kimchi (pickled cabbage).

Alma Llanera Av Churchill just south of 27 de Febrero. A small spot that you could easily walk past without noticing, this little kitchen serves tremendous Venezuelan dishes like shredded beef in creole sauce and a variety of *cachapas* – cornbread pancakes stuffed with beef, chicken, shredded pork or cheese. A nice find, and good for those on a tight budget.

Bagels 'N More Plaza Criscar, Fantino Falco 57. Traditional New York bagels, plus some more unorthodox bagel sandwich concoctions. A remarkably popular stopover for expat bagel lovers across the island.

Chino de Mariscos Sarasota 38A ☎533-5249. Authentic Hong Kong dining room with excellent Chinese seafood dishes. Start out with one of the seafood soups and move on to the black bean lobster or garlic shrimp. Expect to spend RD$300 or so on dinner for two.

David Crockett Ricart 34 ☎547-2999. Excellent steak house with corny "Wild West" decor, which makes it quite popular with kids. The massive porterhouse steaks go under the name "Cowboy Filet"; rack of lamb and prime rib are also favourites.

Lumi's Park Av Lincoln 809 just north of 27 de Febrero. Fun outdoor, tropical garden atmosphere in which you can enjoy home-style Dominican *mofongo* and grilled steaks. A little more expensive than the homespun *mofongo comedores* out in the barrios, but not very expensive nonetheless.

Meson de la Cava Av Mirador del Sur at eastern end of park ☎533-2818. Funky restaurant set in a large Taino cave, with lobster, shrimp *ajillo* and rib-eye steaks. The food is good enough, but it's more notable for the unique atmosphere.

Samurai Av Lincoln 902 and Inchaustegui ☎565-1621. Authentic Japanese sushi bar, definitely a rarity in these parts and surprisingly satisfying, with shabu shabu, mixed sushi and sashimi platters, hibachi platters and sake. Surprisingly inexpensive considering the high quality. Open from noon Mon–Sat, dinner only Sun.

Scheherezade Pastoriza 226 and Lincoln ☎227-2323. Great Middle Eastern cuisine in a mock mosque with occasional belly dancing. Best are the vegetable couscous and lobster in a caviar salsa.

Tacos del Sol Av Lincoln 609 and Locutores ☎541-7870. Popular outdoor Mexican joint with tacos, burritos and fajitas, though the opportunity to drink frozen daiquiris and tequila sunrises in a pleasant outdoor plaza is what attracts the crowds.

Todo Pollo Calle Winston Churchill at Parque Mirador del Sur. The best of the *pollo al carbón* kitchens that line the east end of the park, served in an open-air shack with merengue blasting from the stereo.

Yogen Fruz Plaza Andalucia II, Av Lincoln and Ricart, and at Plaza Unicentro, Av 27 de Febrero and Gerardino. Fresh tropical fruits like mango and papaya blended into frozen yoghurt, a refreshing and relatively inexpensive snack.

Drinking, nightlife and entertainment

Santo Domingo's Malecón is the traditional focus of **nightlife**; along with some of the city's finest dance halls, the boardwalk is crowded with outdoor restaurants and food shacks that slowly start getting crowded around 10pm and stay open into the early hours of the morning. Less known to outsiders are the nightclubs along Avenida Venezuela 1km east of the Río Ozama, and Avenida Abraham Lincoln north of 27 de Febrero. There are also several clubs across the city that specialize in **son** – a slow, melodious Cuban groove with acoustic guitars and percussion that many Dominicans claim was born here – long popular and enjoying unprecedented respectability, highlighted by a citywide festival in March. Another singular Santo Domingo experience is *La Guácara Taina*, a nightclub set in an enormous cave once inhabited by Tainos. More downhome are the informal **merengue périco ripao** bands that wander the crowded *colmados* along Avenida Duarte in the early evening. The **performing arts** are also well represented in the capital, with full orchestra, opera and ballet seasons in the National Theatre and visiting orchestras and chamber groups in the Palacio de Bellas Artes.

Bars and cafés

The **Zona Colonial** is the place for bar-hopping: at night the ruins are especially atmospheric, and dotted around them are a variety of working-class neighbourhood joints, jazz bars and slick clubs. The other major centre of activity is the **Plaza Central shopping district** in Arroyo Hondo, where most wealthy young Dominicans hang out. The best and busiest night for heading out to these bars is Monday, preferably after midnight. The **Malecón** also has a number of informal set-ups with a liquor shack surrounded by tables and chairs.

Zona Colonial

Agua Lounge second floor of *Caribbean Blue* (see p.91). Super-hip, tremendously popular cocktail bar that's completely packed on weekends starting at midnight with the local twentysomething set. Has a definite "trendy New York" feel to it.

Café del Teatro Arz Meriño 110 ℡689-3430. Weekend courtyard café in Casa de Teatro, a nineteenth-century drama venue, with live jazz and jazz-influenced Latin combos.

Copacabana Barco Paco Rabanne, second floor, Av del Puerto, Puerto Las Atarazanas. Unique party atmosphere on the second floor of the large boat that's permanently parked in front of the old city's San Diego gate. Features a mix of top American, Dominican and techno hits. RD$50 cover and one-drink minimum.

Ese Bar Billini and Sánchez. A hip new entry to the crowded field of bars in the Zone, this place manages to be stylish without taking on any airs. A good place for a newcomer to plug into the scene, and a must on anyone's ZC bar-hopping itinerary.

K-Ramba Isabela and Arz Portes. Eclectic little place beside the San José fort, with a mix of merengue and rock. The inhabitants of the row-houses next door set up tables and chairs all along the abutting plaza, and the two crowds tend to blend as the evening wears on.

Meson D'Bari Hostos and Ureña. Do not miss this atmospheric after-work gathering place, notable for its soundtrack of traditional *bachatas*, Sinatra, jazz and old-style Cuban *son*. The seafood dishes are quite good here as well (see p.91).

Nicolás Hostos 352. Unpretentious and pleasant watering hole in the parlour of a private house. Quirky place to hang out for an hour, looking out on a view of the San Nicolás hospital ruins.

Ocho Puertas José Reyes 107. Set in a gorgeously restored colonial warehouse with several luxurious rooms, including a lounge with couches, an outdoor plaza and a standard bar, this Santo Domingo mainstay has become established as the centre of the local rave scene, and is occasionally closed down for drug violations. When open, it's a lot of fun – and a great place to find out about raves taking place all across the country.

Patín Bigote Arz Nouel and Meriño. Funky bar decorated with massive photos of various world celebrities with outrageous moustaches, including Dali, Einstein, Chaplin and Frida Kahlo. A favourite with the college crowd and designed to be a comfortable hangout.

Proud Mary Duarte and Portes. The Zone's main expat hangout, known locally as *Bar de Marie*, features American music exclusively. Can be fun or depressing, depending on the crowd, but it's typically a good place to meet people.

El Sartín Hostos 138. An informal place with a rather erratic schedule, so look for the old blue light in front of the building – when the light is on, customers are welcome. When open, it's a pretty fun place to hang out, featuring great Latin hits from yesteryear and a middle-aged crowd of mostly men hanging out and having a good time.

Malecón

La Ruta Cerveza Plaza D'Frank just west of the *Hotel Inter-Continental*, Malecón. The most popular of the outdoor beer joints dotting the boardwalk and a favourite hangout of Sammy Sosa. They've recently added a roof and a large neon sign, and are reputed to have the coldest beer in town.

Plaza Central and Arroyo Hondo

Beer House Churchill two blocks north of 27 de Febrero. Beer bar with a big patio and a jungle gym for the tykes to play in while mommy and daddy get hammered.

Monte Cristi Lincoln and José Amado Soler. Great little outer-barrio bar with red billowing curtains and a surprisingly hip crowd split pretty evenly between men and women. The red drapes strung along the outside of the booths allow you to close them for greater privacy. Sharp dress required.

Mrs. Teapot GM Ricart and Av Lincoln, Plaza Andalucia I, second floor. Afternoon hangout for wealthy kids, with forty different high-quality teas along with dozens of coffees, iced coffees and ice cream coffee drinks. Closed Sun.

Punto Corcho Av Lincoln and GM Ricart, Plaza Andalucia II. Mellow, ambient wine bar with a broad range of Spanish, French, Italian and Chilean selections.

Discos and live music

Weekends see plenty of activity, but the busiest night for local **clubs** is Monday, when most are booked with big-name acts; street-side banners across the city advertise any notable concert, which will raise the cover charge by RD$50.

Zona Colonial

Aire Mercedes 313 ⓦ www.aireclub.com. Playground of the beautiful people, this hipper-than-thou nightspot boasts a serious scene and an evenly mixed straight and gay crowd. Set in a colonial mansion with multiple rambling rooms, each with a strikingly different ambience and decor. Don't miss Wednesday, which is "Foam Night", when hundreds of square feet of foam the consistency of shaving cream is spewed onto the dance floor. Gay night is Monday (see opposite). Closed Tues.

Malecón

Bella Blu Malecón 165 just west of Máximo Gómez ☎689-2911. Popular oceanfront disco with music at tolerable decibels. Good place for couples to drink and dance. RD$50 cover.

Fantasy Héroes de Luperón and Malecón. Small disco frequented by Dominican couples, but also with some suspect "waitresses" whose virtues are touted by guides along the Malecón. The club fronts a baseball field where games are held most evenings (see p.98).

Jet Set Independencia 2253 ☎535-4145. Very nice, medium-sized seventh-floor disco with great views of the city. Notable because it's so jam-packed with locals every night. RD$50 cover.

Jubilee Malecón 367, *Renaissance Jaragua Hotel* ☎688-8026. Large, luxurious hotel disco featuring top-notch sound and light systems, though serving quite expensive drinks. RD$100 cover.

Mauna Loa Calle Héroes de Luperón at Malecón, Centro de los Héroes ☎533-2151. Super-suave, gorgeous nightclub and casino with two floors of tables looking out onto a big-band stage reminiscent of the Roaring Twenties. Saturday is bolero night with the Francis Santana orchestra. Sunday nights are the best: *son* night with Chichi y los Soneros de Haina. Monday nights feature maestro Anthony Ríos. The club opens at 6pm, but the music doesn't start until 11pm. Whatever you do, don't miss this. RD$25 cover, and one drink minimum.

Merengue Bar Malecón 367, *Renaissance Jaragua Hotel*. Though smaller than most of the other seafront discos, the live nightly merengue, fancy interiors, and lack of cover help bring in a large local crowd.

Napolitano Malecón 101, *Hotel Napolitano*.

Surprisingly, the mid-range *Hotel Napolitano* actually has the most popular disco on the boardwalk these days – in large part because working-class twentysomethings can come here without paying a steep cover charge. Always fun, but especially so on Thursdays – which feature bolero star Antony Ríos.

Outer barrios

La Guácara Taina Av Mirador del Sur ☎530-2666. Probably the most famous club in the city, set in a huge, multi-level natural cave with top live acts and early evening *périco ripao* shows. Truly wild. RD$100 cover.

Monaco JFK and Gracifa Alvarez, just east of Lope de Vega. Not to be confused with an overpriced brothel that bears the same name on the Malecón, this is the newest and most luxuriously apportioned disco in town – and the city's current hot spot. The soundtrack is hip-hop leavened with trance and other forms of electronica. Dress especially sharp or the house diva at the entrance won't let you in. RD$80 cover.

Schizo Plaza Andalucia II, Av Lincoln and GM Ricart. This small disco was the first to introduce techno to young, upper-class Dominicans, and though it's no longer the trendiest spot in town it does still pull in decent crowds.

Vieja Havana Av Máximo Gómez, Villa Mella. Great outdoor *son* hall that's best on Thursday and Sunday nights, when they hold old-style dance contests, with elderly Dominican couples cutting brilliant moves.

East of the Ozama

D'Angel Car Wash Av Venezuela and GM Ricart. The car wash has long been a staple of rural Dominican nightlife, and D'Angel transfers this tradition to the inner city – with big crowds hanging out along the bar, dancing in the odd open spaces and shooting pool on the second floor.

D'Caballeros Av Venezuela and José Cabrera. Unpretentious nightclub with live merengue and televised baseball at the bar.

Eclipse Av Venezuela and Bonaire. The hottest spot on Venezuela, this new club seems to net major live acts every weekend. Should be the first stop on your Av Venezuela itinerary, though the cover charges for live acts can be steep, RD$150–200. Closed Mon.

Latino Liquor Store Av Venezuela and Cabrera. Glittery, mirror-filled bar with a mostly male crowd and a strictly enforced dress code.

Monumento del Son Av Charles de Gaulle and

Los Restauradores, barrio Sabana Perdida ☎590-3666. Famous outdoor *son* hall set in a safe neighbourhood 5km north of the Las Américas highway, with live music Fri–Mon. Well worth the detour.

Gay and lesbian nightlife

Homophobia and official disfavour keep the **gay and lesbian club scene** mostly underground, but there are a handful of places in Santo Domingo with an established and fun reputation. You should, however, be wary of being accosted by local hustlers, and also know that male gay clubs are a major target for bashings; it's definitely safest to arrive and depart by taxi. The main cruising grounds are in the Zona Colonial: along El Conde, in front of the cathedral and at Plaza España.

Aire Mercedes 313 ⓦwww.aireclub.com. The hottest gay club in Santo Domingo is also the hottest club period on the entire island, and a definite must-visit. Sunday is Tea Party night, Monday is gay night, and the rest of the week features a mixed crowd. Closed Tues.

Atlantis Malecón 555 ☎685-2011. Very classy club with good (but pricey) mixed drinks, a large dance floor and weekend stripper shows.

Bar Phoenix Polvorín 10 and Juan Isidro Pérez ☎689-7572. English-operated gay bar near the Parque Independencia. Best place to get oriented to the scene, as the proprietor is well connected and the bar sports a perpetually crowded party atmosphere. Closed Sun.

Glop Hostos and Arz Nouel. Gay-run tapas bar in the heart of the Zona Colonial, with great regional cocktails like Brazilian caipirinhas. Mixed gay, lesbian and straight crowd.

Lido Av Mella 414. X-rated gay cinema in a *very* rough neighbourhood north of the Mercado Modelo, with some cruising in the bathrooms and just outside. Do not hang out here late at night (after 9pm) as muggings are commonplace.

Llego Bar José Reyes 10 ☎689-8250. Piano bar just off El Conde with male strippers on weekends and an entertaining owner who keeps things hopping. Gets a lot of hustlers, so ask the owner first for the scoop on anyone you're interested in. Closed Mon.

O'Hare's Place Danae 3 and Independencia. Unmarked, informal outdoor bar frequented mostly by lesbians, but also with a small gay male crowd. Decorated like an Irish pub and sheltered by a canopy of flowers, it's basically 100 percent Dominican.

Classical music and theatre

Classical music is well funded by Santo Domingo's upper classes and regarded proudly as a manifestation of their European roots. The national symphony, opera and ballet companies are all quite competent, but visitors may find more of interest in the occasional concert hall performances of local merengue and jazz-influenced composers like Dario Estrella in the Palacio de Bellas Artes; tickets for these events are usually still available the night of the performance and run RD$150–500. The **theatre** circuit is small but boasts a vibrant experimental scene that uses Casa de Teatro as its main venue; all performances are, of course, in Spanish. Consult *Diario Libre* – available free in most Zona Colonial shops – for listings of cultural events.

Venues

Casa de Teatro Arz Meriño 110 ☎689-3430. A great courtyard venue for small theatre productions; also showcases live jazz on weekends. RD$30 cover.

Centro Cultural Español Arz Meriño and Arz Portes ☎686-6212. Free lectures, art exhibitions and chamber performances by contemporary artists from Spain, funded by the Spanish embassy and with a loyal local following.

National Theatre Máximo Gómez 35 ☎687-3191. A lush palace, built by Trujillo, that features seasons by the national symphony, ballet and opera companies, along with a regular influx of visiting artists.

Palacio de Bellas Artes Máximo Gómez and Independencia ℡687-3300. Official guardian of the nation's high culture, this beautiful auditorium hosts touring international orchestras and major jazz artists, along with ballet, theatre and orchestra performances by students from the National Conservatory.

Parque Independencia Free military concert band performances are given in the park year-round every Sunday afternoon at 3pm.

Plaza Central 27 de Febrero and Troncoso. Live concert band performances Sunday afternoons at 6pm along the outdoor promenade on 27 de Febrero that fronts the mall.

Cinema

Most Santo Domingo **cinemas** focus on first-run American action flicks, which hit the screens at the same time here as they do in the States; unfortunately, almost every theatre in the city shows the same two or three Hollywood blockbusters at the same time. Check first at the ticket booth to see if the movie is English with Spanish subtitles or dubbed. Either way, expect the audience to be as much a part of the show as the movie – locals often derive most of their pleasure from making fun of the action on screen. You'll find most venues in the major shopping malls and on the Malecón; check local newspapers for places and times.

Broadway Cinema Plaza Central, 27 de Febrero and Churchill ℡526-7171. Offers alternative films unavailable elsewhere, along with the usual hits.

Casa Francia Vicioso 103 and Las Damas ℡532-2844. Runs a wide-ranging French cinema series; movies Wed–Fri 8.30pm; closed July.

Casa Italia Calle Hostos and Luperón ℡688-1497. They've just begun an Italian cinema series in imitation of Casa Francia.

Centro Cultural Español Arz Meriño and Arz Portes ℡686-8212. Film series from Spanish directors, always with a generous sprinkling of Almodóvar.

Cinemax Biblioteca 3 ℡566-0567. Standard Hollywood hits in a comfortable, well-maintained theatre.

Issfapol Núñez de Cáceres behind the Supermercado Nacional, two blocks north of 27 de Febrero ℡541-3255. Huge old film venue, sometimes with alternative and European fare alongside the big-budget Hollywood flicks. Ample parking.

Palacio del Cine 27 de Febrero and Gerardino, one block east of Plaza Central ℡567-2960. The best of the bunch in terms of cleanliness and concessions. Large screens, too.

Sports and other activities

Baseball is the most exciting spectator sport in Santo Domingo; two separate professional teams, **Licey** and **Escogido**, play in the winter professional league from mid-November through early February; games are at Estadio Quisqueya, Máximo Gómez and Kennedy (tickets RD$50–150; ℡565-5565 or 567-6371). You can purchase tickets on Wednesday for the weekly Sunday games in winter at locations across the island – see local newspapers for current ticket purchasing locations. Though more and more Dominican major-leaguers are opting out of the winter season, you'll still find a few famous Dominican players on the rosters (star Red Sox hurler Pedro Martínez still pitches for Escogido, for example), along with some of America's top minor-league prospects. The rest of the year you can catch Santo Domingo intramural-league games at the baseball field behind the *Fantasy Disco*, Héroes de Luperón and Malecón.

Most foreign visitors find **cockfighting**, the other local obsession, less easy to stomach, but it's a critical part of Dominican culture. The city's grand **Coliséo Gallístico**, Avenida Luperón just south of the Autopista Duarte (RD$100 for ground floor, RD$30 for second-floor bleachers; ℡564-3844),

Santo Domingo festivals

February
Carnival
Partying, live music and elaborate costumes along El Conde and the Malecón every Sunday, especially the last of the month. Expect to be pelted with inflated sheep bladders and balloons.

February 27
Independence Day
A citywide celebration that's the culmination of Carnival, with a raucous re-creation of the Trinitarians' 1844 torch-lit march to El Conde, to the tune of the *1812 Overture*, accompanied by live cannons. Afterwards head to Puerta San Diego, where you'll hear big-name merengue acts.

Last two weeks of March
Son Festival
Dozens of events celebrating this popular Cuban musical form that many Dominicans claim as their own. *Meson D'Bari* (see p.95) posts a list of all events on its wall in early February.

Variable (usually in April)
Semana Santa
The holy week of both Christianity and Voodoo. Most Dominicans celebrate by shutting down the city for a week and heading to the beach. In Haina, on the city's western outskirts, you'll find a Hispanicized version of the Haitian Semana Santa festivities also found in the *bateyes*. On Ash Wednesday, go in the morning to the Zona Colonial's Iglesia del Carmen, where a statue of Christ is paraded through the streets, serenaded and draped in money.

Seven weeks after Semana Santa
Espíritu Santo
A full week of religious processions and conga drums in Villa Mella.

First weekend of July
Running of the Bulls
Worth checking out for a hearty laugh, this event was recently created by a local organization wishing to celebrate the Dominican Republic's Spanish heritage. A herd of local bulls "run" along Las Atarazanas in imitation of the more famous festival at San Fermín. Unfortunately, the Dominican bulls they round up are just not as frisky as the ones back in the home country – and most of the effort is exerted in getting the bulls to move at all. On the bright side, there's little chance you'll be gored to death.

Last two weeks of July
Merengue Festival
Loud outdoor concerts on the Malecón by big-name *merengueros*, plus traditional accordion merengue groups performing at the Palacio de Bellas Artes and merengue-based "folklore" shows at the National Theatre that feature the Vodú-based palos musicians of Villa Mella with the National Folklore Ballet.

August 14–17
Restoration Festival
Another major Malecón celebration in honour of the war for independence from Spain, with bandstands, foodstands and liquor shacks set up along the boardwalk.

SANTO DOMINGO AND AROUND | Santo Domingo: Sports and other activities

continued overleaf

September 15–24

Virgen de las Mercedes

Syncretic religious ceremony/neighbourhood block party in Mata Los Indios near Villa Mella. Famous for its African-style drumming and music.

September 29

San Miguel

Fiesta patronal in honour of one of the country's most important deity/saints, celebrated in Villa Mella and the Zona Colonial's barrio San Miguel. Expect to see a large procession carrying an effigy of the saint accompanied by drums and *gagá* band.

October 7

Fiesta Oriental

The eastern side of the city had the first recorded Dominican carnival (1520), and in recent years the Zona Oriental has finally gotten its share of festivities again. This massive carnival in honour of the barrios east of the Ozama is heavier on the African syncretic elements of Dominican culture than the February event, including traditional local dances like the *mandinga* and *bailan pri-pri*, as well as *guloya* performances from the Cocolos of San Pedro. Runs the length of Avenida Venezuela and ends up in Parque Mirador del Este.

December 31

New Year's Eve

Head directly for the Malecón, where over 250,000 people cram in to watch the proceedings at a dozen different bandstands.

practically transforms this traditionally rural pastime into something of an upper-class diversion; indeed, semi-formal dress is required. There are also plenty of other, smaller venues spread across the city's outer barrios, but this is by far the best and most accessible place for visitors to come.

Otherwise you can head towards the airport to the side-by-side horse-racing and auto-racing venues. The **Hipodromo** horse track, Carretera Las Américas Km 11.5 (Wed & Thurs 5pm–midnight; ☎687-6060), is very popular locally. Most come to gamble, and a rowdy party atmosphere pervades the place between races. Next door, a new auto racetrack, the **Autodromo**, Carretera Las Américas Km 12 (Sat & Sun 8am–4.30pm), has recently opened and attracts a mid-sized crowd of hard-core middle-aged gamblers and teenage boys hoping to see a major accident. Other gambling opportunities lie in the various **casinos** spread along the Malecón. The various hotel casinos are virtually interchangeable; they can be found at the *Hotel Intercontinental, Hotel Hispaniola, Hotel Napolitano, Hotel San Geronimo, Hotel Santo Domingo, Jaragua Renaissance Hotel* and *Melía Santo Domingo*. All are open from 4pm to 4am. Far classier, though, are the gaming tables at the *Mauna Loa Club* on Avenida Héroes de Luperón and Malecón (no slot machines), which are frequented almost exclusively by upper-crust Dominicans; their hours are 8pm–4am.

If interested in more **participatory sports**, you can try the **go-kart track** at the Shell Kartodromo, Malecón just west of Avenida Héroes de Luperón (RD$150 for 15min; ☎532-0552), set right on the ocean. Vehicles and facilities are very well maintained, but the course is pretty small and it's really better for kids. On the southwestern edge of Parque Mirador del Sur, you'll find some cliffs that locals use to practise their **rock climbing**, and there is an exclusive **golf course** at Santo Domingo Country Club, at the west end of town, which you can arrange to visit through Golf Holidays Travel, *Plaza Hotel Embajador* (☎534-6606); the same company organizes excursions to the legendary "Teeth of the Dog" golf course at *Casa de Campo* in La Romana (see p.129). If you're not worried about getting in some aerobic exercise, you can instead try your hand at **bowling** at the Sebelen Bowling Center in Plaza Bolera on Avenida Lincoln and Pastoriza (daily; 9am–midnight), which is a fun, family-oriented place that also has a video arcade, pool tables and concessions. A game costs RD$150 9am–4pm, RD$200 4pm–midnight. Finally, the entire city is dotted with **pool halls**, which is a bit of a local obsession. The best places to shoot a few games are the second-floor halls that you'll find all along El Conde – though as with all Dominican pool halls, the atmosphere is hyper-macho and thus the denizens are all men.

Shops and galleries

The city's high-end shopping district consists of the clothing boutiques and shopping plazas that spread outward from the **Plaza Central** at 27 de Febrero and Troncoso. More tourist-oriented shops can be found along **El Conde** in the Zona Colonial and at the **Mercado Modelo** on Avenida Mella (see p.81), which vend an impressive array of Dominican and Cuban cigars, mahogany humidors and jewellery made from local larimar, amber and colonial Spanish coins. El Conde is also home to the city's best **bookstores,** with dozens of new and used shops – though book prices in the DR are pretty steep and English-language literature is hard to find. Meanwhile, most Dominicans shop for clothing and electronics at the budget stores that line **Avenida Duarte**, especially La Sirena, Mella 358 and Duarte, which has inexpensive counterfeit designer clothes purchased en masse at the markets along the Haitian border (see p.277). **Art galleries** are spread throughout the city; of special note is Galería Elín, the outstanding Haitian art gallery in the Zona Colonial.

   Hours for stores and shops in Santo Domingo are typically Mon–Sat 9.30am–noon and 2.30–5.30pm. Most (though not all) are closed on Sunday.

Clothing, jewellery and accessories

El Mamey Isabela 110 ☎689-0236. Otherwise humdrum gift shop that's a good place to find authentic Carnival masks from La Vega.

Museo de Ámbar El Conde 107 at Parque Colón ☎221-1333. Excellent but pricey jewellery shop with the highest-quality amber and larimar pieces in the city, including some amber with insects suspended inside them and knock-off colonial coins made into necklaces and bracelets. There's also a museum on the second floor (see p.73), and it's set in the oldest colonial home on the park.

Museo Larimar Dominicano Isabela la Católica ☎689-6605, ⓦwww.larimarmuseum.com. A generous selection of all manner of quality larimar jewellery; see p.75 for more on the museum itself.

Museo Mundo de Ámbar Meriño 452 and Restauración ☎682-3309. Open 9am–6pm (closed Sun), this new amber museum actually has a better exhibit than the one on Parque Duarte, and a comparable gift shop stocked with all sorts of amber jewellery. See p.73.

Plaza Central 27 de Febrero and Troncoso. Large shopping mall with all the standard shops and a large cinema. The promenade out front on 27 de Febrero has recently been renovated, with a gated walking path, modern sculpture, a funky Eiffel-style clocktower like the one in Monte Cristi and live concert band music on Sundays at 6pm.

Rinascimento Billini 153, Plaza Padre Billini. This is the place to come for top designer labels, including Dominican designer Oscar de la Renta, as well as top Italian brands like Prada and Versace.

Speciality shops

Casa Francia Cigar Shop Vicioso 103 and Calle de las Damas. Small set-up in the lobby shows the entire process of growing and rolling cigars, with boxes of cigars for sale.

Casa Weber Meriño and Restauración. Speciality bookstore set in a beautiful old building, catering to local intellectuals, with good sections on Spanish poetry, Dominican history and the history of the local feminist movement.

Cigar King El Conde 458 ☎689-2565. The best Dominican and Cuban cigars (not cheap, though), plus humidors and other accoutrements. Also sells foreign cigarette brands that you can't find elsewhere, though these are also quite expensive.

Cohiba Hecho a Mano El Conde 109 at Parque Colón ☎685-6425. Cohiba outlet has a variety of top cigars at reasonable prices. There's also a cigar roller on the premises who will teach you to roll your own cigar if you'd like.

Geyda Centro Comercial Naco, Av Tiradentes. Magazine store in the Naco shopping mall that has all the standard North American and European magazines and newspapers – and only charges the cover price. One of the few places where you can get international daily newspapers on the day for which they were intended (not a day or two late). Open 8am–8pm.

Karen CD Store El Conde 251 ☎686-0019. Outlet for the major Dominican distributor, with all of the great contemporary Dominican music and a good archive of the older releases of Karen stars like Juan Luis Guerra.

Librería America Arz Nouel 251. All sorts of second-hand books, some tourism-oriented, others on all aspects of Dominican culture and letters.

Librería La Trinitaria Arz Nouel 255 and José Reyes. Best of the many small bookshops that surround El Conde, with a host of great Spanish-language tomes on every aspect of Dominican life and culture imaginable.

Musicalia El Conde 464. This record store was once the famous record outlet through which *bachata* was first transmitted to the masses of *capitaleños*, who eventually adopted it as their new national music. Today it has the best of the Dominican golden oldies, from operatic favourites like Eduardo Brito and María Montéz through old *bachateros* like Luis Segura and *típico merengueros* from Francisco Ulloa to Tavito Vasquez.

Naturavida O. Báez 13 ☎476-7765, ✉inginsa@tricom.net. Well-stocked health store with a variety of vitamins and homeopathic medicines, as well as incense and other new age accoutrements.

Galleries

De Soto Galería Hostos 215 and Luperón ☎689-6109. Haphazard, homey shop full of all kinds of curiosities and knick-knacks, including 1900 cash registers and various items salvaged from a World War I German shipwreck. Also has some quality examples of pre-Suró Latin Cubism. Unlike the other galleries, this one is open on Sundays.

Elín Gallery Meriño 203 and El Conde ☎688-7100. The best Haitian paintings in the country, with prices half what you would pay in North America or Western Europe and covering a broad spectrum of media and styles. The paintings are simply stacked up in rows all along the shop, but don't let the humble presentation fool you. This is the first place to look for serious Haitian art.

Galería Candido Bidó Dr Báez 5. Art gallery set on a residential block, run by the famous Dominican painter, with a selection of his own work and exhibits from other Dominican modernists like Picasso-influenced Cristian Tiburcio – whose massive sculptures of musicians flank the gallery's front door. See p.87 for more information.

Galería de Arte Arawak Rafael Sánchez 53 ☎565-3614. Taino pieces and regular exhibitions of contemporary Dominican artists.

Galería de Arte Nader Rafael Sánchez and Geraldino ☎544-0878. Most prestigious of the Gazcue art galleries, displaying big-name contemporary Dominican painters.

Llarama Galería Hostos and Arz Nouel. There's always something interesting at this contemporary gallery focusing on experimental photography, installations and other conceptual art. Worth checking out if you have any interest in modern art.

Toledo Gallery Isabela la Católica 163 and Luperón, Plaza María de Toledo ☎688-7649. An excellent selection of Haitian painting, metal sculpture, beaded Vodú flags and crafts. The prices for paintings are way higher than what you will find at Elín, but this is the place to go if you want other Haitian visual arts. They also have some reasonably priced Dominican Carnival masks.

Listings

Airlines In the city: Air Canada, Ricart 54 (☎567-2236); Air France, Máximo Gómez 15 (☎686-8432); Air Santo Domingo, 27 de Febrero 272/Seminario, 2nd Floor (☎683-8006, ⓕ381-0080); ALM, Navarro 28 (☎687-4569); American, El Conde 401 (☎542-5151); Caribair, Av Luperón (☎542-6688); Continental, Edificio In Tempo, Av Churchill (☎562-6688); Cubana, 27 de Febrero and Tiradentes (☎227-2040); Iberia, Lope de Vega 63 (☎508-0188); LTU, Plaza Colonial Duarte (☎571-2403); Lufthansa, Malecón 353 (☎689-9625); TWA, 27 de Febrero and Dargán, Plaza Jomi, Ste 203 (☎732-5000); United, Ricart 54 (☎541-8072); US Air, Ricart 54 (☎541-5159).

Ambulance Dial ☎911 in case of emergency; for private ambulance call Movimed (☎535-1080).

American Express Banco Dominicano del Progreso, Av Kennedy 3 (Mon–Fri 8.30am–3pm; ☎563-3233).

Banks Banco BHD (with Visa advance machines), Arz Nouel 456 at Parque Independencia; 27 de Febrero and Churchill. Banco de Reservas, Av Duarte and Mella; Calle Mercedes and Isabela la Católica. Banco del Progreso, Independencia 509; Av Duarte 200 and Jiménez; Av Tiradentes at Plaza Naco. Banco Mercantil, Bolivar 308. Banco Metropolitano, Calle Ricart and Lope de Vega; 27 de Febrero 385A. Banco Popular (24-hour ATM machines), Calle Isabela la Católica and Tajeras; Calle Duarte and Mella. Baninter (24-hour ATM machine), El Conde at Parque Colón. Citibank, Av Independencia 557. Scotiabank (24-hour ATM machines), Av Duarte and Mella; Calle Isabela la Católica and Mercedes.

Car rental Alamo, Lincoln/Kennedy (☎562-1444, ⓕ227-9015); Dollar, Independencia 366 (☎221-7368, ⓦwww.dollar.com.do); Hertz, Independencia 454 (☎221-5333); Honda, Kennedy and Pepillo Salcedo (☎541-8487); National, Lincoln 1056 (☎562-1444); Payless, Ricart 82 (☎563-4686).

Cell phone Codetel (☎220-1111). Consultel, Lincoln 412 (☎566-0652). World Communication, Independencia 15 (☎688-9559). RD$900/month phone rental, with 100 free minutes. RD$3.9 per minute locally, much higher international.

Currency exchange There are plenty of small exchanges in the Zona Colonial, though withdrawing out of an ATM bank machine will get you a better exchange rate. If you don't have a bank card, go to the exchange desk at Caribe Tours, 27 de Febrero and Navarro, who offer the city's best rates. Avoid any dealings with exchangers who approach you on the street, as rip-offs and coun-

terfeit pesos are standard practice.

Dental Try Dr Luis Gonzalez Canahuate, Edificio El Palacio, El Conde and 19 de Marzo, Apt 204 (☎688-1194; night emergency ☎566-1901); or Clinica Dental Dr Marcos Diaz, Monción 213 (☎686-0561).

Embassies Canada, Máximo Gómez 30 (☎685-1136); United Kingdom, Av Lincoln 552 (☎540-3132); United States, Calle Nicolás Pensión and Navarro (☎221-2171). There is no consular representation for Australia or New Zealand.

Film processing Enfoca, El Conde 351; and Fotosol, 219 Bolivar; both offer 24-hour developing and have an array of film for sale.

Hospitals Good facilities at Centro Médico Semma, Perdomo and Joaquín Peres (☎686-1705), and Clínica Abreu, Beller 42 (☎688-4411).

Internet Deremate Internet Center, Mercedes and Meriño (daily 9am–10pm, DSL, RD$35/hr); Mundo Internet, 27 de Febrero and Lincoln (Mon–Sat 9am–7.30pm, RD$30/hr); Servir.net, El Conde/José Reyes (daily 8am–10pm, RD$35/hr; ⓦwww.enelconde.com.

Laundry Castillo, Ricart 162; Lavaseco, Independencia 208; Nacional, Santomé 401; San Miguel, 27 de Febrero 21. Count on around RD$40 per large load. Otherwise you can use your hotel's laundry service, though they generally charge by the piece and are much more expensive.

Pharmacies There are 24-hour pharmacies at Carol, Ricart 24 (☎562-6767) and Duarte 305 (☎536-4148), San Judas Tadeo, Independencia 33 (☎685-8165) and Vivian, Independencia/Delgado (☎221-2000). Other locations can be found across the city, especially around Plaza Central in Arroyo Hondo.

Police The central police station is at Independencia (☎533-4046 and 682-3151 or 5423). More convenient is the station on El Conde at Parque Colón. Dial ☎911 in case of emergency.

Post office The main office is on Av Héroes de Luperón just off the Malecón (Mon–Fri 8am–5pm, Sat 8am–noon; ☎534-5838). You may also try the office at Casa de Abogados on Parque Colón (Mon–Fri 8am–5pm, Sat 8am–noon).

Taxis Atupal (☎554-0922), Cristiano (☎594-2049), El Refugio (☎687-1572), Super (☎684-9050), Tropical (☎334-6886).

Telephone Telephone centres are spread throughout the city and are open daily 9am–10pm, including Codetel, El Conde 137, Malecón at *Hotel Napolitano*, and Bolivar and 30 de Marzo; Televimenca, Av Lincoln 306 and Sarasota; Tricom,

Hermanas Mirabal 127, and Máximo Gómez one block south of Bolivar; and Turitel, Casa de Abogados, Parque Colón.

Travel agents Santo Domingo Tours, Bolivar 7 (☎689-4745), offers good city tour packages and can also arrange air travel. Reliable agencies for flight and hotel arrangements include IATA, Ricart

69 (☎562-4282); Scala Tours, Av Kennedy (☎549-3244); Thomas Cook, Av Lincoln 306 (☎532-7381); Viajes Internacionales, El Conde 105 (☎689-3373).

Wiring money Western Union, Av Lincoln 306 and Sarasota (Mon–Sat 9.30am–noon & 2–5pm).

Around Santo Domingo

Beyond the belt of industrial barrios that encases Santo Domingo are a variety of **day-trips** within easy striking distance, none of them on a list of top must-dos, but good diversions nevertheless. History buffs will enjoy scavenging the western barrios for the impressive bits of colonial architecture that still stand, mostly in the form of the substantial ruins of four separate sixteenth-century **sugar mills**. You'll need your own wheels to get there, though, tucked away as they are in relatively out-of-the-way places. Baseball fans should head to **Campo Las Palmas**, the Los Angeles Dodgers training facility directly east of town, a professional baseball camp that welcomes visitors with a little advance notice. Those looking for a bit of Caribbean beach should head to **Boca Chica**, an overcrowded resort town 10km east of the airport, about halfway between Santo Domingo and San Pedro de Macorís; further along the same highway is **Juan Dolio**, more beachfront with fewer hassles, though still dominated by all-inclusive hotels.

West of Santo Domingo

Four remote **colonial ruins** lie hidden among the rambling, semi-rural barrios west of the city, nearly impossible to reach via public transport. West of barrio Manoguayabo, the ruins of the grand **Palavé manor**, a typical sixteenth-century sugar hacienda, are the best-maintained of the bunch. Named Palais Bel during Haitian rule, its masonry and brick facade were restored in the 1970s, and still boast bits of the old Andalucian whitewash and a prominent parapet. Three Romanesque portals lead into the large, central room; the beam above the doorways once supported a second-floor balcony. The easiest way to get there is to take the Autopista Duarte and make a left at the Manoguayabo turnoff. Just past the town, take a right at the fork in the road and head 3km beyond Hato Nuevo to the village Buena Noche; a left at the kerosene station leads 100m to the ruins.

Overgrown with weeds are the extensive remains of another sugar mill, **Engombe**, on the Río Haina. Mentioned by Oviedo in his 1534 *History of the Indies* as the colony's leading mill, the manor and adjoining chapel are for the most part still intact. The mansion's militaristic, rectangular facade was originally fortified to protect against slave rebellion – here and there along the wall you'll see foundations of the spiked limestone barrier. The double Romanesque portals on both floors lead to the open main room, which is connected to two galleries

△ Benches and trees on Santo Domingo's Malecón

and an interior staircase that now leads to nowhere. Beside the house is the large chapel with two frames – a polygonal apse and a leaning sacristy. A brief spate of renovation by Santo Domingo's Catholic University in 1963 restored its original Moorish tiled roof, but the buildings have since fallen back into neglect. Fifty metres further down the road you'll find the scattered ruins of the slave barracks and the mill in a family's backyard. The easiest way to Engombe is to take the Carretera San Cristóbal west from Santo Domingo and make a right turn on an unmarked dirt turnoff just before the Río Haina (for which you'll have to keep a very careful eye out), then a left at the fork in the road.

Directly west of Santo Domingo, 13km along the coast, **Boca de Nigua** holds the ruins of two more colonial sugar mills. The 1785 **Hermitage de San Gregorio**, a simple church that's still the local parish, was the site of prayer for both owners and slaves of the **Ingenio Boca de Nigua**, another 250m south past the town cemetery, an enormous mill and boiling room for extracting juice for rum. Back up to the hermitage, head 1km west and then turn off at the Pepsi sign to reach **Ingenio Diego Caballero**. It is fenced off while excavations are under way, but you can still see the foundations of the manor and – if you follow the dirt path that skirts the grounds for 50m – the mill. Built in the early sixteenth century by Caballero, Secretary of the Royal Audience during Diego Columbus's reign, the mill was initially powered by a canal dug in from the nearby Río Nigua, and had to be temporarily closed down in the 1600s when the course of the river changed. The canal has been excavated along with three arched bridges that were built to transport sugar cane from the fields to the mill.

Boca Chica

Once one of the island's prime swimming spots, **BOCA CHICA**, 25km east of Santo Domingo, curves along a small bay protected by shoals, with wonderfully transparent Caribbean water paralleling a long line of beach shacks serving excellent food. Unfortunately, the town that surrounds it has become so epically crowded with freelance guides, sex workers and over-persistent touts that it's impossible to walk more than a few feet without being accosted by some enterprising new individual hell-bent on attaching himself to you for the duration of your stay. As a result, Boca Chica is really not as fun as it once was, and is probably best avoided. If you do decide to visit, try a day-trip during the weekend, when the beach is jam-packed with thousands of day-tripping city-dwellers swimming in the sea and dancing to a cacophony of car stereos – an unforgettable beach party scene. At night, after the Dominicans leave, it becomes little more than a gringo brothel.

Before Columbus this was the major centre of Taino civilization on this part of the island, and archeologists still call the Taino culture that extended from San Cristóbal to Macao the "Chicoid Culture". From the 1860s onward it was an undistinguished sugar-mill town, before rising to prominence as a resort village and weekend getaway for wealthy Dominicans from the capital during the Trujillo era. Tourists began coming here in the 1970s, though the spate of all-inclusive resort areas in other parts of the country has caused a decline in visitation over the past decade, if not a similar dip in the town's traditionally hard-drinking nightlife.

Sitting on the **beach** is the main attraction, and the waters are low and calm enough to walk out to the bird-inhabited mangrove island **La Matica** just off

shore. If you tire of swimming and sunbathing, you could opt for a more rigorous activity like **scuba diving**. Regular trips are led by Orca Divers on Playa Boca Chica at Nuñez 27 (☏ 323-5369, ⓦ www.orca.divers.de; US$29–65), a PADI and PDIC-certified outfit. Dives head out to **La Caleta Submarine National Park**, a protected nearby coral reef at the bottom of which lie two sunken ships: the *Hickory*, once a treasure-hunting ship that salvaged two Spanish shipwrecks but now home to thousands of tropical sea creatures; and a bizarre-looking vehicle called "The UFO" which is touted on the tour as being potentially extraterrestrial, but in fact is an old oil rig. Other diving excursions go to the waters off Bayahibe, Isla Catalina and a cave dive near Santo Domingo; they also do deep-sea fishing excursions and watersports such as sailing, surfing and snorkelling. Other local diversions include **horseback riding**, organized by Crazy Horse Ranch, 20 de Diciembre 1 (☏ 523-4199; US$20); or catching one of the daily **baseball games** at the field on Calle del Sur.

Getting around and other Boca Chica practicalities

It's quite likely you'll have arrived in town by rental car from the capital, but if you need transportation while you're in town, the taxi stand is on Duarte and Hungria on the west side of the town strip. If you have your own car, there is cheap, safe parking (RD$25) in the parking lot on Duarte next to Codetel. Calle Duarte also holds all the major services you might need while in town: a Banco Popular ATM machine, several phone centres, Western Union, a supermarket, a pharmacy and a clinic. The best internet access is also on Duarte at the Boca Chica Gallery Shop (DSL; RD$50/hr). The tourist office is on Vicini and 20 de Diciembre, while the police station is on Mella on the parque central.

Accommodation

There are certainly plenty of hotels in Boca Chica, and these are rarely full; the only time you might have trouble finding a room in the hotel of your choice is in January or February, traditionally the high season in the DR. Of the three **all-inclusive** hotels, only two are set directly on the beach, though the third, the *Boca Chica Beach Resort*, is far nicer. More plentiful (and cheaper, too) are the small **hostels** set up by both European expats and locals all across town. If you're willing to haggle a bit, you can often get RD$50 knocked off the price.

Boca Chica Beach Resort Vicini and 20 de Diciembre ☎523-4521, ℗523-4438, ✉b.resort@codetel.net.do. Best of the local all-inclusive resorts, with beautiful grounds, the cleanest and most modern rooms, helpful service and good buffet food. Set back two blocks from the beach, which is a bit of a disadvantage, but it's much quieter as a result. ❺

Casa Coco Dominguez 8 ☎523-4409, ℗523-4216, ✉hotelcasacoco@codetel.net.do. Nine basic but clean rooms with double beds. There's also a relatively peaceful pool area and *Cocobar*, a little bar/restaurant that's fun to hang out in at night. Rooms have cable TV. ❸

Don Paco Duarte 6 and Vicini ☎523-4816. The best low-budget option, just off the water and surrounded by a garden that buffers the street noise. Friendly proprietors and clean rooms (a/c and hot water), with a good breakfast included in the price. No guests allowed due to the booming local sex business. ❷

Europa Dominguez and Duarte ☎523-5721, ✉htleuropa@codetel.net.do. Highly recommended French-run hotel right on the beach with sociable and efficient proprietors who keep the place up to the highest standards and make everybody feel at home. The 33 comfortable rooms (five with sea view) have king-size beds, but beyond that each is uniquely decorated. There's one three-bedroom for large groups, and several cheap economy rooms. Definitely the nicest hotel in town. ❸–❺

Garant Sánchez 9 ☎523-5544, ℗523-6644. Modern rooms with a/c, strong hot water and cable TV, a block away from the sand. The restaurant is quite good and serves as a major expat hangout. ❹

Hamaca Av Hamaca Beach Resort ☎523-4611, ℗523-6767. Decent all-inclusive but hardly outstanding, split between a main building and *Hamaca Gardens*, a complex of beachfront villas. They do have private balcony rooms, a/c and cable TV; if you're travelling with a group of four or more, book rooms 330, 331 and 343, which connect onto an enormous veranda and have a common living room. Other amenities include a casino, five bars, good food for an all-inclusive and free snorkelling equipment. ❼

Magical Tropical Dibisoria and Sur ☎523-4254. Pretty scruffy, but some rooms have a kitchen – which will help you cut down on costs. Otherwise a bearable bargain option if the other cheap hotels are full. ❷

Romagna Mia Duarte 1 ☎523-4647. Simple rooms just off the main drag, and fine meals at the downstairs restaurant. Nothing to write home about, but does have a/c, hot water and a helpful staff. ❸

San Soucy Vicini 48 ☎523-4461, ℗523-4136. Homey, small hotel a few blocks off the water, with well-kept rooms, pleasant grounds, swimming pool and restaurant. Good value for the money, but no generator. Breakfasts here are delicious and cheap. ❸

Terrazas del Caribe Sánchez 7 ☎523-4488, ℗523-4444. Contains ten scruffy rooms that can fit several people if comfort is not a concern. The grounds, though, boast a secluded swimming pool and a small bar. ❹

Tropic Lost Paradise Vicini and Del Sur ☎523-4424. Check here first if you're on a rock-bottom budget. They have very clean, if basic, rooms and a nice staff, but the hotel is unfortunately often full. ❶

Villa Serene Del Sur 22 and Vicini. Comfortable rooms but at pretty close quarters with a friendly local family. You'll get a good night's sleep, but don't count on much privacy. ❷

Zapata Abraham Núñez 27 ☎523-4777, ℗523-5534, ✉g.zapata@codetel.net.do. This hotel has some serious upside for independent travellers, including a huge, secluded beachfront bar, doorman, strong showers and free breakfast if you're staying two nights or more. Gay clients have recently had some attitude problems from the staff here, though. ❺

Eating and drinking

There are several quality **restaurants** in Boca Chica, but the very best place to eat during the day is at one of the food shacks that serves fresh seafood dishes on the beach; if you go to one of these, try the great local *lambí criolla* (creole conch). If you're staying at the all-inclusives, of course, you'll be stuck with the hotel's buffet food. *Boca Chica Beach Resort* has the best, with *Hamaca* a close second. As for the **bars**, they're all along the festive main strip Calle Duarte, but come in and out of business with alarming rapidity – usually because of intermittent police raids. The **nightlife** scene here is quite rowdy, and focused primarily on sex tourism; popular choices include rock bar *Route 66* and local merengue dance hall *Zanzibar*. The only part of the beach that's particularly safe at night is the row of impromptu bars just east of the *Don Juan Beach Resort*, where a few stragglers from the capital sip rum around tables and play music until midnight. The rest of the beach becomes somewhat of a gay cruising ground after dark.

D'Lucien Duarte 69. Pricey patio restaurant with views of the promenade and fresh seafood displayed on ice at the entrance. Best are the mixed fried seafood and *langosta a la plancha*.

D'Manu Vicini 15 ☎ 523-4616. Great restaurant/bar with heaping grilled platters of chicken ribs and steak in a fun, open-air atmosphere. Moderately priced.

Il Castillo Vicini and Del Sur. Top-notch little Italian restaurant with a good selection of pastas and excellent pizza.

Le Provence Duarte and Dominguez. Pleasant little informal French restaurant that boasts a highly recommended seafood salad, whole creole red snapper and grilled *langostinas*.

La Mama de Tarzan Vicini 12. Good seafood restaurant specializing in shrimp dishes (*ajillo*, *criollo* or *al horno*). Relaxing atmosphere, though the service is a bit too laid-back.

Neptuno Av Hamaca Beach Resort ☎ 523-4703. Popular gourmet seafood restaurant with great views of the ocean. Terrific mixed seafood platters, lobster ravioli and prawns. Reservations are a good idea on weekends.

Pequeña Suiza Duarte 56 ☎ 523-4619. Pleasant spot for a snack, with an eclectic mix of antipasto, fondue and cappuccino. Also good for a croissant or brioche with fresh orange juice at breakfast.

Romagna Mia Duarte 1. Best pizzas in town and surprisingly good pasta in this unpretentiously elegant terrace restaurant that looks out onto the main strip. Try the margherite pizza, pasta arrabiata with shrimp or a grilled dorado filet.

Terraza Quebec Vicini 45. Good French-Canadian restaurant with filet de poisson, a good house lasagne and fresh seafood.

Juan Dolio

Just east past Boca Chica begins a 25-kilometre-long line of rocky coast that holds a strip of vacation homes and all-inclusives collectively referred to as **JUAN DOLIO**. This package resort area was created in response to the wild success of Playa Dorado in the early 1980s, but has never quite matched its northern rival. There has been some recent investment in the area, though, and a couple of new resorts are the equal of any all-inclusives in the country – that is, if it weren't for the beach. Though the sand here is perfectly acceptable, the expanse of dead coral under the water makes swimming and walking in the water uncomfortable, and the private hotel beaches are isolated, small pockets of sand – simply no match for what you'll find further east at Punta Cana and Bávaro (see p.139).

That said, Juan Dolio does have a few advantages over its regional competitors. There's none of the large-scale harassment of Boca Chica, and wandering around the strip is relatively hassle-free. Unlike Bávaro, there are a number of quality restaurants and budget hotels geared towards independent travellers,

Hotel casino rip-offs

If you frequent the casinos of the Dominican Republic's all-inclusive hotels, you should be aware of a series of **casino-based frauds** that have taken place across Juan Dolio, Boca Chica, Punta Cana/Bávaro and the north coast. Sometimes it is called "Progressive Roulette", sometimes "Super Keno", and the wheel on which you play generally looks very cheap – as if it belonged at a church carnival rather than a professional casino. Generally, the casino employees will tell you that this new game is being tried out for the first time at the casino, that it is a sure-win game, and will give you a free chip to begin betting – provided you give them a credit card number. In order to avoid getting scammed yourself, never play a casino game that accepts credit cards.

the nightlife is good, and the strip is still in shouting distance of Santo Domingo, accessible via a one-hour, RD$20 guagua ride.

There's little in the way of sights along the long, paved seaside road that constitutes Juan Dolio. The main drag is located at Villas del Mar, about 12km east of Boca Chica, and is lined with hotels, internet kiosks, souvenir shops and the like. If you get bored wandering back and forth, head 7km east along the Carretera Las Américas to **Guayacanes**, a small, impoverished town that has a tremendous expanse of beach along it that is used by both tourists and locals. If you're up for some out-of-the-way natural beauty, head 3km further west from Guayacanes (the spot is marked by a highway overpass on your right) and you'll find a long-abandoned beach home with a **natural swimming pool** that was carved into the rock by its former owners. It's perfectly safe to swim in the pool, which has rough-hewn steps leading into it from the ground, and from here you can look out onto the Caribbean crashing against high, jagged cliffs. While you're there, stop by the house next door if you'd like to meet María – a famous local *Vodú* priestess who maintains a fascinating syncretic altar with all of the major pantheon members, and is always happy to explain the local folk religion. You can also get a card reading for US$15. If you're in the area on January 5, don't miss her *velación* (see p.81) in honour of patron saint San Miguel.

Accommodation

There are two classes of **hotel** in Juan Dolio: the all-inclusives catering to package tourists and the smaller independent hotels. Of these, the independents win out on both atmosphere and quality of food – and provide you with greater freedom of movement. The all-inclusives, though, do have their own advantages for those who can choke down the buffet food – everything you'll need is provided free of charge inside the compound and they even have free transport from the airport. Addresses on the Carretera Las Américas reflect distance, in kilometres, from San Pedro de Macorís to the east.

Barceló Capella Villas del Mar, Carretera Las Américas Km 14 ☎526-1080, ☎526-1088, @h.capella@codetel.net.do. Expansive grounds, 500 quality rooms with private balcony, friendly service and a casino. But the "beach" is a small strip of cement covered in sand, the food is frankly abysmal and stomach problems are alarmingly common (though this is probably from the water). Still, it's probably the best of the all-inclusives along the strip. Keep in mind, though, that a reservation here does not guarantee you'll be staying here. They routinely overbook and then ship the excess guests off to the lesser Barceló hotels in Juan Dolio. If you stay here, always put a doorstop on your balcony door, or you may well be locked out. ❻

Barceló Decameron Carretera Las Américas Km 13 ⓣ526-2009, ⓕ526-2310, ⓔbarcelodecamero @codetel.net.do. A popular cheapie that can save you a bit of money, though you pay for it in the low quality of the bathrooms – often no hot water, often off-colour, sometimes completely non-functional. Nevertheless, they have a number of amenities, including a good-sized beach, tennis courts and free watersports. It's worth getting up at 7am to reserve a spot at the Brazilian restaurant – by far the best on the compound. Avoid the casino at all costs due to their omnipresent rip-off scams (see box p.110). ❺

Barceló Talanquera Carretera Las Américas Km 13 ⓣ526-1510, ⓕ526-2408, ⓔMschoebel@casamarinaresort.com. Palatial grounds and friendly service, though the rooms are only acceptable and the food – as with many resorts from this chain – is not very good save for one excellent seafood restaurant L'Ecrevisse (reserve early in the morning). Only worth doing if you get a great deal here. ❻

Coral Costa Caribe Carretera Las Américas Km 14 ⓣ526-2244. Nice motel rooms decked out in garish purple, with double beds and all standard amenities. The food here is far better than what you'll get at most all-inclusives, but the place is run like a factory – so you shouldn't expect great service. There's also a 24-hour sports bar and a casino. ❼

Costa Linda Carretera Las Américas Km 18 ⓣ526-2161, ⓕ526-3601. Not the best looked-after resort, with somewhat shabby grounds and small rooms, reflected in the relatively inexpensive prices. ❹

Don Pedro Marina 50 ⓣ526-2147. A very basic, independent cheapie geared toward backpackers who don't mind the spartan rooms. US$15 extra for hot water and a/c. ❷

Fior di Loto Calle Central 517 ⓣ526-1146, ⓕ526-3332, ⓔhfdiloto@codetel.net.do. Best hotel in Juan Dolio by a long shot, and a major

hangout for independent travellers. The India-themed rooms are simple but comfortable and fun, with visitors adding to the ornate Far Eastern patterns painted on the walls – which are based on the lattice-work of a palace in Rajasthan. All rooms have hot water, cable TV and fan; some also boast kitchenettes. In addition to the usual hotel amenities, they host yoga, meditation, martial arts and massage sessions – plus a large gym, a hot tub, a very private sun deck and a small multi-faith chapel. All in all, a tremendously fun place to stay. ❷–❸

Marena Villas del Mar, Carretera Las Américas Km 14 ⓣ526-2121, ⓕ526-1213, ⓔmarena @codetel.net.do. Cheap for an all-inclusive but with claustrophobic grounds and cramped, unattractive rooms. The staff are certainly pleasant and eager to assist, but you should only come here if you don't mind cramped, characterless rooms. ❹

Playa Esmeralda Carretera Las Américas Km 36 ⓣ526-3434, ⓕ526-1744, ⓦwww .hotel-playaesmeralda.com. Extremely nice, quiet hotel way off the main Juan Dolio strip, and closer to the village of Guayacanes. The beach here is far better than what you'll find in the main resort zone (with plenty of good snorkelling), and the grounds are quite private and swarming with songbirds. The rooms are spacious, well kept and have all the usual amenities. ❻

Plaza Flamingo Calle Central 686 ⓣ223-0477. Small beachfront building with six studio apartments for rent at US$150/week. They're not exactly luxurious, but they're clean and fully functional. You'll get a lot more privacy and tranquillity here than you will at most of the big hotels. ❸

Villa 2000 Calle Central ⓣ526-2505, ⓔcindynina @yahoo.com, ⓦwww.tiesse.net/hotel/20020. Modest, inexpensive habitations one notch above Don Pedro, with a/c, private bath and mini-bar. Also a decent little restaurant with reasonably priced pastas and an RD$100 steak. ❷

Eating and drinking

Outside of the all-inclusives, the **food** in Juan Dolio is actually quite good, with three separate Italian restaurants of some merit along the main road. You can also find plenty of little espresso bars in the morning, and there's a half-dozen dance halls and bars that become popular on different days of the week. Even if you're in one of the resorts, you should bring along some extra cash to sample the food and drink available outside your hotel walls. **Groceries** can be found at the small supermarket inside Plaza Chocolate on Calle Central.

Café Giulia Vila del Mar 288. The major Juan Dolio hangout on Monday nights, this is a very nice little bar with a small dancing area. Features mostly American music with merengue thrown in here

and there.

El Batey Posada El Batey, Calle Central 84. Juan Dolio's one disco, with a pretty mixed crowd of locals and tourists. The time to come here is

Saturday, when the place is jam-packed and a lot of fun. The rest of the week you'll find it's only moderately populated.

Chocolate Bar Calle Central 127. Outdoor terrace fronting the Plaza Chocolate (where you can find phone service, souvenir shops and pharmacy) with a pool table and big crowds on weekends.

Delicius Calle Duarte at the beach, Guayacanes. A rather modest-looking fish eatery in the village of Guayacanes, with grilled fish platters guaranteed to have come out of the ocean that very day.

Fior di Loto Calle Central 517 ☎ 526-1146, ✆ hfdiloto@codetel.net.do. The best pastas in town (aglio olio, carbonara, arrabiata, you name it), several excellent shrimp dishes and Indian curries suitably priced for budget travellers, and in an amiable Far East atmosphere. Check before you arrive to see if they're holding one of their bi-monthly Hindu dinner parties, which feature multi-course gourmet Indian meals served in the traditional manner (reservations required in advance

for this). They also have free yoga classes on Mon, Wed and Fri at 5pm.

Grotta Azzurra Calle Central 326. Italian restaurant notable for its singular seaside ambience, which is indeed evocative of the Isle of Capri. Specialities include grilled lobster, spaghetti al vongole and the obligatory caprese salad of fresh mozzarella, tomato and basil. Relatively pricey because of the setting.

Horoscopo Calle Duarte, Guayacanes. A grungy bar in Guayacanes frequented by locals, Italian expats and the occasional adventurous traveller. Good for meeting locals,

Restaurant El Sueño Calle Central 330. The most elegant Juan Dolio restaurant, and a bit more expensive than its competitors, this impeccable little restaurant is set on an outdoor patio with white linen tablecloths and impeccable service. Try the chicken scallopini in white wine sauce, filet of bass in mushroom sauce or grilled dorado.

Campo Las Palmas

Baseball fans shouldn't miss a day-trip to **Campo Las Palmas**, 18km northeast from Santo Domingo on the Carretera 23 (☎687-8350), the Dominican headquarters of the **Los Angeles Dodgers**, especially during the summer when up to two hundred recruits from across Latin America come to be evaluated by Dodger scouts. In addition to having the best facilities of all the major-league camps, Las Palmas has been the most productive; no fewer than forty major league ballplayers have graduated from the annual tryouts into the bigs, including Cy Young Award-winner Pedro Martínez, Jose Offerman, Adrian Beltre, and past Dodger greats like Pedro Guerrero and Mariano Duncan. The organization prefers two to three days' notice before visits, but there's no charge; you'll get to watch exhibition games and have lunch with players and coaches in the "Tommy Lasorda" mess hall.

Travel details

Santo Domingo is the transport hub of the country, and even the smallest villages at the far end of the north coast are connected to it by either bus routes or guaguas. Of the formal outfits, **Caribe Tours** has by far the most connections, stopping at towns along the Autopista Duarte on its way to Santiago, then Puerto Plata and Sosúa, as well as nearly every region and peninsula in the country, save some out-of-the-way places in the southeast and past Barahona. **Metro** can take you to Santiago, the Cibao, Puerto Plata and the Samaná Peninsula, while the less luxurious **Transporte del Cibao** stops at all Autopista Duarte towns to Santiago before heading north to Sosúa. In addition to an express route between Santo Domingo and Santiago, **Terrabus** has daily connections from the capital to Port-au-Prince, Haiti. Caribe Tours, Metro and Terrabus have free printed schedules available at their terminals (see p.67 for locations). If you're heading to the southeast, though, or to remote places in the southwest, you'll need to take a **guagua**, which can range in quality from an air-conditioned minibus to a battered van in which the passengers are packed in like sardines and the sliding doors have long been torn off. All guagua journey times given are rough estimates.

If driving, you may have a more difficult time getting out of the city than anticipated as the **traffic** can be tremendously heavy and the highways are insufficiently signposted. To head north and west, take the 27 de Febrero highway west through town until you arrive at the large traffic circle with a bronze monumental arch in its centre and turn north. This road leads to the Autopista Duarte (north), and a turnoff a half-kilometre after the traffic circle will take you to the Carretera 6 de Noviembre, which leads to San Cristóbal and parts west. Those heading east from the city should also get on 27 de Febrero – but this time heading east – which crosses the Río Ozama as the Duarte Bridge and then turns into the Carretera las Américas, which skirts the ocean all the way to San Pedro and beyond.

Buses

Santo Domingo to: Azua (6 daily; 2hr 30min); Barahona (2 daily; 3hr 40min); Bonao (13 daily; 1hr); Cabrera (2 daily; 6hr 30min); Castillo (4 daily; 4hr); Cotuí (3 daily; 2hr); Dajabón (4 daily; 6hr 50min); Esperanza (4 daily; 4hr); Guayacanes (4 daily; 4hr 40min); Guayubín (2 daily; 5hr 30min); Imbert (10 daily; 4hr 10min); Jarabacoa (4 daily; 2hr 45min); La Vega (26 daily; 1hr 45min); Loma de Cabrera (2 daily; 6hr 15min); Manzanillo (2 daily; 6hr 40min); Mao (4 daily; 4hr 15min); Moca (3 daily; 3hr); Monte Cristi (4 daily; 6hr 20min); Nagua (10 daily; 4hr 40min); Pimentel (3 daily; 4 hr); Port-au-Prince (2 daily; 8hr 30 min); Puerto Plata (17 daily; 4hr 40min); Río San Juan (3 daily; 6hr 45min); Salcedo (4 daily; 3hr); Samaná (6 daily; 5hr 40min); Sánchez (6 daily; 5hr 10min); San Francisco de Macorís (16 daily; 3hr 10min); San Juan de la Maguana (4 daily; 3hr 50min); Santiago (46 daily; 2hr 20min); Sosúa (10 daily; 5hr 10min); Tenares (4 daily; 3hr 10min); Villa Tapia (4 daily; 3hr); Villa Vasquez (4 daily; 5hr 50min).

Guaguas

Boca Chica to: Juan Dolio (frequent; 20min); San Pedro de Macorís (frequent; 45min); Santo Domingo (frequent; 30min).

Haina to: San Cristóbal (frequent; 30min); Santo Domingo (frequent; 30min).

Juan Dolio to: Boca Chica (frequent; 20min); San Pedro de Macorís (frequent; 20min); Santo Domingo (frequent; 1hr).

Nigua to: San Cristóbal (frequent; 30min); Santo Domingo (frequent; 30min).

Santo Domingo to: Azua (hourly; 2hr 40min); Baní (hourly; 1hr 50min); Barahona (hourly; 4hr 10min); Boca Chica (frequent; 30min); Bonao (frequent; 1hr); Cabral (hourly; 4hr 30min); Duvergé (hourly; 5hr 10min); Elias Piña (hourly; 5hr); Galván (hourly; 5hr); Haina (frequent; 30min); Jimaní (hourly; 6hr 10min); Juan Dolio (frequent; 1hr); La Descubierta (hourly; 6hr); La Vega (frequent; 1hr 45min); Las Matas de Farfán (hourly; 4hr 30min); Neiba (hourly; 5hr 10min); Nigua (frequent; 30min); Pedernales (hourly; 6hr 15min); San Cristóbal (frequent; 1hr); San José de Ocóa (hourly; 2hr 30min); San Juan de la Maguana (hourly; 4hr); San Pedro de Macorís (frequent; 1hr 20min); Santiago (frequent; 2hr 30min).

Flights

Santo Domingo to: Las Terrenas (daily; 40min); Puerto Plata (4 daily; 30min); Punta Cana (3 daily; 20min); Santiago (daily; 20min).

The southeast

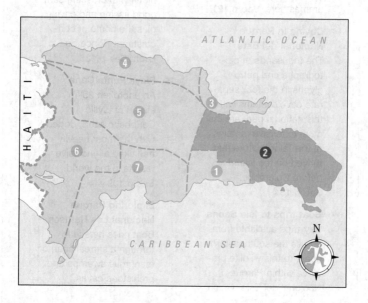

CHAPTER 2

Highlights

* **Cruising the San Pedro Malecón** A bustling promenade that comes alive with music on weekends and during the various Cocolo festivals, when masked groups of dancers perform traditional folk dramas here. See p.121

* **Caving in Parque Nacional del Este** The thousands of pictographs and petroglyphs in the four separate cave systems within this national park are the most extensive remains of the Taino culture that thrived on the island before Columbus. See p.134

* **Boat trips to Isla Saona** Day-trips available from across the southeastern coast to this wildlife preserve within Parque Nacional del Este, which boasts manatees, wilderness hikes and some of the best beaches in the area. See p.135

* **Chilling out in Boca de Yuma** Passed over by package tours, this mellow seafront village owns bluffs with crashing surf, good fishing and caving, plus the home of conquistador Ponce de León. See p.136

* **Playa Punta Cana** An unbroken 25km strand of idyllic Caribbean sand, dotted with the most heavily trafficked all-inclusive resorts in the world. See p.139

* **Exploring Parque Nacional Los Haitises** Boat rides here lead through a surreal snarl of mangrove swamps and prehistoric caves. See p.149

2

The southeast

The Santo Domingo valley stretches east from the capital along the Caribbean coast all the way to the Mona Passage, encompassing vast tracts of sugar cane along the way, once practically the nation's sole source of hard currency. North of these fields roll the verdant high hills of the Cordillera Oriental – really a final spur of the Cordillera Central – which themselves terminate at the bowl-shaped swamp basin of Parque Nacional Los Haitises. This sizeable region is the Dominican Republic's **southeast**, known primarily for its popular resort zones of Bávaro and Punta Cana, bookends of a thirty-kilometre strip of idyllic, uninterrupted sand lined with all-inclusive hotels that are far less expensive than what you'll find around most of the Caribbean. While the remote beaches may not be conveniently located for extensive day-tripping and countryside exploration, they do make perfect spots for utterly relaxing holidays.

Past these newly built attractions, the southeast is fairly poor, rural and, though easy enough to get around, slightly bereft of must-see sights – with the notable exception of the two national parks that help frame the region. One of these, **Parque Nacional del Este**, poking into the Caribbean at the southeastern tip of the Dominican Republic, more or less continues the theme of great beachfront, especially along the remarkable nature preserve on **Isla Saona**. Also here is the most important of the southeast's holy sites, **La Aleta**, the largest Taino excavation yet, though at the time of writing not yet open to the public. Nearby, however, you can visit four **cave systems** – Peñon Gordo, Del Puente, José María and Padres Nuestros – that hold extensive Taino rock art. Not far to the west, the pretty seaside village **Bayahibe**, the latest centre of all-inclusive construction, is really the base from which to visit the park's various points of interest. At the northwestern edge of the region, the mangrove swamps of **Parque Nacional Los Haitises**, on the Bahía de Samaná, hide several Taino caves visited on boat trips organized from towns both in the southeast and on the Samaná Peninsula.

The urban exceptions to the backwater feel of much of the region, **La Romana** and **San Pedro de Macorís**, lie on Highway 3, between Santo Domingo and Parque Nacional del Este, neither city too remarkable or dynamic in itself. The former has benefited quite a bit from Gulf & Western's investment in local industry and has been able to capitalize on some resort build-up, most visible in the vast **Casa de Campo** resort complex just east of town. San Pedro, on the other hand, has acquired fame mainly as a **baseball** town, turning out numerous professionals – such as Chicago Cubs star Sammy Sosa – who often came from the poverty of the sugar *bateyes* which are so prevalent in this area.

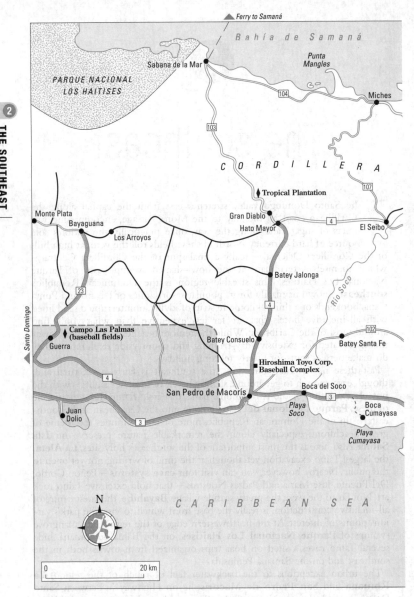

It's not entirely surprising that the southeast, save for a few choice spots, seems slightly left behind – at least when its rocky **history** is considered. Shortly after arriving in Santo Domingo, governor Nicolás de Ovando waged a particularly brutal campaign of Taino extermination in these parts, and the newly cleared land was quickly settled in 1502 by explorers Ponce de León and Juan Esquivel, who established sugar estates and cattle ranches in the area, while at the same time setting up slave-capturing outposts in Puerto Rico and

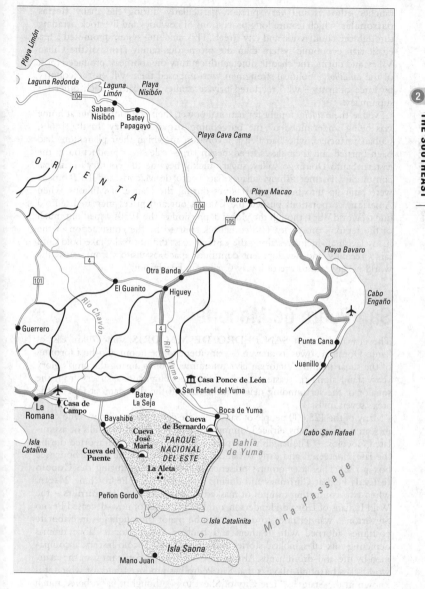

Jamaica. The one notable relic of the era is **Casa Ponce de León**, the forti-fied keep of the famous conquistador near the village of Boca de Yuma. In the late sixteenth century, though, the area was abandoned and became home to roaming herds of wild **cattle** left by the Spanish estates. When the *devastaciones* forcibly moved north coast settlers into Monte Plata and Bayaguana in 1605, the colonists resorted to hunting the cattle for their livelihood, setting up tan-neries and ranches to export leather and beef through Santo Domingo. The rancher ethos is still very present, particularly during the many **fiestas patronales**, which feature long processions of cowboys and livestock parading through the countryside and city streets. This ranching system promoted a less egalitarian economic system than the prosperous family farms of the Cibao Valley, and during the chaotic nineteenth century the southeast produced most of the *caudillos* – political strongmen who imposed their will on the country by force of arms – who recruited private armies and battled each other for supremacy.

Even as the *caudillos* fought for national power, their economic clout at home was being undermined by the burgeoning **sugar industry**. In the 1860s, Cuban financiers, who had fled a revolution in which their plantations had been burned and their slaves freed, began large-scale sugar production in the eastern Santo Domingo valley; sugar quickly became the country's principal commodity. Former fishing villages San Pedro de Macorís and La Romana were built up into bustling port cities during the Dance of Millions, when American corporations pushed the Cubans out and prices increased tenfold due to World War I, though the global depression of the 1930s wiped out much of the region's prosperity. The comeback spurred by the construction of the many lavish all-inclusives along the eastern coast did not really take hold until fairly recently, and development continues apace, as visitors from across the world never seem to tire of lovely Caribbean beachfront.

San Pedro de Macorís

The crowded city of **SAN PEDRO DE MACORÍS**, some 70km east of Santo Domingo, owes its uneven development to the boom-and-bust fortunes of the sugar industry. Victorian civic monuments built during the crop's glory years stand along the eastern bank of the Río Higuamo, a far cry from the squalor of the surrounding neighbourhoods and the shut gates at four of the area's seven mills.

Many of the 125,000 people of San Pedro are descendants of those who came in search of sugar jobs, either Dominicans who worked in the mills or assimilated Cocolos – "The English", as many prefer to be called – imported during the late nineteenth and early twentieth centuries as seasonal field labour (see box p.122). The latter group's presence is most obvious during the **Cocolo festivals** held at Christmas and during the Feast of San Pedro (June 24–30), when two competing troupes of masked dancers known as **mummers** – the Wild Indians of Donald Henderson and Los Momises of now-deceased Primo Shiverton – wander door to door along the major thoroughfares in elaborate costumes adorned with feathers and baubles, and perform dance dramas depicting folk tales, biblical stories and events from Cocolo history, accompanied by fife-and-drum bands. Also from Cocolo ranks come most of the many world-class **baseball players** that San Pedro has produced, and for which it is known in the States as "The City of Shortstops", though it has ushered much more than shortstops through its ranks. Present and former major-leaguers include George Bell, Sammy Sosa, Rico Carty, Pedro Guerrero, Tony Fernández, Juan Samuel and Joaquín Andujar, just for a start.

The decline of sugar prices, continuous urban migration and the devastation of Hurricane Georges have made the bulk of San Pedro a pretty miserable place, and the first view of its smokestacks and sprawling slums is off-putting to say the least. What redeems it for most residents and visitors alike is its

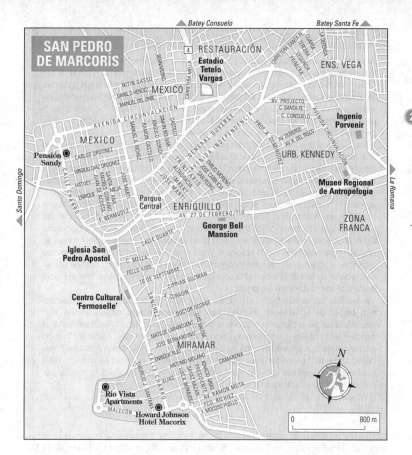

Malecón, a wide seaside boardwalk with modest public beaches at either end, celebrated by *bachata* star Juan Luis Guerra in his song *Guavaberry*: "I like to sing my song/in the middle of the Malecón/watching the sun go down/in San Pedro de Macorís". At night and on weekends, sharp-dressed locals pour onto the promenade or just linger on the concrete benches that line it, while vendors hawk fast food, boiled corn, candy and Clorets, quite the buzzing scene.

Accommodation

Though San Pedro is a fairly large city, there's not much in the way of nice **accommodation**; the plushest hotel in town is the amenity-laden *Howard Johnson Hotel Macorix*, Malecón and Deligne (℡529-2100, ℻529-9239, ✉hj.macorix@codetel.net.do; ❹), which has 170 rooms with balconies, impeccable service and a swimming pool area that thrums with live merengue on weekends. If you have to go cheaper, try the *Pensión Sandy*, Carretera 3 and Deligne (no telephone; ❶), a bit unappealing but with friendly proprietors. *Río Vista*, Malecón 1 at the far western end (℡529-7555; ❸), has full-service apartments available for rent by the week, though they're often sold out. If the city

The Cocolos

When the Dominican sugar industry was nearing its zenith in the late 1800s, plantation owners began to employ migrant labourers from a number of islands in the British Antilles to meet the increased work demand. These black English-speakers were termed **Cocolos**, a bastardization of Tortola, one of the islands from which the workers arrived. While many of them returned home to their respective islands each year with their harvest season earnings, increasingly large numbers began to settle permanently in camps around San Pedro de Macorís.

The Cocolos lived in squalid **bateyes**, shantytowns which were vermin-infested and tended to lack running water. Disease – malaria, cholera and leprosy mainly – was widespread, and residents often starved during the off-season. They were also the victims of widespread **racism**, which led many to embrace the pan-Africanism of **Marcus Garvey**, a Jamaica-born activist who moved to New York's Harlem to spread his message of black empowerment. Thousands joined his Universal Negro Improvement Association (UNIA), which encouraged community self-reliance and provided disability benefits for those injured in the mills, and donated a portion of their paychecks to the Black Star Line, a black-owned and operated fleet meant to one day repatriate New World blacks to West Africa. In August 1921 the Garveyites organized a strike to protest the inhuman conditions of the *bateyes*, but the unrest was broken up by US Marines who occupied the Dominican Republic, and the local leaders of the UNIA were deported.

Interest in Garveyism faded after the intervention, but the community infrastructure begun by UNIA soon evolved into **self-improvement organizations** that pooled resources to better conditions in the *bateyes*, establish and enforce codes of conduct and provide medical care. During non-working seasons, members formed cricket teams that evolved into the sugar mill baseball squads, which eventually produced some of the world's finest players. Labour unrest continued as well – in 1946 the Cocolos staged the only successful strike of the Trujillo era – which made sugar companies turn westward to Haiti for cheap migrant labour.

traffic is a bit much at night and you're looking for a great deal more seclusion, you can head out instead to the *Santana Beach Resort* (T412-1010, F412-1818, Wwww.playasantana.com; ❺), which is just 5km east of town. You'll find an all-inclusive hotel comparable to the ones at Juan Dolio, with spacious, motel-like rooms, immaculate grounds, a casino and manageable buffet food – but set in a much more secluded location and with a far better beach that what you'll find west of San Pedro.

The City

Head north of the Malecón on Avenida Charro to get a quick glimpse (which is all you'll probably want) of some of the Victorian architecture that was built during the city's heyday in the first half of the twentieth century. The foremost example is the 1911 **Iglesia San Pedro Apostol**, avenidas Charro and Independencia, a wide whitewashed church with a lovely mahogany altar and prominent bell tower. Time has been less kind to the old **town hall** a block south of the church, partially in ruins and occupied by a metalwork factory. Not far off, the c.1900 port authority has been renovated into the concrete **Centro Cultural Fermoselle**, Charro at 10 de Septiembre (Mon–Sat 9.30am–noon & 2–5pm; free), a block-long, pastel-pink monster that showcases rotating exhibits of local artists alongside a permanent collection of old San Pedro photographs. From here head east down Duarte two blocks past the parque central – where you'll find a **bank** and local **Codetel** – to San Pedro's fanciful cast-iron **fire station** at Duarte 46. Built in 1903, it's a bit run-down but still quite striking; ask to climb the circular iron staircase to the top of the building's high lookout tower. It's worth going out of your way on Mondays to the parque central itself, as traditional Cocolo bands gather there in the morning and play until noon – the only way to hear the great local *momise* music if you're not in town for a festival. If in town on a Saturday, stop off at the small **Museo Regional de Antropología** on the city's east side, Universidad Central del Este, Carretera Romana and Avenida Circunvalación (Sat only 8am–2pm; free; ☎529-3592). Inside is an intriguing display of Taino stone statuettes, pestles and clay pot shards collected from caves along the Río Soco, and *guloya* costumes and art from the Cocolo festivals.

Above any building, though, San Pedro is famous for its baseball players, and a pilgrimage here is compelling for serious fans. Record-breaking Sammy Sosa was once one of the dozens of kids pestering adults for shoeshines and spending his free time playing stickball with a modified milk carton for a glove. Start your tour at **Estadio Tetelo Vargas**, Avenida Circunvalación and Carretera Mella, a spacious, tattered concrete temple to the sport, squat in the centre of the city. Named for one of the first great Dominican baseballers, its patchy natural-grass diamond serves as venue to minor-league games in the summer and Dominican professional games in winter. Check Santo Domingo newspapers for schedules (see p.67); tickets are available the night of the game for RD$85–115, or walk into the stadium for free during the day and watch various major-league teams work out their prospects. The concessions here are unique but surprisingly good; highly recommended is the pizza with corn, peas and jalapeños.

A few blocks east of the stadium, **Ingenio Porvenir**, at Independencia and Avenida Porvenir, is the largest of the nearby sugar mills, still in operation and open for visits (Mon–Fri 9am–noon & 2–5.30pm; free). A state-of-the-art complex when it was built by Cuban refugees in 1879, it looks positively archaic today, with its enormous grinding wheels pulping the cane and congealing the juice into sugar and molasses, run by peasant workers with little safety gear. Go round the complex and to the east to reach the **San Francisco Giants baseball complex**, where hundreds of local kids are tested and trained each year. The Giants have the longest history of US teams in the Dominican Republic, having signed Ozzie Virgil, Juan Marichal and the Alou brothers. Also worth a look if you've the time are the palatial **mansion** of local baseball hero George Bell (called Jorge Bell locally), which lies on Avenida Independencia two blocks south of Circunvalación and across the street from the *Ferretería Villas* sign. It's certainly one of the city's most ostentatious buildings, an enormous, coral-coloured behemoth adorned with castle turrets, drawbridge and a moat.

The outskirts

On the fringe of San Pedro begins *batey* country, where most of the baseball players grew up, in the midst of seemingly endless fields of sugar cane. Several foreign teams have set up training complexes in the area, the most impressive of which, the **Hiroshima Toyo Carp**, 3km north of town on the Carretera Mella (Mon–Fri 9am–5pm; ☎529-5040), is run by a professional Japanese team that shares its space with the Boston Red Sox. Both clubs work out players on the four baseball diamonds year-round, though the camp is busiest during the summer. It gets few visitors, but management is happy to let you wander around and talk to the players – provided you're escorted by one of the Dominican staff (RD$50 tip).

From the Toyo Carp complex the road leads 8km north to Batey Consuelo, home to hundreds of Haitian cane cutters and a smattering of remaining English – on Sundays you'll see them lined up at the entrance waiting for guaguas to take them to the Anglican church in La Romana. Its century-old sugar mill, no longer in operation, harkens back to the dawn of the machine age; tip one of the security guards to enter and head to the back to see the machine shop where Cuban mechanics kept it running by forging replacement parts for its broken-down components.

The *batey* that surrounds the mill, just a collection of clapboard shacks, was the childhood home of baseball players Rico Carty, George Bell, and Julio Franco, among numerous others. It's at its liveliest during **Semana Santa**, when a Haitian carnival with parades and traditional *gagá* music played on keyless wooden tubes heralds a bawdy religious ceremony (see p.127 for a description of the festivities). Even more famous among Haitian musicians are the superb Semana Santa festivities held at smaller **Batey Santa Fe**, 5km northeast of San Pedro via the Carretera Santa Fe (Highway 102) that turns off from Avenida Circunvalación.

Playa Soco, two bars of sand extending east and west from the mouth of the Río Soco 5km east of San Pedro, wins for top local beach, though in truth it's fairly unremarkable and the waves can get kind of rough. Many locals prefer to swim a few metres upriver where it's muddier but much calmer. Further north on the river are a series of hard-to-access caves that bear Taino petroglyphs; one of them, **Cueva de las Maravillas** in Boca del Soco, can be visited on jeep tours from Juan Dolio. There are hundreds of Taino petroglyphs on the cave, but many have been defaced by graffitti over the years, making it less than ideal. Many visitors spend more time sliding down the "toboggan slide" groove that's been formed in the rock face, leading down to the Río Soco. If you want to check the caves out on your own, you can ask directions within Boca del Soco (15km east of San Pedro), or enquire before setting out at San Pedro's Martínez Travel Agency, Duarte 33 (☎529-3515); the proprietor's sons make regular excursions to the caves and know the area well.

Eating and drinking

The *Hotel Macorix* contains a fine **restaurant**, but the best food in town is at *Roby Mar*, a superb seafood restaurant on Avenida Charro across the street from the cathedral. Given that it's tucked away behind the brightly coloured stalls where fishermen sell the day's catch to city residents, the restaurant has a remarkably romantic ambience, with candlelit outdoor tables that look out on the river. The prices are reasonable, and every menu item is worth trying, including a variety of local shrimp, lobster and grilled fish dishes. You can also find good food at the less-atmospheric *Apolo*, Independencia 53 at Parque Duarte (☎529-3549), which grills the best steaks in town, has fresh seafood and also serves decent Chinese dishes like Moo Goo Gaipan. If looking for some grub on the Malecón, try the cheap and popular patio restaurant *Portofino*, which features fine Italian food and a couple of Greek seafood dishes. San Pedro's **nightlife** is also clustered along the boardwalk, with some very popular discos further inside the city. The current hot spot is Sammy Sosa's disco *Subway*, playing mostly techno and house and located on Avenida Independencia at the Plaza 30/30 shopping mall, not far from Avenida Circunvalación. Other major discos are *Lexus* and *Café Caribe* – both on the west end of the Malecón – and *7-14* on Avenida 27 de Febrero about a kilometre east of the parque central, which has traditional acoustic *bachata* sets on Friday afternoons. The *Hotel Macorix* also has a popular disco, and there's a sports bar called *Phillies* on Av Independencia 64, the best place to watch televised baseball and have a few beers.

West of San Pedro

Thirty kilometres west of San Pedro, Carretera 23 heads north to **Bayaguana** and **Monte Plata**, a pair of sedate cattle towns created during the *devastaciones* of 1605, when the Spanish government forcibly removed all settlers from the north coast. Residents of Monte Cristi and Puerto Plata were sent to Monte Plata (hence the name), while colonists in La Yaguana and Bayajá (today Port-au-Prince and Fort Liberté, Haiti, respectively) were shipped to Bayaguana. Most settlers' property and livestock were lost along the way, and they survived on subsistence farming and hunting wild livestock.

Bayaguana, 25km north of Highway 4, past lush countryside dotted with ranches and pineapple plantations, has little to recommend it beyond its December 28 **fiesta patronal**, when several horseback processions from the surrounding pueblos converge on the town at 11am. Herds of livestock are then paraded through the streets, serenaded by brass bands trumpeting out traditional songs that entreat them to be fruitful and multiply, and blessed by a local priest from the balcony of the church – who then collects several head of cattle for himself at the expense of the townsfolk.

Another 17km west along Carretera 23 lies Monte Plata, only slightly more substantial than its sister town. In colonial days, the fiesta patronal here (January 11–21) was a sort of mini-Pamplona, with livestock goaded into chasing people along the streets, but today the festivities are more tame processions similar to those in Bayaguana. Otherwise, the only thing to check out is the Ramírez **coffee warehouse** at the town's western end, a Dominican agricultural middleman where you'll see campesinos haggling with the proprietors over a fair price for their beans – the traditional method of agricultural exchange here. There's little to keep you in town for the night, but on the off chance that you're stuck here, head to *Restaurant/Hotel El Toro*, at Duarte and Meriño, which has clean, basic rooms with cold water and fan (❶), and delicious, inexpensive beef dishes along with fruit shakes.

La Romana

LA ROMANA, 37km east of San Pedro, has been a one-company town since the South Porto Rico Sugar Company built the mammoth Central Romana mill in 1917; it was the only sugar operation not taken over by Trujillo during his thirty-year reign. The mill was sold to multinational Gulf & Western in 1967, who used the substantial profits to diversify their holdings in the area, constructing the lavish *Casa de Campo* resort (see p.128) and convincing the government to open the first of the country's industrial free zones here. The mill and the resort, sold in the 1980s to the wealthy Fanjul family of Cuba, helps make this one of the most highly employed parts of the country, though Hurricane Georges set the city back a few years; the free zone was battered heavily, and a quarter of the sugar crop destroyed.

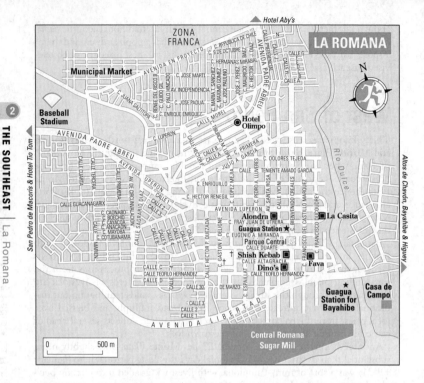

The town itself is not especially interesting, though the **nightlife** is good and a walk along the rambling pastel barrio that borders the river's western bank makes for a pleasant hour. The parque central is the major meeting place, and at its northwestern corner begins a sprawling outdoor market that stretches north for several blocks, chock-full of fresh produce, household wares and cheap knick-knacks. More popular with travellers are the various **jeep and river tours** along the nearby rivers Soca and Chavón that are available at all of the various all-inclusive hotels from Juan Dolio to Punta Cana. You can also book the tours independently through *Cocotours* (☎586-1311, ⓦwww .cocotours.com) and *Turinter* (☎686-4020, ⓕ686-3890, ⓦwww.turinter.com), both with offices in La Romana. Trips generally run a full day and involve a boat cruise up the river past mountains and rainforest, with stops at a typical Dominican campo and sometimes Cueva de las Maravillas (see p.124); expect to pay US$65–85, with lunch included.

Worth a visit in winter is the **Michelin baseball stadium**, located at Abreu and Luperón on the city's west end. As the home field of the hapless La Romana Azucareros, the whipping post for the rest of the Dominican Winter League in recent years, it's well worth a go as long as you won't be crushed if the home team loses; check Santo Domingo newspapers for schedules (RD$50–150 for tickets). Just west of the arena the **municipal market** sells bountiful produce and meat; look also for the several small *botánicas* selling various items related to *Vodú dominicana*. Further west, about 3.5km past the baseball stadium along the carretera, **El Artesano**, the shop of local sculptor José

Semana Santa

The Haitian *bateyes* that surround La Romana and San Pedro hold exuberant **Semana Santa** festivities during the Christian Holy Week, which is also the most important Voodoo celebration of the year. The various satellite *bateyes* that surround a sugar mill each have their own religious brotherhoods, headed by a medium known as a *houngan* (male) or a *mambo* (female). Each worships a patron deity and has its own **gagá** band – called *rara* in Haiti – which plays a repertoire of religious and carnival songs on an orchestra of one-note trumpets and bamboo tubes, both by blowing through them and drumming on them with sticks. *Gagá* processions zigzag across large tracts of territory surrounding the *bateyes*, sometimes lasting all night long.

On **Ash Wednesday**, the groups carry their senior officers on their shoulders in chairs, accompanied by *gagá*. This is just a warm-up to **Good Friday** when, just before dawn, four shrouded dancers parade into the *perestil*, where religious services are performed. The *houngan* "breathes life" into them one at a time, and they throw off their shrouds and lead the *gagá* bands in a parade around their *batey*, playing, singing and dancing to songs with lascivious lyrics, in keeping with the festival's theme of regeneration and fertility. On Saturday and **Easter Sunday**, they head out onto the road towards the sugar mill. Upon encountering another group along the way, a competitive jam session begins, which can, in cases, lead to fisticuffs. Though anyone is welcome to attend Semana Santa, if you look like you have money the *gagá* bands will repeatedly play for you, seeking money and rum in return; you're best off bringing plenty of small bills for tips to the band, and arriving in a small group.

If you want to familiarize yourself with the music of Semana Santa, you should purchase two things: the Smithsonian Folkways CD "Caribbean Revels: Haitian Rara and Dominican Gagá", which features live recordings from Semana Santa festivals across the island, and *Rara!* by Elizabeth McAlister, a terrific book with companion CD on the music and the culture that surrounds it.

Ignacio Morales, holds a number of his fanciful metal sculptures and Deco furniture, intriguing enough to merit a look. Continue west to reach **Playa Cumayasa**, a decent public beach 10km beyond town – the turnoff is marked "Boca Cumayasa".

Back the other direction, and of interest to those wishing to get more closely acquainted with local culture and customs, **Batey La Seja**, 18km east of La Romana along the road to Higuey, is a fairly welcoming place to enjoy Semana Santa celebrations (see above), mostly because the denizens have been thoroughly recorded by anthropologists and are used to outside visitors. To get there turn right onto the unmarked dirt road exactly 1km after the town of Benerito on the road to Higuey.

Practicalities

Most who **arrive** in La Romana (except those staying at *Casa de Campo*) arrive via guagua en route to more exciting destinations like Santo Domingo or Punta Cana. Most guaguas let you off in the city's parque central, though guaguas from Bayahibe stop at the town's east entrance on the main highway, on the west side of the bridge that leads to *Casa de Campo*. Unless you're staying at *Casa de Campo* or one of the resorts in Bayahibe, it's unlikely you'll make use of the small La Romana airport (see p.130).

Nearly everything you might need while in town can be found around the parque central, including the local phone centres, Western Union and banks.

For in-town travel, it's best to avoid driving within city limits, as there are a number of unmarked one-way streets and traffic accidents are frequent. **Taxis** can be picked up at the south end of the parque central or called from other locations (☎550-1126), and should set you back no more than RD$30.

There's no real reason to **stay the night** in town if you're not booked at *Casa de Campo*, but there are a few decent hotels in the area. Within town, solid but somewhat drab *Olimpo*, Abreu and Llúberes (☎550-7646, ℉550-7647; ❸), qualifies as most convenient, with good service, a/c, phone, cable TV and Continental breakfast. For something nicer, head to *Aby's*, Amatista 6, Urb Las Piedras (☎556-5887, ℉556-5047, ℮hotelabys@hotmail.com; ❹), which is far north of downtown but extremely nice, with great mountain-top views, swimming pool and decent rooms. There are other hotels east of town towards Playa Cumayasa, including the basic *Tío Tom*, Carretera Romana Km 4 (☎556-6201; ❸), which has hot water and a/c and is the best local option for budget travellers.

One of the finer **places to eat** in town is *La Casita*, Richiez 57 and Doucuday (☎223-0568), where the Italian menu includes seafood pastas, lobster in cognac and a mushroom risotto. For cheap eats go to *Shish Kebab*, a terrific little Lebanese kitchen just off the parque central on Calle Creales; or head instead to the outdoor pizza patio *Alondra* on Calle Vicini, one block north and another block west of the parque central. For breakfast, try the fresh squeezed juices and breads at *Dino's* on Gonzalvo and Altagracia (☎550-8100). La Romana's **nightlife** draws few tourists but nonetheless can be a lot of fun. The first place to head should be the *Fava* disco on Gonzalvo just off the park. The other hot spot is the *Club Genesis* in Altos de Chavón (see p.130).

Casa de Campo and Altos de Chavón

The **Casa de Campo** resort (☎523-3333, ℉523-8548, ⓦwww.casadcampo.com; ❼–❽), just east of La Romana off Highway 4, is a truly massive resort – really a sight unto itself, and worth a visit even if you're not staying there. If you are you'll fortunately be spared the security paranoia, compulsory plastic wristbands and terminally bland buffet fare of most deluxe Dominican accommodations. The complex encompasses seven thousand meticulously manicured acres of rolling hills set along the sea and boasts two golf courses – including Pete Dye's famous "Teeth of the Dog", with eight of its holes right along the oceanfront – a 24-hour tennis centre, fourteen swimming pools, equestrian stables with horseback riding and polo grounds, a sporting clay course, personal trainers, a beauty spa and so forth; see box opposite for details. In addition to the spacious, comfortable rooms, there are 150 luxury private villas with butler, private chef and maid, used by (among others) Madonna, Elizabeth Taylor and Henry Kissinger. If you're staying here, you're best off renting a car (which can be done at the resort or from the airport), as the system of shuttle buses that ferry visitors back and forth across the sprawling resort are notoriously slow. The crowning pleasure is **Playa Minitas**, a gorgeous strand of beach protected by a shallow coral reef – nice enough that some spend their whole vacation on it; it's not technically open to the public, but you won't be questioned unless you ask for a towel (lifeguards are present 9am–6pm). Just as nice is nearby **Isla Catalina**, a small island 2km offshore reachable by shuttle boats, where *Casa de Campo* has set up a small dock, a few pavilions and a shaded restaurant/bar. Several local tours and cruise ships drop anchor just off the island and ferry thousands of passengers back and forth

Casa de Campo sports

Casa de Campo boasts a remarkably broad range of **sports and activities**. The following is a rundown of the most interesting. Most sports are off limits to non-guests, though the golf courses and shooting ranges are open to all – and no one will check for ID if you drive in to watch a game of polo. All of the sports below should be booked directly through the hotel (☎523-3333).

Deep-sea fishing Half- (RD$350) and full-day (RD$500, lunch included) expeditions depart daily at 8.30am. This is serious sport fishing: expect to catch wahoo, dolphin, kingfish, sailfish, marlin and barracuda.

Golf The resort boasts one of the world's top golf courses, Teeth of the Dog, with two-thirds of its holes set on open oceanfront. Costs RD$2460 for 18 holes, including golf fees, green fees and shared cart, though at twilight rates drop to RD$1312. The lesser, land-locked Links course runs RD$1640 for 18 holes. Club storage is RD$50/day, club rental RD$656. A caddie will set you back another RD$200–330, depending on the caddie's experience. Balls at the driving range are RD$74/bucket, while golf lessons cost RD$740.

Horseback riding Guided wilderness horseback rides are offered 8am–noon and 2–6pm; RD$400/hr or RD$800/3hr.

Polo You can watch weekly games from November through May. Polo lessons take place in the same time frame, and cost RD$656 per lesson. If you want to participate in the weekly game, it will cost you RD$738.

Riverboat fishing Excursions depart daily at 8.30am. Expect to spend three hours trolling the extremely scenic Río Chavón performing light-tackle angling for championship snook. RD$410.

Scuba diving The in-house Circe Dive Shop (☎246-3115, ⊛www.circewatersports .com) is one of the best on the island, running outstanding dives all across the south coast, including two deep wrecks in Juan Dolio, cave diving in Bayahibe (experts only) and an artificial reef created by the wreck of the *St George* cargo ship off the coast of Parque Nacional del Este. Equipment rental runs US$35/day, and dives are US$28 with discounts for multiple dives. They also offer a full PADI course.

Shooting The resort has a full 350-acre course with 150 shooting stations that's rated one of the best on the planet. You can skeet shoot (RD$390/round), trap shoot (RD$1900/round), or blast away at sporting clays from a 110-foot tower (RD$1900/round).

Tennis 24-hour courts, both clay and grass. Costs RD$328 during the day, RD$410 at night.

Tours Among the many tours on offer are a boat cruise up the Río Chavón (RD$410), snorkelling at Isla Catalina (RD$492), and a romantic sunset cruise along the coast (RD$410).

Watersports At Playa Minitas snorkelling gear, hobie cats, sailboats, windsurfers, sunfish sailboats and paddleboats are all available. Rental prices range RD$200–500, depending on the item.

via speedboats, so expect big crowds. The island does, though, have the southern coast's best coral reef, and the fish have grown tame enough that schools of them swim up and eat food literally out of your hands. This makes it one of the island's prime spots for scuba diving as well; various dive shops, including *Casa de Campo*'s own Circe Divers (see above), lead trips to a steep underwater dropoff called "The Wall", which holds an enviably intact coral reef that's habitat for a virtual underwater zoo. There is also one place on a virgin beach far from the main dock where you can camp for the night; to do so, you'll need to get a permit from the national park office for Parque Nacional del Este in Bayahibe's main parking lot (see p.135). Otherwise, tour companies across the island offer Catalina day-trips.

Flanking the resort to the east is another Gulf & Western brainchild, **Altos de Chavón**, a high-concept shopping mall perched atop a cliff looking out over the Río Chavón. Constructed to the specifications of a sixteenth-century Italian village with artificially aged limestone, it exudes dreary kitsch like few places in the country, its cobblestone streets littered with double-parked tour buses and its "Tuscan" villas crammed to the gills with dimestore souvenirs. That's not to say that the place is totally devoid of merit: the 5000-seat open-air amphitheatre is impressive and the small **archeology museum** (daily 9.30am–5pm; free; ☎682-3111) is quite excellent, with a variety of Taino artefacts, including two intact canoes and a wooden *cahoba* idol culled from Parque Nacional del Este. There's a very good designer jewellery shop, Everett Designs (☎523-8331), which has some unique pieces using amber, larimar and pearl, and several good restaurants on the grounds, as well. The most idyllic time to visit the place is just before dusk, when the hordes have departed and the sunset spreads over the western hills.

Practicalities

Many guests of the resort arrive via the brand-new **Aeropuerto La Romana** (☎556-5565 or 2611), located 8km to the east. Flights arrive twice-daily from San Juan, Puerto Rico and one daily from Miami, Florida via American Airlines (☎542-5151), and frequent charter flights land here from various major cities in Canada and Europe. The airport has an information desk (8am–5pm), phone centre, ATM machine, currency exchange, taxis and ample parking space. The guaguas that stop here are strictly local, and serve mostly the Dominicans who work here; if you're staying at a resort, though, your hotel will arrange for shuttle bus pickup.

Acommodation at *Casa de Campo* (☎523-3333, ⑤523-8548, ⓦwww .casadcampo.com; ❼–❾) won't disappoint, provided you can cover the US$100–140 a night it costs to stay here. The rooms are large, well appointed and include all the amenities one would expect for the price. Decor is more in line with top-flight corporate hotels, as opposed to the dreary motel rooms you'll find in most Dominican all-inclusives. There are also a number of expensive private cottages which can cost as much as US$1500 a night, though many of these are a bit run-down and of more use to those who need to pay big bucks for a bit of privacy – recent tenants include former US President Clinton and actress Elizabeth Taylor.

Casa de Campo used to have far better **food** than the other Dominican all-inclusives, but quality has deteriorated sharply over the past few years. Nevertheless, they do offer meal plans costing US$12 for breakfast, US$50 for breakfast and dinner and US$65 for all three meals. The breakfast buffet at the *Lago Grill* is the best meal on the complex, with all manner of fresh tropical fruits alongside omelettes, pancakes and French toast made to order; for dinner you should head to *El Pescador*, an outdoor patio right on the beach with an array of decent seafood dishes. Altos de Chavón has several restaurants, best of which are pricey *Giacosa*, with its memorable seafood risotto, and the more reasonably priced *Sombrero*, which has good versions of the standard Mexican staples. Even better food can be found in La Romana; see p.128 for recommendations. The most active **nightlife** spot around the resort is the *Club Genesis* in Altos de Chavón, which is open Thursday through Saturday night and gets a pretty upscale crowd.

Bayahibe

The fishing village of **BAYAHIBE** was until recently one of the most pleasant seaside villages on the island, but a seemingly unending series of all-inclusive construction projects have turned the town into a bit of a dump. It's sadly become increasingly poverty-stricken as more and more massive resorts have been built up all around it – and the only public beach access nearby is one thin little strip of sand abutting the town square. Though one would think that such a construction boom would result in an increase in income and jobs, the resorts actually pull in most of their workers from La Romana and Higuey, meaning very little of the income flowing into the area has ended up in the pockets of locals.

Some of the all-inclusives that have sprung up both east and west of town are nice places to spend a relaxing beach holiday, but there's little enticing in Bayahibe itself anymore. The only reason for independent travellers to spend time here is to use it as a base camp from which to visit Parque Nacional del Este (see p.133), a park just east of Bayahibe that holds Taino ruins, secluded beaches and mangrove estuaries.

Accommodation

In the past two years, mass construction has turned Bayahibe into a burgeoning **resort district** that local developers hope will soon rival Punta Cana. As

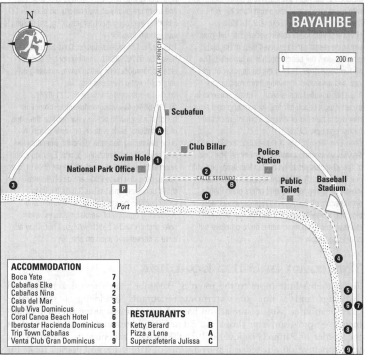

BAYAHIBE

N

CALLE PRINCIPE

Scubafun

Club Billar

Police Station

Swim Hole

National Park Office

CALLE SEGUNDO

Public Toilet

Baseball Stadium

Port

P

0   200 m

ACCOMMODATION

Boca Yate	7
Cabañas Elke	4
Cabañas Nina	2
Casa del Mar	3
Club Viva Dominicus	5
Coral Canoa Beach Hotel	6
Iberostar Hacienda Dominicus	8
Trip Town Cabañas	1
Venta Club Gran Dominicus	9

RESTAURANTS

Ketty Berard	B
Pizza a Lena	A
Supercafetería Julissa	C

131

Parque Nacional del Este ▼

a result, there's a number of large all-inclusive resorts to choose from – though quite frankly there's little to distinguish one from the other. Your decision should be based on the best deal you can find with one of the mass package tour agencies (see p.13). Independent travellers have begun to stay away from the area, but there are still a couple of decent little budget hotels to be found.

Boca Yate Calle Dominicus 10 ℡688-6822, ⓔh.bocayate@codetel.net.do. Very basic accommodations with fan and cold-water bath, right across the street from the *Coral Canoa* resort – and with access to the otherwise private beach on the far side of *Coral Canoa*. Good if you want to stay away from Bayahibe and are just interested in hitting the beach and nearby national park. They also have a good little Italian restaurant (see opposite), with big crowds at the bar on Wednesday and Thursday nights. ❸

Cabañas Elke ℡ & ℱ696-0148, ⓦwww.viwi.it/turvillaggio.htm. A set of *cabañas* (some with kitchen) with a pool and access to meals at the *Club Viva Dominicus* (see below). Much nicer than *Boca Yate*, but looks a bit lost amid all the recent construction, and is not as peaceful a place as it once was. ❹

Cabañas Nina Calle Segunda, Bayahibe ℡224-5431. Simple, clean rooms in town, with breakfast included in the nightly rates. A real bargain and with pleasant, dependable proprietors. ❷–❸

Casa del Mar ℡221-8880, ℱ221-8881, ⓦwww.amhsahotels.com/resorts/casa_del_mar. Very nice resort set up by itself east of Bayahibe, which makes the beach much less crowded. The all-turquoise grounds hold the usual array of services and amenities, including three restaurants (the Thai-oriented one is best), a disco, horseback excursions, a beach bar and an amazing pool area. Has won a number of awards from international tourism groups. ❼

Club Viva Dominicus ℡686-5658, ℱ687-8583, ⓦwww.vivaresorts.com/eng/dominicus. The first of the all-inclusives to be built in this area, and still one of the best. A lavish compound frequented mostly by Italian tourists that offers good food, a great beach, numerous watersports, tennis, aerobics and a dive centre. You can choose between a standard a/c hotel room and a more primitive but private bungalow. ❼

Coral Canoa Beach Hotel ℡682-2662, ℱ688-6565, ⓦwww.coralhotels.com.do/english/canoa.htm. New resort with an odd interior design that's meant to be evocative of the Taino Indians but instead looks like an Arizona suburb, with the usual all-inclusive amenities and downsides, including nice but not luxurious rooms with private balconies, an enormous swimming pool with two "islands", hot tub, archery range, mini-golf and tennis courts. The beach is private and there are plenty of chairs, which means you won't have to get up so early in order to reserve one in advance. ❼

Iberostar Hacienda Dominicus ℡688-2576, ⓦwww.iberostarcaribe.com/dominicusing.html. An excellent thirty-acre all-inclusive in the Iberostar tradition, with a great beach with kiosk bars, three separate swimming pools, a rambling, pastel outdoor shopping mall and 500 very large, comfortable rooms with balcony. The food is acceptable and there are plenty of watersports on offer, including free equipment for kayaking, snorkelling and windsurfing. ❺

Trip Town Cabañas Malecón, Calle Segunda, Bayahibe ℡707-3640. Nondescript but comfortable accommodations within town, including private cold-water bath and fan. ❹

VentaClub Gran Dominicus ℡221-6767, ℱ221-5894, ⓦwww.grandominicus.com. Four hundred rooms with ocean view right on the edge of the national park, with an enviable beach, a huge swimming pool and standard amenities like a/c, cable TV and direct-line phone. Evening entertainment features the usual off-Vegas cheese, but takes place in a huge 900-seat amphitheatre that's genuinely impressive. Sports facilities include tennis courts, sailing, windsurfing and snorkelling equipment, aerobics classes, water polo, archery and a beach volleyball net. They also have a decent dive shop on site. ❼

The town and the beaches

Today there's little more to the town of Bayahibe than a few dozen cramped dwellings and a line of waterfront restaurants straddling a spectacular Caribbean vista. Most of the action has moved a bit east along the strip of all-inclusive hotels, souvenir shops and cafeteria-style restaurants on the beach at the border of Parque Nacional del Este. That said, this new main strip is not very attractive, dominated as it is by a series of strip malls, and doesn't make for a pleasant place to hang out. Though your hotel may be here, a more relaxing time can be spent hanging out at one of the beachfront establishments within the town, which are quieter and have a better view of the waterfront.

Worth seeking out are the patches of **undeveloped beachfront** west of the *Casa del Mar* resort. A small port lies at the end of Bayahibe's Calle Príncipe, from where you can hire a boat (see Parque Nacional del Este's "Practicalities" p.135) to the two western sand coves, one of which is occasionally used by Oscar de la Renta, who has set up a boat ramp and a shaded hut with bamboo chairs that go mostly unused. There's also a good patch of coral reef nearby, or you can skip the boats altogether and walk past the eastern resorts to the undeveloped beach abutting the national park.

Eating and drinking

There are a handful of decent **dining** options in Bayahibe itself. The most popular lunch spot for locals is the small, unmarked *comedor* on Calle Segunda across from the town's police station, where you can get genuinely delicious chicken and fish dishes (depending on what the chef cooked that day) for RD$30, often washed down by regulars with a shot of rum. At night, try *Pizza a Lena,* a candlelit pizzeria on Calle Príncipe (closed Mon). The modest *Supercafetería Julissa,* right on the village's Malecón, does a decent breakfast and also serves daiquiris at night. Away from town alongside the western row of resorts is *Boca Yate* (see opposite), with a restaurant serving high-quality Italian specialities and fresh fish; specialities include penne with lobster meat and king-fish filet in a mushroom sauce, and the bruschetta appetizers are worth trying as well. The bar here is also a major hangout, particularly on Wednesday and Thursday nights, when masses of hotel staff come here. Aside from this one spot, there's little in the way of **nightlife** outside of the resorts – which feature the standard floor-show entertainment – though *Ketty Berard*, within the village itself on Calle Segunda, is a pleasantly low-key local hangout that features ice-cold beer, local rum drinks some good Haitian food.

Parque Nacional del Este

Bayahibe sits on the very northwest edge of expansive **PARQUE NACIONAL DEL ESTE**, a peninsula jutting south into the Caribbean and also encompassing Isla Saona, just across a small bay and easily accessible by boat. The national park maintains a maze of forests, trails, caves and cliffs, home to an impressive array of birdlife and, on the cultural side, some signs of early Taino activity. Not much of the park, however, is conveniently accessible; in fact, no roads lead directly into its interior, and the best method of approach is to hire boats from Bayahibe to hit specific points along the rim, from where you can hike inland. Wherever you go in the park, wear plenty of mosquito repellent, as wasps are fairly prevalent here. Watch out, too, for tarantulas, though they won't bother you unless they're antagonized.

The most popular part of the park – and rightfully so – is **Isla Saona**, an island off the southern coast lined with alternating stretches of idyllic, coconut tree-backed beachfront and mangrove swamp, unpopulated except for two fishing hamlets. That said, the traffic at Saona has increased exponentially in recent years, and despite its reputation as a pristine natural oasis, the most popular stop-off points for boat tours have begun to feel more like high season at Miami's South Beach. The largest ships stop off at **Mano Juan**, a strip of pastel shacks with a four-kilometre hiking trail that leads inland, an expensive restaurant run by *Club Viva Dominicus* and a long line of beach chairs and umbrellas; or **Piscina Natural** (known locally as Laguna Canto de la Playa), a sand bar with a clear lagoon behind it good for splashing about. If you use one of the independent boats, avoid the hordes and head to one of the many more isolated stretches of beach that dot the entire island, where you can still get the white sand and transparent water to yourself. Another option is to have your boat captain skip Saona altogether, head into the Catuano Canal that separates Saona from the mainland, and stop off at the small island of **Catalinita**, which gets little tourist traffic and has some excellent reefs for snorkelling. In winter, you'll often see humpback whales and dolphins, and it's possible to spot the occasional manatee year-round.

Boats can also be hired to **Peñon Gordo** on the national park's west coast (2hr each way), which has a nice little isolated beach of its own, as well as a large **cave** 2km inland that's good for exploring. It used to have a 600-year-old large guardian pictograph etched at its entrance – a reference to a Taino myth in which the sun turned a man into a stone – but this priceless treasure was defaced with spray paint by a local tour operator wanting to make it more "dramatic". Still, the cave is good for exploring, and there are scattered Taino glyphs throughout its second level; if you head out here bring a flashlight and boots. Also watch your step at the entrance, which is basically a large, slippery hole in the ground.

Two other cave systems in the park are also well worth the trouble it takes to get to them. You'll have to hire one of the rangers to guide you from the national park outpost a kilometre southeast of *Club Dominicus*; it's a three-kilometre walk to the first, **Cueva del Puente**, a fairly easy two-hour hike down a narrow, signposted parting in the stunted treescape (look for the bromeliads and orchids that hang from the branches), that passes a high ancient sea-ridge escarpment before veering inland. The system consists of three separate levels of caverns (the first has been caved in and thus gets some sunlight) with thousands of stalagmites and stalactites along with hundreds of bats and sparkling seams of bright, crystallized minerals. There are also Taino pictographs on the second level, though they're not accessible via the entrance used by local tour operators: if you pester one of the park rangers to take you, scattered images of bats and birds can be seen, including one image of a small-eared owl – a bird that was thought by the Tainos to ferry dead souls to the afterlife.

The next system, **Cueva José María**, lies another 2km along the same path, no longer signposted but well known to the park rangers, who will also help navigate the narrow opening along a steep, guano-encrusted ledge that serves as its entrance. Inside, the cave bears some 1200 pictographs depicting the major events of Taino mythology and some historical events, including a reputed recording of Columbus's 1492 voyage (three Spanish caravels with white sails), and a bearded Spanish soldier wearing a metal helmet. The most significant, at the far end of the main cavern, is the documentation of a 1501 peace treaty with the Spaniards, in which the two parties agreed to co-exist in peace provided the natives gave the colonists cassava bread; look near the back of the cave for the scribbly depiction of a cassava grinder, a yucca root, a barbecue grill, the stick-figure *cacique* and a Spanish ship. The peace fell apart when a Spanish soldier unleashed his dog on a Taino in 1502.

Also worth a visit if you're here for a few days are the **Cuevas Padres Nuestros**, a remote cave system with four perfectly clear, deep fresh springs that have been a source of potable water since pre-Columbian times. Today local kids swim in Cueva Chico, the cave with the easiest access, while archeologists scour the others for Taino relics. Hire a motoconcho if you want to get there, as the muddy dirt road leading to it is impassable by car. Along the road to Bayahibe, turn off east onto an unmarked dirt path for 15km to the village of Padres Nuestros, then continue 2km south; the caves are at the end of this dirt road.

Practicalities

The majority of **boat tours** into the park take off from the carpark at Bayahibe's main pier. This is also where you'll find the **national park station** (daily 9am–noon), little more than a small green booth but a necessary stop if you're headed into the national park, either by boat or by foot – or for a camping permit on Isla Catalina (see p.128).

As dozens of tour companies from across the island use this as their setting-off point for Isla Saona, boat tours from here tend to visit the most crowded parts of Saona, making it hard to appreciate the island's tranquil beauty. One good solution is the inexpensive (RD$100; breakfast included) boat trips run daily (8.30am) by the *Boca Yate* hotel (see p.132), which head to an empty beach on the northern side of Saona. Make sure that you reserve at least two days in advance. Another option is the tours run by Scubafun (Calle Príncipe 28, Bayahibe ☏301-6999 or ☏833-0003, ⓦwww.o-markt.de/scubafun.com), a top-notch dive shop that also runs hiking and caving excursions. Their

La Aleta

On an expedition deep in the heart of Parque Nacional del Este, a team of archeologists from Indiana University recently discovered the most significant and extensive Taino excavation yet on record, four ceremonial plazas surrounding a cenote (a natural well) – a site referred to as **La Aleta**. Evidence shows that natives came to this well to worship during pre-Columbian times from across the countryside, even as far away as the Tetero Valley near Pico Duarte.

In his *History of the Indies*, Spanish priest Bartolomé de Las Casas recorded a journey to La Aleta in the late fifteenth century, noting that the natives lowered bowls into the well via a piece of rattan rope to pull up water, which was sweet at the surface and salty at the bottom – a stratification that still exists. He also described the slaughter of seven hundred people at La Aleta in 1503, the culmination of Nicolás de Ovando's campaign of Taino extermination, which he started after the Tainos killed three Spaniards on Isla Saona, itself a retaliation for an attack by a Spanish soldier. Bones from the mass killing have been found scattered throughout the site and within the well.

For the Tainos, caves served as the gateways to an underground spirit world. The well was apparently a site for subterranean ceremonies: fragments believed to have been parts of rafts lowered into the well have also been discovered. Other artefacts recovered from the site include clay pots and one straw basket, thought to contain offerings of food; a cassava cooking pan; axes and clubs; and an intact wooden *duho* (the seat from which the *caciques* prophesied to their people). In addition to the cenote, there is a series of four ceremonial plazas at the site – bounded by monumental limestone pillars – where a ball game similar to modern-day soccer was played by those who attended the rituals.

The government hopes one day to blaze a trail here from Peñon Gordo and open La Aleta to the public, but for now archeologists have to use a helicopter to get in, and no one else is supposedly allowed admittance. Still, the place has been ransacked twice by treasure hunters, and Dominican soldiers have been posted to prevent further looting.

scuba programme includes PADI certification (US$180), dives to local coral reefs (US$85; or US$100 for two trips) like the El Toro wall off of Saona, plus advanced adventure dives into caves and at night along the coast of the park (US$185). Equipment rental costs another US$15 per day. Their boat excursions (US$75) head to Isla Saona, Isla Catalina and the little-visited Isla Catalinita – which is where you'll get the remote sands mostly to yourself. Guided caving trips head to Peñon Gordo (US$40) and Cueva del Puente (US$35), though they don't visit the Taino rock art deep in del Puente, focusing instead on the cave system's otherworldly beauty. All trips depart daily between 8am and 8.30am.

You can alternately hire a **private boat** and captain either at the Bayahibe car park or at one of the overpriced restaurants that line the waterfront, which will take you to one of the park's best beaches. You should expect to haggle quite a bit over the price; a trip to Peñon Gordo should run about RD$500 per person; the going rate for Saona is RD$300–500 depending on the boat, and RD$200 for a half-day to the de la Renta beach cove.

If you're on your own and **hiking** into the park, you'll first have to get the RD$50 entrance ticket at the park station and then drive to the far southern end of the western resort strip. From there, walk another kilometre along the beach until you arrive at the entrance to the park. There you'll be required to hire one of the park rangers as a guide, which will cost another RD$100–150, depending on the hike. Tell the park rangers which cave system you want to visit before departing – if they don't recognize the name José María, try "Guaragao", another local name for the same cave system.

Camping in the park is permitted only to archeologists involved in the ongoing excavation of La Aleta and related sites, and the only place to **eat** is at Mano Juan on Isla Saona. You're therefore best off basing yourself in Bayahibe.

Boca de Yuma and inland

On the northeastern tip of Parque Nacional del Este sits **BOCA DE YUMA**, a pueblo that for the most part has been passed over by mass tourism because of its lack of spectacular beachfront, though there is one fairly nice beach across the river. Regardless, the town's setting along squat, ocean-pounded bluffs is undeniably impressive and as such it makes a pleasant stop for independent travellers seeking to escape the frenzy of all-inclusive construction and discover the Dominican Republic as it is away from the resort zones. It also makes a good alternate entry point to many of the sights within Parque Nacional del Este, and from here you can also take in the nearby home of conquistador **Ponce de León**.

Within the tiny town it's possible to wander along the shore, which has several surf-crashing grooves cut into the rock, or pay a local fisherman RD$10 to ferry you across the Río Yuma to a pretty little beach called **Playa Borinquen** that you'll share only with a couple of grazing cows. A short walk west of town along the waterfront is the national park station at the eastern entrance to Parque Nacional del Este (RD$20), from where you can hire horses (RD$100) or walk for an hour along the water to a natural land bridge from which turbulent jets of sea water rocket into the air. Just 100m north of this park station, the cavernous **Cueva de Bernardo**, a large cave once inhabited by Tainos, makes for an alternate, if less spectacular, goal than the caves near Bayahibe. Along with hundreds of bats and small birds, you'll see Taino *caritas* (little faces) carved on the walls, though some have been defaced by graffiti. If you want more caves, hire one of the park rangers (RD$100) to take you to three other local caves that bear modest Taino rock art that has yet to be defaced.

As with Bayahibe, boat tours of the national park are offered in Boca de Yuma, heading to islas Saona and Catalinita (see p.133); prices are a bit lower here, in the range RD$300–400. Anglers may also want to hire a local boat captain for some deep-sea **fishing** in the Catuano Channel between Saona and the mainland, where there's a tremendous variety of large fish. The best place to book a tour here is local hotel/restaurant *El 28*; rates range RD$250–500, depending on the trip. A less expensive alternative from the same hotel is an RD$100 trip up the Río Yuma.

Casa Ponce de León

Northwest of town, approximately 9km, in pueblo San Rafael de Yuma, fortified **Casa Ponce de León** (Mon–Sat 9am–5pm; RD$10) is the area's main attraction, a remote medieval keep built by Taino slaves for the noted explorer, who established a working farm and sugar plantation here during his rule of nearby Higuey at the beginning of the sixteenth century. Ponce didn't stay here for too long, however; in 1508 he increased his holdings by setting up a slave-catching outpost in Puerto Rico, which quickly grew into a colony in its own right, proving more profitable than his Dominican estate. Following this venture he set off to Florida, where he died at the hands of natives while searching for the Fountain of Youth. His former residence is now maintained by the parks department, who have renovated the two-storey house into a museum meant to evoke de León's life and times; inside you'll find original mahogany furnishings and the restored mahogany floor, along with de León's suit of armour and bulky treasure chest. The caretaker takes visitors on a guided tour in Spanish (for which he expects an RD$40 tip), dispensing a lot of information about both the construction of the house – note the massive stone walls – and de León's exploits.

Practicalities

There's not much choice of **accommodation** in Boca de Yuma, but fortunately the one hotel in town is a good one. *El 28* (Duarte 1 ☎476-8660 or 223-0503; ❷) is an Italian-run set of bungalows with hot showers, a/c and a swimming pool. The chef at the hotel's restaurant is the proprietor's 70-year-old mother, who makes home-made pastas, antipastos and Italian bread, and melt-in-your-mouth fresh fish. The food here alone is reason enough for making the trip to Boca de Yuma. They also rent 4WDs for US$40/day with full insurance, and their Tricom booth is the only public **phone** centre in town.

Higuey

Cramped, dusty and one hundred percent concrete, **HIGUEY** is an unpleasant town of 150,000 that's best passed through quickly on your way to the eastern coast. Despite the uninviting setting, it's famous throughout the country as a Dominican holy city, and tens of thousands gather here each January 21 for a mammoth procession and prayer of intercession to the nation's patron saint, the Virgin of Altagracia, who supposedly provides miraculous healing to those who make the pilgrimage.

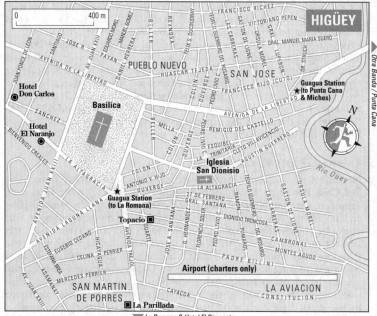

La Romana & Hotel El Diamante

The eighty-metre arch of the modernist **Basílica de Nuestra Señora de la Merced**, centre of the town's religious activity, is visible from the entire city. There's no real need to go inside; the basilica is actually most impressive when viewed from a distance, as the grounds around it are garbage-strewn and inhabited by dozens of the sick and lame, many of whom display their deformities to passers-by for pesos. At the parque central, you can check out the pretty sixteenth-century **Iglesia San Dionisio**, goal of the annual pilgrimage before construction of the basilica in the 1950s.

Just north of town, things brighten slightly in **La Otra Banda**, an attractive residential neighbourhood full of colourful gingerbread houses; you could easily spend a little time admiring the wares in Harrison's, an excellent jewellery shop right on Highway 104.

Practicalities

Hotel options in Higuey are pretty dire, but there are a few tolerable spots. *Don Carlos*, Ponce de León and Sánchez (☎554-2713; ❷), has clean rooms with a/c, cable TV, and hot water, plus a decent restaurant, while *El Naranjo*, Altagracia 23 (☎554-3400, ℱ554-5455, ✉bavaro@codetel.net.do; ❹), is modern, if somewhat pricey for what you get. More basic is *El Diamante*, Avenida Trejol and Cayacoa (☎554-2754; ❷), which has a worthwhile restaurant and sits just across the street from Televimenca and Western Union. If you've come for the Altagracia procession, though, all of these hotels will be booked unless you reserve a year in advance. There's not too much in the way of **eating**, either; try *xf*, at Duarte and Cambronal, or *La Parillada*, an excellent Argentine grill at the town entrance from La Romana, right across the street from the

Coca-Cola plant. Good Dominican food and ice-cold beer can also be found at *El Canuto*, Altagracia and Duarte, a lively local bar. There are also plenty of dance floors and beer halls spread throughout town, though nightlife in Higuey is of the traditional, male-dominated hard-drinking variety. **Codetel** is right in front of the basilica on Altagracia and Duarte.

Punta Cana and Bávaro

From La Otra Banda, a paved road winds 35km east to the tropical playlands of **PUNTA CANA** and **BÁVARO**, two resort areas on either end of a long curve of coconut tree-lined beach. Go elsewhere if you want to explore the country: the individual resorts tend to be cities unto themselves, encompassing vast swaths of beachside territory, expansive tropical gardens and several separate hotels. Fortunately, the beach is big enough that it doesn't get overly crowded despite the 700,000 visitors each year; with enough fortitude you could walk some thirty kilometres without seeing the sand interrupted once. At points where resorts have cropped up, you'll find the requisite concentration of umbrellas, watersports outfitters and beach bars, with occasional souvenir shacks set up in between. Aside from the glass-bottom boat operators trying to drum up business here and there, though, there's relatively little hassle – and the all-inclusives here are the nicest on the island; budget travellers, however, will find themselves restricted to one small *pensión* in the village of **Cortecito**.

Arrival and getting around

If you're not flying to the resorts via charter (or, less commonly, via Air Santo Domingo) arriving at **Aeropuerto Punta Cana** (☎688-4749 or 686-8790), from where you'll be ferried to your hotel in an air-conditioned bus, you'll have to get here by private car or guagua. **Taxis** are usually waiting at the airport and the entrance to the resorts; otherwise, call ☎552-0617 for pickup. Guaguas head to Punta Cana hourly from the bus station in Higuey (across the street from the basilica), with connections from Santo Domingo, San Pedro and La Romana. From Santo Domingo the cost should be no more than RD$100, RD$80 from San Pedro, RD$60 from La Romana and RD$50 from Higuey. The dropoff point for most guaguas is the Caribe Tours terminal, well away from most of the resorts, but from there you can catch a local guagua (used mostly by local resort staff) with stops at each hotel.

Once you arrive, all the resorts save *Club Med* have **car rental** agencies, though there's also a National Car Rental in Plaza Bávaro, just north of the *Fiesta* resort complex (☎221-0286, ⓦwww.nationalcar.com). The same plaza is also home to a Televimenca, Western Union, internet café (RD$30/hr; printing available) and Banco Popular's currency exchange and cash machine, as well as the only dentist this side of Higuey. Most hotels also offer free internet access, but their rates for phone calls and currency exchange are exorbitant – so come to Plaza Bávaro for these services. If you're looking to rent a cell phone or a laptop, contact PCs Solutions in the Plaza Riviera (☎552-1099, ⓕ552-0818).

Your resort will have plenty of **tours** on offer, but you can also book directly through an independent operator. For deep-sea fishing excursions, try RED Coral Diving and Fishing Centre in Plaza Bávaro (☎552-0740, ⓔcobupesa @hotmail.com; US$80), which specializes in water-based activities, and also has a scuba centre (US$300 for PADI course, US$75 per dive). A better dive

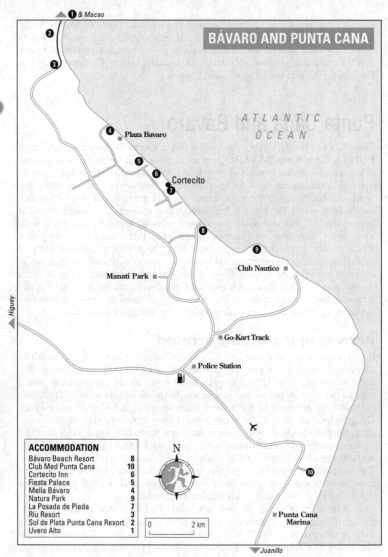

BÁVARO AND PUNTA CANA

ATLANTIC OCEAN

1 & Macao

2

3

4 ◻ Plaza Bavaro

5

6 ◻ Corticito

7

8

9

Club Nautico ◻

Manatí Park ◻

■ Go-Kart Track

■ Police Station

✈

10

■ Punta Cana Marina

ACCOMMODATION

Bávaro Beach Resort	**8**
Club Med Punta Cana	**10**
Cortecito Inn	**6**
Fiesta Palace	**5**
Melía Bávaro	**4**
Natura Park	**9**
La Posada de Pieda	**7**
Ríu Resort	**3**
Sol de Plata Punta Cana Resort	**2**
Uvero Alto	**1**

N

0   2 km

▼ Juanillo

shop is Pelicano Sport, at the *LTI Punta Cana Beach Resort* (☎688-6820,
Ⓦwww.pelicanosport.com), which boasts low-priced dives to local reefs
(US$35) as well as excursions to reefs and wrecks around Parque Nacional del
Este (US$75) and seven-day scuba safaris to the best reefs and cave dives along
the south coast (US$300). Back on dry land, Bávaro Runners (☎552-1035,
Ⓕ688-5732, Ⓦwww.bavarorunners.com; US$60–80) does well-regarded
horseback-riding and jeep excursions of the surrounding countryside. Within
the all-inclusives, look out for Rancho Capote's (☎553-2812, Ⓕ553-2656)
caving excursions to Parque Nacional Los Haitises (see p.149).

Accommodation

Most people staying in the **all-inclusives** are on package tours, so it's rare to actually call up such a hotel and request a room for the night. You'll get much better deals in any case if you book at home through a travel agent. You won't have much luck finding **budget lodging** unless you're interested in staying with a Dominican family in Cortecito.

Bávaro Beach Resort ☎ 686-5797, ⓕ 686-5859, ⓦ www.barcelo.com. Lovely grounds and 2000 spacious rooms, though there are no children's activities and the buffet food is lacklustre. Book a room in the Beach or Garden complexes, closer to the water, or the Palace, which is not all-inclusive, though slightly more expensive. The nine-hole golf course is free if you stay in the Golf hotel. ⑦

Club Med Punta Cana ☎ 687-2767, ⓕ 589-6086. More akin to a summer camp than a luxury hotel, this downscale resort – one of the first on the entire strip – is a good place for those who don't need luxury and are looking for a singles atmosphere. The beach is pleasantly underpopulated, and there are plenty of sailing, snorkelling, kayaking and windsurfing opportunities. ⑦

Cortecito Inn Calle Playa, Cortecito ☎ 552-0639, ⓕ 552-0641. This is the place if you don't want to go all-inclusive. It's right by the beach in the heart of Cortecito village, and has better accommodations than the larger resorts. Some rooms have private balconies, and there's a swimming pool and restaurant too. Breakfast included. ⑤

Fiesta Palace ☎ 221-8149, ⓕ 221-8150, ⓦ www.fiesta.hotels.com. Very nice all-inclusive with excellent service, decent food, tennis courts, football pitch, outstanding watersports facilities and two kiosk bars on the beach. The rooms are set in small villas rather than large concrete apartment complexes (as with most other local options), there's a nice tropical garden surrounding the place and it's over 2km to the next resort – all in all, an idyllic setting. ⑦

Iberostar Dominicana Hotel ☎ 221-6500, ⓕ 688-9888 or 221-7030, ⓦ www.iberostar.com/home_i.htm. Enormous complex with extremely large and comfortable rooms, great service and an attractive beachfront area – perfect for an all-inclusive vacation, provided you don't mind the frankly mediocre food. Get up early to reserve a seat at the steak house for dinner, the best restaurant on the complex. There's also a spa with hot tubs (though you have to pay extra for it) and a casino. Keep in mind that most guests here do not speak English, so picking up a bit of Spanish beforehand will hold you in good stead with the staff. ⑦–⑧

Meliá Bávaro ☎ 221-2311, ⓕ 686-5427, ⓔ hotelmelia@codetel.net.do. The very best of the

resorts, slightly more expensive but well worth it, with opulent contemporary architecture, sculpted tropical gardens, and the option of suites or bungalows. Luxurious amenities include bathrobes, a daily newspaper of your choice and a glass of champagne. Sporting options include volleyball, a large gym, water polo, beach soccer, horseback riding, tennis and a dive shop. Waterfront *Licey* is the best of the restaurants. ⑦–⑧

Natura Park ☎ 221-2626, ⓕ 221-6060, ⓔ hotel.natura@codetel.net.do. Resort with a New Age sheen that bills itself as eco-oriented but is largely indistinguishable from its competitors, aside from the plethora of birds on the compound. The beauty spa is tops in Bávaro and the large tropical garden is perfect for a shady afternoon walk. Price includes one free hour of horseback riding daily, and free water taxis to several other resorts. As usual, the food is not especially great – also watch out for the geese at the outdoor grill, as they often try to grab food right off of your plate. ⑥

La Posada de Pieda Calle Playa, Cortecito ☎ 221-0754. One of the few budget options, in the large beachfront home of a local family. Simply appointed private rooms with water views, shared cold-water bath and only limited privacy. ③

Ríu Resort ☎ 221-7515, ⓕ 682-1645. Classy Julio Iglesias brainchild with swimming pools punctuated by artificial palm islands, great food and service. Some rooms come with a private hot tub. The Taino, Naiboa and Melao compounds are all-inclusive, but the pricier Palace is not. Extras include a casino, tennis courts, dive school, windsurfing and deep-sea fishing. Melao's *La Proa* restaurant is particularly good. ⑦–⑧

Sol de Plata Punta Cana Resort ☎ 221-6640, ⓕ 221-4658, ⓦ www.lti.de. A new LTI-run resort comparable to what you'll find in the other resorts. The food is awful, and there's no night activity to speak of, but the rooms are spacious and the grounds well cared for. Worth trying only if you get a great package deal. ⑦

Uvero Alto ☎ 685-9880, ⓕ 685-4657, ⓦ www.royaluveroalto.com. Set seven kilometres north of the main strip, this is one of the better resorts in the area, with hot tubs in each of the 446 rooms and free TV movies and 24-hour room service. That said, the beach here is prone to nasty attacks of sand fleas at dusk, which will make you miserable if you don't wear ample quantities of repellent. They also have a sizeable ranch, and daily horseback excursions are included in the price. The buffet food – as usual – is bad, but if you reserve early you can eat at the excellent *Quisqueya* restaurant, which has delicious entrees like rack of lamb, stuffed peppers and roast duck. ❺

The beaches and inland

If you're not staying at one of the resorts, head to **Cortecito**, a kilometre north of the first Bávaro turnoff from the highway – the only village left along the entire stretch. It's an agreeable hangout populated by backpackers, independent European vacationers and a slew of Dominican vendors, with souvenir stalls set up along the public-access beach. Many travellers congregate around the beach volleyball net at the north end of town, and there are often bonfire beach parties here at night. If even this is too much, head 6km south from Punta Cana to pueblo **Juanillo**, a fishing village with no amenities that sits on equally superb waterfront. This is the favourite local beach spot for Dominicans, so on weekends you should expect to share the sands with hundreds of locals; you can also buy fresh grilled fish here from a couple of beach-stands for around RD$40. A kilometre further and you'll have the beach completely to yourself.

Away from the water, activity slows down quite a bit and the landscape becomes rather bleak. One option is the **Tropical Racing** go-kart track at the turnoff that separates upper and lower Bávaro (daily 5–10pm; US$10 for 15min; ☎707-5164), most exciting when it's crowded with daredevil Dominican teenagers taking the corners too fast. Also nearby, the much-advertised **Manatí Park** (daily 9am–7pm; US$25, US$15 for children, plus additional fees to swim with the dolphins ($70) or attend the Dancing Horses show (US$35); ⓦwww.manatipark.com) bills itself as an eco-theme park but is best avoided unless you're travelling with kids and looking for something to pass the time. Its tropical garden holds a crocodile cage, aviaries for parrots, flamingos and ducks and a show of sea lions and dolphins performing circus tricks. You can also swim with the dolphins for five minutes if you book at your resort a day in advance, but keep in mind that the park has been subject to extensive lawsuits by animal rights groups seeking to keep the dolphins' workload down. As it stands now, they are forced to perform five shows daily and be touched by 200 people. Three dolphins have reportedly died prematurely already, so it's probably best if you don't add to their woes by attending. A local NGO, Fundemar (ⓔfundemar@codetel.net.do), collects email petitions asking the Dominican government to stop the mistreatment of dolphins at the park.

Eating and drinking

In the unlikely event you'll be **eating** outside of the resorts, go to *White Sands*, 1.5km north of *Melía Bávaro*, with a beachfront patio where you can feast on barbecue and great paellas. The budget-minded can also try *Tropical Bávaro Restaurant* in Cortecito, which offers fresh fish dinners nightly for RD$150. **Nightlife**, too, is concentrated in the resorts, but *Disco Mangú* is a dance hall/sports bar near the *Flamenco Bávaro* resort that stays pretty crowded all night, and Cortecito's seedy *Coco Disco* sometimes features major merengue acts.

△ Mangroves

Macao to Miches

The resort hotels stop at the northern end of Bávaro, but the spectacular beach ploughs on with little interruption all the way up to the Limón and Redondo lagoons. The problem here is not getting the beach to yourself, but getting yourself to the beach; most of the paved roads end at Bávaro, and aside from the entrances at Macao and Laguna Nisibón, you'll need a decent 4WD to explore much of the coast.

Only 9km north of the Bávaro resort chain, **MACAO** already feels remote, its pounding, dangerous surf warding off the hotel chains and many would-be vacationers. A rusty sign points to the sand road that leads to Macao from just north of the *Ríu Resort*; if arriving from Higuey, you can take the extremely rocky fifteen-kilometre-long road that turns off east from Highway 104, 6km north of Higuey. Once there, you're best off swimming at Macao's southern cove, which is framed by majestic bluffs that themselves make for a diverting hour's hike. The only nearby building is the downscale *Cabañas/Restaurant* (no phone; ❶), with modest accommodation (cold-water bath, fan and not much else) and a not very notable lunch.

North from the Macao turnoff, Highway 104 skirts the Mona Passage – the channel that separates the Dominican Republic and Puerto Rico – a kilometre inland, remaining paved for 60km to Miches and passing a series of small towns along the way. About a third of the way up, a marked turnoff within the town of Laguna Nisibón leads east to **Playa Nisibón**, the entry point to an extraordinary uninterrupted strain of sand – picture Punta Cana and Bávaro without a single hotel. Once you've spent the day here, though, you'll be hard-pressed to scrape together any decent local accommodation. In case of emergency you can bunk down at the *Hotel/Restaurant Mercedes* in Laguna Nisibón (☎558-7225; ❶), but the place is so cramped and basic that you're unlikely to get a good night's sleep.

Lagunas Redondo y Limón

The beaches are finally cut off by twin mangrove lagoons protected as a single national park of interest mostly to serious birdwatchers, some 20km northwest of Varma via Highway 104. The westernmost, **Laguna Redondo**, is especially difficult to reach – though a rusted sign points to the turnoff – and you can only get to its banks with a 4WD. There are no boats dedicated to taking travellers out, though occasionally a fishing boat nearby can be enticed to do the job for RD$100. Even if you're stuck on shore, you'll see a number of birds, including the predatory osprey, egrets, horneate spoonbills and herons.

More accessible is the especially beautiful and serene **Laguna Limón**, which feels extremely pristine and remote but has a couple of small outfits around it dedicated to tourism. Two separate entrances lead to it from the highway, the first of which is marked by a small **national park station** (9.30am–noon & 2–5pm; RD$15), where a local guide with a boat can be hired (RD$250 for three to four people). The second entrance is 2km further west; there's no park station here, so you won't be asked to pay the fee. Another 2km on stands *La Cueva* (☎689-4664; reservations necessary), a restaurant with fresh seafood and lobster that caters mostly to passing tour buses on their way to Los Haitises and guests of the nearby hotel. A hundred metres further on, the road veers right at **Playa Limón**, another of the spectacular area beaches, though the undertow is strong enough to preclude swimming and it's plagued by sand fleas at dusk. It does, though, make for a scenic walk, and sea turtles lay their eggs here in the spring; take a left to reach the mouth of a local river, where the surf churns sea water into the brackish lagoon and the beach is adorned with patches of mangrove. To the right of the beach entrance, the road turns to sand, leading to the *Tortuga Bar and Cabanas* (☎ & ⓕ689-4664; ◑), a pleasant set of thatch huts with hot water and fan. The restaurant here has recently closed down, but guests are entitled to take their meals at *La Cueva*. It's another kilometre down the beach to the lagoon (accessible only by 4WD, though if you're staying at *Tortuga*, the owner will take you), where you can hire a fishing boat at the narrow, mangrove-lined estuary that connects it to the ocean.

Miches

MICHES is a seedy little town on the Bahía de Samaná notorious as the setting-off point for illegal immigration to Puerto Rico. Dominicans pay RD$15,000–25,000 to local boat captains to be smuggled in small fishing vessels across the shark-infested Mona Passage. For visitors, however, the lone attraction is **Costa Esmerelda**, a series of sandy beaches that extend for several kilometres east of town. Enter at **Playa Miches**, directly across the Río Miches from town and accessible by a marked dirt path (you can either walk or drive); from here the sand continues 8km further, though there are a couple of small rivers to ford. You can also get local fishers to take you out to **Media Luna**, a half-moon of sand that peeks out of the ocean at low tide, several kilometres offshore. Trips will generally cost RD$200 or so; make sure yourself that the ship is quite sturdy, and it's recommended that women not go out alone in a local boat.

There's less to entice you within town, though the seaside **parque central** has a basketball court with popular nightly games. You can find live music on weekends – sometimes big-name acts – at the cockfighting arena just east of town.

Practicalities

Guaguas approach Miches from all directions, though the highways to El Seibo and Sabana de la Mar are only half-paved, and the road to Higuey is currently undergoing extensive renovation. Public transport lets you off at the petrol station on the east side of town; if you're heading to the beachfront *cabañas* (see below), you can catch a motoconcho here that will take you to them for RD$50.

In and of itself, Miches isn't an especially compelling destination, but just outside the town of Las Minas de Miches – 10km east of Miches proper – you'll find two sets of **thatched hut cabañas** along a very isolated beach that make a perfect place for independent travellers to spend the night. The better of the two is *Campo la Concha* (☎248-5884; ◑), six *cabañas*, well maintained with fan and shared cold-water bath, a library full of eclectic books and CDs and a nice little restaurant. The proprietor also owns a couple of well-groomed horses used for rides along the beach. Right next door, *Cabañas de Leo* (☎248-5888, ⓕ533-5222; ◑), is run by a long-term expat who knows the area well. His *cabañas* are comparable in amenities to *Campo la Concha*, but not quite as well maintained; there are, though, some funky perks like a trampoline, hammocks set up along the water and daily trips to Laguna Redondo with package tourists from the Bávaro resorts. To get to either establishment, head 10km east of Miches to Las Minas de Miches and turn left onto the dirt road at the western end of town. From there you'll need to make a left at the fork in the road, a right at the beach and then a kilometre further along the sand. Before you arrive, stock up on plenty of insect repellent, as the beach is plagued with nocturnal sand fleas.

In the event you want or need to **stay the night** within town, try *Bahía del Este*, Deligne and San Antonio (℡553-5834; ❸), which has modern rooms, a swimming pool and restaurant (try the crabmeat with rice), but can get noisy at night thanks to two nearby discos; or clean pensiónes *Quiles* (❷) and *Orfelina* (❷), both on Duarte off San Antonio, which have rather homey restaurants attached serving edible breakfasts.

El Seibo

Well off the beaten path, the pleasant cattle town of **EL SEIBO**, smack in the middle of the Cordillera Oriental and a bumpy forty-kilometre drive south of Miches, was once the stomping ground of nineteenth-century *caudillo* Pedro Santana, who ruled the Dominican Republic off and on during the period of internecine strife that followed independence from Haiti and continued until annexation by Spain. Whenever Santana was booted out of office by his rival Buenaventura Báez, Santana would retreat here until the next Haitian invasion, when he would be called back to lead the nation's military defence.

The only sight here is the squat **Iglesia Santa Cruz** – which stands beside the parque central along the winding main road that bisects El Seibo – a preserved piece of colonial architecture that's still used as the local parish. Occasional renovations have kept its red-brick dome and partially whitewashed limestone facade in good shape, though one of these "improvements" also resulted in the unfortunate plaster Victorian top to the bell tower. Otherwise, you may wish to head to the eastern end of the highway that runs through town, where there's a **balneario** tucked beneath the Seibo Bridge, crowded with local kids.

Spreading out along the main road from either side of the church are dozens of bars, dance halls and restaurants – surprising for such a seemingly out-of-the-way town. The best of the **restaurants** is *New York*, though it's less cosmopolitan than the name might suggest, and discos include *Topacio* and *Genesis* on the Higuey side, and on the main strip *Metropolis* and *El Lugar*. Also on this road, *Paraíso* (no phone; ❶) offers the cleanest of the very basic, cold-water-only **accommodation** options in town.

El Seibo festivals

The May 1–3 **fiesta patronal** in honour of Santa Cruz sees a spirited celebration converge on the otherwise downbeat and slow-moving town. Cattle are paraded along the main road, serenaded with song and eventually blessed at Iglesia Santa Cruz. The nine nights leading up to the fiesta are known as **novenas**, similarly festive evening celebrations worth a pass if you're in the area.

North of the city a spottily paved road leads through the most scenic part of the unspoilt Cordillera Oriental mountain range to Miches (see p.144); the peaks here are shaped into surreal spires and cones draped with a thick canopy of greenery. You can get here by guagua from El Seibo – one traverses this road each morning – but otherwise you'll have to drive it, which is no problem provided you go slowly over the unpaved patches.

Hato Mayor to Sabana de la Mar

Despite its lush surroundings, in the pretty rolling hills and orange groves of the Cordillera Oriental, overcrowded **Hato Mayor** is one of the poorest towns in the region and has little of interest for visitors. Most get just a passing glance anyway while taking Highway 103, the only paved road to Sabana de la Mar and Parque Nacional Los Haitises. If you don't have your own transportation, guaguas take off from the corner of San Antonio and the highway.

Just 8km north of Hato Mayor is pueblo **Gran Diablo**, which holds an extremely rocky dirt road that leads 5km northeast to a Cordillera Oriental cave system used for spelunking by Rancho Capote (☎553-2812, ☞553-2656; US$55), an adventure tour outfit in Higuey. Tours take in stalactite-ridden **Boca de Diablo** (which was recently officially renamed "Cueva Fun Fun" by the tourism-conscious national government), a huge cave system at the south end of the park that holds several separate chambers and an underground river. Many of the tour operators in the Punta Cana/Bávaro resorts book their tours; otherwise, it's best to reserve well in advance, as the office can be hard to reach by phone.

Some 12km further north on Highway 103, the so-called **Tropical Plantation** (daily 9am–6pm; RD$100; ☎470-9673), the Caribbean's largest anthurium farm – which also produces a good number of orchids, heliconias and a hundred species of bromeliad – sits nestled among local coffee and cacao plantations. Tours take you through a large forest with examples of most trees found on the island, a butterfly house, a beehive and an aviary. Near the end of the trek, you'll navigate a labyrinth of manicured shrubs to reach a traditional campesino dwelling and farm, which – basically for show – grows coffee, citrus, pineapple, agave, peanuts and tobacco. The price of the tour also includes a modest lunch.

You're unlikely to want to **spend the night** in Hato Mayor, but in a pinch you can head to *Centenario*, Mercedes and Hincado (☎553-2800; ❷), the only formal hotel in town, with clean rooms and private bath but no hot water. For **food** try *Azotéa*, on Hincado and San Antonio, which does above-average versions of Dominican staples. A surprisingly pleasant series of outdoor bars stand just east of town along Highway 4, the best of which is a combination restaurant/dance hall called *La Hora Azul*.

Sabana de la Mar

SABANA DE LA MAR is a dusty little port unremarkable but for its use as a setting-off point for the highly recommended boat tours of Parque Nacional los Haitises (see p.149). It also happens to be fairly convenient to the Samaná

Over the past century, a lot of impassioned debate has gone into the question of whether or not the **Tainos** who once inhabited Hispaniola – along with Puerto Rico and Cuba – were exterminated during the initial period of Spanish colonization. Certainly the majority were wiped out – by war, slave labour and epidemic smallpox – but a growing body of evidence points to the fact that some Tainos (perhaps quite a number of them) survived throughout the colonial era and inter-married with the Africans and Europeans who lived on the island from Columbus onward.

The primary evidence for complete **genocide** comes from Spanish authors such as Las Casas and Montesino who wrote of the absolute devastation wreaked upon the Tainos in the early years of European colonization. According to Las Casas, only a few thousand remained as long ago as 1518, and early sixteenth-century sugar mill owners such as Juan de Viloria claimed that their entire Taino slave workforce had been destroyed by smallpox. Counter-evidence, though, can sometimes be seen at the margins; when Viloria died, his wife claimed that he had 300 Taino slaves as part of his property, and it seems a reasonable assumption that he hid them in his report to the Crown in order to get a free allotment of several hundred African slaves as an additional labour force. In addition, early colonial records show that most of the first male colonists intermarried with locals; some records suggest that as the sixteenth century wore on, Tainos who married Europeans and converted to Catholicism began to be considered Spaniards.

At the very least, the historical record is confused. Various wills and court documents continued to refer to "Indians" in a variety of contexts, and a **1545 census** claimed that over half of the sugar mill slaves were Indian – twenty years after the Tainos' supposed extermination. In addition, the vast majority of the island was not under European control and thus would have served as a safe harbour for Taino communities as well as *cimmarones*; in 1555 four large Taino villages were discovered along the island's north coast, and there were likely many more in the isolated mountain regions.

As a result, various tests of Dominican and Puerto Rican **genetics** have been performed in order to establish to what extent the current inhabitants of the Greater Antilles are descended from Tainos, and some have purported to find definitive traces of Taino in the current population. A recent study of DNA in hair samples of Puerto Rican citizens found that about half of them had some Taino heritage, while a study of blood types in the Dominican Republic indicated that today's Dominican people get around 15 percent of their genes from the Tainos.

The question of the Dominican Republic's continuing Taino heritage is a lot trickier than it looks at first sight, though, in large part because the Tainos have been used by Dominican intellectuals in the past to cover up the nation's more extensive **African** background. Dominican mulattos, for example, are still officially classified as "Indios", and many mainstream anthropologists become understandably suspicious whenever they hear someone pressing the case for the Taino heritage of the Dominican people. Even though it now appears that the Dominican people do possess significant Taino heritage, the African debt is much greater, and much harder for many to admit due to racism and widespread mis-education in the schools.

Regardless, Dominican culture owes a profound debt to the Tainos. Dominican Spanish is interspersed with hundreds of Taino words and inflections, the pantheon of spirits in *Vodú dominicana* – a largely African religion – includes several divisions of Taino spirits, and the Taino methods of farming, cooking, weaving and boat-building are still widely performed throughout the country even today. In the most rural campos, villagers still call to each other from hill to hill with signals blown through conch shells whenever fresh meat or ice has arrived for sale.

Peninsula; **ferries** depart regularly from the wharf at the northern end of town to Samaná itself, and the recently renovated town port allows the ferries now to transport vehicles as well (daily 11am & 5pm; RD$50; RD$250 for cars; RD$350 for trucks).

You won't really want to use Sabana de la Mar as a base for anything – the hotels are pretty substandard – but just east of the town (and close to the entrance of Los Haitises) is *Paraiso de Caña Hondo* (℡556-7483; ❹), which has a small restaurant and a very nice set of rooms with a/c and private cold-water bath, plus a natural pool with cascades. A cheaper alternative is *El Tres* (℡556-7575; ❶), a decent hotel 2km south of town along the road to Hato Mayor, with rather plain rooms – some with private bath – on rambling rural grounds, and with a restaurant that serves typical local seafood dishes like fish cakes and crabs in coconut stew. The best part about the place is that they also run three-hour-long horseback excursions for groups of ten or more into the nearby mountains, visiting a typical Dominican campo and a remote waterfall within Los Haitises that has an ice-cold freshwater pool at its base (RD$200 per person, lunch included). Within town, you can get good fresh seafood at *Parador del Mar* on the town wharf.

Parque Nacional Los Haitises

PARQUE NACIONAL LOS HAITISES, a massive expanse of mangrove swamp that protects several Taino caves, 92 plant species, 112 bird species and a wide variety of marine life, spreads west of Sabana de la Mar around the coastal curve of Bahía de Samaná. Though twelve hundred square kilometres in total, only a small portion of that is open to the public, most of that accessible by organized tours (see "Practicalities" p.150).

Along the coast it holds the country's largest unblemished expanse of red and white mangroves; in the near-impenetrable interior, dense, trail-less rainforest predominates, punctuated by the ruins of long-abandoned sugar plantations and numerous cave systems. What you'll see on the boat tours is a series of virtually untouched mangrove rivers along with small islands and coastal caves that provide habitat for untold numbers of tropical birds; some of the caves, too, bear Taino petroglyphs.

The 2.5-hour **Ruta Litoral**, or standard boat trip, hits three main areas of interest within the park. First up is **Cueva Arena**, a large grotto that has numerous Taino drawings of families, men hunting, supernatural beings, whales and sharks. You can stop briefly at the beach cove here if you'd like to get a good look at **Cayo Willy Simons** – once a hideout for the infamous pirate – recognizable by the dozens of birds circling around: pelicans, herons, terns, frigates, even an occasional falcon. The next stop is grottoes **San Gabriel and Remington**, both with Taino faces carved into their walls. The two caves were also known as temporary homes of various pirates, including Cofresí, Jack Banister and John Rackham. From here you'll pass the ruins of a 100-year-old banana wharf, with pelicans perching on the remaining wooden supports, to reach **Cueva de la Linea**, which was once intended to hold a railroad station for the sugar cane that was grown in the area. In pre-Columbian times, the cave was a Taino temple; look for the guardian face carved at the entrance, residues of ancient campfire smoke and the innumerable pictographs along the inside walls.

Practicalities

Almost everyone who comes to Los Haitises chooses to **explore the park** by boat, mostly because this is doable in a half-day trip. It is, though, perfectly possible to explore the interior of the park with a bit of advance planning and pluck. For the **boat tour**, you'll need to hire a guide from Sabana de la Mar; this runs around RD$800 for up to six people, plus RD$300 for the guide and an RD$50 park fee. Guides can be picked up at the national park office (☎556-7333) at the town port on the east end of town. The park rangers also run a training seminar for the guides that teaches them a great deal about flora, fauna and the Tainos, so ask to see their certification before you set off, and remember to bring insect repellent.

The port of entry to the park – which is accessible only by sea – is a tiny pier called **Caña Hondo**, entered via a signposted turnoff on the road to Hato Mayor at the village's southern end. From there you'll travel 12km along a bumpy dirt road to the pier before you set off along a mangrove-lined canal and into the bay. There's also a park ranger station at Cueva Arena where you'll pay the RD$50 entrance fee.

If looking to **explore the interior** of the national park, your best bet is to book a horseback excursion. *El Tres* (see above) does good trips into Los Haitises, but they require groups of ten or more. If you can't get that many people together, an alternative is to look for a gentleman nicknamed Montezuma at the national park office; he's a bit of a local legend and is said to have swum the entire Samaná Channel in his youth, from Samaná city to Sabana de la Mar. With a day's notice, Montezuma can arrange horseback excursions that run RD$500 per day for the guide, plus RD$200 per person for the horses. Trips typically follow the old banana plantation train tracks that snake through the swamps and the mountains toward Sánchez, passing a series of abandoned plantations in ruins and a remote mountain balneario. If you decide to do a multi-day excursion, make sure to bring your own tents and camping gear, though you could sleep with campesinos in their extremely modest dwellings if you preferred.

Travel details

There are no formal bus company routes that will take you to the southeast, but the region is served by a network of **guaguas**, which range in quality from air-conditioned mini-vans to battered trucks in which you'll be squeezed with as many other passengers as can fit. You'll have to switch vehicles in most major towns, though one guagua line goes all the way from Higuey through Miches to Sabana de la Mar. Journey times given for guaguas are rough estimates.

Guaguas

Bávaro to: Higuey (hourly; 1hr 15min).
Bayaguana to: Monte Plata (6 daily; 45min); Santo Domingo (5 daily; 2hr 20min).
Bayahibe to: Higuey (8 daily; 1hr 40min); La Romana (hourly; 25min).
Boca de Yuma to: Higuey (10 daily; 1hr 25min); La Romana (5 daily; 1hr 25min); San Rafael de Yuma (hourly; 20min).

El Seibo to: Hato Mayor (10 daily; 40min); Higuey (hourly; 1hr 15min); Miches (daily; 1hr 45min).
Hato Mayor to: El Seibo (10 daily; 40min); Sabana de la Mar (hourly; 1hr); San Pedro de Macorís (hourly; 1hr 10min).
Higuey to: Bávaro (hourly; 1hr 15min); Bayahibe (8 daily; 1hr 40min); Boca de Yuma (10 daily; 1hr 25min); El Seibo (hourly; 1hr 15min); La Romana (hourly; 2hr); Macao (4 daily; 2hr); Miches (hourly; 3hr); San Rafael de Yuma (10 daily; 1hr 5min).

La Romana to: Bayahibe (hourly; 25min); Boca de Yuma (5 daily; 1hr 25min); Higuey (hourly; 2hr); San Pedro de Macorís (frequent; 50min); San Rafael de Yuma (5 daily; 1hr 10min).

Macao to: Higuey (4 daily; 2hr).

Miches to: El Seibo (daily; 1hr 45min); Higuey (hourly; 3hr); Sabana de la Mar (hourly; 1hr 15min).

Monte Plata to: Bayaguana (6 daily; 45min); Cotuí (daily; 2hr 15min); Santo Domingo (5 daily; 3hr).

Sabana de la Mar to: Hato Mayor (daily; 1hr); Miches (hourly; 1hr 15min).

San Pedro de Macorís to: Boca Chica (frequent; 45min); Hato Mayor (hourly; 1hr 10min); Juan Dolio (frequent; 20min); La Romana (frequent; 50min); Santo Domingo (frequent; 1hr 30min).

San Rafael de Yuma to: Boca de Yuma (hourly; 20min); Higuey (10 daily; 1hr); La Romana (5 daily; 1hr 10min).

Ferries

Sabana de la Mar to: Samaná (3 daily, 45 min).

Flights

La Romana to: Las Terrenas (daily; 40min); Puerto Plata (daily; 40min); Punta Cana (daily; 15min); Santiago (daily; 50min).

Punta Cana to: La Romana (daily; 15min); Las Terrenas (daily; 30min) Puerto Plata (3 daily; 45min); Santiago (daily; 30min); Santo Domingo (3 daily; 20min).

The Samaná
Peninsula

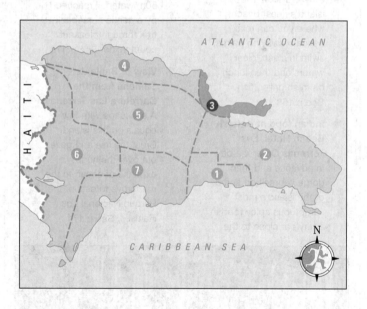

CHAPTER 3

Highlights

✳ **Whale watching, Samaná** One of the world's finest, most dependable wildlife spectacles. More than 12,000 humpback whales visit Dominican waters from mid-January through mid-March, during which time you're almost guaranteed a sighting. See p.160

✳ **Playa Rincón** The island's finest beach, where you can relax beneath swaying palms, swim in clean, clear waters and then lunch on fresh grilled fish. See p.169

✳ **Indian food at Kanesh Beach Hotel, Las Terrenas** Order it a day in advance and then gorge yourself on some of the island's most sumptuous spicy food in a tiny bar close to the beach. See p.175

✳ **Playa Cosón** An unspoilt, uninterrupted strip of white sand dropping down into a turquoise ocean just a stone's throw away from the bustle of Las Terrenas. See p.176

✳ **Salto El Limón, El Limón** An impressive 50m waterfall reached by a gentle horseback trek through pleasant countryside. See p.179

✳ **View of Bahía de Samaná from the Carretera Las Terrenas** A seascape with few equals on this island. Crest the rise and gaze out over the huge expanse of ocean to the mangrove forests of the Parque Nacional Los Haitises. See p.171

The Samaná Peninsula

t's not hard to appreciate the beauty of the **Samaná Peninsula**, a thin strip of land poking from the Dominican Republic's northeast out into the Atlantic Ocean. Perhaps the most appealing part of the whole country, the region boasts a coast lined with spectacular beaches that conform strictly to the Caribbean archetype of powdery white sand, vast banks of swaying coconut trees and transparent green-blue sea. Away from the water, the Cordillera Samaná, an imposing mountain range thick with sixty different types of palm tree and possessing a few spectacular waterfalls, supports the peninsula, most of it penetrable only by horse.

Perhaps more than for the beaches and spectacular geography, visitors come for the opportunity to see up close the thousands of **humpback whales** that migrate to the Bahía de Samaná during the winter. **Whale watching** has become a thriving local industry – with tough regulations in place to preserve the safety of the whales – peaking between mid-January and mid-March, when sightings are virtually guaranteed. Most whale boats depart from the city of **Santa Bárbara de Samaná** (generally shortened to "Samaná"), the largest on the peninsula, and within easy shouting distance of several terrific beaches – including **Cayo Levantado**, the original Bacardi Island. If the hustle and bustle of the more typical Dominican towns becomes too much, head east to **Las Galeras**, a pristine horseshoe of sand that, despite considerable development in recent years, still maintains an air of tranquillity. A short drive away are the **Cuevas de Agua**, the peninsula's most impressive Taino archeological site; alternatively, hop on one of the daily ferries heading north to isolated **Playa Rincón** – rated one of the world's ten best beaches by *Condé Nast Traveler*. Along the peninsula's north coast you'll find the remote expat colony of **Las Terrenas**, a burgeoning hangout for independent travellers set on its own spectacular beach and with a decent nightlife scene. Day-trips easily made from here include untamed **Playa Bonita**, the biggest Samaná beach of all, and horseback excursions to the remote and thundering **El Limón waterfall**.

Until the late nineteenth century, a narrow channel separated Samaná from the Dominican mainland, making it a hotbed for pirates during colonial days, whose smaller ships used the channel to evade the bulkier galleons that couldn't make it through. Since then, sediment has slowly glued the peninsula onto

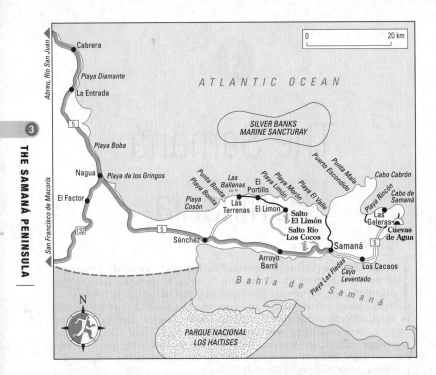

the mainland; the old channel area is now a fertile flood plain packed with rice paddies. The peninsula's gateway city **Sánchez** lies here, with little of intrinsic interest but a popular setting-off point for boat tours of **Parque Nacional Los Haitises**, an enormous mangrove preserve across the bay (covered in Chapter Two, "The southeast"; see p.149).

Getting around the peninsula

The **Carretera 5 (C-5)** that skirts the Dominican north coast leads all the way from Puerto Plata to Santa Bárbara de Samaná and on to Las Galeras. The only other well-paved road in the region traverses the short trek from Sánchez to Las Terrenas. The major bus companies ply the C-5, as do a number of guaguas, and pickup trucks also make the run out to Las Terrenas every half-hour during the day. Getting around the rest of the peninsula is a bit more difficult: aside from those two roads, it's rough-and-tumble dirt track between towns, often barely navigable by car. There's a guagua route from Samaná to Las Galeras, but you'll likely rely more on motoconchos to get you from place to place. Meanwhile, a new **airport** is under construction in the town of Arroyo Barril (16km west of Samaná). Originally planned to take international flights, development has been slow and it's looking more likely that it will handle mainly internal traffic. A **new highway** from Santo Domingo to Samaná is also in the pipeline and, once finished (target date 2005), it should offer significant savings in both time and fuel in getting to and from the capital.

Samaná and around

Protected on its southern side by an elongated strip of land that breaks apart into a series of small islands, **SANTA BÁRBARA DE SAMANÁ** possesses a remarkably safe harbour, giving the city a tremendous strategic potential that's never been fully realized. The barrier blunts the impact of hurricanes and tropical storms, and the shoals and breakers allow entry via only one small bottleneck, the perfect spot to ward off unwelcome intruders. Despite the international political wrangling that has occurred here over the last five centuries, the town is now more of a focus for travellers wishing to get away from the all-inclusive vacations other coastal spots are known for. Many use it as a base to **whale-watch** and explore the area beaches, returning at night for the busy outdoor nightlife along the **Malecón**. Worth going out of your way to discover, though, is Samaná's English-speaking community descended from African-American freemen, who hold a series of interesting **harvest festivals** from August through October (see p.162).

Before European colonization the harbour was one of the settlements of the **Ciguayos** – one *cacique* within the Taino culture – that dotted the peninsula's south coast. The Ciguayos lived in close proximity to the Caribes, and borrowed some aspects of Caribe culture, including the bow and arrow, elements of their language, and black and red body paint. When Columbus landed at Playa Las Flechas just east of town in January 1493, the Ciguayos greeted his men with a flurry of arrows that forced the Spaniards back to their ships. A week later, the Admiral met with Chief Cayacoa, aboard the *Niña*, repaired their differences and formed an alliance; the Ciguayos later assisted in subjugating the remaining four Taino *caciques*, only to be pacified themselves in the early sixteenth century.

Spain officially founded Santa Bárbara de Samaná in 1756 with transplants from the Canary Islands. In 1795, though, Spain handed the entire island over to **Napoleon Bonaparte**, in exchange for territory he controlled in Spain. Bonaparte quickly had blueprints drawn up of his dream New World capital,

Piracy in the Samaná Bay

The Spaniards made little use of Samaná harbour for the first two centuries of their rule, paving the way for **pirates** to take advantage of the narrow Samaná Channel and the snarl of limestone caves within the dense swamps of Los Haitises. The most notorious of these ne'er-do-wells was Britain's **Jack Banister**, an official government privateer condemned to outlaw status by the 1670 Treaty of Madrid between Britain and Spain. In 1690 Banister was anchored at Samaná with a frigate and another smaller vessel when two British warships tried to enter the harbour to arrest him. Banister took his boats to the nearby island of Cayo Levantado, and moved his men ashore along with some heavy artillery. The incoming warships were thus put directly in the line of fire, and 125 British soldiers were killed as they cruised into the teeth of Banister's defences. Banister's large vessel was also destroyed in the melee; when his two-hundred-man crew found out that the ship was gone – and that the smaller one could accommodate only a quarter of them – they stampeded aboard the light craft, forty of them killed in the process. Banister, though, got away, and the islands surrounding the Samaná harbour have been known ever since as the Banister Cays.

to be set in Samaná, but widespread chaos on the island – including a revolution in Haiti, two British invasions and civil war among the French commanders – prevented Bonaparte from taking control of the Dominican Republic for almost a decade. When the French finally received their colony in 1802, they were besieged by both a well-organized Haitian force and a British invasion, and they soon capitulated.

The United States, too, went to some effort to acquire Samaná, inadvertently toppling two regimes in the process. In 1855, General Pedro Santana entered into formal negotiations with the Americans to annex the peninsula and its harbour, a move that proved fatal to his government as – eager to prevent the US from gaining a foothold here – Haiti invaded and Spain sent aid to local rebels. Santana's successor Buenaventura Báez reopened negotiations in 1870 with President Ulysses S. Grant, who wanted Samaná to become the US's main Caribbean port, finally agreeing to annex the island for US\$150,000. The treaty was rejected by the isolationist US Senate, so the desperate Báez turned instead to private American investors, who signed a 99-year lease with him that gave them total political control over Samaná. Before the Americans were able to take it over, though, Báez was deposed and the contract was rescinded.

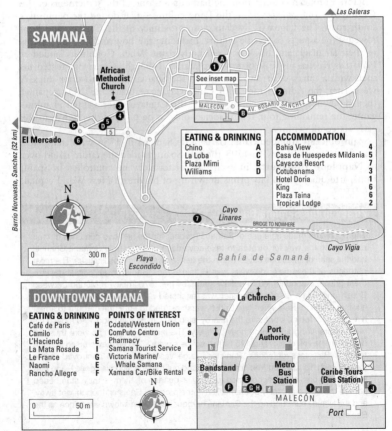

SAMANÁ — Las Galeras

Barrio Norueste, Sanchez (32 km)

African Methodist Church

See inset map

MALECÓN — AV. ROSARIO SANCHEZ — 5

El Mercado

EATING & DRINKING
Chino	A
La Loba	C
Plaza Mimi	B
Williams	D

ACCOMMODATION
Bahia View	4
Casa de Huespedes Mildania	5
Cayacoa Resort	7
Cotubanama	3
Hotel Doria	1
King	6
Plaza Taina	6
Tropical Lodge	2

N

Cayo Linares

BRIDGE TO NOWHERE

Cayo Vigia

0 — 300 m

Playa Escondido

Bahía de Samaná

DOWNTOWN SAMANÁ

La Churcha

EATING & DRINKING
Café de Paris	H
Camilo	J
L'Hacienda	E
La Mata Rosada	I
Le France	G
Naomi	E
Rancho Allegre	F

POINTS OF INTEREST
Codatel/Western Union	e
ComPuto Centro	a
Pharmacy	b
Samana Tourist Service	d
Victoria Marine/	
Whale Samana	f
Xamana Car/Bike Rental	c

N

Port Authority

CALLE SANTA BARBARA

Bandstand

Metro Bus Station

Caribe Tours (Bus Station)

MALECÓN

Port

0 — 50 m

Look out over Samaná harbour today and you can still envisage the great Napoleonic city destined to remain an emperor's dream. A flotilla of sailboats stands behind the palm-ridged island chain; the port and the wide-open promenade bordering the water hustle with activity; and in place of the impenetrable French fortress that was to jut atop the western promontory is the whitewashed *Cayacoa Resort* with a bridge extending from it to the two nearest cays. In part this is due to French-descended President Joaquin Balaguer's own failed act of hubris – the transformation of this sleepy town into the largest resort complex on the planet, its design mirroring Napoleon's to the letter. A Samaná native himself, in the early 1970s he tore down the city's remaining Victorian architecture, widened the streets, built three large resorts and secured a World Bank loan to construct several more hotels and an international airport. A bridge was constructed that extended from the eastern point across two of the small islands, in line with the vision of Napoleon, and a restaurant was built on the second. When he lost the election in 1978, though, the project was scrapped and the tourism complex was moved to Playa Dorada near Puerto Plata (see p.200). The restaurant never opened and the bridge leads merely to its ruins.

Arrival, orientation and information

The C-5 that stretches along the country's north coast leads into Samaná's Malecón. Together, the C-5 – known locally as Avenida Rosario Sánchez – and the Malecón are the only major thoroughfares in the city. Incoming **buses** stop in the centre of the Malecón, easy walking distance from most hotels, while guaguas stop and set off from the large city market (El Mercado), right on the C-5, close to a few budget accommodations but a half-kilometre north of the Malecón. Numerous motoconchos and motorcycle rickshaws also gather at the market for those heading into town with luggage. If **sailing**, the port of Samaná makes a good safe place to dock but you'll have to get a permit from the Port Commandant immediately upon arrival, and another before disembarking.

Once you arrive on the Malecón, you'll be immediately beset by a number of the local *buscones* (literally "finders"), freelance assistants who speak fluent English and will help you find whatever you need – hotel, restaurant, and so on. If you're looking for good, cheap accommodation upon arrival, they can make life a bit easier even if they do have a vested interest in the places that they point you to otherwise; they'll usually take a polite no for an answer.

The official **tourist office** (☎538-2332) is located in the government offices on Calle Santa Bárbara but you'll probably get more information from the cleverly named Samaná Tourist Service (☎538-2740) on the Malecón, which is actually a travel agency offering package tours of the peninsula.

Accommodation

Samaná has a wide mix of **accommodations**, from luxury resorts to dirt-cheap options, but many of the latter are not quite as comfortable as you'll find in nearby Las Terrenas (see p.170). If on a tight budget you'd therefore do well to check out one of the very homey local **pensiónes**. The three all-inclusives

– the best of which is *Gran Bahía* – offer fairly good deals, though the constant undercutting of prices has resulted in some deterioration in the quality of food and service. If it's comfort within the town limits you're after, head for the seaside *Tropical Lodge*.

Bahia View Av Circunvalación ☎538-2186. Exceptionally clean budget hotel with a friendly proprietor and better than average rooms, private showers and, as the name suggests, a good view over the bay. ❷

Casa de Huespedes Mildania Calle Fco. Del Rosario Sánchez 41 ☎538-2151. Clean and tidy rooms with private showers in an immaculate Dominican house make this the best of the pensiónes in town, though the street can be noisy. ❷

Cayacoa Resort Calle Cayacoa ☎538-3111, ℱ538-2985. All-inclusive beach resort perched on the harbour's western promontory, with great views of the city and the Bahía de Samaná. There's a swimming pool and an impressive dining

Whale watching

Humpback whales have used the Dominican Republic's Samaná Bay and Silver Bank coral reef sanctuary as a nursery and breeding ground for untold millennia. Taino drawings on the limestone caves of Los Haitises depict breaching whales in the Bahía de Samaná, and Columbus made note of their presence here in 1493. The whales return each December after spending nine months fanning out across the North Atlantic in search of enormous quantities of food; by late January, more than twelve thousand of them, the entire northern Atlantic population, move around the waters of the country's northeast coast. They're at their liveliest in Samaná's tepid depths, as males track females, compete for attention and engage in courting displays, while mothers teach their calves basic survival skills. Don't allow yourself to come here during the winter without taking an expedition to see them; the **season** generally runs from mid-January to mid-March.

Adult humpbacks grow to nearly fifteen metres long and forty metric tons, and are black with distinctive white patches. Their name comes from the singular arching of their backs when they dive. Like all whales, they breathe through blowholes that are sealed airtight while under water. If your boat gets close enough to them while they're breathing, you'll definitely notice the notoriously rancid vapour exhaled from their lungs. Their teeth have long been replaced by **baleen**, hundreds of fibrous sheets that hang from the upper mouth and act as a sieve that traps tiny crustaceans. On their bellies are **ventral folds** – retractable pleats that extend the length of their bodies – used to hold massive amounts of food and for courting displays. The enormous **tail** possesses a unique pattern of white blotches that marine biologists use to identify individual whales in a similar way to human fingerprints.

Among the behaviours that you may see while whale watching are: **breaching** – hurtling the entire body above the surface before landing back down in a spectacular crash; **chin breaching** – bringing the head above water and slapping the chin against the surface; **lobtailing** – raising the tail and smacking it against the water; **flippering** – rolling the body and slapping the flipper against the water; **diving** – arching the back and then sticking the tail straight up in the air in preparation for a deep descent; and the **trumpet blow** – a tremendous, low blast that can be heard from several kilometres away.

Humpbacks also engage in the **whale songs** for which the species is well known – an eerie combination of moans and chirps formed into short phrases that are shuffled and put together in a basic form of communication. Their songs were long a legend among mariners, but until recently were thought to be mythical. Only males sing, and they do so far more frequently here than in the North Atlantic – which leads to speculation that songs are used to find a mate. Humpback groups in each region of the North Atlantic develop their own distinctive music, but a single song prevails while around the Dominican Republic. This is constantly evolving, probably due to room, but the food served up isn't quite as inviting as the digs and the grounds are growing a bit worn. Reasonably priced though. ❹

Cotubanama Av Rosario Sánchez and Santa Bárbara ☎538-2557. Traditional backpacker hangout, offering very basic, though somewhat overpriced, rooms with cold water and minimum atmosphere. ❸

Hotel Doria Duarte 1 ☎538-2041. Wildly popular small hotel just off the Malecón. Clean, modest and well placed, it's the most convivial spot for budget travellers. It's often full, though, so it's best to call ahead. ❷

Gran Bahía Samaná–Las Galeras road ☎538-3111, ℻538-2764, ℗www.occidental-hoteles .com. One of the great gems among Caribbean resorts, with a majestic oceanfront setting around 6km east of town, immaculate grounds, well-maintained rooms, a swimming pool, watersports equipment and horse stables. Reasonably priced, too, considering the quality, and you can sometimes get a room even cheaper through a package deal. ❺

King Av Rosario Sánchez at La Loba traffic circle ☎538-2353. Not the best-maintained of the budget choices, but with nice views from the rooms

the breeding success of the males who deviate from the original. Therefore, each winter is started with last year's song but this is slowly revised over the course of the ensuing three months.

All of this is done to advance the serious business of **mating and birthing** that takes place in Samaná. The female gestation period is a full year, so calves that are conceived in the bay one year are given birth here the next; there's a good chance you'll see at least one of the babies, which can weigh over a ton and are light grey. Mothers give birth at two-year intervals, and shed up to two-thirds of their body weight while nursing; if twins are born – as they sometimes are – the mother is forced to choose between them, as her body cannot feed them both. The thick milk enables infants to grow at the astonishing rate of over 40kg per day.

Whale watching as a local tourist industry was begun in the 1970s by Kim Beddall, then an itinerant scuba instructor with no formal training as a marine biologist. She's spent the subsequent twenty-plus years lobbying for government protection of the whales and creating an economic incentive that will protect them should the international whaling ban ever cease. As a result, there are more than forty boats in Samaná city offering whale-watching tours every winter, and regulations, again instigated by Kim Beddall, are strictly enforced to ensure that the vessels don't harass the animals.

Beddall still runs excellent **whale tours** through her Whale Samaná/Victoria Marine operation, Malecón (☎ & ℻538-2494; US$38), though she's no longer the only operator who respects the rules governing the creature's wellbeing. There are a number of vessels that depart from the Samaná port, as well as three that leave from Simi Baez Port at Playa Las Flechas just east of town. *Cayacoa Resort, Cayo Levantado Hotel, Gran Bahía* and Samaná Tourist Service are all good places to sign on with a whale boat. Each vessel generally does two tours a day, at 9am and 1.30pm, costing US$30–40. Before you sign on, get a sense of what the tour's going to be like – trips vary in size and degree of scientific orientation. Most whale-watch on the Bahía de Samaná, though three operators offer **week-long expeditions** to the country's Silver Banks Sanctuary just north of the peninsula. Aquatic Adventures (☎305/027-0211, ℻027-0212, ℗www.aquaticadventures.com; US$2295) are based in Florida but sail out of Puerto Plata, as do Bottom Time Adventures (☎1-800/234-2464, ℻950/924-5578, ℗www.bottomtimeadventures.com; US$2000) who are also based in Florida. Both offer the opportunity for "soft encounters" with the whales, setting aside time for swimming and snorkelling in the waters around them. The Aggressor (☎1-800/348-2628, ℗www.turksandcaicosaggressor.com; US$2000) sails to Silver Banks from Grand Island in the nearby Turks and Caicos Islands, but otherwise offers a similar excursion.

facing the ocean. Rooms with shared bath cost even less. ❷

Plaza Taina Av Rosario Sánchez at La Loba traffic circle (no phone). Last-ditch bargain-basement option for those who don't mind roughing it. Some rooms have private cold-water baths. ❶

Tropical Lodge Malecón, just east of downtown ☏538-2480, ⓕ538-2068, ⓦwww.tropical-lodge .com. Easily one of the best hotels on the peninsula, with modern rooms, hot showers, bay views and attentive service. Set right on the water near the centre of town, just far enough away from the noise. ❹

The Town

Samaná may not be the military powerhouse or engine of wealth that Balaguer, Grant and Napoleon imagined, but it's undoubtedly far more charming than it would have been, with pretty, spacious neighbourhoods, winding streets that amble up the hills and a warm sense of community. The centre of activity is the city's **Malecón**, a broad, concrete boardwalk dotted with outdoor cafés, storefront shops and patches of park. At night, during the busier seasons, the Malecón's restaurants and bars buzz with activity and music, a fairly mixed scene of Dominicans, expats and foreign visitors that manages to be lively but not at all overwhelming.

The **Samaná port** at the Malecón's centre is a good place to begin exploring. Not only is it equipped with elevated balconies from which to view the scenic harbour, but it is also the departure point for ferries to Cayo Levantado or Sabana de la Mar across the water and whale-watching boats that cruise the bay in winter. At the harbour's western promontory begins the so-called **Bridge to Nowhere**, linking the town to Cayo Linares and Cayo Vigia.

African-Americans in Samaná

A large portion of Samaná's residents are descendants of **African-American freemen** who emigrated here during Haitian rule in 1824–25. At the time a movement in the United States worked to repatriate thousands of freed slaves – seeking to escape the pervasive racism in the States – to Liberia, but stories of malaria epidemics in West Africa made Haiti, the world's only black republic, a more attractive option for many. Six thousand emigrants were temporarily housed in Santo Domingo's Iglesia Las Mercedes before being shipped to various points across the country in need of economic development. About half ended up in Samaná, which the Haitians wanted to develop into a naval base. The settlers have since, for the most part, managed to maintain their culture despite sustained persecution by Trujillo, whose troops beat anyone caught speaking English on the streets and torched the town in 1946, and despite a general lack of interest these days in the younger generation carrying on the traditions.

Samaná's older African-American population – much of it clustered within the sprawling **barrio Noroueste** that borders the C-5 – preserves an antiquated form of English, an oral history of the community's struggles and an array of folk tales and legends. One ongoing custom is the series of yearly **harvest festivals**, community feasts with African-American church music held every Friday from late August to the end of October, a tradition that harks back to the Yam Celebrations and Rice Festivals of West Africa. The English-speaking community has several small churches in the surrounding countryside, and the festival is held in a different one every week; check the bulletin board in the back of La Churcha for dates and locations if you're interested in attending. The final festival of the harvest cycle is held in La Churcha at the end of October.

Accessible from an unlocked gate in the car park behind the *Cayacoa Resort*, the rickety bridge – and the graffiti-ridden ruins it leads to – serve as a reminder of Samaná's unfulfilled promise. Still, it's an intriguing spot to wander, taking in spectacular views of the harbour and town, and – at the end – a particularly harrowing stretch up a muddy slope to the ruins of the restaurant that was to open on Cayo Vigia. Just west of the *Cayacoa Resort* is the small city beach, **Playa Escondido**, serviceable enough but underused because of its far more spectacular competitors outside town.

A few blocks back from the waterfront, the old First African Wesleyan Methodist Church of Samaná popularly known as **La Churcha**, Santa Bárbara and Duarte (daily 9am–6pm), tangibly maintains what African-American culture is left in Samaná (see box p.162). The prefabricated, tin-roofed structure was originally shipped over by the English Methodist Church in 1823, in support of a recently emigrated African-American community that still remains here. These days it's known as the Dominican Evangelical Church and often works harmoniously with the African Methodist Episcopalian Church, another interesting building a few blocks further back. North of this church, a series of winding streets move up the hills through residential neighbourhoods filled with clapboard shacks, muleback *caballeros*, schoolkids playing stickball and the occasional grazing cow.

Eating and drinking

Most of Samaná's best **restaurants** are concentrated on the four blocks of the Malecón around the port, with waterside expat joints serving great French and Italian, several good spots for Dominican food, and even a decent Chinese restaurant. A few more local establishments operate just north of the Malecón on Avenida Rosario Sánchez. The expats have also opened a numbers of **bars** along the waterfront, while locals have set up a festive clutch of beach shacks serving beer, rum and fried chicken on the Malecón just west of the port, as well as the *Williams* complex at the far western end of the harbour, with several cheap eateries, a couple of shacks selling liquor and a small dance floor.

Café de Paris Malecón 6. French-run expat hangout serving up delicious pizzas and crepes from around RD$80, amid colourful, Pop Art decor.

Camilo Malecón. Classy, reasonably priced Dominican restaurant on the waterfront. Specialities include chicken and rice, chicken *asopao*, creole-style sea bass and *mondongo*.

Chino Calle Santa Bárbara. Perched on a high hill overlooking the bay, *Chino* serves good but greasy Chinese and terrific Dominican food, including tasty *pescado con coco*.

Le France Malecón. Reasonably priced gourmet Dominican dishes with some French fare as well, in a quiet indoor dining room. The Gambas are wonderful and the chocolate cake's to die for.

L'Hacienda Malecón. Affordable French seafood – including a terrific shellfish bouillabaisse – and excellent steaks, in an outdoor café setting below

Naomi disco (see overleaf). The chocolate mousse is a house speciality. Closed Wed.

El Manantiel Av Rosario Sánchez. Good, cheap Dominican staples like rice, beans and chicken, in an unassuming little kitchen with just a half-dozen tables.

La Mata Rosada Malecón. Excellent high-end Italian cuisine – seafood is best here – that can be enjoyed in either an indoor dining room or outdoor patio.

Plaza Mimi Malecón. Probably the tops of the modest beachfront shacks on the Malecón, just west of the port. Chicken, pork and fish dishes are most popular, generally costing less than RD$60 a throw.

Williams Av Rosario Sánchez, 100m north of the Malecón. Modest-looking outdoor creole restaurant with definite shades of soul food, including great collard greens.

Nightlife

Samaná has a great **nightlife** scene, with three crowded discos open until dawn and dozens of outdoor restaurants along the Malecón that become especially lively late at night. The scene extends down the C-5 for 500m with a bank of outdoor establishments surrounding *Williams* restaurant and the packed *La Loba* disco further down. These places net enough travellers that they're welcoming spots for visitors to hang out, with the exception of highly popular, mainly male *Almendro*.

Almendro Av Rosario Sánchez. A packed local hangout blaring merengue and pervaded by a heavy dose of machismo.

La Loba Av Rosario Sánchez. A fun, massive rough-and-tumble Dominican dance floor with a smattering of foreigners and some prostitution. During the week the smaller *La Lobita* dance floor next door is used. A food stand outside sells RD$20 pulled-pork sandwiches. RD$20 cover.

Naomi Malecón. Slick, dark and bustling meat market with great light shows and sound system, playing a mix of merengue and European techno. RD$40 cover.

Rancho Allegre Malecón. Traditional outdoor dance floor, with the familiar sounds of merengue and *bachata*, in the centre of the Malecón.

Listings

Banks and currency exchange Banco Popular, Malecón (Mon–Fri 9am–noon & 2–5pm, Sat 9am–noon), has a 24-hour ATM and even a drive-thru section. Baninter, near the market, also has an ATM. There are also well-marked exchanges on the Malecón (Mon–Sat 9am–5.30pm).

Car and motorcycle rental Samaná Moto Rent, Malecón (9.30am–noon & 2–5pm, closed Sun; ☎538-2380) offers cycles; J.A. Rent-A-Car, Malecón 5 (daily 9am–5pm; ☎538-2940) rents both cars and 4WDs.

Internet Computo Centro, Santa Bárbara and Lebantiel (Mon–Sat 9am–5.30pm).

Laundry There are no laundromats in Samaná. One of the house cleaners at your hotel will generally wash laundry for RD$50 per load in the mid-range hotels, RD$120 per load in the all-inclusive resorts.

Medical Dr Ernaldo Caccavelli, MD, Malecón beside Victoria Marine (Mon–Fri 2–6pm; ☎538-2589). For dentistry try Dr Leonardo Ferrand

(Mon–Fri 2.30–7pm; ☎538-2391). There is also a public 24-hour emergency medical facility, Hospital Leopoldo Pou, at Calle Maria Trinidad Sánchez.

Pharmacy Giselle Pharmacia, Santa Bárbara and Lebantiel (Mon–Sat 8am–noon & 2–6pm).

Post office Calle Santa Bárbara behind Victoria Marine (Mon–Fri 8.30am–noon & 2–5pm, Sat 8.30am–noon).

Telephone Codetel, Santa Bárbara and Lebantiel (daily 8am–10pm).

Travel agents Samaná Tourist Service, Malecón (daily 8.30am–4pm; ☎538-2740), books organized tours across the island, including peninsula trips that go whale watching or to El Limón, Las Galeras or Los Haitises. They can also help you with airline tickets and travel changes. Victoria Marine, Malecón (☎ & ☎538-2494), offers tours of Parque Nacional Los Haitises (see p.149) in the whale off-season.

Wiring money Western Union, Malecón (Mon–Sat 8am–noon & 2–5pm).

Around Samaná

Samaná's best attribute may well be its convenience as an inexpensive base from which to explore some of the peninsula's more compelling sights. Three ferries a day head to the nearby desert island **Cayo Levantado**, while along the eastern tip of the peninsula, easily reachable by guagua, a series of attractive beaches lead towards untainted **Las Galeras**, a pretty spot tailor-made for those looking to avoid the crowds, and the even better beach at **Playa Rincón**. West of Samaná, the C-5 guides you past an uninspiring stretch to **Sánchez**, where you can sign on for a boat tour of Parque Nacional Los Haitises (see p.149).

Cayo Levantado

CAYO LEVANTADO is the original Bacardi Island photographed in the 1970s rum campaign, though the famous swaying palm from the ad has since been uprooted in a tropical storm; fortunately, hundreds of others still line the white sands. The resort hotel that once dominated the island has long been closed but ferries, which cost around US$20 each way and leave from the main port in Samaná, still drop off hundreds of day-visitors, so be prepared for crowds at the main beach. It's possible to find a bit more solitude by following the path extending inland across the island to the smaller beaches on the opposite side. But with constant hassling from vendors and extortionate food and drink prices across the island, it's definitely a case of paradise ruined and, unless you're visiting as part of a whale-watching tour, there are many better places on the peninsula to spend a day on the beach. At night Cayo Levantado sees much less traffic, and it's possible to **camp** on the more remote side – though you'll need permission from the port officials first, which will cost you RD$100. You can ask them directly at the Samaná port, but your best bet is to go through Victoria Marine (☎ & ⓕ 538-2494), who are used to setting up Cayo Levantado camping.

East to Las Galeras

Just east of Samaná along the Carretera Las Galeras, a signposted turnoff leads 11km north up a tortuously bad road to **Playa El Valle**, an entirely isolated beach cut off by steep mountains. A 4WD is recommended, as you'll have to ford a small river, but you're pretty much guaranteed to share the beach with only the inhabitants of the small fishing village on its western bank. A couple of shacks in the village serve good fish with rice and plantains for RD$80.

Back along the Carretera Las Galeras, it's 5km east to **Playa Las Flechas**, a fairly quiet beach that was the site of the first battle between Native Americans and Europeans, though there's nothing here to mark this momentous event. At the western end of the beach is the tiny **Simi Baez** Port, embarkation point for a few whale-watching boats and ferries to Cayo Levantado for RD$50 – less than what you'll pay in town. The modest *Anacaona* restaurant, optimistically billed as a resort, is the one spot for **lunch**, serving burgers, hot dogs and a few Dominican dishes.

East of Las Flechas, a beautiful stretch of tree-lined road – the boughs arching over the avenue – leads to the Victorian splendour of the renowned *Gran Bahía* resort (see p.161), with stables and an immaculate tropical garden along the road. Three kilometres further, pueblo **Los Cacaos** is notable for a seventy-metre waterfall in the mountains just beyond it – look for the small, unmarked dirt path that leads to it, which commences from the village's only *colmado* (grocery shack).

Ten kilometres east of Los Cacaos, a turnoff, marked only by a small cockfighting arena, leads down to clifftops, with great views over the bay and an opportunity to spot whales without taking a boat trip. Between the end of January and early March, you are virtually guaranteed a sighting. The road veers east from here passing between the bay and a series of prominent limestone caves, collectively known as **Cuevas de Agua**, which once served as homes for the local Ciguayo population. The tiny farms adjacent contain some of the most extensive archeological sites on the island. Current residents use the caves as kitchens, roasting meat there to keep the smoke out of their homes, and a family has even put a fence around one with several Taino faces carved into it, charging RD$50 for entrance. They'll also take you to see an even better cave at low tide, set just over the ocean and with dozens of petroglyphs. Another local has a hand-painted sign up in front of his house advertising his souvenirs (RD$50–200), perfect clay re-creations of the hundreds of small Taino *cemi* sculptures that have been unearthed at the site. The road continues for another half-kilometre, ending at a high limestone cliff with more ocean views. Over millions of years, a blowhole, known locally as **Boca del Diablo**, has been gouged out of the cliff; the intense surf thunders up 50m and sprays you where you're standing. From here a walking path leads 2km further to the beautiful remote beach of **Playa Fronton**.

Las Galeras

Set in a horseshoe-shaped cove at the eastern end of the peninsula, the sleepy outpost of **LAS GALERAS** has seen considerable changes over the last few years, including *Casa Marina Bay*, a large all-inclusive resort just east of town, and numerous other hotels near the main beach entrance. Despite this construction, the small village has managed to maintain its peaceful and timeless ambience. In short, while it may no longer be the undiscovered gem it was only a few years ago, the village's main attraction, a sweeping curve of pure

LAS GALERAS

Playa Las Galeras

Caribe Fun
(Car & Bike Rental)

Centro
Commercial

Xamana
Bike Rental

Codetel

Western
Union

CALLE LAS GALERAS

N

0   200 m

ACCOMMODATION	
Casa Lotus	1
Casa Marina Bay	11
Casa Por Que Non	4
Club Bonito	5
El Marinique	3
Juan y Lolo Rent House	12
La Plantacion	7
Moorea Beach Hotel	9
Paradiso	10
Plaza Lucitania	8
Todo Blanco	6
Villa Serena	2

BARS, RESTAURANTS AND CLUBS	
Casa Por Que Non	B
Chez Denise	F
Indiana	I
El Marinique	A
El Pizzeria	C
Gri Gri	D
Liadventure	H
Patiserrie	E
Pescador	J
Zozo	G

▼ *Samaná*

white sand, upon which an almost unbelievably turquoise sea laps gently, remains as beautiful as ever.

The road into town, the Carretera Las Galeras, leads right to the beach entrance, where there's a cluster of beach shacks and restaurants as well as a volleyball court. Most of the restaurants and bars line the road near the beach, with the area around the Centro Comercial being the closest that Las Galeras has to a social focal point. If you're looking to get in the water and do a bit more than swim, Dive Samaná (☎538-0210; RD$525/dive), who operate out of a beach shack by the *Casa Marina Bay Resort* but are totally independent, organize **diving** trips around the tip of the peninsula to reefs, wrecks and even caves, including an underwater cave with an air pocket known as La Catedral,. They also offer **boat trips** to Playa Rincón (see p.169) for US$10. By the beach, Rancho Thikis (☎223-0035) offers **horseriding** trips along the shore for US$10/hr as well as whole and half day-trips. It's also possible to walk to Playa Fronton and the paradise-like Playa Madama from Las Galeras, but it's advisable to organize a guide the first time as route finding can be a little daunting – ask in the hotels for details.

Accommodation

Most of the **accommodation** options are scattered along the beach end of the main road and also on either side of the dirt roads that run parallel to the beach to the east and west. There's something for every budget and preference, from the unadulterated and pricey luxury of *Villa Serena* to a number of simple garden cabanas.

Casa Lotus Beach Rd West ☎538-2545. Superb, untamed but beautiful terraced gardens and the kind of tranquil karma usually reserved for Buddhist monasteries make this the place for those wanting absolute serenity. Inside, the *Lotus* offers choice rooms with hot-water baths in a beautiful beach home adorned with New Age paraphernalia. Vegetarian meals are a speciality and available upon request. ❺

Casa Marina Bay Beach Rd East ☎538-0020, ⓕ538-0040, ⓦwww.amhsamarina.com. A large, but tasteful, all-inclusive one mile east of the main road. The 200 rooms are well equipped and smartly decorated, scattered about nice gardens and a large pool area in a selection of mainly low-level buildings. The standard buffet fare isn't that inspiring but the white-sand beach is stunning. ❻

Casa Por Que Non Calle Las Galeras ☎538-0011 or 514/661-9013 (Montreal). Two light and airy rooms attached to a private house with a lovely garden. Excellent breakfasts every day and home-cooked dinners by arrangement. Open during winter only. ❸

Club Bonito Beach Rd East ☎538-0203, ⓕ538-0061, ⓦwww.club-bonito.com. A beautifully designed and decorated establishment littered with odd maritime artefacts and boasting large rooms and a colourful garden. It occupies perhaps the prime beachfront, and can also boast a good restaurant, bar and swimming pool. ❻

Juan y Lolo Rent House Beach Rd West ☎&ⓕ538-0208, ⓔjuanylolo@hotmail.com. A selection of rustic but rather attractive thatched, creole-style self-contained houses that sleep two, four or even six people. Well equipped, with spacious lounges, full-size bathrooms and fully functional kitchens, and wonderfully peaceful. ❹

El Marinique Beach Rd West ☎538-0262, ⓦwww.elmaranique.com. One of the first hotels in Las Galeras, *El Marinique* features four very basic cabins set in a garden a few minutes from the sea. There are, though, better options for the money. ❹

Moorea Beach Hotel One block inland from the beach ☎538-0007, ⓕ538-0202, ⓦwww.hotelmooreabeach.com. An old and reasonably priced hotel that remains incredibly popular. It doesn't have many frills but it's well maintained with clean rooms, a bar downstairs, a pool, a few hammocks and an entertaining array of cats and dogs. ❹

Paradiso Bungalows Calle Las Galeras ☎538-0210. The best of the several private budget cabanas in the village, offering private cold-water facilities and a cosy, tropical communal garden close to the beach. Not luxurious but well priced for long-term stays. ❷

La Plantacion Guest House Beach Rd East ☎538-0079, ⓦwww.laplantacion.com02.com. Four sizeable and clean rooms attached to a modern house belonging to a friendly French couple. Great gardens and very close to the beach. ❹

Plaza Lucitania Centro Comercial ☎538-0093, ℱ538-0066, ✉plazalusitania@hotmail.com. Clean, a/c rooms above shops and restaurants in the very heart of the village. Not cheap but eminently pleasant. ➍

Todo Blanco Beach Rd East ☎538-0201, ℱ538-0064, ✉todoblanco@hotmail.com. Tasteful to the extreme and a genuine haven of tranquillity with huge airy rooms set in a pretty but enjoyably wild garden right on the beach. Run by an incredibly friendly Italian couple, it also boasts a superb and authentic Italian restaurant that is open to non-guests. ➏

Villa Serena Beach Rd West ☎538-0000, ℱ538-0009, ⊛www.villaserena.com. Housed in a beautiful faux-Victorian mansion with a large, manicured tropical garden, this place just screams "honeymoon". Set right on the beach and facing a small desert island, it's difficult to imagine a more idyllic location. The restaurant is one of the best in town (open to non-guests but call first) so, if you have the money, this is the place to spend it. ➐

Eating and drinking

Options for **dining** in Las Galeras have increased as much as places to stay. Most of the hotels will provide food but if you want a change of scenery or menu, there's a mixed bag of eateries dotted along the main road. As far as **nightlife** goes, Las Galeras remains pretty quiet, but if you do fancy living it up a bit then the best bet is *Indiana*, Calle Las Galeras, which pumps out merengue, *bachata* and even the odd dance tune at an incredibly high volume.

Casa Por Que Non Calle Las Galeras. The best breakfasts in town but only available Dec–May. RD$65 for a choice of cooked dishes including French toast and scrambled eggs, served alfresco in a pretty garden.

Chez Denise Calle Las Galeras. Traditional French creperie and seafood restaurant in a small diner with couple of street-side tables. Main courses start from around RD$120, with the grilled grouper being particularly good when available.

Dominican Kitchen Beach entrance. Not so much a restaurant as a collection of thatched shacks serving excellent locally caught seafood dishes. Prices can vary for tourists so check before eating but expect to pay around RD$100 per head for something like red snapper with rice and plantains.

Gri Gri Calle las Galeras. Right in the heart of the action, *Gri Gri* dishes out some great fish and meat dishes with rice or pasta from around RD$90. The slow, complacent service can be tiresome.

L'adventure Calle las Galeras. French-run pizzeria with excellent food, though the experience can be dampened by an annoying television blaring in the background. The menu features all the usual toppings but the spicy pepperoni is excellent at RD$80.

El Marinique Beach Rd West. International food with a touch of Dominican flavour, set back from the beach. Steaks are the highlight of a menu that changes daily. Check the blackboard in front of the restaurant for the specials.

Patiserrie Calle Las Galeras. A great breakfast spot with a good selection of pastries and croissants, real orange juice and strong coffee, served in a cramped but pretty courtyard, just off the main street.

Pescador Calle Las Galeras. The best fish in town served out on a friendly outdoor patio, 500m from the beach. The friendly Spanish proprietor is well known for his excellent hospitality and will probably join you for a customary tipple of local firewater.

El Pizzeria Calle Las Galeras. An outdoor patio pizzeria attached to the Centro Comercial. Excellent pies – try one with shrimp – and a good selection of pizzas from around RD$60 upwards. It's a lively spot with a fun atmosphere and very friendly proprietors.

Death by coconut

If you're in the vicinity of **coconut trees**, be careful where you park your car. All Dominican car rental agreements have a provision explicitly stating that insurance will not cover damage – usually shattered windshields or dented hoods – inflicted by a falling coconut. More unfortunate, an average of six people per year in the Dominican Republic die from being hit by one of the plummeting fruits. Tropical storms are the most frequent culprits; the high winds sometimes launch dozens of them through the air like cannon shot.

The RD$160 *chillo* (red snapper) is wonderful. **Todo Blanco** Beach Rd East ☎538-0201. Superb hotel (see p.168) restaurant specializing in Italian food cooked from imported ingredients and served in a wonderfully elegant setting. Call ahead for reservations. The menu changes regularly but

expect to pay around RD$200 for two courses. **Zozo** Calle Las Galeras. Small outdoor spot near the beach, less expensive than the other French and Italian restaurants but quite good, with a variety of pastas, crepes, seafood and, on occasion, *lambí criolla*, which is not to be missed.

Listings

Banks and currency exchange There's a Baninter (Mon–Fri 9am–noon & 2–5pm, Sat 9am–noon) in the Centro Comercial which also has a 24-hour ATM. Telecom Samaná, also in the Centro Comercial (see below), will also exchange travellers' cheques and cash.
Car and motorcycle rental Caribe Fun Rentals, Calle Las Galeras (☎538-0109, ℮caribefun_wy@hotmail.com) for jeeps and motorcycles. Xamana, Calle Las Galeras (☎538-0208) has decent-size motorcycles for rent and also arranges excursions on four-wheelers to near-

by beaches and mountains.
Internet Telecom Samaná, Centro Comercial (see hours below) has good connections at RD$15 per 15min.
Laundry With no laundry service available, your best bet is to use the hotels.
Telephone Telecom Samaná, Centro Comercial (☎538-0232; Mon–Sat 9am–7pm, Sun 9am–12.30pm); Codetel, Calle Las Galeras (daily 8am–10pm).
Wiring money Western Union, Calle Las Galeras (Mon–Sat 8am–noon & 2–5pm).

Playa Rincón

Hidden from the rest of the peninsula by the upper prong at its easternmost end, **PLAYA RINCÓN** boasts the top Samaná beach bar none; a pity then that it's so inaccessible, with only one rocky road leading to it from Las Galeras (or ferry ride, departing at 9am from Dive Samaná, Calle Las Galeras; US$10). Still, this has kept development mostly at bay, though rumour has it that one hotel chain has purchased most of the land behind it and is lobbying the government for permission to construct the next choice Caribbean resort.

Tucked away at the base of the Bahía de Rincón – which is buttressed on both sides by enormous capes – the beach has long been a favourite of wealthy Dominican city-dwellers who camp out here with their families for the night. Of all the warm, clear waters on the island, Rincón has the very finest – moderately deep with manageable waves and a bright turquoise transparency that can't be matched – combined with a four-kilometre stretch of whiter-than-white sand and a sprawling coconut forest behind it.

Both ferries and cars approach the beach near its western end, which is bordered by high cliffs. From here it's another 1km west to **Río Frío**, a freezing-cold river popular for washing off the salt at the end of the day. To the east, the beach stretches uninterrupted for another 3km – you're likely to find nary another soul as you walk its length. There are a few shacks set up by the Río Frío and also one to the east of the entrance. These all sell great-value fresh fish lunches which are usually accompanied by rice and plantain. All are good, though one to the east, run by Mimi, is the most popular. Expect to pay around RD$100 per head.

West of Samaná: Sánchez

The uninspiring stretch of C-5 between Samaná and Sánchez is unavoidable for all except those who fly into El Portillo, near Las Terrenas. Nine kilometres west of Samaná, you'll see a sign marking the turnoff to the eminently missable **Río Coco waterfall**, where the base of the falls has been cemented into a rather unappealing swimming pool (RD$40 entrance fee).

Further down the road, the growing transportation hub of **SÁNCHEZ** was once a wealthy, cosmopolitan rival to Puerto Plata, when it served as the eastern end point of the now-defunct railroad that transported the Cibao Valley's agricultural riches to the coast. In the 1920s a flood mired the port in mud and silt, and twenty years later Trujillo tore up the local train track in order to build a railroad line for his sugar estates in the southwest. Today the local economy revolves around the unglamorous trade of shrimp harvesting. Regardless, the town is unavoidable if you're heading to the Samaná Peninsula by land; Sánchez is the stopping point for all guaguas, and it is here that the pickup trucks to Las Terrenas set off.

In Sánchez proper, what little there is to see centres around the old **port**, at the waterfront on the western side of town. The views are pretty and you'll find a couple of the remaining Victorian gingerbreads facing the water just east of the port, including the nineteenth-century **City Hall**, a peeling white gingerbread with a small central dome, though it's not open and looks ready to collapse. A block north of the port is the **parque central**, bordered to the west by the old **railway station**, a glorious three-storey structure gone to seed, its impressive glass ceiling caked over with dirt. Squatters sell produce from its main entranceway and doorway stalls, even occasionally holding a large produce market inside, an incongruous sight amid the marble ruins.

You may wish to use Sánchez as a base for day-trips to **Parque Nacional Los Haitises** (see p.149), the mammoth mangrove swamp on the opposite side of the bay. Trips depart daily at 10am from the popular restaurant of *Amilcar* (see below) just south of the town's eastern entrance (☎552-7664; RD$500). Reservations are recommended; the trip includes a buffet lunch upon your return.

Practicalities

In the odd event you've got a layover here, Sánchez has several inexpensive, no-frills **hotels**; the cleanest among them is probably *El Patrio*, Calle San Tomé (❶), which has private cold-water baths. Surprisingly, the city is home to one of the best **restaurants** in the area, *Amilcar*, Duarte and Colón, which features spectacular shrimp dishes in pleasant dining rooms for around RD$200.

Las Terrenas and around

Set midway along the peninsula's remote northern coast, former fishing village **LAS TERRENAS** has grown over the past twenty years from backwater to an expat-dominated resort town renowned for its buoyant nightlife. No village existed here at all until the 1940s, when Trujillo began, in a misguided effort to alleviate urban poverty, to forcibly move the lower classes from Santo Domingo to the countryside, in order that they fish and farm the land; thirty such families wound up in present-day Las Terrenas. Their quiet settlement was interrupted in the 1970s by an influx of French expats searching for a secluded patch of paradise; these "intruders" were soon followed by waves of Swiss, Canadians, Germans and English. Though development has led to a new paved road from Sánchez which – along with the beach – is lined with restaurants, bars and shops, the inland Dominican barrio remains much the same as it was, small clusters of clapboard shacks punctuating fenced-off pasture land. The increase in expatriation and tourism has fuelled some resentment between the Dominican and foreign communities, centred on the growing prostitution trade in the discos and on the well-founded perception that the expats are making all of the money off the booming tourist business.

Terrenas sees its busiest time in the summer when, during July and August in particular, it's swamped by mainly Europeans. The larger hotels and resorts catch most of the traffic but there are enough independent travellers and backpackers to keep the smaller bars and restaurants busy and everybody tends to come together later in the evening to crowd out the livelier bars and discos to the early hours.

Las Terrenas also makes for a pleasant base camp from which to explore the northern part of the Samaná Peninsula, including the less developed beaches on either side, such as **Playa Bonita** and **El Portillo**, that hold even more appeal than the one in town. Aside from exploring these, a day-trip to the **El Limón waterfall** is highly recommended both for the horseback ride out and the view of the fall itself.

Arrival, information and getting around

The only way to get to Las Terrenas **by road** if you don't have your own car is an RD$40 pickup truck leaving every half-hour from the Texaco station at Sánchez. Though in great condition, the road passes through the centre of the Cordillera Samaná, and thus is incredibly curvy and steep, so it's fairly slow going – allow a half-hour for the trip. At least it's scenic, with stunning views of the bay and, closer to Las Terrenas, Playa Bonita and the three small islands known as Las Ballenas. Alternately, you can **fly** into El Portillo Airport, 6km east of town, on Air Santo Domingo (☎240-6094), which has daily flights from Puerto Plata, Punta Cana, La Romana and Santo Domingo. You'll usually find a motoconcho waiting at the airport – an isolated airstrip in the wilderness – or at the *El Portillo Beach Club* beside it; if not, wait by the side of the road for a guagua heading to Las Terrenas.

There is an official government **tourist office** (Mon–Fri 9am–noon & 2–5pm) at the end of the Carretera Las Terrenas, also the town's one major intersection, but while its employees are quite friendly, they offer little in the way of practical information. The privately run Sunshine Service Tourist Information, off Calle Playa Cacao (☎240-6184, ℗240-5157), is a better bet, offering a range of excursions as well as exchange and general advice.

You probably won't have too much trouble just **walking** where you want to go – the layout of the town is exceedingly straightforward, built around Carretera Las Terrenas – but if you need a lift anywhere, motoconcho rides within town are RD$10 during the day, double that at night. **Private taxis** and **guaguas** to El Portillo, El Limón and Sánchez are also available at the crossroad. No trip should cost you more than RD$40. There are no guaguas to Punta Bonita, so you'll have to catch an RD$20 motoconcho. You can also hook on with several **tour operators** in town if you're looking to hit Los Haitises or see the whales, but be aware that prices will be higher than you'll pay elsewhere – though transport back and forth is included.

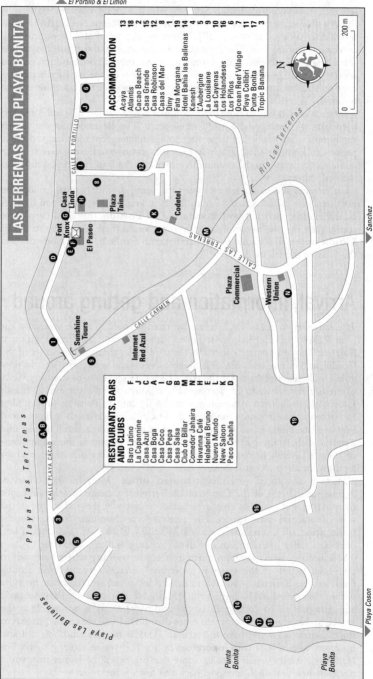

LAS TERRENAS AND PLAYA BONITA

El Portillo & El Limon

ACCOMMODATION

Acaya	13
Atlantis	18
Cacao Beach	2
Casa Grande	15
Casa Robinson	12
Casas del Mar	8
Diny	1
Fata Morgana	19
Hotel Bahia las Ballenas	14
Kanesh	4
L'Aubergine	5
La Louisiane	9
Las Cayenas	10
Los Holandeses	16
Los Piños	6
Ocean Reef Village	7
Playa Collibri	11
Punta Bonita	17
Tropic Banana	3

0   200 m

N

RESTAURANTS, BARS AND CLUBS

Baro Latino	F
La Capannine	J
Casa Azul	C
Casa Boga	A
Casa Coco	I
Casa Pepa	G
Casa Salsa	B
Club de Billar	M
Comedor Jahaira	N
Havanna Café	H
Heladeria Bruno	E
Nuevo Mundo	L
New Saloon	K
Paco Cabaña	D

Playa Las Terrenas

CALLE PLAYA CACAO

Playa Las Ballenas

CALLE EL PORTILLO

CALLE CARMEN

Sunshine Tours

Internet Red Azul

Fort Knox   Casa Linda

El Paseo

Plaza Taina

Codetel

CALLE LAS TERRENAS

Plaza Commercial

Western Union

Río Las Terrenas

Sanchez

Punta Bonita

Playa Bonita

Playa Coson

It's worth noting that Las Terrenas has been subject to frequent burglaries in the past so it's best to keep your valuables and passport in the aptly named Fort Knox, Carretera Las Terrenas (daily 8.30am-8.30pm), a storefront shop that rents **safety-deposit** boxes for a few pesos a week.

Accommodation

Continual development in Las Terrenas has meant the loss of most of its rock-bottom **accommodation** options, unpretentious shacks along the water like the legendary *Pensión Doña Nina*, where tadpoles swam in the toilet and breakfast was RD$5. What remains are pricier inns and cabanas, though none that should be too much of a strain on anyone's budget. Still, it's best to make reservations before you arrive – the cheaper places get booked up quickly. The beachfront east and west of town has also seen its fair share of development in recent years, particularly around Playa Bonita, which remains much quieter than Las Terrenas but now offers accommodations to suit most budgets.

Cacao Beach Calle Playa Cacao ☎240-6000, ℗240-6020, ⓦwww.samana.net/cacao-beach .html. Tasteful all-inclusive with a deceptively large and very grand reception area and peaceful grounds with a nice pool and hot tub. The air-conditioned, attractive rooms are in small cabanas scattered around the gardens. ❻

Casa Robinson Calle El Portillo ☎240-6496. Small, clean and cheerfully decorated rooms in a number of two-storey cabins dotted about a shady and quiet garden. Not as nice as *Kanesh* but ceiling fans and hot water make this one of the best options in this price range. ❸

Casas del Mar Calle El Portillo ☎360-2748, ⓔcasagigi@yahoo.fr. Clean cabanas with welcoming proprietors, access to the beach and a scenic location slightly away from the main part of town. Hot water and ceiling fans plus a dedicated laundry area make this justifiably popular with backpackers. ❸

Las Cayenas Calle Playa Cacao ☎240-6080, ℗240-6070. A popular American hangout, *Las Cayenas* is an authentic-looking beachfront manor that resembles a grand old plantation house, with a sleepy palm-shaded patio area. Basic but elegant rooms with ceiling fans, hot water and great sea views. Powered by solar panels. ❹

Diny Calle Playa Cacao ☎240-6113. Highly recommended budget hotel directly on the water, though you should be prepared to put up with some motorcycle noise, particularly early in the morning. ❶

Fata Morgana Playa Bonita Rd ☎752-4231, ⓔeditdejong@hotmail.com. Real basic budget cabins with a shared, fully functional kitchen, set in the garden of a house in a quiet residential area, some way from the beach and centre.

Cheapest deal in town and ideal for backpackers or long-term stays. ❷

Kanesh Beach Hotel Calle Playa Cacao ☎240-6187, ℗240-6233, ⓦwww.samana-lasterrenas .com/kanesh. Excellent-value beachfront hotel with basic but cheerier than average rooms, small balconies and sea views. Very good Indian food is available in the restaurant as well (see p.175). ❸

La Louisiane Calle Playa Cacao ☎240-6223. Well-kept, decent-sized, unpretentious rooms with mosquito nets, fans and small kitchenettes, set in a slightly scruffy, dusty courtyard just off the main drag. Some with sea views. ❸

L'Aubergine Calle Playa Cacao ☎240-6167, ℗240-6070. Three no-frills rooms above a restaurant, close to the beach. Comfortable and well decorated for the money, with hot water and a decent sitting area, but it can be noisy at night due to the restaurant and even more so in the morning with motorcycle traffic. ❸

Ocean Reef Village Calle El Portillo ☎240-6457, ⓔinver.komare@codetel.net.do. Well-maintained, large resort-style hotel with 100 sizeable rooms, featuring ceiling fans, fridge and hot water, set in small terraced blocks around a clean and restful pool area. Full kitchen option available as well. ❻

Los Piños Calle El Portillo ☎240-6168, ℗240-6197, ⓔhotellospinos@codetel.net.do. Highly recommended Swiss-run inn with nice rooms in the main building along with a few private bungalows, some with water views. The grounds feature a pleasant outdoor terrace and a tropical garden, and the service is outstanding. ❸

Playa Colibri Calle Playa Cacao ☎240-6434, ℗240-6917, ⓔcolibri@codetel.net.do. A variety of tasteful and spacious self-catering apartments set in a new three-storey complex around an immaculate pool area. Good-sized rooms with a full kitchen, cable TV and spacious balconies. Some larger apartments suited to groups or families. Good bar and restaurant too. ⑤

Tropic Banana Calle Playa Cacao ☎240-6110, ⓕ240-6112, ⓔhotel.tropic@codetel.net.do. The oldest hotel in Las Terrenas, and still one of the very best. The well-kept rooms are large, with private balconies, and the extensive palm-covered grounds include a swimming pool and tennis court. It's also attached to a diving centre and has a peaceful bar/restaurant area. ⑥

The Town

Aside from spectacular day-trips to the surrounding countryside, the **beach**, which stretches uninterrupted 2km in either direction from town, is the focus of daytime entertainment. Several old fishing shacks have been renovated to house a cluster of restaurants, but they stand far enough away to leave the sand undisturbed. The ocean here is calm and perfect for swimming, with a coral reef 100m out that provides decent snorkelling.

Just west of the Carretera is the less lively beach area, which stretches a full 2km to **Playa Las Ballenas** – a section of the beach named for three oblong islands in the waters just beyond it that resemble breaching humpback whales – before ending in a patch of swamp. The beach east of the intersection has just recently been built up, and has a slightly funkier feel, dominated by low-end cabanas and bars until the construction peters out entirely.

The newly developed malls of **El Paseo**, **Plaza Taina** and **Plaza Linda** dominate the main intersection and there are a number of **souvenir shops** tucked away in their corners. The most interesting is **Haitian Art Gallery**, Plaza Linda (10am–8pm, closed Sun), with the best selection of Haitian Naivist art and folk crafts outside of the capital. Also worth exploring is **Nativ'Art**,

---

Las Terrenas adventure outfitters

Diving

Stellina Dive Centre Hotel Cacao Beach (☎240-6000, ⓕ240-6149, ⓦwww .stellinadiving.com). Runs PADI Open Water Courses for US$320 and single dives to local reefs and wrecks from US$35.

The Tropical Dive Centre Tropic Banana Hotel (☎481-0178). Features CMIS courses along with scuba dives to the reefs and underwater caves at Cabo Cabrón just north of Playa Rincón. CMAS courses for US$400, US$40 for a dive.

LT Divers Playa Bonita (☎727-5686, ⓕ240-6070, ⓦwww.ltdivers.com). Dives across the northern coast of the peninsula, including the caves, as well as the usual PADI, CMAS courses. Charges range from US$30 for a single dive to US$345 for a PADI Open Water Course.

Horseback riding

Rancho de la Playa Calle Playa Cacao (☎240-6501). A very good outfit worth trying. They not only provide an extensive list of services for tourists, but also run the best equestrian competition school on the north coast, catering to the children of the French expats. The horses are in excellent condition and are a pleasure to ride. As well as short rides along the beach they also organize two-day trips into the Cordillera Samaná beyond El Limón for US$200 and six-day trips around the peninsula for US$600.

just across the street (9.30am–7pm, closed Mon), with imitation Taino sculpture, amber and larimar jewellery and sarongs.

Further south up the Carretera Las Terrenas, you'll enter the original Dominican **barrio**. There's much more local flavour to the streets here but the heady cloud of exhaust fumes that fills the air can be a little stifling at times.

Eating and drinking

There's a pretty decent variety of **restaurants** in Las Terrenas, quite a few of which serve up the kind of international cuisine you might only expect to find in bigger cities. You can find Spanish tapas, pizza and other Italian dishes, French food, even Indian fare. Accompanying these is *La Gaterie* (Tues–Sun 9am–6pm, closed Mon), a pricey **grocer** with gourmet meats and spices, catering to the large expat community, plus a few smaller fruit markets, fishmongers and butchers. There are a few **supermarkets** south of the beach on the main road. The most pleasant places for **drinking** are the beachside restaurants mentioned below, though if you wander around the Dominican barrio you'll also find several small liquor shacks where locals hang out drinking dixie cups of rum.

Baro Latino Calle Playa Cacao. Bustling café in the heart of the village with a huge menu including filling breakfasts, burgers and pizzas. Good for people-watching too.

Casa Azul Calle Playa Cacao. Part of the redeveloped fishing shacks, serving terrific, if pricey seafood along with burgers and more exotic dishes like grilled beef tongue.

Casa Boga Calle Playa Cacao. Another of the popular beachside shacks. Not cheap but it serves the best fish in town: try the red snapper (*chillo*) if it's on (RD$180).

Casa Coco Calle El Portillo. Reasonably priced pizzeria with a candlelit outdoor seating area. The lemon herb chicken is also worth ordering.

Casa Pepa Calle El Portillo. Traditional Spanish tapas bar on the beach, with an assortment of appetizers – including *lambí* in tomato sauce, chorizo and octopus with paprika – and a good paella.

Casa Salsa Calle Playa Cacao. Expensive but worthwhile seafood restaurant located on an outdoor beach patio at the western end of the refurbished row of old fishing shacks. Try the creole sea bass or the garlic *lambí*.

Comedor Jahaira The only place to go for *cómida criolla* in Las Terrenas, and incredibly inexpensive.

Best are Dominican standards like rice with beans and chicken, but the *mofongo* and *pescado con coco* are excellent as well. From the town centre, head up the Carretera Las Terrenas and take the 2nd dirt track on the right after the Centro Comercial. There are three small *comedores* on the block – *Jahaira* is the one in the pink building.

Havanna Café Plaza Linda. Expensive but classy bar and restaurant. Try any of the chicken dishes and you won't be disappointed. It also gets pretty lively later on.

Heladeria Bruno El Paseo. The best coffee on the beach as well as a selection of ice creams and other snacks.

Kanesh Beach Hotel Calle Playa Cacao ☎240-6187. A varied menu close to the beach but best known for its excellent and authentic-tasting Indian food that needs to be ordered at least one day in advance.

La Capannine Calle El Portillo. Good but expensive Italian fare with a beach view. Lobster is a house speciality, as are the pastas and the octopus in ink.

Paco Cabaña Calle Playa Cacao. A little pricey, but a pleasant bar and grill with tables right on the sand and a beach volleyball net. Located at the eastern end of the old row of fishing shacks.

Nightlife

Nightlife in Las Terrenas has actually quietened down a little over the last few years with the burning down of one of its major nightspots and the closure of a couple of others. That said, there's still plenty going on to keep the large numbers of independent travellers visiting occupied through the early hours. Besides the discos and bars, there's also the festive **Night Market**, in the Dominican barrio, south of town, a weekend tradition where locals sell food and liquor out of stalls, hang out along the road and play drums on Friday, Saturday and Sunday – a memorable rural Dominican experience.

Club de Billar Carretera Las Terrenas. Divey local pool hall 1km south of the beach.

New Saloon Carretera Las Terrenas. A new guise for *El Tiburón*, one of the most popular of the Las Terrenas discos. It seems to be permanently troubled, but when open it's typically heaving.

Nuevo Mundo Carretera Las Terrenas. Very popular disco a few metres south of the main crossroads, sporting a dark, modern look and spinning a jarring mix of merengue and European techno.

Listings

Airlines Air Santo Domingo (℡ 240-6094) fly out of the El Portillo airport.

Banks and currency exchange All of the main banks have a presence in Las Terrenas these days. Progresso, El Paseo (Mon–Fri 9am–3.30pm) has an ATM, as does Baninter in the Plaza Comercial, south on the main road. There are plenty of storefront exchanges too. Best bets are Sunshine Services and Western Union, Carretera Las Terrenas. Fort Knox (daily 8.30am–8.30pm), El Paseo, gives competitive rates as well as renting safe boxes.

Car and motorcycle rental Plenty of choice so worth shopping around. Car Silver, Carretera Las Terrenas (℡ & ℻ 240-5488, ℮ carsilver@hotmail .com), is pretty central and has a good selection of cars. Jessie Car Rental, Calle Playa Cacao (℡ & ℻ 240-6415, ℮ jessiecar5@hotmail.com), has everything from jeeps to four-wheelers. Sebaja, Carretera Las Terrenas, opposite the main petrol station (℡ & ℻ 240-6343), specializes in jeeps.

Film processing The place to go is Ivan Colour, Carretera Las Terrenas (Mon–Sat 9.30am–1pm & 4–8pm), for one-hour photo processing or to purchase film.

Internet Red Azul Internet Café, Calle Carmen. RD$15 for 15min.

Laundry Nora Lavendería (Mon–Sat 8am–6pm) on the main road is the only automated laundromat in town. They charge RD$60 per load. Lavendería Helena on the La Louisiane road does a good job of hand washing for RD$6 per item.

Medical Las Terrenas has a 24-hour medical hotline (℡ 543-3727) that will hook you up with a doctor within minutes. There is also a small 24-hour clinic (℡ 240-6032) within El Paseo.

Pharmacy Farmacia del Paseo (℡ 240-6497; daily 8am–8pm). There are also two other well-stocked shops: Farmacia la Patrona, Centro Comercial, Carretera Las Terrenas (℡ 240-6129; daily 8am–8pm) and Farmacentro Principal, Carreterra Las Terrenas (℡ 240-6199; daily 8am–8pm).

Police The police station (℡ 240-6022) is on Calle Playa Cacao beside the *Hotel Diny*.

Post office El Paseo, Carretera Las Terrenas

Telephone Codetel (daily 8.30am–9.30pm) is located a few metres south of the main crossroads. Televimenca (8am–6.30pm, closed Sun) is a half-kilometre further south along the Carretera.

Travel Agents Bahia Tours, Plaza Linda (℡ 240-6088, ℻ 240-6297, ℮ bahia.tours@codetel.net.do), can help with flights, tailor-made excursions and hotel reservations.

Wiring money Western Union is housed within the Televimenca office on the Carretera a half-kilometre south of the beach (8.30am–6.30pm, closed Sun).

West from Las Terrenas: Playa Bonita and Playa Cosón

Playa Bonita, 13 km of uninterrupted beach that begins just west of Playa Las Ballenas, boasts the kind of powdery white sand you might expect to see only in tourist brochures, plus the offshore reef provides the best snorkelling on the peninsula. It's seen a fair bit of development over the past few years, but most of it has thankfully been discreet and tasteful, increasing the number of places to stay and eat without detracting too much from the unspoilt character. Stay the night and the sunset will leave you reeling, as will the canopy of stars.

From Playa Bonita's entrance, a sand road provides access for four-wheel-drives and motorbikes, past the front of what hotels there are and behind a beachfront populated at most by one or two people taking advantage of the isolation to swim or sunbathe nude. Six kilometres down the coast is **Playa Cosón**, a small fishing village holding two gourmet beach shacks with tables and chairs on the sand, serving grilled, fresh-caught fish for a few pesos. From Cosón the splendid beach continues east uninterrupted for another 7km with no human outposts to speak of, before running smack into the Cordillera Samaná. At the end there are a few fishing huts and a walking path leading into the mountains and to the beaches south of Nagua – the trail is a full day's trek with a number of false turns, so don't strike out without a local. If you're determined to cross, your best bet is to book a horseback excursion with Rancho de la Playa (see p.174).

It's also possible to walk along the water from Punta Bonita, the point between Playa Bonita and Las Terrenas, to Las Terrenas, though it's a sticky trek through a marsh. To the east, Punta Bonita is bounded by a tall, rocky outcrop; a hiking trail over the hill leads to a tiny beach hemmed in by rocks. From here the path becomes less than ideal, as you'll have to wade knee-deep through a partition of reeds in the marsh to refind the trail, by now quite narrow.

Just south of Punta Bonita, off the road to Las Terrenas, stands a **1000-year-old ceiba tree** (also known as a cotton tree), one of the largest and oldest documented trees on the island, a gnarled monstrosity good for climbing. From the beach entrance, go 200m to the bar *Tres Locos Amigos* and head east 500m along the dirt path that begins there.

Practicalities

Playa Bonita is most easily accessible from Las Terrenas via a marked turnoff from the Carretera. There are a few prime **places to stay** here, all of them excellent value for the money. Each has good restaurants attached, and if you're looking for natural beauty, peace and quiet, you're far better off staying here than in Las Terrenas. The best of the bunch is *Atlantis Hotel and Restaurant* (☎240-6111, ☏240-6205, ⓔhotelatlantis@codetel.net.do; ❹), whose pretty rooms are palatial; try to book either the Jamaica or the Grenada room, both with panoramic views of the beach. The French restaurant on the grounds is run by the former chef of President Mitterand – at the very least try breakfast, as it's included in the price. Also nice is the *Acaya* (☎240-6161, ☏240-6166, ⓦacaya.free.fr; ❹), a modern hotel with a/c and all the amenities, including swimming pool, free snorkelling gear and a thatch-roofed beachside restaurant with good seafood; go for the second-floor rooms, which are cooler and have a better view. The *Hotel Bahia las Ballenas* (☎240-6066, ☏240-6107, ⓔb.lasballenas@codetel.net.do; ❺) is also something special with beautifully decorated individual cabanas set in a brilliant garden. Highlights include open-air showers and carefully thought-out lighting in each room. Slightly more downscale but still pleasant is *Los Holandeses* (☎248-5104; ❸), a well-kept set of cabanas that offers free watersports equipment. If you're looking for an all-inclusive, try the *Punta Bonita Beach Resort* (☎240-

△ Man on donkey, Las Galeras

6082, Ⓕ240-6012; ❹), less frenetic and walled-off than most, and with beautiful, bungalow-dotted grounds, a swimming pool and good buffet food. The cheapest place on the beach and excellent value is *Casa Grande* (Ⓣ & Ⓕ240-6349, Ⓦwww.casa-grande.de; ❸), five good-sized rooms in a large house.

East from Las Terrenas: El Portillo and El Limón

East from Las Terrenas the development slowly winds down again until you're on unblemished beach bordered only by coconut forest. Six kilometres down the road lies the secluded **El Portillo Beach Club** (Ⓣ240-6100, Ⓕ 240-6104; ❼), one of the largest all-inclusives in the country, with tennis courts, swimming pools, beach volleyball, horseback riding, scuba diving, two restaurants (plus weekly outdoor barbecues), a high-tech disco and its own private airstrip. The grounds are walled-off from outsiders, but you can easily step onto the beach from the west of the resort, where a small pueblo boasts a couple of *colmados* and a bar.

The beach extends 2km east beyond *El Portillo* before being cut off by high rocks. At low tide, it's possible to walk all the way to Playa El Limón 5km further east, and from there to Playa Morón and a series of other small beaches all the way to El Valle – though you'll have trouble walking back if you don't set out at dawn.

Little more than a crossroads with a few shacks attached, dusty **EL LIMÓN**, 5km east of El Portillo, seems unpromising at first, but it does make an ideal base for excursions to the magnificent **El Limón waterfall** to the south and two isolated beaches to the north. Upon arrival you'll be beset by several local *buscones* trying to steer you to one of the excursion outfits; best is Casa Santi, just south of the crossroad on the road to Samaná (Ⓣ240-6261; RD$350), who include an enormous lunch in the price. The waterfall is accessible by horse from the town and takes 2.5 hours round-trip. The path cuts across a broad river before climbing into the palm-thick mountains. As the waterfall comes into sight, the horses are tethered at a small way station where you can have a drink before walking the rest of the way. The walk is well worth the effort to see the 50m of torrential white water dropping precipitously off a sheer cliff in the middle of the wilderness. At the base of the falls is a large swimming hole. Between El Limón and Samaná, there are a number of small *paradas* (stop-offs) which offer a variety of horseback excursions to the falls. Despite the obvious competition between them, the businesses all work closely together to ensure high standards are maintained and costs are kept to a minimum. Highly recommended comes Parada Manaza, ran by Antonia, who, in addition to organizing a good trip, can also prepare an excellent traditional lunch. Expect to pay around RD$350 for the round trip plus lunch.

Also within striking distance – some 3km from the hamlet – are sister beaches **Playa El Limón** and **Playa Morón**. Casa Santi does horseback excursions to the beaches, but it's also possible to walk from town, setting off on the small path just east of the main crossroads. Playa El Limón comes first, a beautiful, abandoned beach from which it's another 1km east along the shore to Playa Morón – even better and surrounded by rocks, with a large mountain cave on its eastern end into which the waves crash, safe to clamber around in at low tide.

Practicalities

El Portillo Beach Club arranges regular outings to the waterfall for its customers, as do the top Las Terrenas tour organizers and a number of island-wide operators. From Las Terrenas, a motoconcho costs RD$50, and, during the day, the guaguas that ply the route will cost approximately RD$30. Getting back is more of a problem if you're depending on public transport – it's standard practice (and safe) to hitchhike from here. Every hour or so, a guagua will pass by. You can also get here directly from Samaná via motoconcho, a much longer trip that will cost you RD$150–200 for the day.

If you decide to **stay the night**, *Casa Santi* (T240-246; ❷) has a few basic but clean cabanas for rent. *Rancho Casa Berca* is the place to eat in town, with RD$75 dinners of creole chicken, rice and beans, plantains, salad and beer.

The coast to Cabrera

The coastal stretch just west of the Samaná Peninsula holds a series of excellent beaches, most of them surprisingly untouched by tourism. There are two sizeable towns at either end of this strip, **Nagua** and **Cabrera**, the latter a focus of French-Canadian tourism and the more diverting destination: just south of town are a waterfall, an eerie twilight meeting spot for thousands of egrets, and a working coffee farm. Between the two, consider stopping at **Playa La Entrada**, a little-used strand of beach with the ruins of an abandoned village on its far end, and **Playa Diamante**, a turquoise inlet with views of the pounding surf just beyond its sheltering coral reef.

Nagua

Below sea level and often stiflingly hot, **NAGUA** is typically Dominican and surprisingly large for a seaside town. Once known as a bit of a political hot spot due to frequent labour strikes, it's peaceful enough these days although the workforce will never be slow to down tools if the need arises. Perhaps not surprisingly, few visitors stop off at this industrial town, with its cement factory and federal penitentiary (the country's largest) providing a not-so-scenic backdrop. There's little to detain in any case, the lone "sight" being the statue of **María Trinidad Sánchez** – who designed and sewed the first Dominican flag – in the parque central. The waterfront, north of the park, is fairly sedate, save for the annual **fiesta patronal**, January 14 to 21, in honour of the Virgin of Altagracia.

The beaches that extend out both ways from the city brighten the mood a bit, though they're better for **surfing** than swimming. The first of these, on the south side, **Playa de Los Gringos** – with no gringos in evidence – sees slightly more use by townsfolk than the beach to the north, **Playa Boba**, seven solid kilometres of sand and intimidating surf at the end of which the Río Boba meets the sea.

An excellent road extends from Nagua inland to San Francisco de Macorís (see p.267) and the Cibao Valley, quite scenic as it winds through the far end of the palm-covered Cordillera Septentrional, before plunging into some of the most verdant farmland in the world. Along the way you'll pass coffee, rice and cocoa farms, plus a number of small pueblos that see virtually no tourist traffic; the people here are among the DR's nicest. Metro and Caribe Tours both do the run, and from Samaná it's the fastest route to Santo Domingo. If you're driving the C-5 east, along the north coast, watch for the marked turn at the eastern end of town; otherwise you'll be taking the road to San Francisco de Macorís accidentally.

Practicalities

Nagua doesn't receive a lot of visitors, but there are usually a few foreign surfers in town taking advantage of Playa Boba's tremendous waves. If you need to **stay the night**, the hotels are a lot better than one perhaps would imagine; try the *Aparta Hotel Central*, Calle Mella (T584-4255, F584-4384, Wwww.hotel.central.com.do; 3), a particularly clean and tidy hotel with private facilities and a good restaurant. The other good option is *Hotel Sweet Dreams*, Calle Mella 46 (T584-4971, F584-4970; 3), which is also clean and tidy with all mod cons. Outside of the hotel restaurants, there are a number of modest **eating** options in town including a Mexican joint next to the *Aparta*, which does excellent burritos, *Escosa*, an Italian option right by the parque central and a few Dominican *comedores* scattered about. **Nightlife** is centred around Nagua's two big discos, *Menci's* and *Yana Cona*, both just off the park.

North to Cabrera

Fifteen kilometres north of the Río Boba's mouth is sparsely populated **Playa La Entrada**, with a small town of the same name perched at its northern end. From the entrance, at the corner of the C-5 and Calle Príncipe, roam 250m down to get to the picturesque mouth of the Río La Entrada. Just beyond you'll see a beautiful, rocky island on the water, though don't try and swim out to it – the water here is known for its riptides. It's worth hiking to the south end of the beach to see the so-called **Lost Village**, a small pueblo that was all but destroyed thirty years ago by a hurricane. The remains of thatch houses with bamboo supports and various household utensils still litter the area directly behind the sand.

There's very little in the way of **accommodation** – or anything else – at La Entrada, but most of the beach is abandoned enough to make **camping** a tempting (if unregulated) option. For **food**, try the *Parador* restaurant, a half-kilometre north of town on the C-5; drinks and dancing can be had at *La Entrada Disco* on Calle Príncipe or the garish *JM Disco*, an indoor club on the corner of Calle Príncipe and the C-5.

The *Parador* also sells RD$20 tickets to **Lago el Dudu**, a freshwater sinkhole just behind the restaurant created by drooping volcanic rock, and used as a local swimming hole. Surrounded by dense rainforest vegetation and accessible by a series of rough steps hewn into the rock face, the place has the feel of a Tarzan movie set.

Continuing north, the riptide-laden waters are safe only for exceptionally strong swimmers until you reach **Playa Diamante**, located at the end of a dirt road, off the C-5, next to the *Diamante* restaurant, 3km north of La Entrada and a good bet for lunch. Diamante consists of a placid, blue beach cove set off from the ocean by a rock outcrop at its mouth. Several hotel chains are elbowing each other for permission to develop the site, but nothing has disturbed the surf yet.

Cabrera

CABRERA, 5km north of Playa Diamante, is the most visibly prosperous outpost along this part of the coastline – clean, uncongested and dotted with a number of attractive, pastel-coloured homes – but there's still precious little to it. Its city beach, **Playa Clara,** at the north end of town isn't bad, though no competition for Playa Diamante and Playa El Bretón (see p.221), each within easy striking distance.

Better is the large **waterfall** just west of town, hidden off an unmarked dirt road across the C-5; the pool at its base is swimmable when the water level is high enough. You'll also see a steep embankment – passable only by four-wheel-drive – that leads through a few small subsistence farms to a condominium complex and the *La Catalina* hotel before reconnecting with the C-5.

Further into the mountains, a large tree 3km west of the *La Catalina* hotel down a dirt road serves as the nightly gathering point for thousands of **African egrets** that populate Dominican pastures. The birds arrive every night around 6pm without fail. Once the convocation is complete, the massive tree – identifiable by the enormous sheet of rock-hard guano that surrounds it – is abuzz with frenetic white motion and noise.

La Catalina also arranges a two-hour tour (RD$275) every Wednesday at 10.30am to **Chez José,** a large working tobacco and coffee farm 4km east of Cabrera in the Cordillera Septentrional. The owner will take you to see field hands picking coffee beans from shrubs, explain the three-year process of cultivating them, and show you the tobacco being harvested and dried out in thatch sheds. A large lunch is included in the price.

Practicalities

Cabrera itself doesn't offer too much on the **accommodation** front, just a few in-town budget options such as *Hotel/Restaurant El Dorado*, a few sparse rooms above *Pizza El Dorado* at the town's western entrance (no phone; ❷), and *Hotel/Restaurant Julissa*, at its eastern entrance (no phone; ❶). Better to head just out of town, about 3km west to a small pueblo and then south up a dirt road to *La Catalina*, Calle La Catalina (☎589-7700, ℱ589-7550, Ⓦwww.lacatalina.com; ❹), a large country inn perched atop a steep cliff that overlooks Cabrera and the sea. The outdoor patio dining room serves excellent, pricey French cuisine (reservations necessary). Outside of **eating** at *La Catalina*, you may wish to try less the pricey pizzas at the aforementioned *Pizza El Dorado*. If you have your own transport, *Virginia* – a terrific local seafood restaurant – is a must; it's 3km west of town in Abreu (see p.221).

Travel details

The domestic **flight** details given opposite don't take into account the impending opening of the airport at Arroyo Barril. The only formal **bus com-**

panies that go to the peninsula are Caribe Tours and Metro. Both have connections to San Francisco de Macorís and the Cibao heartland, and Caribe Tours has an additional trip that heads west along the north coast to Puerto Plata. Far more frequent from Samaná town are the **guaguas** that gather at El Mercado, which is the mode of transport you'll have to take if you're heading to Las Terrenas. Most of the guaguas that do the Sánchez–Las Terrenas road are pickup trucks where you'll be perched in the back along with your luggage. Once you arrive you'll find a guagua that leaves from the town centre to pueblo El Limón.

Buses

Cabrera to: Cabarete (daily; 1hr 15min); Nagua (2 daily; 35min); Puerto Plata (daily; 2hr 15min); Río San Juan (daily; 30min); Samaná (2 daily; 1hr 45min); Sánchez (2 daily; 1hr 15min); Santo Domingo (daily; 6hr 35min); Sosúa (daily; 1hr 35min).

Nagua to: Cabarete (daily; 1hr 50min); Cabrera (2 daily; 1hr 15min); Castillo (4 daily; 30min); Pimentel (3 daily; 45min); Puerto Plata (daily; 2hr 45min); Samaná (8 daily; 1hr 5min); San Francisco de Macorís (12 daily; 1hr 20min); Sánchez (8 daily; 35min); Santo Domingo (12 daily; 4hr 40min); Sosúa (daily; 2hr).

Samaná to: Cabarete (daily; 3hr); Cabrera (daily; 1hr 45min); Castillo (4 daily; 1hr 40min); Nagua (7 daily; 1hr 5min); Pimentel (3 daily; 1hr 55min); Puerto Plata (2 daily; 4hr 15min); Río San Juan (daily; 1hr 45min); San Francisco de Macorís (6 daily; 2hr 30min); Sánchez (8 daily; 30min); Santo Domingo (8 daily; 5hr 40min); Sosúa (2 daily; 3hr 35min).

Sánchez to: Cabarete (daily; 2hr 30min); Cabrera (daily; 1hr 15min); Castillo (2 daily; 1hr 10min); Nagua (7 daily; 35min); Pimentel (3 daily; 1hr 15min); Puerto Plata (daily; 3hr 45min); Río San Juan (daily; 1hr 15min); Samaná (8 daily; 30min); San Francisco de Macorís (6 daily; 2hr); Santo Domingo (6 daily; 5hr 10min); Sosúa (daily; 3hr 5min).

Guaguas

Cabrera to: El Bretón (35 daily; 15min); La Entrada (35 daily; 15min); Nagua (35 daily; 35min); Río San Juan (35 daily; 30min).

El Limón to: Las Terrenas (8 daily; 45min).

La Entrada to: Cabrera (35 daily; 15min); El Bretón (35 daily; 30min); Nagua (35 daily; 20min); Río San Juan (35 daily; 40min).

Las Galeras to: Samaná (14 daily; 1hr).

Las Terrenas to: El Limón (8 daily; 45min); Sánchez (26 daily; 35min).

Nagua to: Cabrera (35 daily; 35min); Castillo (11 daily; 30min); El Bretón (35 daily; 45min); La Entrada (35 daily; 20min); Pimentel (11 daily; 45min); Río San Juan (35 daily; 1hr); San Francisco de Macorís (11 daily; 1hr 15min); Sánchez (35 daily; 35min).

Samaná to: Las Galeras (14 daily; 1hr); Sánchez (20 daily; 30min).

Sánchez to: Las Terrenas (26 daily; 35min); Nagua (35 daily; 35 min); Samaná (20 daily; 30min).

Ferries

Cayo Levantado to: Samaná (3 daily; 15min).
Las Galeras to: Playa Rincón (daily; 25min).
Playa Rincón to: Las Galeras (daily; 25min).
Samaná to: Cayo Levantado (3 daily; 15min); Sabana de la Mar (2 daily; 1hr).

Flights

Las Terrenas to: La Romana (daily; 40 min); Santo Domingo (daily; 45min); Puerto Plata (daily; 30min); Punta Cana (daily; 30min).

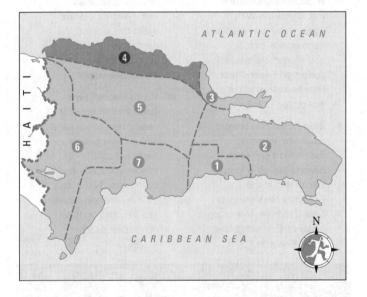

The Silver Coast

CHAPTER 4

Highlights

✳ **Isabela de Torres Cable Car, Puerto Plata** There's no better way to view the north coast than from the summit of La Isabela de Torres; there's no easier way to get there than on the Puerto Plata cable car. See p.199

✳ **Windsurfing/kitesurfing, Cabarete** With warm water and such a huge choice of tuition and equipment available, surfers and riders flock here from around the world. See p.212

✳ **Blue Moon Restaurant** Exquisite authentic Indian food served on banana leaves in temple-like setting in the Cordillera Septentrional near Cabarete. Evenings usually finish with a fine party. See p.217

✳ **Mountain biking in the Cordillera Septentrional** A fabulous way to get deep into the country-side and there are plenty of trails to suit riders of any ability. See p.217

✳ **Snorkelling near La Isabela/Monte Cristi** Pristine coral, clear water and no crowds make this area off the north coast the best snorkelling spot on the island. See p.223

✳ **Punta Rucia/Playa Ensenata** Tranquillity personified; white sand and shallow turquoise water set against an imposing backdrop of rolling hills. Two of the quietest and most beautiful beaches on this coast. See p.227

The Silver Coast

The Dominican Republic's so-called **Silver Coast**, 300km of mostly prime waterfront property on the country's northern edge, hemmed in to the south by the **Cordillera Septentrional** mountain range, is without a doubt the most popular tourist destination in the Caribbean. With a seemingly unending supply of great beaches, such a designation is no surprise, though away from the heavy traffic of the resort towns – mostly around Puerto Plata and parts east – you may well be surprised by the coast's unspoilt character and the diversity of its geography. The place has historic resonance as well, as the first shore that Columbus settled, though the colony later grew up around Santo Domingo.

Columbus envisioned the coast as a shipping-off point for vast deposits of gold that proved to be a product of his imagination; the sobriquet originated a few decades later when armadas bearing Mexican silver skirted the fortified shore to protect themselves from the pirates of the old Cannibal Sea. The word "cannibal" is a corruption of "Caribbean", after the Caribe Indians, who were reported practitioners of cannibalism; indeed, sixteenth-century maps of the region invariably bore illustrations portraying natives roasting missionaries on a spit.

A century after Columbus's discovery, Cuba supplanted the north coast of the Dominican Republic as favoured way station for Spanish booty plundered from Mexico and Peru. The region soon after began to rely on contraband trade with the very pirates it once fought, and the major settlements were razed to the ground by the Spanish crown in 1605 as punishment. At the mercy of world price fluctuations that have taken their toll on a series of one-crop economies, the last four centuries proceeded much as the first, with periods of short-lived prosperity followed by long decades of subsistence. You'll see evidence of the occasional construction booms embedded in the major towns like geological strata.

Nowhere is this better seen than in **Puerto Plata**, a bustling city packed with atmospheric nineteenth-century architecture located just about halfway between the Samaná Peninsula and the Haitian border. Though it's an interesting place to explore, most visitors tend to bypass it entirely in favour of the titanic resort flanking it to the east, **Playa Dorada**, the largest all-inclusive resort complex in the world, and as such home to a dizzying array of organized activities. Further east are more resort towns, linked by the coastal Carretera 5: **Sosúa**, a former sex-tourism centre that over recent years has cleaned up its image, with three separate beaches and an old Jewish quarter founded by World War II refugees; and **Cabarete**, the windsurfing capital of the Americas, an internationally flavoured village erected over a

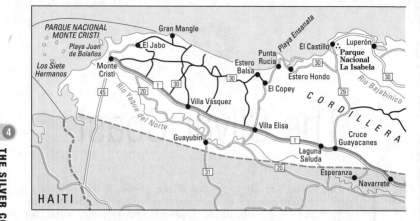

cow pasture during the past fifteen years. Even further east, things quieten down with no huge developments until you reach the Samaná Peninsula, although there are some interesting diversions along the way. The best of these is sleepy **Río San Juan**, a small town bordered by the thick mangrove swamps of **Laguna Gri-Gri** and a glorious two-kilometre beach known as **Playa Grande**.

Back west of Puerto Plata lie a series of remote pueblos linked by unpaved roads, where campesinos live much the same as they have for the last five centuries. Of interest here are **La Isabela** and **El Castillo**, site of Columbus's first permanent settlement, which sit behind an immaculate bay with the best snorkelling on the island; the remote beaches **Playa Ensanata** and **Punta Rucia**, as beautiful as any on the island; and at the far western end **Monte Cristi**, a remote, dusty border town flanked on both sides by a national park that protects a river delta, a collection of desert islands and a strip of cactus-laden mountain landscape.

The C-5 makes **getting around** by car easy east of Puerto Plata. The country's two major bus companies ply the highway, along with guaguas and plentiful *público* taxis. Getting around west of Puerto Plata is more of a challenge (but not impossible) if you don't have a four-wheel-drive. From the Carretera Puerto Plata that heads south towards Santiago, you'll find a number of turnoffs that lead successively to Guzmancito, Luperón, La Isabela and Punta Rucia, hellish pot-holed moonscapes for the most part, but slowly in the process of being paved. Guaguas run along each of these roads during the day. Beyond Punta Rucia are mule tracks; if you don't have a motorcycle, you'll have to head south to the Carretera Duarte that stretches along the western Cibao Valley to reach Monte Cristi.

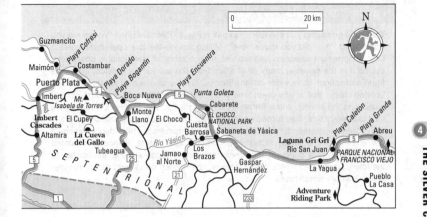

Puerto Plata and Playa Dorada

PUERTO PLATA and **PLAYA DORADA** comprise the mass-tourism capital of the Caribbean, and most of the half-million-plus tourists who visit each year are here on package tours to the walled-off vacation factory of Playa Dorada. Not be overlooked, though, is Puerto Plata, whose city limits lie a kilometre east of the beach. A vibrant Dominican town of 200,000, it's well worth exploring for the historic architecture and great nightlife. Its core, the **Old City**, borders the port to the east, a narrow grid of streets that was once the most stylish neighbourhood in the country. Around the original town sprawls a patchwork maze of industrial zones and concrete barrios known as the **New City**, formed over the past century with the growth of the town's main industries outside of tourism, namely tobacco, sugar and rum. More relaxing than either the city or Playa Dorada is **Costambar**, a small cluster of condos and other beachfront accommodations, 1km west of town.

One of the oldest European settlements in the New World, the city's **San Felipe** fort is the one impressive vestige of colonial times. More prominent, if not quite as atmospheric, are the scores of Victorian **gingerbread mansions** that make an outdoor museum of the Old City. Along the Atlantic Ocean is its deservedly famous **Malecón**, a two-kilometre stretch of boardwalk lined with discos, outdoor bars and bonfire beach parties. Other sights of interest include the **Museo Ámbar**, with an impressive display of insects trapped millions of years ago in the half-clear sap, and the cable car ride to the summit of **Mount Isabela de Torres**, the flat-topped behemoth that lords over the city from the south.

④

The worst questions you can ask an **expat** in Puerto Plata are often "Where are you from?" and "Why did you move here?" Milling among the tour operators, itinerant sailors, timeshare salesmen and retirees are a number of questionable characters, colourful in the extreme, many on the lam from the law for tax evasion, insurance fraud and various other white-collar offences. The Caribbean adjuster for Lloyd's of London claims that at any given time you'll find five of Interpol's ten most-wanted wandering the streets, and a British crew filming a documentary on English expats said that every time they turned on the camera inside one popular watering hole, a half-dozen people ran for cover. The fugitives tend to attract a bewildering variety of law enforcement officials, including undercover FBI agents, Canadian Mounted Police, international spies and insurance detectives. It lends an eerie film-noir feel to the town, augmented by the placid, narrow streets lined with slowly decaying nine-teenth-century warehouses.

Some history

Christopher Columbus sailed past the city's harbour on his 1492 voyage and gave the Silver Port its name. The settlement established here in 1502 by colonial governor Nicolás de Ovando for a time served as resupply point for armadas bearing silver from Mexico to Spain. As the sixteenth century wore on, though, it was bypassed by the main routes due to increasing piracy and the importance of Havana further west. The absence of Spanish ships created a big problem as both a royal monopoly forbade commerce with foreign powers and hostile bands of escaped slaves in the mountain passes made it impossible to transport local goods to Santo Domingo. To survive, the town became a centre for **illegal trade**, providing leather hides to French, English and Portuguese ships in excange for bolts of fabric, casks of wine and slaves until the Spanish-controlled government in Santo Domingo destroyed all settlements along the north coast, forcibly deporting residents of Puerto Plata to Monte Plata just east of the capital.

The ensuing depopulation was a disaster – pirates made a base of the coast, ravaged Spanish colonies and assisted the French in their efforts to gain a foothold on the island. Puerto Plata was abandoned until 1737, when the site was repopulated with Canary Islanders to prevent further French encroachment. It stayed a backwater until 1751, when entrepreneurs from the capital rebuilt the port and began exporting mahogany and other precious woods, but in 1864–65 during the **War of Restoration**, it was virtually demolished by nationalist guerrillas intent on driving out the occupying Spaniards. Quickly reconstructed, in the 1870s it became the main shipping point for Cibao tobacco.

The **tobacco boom** was Puerto Plata's golden age, when for a few decades it was the wealthiest, most cosmopolitan town in the Caribbean. The burgeoning merchant class – many of them German exporters – built dozens of fabulous mansions, some of which remain to this day. By the beginning of the twentieth century, though, the United States took control of Dominican customs receipts and awarded themselves preferential trade status. Puerto Plata's German market shrank, and American barriers to tobacco sank the economy. In 1910 skyrocketing sugar prices (caused by the destruction of French beet farms) resuscitated the port. In the following decade, dubbed **The Dance of Millions**, Puerto Plata took on more of a modern urban air with dozens of new factories and a population explosion, snuffed out a few years later as

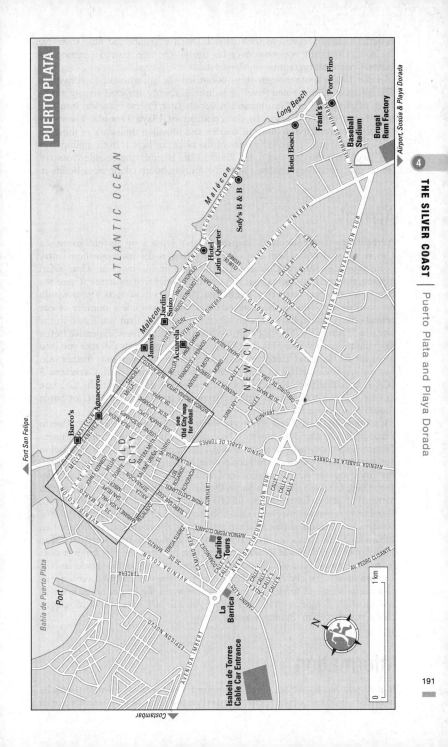

Airport, Sosúa & Playa Dorada

Porto Fino

Long Beach

Frank's

Brugal
Rum Factory

Baseball
Stadium

AV. HERMANOS MIRABAL

Hotel Beach

Malecón

Sofy's B & B

AVENIDA CIRCUNVALACIÓN NORTE

AVENIDA LUIS GINEBRA

CLUB DE
LEONES

Hotel
Latin Quarter

CALLE A1
CALLE B1
CALLE A
CALLE B
CALLE C

AVENIDA CIRCUNVALACIÓN SUR

ATLANTIC OCEAN

Malecón
Jardín
Suizo

Acuarela

Jamvis

VISTA ALEGRE
HUGO KUNHARDT
VINCS SPOONDLIU
PROF. JUAN BOSCH SABE

CALLE 27 DE AGOSTO

CALLE

PROF. CERRADO

AVENIDA LUIS GINEBRA

FRANCISCO J. PEYNADO

RAFAEL AGUILAR

NEW CITY

Barco's

Aguaceros

Malecón

SÁNCHEZ
MELLA
12 DE JULIO
30 DE DICIEMBRE
SEPARACIÓN
FABRICIO DESCHAMPS
JOSÉ RAMÓN LÓPEZ
DR. ZAFRA

BELLER
ANTERA MOTA
EL MORRO
VILLANUEVA
VIRGINIA ORTEA

ANTERA MOTA
MOTA

CALLE 2
CALLE 3

AVENIDA 27 DE FEBRERO

OLD
CITY

see
'Old City map
for detail'

20 DE MAYO

GREGORIO DE LORA

AVENIDA ISABELA DE TORRES

Fort San Felipe

AVENIDA COLÓN
30 DE MARZO
JUAN KENNEDY
IMBERT
SAN FELIPE
VILLA NUEVA

JUAN LARA
J. E. KUNHART

JUAN KENNEDY
ARIZA MOTA
SALOMÉ UREÑA
ALTAGRACIA
SUPR. SAN JOSÉ
PADRE CASTELLANOS
MA. TERESA SUÁREZ

EUGENIO PERDOMO
DUARTE
SAN FELIPE
JOSÉ DEL CARMEN ARIZA
BEGALADO
SEPARACIÓN
LOS ROSARIOS

AVENIDA ISABELA DE TORRES

AV. PEDRO CLISANTE

Bahía de Puerto Plata

Port

TERCERA
ESPISON NUEVO

AVENIDA COLÓN
30 DE MARZO

CAMINO REAL
ZÓNDOMÍNGUEZ

MA. TERESA SUÁREZ
MARIANA LAYDA HLL

AVENIDA PEDRO CLISANTE

Caribe
Tours

La
Barrica

CALLE 1
CALLE 2
CALLE 3
CALLE 5
CALLE 6
CALLE 4

AVENIDA CIRCUNVALACIÓN SUR

CAMINO A LOS

Isabela de Torres
Cable Car Entrance

AVENIDA TIMBERT

Costambar

N

0 ____ 1 km

America's Great Depression took its toll. Dictator Trujillo did little to revive the town's stagnant economy over his thirty-year rule, instead centring his industrialization programme on the capital.

In the 1960s, another sugar mini-boom led the government to revive the decrepit port, and the new level of industrial activity attracted tens of thousands of additional rural immigrants. A decade later, Puerto Plata was insulated from fluctuating crop prices by the **creation of Playa Dorada**. The resort complex has attracted millions of tourists and provided thousands of jobs, but the self-sustaining, walled-off nature of the place has kept it from spilling over too much into the city, and today Puerto Plata is a thriving, seaside industrial centre that is relatively insulated from the tourism boom taking place beside it.

Arrival

Aeropuerto Internacional Luperón (also known by its old name, La Unión; ☎586-1992), 18km east of Puerto Plata, is the main northern entry point into the country. Uniformed guards identifiable by their white safari helmets are scattered throughout the airport to offer free assistance. There is a Banco de Reservas **currency exchange** (Mon–Fri 8.30am–6.30pm) within the strip of shops lining the front of the airport, alongside a number of **car rental** offices, which have a better selection of vehicles than you'll find in the city (see "Listings", p.203 for details). While most of the more expensive hotels have shuttle buses waiting for their clients, motoconchos can also take you into town for RD$20, and there are plenty of taxis heading to points further out. Just outside the entrance to the airport is the main coastal road, **Carretera 5 (C-5)**, stretching from Puerto Plata all the way to Samaná. From the C-5 you can catch a guagua going in either direction; a trip to Puerto Plata or Sosúa should cost around RD$10.

If coming **by car**, you'll arrive via either the C-5 or the Carretera Puerto Plata, which heads south towards Navarrete before ending at the Carretera Duarte. The two roads meet at the bleak, congested Avenida Circunvalación Sur, which marks the city's southern border. Arriving **by bus** is another option; the city is a major junction point for Caribe Tours and Metro, whose vehicles arrive here from the south (via Santo Domingo and Santiago) and the east (via Samaná). Caribe Tours (☎586-4544) has its terminal on Avenida Pedro Clisante, between the parque central and the C-5. The Metro terminal (☎586-6062) is in a residential part of town well east of the centre of activity, though still accessible by motoconcho, at Beller and 16 de Agosto. Transporte del Cibao (no phone) uses Sosúa as its main north-coast link, but the few buses it does have to Puerto Plata let you off just west of the traffic circle at the Circunvalación Sur and Avenida Colón, from where you can take a motoconcho to the centre of town. The **guaguas** that travel the length of the coast all end up at the parque central, from where you can pick up a taxi or motoconcho if your hotel isn't within walking distance.

Information

If at all possible, book your hotel beforehand. Once you hit town, you may be pounced on by one of the **local "guides"**; using them to help orient yourself and find accommodation is not recommended. If you feel pressured, a firm refusal is the only way to save yourself having to hand out large amounts of money in the long run. The government **tourist office**, Malecón 25 (Mon–Fri 9am–5pm, though hours can sometimes vary), is not really worth even a cursory visit. Better sources of information are the **expat hangouts**, such as *Cafe Cito* (see p.201), owned by Canadian Consul Tim Hall, and *Sam's Bar and Grill* (see p.201), which also has a few basic rooms for rent above the restaurant. Both have noticeboards and a good amount of visitor traffic. Puerto Plata also boasts a weekly rag, *El Faro*, which offers some listings. Other information can be obtained from Ⓦwww.puertoplatainfo.com or by watching out for large neon banners and the like when major acts hit town.

If you've arrived in Playa Dorada and find your hotel does not have all your needs, head to the shopping plaza at the centre of the complex; you'll find banks, car rental and the like there.

City transport

Central Puerto Plata is compact enough to make **walking** your best option. Keep to the extremely narrow sidewalks; **motoconcho** accidents involving pedestrians are frequent. If heading to Playa Dorada or Costambar, you may want to take one of these ubiquitous motoconchos, which should cost RD$30 (RD$10 within town). Cheaper but far slower are the **public buses** shuttling between Playa Dorada and the parque central. The price is RD$3 but it can take up to 45 minutes to get from one side of town to the other. The A bus goes down Circunvalación Sur to Colón, winds through the dockyard barrio and heads to the park, while the B heads down Avenida Kunhardt – which slants from Circunvalación Sur to the Old City – and hits a few side streets in the New City. **Taxis** are relatively expensive (RD$60 to Playa Dorada), but are the fastest mode of transport and far safer than motoconchos. It's best to pick them up at one of their main gathering points: parque central, Long Beach, the traffic circle at Circunvalación Sur and Colón, or the entrances to Playa Dorada and Costambar. The taxis don't have meters – settle on a fare before you get in, and don't be afraid to bargain. To call ahead for a pickup, try Central (Ⓣ586-7498), Servi (Ⓣ971-6737), or Tecni (Ⓣ320-7621). If shuttling back and forth from Costambar or Playa Dorada, **renting a car** can spare you the hassles of public transportation. You're best off renting at the Puerto Plata airport; the rental outlets along the eastern end of the Circunvalación Sur are just as expensive and tend to have fewer vehicles. If you do drive, prepare for a bit of an adventure as the city streets are quite crowded.

Tours

The popularity of Playa Dorada has attracted some excellent **tour operators** offering a variety of interesting day-trips. Outback Safari, Plaza Turisol, Local No. 7, Av Luperon Km 2.5 (Ⓣ244-4886, Ⓦwww.outbacksafari.com.do), is the best of the adventure **jeep tour** outfits, with a tour (US$69) that includes coffee with a local family, swimming in a clear Cordillera Septentrional stream and boogie-boarding on a less popular north coast beach. There's always a bit of rum flowing so expect it to become quite lively as the day wears on. Freestyle Catamarans (Ⓣ586-1239, Ⓕ586-6668, Ⓦwww.freestyle-catamarans.com; US$69) does a well-run, full-day **catamaran** trip that goes from Puerto Plata to Sosúa and back and includes snorkelling and free drinks. Go Caribic, Plaza

Turisol 55 (☎586-4075), is the largest tour operator in the country and can help out with any other possibilities on the island. Check out too, Iguana Mama (see page 000), who operate out of Cabarete, but run mountain-bike trips and the like in the mountains south of here.

Accommodation

The best luxury **hotels** are east of town within Playa Dorada, but these are of course **all-inclusives**, which limit your freedom a bit. Most of the downtown options are at the **budget** end of things but *Sofy's* is notch up for those who want a quiet base and *Porto Fino* is also quite comfortable, ideal for good nightlife options but a motoconcho ride from the parque central.

As most people staying in Playa Dorada are on **package tours**, it's rare to actually call up the hotel and request a room for the night; you'll get much better deals, anyway, if you book at home through a travel agent. With all-inclusive resorts, remember that what glitters on the cover of a glossy brochure is not necessarily gold. The majority of the resorts are quite similar, though, with service levels varying more due to the staff and management on duty at the time than the quality and star-rating of the resort itself. Nevertheless, they all offer an expansive list of facilities, including a/c, swimming pools, tennis courts, watersports, horseback riding, and access to the golf course and the beach.

Another possibility is **Costambar**, a maze of townhouses and condos, many available for rent, and just a short motoconcho or taxi ride away from the parque central. The best way to find an apartment here is to drive around and peek in the various places with "For Rent' signs out front. You're likely to turn up something good for RD$1500 a week (rates are advertised in pesos, but you can also pay in US dollars). If you want to reserve ahead of time, call *Villas Olas Tropicale*, Duarte 53 (☎970-7132, ☎970-7342; ⑤), a beautiful bed-and-breakfast on the beach, with water views and good food (RD$75 for breakfast if you don't have a room).

Puerto Plata

Hotel Atlantico 12 de Julio 24 ☎586-2503, ☎586-6108. Decent downtown budget accommodation with average but clean rooms and a pretty courtyard area. ②

Hotel Beach Malecón at Long Beach ☎586-2551. This run-down hotel has long been a backpacker hangout because of its dirt-cheap rates. Right on Long Beach with very basic facilities, and strictly for those determined to rough it. ①

Ilra Villanueva 25 ☎586-2337. A sombre Victorian building with enormous rooms sharing a single bath with hot water. It's not the cleanest place in town and definitely not a first choice. ①

Indio 30 de Marzo 94 ☎586-1201. A good midrange accommodation with private baths, hot showers, mosquito nets and communal courtyard in a fairly quiet location. ③

Latin Quarter Malecón ☎586-2588, ☎586-8646. A modern, box-like building with clean if somewhat soulless rooms, right across the street

from the beach. The enclosed courtyard with pool is a definite plus. Rooms with water views are tempting, but much noisier than those in the back. ④

Porto Fino Av Hermanas Mirabal ☎586-2858, ☎586-5050. Clean and comfortable air-conditioned rooms, way nicer and quieter than the *Victoriano* for only a few bucks more. A kilometre or so from town at the eastern end of the Malecón. ②

Sofy's Bed and Breakfast Las Rosas 3/Ginebra ☎ & ☎586-6411, ✉gillin.n@codetel.net.do. A cozy private home with a hibiscus-filled courtyard patio and two large rooms rented to travellers. Price includes free laundry service and a terrific breakfast, including pancakes, eggs, Canadian bacon, fresh fruit and coffee. ④

Victoriano San Felipe 33 ☎586-9752. The best of the *really* budget options with clean but depressingly plain rooms and warm water. Can be very noisy at night. ②

Playa Dorada

Caribbean Village Club on the Green ☎ 320-1111, 🖷 320-5386, 🖳 www.allegroresorts.com. A collection of unobtrusive two-storey villas scattered around a pleasant garden about as far from the beach as you can get within the resort walls, though the golf course is nearby. The decor is tasteful and the restaurants are excellent, particularly the grill. ⑦

Delta Dorado Club Resort ☎ 320-2019, 🖷 320-3608, 🖳 h.dorado@codetel.net.do. One of the smaller complexes with non-themed buffet food and a reasonable grill restaurant for when you feel like a change. Service levels seem to be pretty variable and the entertainment programme can grate after a while. Nothing special but close enough to the beach and perfectly functional; ideal if you can get a good deal. ⑦

Dorado Club Resort ☎ 320-2019, 🖷 320-3608, 🖳 www.hotetur.com. Quite small by Playa Dorada standards, the *Club Resort* has 165 decent-sized rooms in nine buildings close to both the ocean and the shopping mall. Two à la carte restaurants offer a break from the usual buffet food which can get a bit bland. All non-motorized sporting facilities are included and there's also a great programme for kids. ⑦

Gran Ventana ☎ 320-2111, 🖷 320-2112, 🖳 www.victoriahoteles.com.do. The newest and simply the very best of the resorts in Playa Dorada, though there is the occasional water pressure problem in the bathrooms. The grounds are absolutely gorgeous, with tropical gardens, baroque fountains and meticulously groomed beach, plus extensive sports and impeccable service. In addition to the buffets, you can reserve a table at the top-notch *Octopus* seafood restaurant. ⑦

Inter Clubs Fun Royale/Fun Tropical ☎ 320-4054, 🖷 320-5301, 🖳 www.interclubresorts.com. Two adjacent resorts under a common, Dominican ownership. There's a leaning towards family vacations here with childcare facilities and plenty going to entertain kids of all ages. The *Royale* has slightly larger rooms but be aware that they don't all have balconies. The resorts share the pool areas and restaurants, which certainly adds to the variety, but most of the latter do need to be booked in advance. ⑦

Jack Tar Village ☎ 320-3800, 🖷 320-4161, 🖳 www.allegroresorts.com. The oldest of the Playa Dorada resorts and long highly regarded, though under new management the service isn't what it used to be. Still not bad, considering the two large swimming pools, one with hot tub. For each week you stay here, you're entitled to eat once at each of the à la carte restaurants, which specialize in Caribbean, Italian and seafood respectively. ⑦

Occidental Flamenco Beach Resort ☎ 320-5084, 🖷 320-6319, 🖳 www.occidental-hoteles .com. A set of somewhat weather-beaten faux-Moorish villas that contain large suites with private balconies, some overlooking the ocean. The gardens are delightful but the service is pretty ordinary and some of the facilities need renovation. The buffet food is mediocre. ⑦

Occidental Playa Dorada ☎ 320-3988, 🖷 320-1190, 🖳 www.occidental-hoteles.com. Sister hotel to the *Flamenco Beach* but very different in character. The three-storey building offers the best sea views of the whole complex and the choice of restaurants is appealing too, especially the gourmet *La Palma*. Full watersports package and a great pool to relax by as well. ⑦

Paradise Resort ☎ 320-3663, 🖷 320-4864, 🖳 www.amhsamarina.com. Known for their excellent restaurants (especially *Michelangelo*), sports facilities and children's programme. The rooms and grounds are in perfect condition, and ethnic "theme nights" like Mexican, Chinese and Italian keep the buffet food varied. This is the closest hotel to the beach and it's very popular with the British. ⑦

Playa Naco ☎ 320-6226, 🖷 320-6225. Enormous, glittery prefabricated palace with a large shopping arcade bordering a nice pool area. It's not the grandest of the resorts but the gardens are great, with plenty of features, including a waterfall, and the beach really is only a short walk away. Service is fast and polite and there's a choice of three restaurants, including Mexican and Italian, two bars and a small disco. Some rooms feature kitchenettes. ⑦

Puerto Plata Village ☎ 320-4012, 🖷 320-5113, 🖳 www.ppvillage.com. A large, quiet compound of cottages, supposedly based upon the town of Puerto Plata itself, for those who want to escape the frenzy of the rest of Playa Dorada. The hotel grounds are a bit worn, but the rooms are clean and well maintained, if a little tacky. It's a long walk from the beach but there's unlimited non-motorized watersports when you do get there and it's right by the golf course. In addition to the decent buffet food, guests can dine free at an excellent beachfront pizzeria. No children's programme, though. ⑦

Rhumba Heavens ☎ 562-6725, 🖷 562-0660, 🖳 www.coralhotels.com.do. A mixture of clean but ordinary rooms and larger suites in the heart of the complex. The onsite *Andromeda* disco (p.202) is about the best spot for nightlife in the whole complex and the Italian restaurant also stands out from the crowd. Other than that, all the usual water-sports and facilities and good value for a three-star property. ⑦

Victoria Resort ☎320-1200, ⓕ320-4862, ⓦwww.victoriahoteles.com.do. Generally the cheapest of the Playa Dorada resorts, the *Victoria* is pretty basic with limited watersports facilities and a small pool. It's well kept, with a large tropical garden and palatable buffet food. Being one of the furthest resorts from the beach it's certainly fairly quiet. ⑦

Villas Doradas ☎320-3000, ⓕ320-4790. Another of the smaller complexes but the rooms are large and the usual buffet food is complemented by a choice of Chinese and seafood restaurants that can be visited once a week. All the usual sports and entertainment are available but service levels can vary considerably. Often available at bargain prices and certainly very pleasant if you just want to get a bit of sun on your skin. ⑦

Puerto Plata: the Old City

The once-exclusive **Old City** of Puerto Plata, a compact area bounded by Avenida Colón, the Malecón and Calle López, visually retains much of the Victorian splendour of its past, when it was populated by wealthy landowners, dock workers and European merchants who made their fortunes exporting tobacco and cocoa. The elaborate gingerbread houses they built – Victorian mansions with fanciful ornamentation in the doorframes, window frames and fences, and second-floor balconies with stilt supports – still survive for the most part even though time hasn't been kind to the majority of them.

Fort San Felipe

A good place to begin wandering is the colonial-era **San Felipe** fort (9am–noon & 2–5pm; closed Wed; RD$50), an orange-tinted limestone edifice perched atop a rocky point at the seaside Malecón just west of Avenida Colón. The Spaniards constructed it in 1540 as a defence against corsairs and a prison for smugglers; when the city was torched in 1605, it was the lone struc-

PUERTO PLATA: OLD CITY

ACCOMMODATION

Atlantico	1
Ilra	2
Indio	4
Victoriano	3

EATING & DRINKING

Orión	A
Polanco	C
Roma II	D
Sam's Bar & Grill	B

ture to survive. Once past the phalanx of unnecessary freelance tour guides who now surround it, you can climb up several of the towers and gun turrets, or down into the old prison cells that were in use through the time of Trujillo. Some of the most esteemed figures in Dominican history have been imprisoned here, including Father of the Country Juan Pablo Duarte (incarcerated in 1844 after a bungled attempt to declare himself president) and the husbands of the national martyrs, the Mirabal sisters, who were gunned down by Trujillo's secret police after visiting their spouses in prison. The old prison houses a small **museum** with artefacts such as prisoner's shackles, cannonballs and coins. The museum guard will provide you with an overacted recitation of the fort's history, and will expect an RD$5 donation. Regardless of whether you take advantage of this, be sure to check out the views. During the c.1900 tobacco boom, the harbour to the west was too shallow for boats to dock, and arriving German merchants were carried ashore on the backs of local porters. Today, though, it's been dredged and has a massive, floating power station docked in its centre. You'll find the area to the east more idyllic, where seaside **Parque Luperón** borders the fort, highlighted by a horseback bronze statue of the general who ruled the country for a year from Puerto Plata.

The parque central and around

The heart of the more extensive Victorian city is the **parque central**, at the corner of Separación and Beller, fast-paced focal point for transportation and tourism, where taxis, guaguas, motoconchos and public buses vie for space along the curb. Beside them on the sidewalks are carts selling sugar cane, peeled fruit and all manner of cheap souvenirs. Other vendors crowd the rest of the park, including suited men selling lottery tickets and local tour guides spinning tales of Taino caves just outside town to newcomers. Better to head for the small patches of tranquillity among the shaded benches and the central **gazebo**, a 1960s replica of one that stood here a century earlier.

South of the park across Calle Duarte looms the large **Catedral San Felipe**, which manages to successfully blend Spanish colonial and Art Deco influences. When not in use it's usually locked tight, and the unexciting interior isn't worth the effort it takes to get the caretaker to open it. The remaining three sides of the park are surrounded by some of the best **Victorian architecture** in the city, notably a colossal white gingerbread mansion on the northwest corner that now serves as a Pentecostal church. Its sweeping, elevated first-floor porch spans an entire city block. On the southeast corner, the pink gingerbread at **Separación 22**, former home of a wealthy German merchant, is the city cultural centre and houses occasional local artist exhibits. The old Moorish **town hall** next door, which still serves as the office of the mayor, is the most fanciful of the park's edifices, a battered, dime-store mini-Alhambra adorned with two mock minarets. Stroll down most any nearby street to see more such buildings, though many are in partial or complete disrepair.

If you're looking for a token reminder of the DR to take home, you could do worse than to visit one of the gift and craft shops north of the parque central. The **Canoa**, on Beller, is probably the best of the bunch where, as well as wading through the chaff to find the grain, you'll also get the chance to see some local artists at work.

Museo Ámbar and the mercados

One block east of the parque central on Duarte and Castellanos, the popular **Museo Ámbar** (Mon–Sat 9am–6pm; RD$30) comprises two floors of insects trapped in amber and various other amber-related exhibits in a renovated c.1900 mansion called Villa Berz, built by one of the town's wealthiest German tobacco families. At the entrance, a few artefacts give you a sense of how the family lived: outside of photographs, objects on display include flower-painted porcelain, monogrammed silverware and a colourful, glazed tile corner from the original floor. The second-floor museum, though, is the main draw, a collection culled from the amber mines in the Cordillera Septentrional south of Puerto Plata (see p.248), consisting of Jurassic and Triassic leaves, flowers, spiders, termites, wasps, ants and other insects, along with one small several-million-year-old lizard identical to those on the island today. There's also a gift shop with polished jewellery and chunks of raw amber for sale.

More opportunities for shopping can be found at the old and new markets, several blocks away in opposite directions. The **Mercado Nuevo**, Calle Isabela de Torres and Villanueva (daily 8am–9pm), is housed in a decaying, concrete, star-shaped structure crammed with colourful, crowded stalls. Among the mass-produced Haitian paintings, T-shirts, lewd novelty items and maracas you'll find quality rums, Cuban cigars, and some good wicker furniture, all fairly cheap if you're willing to haggle. The **Mercado Viejo**, at Calle Ureña and Separación (daily 8am–6.30pm; prices not negotiable), spills onto the sidewalk from a series of former private homes and is more utilitarian, containing hardware, furniture, lawn flamingos and a **botánica**, a shop dedicated to syncretist religious items, marked by pictures and icons propped along the outside wall. This is as good as any place to learn about Dominican folk religion; ask and the owner will give you the address of one of the old-fashioned *brujos* who live in the outer barrios, syncretist folk healers who are still a staple of rural Dominican life.

Avenida Colón and around

Avenida Colón marks the Old City's western boundary, with nothing too much of interest beyond it – just the port and the extremely poor barrio Agua Negra. Along Colón you'll find decrepit Victorian warehouses that once held enormous loads of cargo waiting to be shipped to Europe. Despite thorough decay, much of their original ornamentation is still visible, including elegant, dangling icicle awnings on a few. At the corner of Colón and Duarte is the century-old **immigration centre**, a boarded-up one-storey building of crumbling bricks, though plans are in the pipeline to renovate and turn it into a museum. There's not much to see for now except a railroad car that stands on its front lawn as an informal monument to the long-gone railway that transported tobacco from the Cibao region. The former warehouses a block east of Colón along 30 de Marzo are less ornate but better maintained, many having been converted into offices and banks. Back to the east, **Plaza Arawak**, San Felipe and Beller (Mon–Fri 8.30am–5pm), is an office building with a pleasant central plaza that displays a modest collection of stone Taino sculptures known as *cemis*, notable for their grimacing features and inward-spiralling eyes. Discovered just west of Puerto Plata and at Samaná's Cuevas de Agua, the artefacts were physical embodiments of the Taino gods used in ecstatic religious ceremonies.

Puerto Plata: the New City

Puerto Plata's **New City** spreads outward in three directions from the Old, roughly bounded by the port, Circunvalación Sur and Avenida Hermanas

Puerto Plata festivals

Puerto Plata holds the usual Dominican festivals, a **fiesta patronal** – this one in hon-our of patron San Felipe on July 5, featuring large crowds drinking and dancing along the Malecón – and **Carnival**, in February, when hundreds of townsfolk parade around in full regalia and thwack passers-by with inflated balloons. Perhaps better than either of these, however, is the renowned **Merengue Festival** – typically split between a band shell at Long Beach and parties along the Malecón – often held dur-ing the third week of October, though the exact timing varies slightly from year to year.

Mirabal, though additional, less developed barrios exist beyond this convenient circumscription. The majority of the area is taken up by residential neighbour-hoods and heavy industry, and particular sights of interest lie much further apart than in the Old City, so you'll need to take a motoconcho or taxi to get from place to place.

The centre of social life is the two-kilometre-long **Malecón**, a sunny, spa-cious boardwalk lined with hotels and all manner of commerce. During the day it's a popular spot for locals to hang out, lie on the beach and picnic. At night a strip of bars opens up along with numerous restaurants and outdoor shacks selling Dominican fast food. At one time the entire boulevard was packed with these food stands, but police crackdowns – misguided attempts to beautify the promenade – have thinned things out considerably. Most of the new breed stick to bicycle carts, making it easier to flee. The Malecón begins at **Long Beach**, on the town's far eastern end, not the most picturesque beach by any stretch, but with a convivial mood, peopled largely by merengue-blar-ing teens. Behind the sand is a concrete plaza with a tower you can climb for a wide-angle view of the coast, although this is probably not the place to hang around after dark. A row of **outdoor bars** extends for several hundred metres down Avenida Hermanas Mirabal, quite fun at night, though increasingly the domain of prostitutes.

Just east of Hermanas Mirabal is the **Brugal Rum bottling factory**, Circunvalación Sur across from the Plaza Turisol (Mon–Fri 9am–noon & 2–3.30pm; free), a popular stop-off for tourists, though really little more than a PR exercise for this local rum company. Better than the quick glance at the bottling and packing operations are the free rum-based margaritas on the out-door patio that follow the tour.

Puerto Plata's crowning attraction is the suspended **cable car ride** (Mon–Sat 8.30am–3.30pm; RD$50) that goes to the top of Mount Isabela de Torres. The entrance is at the far western end of town past the port, just off the Circunvalación Sur on Avenida Teleférico. Though the ride has been only spo-radically operational over the last few years, it had been running reliably for some time at the time of writing. It's definitely not to be missed; the views of the city on this 25-minute trip are stupendous. At the summit a statue of **Christ the Redeemer**, a slightly downsized version of the Río de Janeiro landmark with its arms spread out over the city, crowns a manicured lawn. Also on the grounds are a tropical garden, a pricey café and a souvenir shop. The mountain is now a protected national park, covered by rainforest on its far side and inhabited by 32 species of indigenous birds. Don't wander too far beyond the area marked off for tourists, as Mount Isabela is in the process of splitting in two. The brown splotch along its face, visible from the city, is a landslide cre-ated by the split, and there are a number of deep fissures at the summit.

Climbing Mount Isabela

Climbing Mount Isabela de Torres is a challenge that some can't resist, especially attractive when the cable car isn't running. Iguana Mama (℡571-0908, ℻571-0734, ⓦwww.iguanamama.com), an adventure outfit based in Cabarete, features regular hiking excursions to the top that commence in Puerto Plata. If you want to make the trek on your own, there's a well-marked path on the opposite side of the mountain, starting at the pueblo **El Cupey**. Head east on the C-5 to the junction of the Carretera Turística and turn right. Just beyond the intersection is a marked dirt road leading to the pueblo – an isolated outpost tucked between two mountains and with few facilities, though a couple of local farmers do rent horses and guides for the ascent. The Isabela hike is an arduous four-hour trek one way through a canopy of rainforest, so you'll have to start early. If lucky you may catch sight of the endangered Hispaniola parrot or the red-tailed hawk. There's also a small system of **Taino caves** with petroglyphs near the summit, an hour's hike west off the main path. Look for a guide in El Cupey if you want to see them; either trip should cost you no more than RD$250. Another great hike from the town is the trail that leads away from Mount Isabela up to the Río Camú and **La Cueva del Gallo**, an underground river cave several hundred metres long that traverses the side of the mountain to the south of El Cupey. Just 3km from the pueblo, it's a less rugged hike than the Isabela trek and can be done in half a day.

Playa Dorada

PLAYA DORADA, just 1km east of Puerto Plata on the C-5 but truly a world away, is walled off from the outside universe; inside its confines are fourteen separate resorts, each an entity unto itself, with restaurants, discos, swimming pools, hot tubs and an array of sports facilities. Meandering between them is one of the best golf courses in the country, designed by Robert Trent Jones. Frequented by a half-million package tourists per year (the majority of them from Canada and Europe), Playa Dorada is the perfect place to lie for a few days on a hassle-free beach, though those seeking more than a cruise ship on sand may find its alluring promotion campaign – like the city of gold for which it was named – a mirage.

The **beach** is the main draw, 2km of impeccably white sand from which you're treated to terrific views of Mount Isabela. The **hotels** offer a variety of activities that take up much of the space, including beach volleyball, spaghetti-eating contests, merengue lessons, parasailing and group aerobics. All of this plus the numerous local souvenir vendors and hair braiders makes for a frenetic scene, but there are still places reserved for tranquil sun worship. It's standard practice here to reserve a beach chair or a spot near the swimming pools by laying down your towel, so best follow suit early in the morning if you want a prime spot.

Even if you're not staying at Playa Dorada, getting through the front gate should be no problem; choose either from the two easy points of sneak entry onto the beach, one beside the *Dorada Naco* complex and the other just east of the *Playa Dorada Hotel*, or from the array of **day passes**, available from each resort, from US$45 to US$60, and entitling you to five hours on the grounds, including meals and drinks.

Costambar

Costambar, 1km west of Puerto Plata on the C-5, is a rambling settlement of townhouses and private homes, timeshared, rented or owned by expats and well-to-do Dominicans. Once you make your way through a spaghetti bowl of ever-curling lanes, you'll find a lightly populated **beach** far better than the one in Puerto Plata, though it offers little shade. Only an RD$30 motoconcho ride from the parque central, it has a couple of restaurants right on the water offering pizza and sandwiches, and views across the harbour of the city lights are an added bonus at night.

Eating

Puerto Plata has several outstanding **restaurants**, from mom-and-pop rice-and-bean *comedores* and burger shacks to upmarket places offering mouth-watering, budget-busting international cuisine; most of them are scattered within the Old City and along the Malecón. Those on a tight **budget** can also try one of the plentiful and cheap food shacks that line the Malecón. If staying at an all-inclusive at Playa Dorada, you're restricted to whatever restaurant is run by your hotel. The quality of the buffet food is generally bearable but tasteless; however, at most of the Playa Dorada hotels you also have the option of eating at a better à la carte restaurant – seating at these is limited, so you should make a reservation very early in the morning. The mid-range restaurants that dot Costambar are also a good option for dinner. If cooking for yourself, look for **groceries** in town at Supermercado Messon, Separación 35 (daily 8am–noon & 2–7pm), and José Luis, Calle Circunvalación Sur Km 2 (same hours). Phone numbers are provided for restaurants where there's a chance you'll need reservations.

Puerto Plata

Acuarela Professor Certad 3 ☎586-5314. Expensive by Dominican standards but more than worth it; in the elegant dining room, feast on outstanding international dishes like rack of lamb, lobster *criolla*, garlic shrimp and *lambí*. Don't arrive in T-shirt or shorts.
Aguaceros Malecón 32. Dominican dishes served in a festive, oceanfront barn. The *lambí* is reasonably priced and as good as in the more expensive restaurants.
Barco's Malecón 6. A great people-watching spot on the Malecón with a sidewalk patio and a second-floor terrace. They serve good pizzas, lamb and goat dishes, along with steak *criolla* and grilled dorada.
Cafe Cito Sosúa Highway Km4 ☎586-7923. The best restaurant in town has recently moved and is now situated 500m west of Playa Dorada. Great food – try the filet mignon (RD$160) or the curried chicken (RD$110) – and a pleasant accompaniment of jazz or blues.

Jamvi's Malecón 18. Clean and efficient pizza joint right by the beach with a children's playground and a terrace above that makes a great spot for watching the world go by. A pie runs around RD$70.
Jardin Suizo Malecón 13 ☎586-9564. Top-end international fare in a smart but relaxed building close to the water's edge. The seafood specials include excellent tuna steaks.
Polanco Calle Kennedy and Ariza. Quality budget Dominican fare served in an open-air enclosure near the parque central. Also a good spot for breakfast.
Roma II Beller 43 ☎586-8358. Tasty international food with Italian dishes dominating the menu. The lasagne is spot-on and there are plenty of seafood choices too. One of the smartest options in town, so best to book ahead.
Sam's Bar and Grill Ariza 34. Established meeting place for fellow travellers, with good-value daily specials. The philly cheesesteak, made with filet mignon, is highly recommended. American breakfasts served as well.

Costambar

El Carey Beach Bar Costambar Beach. A bustling lunch spot on the beach, good for burgers, soft-shell tacos and grilled fish.

Le Café Main Costambar Rd. Trendy terrace café on the main road into Costambar, with the standard fare and a TV devoted to sports.

Pizzeria Sole Mio Costambar Beach. Easily the best pizza you'll find in these parts and a great bargain. Tables are right on the beach.

El Portal Costambar main entrance. Excellent home-cooked Dominican fare in a thatch-roofed patio setting at the Costambar gate. The fish is tender and fresh, and the *sancocho* and *mofongo* are sublime.

Drinking and nightlife

Fed by a metropolis full of dance-crazy Dominicans and vacationing foreign hordes, a slew of Puerto Plata **nightlife** establishments are crammed with dancers until dawn. You won't find a lot of local live music, but big-name merengue acts come through the major discos on a regular basis. The bar scene is dominated by expat establishments, which can be fun places to meet some colourful characters. In addition to the clubs listed below, the outlying barrios south of the Circunvalación Sur generally feature a small *colmado* equipped with cassette player, tables and chairs, providing a more laid-back rural feel.

While **Playa Dorada** resorts and their restaurants are off limits to non-guests, the discos are open to all. Most, though, are pretty boring and half-empty; try one of those listed below, which are more often than not crowded with a mix of foreign visitors and Dominicans.

Puerto Plata

La Barrica Circunvalación Sur 35/Av Colón. Hip, strictly Dominican music disco catering mostly to indigenous city-dwellers cutting vicious moves. There are no lights in the entire club – the waiters use flashlights. The standard drink order is *Cuba libre servicio*: two cokes, one bottle of dark rum and a pitcher of ice.

Cafe Cito Sosúa Highway Km4. You're more likely to hear Billie Holiday or Charlie Parker than merengue or *bachata* in this ambient restaurant. They serve the best mixed drinks in town, including positively addictive "rum mudslides".

Frank's Av Hermanas Mirabal. Iranian-owned outdoor biker bar just south of Long Beach. Merengue pours out of the radio, pedestrian traffic glides along the street, and the long-suffering bartender clangs a large bell every time she gets a tip. Avoid mixed drinks with "fruit juice", which are made with Tang.

Orión 30 de Marzo and 12 de Julio. Slightly seedy and intimidating, but the most popular dance spot in town, featuring strictly merengue and *bachata*.

Playa Dorada

Andromeda *Rhumba Heavens Hotel.* Large, modern dance floor with mostly Dominican music despite the foreign clientele. Has a meat-market reputation.

Crazy Moon *Paradise Resort.* Dark, purple neon nightclub mixing the occasional merengue with a healthy dose of techno and pop.

Hemingway's Cafe *Playa Dorada Plaza.* Haven for crazed drunken tourists intent on having a good time. Friday's ear-splitting karaoke night is the most popular; Thursdays and Saturdays feature a good rock'n'roll band. The food is good but expensive.

Sports and entertainment

Puerto Plata is no cultural centre, but there are plenty of diversions for those willing to keep their expectations down. Foremost among the more lowbrow activities are **spectator sports**, particularly professional **baseball** games – held between November and early February – at the Puerto Plata Baseball Stadium, intersection of Circunvalación Sur and avenidas Ginebra and Hermanas Mirabal. The games are memorable for the operatic passion of the crowd as much as the high level of play; teams usually include a few American players and are coached by big-name, retired Dominican stars (see p.357 for more on baseball's importance in the DR). Advance purchase of tickets isn't usually necessary; consult the posted schedules at the stadium or the parque central gazebo for game times.

There are two *club gallísticos* with regular **cockfighting** – one at Parque Duarte on Calle Hernández (Tues & Sun 2–6pm), the other on Circunvalación Sur across the street from the Brugal Rum plant (Fri–Sun 1.30–5.30pm). If you don't want to be a spectator, **golf** is a popular option; Costambar has a modest nine-hole course, but virtually everyone goes to the magnificent Robert Trent Jones course at Playa Dorada (☎320-3803), with exquisitely maintained lawns and several holes set on the ocean. The price is RD\$450 for eighteen holes, RD\$350 for a cart and around RD\$200 for the required caddie.

More sedentary pastimes include Cine Roma, Beller 35 (no phone; RD\$30), a recently refurbished and noisy **cinema**, featuring subtitled second-run American shows daily at 5.30pm and 8.30pm. There are also three large, neon **casinos** in Playa Dorada at *Paradise Resort*, *Playa Dorada Hotel* and *Jack Tar Village*, all with the same standard set of slot machines, blackjack, roulette and craps tables. All are open from 4pm to 4am.

Listings

Airlines Air Santo Domingo (☎586-0385); American (☎542-5151); Continental (☎541-2000); LTU (☎586-0281); Martin Air Holland (☎586-0289).

Ambulance Dial 911 in case of emergency.

Banks and currency exchange The following banks all have 24-hour ATMs: Banco Popular, Calle Duarte at parque central (Mon–Fri 9am–5pm); Banco Mercantil, Calle Separación at parque central (Mon–Fri 9am–5pm); Scotia Bank, Calle Beller and San Felipe (Mon–Fri 9.30am–5pm). The best rates for currency exchange are at the shop above the Cibao Fine Gift Centre, 12 de Julio and Ariza (Mon–Sat 9am–5.30pm).

Car rental Reputable operators at the airport include Alamo (☎586-1444); Avis (☎586-4436); Budget (☎586-0284); National (☎586-0285).

Consulates Canadian Consulate, Beller (Mon–Fri 9am–5pm, ☎586-5761); UK Consulate, Beller 51 (Mon–Fri 9am–5pm; ☎586-4244); US Consulate, 12 de Julio 55 (Mon–Fri 9am–5pm; ☎586-3143).

Dental Clínica Dental, Calle Duarte (☎971-5689), is open 24 hours.

Film processing Foto Plaza at the Plaza Turisol, Av Circunvalación Km 2, has one-hour developing for RD\$50.

Hospital Clínica Dr José Gregora Hernández, 27 de Febrero 21 (☎586-1166); Clínica Dr Brugal,

Ariza 15 and Kennedy (☎586-2519). Both have 24-hour emergency facilities.

Internet You can get access for RD\$35/hr at *Sam's Bar and Grill*, Ariza 34 (daily 9am–midnight). Also available at @Internet Connection, on Separación south of the parque central.

Laundry Most hotels have laundry service; otherwise, go to Lavendería Rosa, on Circunvalación Sur, just west of Brugal Rum (Mon–Sat 8am–6.30pm).

Pharmacy Of the numerous pharmacies scattered around town, the best-stocked is Pharmacia Drugstore Popular, Kennedy and José Ramón López (open 24 hours).

Police Central station at Carretera 5 Km 1 (☎586-2331).

Post office Puerto Plata has an inordinately efficient postal service; main office is on the corner of 12 de Julio and Separación. EPS is at Carretera 5 Km 3, Plaza Turisol (☎586-7185).

Telephone Televimenca, Kennedy and José Ramón López (Mon–Sat 8am–10pm; closed Sun); Tricom, 27 de Febrero 45 (daily 8am–10pm).

Travel agents Cafemba Tours, Separación 12 (☎586-2177); Viatur, Beller 116 (☎586-2990).

Wiring money Western Union, Kennedy and Ariza, is in a furniture store near the parque central (Mon–Fri 8am–5pm, Sat 8am–3pm).

Around Puerto Plata: Cofresí, Ríu Merengue and Ríu Mambo

A small group of resort complexes lie along the coast just west of Puerto Plata. From Costambar, it's 2km to **Playa Cofresí**, named for an infamous Puerto Rican pirate Roberto Cofresí (born Robert Kupferstein), though there's no documented link between them. Once backed by a small fishing village, Cofresí is one of the most stunning beaches on the island, home to the deluxe *Hacienda Resort* (☎586-1227, ℗970-7100; ➐), a complex of five separate hotels; of these the *Villas* is best and by far the most expensive, while *Tropical* has the best food and location of the other four. The ocean near here gets extremely choppy, better for bodysurfing and boogie-boarding than a pleasant swim. For better food than you'll find at the hotel restaurants, walk about ten minutes west down the beach to *Chris and Mady's*, a casual eatery with excellent sandwiches and seafood, including boiled lobster and grilled mahimahi; or across the highway to more formal *Papillon*, with a varied and ever-changing Sunday brunch menu.

Just beyond Cofresí on the C-5 are two resorts, **Ríu Merengue** (☎320-4000, ℗320-5555, ⓦwww.riu.com; ➐), and **Ríu Mambo** (☎320-1212, ℗320-1118, ⓦwww.riu.com; ➐), a steadily growing hotel complex owned by the same company. Ongoing construction detracts from the peacefulness, but the grounds are still pretty, with a nice beach, tennis courts, horseback riding, watersports, children's facilities and a row of mock gingerbread souvenir shops – plus the best deal on **day passes** of the area's all-inclusives, US$50 for a pass that lasts from 9am to 9pm, encompassing all three meals and drinks. Of the restaurants, *Macumba* is by far the best – and you're allowed to eat there every night provided you make reservations very early in the morning. Just west of the resorts, the fishing village **Maimón** has its own small beach, accessible via the C-5's Guzmancito turnoff.

East of Puerto Plata

Resort development around Puerto Plata has gobbled up most of the prime beachfront east of the city; as such, you'll have to trawl the coast all the way to **Río San Juan**, some 70km away, to find anything approaching unspoilt coastline – though even that may be on its way towards being developed. If you're up for a bustling resort town with some adventure sports, though, you couldn't do better than burgeoning **Cabarete**, a windsurfing enclave that's quickly being swallowed by tourism construction. Just west of Cabarete, **Sosúa** is a bit less appealing, but does boast three separate beaches, plus a plethora of hotels, restaurants and nightspots. Wherever you go, there are plenty of hidden pleasures in the **Cordillera Septentrional** mountains that border the coast, including a secluded gourmet Indian restaurant, several horse ranches with rides into mountain wilderness and cascade trips down a steep waterfall.

Sosúa

Set along a sheltering horseshoe inlet impressed into the eastern end of Bahía de Sosúa, the large resort town of **SOSÚA** has a bit of a bumpy history, somewhat hard to detect without some exploration as few visitors make it past the inviting beaches. It was created in the late nineteenth century by the **United Fruit Company**, who used it as a port for their extensive banana plantations along today's El Choco Road. In 1916, United Fruit abruptly abandoned their operations in the Dominican Republic, and Sosúa lay mainly derelict until the early 1940s, when Trujillo provided refuge for several hundred Jews fleeing from Nazi Germany. In truth this was no great philanthropic gesture on his part, more a convenient element of his vision to both stimulate agriculture and "whiten" the Dominican population. The refugees settled just east of Playa Sosúa and created the barrio known as El Batey, where they formed a successful dairy farming co-operative – Productos Sosúa – which operates to this day.

The first stirrings of tourism came in the 1970s, when wealthy Dominicans and retiring foreigners attracted to its fine sands turned it into a centre for winter beach homes. The real boom began in the 1980s with the explosion of **sex tourism**, with tens of thousands of travellers coming exclusively for the prostitution: hundreds of young Dominican women from the outlying rural districts worked here to support families back home. Massive hotel build-up ensued, and much of the traditional fishing and agriculture was abandoned. This kind of atmosphere did not sit well with the wealthy retirees who had bought beach homes in town, and after several years of petitioning the government, they convinced President Fernández to act. In 1996, the national police poured into Sosúa and shut down every bar in the city for a year; with its controversial lifeblood squeezed dry, the local economy promptly collapsed leaving an abundance of empty hotel rooms and restaurants with no clientele. Slowly but surely the town has risen from its ashes, helped in no small part by

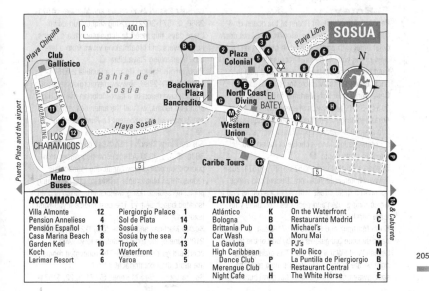

ACCOMMODATION

Villa Almonte	12	Piergiorgio Palace	1
Pension Anneliese	4	Sol de Plata	14
Pensión Español	11	Sosúa	9
Casa Marina Beach	8	Sosúa by the sea	7
Garden Keti	10	Tropix	13
Koch	2	Waterfront	3
Larimar Resort	6	Yaroa	5

EATING AND DRINKING

Atlántico	K	On the Waterfront	A
Bologna	B	Restaurante Madrid	C
Brittania Pub	O	Michael's	I
Car Wash	Q	Moru Mai	G
La Gaviota	F	PJ's	
High Caribbean		Pollo Rico	N
Dance Club	P	La Puntilla de Piergiorgio	B
Merengue Club	L	Restaurant Central	J
Night Cafe	H	The White Horse	E

low prices but also because it really is a pleasant little town with a great beach. Today, it's buzzing with tourists again and while not completely devoid of prostitution, it's no more noticeable here than in any other Dominican resort.

Arrival, orientation and getting around

Many who come here arrive directly from **Aeropuerto Internacional Luperón**, 9km west (see p.192). **Taxis** into town should cost around RD$150. You can also take a **motoconcho** for RD$50, or walk onto the C-5 and flag down a **guagua** for RD$20. The **bus stations** are on the C-5 at the town entrance, and if you don't fancy walking the rest of the way, you'll find plenty of taxis and motoconchos waiting.

Sosúa is divided in two by 500-metre-wide Playa Sosúa and the bay in front of it. **Los Charamicos** to the west is a traditional Dominican neighbourhood, with two entrances from the C-5 at its eastern and western ends – both of them crowded with motoconchos. At the east entrance you'll find the informal stations for Caribe Tours and Transporte del Cibao. East of Playa Sosúa, **El Batey** was the Jewish quarter and is now the tourism hub. There is one entrance to it from the C-5, marked by a Texaco station. Walking is your best option for **getting around** within the neighbourhoods. For travel between the two barrios, motoconchos are more convenient and very cheap; you should have no trouble finding one at the C-5 town entrances or in El Batey. For travel further out, there's the El Batey taxi stand, corner of Martínez and Pedro Clisante. Rates are posted on the operator's booth.

Accommodation

Sosúa has plenty of **accommodation** options, and many of those hotels have more than their share of empty rooms. For this reason, prices in all but the all-inclusive resorts tend to be negotiable, even in high season. Most tourist hotels are in El Batey, but there are also several budget options in Los Charamicos.

El Batey

Pension Anneliese Dr Rosén at the ocean ☎ & ℻ 571-2208, ✉ analise.pension@codetel.net.do. A quiet hotel with pretty, fenced-in grounds and a view of the water. The large rooms have ocean-front balconies, and there's a secluded pool in back. Breakfast is available for RD$60. ❹

Casa Marina Beach Martínez ☎ 571-3690, ℻ 571-3110, ⓦ www.amshamarina.com. Amazingly large all-inclusive complex squeezed into a small beachfront plot. Usual high standard accommodations and a choice of Italian and Mexican restaurants. ❼

Garden Keti Dr Rosén ☎ 571-1557, ℻ 571-2055, ⓦ www.hotelgardenketi.com. Decent mid-range option in a quiet street, with spacious rooms and a welcoming garden and pool area, complete with tame parakeets. ❹

Koch Martínez and Duarte ☎ 571-2284. Clean, basic seaside bungalows run by one of the former Jewish World War II refugees. The grounds are right on the water at the town's most peaceful spot, away from the traffic and general bustle. ❷

Larimar Resort Av Kunhardt and Martínez ☎ 571-2868, ℻ 571-3022. Looking slightly run-down these days, this resort features modern a/c rooms, hot showers and breathtaking views from a terrace overlooking Playa Libre. ❺

Piergiorgio Palace Hotel La Puntilla 2 ☎ 571-2215, ℻ 571-2786, ⓦ www.piergiorgiohotel.com. All-inclusive resort in a faux-Victorian manor. High-standard rooms, with all the amenities, and two meals daily at the excellent La Puntilla restaurant. ❼

Sol de Plata Beach Resort Carretera 5 ☎ 571-3600, ℻ 571-3380. All-inclusive beachfront compound 2km east of town, featuring immaculate rooms, three restaurants, tennis courts, swimming pools, horseback riding, watersports, disco and an isolated beach setting. The best choice if you want luxury. ❻

Sosúa Martínez and Duarte ☎ 571-2683, ℻ 571-2180. One of the oldest hotels in town, with a courtyard garden and pool. The renovated rooms are more than comfortable. ❹

Sosúa by the Sea Martínez ☎ 571-3222, ℻ 571-

3020. Very clean and tidy all-inclusive with a decent strip of beach and a selection of airy air-conditioned rooms. Not as nice as the *Casa Marina* but good value nonetheless. ⑤

Tropix Libre near C-5 ☎ & ⓕ 571-2291, ⓦ www.tropixhotel.com. Small and intimate hotel run by the descendant of one of the original settlers. Ten cosy rooms, including a few suites that sleep up to five. Extras include ceiling fans, refrigerators, use of a shared kitchen and a shady pool area. ④

Waterfront Dr Rosén 1 ☎ 571-2760, ⓕ 571-3586, ⓦ www.hotelwaterfront.com. Modern bungalows with private hot-water bath in a stunning position just off the sea. The sweeping ocean terrace with swimming pool is a big plus. ④

Yaroa Dr Rosén ☎ 571-2651, ⓕ 571-3814, ⓦ www.hotelyaroa.com. Quiet hotel near the waterfront. A restful pool area and decent-sized air-conditioned rooms make it good value. ④

Los Charamicos

Pensión Español Calle Prica ☎ 571-3187. Decent rooms on the top floor of a local family's three-storey home with shared, cold-water bath. ①

Villa Almonte Calle Arzeno at beach entrance ☎ 571-2256. Several spacious apartments – some with kitchens and balconies with water views – that vary in size and price. Easily the best value in the barrio. ②

El Batey

El Batey maintains a bright and somewhat jovial disposition despite its troublesome past. The main epicentre follows **Calle Pedro Clisante** west from **Calle Dr Rosén** to **Calle Duarte**, with most of the action focused on and around the junction. The surrounding streets are peaceful and tidy with well-established gardens, and in recent years malls have been going up in place of some of the town's oldest buildings. The biggest such changes have been the demolition of the original **United Fruit Company warehouse**, at the western end of Duarte and its replacement with banks and stores, and the old **Refugees Barracks** on the junction of Martínez (not to be confused with Martínez 1) and Duarte.

The Jewish legacy still remains, though, and one block east of Duarte, on Martínez and Dr Rosén, you'll find the old **synagogue**, a simple wooden structure adorned with a 50-year-old Star of David, and still used by a number of practising Jewish-Dominican descendants of the settlers. There's a small museum attached, **El Museo de Sosúa** (Mon–Thurs & Sun 6–11pm; free), which recounts the early experiences of the refugees and the development of the agricultural co-operative through photographs and a few of the settlers' personal effects. The settlers' enormous pasteurizing plant is next door and still in operation; indeed, Productos Sosúa remains the largest dairy producer on the island.

East of the dairy plant, a walkway leads to **Playa Libre** and its all-inclusive hotels. A several-hundred-metre sandy cove enclosed by a cliff, the beach has become a haven for package tourists who want to avoid the hassles of Playa Sosúa. Atop the cliff is a large, communal **terrace**, a pleasant place from which to admire the bay.

Playa Sosúa

Crescent-shaped and bounded by cliffs, 250-metre-long **Playa Sosúa** separates the town's two barrios. The small bay's water is completely placid and transparent, a contrast to the crowded beach and, just behind the sand, the busy row of bars, lobster-tank restaurants and souvenir shops, with some colourful, itinerant vendors lurking among them. Some stalls rent snorkelling equipment for the **reef** just outside the inlet, which isn't especially spectacular but does hold some tropical fish. For better snorkelling options, contact the local Northern Coast Divers shop (see box on p.208).

Diving from Sosúa

Sosúa is home to one of the finest diving outfits on the Island, **Northern Coast Divers**, Pedro Clisante 8 (T571-1028, F571-3883, Wwww.northerncoastdiving .com). The multi-lingual staff run daily boat trips to several local hot spots, including the Airport Wall, a 33-metre wall dive with tunnels, and The Canyon, two walls formed by the splitting of the reef only 2m apart. They also head further afield to the mangroves of Río San Juan (see p.218) and the Caverns of Cabrera. First-timer dives start from US$60, with PADI Open Water courses from US$325. The shop can also arrange **snorkelling** trips as well as pickups from nearby resorts.

Los Charamicos

West of Playa Sosúa spreads the Dominican barrio of **Los Charamicos**, a tangle of narrow streets lined by musky shacks selling food supplies and rum, motoconchos manoeuvring past stickball-playing children, and some of the older locals taking it all in from their front-door stoops. **Calle Arzeno** skirts the barrio's eastern edge, boasting several good open-air restaurants and great views of the beach below. At the far western end of town on Calle Morris Ling, the local **cockfighting arena**, Club Gallístico Los Charamicos (Tues & Sat 3–7pm; RD$60 for gallery standing room, RD$100 for a ground-floor seat), is undoubtedly one of the most authentic places to observe this violent ritual and the enthusiastic crowds it attracts. Four blocks east, Calle Playa Chiquita turns sharply down to rubbish-strewn **Playa Chiquita**, the locals' beach of choice, full of families and teens barbecuing pigs over bonfires and engaging in general merriment. Sosúa's **fiesta patronal**, in honour of San Antonio, is held on June 13 in Los Charamicos.

Eating

Sosúa's tourist-heavy days have left it with more than its share of **restaurants**, from the simple *pica pollo* establishments in Los Charamicos to reasonable seafood spots and elegant waterfront dining rooms. Also around Los Charamicos are several stand-up **cafeterias** serving typical Dominican meals at around RD$30; best to go during lunchtime, when the food is freshest. Elsewhere, prices are fairly reasonable, and reservations are rarely necessary, even in the best eateries. The largest supermarket is El Batey's Supermercado Playero, on Calle Duarte (daily 8.30am–6pm), but you'll find far cheaper groceries in the many small shops of Los Charamicos.

El Batey

Bologna Martínez/Ayuntamiental. Lively patio restaurant serving up some excellent staple Italian dishes and pizza at very good prices.

La Gaviota Calle Duarte just south of Clisante. Moderately priced Italian restaurant dishing up good meals in an open-air, intimate candlelit setting.

Moru Mai Pedro Clisante. Decent affordable international fare in a smartly decorated diner. The chic and convivial atmosphere makes it popular with the twentysomething crowd, and the service is excellent.

Night Cafe Av Kunhardt just south of Clisante. An unassuming spot with home-cooked *cómida criolla* and great breakfasts with fresh-squeezed juice.

On the Waterfront Dr Rosén 1. Terrific seafood restaurant on a sweeping oceanfront patio; choose from fresh lobster, red snapper, sea bass, *lambí* and calamari. Not as pretentious as *La Puntilla* but just as good, with main courses from around RD$150.

PJ's Duarte and Clisante. A popular, unpretentious burger establishment located on the busiest corner in town. The outdoor patio is particularly good for people-watching.

Pollo Rico Dr Rosén and Clisante. High-turnover fried chicken joint that serves good, cheap food into the early hours. Lively and even rowdy at times.

La Puntilla de Piergiorgio La Puntilla 1. Sosúa's best-known restaurant, though standards have slipped in the past few years. Set along a series of seven grand waterfront patios that afford jaw-dropping sunsets; the seafood is usually the best choice, particularly lobster. It's the dearest option in town, though a free aperitif is included in the meal.

Restaurante Madrid Dr Rosén 6. Cosy and immaculate Spanish-inspired dining room just up from the seafront. Lobster in Spanish sauce (RD$195) is the highlight of an extensive menu.

The White Horse Duarte and Martínez. Internet café (RD$15 for 15min) with a few outdoor tables on a lively street corner and the best cappuccinos in town.

Los Charamicos

Atlántico Arzeno at beach entrance. Popular seafood restaurant and bar with great views that attracts crowds from the beach.

Michael's Arzeno at beach entrance. Good, inexpensive seafood spot frequented mostly by locals, with a pleasant, low-key atmosphere and more great views of the beach. Fish of the day specials are good value.

Restaurant Central Kunhardt and Arzeno. A phenomenally popular little Dominican fish restaurant. It's well worth the wait (up to a half-hour), though, for the specialities with *criolla* sauce.

Drinking and nightlife

The **discos** and **bars** of Sosúa have slowly reopened over the past few years, and dark, ear-throbbing clubs and boozy German beer halls once more dominate the western end of Pedro Clisante. If you want to see **live music**, stay on the lookout for the banners that are spread across the streets whenever a good merengue band comes to town.

Brittania Pub Clisante and Dr Rosén. Rowdy, narrow English pub catering to tourists; somewhat nondescript, but still a decent place for a few drinks.

Car Wash Carretera 5 at El Batey entrance. Reputable pool hall with no hustlers. Play is free, so it's possible to nurse a beer and shoot for hours.

Dollaras Calle Príncipe, Pueblo Monte Llano. Located 10km west of town, just off the Carretera 5 in the town of Monte Llano, this friendly rural Dominican *típico* disco is frequented by field hands and factory workers after a hard day's labour. A perfect place to see how people in the pueblos kick back.

High Caribbean Dance Club Clisante and Martínez, just east of town. High-tech nightclub with a circular dance floor and an indoor swimming pool, around which patrons gather to sip their drinks.

Merengue Club Clisante and Dr Rosén. Outdoor dance floor, meat market and bar with a second-floor terrace from which to watch the action. Things don't get hopping until after 2am.

Willy's Carretera 5, 1km west of El Batey entrance. Welcome to Hell. This garish disco features long wooden snakes carved into the walls, with glowing red eyes, along with various other ostensibly Satanic touches.

Around Sosúa

A couple of kilometres west of town along the Carretera 5 is the **Columbus Aquapark** (daily 10am–6pm; RD$150 for a full day, RD$90 after 1pm; ☎571-2642), an impressive water park with 25 different rides, including a number of slides and a thrill ride that hurls you through pitch darkness. There are also two dramatic high drops and a slower, winding raft ride that traverses the length of the park. It's best to go on weekdays, when the place is less crowded.

Five kilometres further west on the C-5, the rural sugar town of **Monte Llano** holds a Haitian sugar-cane *batey* and an enormous mill. The **sugar refinery** is worth visiting if interested in the industry. Here you'll see the cane hauled into the factory on enormous carts followed by the two-fold extraction process: the bundles of cane are laid out flat on a press and squashed, then the pulp is soaked in water for a few hours and re-mashed. The waste material is used as fuel for the factory's furnace. The only way that you'll get into the plant is through Extra Tours (℡571-3106; RD$600) in Sosúa, who stop here on one of their jeep tours. Otherwise, the town's only other real draw is the annual **Semana Santa** proceedings, during which a traditional Haitian *gagá* celebration (see p.127) takes place.

A well-marked turnoff just south of Monte Llano leads to the **Carretera Turística**, a scenic road that winds past lush coconut plantations, rivers and remote mountain pueblos on the way to Santiago. Tiny **Tubeagua**, 18km down the road, has no real facilities or tourist structure, but if you're interested in **caving**, this is the place. Be warned, though, the extensive underground system, accessible via a dirt path from the town, is totally uncharted and should only be approached with the aid of a local guide – ask at the town's small *colmado* on the main road.

Listings

Banks and currency exchange The large Banco Popular (Mon–Fri 8.30am–5pm) is in one of the old refugee barracks on Calle Martínez just off Duarte. It exchanges currency and has a 24-hour ATM machine. The new Bancredito, Pedro Clisante and Duarte (Mon–Fri 9am–5.30pm), also has an ATM. If looking to change money on weekends, there are a number of storefront exchanges on Calle Duarte and Pedro Clisante.

Car rental Best bets are the international companies located at the airport. There are, though, a few reliable agencies in town, including Honda (℡571-3690); El Chaval (℡571-2160); Freddy's (℡571-3146); and Lucho (℡571-3596).

Emergency Dial ℡911

Film processing The most dependable place to buy or get film developed is Planet Foto, on Duarte, just south of Clisante.

Internet *The White Horse* café (see p.209).

Laundry Lavendería Agua Azul, Pedro Clisante, just east of main entrance (Mon–Sat 8.30am–6pm; RD$70 per load).

Medical Servi-Med, Beach Rd, El Batey (Mon–Fri 9am–5pm & 24-hour emergency; ℡571-0964).

Pharmacy Farmacia Sosúa, Pedro Clisante (Mon–Sat 8am–7pm).

Police The police station is at the entrance to El Batey across the street from the Texaco station.

Post office Instead of chancing the main office's erratic service, head to EPS, Sosúa Business Services, Pedro Clisante 12 (℡571-3451).

Telephone Codetel has a monopoly here; offices are located in El Batey at Calle Martínez and in Los Charamicos next to Caribe Tours on the C-5, at the entrance to the barrio.

Travel agents Melissa Tours, Calle Duarte 2 (℡571-2567), operates a number of tours across the island, and can help you make travel arrangements and flight changes.

Wiring money There's a Western Union on Carretera 5 at the El Batey entrance (Mon–Sat 9am–5pm).

Cabarete

Stretched along the C-5 between the beach and lagoon that bear its name, **CABARETE** is a crowded international enclave that owes its existence almost entirely to **windsurfing**. There was no town to speak of in 1984 when legendary windsurfer Jean Laporte discovered its near-perfect conditions (see box on p.212). The town then became a haven for sculpted surf bums debating the nuances of gear between death-defying feats. The multicultural cross-section of aficionados of the sport attracts a growing community of people from across the globe, which has in turn attracted hotel chains and an assortment of adventure sports outfits. In more recent years, a spate of all-inclusives on the fringes of the resort has led to a lot more traditional tourism, but apart from the boisterous nightlife, the two tend to mix like oil and water.

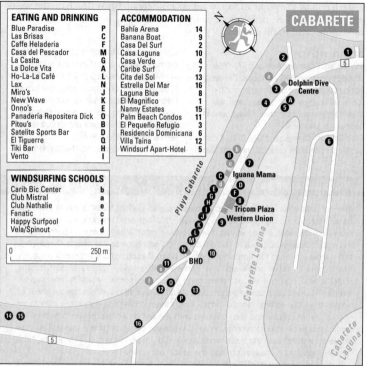

EATING AND DRINKING

Blue Paradise	P
Las Brisas	C
Caffe Heladeria	F
Casa del Pescador	M
La Casita	G
La Dolce Vita	A
Ho-La-La Café	L
Lax	N
Miro's	J
New Wave	K
Onno's	E
Panadería Repositera Dick	O
Pitou's	B
Satelite Sports Bar	D
El Tiguerre	Q
Tiki Bar	H
Vento	I

ACCOMMODATION

Bahía Arena	14
Banana Boat	9
Casa Del Surf	2
Casa Laguna	10
Casa Verde	4
Caribe Surf	7
Cita del Sol	13
Estrella Del Mar	16
Laguna Blue	8
El Magnifico	1
Nanny Estates	15
Palm Beach Condos	11
El Pequeño Refugio	3
Residencia Dominicana	6
Villa Taina	12
Windsurf Apart-Hotel	5

WINDSURFING SCHOOLS

Carib Bic Center	b
Club Mistral	a
Club Nathalie	e
Fanatic	c
Happy Surfpool	f
Vela/Spinout	d

CABARETE

Caves, Laguna, National Park & Q

Arrival and city transport

Virtually all of Cabarete is on the **Carretera 5**. Buses, guaguas and motoconchos will all drop you off along the main strip, a crowded patchwork of restaurants and bars, tour operators, and souvenir shops. (Actually, Caribe Tours has no terminal in Cabarete, but its drivers are supposed to stop for passengers flagging them down – either at Tricom Plaza if you're heading east, or at the taxi stand across the street if you're heading west.) The overflow of visitors has led to hotels cropping up for nearly a kilometre on either side, the furthest ones being accessible to the main town through cheap and omnipresent motoconchos. You should never pay more than RD$10 during the day to get from an outlying hotel to the main strip, RD$20 at night although it's worth seeking out a registered operator after dark – easily recognized by their numbered waistcoats. Playa Cabarete stretches out across the length of existing development, with a row of lively outdoor restaurants and bars at the centre.

Accommodation

There is a bewildering variety of **accommodations** available in Cabarete, including small pensiónes, several good mid-range choices, a number of apartment hotels and a couple of all-inclusives. Most lie on or close to the main strip that runs behind the beach, on either side of the C-5 between the Carib Bic Windsurf Centre and Happy Surf, although there's also a small cluster at the eastern end by the point and a few others fronting up Bozo Beach on the western side. Regardless of location, you should definitely book ahead as accommodations tend to fill quickly.

Main strip

Banana Boat Carretera 5 ⓣ & ⓕ 571-0690, ⓔ maribeldelcarmen54@yahoo.com. The oldest and best of the budget accommodations. The rooms are relatively basic but functional, and there's a common kitchen area. Always busy, so book well in advance. ❷

Casa Del Surf Carretera 5 ⓣ 571-0736. A comfortable pensión in the centre of town, with shared cold-water bath. Inhabited mostly by long-termers, but there's usually at least one room open. ❸

Casa Laguna Carretera 5 ⓣ 571-0725, ⓕ 571-0704. A standard all-inclusive resort that has all the amenities, including a/c, TV, manicured grounds, swimming pool and modest children's facilities. Rooms are tasteful and clean, and the service is fast and friendly. ❻

Cita del Sol Carretera 5 ⓣ 571-0720, ⓕ 571-

Windsurfing and kitesurfing

The conditions for **windsurfing** in Cabarete are so perfect that the whole bay may as well have been designed specifically with this in mind. The trade winds normally blow from the east, meaning that they sweep across the bay from right to left allowing easy passage both out to the offshore reefs and back to the beach. Downwind, the waters lap onto the amusingly named **Bozo Beach**, which will catch anybody unfortunate to have a mishap. The offshore reef provides plenty of surf for the experts who ride the waves, performing tricks and some incredibly spectacular jumps. The reef also shelters the inshore waters so that on all but the roughest of winter days the waters remain calm. During the morning the winds are little more than a gentle breeze and this, coupled with the flat water, makes the bay ideal for beginners, especially in summer when the surface can resemble a mirror. Then, as the temperature rises, the trade winds kick in big-time and the real show starts. Take some binoculars if you want to see the action out on the reef.

Two kilometres west of Playa Cabarete, on a white-sand beach hidden behind Punta Goleta, Cabarete is playing its part in the birth and infancy of a new sport – **kitesurfing.** In many ways similar to windsurfing, but relying on a huge kite to provide the power instead of a sail, kitesurfing needs less wind to really get moving and the best riders, as they're called, are performing huge jumps and tricks that would be impossible with a sail.

All the windsurf **outfitters** are based right along the beach, in the heart of the activity. They have a confusing array of pricing structures but there's not really much between them all when you break it down. The main differences are the actual make (rather than quality) of equipment, the amount of gear in stock (important mainly during busier times like Christmas–New Year and July–August), the launch position on the beach, and the languages spoken both by the staff. Most also run kitesurf schools here too, although there are others specializing in the latter on the kite beach itself. If you need some **equipment repaired** while you're here, try Cabarete Sail and Board Repair, beside the *Banana Boat* hotel (no phone); they've been here since the beginning of Cabarete windsurfing, and still do good work for reasonable prices.

Windsurfing schools

Carib Bic Center ⓣ 571-0640, ⓕ 571-0649, ⓦ www.caribwind.com. Slick outfit, with a great equipment shop and a well-trained, friendly staff always willing to give you pointers. US$150 for ten hours of use on the water; US$100 for three-hour classes; US$25 equipment insurance.

Club Mistral ⓣ & ⓕ 571-0770, ⓦ www.club-mistral.com. A well-stocked centre housed in the *El Pequeño Refugio* hotel and benefiting from being part of a huge

0795, ⓦ www.citadelsol.com. A hidden gem, far enough away from the road to cut out most of the chaos yet right on the beach and by several restaurants. Good-size rooms with kitchens and a pleasant pool area. Best in its price group. ❹

Laguna Blu Hotel Carretera 5 ⓣ 571-0659, ⓕ 571-0802. A pleasantly sleepy hotel behind the Tricom plaza, with hot water, average-sized clean rooms with fans, generator, swimming pool, and a nice patio area. ❸

Palm Beach Condos Carretera 5 ⓣ 571-0758, ⓕ 571-0752, ⓦ www.cabaretecondos.com. Full-service apartments right in the middle of the action. Slightly more expensive than *Nanny Estates* and with smaller suites. ❼

Villa Taina Carretera 5 ⓣ 571-0722, ⓕ 571-0883, ⓦ www.villataina.com. One of the best hotels in town with a smart reception area, helpful staff and a selection of very clean, tidy and imaginatively decorated rooms, with a/c, phones, luxurious bathrooms, and good beds. Some have balconies and sea views. ❻

West of the main strip

Estrella Del Mar Carretera 5 ⓣ 571-0808, ⓕ 571-0904, ⓦ www.amshamarina.com. One of

group. Great staff and a less frenetic location than the other centres although the wind can be a bit holey close to the shore. US$200 for seven days' equipment rental; US$30/hr group classes; US$25 equipment insurance.

Club Nathalie ⓣ 571-0848, ⓕ 571-0595, ⓦ www.cabaretewindsurf.com. Set up by a French windsurfing legend and mainly populated by French-speakers, although not by exclusion. Small centre with a decent amount of gear and an attentive staff. Good advanced lessons, including looping. US$210 for seven-day equipment rental; US$30 equipment insurance; US$40/hr private lessons.

Fanatic ⓣ & ⓕ 571-0861, ⓦ www.fanatic-cabarete.com. Another small but friendly operation that gives students a lot of personal attention and has a nice beach bar that serves up tasty cocktails. US$120 for ten hours on the water; private lessons for US$30/hr; US$20/hr in a small group; US$25 equipment insurance.

Happy Surfpool ⓣ & ⓕ 571-0784, ⓦ www.happycabarete.com. Very friendly small centre with a thriving social scene. The clientele is mainly German, but English and French are spoken as well. Not as much equipment as the bigger centres but very personalized, and they'll even take beginners onto a lagoon to start with. US$150 for ten hours on the water; US$30/hr group classes; US$25 equipment insurance.

Vela/Spinout ⓣ 571-0805, ⓕ 571-0856, ⓦ www.velacabarete.com. German-owned and the best-stocked of Cabarete's windsurf centres with free daily clinics and a lively social scene. The small bar is a great place to relax and does great lunches. US$160 for ten hours actually out on the water; US$100 for three-hour classes; US$25 equipment insurance.

Kitesurfing schools

Cabarete Kitesport ⓣ 857-0148, ⓦ www.cabarete-kitesport.com. The new kid on the kite beach, but already doing very well mainly due to the enthusiasm of the young staff. The standard three-day introduction course is US$225, with equipment rental for experienced riders starting at US$250 per week.

Dare2fly ⓣ 571-0805, ⓕ 571-0856, ⓦ www.dare2fly.com. Based at the Vela/Spinout windsurf centre, with equipment rental and lessons given at the kite beach daily. US$298 for a three-day introductory course with equipment; US$250 for a week's equipment hire only.

Kite Excite ⓣ 838-1225 or 571-9509, ⓦ www.kiteexcite.com. One of the original kitesurf schools on the beach. German-run but mainly Dominican staff. US$245 for a three-day introduction course or US$299 for a week's rental.

the first all-inclusives to open up in Cabarete; its designers went to great pains to remain a part of the town, abandoning the usual high walls in favour of an open courtyard entrance. The food's pretty basic but it's close enough to a plethora of other options. Rooms are large and have a/c and TV. **❼**

Kite Beach Hotel Carretera 5 ☎571-0878, ℻571-7417, ⓦwww.kitebeachhotel.com. A large hotel right on the kite beach 3km west of "downtown" and mainly populated by its participants. A mixture of reasonably decorated rooms and suites, some with a/c. Good value but a long way from town. **❹**

Nanny Estates Carretera 5, 1km west ☎571-0744, ℻571-0655, ⓦwww.cabaretebeachhouses.com. Excellent high-end value, especially if you're with a group: these two-storey apartments 1km west of Cabarete's core boast two huge bedrooms, a spacious lounge, well-equipped kitchens and the top floors have private roof terraces. Located on a quiet section of beach with a private pool and a tennis court. **❻**

East of the main strip

Caribe Surf Carretera 5 ☎ & ℻571-0788, ⓦwww.hotel-caribe-surf.com. One of the original windsurfer hotels and still a good bet with good-sized and well-furnished rooms, some with a sea view, and a very relaxed pool and garden area. **❸**

Casa Verde Carretera 5 ☎571-0770. Part of the *El Pequeño Refugio* complex (see below), this is the cheapest accommodation in town, extremely basic dormitory rooms with shared cold-water bath. **❶**

El Magnifico Carretera 5 ☎ & ℻571-0868, ⓦwww.hotelmagnifico.com. Three different beachside buildings with eye-catching architecture and ethnic interiors set around a tranquil pool area. Tranquil, yet it's just a five-minute stroll from the town centre. Perfect for relaxing in the morning and surfing in the afternoon. **❻**

El Pequeño Refugio Carretera 5, off small lane beyond *Casa Verde* ☎571-0770. Popular with windsurfers for its modern, mid-range rooms, all-you-can-eat breakfasts (not in rate), and affiliation with equipment maker Mistral. Has its own windsurfing rental shop and is 90 percent solar-powered. They also run the *Casa Verde* (see above). **❹**

Residencia Dominicana Calle Las Orquideas ☎ & ℻ 571-0890, ℮resdom@hipaniola.com. Small hotel with standard Western-style rooms and a peaceful garden and pool. Located on the Orquideas road, south of the C-5, at the eastern end of town. The place usually fills up, so it's a good idea to reserve in advance. **❸**

Windsurf Apart-Hotel Carretera 5 ☎571-0718, ℻571-0710. Efficient largish hotel with modern apartments, some with a/c and TV, and a nice pool area. **❻**

The town, the beach and the lagoon

What there is of a town consists of the hectic strip of restaurants and hotels along the C-5, just behind the water, with the main Dominican barrio set back towards the lagoon on the western perimeters. As you'd expect from a town that grew up on surfing, the beach, **Playa Cabarete**, is where the real action is. During the day it's crowded with a mixture of windsurfers and sun-worshippers, although if you head out a little way east or west, peace and quiet is easy to find, interrupted only by the occasional horseback rider. At night, the bars and restaurants spill out onto the sand, making for a superb dining scene, where you can eat at a quality restaurant with sand between your toes and the sound of the sea as background music. It also gets pretty lively later as the music gets louder and many of the bars take on the role of discos and clubs.

Behind the town to the south is **El Choco National Park**, a lush green wilderness that contains the lovely **Laguna Cabarete**, home to thousands of birds, but surrounded by dense brush and somewhat hard to get around. The park also holds the **Caves of Cabarete,** a set of holes around the lagoon that have been fenced off and illuminated with electric light. There's a park entrance down a well-marked turnoff just west of town, where you can join an organized tour (Mon–Fri 9am–5pm; RD$195) to the caves and lagoon. You'll see a few "Arawak glyphs", though twentieth-century graffiti is more prominent than Taino art, and get the opportunity to swim in an underground pool. Self-guided exploration of the national park isn't really an option as there's not much way-marking and the odds of ending up lost and confused are relatively high. Iguana Mama (see box on p.215) also run tours of the national park.

Cabarete adventure sports outfits

Dolphin Dive Center ☎571-0842, ✉d.divecenter@codetel.net.do. Well-established scuba-diving school offering PADI Open Water instruction for US$299 and a variety of dives on local reefs and wrecks for US$28/dive.

Get Wet ☎696-9073. One-man band operated by a qualified mountain guide who offers canyoning (walking, swimming and rappelling down a mountain river) trips in the surrounding mountains. The scenery is stunning and the adventure unbeatable. Trips with Get Wet are also bookable through Iguana Mama and some of the windsurf centres. (US$50 half-day.)

Iguana Mama ☎571-0908, 🖷571-0734, 🌐www.iguanamama.com. The very best of the country's adventure operators, with imaginative tours, well-trained, friendly, and incredibly informative staff and an enviable ethical eco-tourism record. They offer a huge selection of US$30 mountain-bike day-trips, suitable for all levels of rider and fitness, as well as week-long bike tours of the island, hikes up Mount Isabela (see p.200) and multi-day treks through the Cordillera Central to Pico Duarte (see p.258). They also rent quality mountain bikes for US$25/day, and do horseback riding for US$20/half-day.

Rancho Al Norte ☎223-0660. A large horse ranch in the nearby mountains (see p.212) with a number of beautiful trails, including one that goes to a remote waterfall. Rides cost US$70/day.

Rancho Montana ☎571-0990. Half-day horseback rides along Playa Cabarete for US$25.

Tropical Wakeboard Center ☎707-0048, 🖷571-0890, ✉tropicwake@hotmail.com. Water-skiing and wakeboarding – water-skiing on a miniature surfboard – along the Río Yasica. Both are a lot easier to pick up in a single day than windsurfing, so if you're a beginner you may want to try them out; they'll pick you up at your hotel in the morning for free. US$120 per day for unlimited sessions; US$450 per week.

Eating

Cabarete has an array of good **dining** options, most of them opened by European expats, and hence with some unusual cuisine for this part of the country. Indeed, outside of Santo Domingo, Cabarete may have the best French and Italian food available in the Dominican Republic. Even with all of these choices, though, a pilgrimage to the wonderful nearby Indian restaurant *Blue Moon* (see p.217) is a must when in town.

Blue Paradise Carretera 5. This French-Canadian joint on the west side of town serves up good, basic breakfasts and burgers, but the service can be infuriatingly slow.

Las Brisas Carretera 5. Loud open-air beach disco dishing out good food, including nightly dinner specials, such as lasagne or steak for a very good price, and RD$150 all-you-can-eat buffets; get there before the music really starts blaring at 10pm.

Casa del Pescador Carretera 5. The best seafood in town in an idyllic candlelit atmosphere right on the beach. All meals come with sides of ratatouille, rice, french fries and a small salad. Watch out for the extremely strong free rum aperitif.

La Casita Carretera 5. Festive main-strip restaurant notable for its gargantuan skillets of grilled langostinas (RD$200), which are not to be missed.

La Dolce Vita Carretera 5. The best pizzas in Cabarate are prepared in a genuine brick oven in a smart setting beneath the *Windsurf Apart-Hotel*. The pasta's also worth trying, especially during Sunday's "2 meals for the price of 1" deal.

Miro's Carretera 5. The best of Cabarete's beach restaurants, on the spot where Jean Laporte founded the first windsurfing school. The blend of Caribbean and African cooking makes for some fabulous combinations, including an exquisite Moroccan tuna for RD$190.

Panadería Repositera Dick Carretera 5. Just the smell of this place will give you a new lease on life, with various gourmet breads for a few pesos, great Danishes and croissants as good as those in Paris. They also have fresh-squeezed orange juice and cappuccinos that taste like French *café crème*. Closed Sun afternoon and evenings.

Pitou's Carretera 5. A favourite with the international workforce, this casual eatery on the beach features a good selection of pizza and Mexican dishes from RD$90, along with great coffee.

Satelite Sports Bar Carretera 5. A festive second-floor sports bar with three TVs and a menu featuring Dominican food. Their speciality is fried chicken with rice.

El Tiguerre Callejon de la Loma. Excellent, inexpensive local cuisine served by a friendly staff in a rustic barrio setting on the outskirts of town. Prices are much cheaper than on the beach and you'll get a real Dominican experience.

Vento Carretera 5. Smart, high-end gourmet Italian fare on the beach. The view of the water is exceptional, as is the cuisine: pastas, lamb and veal dishes, accompanied by an extensive wine list.

Drinking and nightlife

The entire town is packed with **bars**, but a select few garner the majority of the business. Almost all have early-evening happy hours and many feature live music one night a week.

Las Brisas Carretera 5. The town's most popular disco bar is home to a raucous mix of merengue and techno, plus a popular Thursday night beach volleyball game.

Caffe Heladería Tricom Plaza, Carretera 5. Unpretentious outdoor bar serving excellent Italian espresso drinks for a few pesos. Well placed for people-watching, though the small square bar in front of it blasts bad 1980s rock at intolerable decibels. Closed Sun.

Ho-La-La Café Carretera 5. Less chaotic than the main beachfront bars but still popular, with a pool table that takes precedence over the loud music and minimal dancing.

Lax Carretera 5. The latest in-place, at the western end of the beach. Casual and relaxed, it's a great place to chill when the other bars get too loud.

New Wave Carretera 5. The resident rock 'n' roll bar, on the beach and smack bang in the middle of everything, with good food and a loud party atmosphere. Get here before the dancing starts if you want to sample one of their tasty and very inexpensive daily specials, which might include

Indonesian satay or fettucine alfredo with shrimp. Live music Wed and Sat.

Onno's Carretera 5. Lively bar/restaurant, on the beachfront in the centre of the strip, which really gets going in the small hours – plays mainly European and American hits.

Roadhouse Carretera 5. A wild and rocking kind of dive out near the kite beach. Very busy, very rowdy and the roof leaks all over if it starts to rain.

Tiki Bar Carretera 5. Another beachfront bar, in the centre of the strip, with a more congenial setting than the louder dance halls around it, good for hanging out and talking. Live music Fri.

Tricom Plaza Bar Tricom Plaza, Carretera 5. Perpetually crowded outdoor bar located on the inland side of the street, in the centre of the strip. Usually shared between Dominicans and Europeans shouting over the loud music.

Villa Taina Carretera 5. Small beach bar next to *Happy Surfpool* – a huge selection of happy hour (5–7pm) cocktails including excellent piña coladas, make this a great place to start the evening.

Listings

American Express Tricom Plaza, Carretera 5 (Mon–Fri 8am–noon & 2.30–6pm, Sat 8am–noon).

Banks and currency exchange There's a BHD with an ATM at the western end of town and another ATM opposite. Best exchange rates at Western Union (see opposite).

Car and motorycle rental Reputable operators include Arcar (T 571-1282); Autoclínica Cabarete (T 571-0626); Mauri Moto Rentals (T 571-0666); and Tropicar (T 571-0991). Motorcycles can be

rented from Easy Rider (T 571-0825).

Film processing Cabarete Beach Foto, Tricom Plaza, Carretera 5 (Mon–Sat 9am–5.30pm).

Internet Tele Cabarete, Carretera 5, or *Ski Internet Café*, Carretera 5; both have fast enough connections and similar rates of about RD$15 per 15min.

Laundry Just about every hotel has laundry service. *Banana Boat* or *Nanny Estates* will do laundry for non-guests, both RD$50 per load.

Medical Servi-Med, Carretera 5 (☎571-0964; open 24 hours).

Post office There is no post office in Cabarete, but there are a number of small post boxes. The most reliable is maintained by Fuji Photo just to

the right of the small central plaza. EPS is located at the west end of the strip.

Wiring money Western Union, Tricom Plaza, Carretera 5 (Mon–Sat 8.30am–noon & 2–5.30pm).

Around Cabarete

Undeveloped **Playa Encuentra**, 4km west of Cabarete on the C-5, then north on an unmarked turnoff at a metal gate, has massive waves unseen in most of the DR, which attracts a good number of surfers and some of the most highly skilled windsurfers on the planet. It's worth stopping off between 6am and 8am to watch the most daring of them ride atop six-metre waves, execute 360-degree leaps and even ride within the curl of the waves on the rare occasions when the surf is large enough to allow it. Every March the **Encuentra Classic** takes place here, one of the top-rated surfing and windsurfing competitions in the world.

The main attraction in the surrounding countryside is the mountain-biking trail along the old **El Choco** road, which was once used to truck bananas from the countryside to the coast but is now little more than a dirt path. Iguana Mama's (☎571-0908; US$30) half-day **mountain-bike excursion** down El Choco is a fairly challenging trip that steers you through the heart of rural DR. If you want to do the trail on your own, go approximately 4km west of Cabarete and take the dirt road just before the Colmado Beatón. This rough track is known as La Bombita, and after 4km it feeds into the larger El Choco, from which it's 17km past non-stop breathtaking mountain scenery dotted with tiny Dominican outposts and waving kids to the pueblo La Catalina. From there the trip heads down the gorgeous Moca road to Sabaneta de Yásica, then back along the coast to Cabarete.

Sabaneta de Yásica and around

SABANETA DE YÁSICA, a few kilometres southeast of Cabarete, is a non-descript concrete town at the junction of the Río Yásica – a large river with little development along it – and the Atlantic. Islabón Boat Jungle Tours, a few metres west of town (☎696-3253; US$35), operate a **rainforest ecotour** that takes small groups of passengers up a tributary of the Yásica to the large Laguna Islabón, then turns back along the Yásica to the river's mouth. This two-and-a-half-hour ride cruises through otherwise impossible-to-access, dense rainforest and mangrove swamp, home to an enormous variety of orchids, tropical birds and reptiles.

South from Sabaneta de Yásica, the **Sabaneta–Moca road** winds through the heart of the Cordillera Septentrional mountains past a number of relatively prosperous agricultural pueblos. At pueblo Los Brazos, the *Blue Moon Retreat* (☎223-0614, ⓦwww.bluemoonretreat.net; ❸), is an isolated mountaintop compound, with a few brightly decorated cabins, featuring the work of local artists, scattered around a swimming pool. Even more notable is their unique restaurant, which serves delicious multi-course gourmet Indian dinners in an expansive tent on mats and cushions. Reservations, which are for the whole evening, have to be made at least three days in advance, and they only serve parties of ten or more people; if short of the requisite number, see if you can piggyback onto another party (try at Iguana Mama or any of the windsurfing schools). The whole trip including return transport from Cabarete is usually around RD$350. Further on is the town of **Jamao**, with little more than a phone centre, a few houses and a couple of restaurants, nothing to stop for unless you're in need of a bit of rest. A steep turnoff within town heads 1km east up a mountain to **Rancho Al Norte** (☎223-0660; US$70), a large horse ranch utilized by several Cabarete tour companies. They have the best mountain trails of the area ranches, including one that leads to a large waterfall.

Heading east on the C-5 from Sabaneta, the next major town is **Gaspar Hernández**, a bleak, concrete fishing village prone to flooding during heavy rains. Just east of town, though, is lovely **Playa Hermosa**, an abandoned beach that's most pristine at its western end. From Gaspar Hernández, the paved Carretera 233 runs south through the Cordillera Septentrional for 32km towards Salcedo, an excellent entry into the isolated northern mountains, featuring large tracts of virgin forest and great views all the way. If you continue 15km east of Gaspar Hernández, you'll hit tiny **La Yagua**, though the only reason to stop would be to eat at the creole seafood restaurant, *El Pescador de La Yagua*, with its tables set right on the beach.

Río San Juan

The small, friendly fishing village of **RÍO SAN JUAN**, 5km east of La Yagua, borders the large mangrove lagoon, **Laguna Gri-Gri**, as well as several great nearby beaches, including **Playa Caletón, Playa Grande** and **Playa Preciosa**, relatively undeveloped but with a slew of high-end resorts in the works. The impending arrival of the package tourism trade bodes change, something the locals hope will translate into increased prosperity. It's hard to find much fault with that, though you'd be forgiven for wanting its tree-lined streets, easy-going atmosphere and simple reliance on boat building, fishing and dairy farming to remain forever as they are.

The Town

The centre of transportation and activity is the Texaco station on the corner of the C-5 and Calle Duarte, behind which is an **outdoor bar** well placed for people-watching. North up Duarte, the main thoroughfare, which runs from the highway to the lagoon and is lined by shops and hotels as well as exchanges, taxi stands and a post office, you'll hit the part of town most come to see. It's also worth heading west to **barrio Acapulco**, a residential neighbourhood of unpaved roads and front lawns adorned with carved wooden boats, which artisans here craft for local fishermen.

Laguna Gri-Gri, at the northernmost end of Duarte, is the main draw, a magnificent **mangrove preserve** traversed by organized boat tours boarded from a small quay at the road's end. The ninety-minute tours, which cost RD$20–100, begin at the pond on the northern end of Duarte; go early in the morning for better birdwatching and the chance to spot a crocodile. Beyond the lagoon, the boats enter a series of impressive coastal caves, then head along the coast to Playa Caletón for a quick swim. You can also see the lagoon's birdlife by walking east from the *Bahía Blanca Hotel* to the peninsular **bird sanctuary** that the tour skirts.

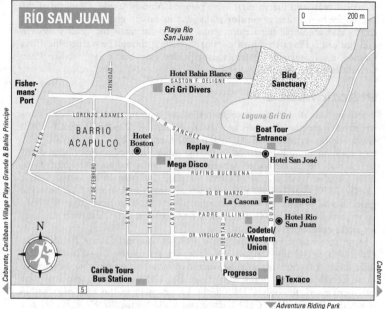

Adventure Riding Park

The beaches

Tiny **Playa Río San Juan** lies within the town limits, though it pretty much disappears at high tide. A five-minute walk west of town is the *Bahía Príncipe* resort's **private beach**, which can be snuck onto from either side of its fenced-off grounds, although better beaches lie east of town. The closest of these is **Playa Caletón**, a small cove surrounded by rocks and safe for swimming, accessible from the C-5 by a marked turnoff. Two kilometres further out is **Playa Grande**, the most spectacular in the area, a long strip of spotless white sand flanked by high cliffs and crashing surf. Unfortunately, there's been a little development here

Riptides

Common on beaches with high surf, **riptides** are dangerous ocean conveyor belts that funnel the water being smashed against the coast back to sea. Surfers and windsurfers actually find them desirable, as they pull you effortlessly out to the big waves, but they can pose a life-threatening problem for less experienced swimmers; indeed, at Playa Grande, a couple of people die each year in the tides. If you're not a strong swimmer, it's best to keep off beaches with high, crashing surf altogether. You can sometimes – but not always – identify riptides by sight as ribbons of sea that don't have any large waves travelling across their surface. At times they'll also have a different colour from the rest of the water. If you're caught in a riptide, do not attempt to swim against the powerful current. Instead, swim to the right or the left – and not directly back to the shore – until you are out of its grip.

in recent years and there's even more planned. Already taking advantage of the people the beach attracts, **vendor stalls** sit at its eastern end, selling sandwiches, snacks and pineapple-filled rum drinks. A lifeguard mans the beach's western end. Just east is **Playa Preciosa**, popular for surfing, though be warned: like Playa Grande, it's renowned for ferocious **riptides** (see box p.219); unlike Playa Grande, it has no lifeguard.

Practicalities

There are two all-inclusive **resorts** in the area, with more slated to begin construction over the next decade. *Bahía Príncipe* (☎226-1590, ℱ226-1991, ⓦwww.bahia-principe.com; ⓪) is the largest, marked by a long row of pastel bars running along its entrance. Inside the inner gates are several hundred villas, a private beach, casino, spa, supermarket, car rental and good children's facilities. On the western end of Playa Grande, *Caribbean Village Playa Grande* (☎582-1170, ℱ582-6094/5585, ⓦwww.allegroresorts.com; ⓪) has beautiful grounds and is skirted by a new eighteen-hole **golf course** (☎1-800/858-2258; rates from the hotel), designed by Robert Trent Jones, featuring ten holes set along bold, open oceanfront.

More convenient for spending time in town, however, is the *Bahía Blanca*, Calle Deligne (☎589-2563, ℱ589-2528; ④), set on the tiny Playa Río San Juan, a view of which is available from the terrace dining room/bar. Besides the quite luxurious large rooms with fridge and ceiling fan, they also have one basement room for only RD$200, the best bargain in the area. Also within town, the *Río San Juan*, Calle Duarte and Calle Billini (☎589-2572; ③), is a well-run family establishment with spacious, nondescript rooms, hot water and pleasant grounds. Less palatable but cheaper are *San José*, Calle Duarte and Calle Mella (no phone; ②), which has some spacious balcony rooms, plus hot water and fan; and *Boston*, Calle Capotillo and Calle Bulbuena (☎589-2921; ②), featuring kitchenettes.

There are a dozen inexpensive **cafeterias** and **open-air cafés** along Calle Duarte that cook decent Dominican cuisine. *La Cosona*, at Duarte and 30 de Marzo, is particularly good for staples like rice and beans. The restaurant at the *Bahía Blanca* hotel serves excellent seafood on a terrace facing out over the ocean. The most popular spot in town is *Replay*, Calle Sanchez just off the lagoon entrance, an outdoor bar with an inexpensive menu of Dominican dishes and American fast food. It's also a popular drinking establishment, with an outdoor patio that plays good music at a moderate volume.

Nightlife in Río San Juan is lively enough, as many of the bars along Calle Duarte stay open late. One block southwest of the laguna entrance is the pueblo's only dance hall, *Mega Disco*, calles Capotillo and Mella (closed Mon; RD$20 cover), which gets crowded every night around 1am. The elegant

Río San Juan tour operators

If looking to hook up with some **outdoor excursions** or **watersports** while in Río San Juan, try one of two reputable operators: Merk & Merk, Carretera 5, 1km east of town (☎248-5263), offers jeep safaris and "funny bike" (all-terrain, three-wheel buggies) tours into the Cordillera Septentrional, along with outings to the new golf course; and Gri-Gri Divers (☎589-2671), Calle Deligne, across the street from the *Bahía Blanca*, is an excellent UK outfit that does scuba dives into several nearby reefs and full PADI training.

oceanfront patio at *Bahía Blanca*'s is also an option, as are the outdoor bars at *Bahía Príncipe*, though you'll need to take a taxi or motoconcho to get out there.

East to Cabrera

East of Playa Grande is the eminently skippable **Amazonia 2** (daily 9.30am–5pm; RD$50), a very miniature rainforest conserved for commercial purposes. It's just the base of a cliff covered by scads of mosquito netting, which you can enter to check out various plants, parrots and a rhesus monkey imported from Brazil. Ten kilometres down the road, between the sister towns Abreu and El Bretón, **Cabo Francisco Viejo** (Mon–Fri 10am–4.30pm; RD$40), a small national park centred on a majestic cape, holds a lighthouse at its far end and is a great place to take a short stroll and look out over the ocean. Just east of the cape and protected from development is the pounding surf of **Playa El Bretón**, a ruggedly beautiful beach backed by high, chalk-white cliffs. If you're hungry, check out *Virginia*, an excellent seafood restaurant just east of El Bretón on the C-5.

Continuing east towards Cabrera, the landscape is marked by more white cliffs and rock formations containing various Taino caves, some said to hold remnants of Indian occupation, but for the most part treacherously hard to reach. One with easy access is the **Cave of the Virgin of the Rock**, 2km east of El Bretón. For RD$10, you can view a "crying" rock formation purported (by the local entrepreneur who has fenced the cave off and charges admission) to resemble the Virgin Mary, though you may have a hard time agreeing with him. Just beyond it, the road rises atop the cliffs; two kilometres before you reach Cabrera, you'll see one place to pull over and check out the stupendous views. Turn to p.182 for more on Cabrera itself.

Inland to the Cordillera Septentrional

South of the C-5, Río San Juan's Calle Duarte becomes a rough 4WD dirt track that heads straight into the eastern end of the coastal mountains. If in a sturdy vehicle, you should have no trouble traversing the mountain road, though in truth there's not too much out of the ordinary to see here – just tiny pueblos and rugged terrain. The road forks after about 10km, its right path heading to **Adventure Riding Park** (☎571-0890, ⓔresdom@dominican-mirror.com), a several-hundred-acre ranch that features horseback riding across isolated mountain trails. In addition to the forty-horse stable, the ranch runs a small guest house known as the *Bush Hotel* (⊙, including meals and riding). Back at the fork in the road, a left turns heads onto a road winding east through the mountains to pueblo La Entrada (see p.181). Several kilometres along the way is **Pueblo La Casa**, a tiny mountaintop village offering views of the distant Cibao Valley to the south. The pueblo consists of only a few shacks but is fastidiously clean; on weekend evenings its *comedor*/bar converts into a rural dance hall, a fun place to experience campesino nightlife. Camping is also an option, provided you ask permission first.

△ Windsurfer in the waters near Cabarete

West of Puerto Plata

The contrast east and west of Puerto Plata couldn't be more striking. In place of the paved highways, resort complexes and golf courses that prevail in much of the east, the west contains vast stretches of small family farms and untrammelled wilderness along rough dirt tracks, though some are slowly being converted into freeways. The view towards foreign visitors is different in the west, too; an old code of warm, formal manners prevails, and strangers will often go to great lengths to assist you out of sheer good nature. One thing that doesn't change, though, is the proliferation of lovely beaches – though these get far more use by locals than tourists. Most **coral reefs** here are still intact, and the island's finest are located between Punta Rucia and Monte Cristi. Fine coastal detours from the Careterra Luperón that heads west from just outside Puerto Plata include **Luperón** itself, a remote seaside village that has a couple of comfortable resorts nearby; **El Castillo**, a scenic fishing village that holds the remains of Columbus's first settlement La Isabela; and the twin beaches **Playa Ensenata** and **Punta Rucia**. Inland a long, fertile strip of verdant rice paddies is set between imposing mountain ranges. At its most western part, towards frontier town **Monte Cristi**, the terrain becomes more like a cactus-dominated desert landscape. If you're heading out this way from Puerto Plata, make sure you keep a close eye on your gas tank; petrol stations are few and far between. If you do get low, look out for the occasional roadside house with litre jugs propped on a table along the road.

Puerto Plata to Luperón

Two routes lead from Puerto Plata to Luperón, the first – and quicker – being the Carretera Luperón, which you can pick up 1km north of **Imbert**, a town marked mainly by its large Texaco station. Just outside town, you can visit a stunning series of **cascades** along the Río Bajabonico, though they're somewhat hard to get to. Seven hundred metres south of the Texaco station, a dirt road leads east – the turnoff is by a local *comedor* – for about a half-kilometre to a parking area, from where you'll be pointed in the direction of the cascades. Here 23 pretty, boulder-strewn waterfalls snake down the side of a mountain wilderness, the water crashing down at a breakneck pace. It's a challenging but safe climb up, with a great hilltop view at the end. You can easily do the cascades as a day-trip from Puerto Plata, but if you want to stay in a more pastoral setting, head to *Rancho Nazdrowie* (☎707-7600, Ⓕ581-2349; ❸), a set of remote bungalows, an outdoor swimming pool and a small restaurant in the mountains east of Imbert. To get to the ranch, head east from the parque central for 6km until you reach **Puente de Hierro**, an old railroad bridge with a floor of loose logs, and make a left.

The rest of the way to Luperón is less interesting, a trip up a paved highway running through the heart of a dozen different pueblos, though none worth a stop. A word of warning; it's worth keeping an eye out for farm animals wandering along the curvy Carretera Luperón.

The **second route** from Puerto Plata to Luperón is a much rougher ride than the first, but offers better scenery and an intimate look at the lives of the

DR's rural peasantry, or campesinos, as you drive through a series of seaside campos – outposts so small they couldn't even be called pueblos – dotted with thatch huts, small vegetable gardens and freely roaming farm animals. From the Carretera Puerto Plata, take the northwest turnoff marked "Guzmancito", 10km beyond Puerto Plata. Just after turning, you'll hit the small beach of **Playa Maimón**, which typically has a smattering of locals. You're better off forging on to **Playa Guzmancito**, a gorgeous, mostly abandoned beach another 10km down the road near the tiny fishing campo Cruce de Guzmán, where you can **camp** if you ask permission from the townsfolk first. From here the road passes through the foothills of the Cordillera Septentrional for 15km, affording occasional spectacular ocean views before ending at La Sabana on the Carretera Luperón.

Luperón

Despite being the most developed of the western beach towns, with a popular all-inclusive resort and a large marina along its outskirts, **LUPERÓN** maintains the dusty, low-key feel of the coast west of Puerto Plata, and there is precious little to see or do in the town itself. The action, as usual, is along the beach, a kilometre of sand lined with sea grapes and palms known as **Playa Grande**. It's not too far off the main road, the Carretera de las Américas, which has a couple of restaurants good for lunch or a drink.

A half-kilometre further down the Carretera de las Américas is the **Puerto Blanca Marina** (☎571-8622 or 8644), a lively mooring spot that acts as a great social centre for expats in the area. The port is usually bustling with numerous world-travelling vagabonds making the most of the bay's ample protection from hurricanes and tropical storms; as a result, it's normally easy to find someone willing to take you on a sailboat day-trip to the hard-to-reach **reefs** around La Isabela and Punta Rucia. A trip should cost you around RD$750. Ask for a recommendation from Lenin, the proprietor of the marina, and make sure that whoever you sign on with has radar, radio, life jackets and an emergency life raft.

Practicalities

Luperón is not a bad place to base yourself in the area, though don't forget that Puerto Plata is just 35km to the east, and has a far greater selection of **accommodation**. Still, at the top end, there are two all-inclusive resorts, run by the same operator and located side by side, 2km west of town near the marina. Both the *Luperón Beach Resort* and *Caribbean Village*, La Isabela Carretera (☎571-8303, ☎571-8180; ❼), have beautiful grounds and rooms and share restaurants, a disco, large swimming pool, horseback riding, watersports excursions and spa. The beach here is truly stunning, but expect a lot of hassles from local vendors. Just west of the resort, *Rusi Mar*, La Isabela Carretera (☎374-5754; ❷), has basic rooms, but the place gets noisy at night, when it doubles as a dance hall. Better are *Casa del Sol*, between the town and marina on La Isabela Carretera (☎&☎571-8403; ❷), with a few decent rooms above a restaurant, and the marina itself (☎571-8622 or 8644; ❷), which has a few basic but liveable rooms. Within town is *Hotel Dally*, Calle Duarte at Parque Central (☎571-8034; ❷), boasting clean and comfortable if not particularly exciting rooms and a smart **restaurant** serving international cuisine and inexpensive seafood, much of which is caught locally. Other food options include the marina's restaurant, a fairly casual affair that does some excellent and cheap daily specials – try the dorado and octopus salad – and the *Chicken Shack*, a small blue building, north of the parque central on Duarte, that excels at fried chicken. Best of the lot, though, is the restaurant in the *Casa del Sol* (see above), which is a smart though informal dining room serving an excellent pepper-steak (RD$100).

There's not too much excitement at **night** in Luperón, though residents do gather outside along Calle Duarte and at the parque central to listen to music streaming from a dozen different car radios. It's at its most festive during power outages – which are infuriatingly frequent in the rural DR – when literally everyone in town heads to the main strip. The marina's bar is likely to be lively if there's a good amount of boats anchored in the bay.

Clustered around the parque central are convenient places to fill most of your other needs, like Codetel, Tricom, Western Union and a pharmacy. If you don't have your own transportation and need to get to El Castillo or Punta Rucia from here, Taxi Luperón (☎280-3164) is a reputable operator.

El Castillo and La Isabela

The Carretera de las Américas heads 13km west from Luperón to sleepy **EL CASTILLO**, a seaside village located on the site of Columbus's first permanent settlement, the remains of which are now nestled inside a small parque nacional just east of the village. The scenery itself makes the trip worthwhile, passing prosperous plantations along rolling hills and breathtaking shots of the sea. Still, the best ocean views are reserved for the town, which is set on a splendid bay of tranquil, blue water and a solid wall of imposing, Olympian peaks stretching in both directions.

The village itself is no great shakes, just a few houses scattered around a grid of tiny dirt roads on a steep hill. Visitors come for the scenery and the peace and quiet rather than the excitement. Entering the town from Luperón, the main road passes the *Rancho del Sol* hotel, which looks out over the beach, on the right. The road then forks and most of the dwellings and the *Miamar* hotel are up to the left on the hillside. **Playa Isabela**, a couple of metres down a marked dirt path just right of *Rancho del Sol*, attracts few beachgoers and is instead marked mainly by the small wooden boats moored just offshore and children fishing at the water's edge. The placid atmosphere is interrupted daily at around 2pm, though, by the *Kon Tiki* party boat that comes here from *Luperón Beach Resort*, blasting steel-drum music. If you have a 4WD you can head about twenty minutes east along the water and through a patch of high grass to a wilderness beach that won't have a single other person on it. A kilometre offshore from El Castillo is an intact, living **coral reef** – rare on this island – where you'll see a healthy, multicoloured reef bed that's home to thousands of tropical fish and sea creatures. Sadly, the local dive centre has closed down, but *Rancho del Sol* can arrange regular scuba and snorkelling trips, and can also take you to other remote reefs west of Punta Rucia (see p.228).

Just west of El Castillo is **Laguna Estero Hondo**, one of the last remaining Dominican homes of the **manatee**, which has been killed off in droves in recent decades by destruction of habitat and speedboat accidents. The hotels in town, and also *Punta Rucia Sol* (☎471-0173) in Punta Rucia, can organize boat excursions into the lagoon though it may be best to give them a few days notice. Even then, sightings are not guaranteed, but you will see a gorgeous mangrove preserve that serves as a haven for tropical birds, such as egrets, wood storks and roseate spoonbills.

Parque Nacional La Isabela and around

Just off the main highway, before you reach town, is the entrance to **Parque Nacional La Isabela** (9am–5.30pm, closed Sun; RD$30), which takes up much of the village's shoreline and preserves the ruins of La Isabela, the first European town in the New World. Centred on the private home of Columbus himself, which is perched atop a prominent ocean bluff, the park also encompasses the excavated stone foundations of the town and a small museum, though to see either you'll need to hire a local guide from the main park office (RD$40 tip). Supposedly there were far more extensive ruins up until 1952, when Trujillo bulldozed the site in a misguided effort to "clean it up" for visiting UN officials. You'll still see two large warehouses, a sentry tower, a chapel, what some assert was a clinic and Columbus's house, which retains a good portion of its walls intact. A number of skeletons have been unearthed from the chapel's cemetery; one – a Spaniard who died of malaria – is rather unceremoniously on display in a box near the museum. The museum itself offers an account of the cultures of both Spaniards and Tainos at the time of their first encounter. Better than the solemn recitations by the guide are the hundreds of excavated artefacts, including a pottery oven, a kiln and several containers that still held mercury (used to purify gold) when they were unearthed, along with

The beginning and end of La Isabela

Founded in 1493 by Christopher Columbus and some 1500 Spanish settlers under his command, **La Isabela** was strategically located on a defensible ocean bluff but far from fresh water and fertile soil, oversights that led to its abandonment in favour of Santo Domingo after only four years. Columbus intended that it would become the gold-bearing capital of Spain's empire, organizing it according to the *factoria* system of Portugal's colonies along the northwest coast of Africa; in these, a small group of entrepreneurial partners forced natives to hand over a valuable local commodity (in this case, gold), either as tribute or in exchange for European goods at a ridiculously low rate.

However, it soon became evident that there was not much gold to be had, and after yellow fever and malaria killed half of the original settlers, the rest became increasingly disgusted. Another sticking point was the tradition of Christian conquest in Spain, which allowed soldiers to enslave Moors on conquered lands. At first Columbus opposed transplanting slavery here, and as hardships mounted he demanded that colonists perform manual labour regardless of rank, alienating the petty nobility. After a failed coup attempt, several nobles stole one of his boats and set off for Spain to complain of the goings-on. In mid-1494, Columbus, perhaps realizing that he was in danger of losing the faith of his men, waged two military campaigns to capture Tainos, allotting slaves to his men in lieu of monthly wages. The Indians were to work the surrounding fields, though many were able to escape.

Two years later Columbus sailed to Spain to request more settlers, leaving his brother Bartolomé in charge of La Isabela. Upon his departure, a group of colonists led by Columbus's personal servant Francisco Roldán revolted and went to settle in the outlying countryside. Bartolomé abandoned La Isabela in 1497 with his few remaining men for the site of Santo Domingo, where one Spaniard had found a large gold nugget. Upon Columbus's return in 1498, his town lay abandoned; two years later, he was removed from command in Santo Domingo and sent back to Spain in disgrace.

smaller items such as a tiny sixteenth-century crucifix, unglazed Moorish-style pottery shards and several Taino religious icons. Just outside the building are small plots where local anthropologists grow samples of the agriculture practised by the Taino and the colonists.

Two ancillary sites have been uncovered outside the park, both rather uninspiring and not really worth the time. One, **Las Coles**, across the bay to the west, has only a few scattered pieces of masonry left, and was quite possibly only built as a temporary shelter. Meanwhile, the unnamed ruins within town have not been thoroughly examined; the few artefacts that have been unearthed are on display in the park's museum.

Across the carretera from the park, **Templo de las Américas** (daily 8.30am–5pm), a spotless neo-colonial church topped by a high central dome, merits a quick look round. It was constructed for Pope John Paul II's visit to La Isabela in 1992 for the Columbus Centenary, and the pope gave Mass there on the anniversary of the admiral's landing; a plaque on the outside commemorates the visit. The interior is simple but striking, with marble floors and red-brick walls; even better is the elevated vista of Bahía de Isabela from the top of the steps.

Practicalities

There are a couple of good-value **accommodations** in El Castillo. *Rancho del Sol*, Carretera de las Américas at the town entrance (☏543-8172; ❷–❸), rents simple but well-maintained duplexes with kitchen and bath. Two have a/c. They also have a great seafood restaurant where the menu varies with the day's catch. On the hill above, with stunning views over the bay, is *Miamar*, Calle Vista Mar (Ⓕ only 471-9157; ❸–❹, breakfast included), a hotel with cold water, swimming pool, bar and enormous rooms with king-size beds, kitchenettes and private balconies. At the time of writing it had been allowed to slip into disrepair a little but plans for a refurbishment are afoot. At the base of that hill, an unmarked blue house has a few basic rooms for rent as well (❶).

Rancho del Sol is the tops for **food** in town but if you fancy a little *cómida criolla*, try *Milagro*, near the entrance to Rancho del Sol, a small and friendly *comedor* with a good selection of local dishes including some great piquant goat.

Punta Rucia, Playa Ensenata and El Pato

From El Castillo the road to Punta Rucia extends west around the lagoon and heads through increasingly arid scrubland to a series of beaches that relatively few foreign visitors make it to. Though the road is graded – flattened out by a bulldozer in preparation for paving – it's mainly dirt and there are two shallow rivers for which bridges have yet to be built. It's usually possible to drive through these and there's never a shortage of locals loitering nearby to assist you if you're not confident. Be aware, though, that they'll want a good tip. After around 10km, a turnoff heads north to pueblo Estero Hondo, a village with no tourist facilities but set in a river delta replete with birdlife and mosquitoes. Four kilometres beyond the town, **Playa El Pato**, a small cove protected by a giant reef that turns it into a large natural swimming pool, is rather sparsely populated, at least much more so than **Playa Ensenata**, 1km further west, where many Dominican families come to take advantage of the shallow waters.

The western end of the kilometre-long beach, where it meets the road, is quieter, with stunning white sand, gently lapping turquoise water and a few small boats bobbing just offshore with the mountains as a background. Turn right to the eastern end of the beach for a totally different cultural experience with radios blasting the sounds of *bachata* and a few shacks selling food and rum. The food's usually excellent and the rum's always cheap. Just around the point from Playa Ensenata, **Punta Rucia** is arguably the most beautiful beach on the north coast, with more bone-white sand and great mountain views. It attracts fewer people than Ensenata but has several informal local places to stop for lunch or a beer, some with live music. The small point that separates the two beaches is bordered by a thriving **coral reef**, which provides good snorkelling.

Practicalities

Punta Rucia is the only one of the three beaches that has any form of **accommodation**. Here, the *Punta Rucia Sol* (☎471-0173; ❸), quite the hidden – albeit basic – gem, oozes a timeless, unhurried tranquillity that's really quite addictive. Run by a pair of New Age hippies, the small and clean cabins, dotted about cool, shady, wooded grounds, with cold-water showers, are all decorated with the proprietors' own paintings. The small collection of dogs that seem to romp endlessly around the grounds only adds to the fun. **Camping** is your only option at the other two beaches, though keep in mind that they're notorious for their nocturnal sand fleas; you're well advised to wear an ample coating of insect repellent. The *Punta Rucia Sol* has an excellent **restaurant**, although the menu's a fairly impromptu affair, and there are a few down-home Dominican seafood restaurants on the beach as well. *Demarís* is the most established but it's not as good as it used to be, catering more for the previously mentioned *Kon Tiki* party boat than for casual visitors. All along both Punta Rucia and Playa Ensenata, vendors sell **fresh oysters** culled the same day from the nearby river's mouth.

In addition to the easier El Castillo road, you can reach Punta Rucia from a once-paved road that leads north from the Santiago–Monte Cristi Carretera; the turnoff is at Villa Elisa, from where guaguas also run on weekends up to Punta Rucia.

West to Monte Cristi

All paved roads come to an end in El Castillo and the condition of the dirt tracks west deteriorates even further beyond Punta Rucia, so if you want to head **west to Monte Cristi**, you'll have a tough, though likely rewarding, time of it. It's not too bad to pueblo El Cupey, where the main road continues south to meet up with the Carretera Duarte (see p.251); but west of this is the arid **La Costa de Buen Hombre**, a long stretch of desert terrain dominated by scrub brush, which you'll need a motorcycle to traverse. The main track soon dissolves into a narrow mule track, intersected at random by others that are equally narrow and badly surfaced. Maps of the area don't do it justice – so be prepared to ask directions from the mule teams you'll encounter along the way. Stick to the coast and you'll find a modest sign marking the turnoff to **Gran Mangle** – one of the most isolated fishing villages in the country. Set on a small, dramatic point, Gran Mangle is mostly rocky coast, but there are a few patches of beach here and there along with an intact coral **reef**. Other great reefs can be found all along the coast here, and much of it is also populated by manatees, but it's extremely remote. The mule trails continue in a similar vein for 25km, leading to the pueblo **El Jabo**, near the base of the towering El Morro mesa. From here you'll navigate around El Morro through the weeds, avoiding the mesa's soggy moat, to get to Playa Juan Bolaños and Monte Cristi, at the DR's northwestern tip.

The Carretera Duarte

Bordering the Cordillera Septentrional to the south is the **Carretera Duarte** – an extension of the Autopista Duarte, which stretches between Santiago and Santo Domingo – a road that provides a far easier way to get to Monte Cristi than the coastal mule tracks. The well-paved freeway stretches from Santiago to Monte Cristi, intersecting the Carretera Puerto Plata at Navarrete, a major tobacco centre. As you move west, tobacco fields quickly give way to banana trees and rice paddies; at Villa Elisa, the land suddenly becomes arid, transforming into a cactus-dominated desert teeming with goats. The towns that line it are all fairly basic, with at most a couple of *colmados* and the occasional cockfighting arena. As far as basic necessities along the way, petrol stations are mercifully posted every 20km or so, and if you have to stop for the night, the small town of **Laguna Saluda**, 20km west of Navarrete, has two no-frills accommodations, *Acapulco* (❶) and *Imperial* (❶), both with shared bath. A little better is *Villa Cactus* (❷), a complex of *cabañas turísticas* just before Villa Vasquez, 27km further on. The best place to eat along the way is *La Sandán*, a restaurant in pueblo Jaibón (just past Laguna Saluda), famous nationwide for its goat dishes. *Mi Casa*, at the Punta Rucia turnoff in Villa Elisa, is another good option. There's also an ATM in Villa Vasquez, the last one out west, so stock up on money before proceeding to Monte Cristi.

Monte Cristi

MONTE CRISTI has the feel of the mythic Wild West, a dusty frontier town bearing the occasional tarnished remnant of its opulent past along wide, American-style boulevards that the sand incessantly tries to reclaim. One of the very oldest European cities in the New World, it was founded in 1501 and became one of the country's most important ports in the eighteenth century, when it shipped out vast quantities of mahogany. The next century saw the port, like Puerto Plata to the east, benefit greatly from the tobacco boom, but its prosperity came to an abrupt end during the era of Trujillo, who shut down its shipping in retribution for local resistance to his rule. The town has never fully recovered, and the only industry of note comes from the large Morton **saltpans** – rectangular pools of the salty local water that are filled from a canal and then harvested by allowing the water to evaporate – just north and south of the city, which supply much of North America's table salt.

There are a couple of century-old mansions worth seeing in town, but most people use Monte Cristi as a base from which to explore the local **beaches** and the **Parque Nacional Monte Cristi**. The latter protects a towering mesa named El Morro, an enormous river delta region with a wildlife-filled mangrove coast and a series of seven nearby islands known as **Los Siete Hermanos**, coral reef-wreathed sand protrusions that sea turtles use to lay their eggs.

The Town

Within town, the charming parque central is worth a look, with a singular Eiffel-style **clock tower**, imported from France at the turn of the century, in its centre and a pretty faux-colonial church across the street. Also at the park on Duarte is the Victorian **Villa Doña Emilia Jiménez**, a palatial old building that was the residence of an early Dominican president and until recently served as the town courthouse; it's been undergoing renovation and may be open for visitation by the time you arrive. In the barrio just south of the park are several c.1900 gingerbread homes worth a look, including one two blocks south on Calle Mella that was owned by Cuban liberator **Máximo Gómez**. It's now a fairly dreary museum (Mon–Fri 9am–noon & 2.30–5.30pm; free), set in a nice garden, with period furnishings, personal mementoes and an account of his fight for the liberation of both Cuba and the Dominican Republic from Spain.

Carnival in Monte Cristi

Monte Cristi is somewhat infamous for its peculiarly violent Carnival celebrations. Each Sunday in February, the locals split into two groups: the **Toros**, who dress in stylized Carnival bull masks and bright cloth outfits decorated with mirrors, whistles and other miscellaneous bangles, and the unadorned **Civilis**. Both parties protect themselves by putting on four or five layers of clothing, including winter coats, then proceed to attack each other in the streets with bullwhips. Police measure the whips beforehand to ensure that they do not exceed a certain length, and combatants are not supposed to hit anyone in the face, though these safety measures don't eliminate the danger. Onlookers are supposed to be safe from the proceedings, but with hundreds of people whizzing deadly weapons through the air, you're better off watching the "festivities" from the second-floor balcony of the *Hotel Chic* restaurant, conveniently located at the centre of the action.

Monte Cristi's beaches

Just north of the city, 2.5km up Calle Bolaños past the saltpans, is **Playa Juan de Bolaños**, the area's most popular beach. At its entrance you'll find a cluster of restaurants; elsewhere it's less populated, and the stark desert whiteness of the landscape makes the water's perfect turquoise even more inviting. East of the restaurants, the beach road passes numerous small fishing boats and the large Club Nautico Marina before arriving at the entrance to the eastern half of Parque Nacional Monte Cristi (see below). A half-kilometre to the west is a river you'll have to ford by foot to reach the beach known locally as **Playa de los Muertos** (Beach of the Dead), its most notable feature the palm trees that have been uprooted and deposited here by tide and tropical storms. To get to Playa de los Muertos by car, drive south of town on Carretera 45 until you arrive at the first bridge. From there take a right, and the dirt road will lead you straight to the beach.

Parque Nacional Monte Cristi

Parque Nacional Monte Cristi is essentially divided into two parts by Monte Cristi's beaches. Its eastern section is often referred to as Parque El Morro, after the flat-topped mesa **El Morro** that takes up a good chunk of it. Climbing the mesa is reasonably straightforward as the park office has built a set of steps up from the road's highest point, near its office at the far eastern end of Playa Bolaños (RD$50 entrance fee). At the foot of El Morro's eastern slope is a lovely and unpopulated **beach** accessible by parking at the end of the same road and continuing down on foot. From there you can swim out to **Isla Cabrita**, a large island punctuated by a lighthouse, some 300m offshore. The waters surrounding the park contain several **shipwrecks**, two of them colonial-era galleons – long plundered – that sought safe harbour from storm in the Bahía Manzanillo just west of here and didn't make it.

The western half of the national park encompasses an inland swath of arid desert environment, a dense mangrove coast dotted with small lagoons, and some desert islands visited by sea turtles. The fairly uninteresting inland section can be reached through the scarecrow-lined dirt roads that lead through adjacent farms and into the park along Carretera 45. The mangrove coast is far more beautiful, though accessible only by boat; informal tours are led from the *Los Jardines* hotel (see below; RD$300), on which you'll see several river deltas thick with mangroves and perhaps a couple of crocodiles. The swamp is also home to innumerable orchids, along with ibises, egrets, pelicans and a host of other birds. The same hotel offers tours to **Los Siete Hermanos**, seven tiny islands a kilometre offshore, with arid vegetation and desolate beaches. By far the most beautiful is known as "Tuna", in honour of the gorgeous, white-flowering tuna cacti that grow here. To see the mangrove swamps or Los Siete Hermanos, you might also try hiring a fishing boat at Playa Bolaños (from RD$250 per person), or a small yacht at the Playa Bolaños (from RD$500 per person).

Practicalities

The best **accommodation** in Monte Cristi is *Cayo Arena*, Playa Juan de Bolaños, 250m west of the beach entrance (☎579-3145, ℗579-2096; ❹). Here you'll find a set of large, full-service apartments on the beach, with ocean-view balconies, a/c, kitchenettes, swimming pool, bar and 24-hour security – they sleep six and are ideal for a family. Also on the beach, a little more basic but better value if travelling alone or with only one other, is *Los Jardines*, Playa Juan de Bolaños (☎579-2091, Ⓦwww.elbistrot.com; ❸), which has simple rooms with cold-water showers. Both of these hotels get busy over the weekend and the rates go up accordingly. Off the water, downtown's rather noisy *Hotel Chic*, Monción 44 (☎579-2316; ❸), maintains somewhat run-down but serviceable accommodations with a good restaurant and outdoor cafeteria next door. The *Don Gaspar*, Jiménez 21 (☎579-2477, ℗579-2206; ❷), is a better choice, though the town noise remains a problem.

At the entrance to Playa Bolaños, *Cocomar* is the best of the beach **restaurants**, with unbelievably good kingfish and crab dishes from around RD$90. The concrete floor and shuttered windows can feel quite sombre when it's quiet but it's friendly and often very lively. *El Bistrot*, on Calle Bolaños (☎579-2091), is the best eating option in town, serving great seafood dishes, particularly lobster (RD$180), in an atmospheric courtyard.

If moving on by **bus**, the Caribe Tours office is at the corner of Mella and Camargo (☎579-2129); most other services, including Codetel, the petrol stations and the pharmacy, are also located on Calle Mella. Tricom is across the street from *Hotel Chic* on Monción and Duarte.

Travel details

The stretch of northern coast between Puerto Plata and Río San Juan is the most heavily trafficked **guagua** route in the country; you'll rarely have to wait longer than five minutes for one to stop and pick you up. It should cost you no more than RD$60 for the full route from Puerto Plata to Río San Juan; be wary if you're quoted anything above that. Guaguas are also the fastest way to get to the area west of Puerto Plata or to the Samaná Peninsula, though **Caribe Tours** do routes to both – if you're heading to Monte Cristi and points west you'll have to change buses in Santiago. Travelling down the Autopista Duarte to Santiago and Santo Domingo is most easily done with one of the official bus companies. Caribe Tours and Metro run south from Puerto Plata, while the downscale Transporte del Cibao does the trip to Santiago from both Puerto Plata and Sosúa. Caribe Tours and Metro have comprehensive, free printed schedules available in their terminals.

Buses

Cabarete to: Cabrera (2 daily; 1hr 15min); Nagua (2 daily; 1hr 45min); Puerto Plata (3 daily; 1hr); Río San Juan (3 daily; 1hr 15min); Samaná (2 daily; 3hr); Sánchez (2 daily; 2hr 30min); Sosúa (3 daily; 20min).

Esperanza to: Mao (4 daily; 30min); Monte Cristi (4 daily; 3hr); Santiago (4 daily; 1hr); Santo Domingo (4 daily; 3hr 20min).

Guayacanes to: Dajabón (4 daily; 2hr 30min); Monte Cristi (4 daily; 2hr); Santiago (4 daily; 2hr 30min); Santo Domingo (4 daily; 4hr).

Guayubín to: Manzanillo (2 daily; 1hr 20min); Santiago (2 daily; 3hr); Santo Domingo (2 daily; 6hr).

Mao to: Esperanza (4 daily; 30min); Loma de Cabrera (2 daily; 2hr); Los Indios de Chacuey (2 daily; 1hr 30min); Santiago (4 daily; 1hr 45min); Santo Domingo (4 daily; 4hr 15min).

Monte Cristi to: Dajabón (4 daily; 30min); Esperanza (4 daily; 3hr); Guayacanes (4 daily; 2hr); Guayubín (4 daily; 1hr); La Vega (4 daily; 4hr 35min); Santiago (4 daily; 4hr); Santo Domingo (4 daily; 6hr 20min); Villa Vasquez (4 daily; 40min).

Puerto Plata to: Bonao (20 daily; 3hr 30min); Cabarete (2 daily; 1hr); La Vega (23 daily; 2hr 45min); Moca (3 daily; 2hr 40min); Nagua (2 daily; 2hr 45min); Piedra Blanca (10 daily; 4hr 30min); Río San Juan (2 daily; 2hr 15min); Samaná (1 daily; 4hr 10min); Sánchez (2 daily; 3hr 35min); Santiago (16 daily; 2hr 10min); Santo Domingo (17 daily; 4hr 30min); Sosúa (2 daily; 40min).

Río San Juan to: Cabarete (3 daily; 1hr 15min); Nagua (2 daily; 45min); Puerto Plata (3 daily; 2hr 15min); Samaná (2 daily; 1hr 45min); Sánchez (1hr 15min); Santo Domingo (4hr 30min); Sosúa (3 daily; 1hr 40min).

Sosúa to: Bonao (20 daily; 3hr 30min); Cabarete (2 daily; 20min); La Vega (10 daily; 3hr); Nagua (2 daily; 2 hr); Piedra Blanca (10 daily; 3hr 45min); Puerto Plata (10 daily; 40 min); Río San Juan (2 daily; 1hr 40min); Samaná (1 daily; 3hr 30min); Sánchez (1 daily; 2hr 50min); Santiago (20 daily; 3hr); Santo Domingo (20 daily; 5hr 10min).

Villa Vasquez to: Dajabón (4 daily; 1hr 20min); Monte Cristi (4 daily; 40min); Santiago (4 daily; 3hr 20min); Santo Domingo (4 daily; 5hr 50min).

Guaguas

Cabarete to: Gaspar Hernández (frequent; 30min); Puerto Plata (frequent; 1hr); Río San Juan (frequent; 1hr 30min); Sabaneta de Yásica (frequent; 15min); Sosúa (frequent; 20min).

El Bretón to: Cabrera (frequent; 15min); Nagua (frequent; 45min), Río San Juan (frequent; 20min).

El Castillo to: Estero Hondo (6 daily; 30min); Luperón (6 daily; 30min).

Esperanza to: Mao (20 daily; 30min); Monción (20 daily; 1hr); Monte Cristi (9 daily; 3hr); Santiago (20 daily; 1hr 30min).

Estero Hondo to: El Castillo (6 daily; 30min); Guayacanes (5 daily; 2hr); Imbert (10 daily; 2hr); Punta Rucia (12 daily; 20min); Villa Elisa (12 daily; 2hr).

Gaspar Hernández to: Cabarete (frequent; 30min); Puerto Plata (frequent; 1hr 30min); Río San Juan (frequent; 1hr); Sabaneta de Yásica (frequent; 20min); Sosúa (frequent; 45min).

Guayubín to: Monte Cristi (4 daily; 1hr), Sabaneta (5 daily; 50min).

Guzmancito to: Puerto Plata Carretera (4 daily; 1hr).

Imbert to: Estero Hondo (10 daily; 2hr); Luperón (15 daily; 1hr 30min); Navarrete (frequent; 2hr); Puerto Plata (frequent; 40min).

Luperón to: El Castillo (6 daily; 30min); Imbert (15 daily; 1hr 30min).

Mao to: Esperanza (20 daily; 30min); Monción (20 daily; 30min); Sabaneta (6 daily; 1hr 15min); Santiago (20 daily; 1hr 45min).

Monte Cristi to: Batey Isabel (10 daily; 45min); Dajabón (12 daily; 1hr 10min); Esperanza (9 daily; 3hr); Guayacanes (24 daily; 2hr); Guayubín (4 daily; 1hr); Manzanillo (11 daily; 40min); Navarrete (12 daily; 3hr 30min); Sabaneta (4 daily; 1hr 40min); Santiago (12 daily; 4hr); Villa Elisa (24 daily; 1hr 30min).

Puerto Plata to: Cabarete (frequent; 1hr); Gaspar Hernández (frequent; 1hr 30min); Imbert (frequent; 40min); Navarrete (frequent; 2hr); Río San Juan (frequent; 2hr 15min); Sabaneta de Yásica (frequent; 1hr 15min); Sosúa (frequent; 40min).

Punta Rucia to: Estero Hondo (12 daily weekends only; 20min); Villa Elisa (10 daily weekends only; 1hr 30min).

Río San Juan to: Cabarete (frequent; 1hr 30min); Cabrera (frequent; 30min); El Bretón (frequent; 20min); Gaspar Hernández (frequent; 1hr); La Entrada (frequent; 40min); Nagua (frequent; 1hr); Puerto Plata (frequent; 2hr 15min); Sabaneta de Yásica (frequent; 1hr 15min); Sosúa (frequent; 1hr 40min).

Sabaneta to: Guayubín (5 daily; 50min); Loma de Cabrera (7 daily; 1hr 15min); Mao (10 daily; 1hr 15min); Monción (6 daily; 1hr 30min); Monte Cristi (4 daily; 1hr 40min); Santiago de la Cruz (7 daily; 1hr).

Sabaneta de Yásica to: Cabarete (frequent; 15min); Gaspar Hernández (frequent; 20min); Moca (15 daily; 2hr); Puerto Plata (frequent; 1hr 15min); Río San Juan (frequent; 1hr 15min); Sosúa (frequent; 30min).

Sosúa to: Cabarete (frequent; 20min); Gaspar Hernández (frequent; 45min); Puerto Plata (frequent; 40min); Río San Juan (frequent; 1hr 40min); Sabaneta de Yásica (frequent; 30min); Santiago (hourly; 2hr); Tubeagua (hourly; 45min).

Tubeagua to: Santiago (hourly; 1hr 15min); Sosúa (hourly; 45min).

Villa Elisa to: Monte Cristi (hourly; 1hr 30min); Navarrete (hourly; 1hr 30min); Punta Rucia (10 daily weekends only; 1hr 30min); Santiago (hourly; 2hr).

Flights

Puerto Plata to: La Romana (daily; 40min); Las Terrenas (daily; 30min); Punta Cana (4 daily; 45min); Santo Domingo (4 daily; 30min).

The Cibao

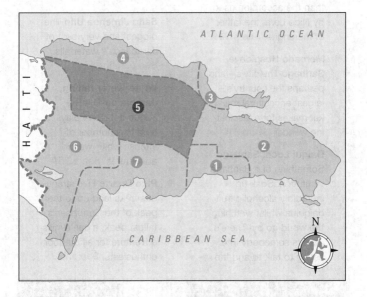

ATLANTIC OCEAN

HAITI

④

③

⑤

②

⑥

⑦

①

N

CARIBBEAN SEA

CHAPTER 5

Highlights

✳ **Museo Folklórico de Tomas Morel, Santiago** A myriad of authentic carnival masks, religious artefacts and the first television, telephone and wood saw in the country. For pure patriotism it's difficult to imagine a greater star of the show than the accordion used by Nico Lora, the father of merengue. See p.244

✳ **Mercado Hospidaye, Santiago** The city's – and perhaps the country's – largest agricultural market makes for a fascinating wander. See p.245

✳ **Daiqui Loco, Santiago** Something of a Santiago institution. Soak up incredibly alcoholic fruit daiquiris whilst watching the world go by. There's always somebody interesting to talk to and the snacks aren't bad too. See p.247

✳ **La Vega Carnival** A highlight of this massive street party held in February is the platoons of rowdy participants roaming the streets in wild hand-crafted masks. See p.252

✳ **Salto Jimenoa Uno** The biggest and very best of Jarabacoa's waterfalls. See p.255

✳ **White-water rafting, Jarabacoa** The Río Yaque del Norte plays host to a number of intense white-water adventures. See p.257

✳ **Pico Duarte** Five strenuous treks lead up to the peak of the Caribbean's tallest peak, a can't-miss adventure for all outdoor enthusiasts. See p.258

5

The Cibao

Cibao (rocky land) is the word Tainos used to describe the Cordillera Central mountain range that takes up much of the Dominican Republic's central interior, ploughs westward through Haiti (where it's called the Massif du Nord) and then pops up again in Cuba and Central America. The Dominican section of these mountains has by far the **highest peaks** in the Caribbean, higher even than North America's Appalachians, with some mountains over 3000m, including **Pico Duarte**, the Caribbean's tallest at 3087m. Today the heart of the range is protected as **Parques Nacionales Bermúdez y Ramírez** and **Reserva Científica Valle Nuevo**, three national parks inaugurated during the 1960s and 1970s to preserve the remaining virgin pine and cloud forest, as well as the many rivers that begin in these parts. The need to safeguard the region's rivers rests in no small part with the fact that they provide ninety percent of the DR's fresh water and a third of its electricity.

Today, though, Dominicans use the term Cibao more to describe the fertile **Cibao Valley** – the island's breadbasket since pre-Columbian times – that lies between the Cordillera Central to the south and the Cordillera Septentrional to the north, the mountain range seen clearly from the north coast. This valley can be neatly divided into two sections: the **western Cibao**, a ribbon of farmland north of the central mountains, and the prosperous **Vega Real**, a triangle of alluvial plain between **Santiago, Cotuí** and **San Francisco de Macorís** that contains some of the deepest topsoil in the world. During the nineteenth century the Vega Real's agricultural middle classes were the country's primary exponents of democracy and engaged in a century-long struggle for power with the demagogic cattle ranchers of the southeast.

The appeal of the Cibao is not as obvious as that of the coastal resorts, but you'll still find plenty to do, especially in **Santiago**, the country's second largest city after Santo Domingo. Besides its legendary nightlife scene, Santiago is well positioned for short excursions into the neighbouring farmland, which produces some of world's best **cigars** – you can easily see the process firsthand. Likely, you'll head south from Santiago on your way to Santo Domingo, past a chain of Cibao towns that Columbus founded as gold-mining outposts. Of these, **La Vega** is the choice stop, holding as it does the DR's largest **Carnival** celebration and the ruins of Columbus's colony La Vega Vieja, east of the present-day city.

For most, however, the first priority is the **mountains.** Surrounded by dense alpine vegetation, the small but bubbly town of **Jarabacoa** is the most set up for tourism, with a nice, though limited, array of hotels and restaurants, plus plenty of adventure-tour outfits offering everything from white-water rafting,

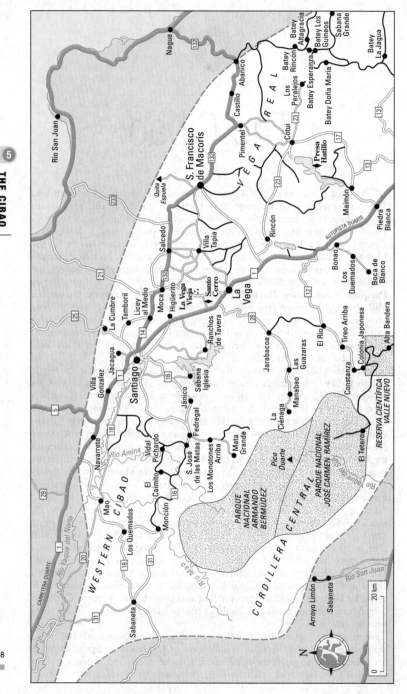

kayaking, and cascading to three-day treks up bald-headed **Pico Duarte**. Another Pico Duarte trail begins near **San José de las Matas**, a mellow mountain village that makes a pleasant day-trip from Santiago; while one of the most difficult – a gruelling five-day jaunt – sets off from **Constanza**, a circular Shangri-La valley in the heart of the highest part of the range. Aside from the isolation and fresh air, Constanza's attractions include several hiking trails, another impressive waterfall and a jagged but scenic road that leads south through **Reserva Científica Valle Nuevo** to **San José de Ocóa** at the southern end of the range. Wherever you go, remember that these are big mountains and should be explored only with hiking boots, winter clothing and a waterproof coat.

If you want to get away from where everyone else is headed, look no further than the farming towns in the Vega Real, like **Moca**, **Cotuí** and San Francisco de Macorís. Though not necessarily teeming with things to do, the rural towns east of the mountains in fairly fertile flatland are pleasant and easy enough to reach.

The western Cibao

The **WESTERN CIBAO** is the less fertile of the valley's two halves, increasingly arid as it approaches the Haitian border. Extending in a narrow ribbon between two mountain ranges, its fields are given over to tobacco near **Santiago**, the heartland city that separates it from the Vega Real; to rice paddies in the quieter districts surrounding **Mao**; and to irrigated banana plantations as it devolves into a desert from **Sabaneta** onward. Outside of Santiago the main interest will come from some **beautiful mountain scenery** and an opportunity to rub shoulders with the locals away from the traditional tourist trail. If you need something to aim for, consider a short jaunt to **San José de las Matas** or **Monción**, villages in the northern foothills of the Cordillera Central, easily accessible from both Santiago and Mao.

Santiago

For five centuries **SANTIAGO** has been the main transport point for Cibao tobacco, bananas, coffee and chocolate; farmers still truck the lion's share of their produce here, from where it is shipped to Puerto Plata and Santo Domingo for export. Set at the intersection of the western Cibao and the Vega Real, and with easy access to the country's two major ports, its prime location has brought settlers back time and again – Santiago's population of 800,000 trails only that of Santo Domingo – even after destruction by various earthquakes, invading armies and fires.

Founded in 1504 as a mining town and demolished by an earthquake in 1562, Santiago has been associated with tobacco since it was introduced for export to the French in 1679. The Haitian army slaughtered most residents

Cibao tobacco

Tobacco was first cultivated (and given its name) by the Tainos, who pressed the leafy plant into a rock-hard substance to be smoked in pipes. Many Cibao peasants still make this form of tobacco – called *andullo* – which you can find if you ask around in Tamboril, Navarrete or Villa González; it's sometimes even for sale in local *colmados*. Export began in 1679, when Cibao farmers started growing it for the French colony on the western side of the island. For two centuries, Dominican tobacco was widely praised as top quality, but when large-scale export to Germany for cigarette filler began in the mid-nineteenth century, that quality soon began to erode.

Tobacco was traditionally farmed by local peasants, who grew small plots of it alongside their vegetable gardens and sold the dried leaves to local middlemen for cash, who then transported it to Puerto Plata and sold it at a profit to large German export firms. When the US took over customs receipts in 1907, the Germans imposed tariffs that eradicated the old market, and many of the former middlemen opened **cigar factories** for export to the States. Cigar quality wasn't top-rate, though, until revolution sent many prominent Havana tobacco men to the Cibao, where they developed an industry that today sells more cigars than Cuba's, and just as good ones. During the 1990s, more and more small-scale businessmen have tried to take advantage of the high profile of Dominican cigars by opening up factories of their own, but they've had a hard time equalling the quality of more established firms: many are now going out of business.

If you're in the region to **purchase cigars**, don't be surprised to find that many of the best-known DR brands are not readily available locally. This is because companies dedicated to export are usually not involved or interested in regional distribution. The bad news is that this puts the visitor in the difficult position of identifying good quality without the benefit of recognizable brand names. The good news is that regional product is often as good or even better than the famous brand names, and usually much cheaper because of its anonymity. If you're not a connoisseur, though, and are looking to buy cigars without first smoking a tester, there are two nationally available brands that shouldn't let you down: Carbonell and Leon Jimenez. The latter also markets a secondary quality brand widely available called Aurorais. All three are respectable, consistent in quality, reasonably priced and should be available for purchase nearly everywhere.

during an 1805 invasion, but the city was again rebuilt and served for the rest of the century as transport hub for tobacco headed to Puerto Plata and Germany. During this time *merengue périco ripao* – the classic Dominican music using accordion, tambora and güira – evolved in Santiago, and the city has since produced many of the DR's top musicians, giving it a bit of cultural flair amidst agriculture's pre-eminence.

As well, there's a good club scene, based mostly around this indigenous music, so you won't lack for fun at nights. Otherwise, it's worthwhile to spend a few days, certainly no more, browsing around **downtown Santiago** and its surrounding barrios. Downtown holds the most of interest, both in a busy street life and a collection of fine **museums**, devoted to tobacco and folkloric art, and architecture. On the edge of downtown looms the mighty **Monument a los Héroes de la Restauración**, visible from pretty much anywhere in the city. Further out, you can opt for a few nice factory tours, either to check out the local **tobacco** product or to see how **rum** is made.

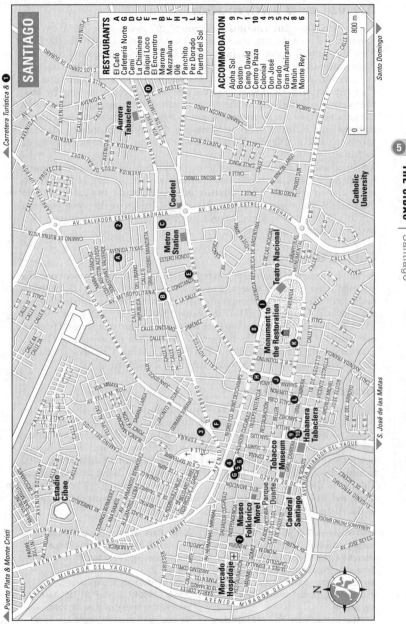

SANTIAGO

RESTAURANTS

El Café	A
Cafetería Norte	G
Cemi	D
La Chiminea	C
Daiquí Loco	I
El Encuentro	B
Maroma	F
Mezzaluna	H
Olé	J
Panchito	L
Pez Dorado	L
Puerto del Sol	K

ACCOMMODATION

Aloha Sol	9
Boston	7
Camp David	1
Centro Plaza	10
Colonial	4
Don José	3
Dorado	5
Gran Almirante	2
Matún	8
Monte Rey	6

▲ Carretera Turística & ❶

◀ Puerto Plata & Monte Cristi

Santo Domingo ▶

S. José de las Matas ▶

0 · 800 m

Catholic University

Estadio Cibao

Aurora Tabaclera

Codetel

Metro Station

Teatro Nacional

Monument to the Restoration

Habanera Tabaclera

Tobacco Museum

Museo Folklorico Morel

Mercado Hospidaje

Catedral Santiago

Parque Duarte

AVENIDA MIRADOR DEL YAQUE

N

THE CIBAO | Santiago

5

241

Arrival and information

The new **Cibao International Airport** (☎226-0664) is just a twenty-minute drive from the city, and receives American Airlines flights directly from New York as well as domestic flights from Air Santo Domingo and American Eagle. You're more likely, though, to be arriving by land, and all three highway entrances to town – the Autopista Duarte, the Carretera Duarte and the Carretera Turística – lead directly to the city centre. If you're arriving **by bus**, your station will likely be on the north or east side of town, from where you can get an RD$40 taxi closer to the heart of downtown. There are also **guagua stations** on the corner of 30 de Marzo and Cucurullo (guaguas to Mao and Monción), and on Calle Valerio a block west of Parque Valerio (to San José de las Matas).

Nacional and *La Información* are the two major Santiago daily **newspapers**, with useful local phone numbers on the second page, a listing of local events and a cinema schedule. The **tourism office**, JP Duarte and Estero Hondo (Mon–Fri 9.30am–noon & 2–5pm; ☎&ⓕ582-5885), is on the second floor of city hall; though they're friendly, they have little in the way of information likely to be relevant to your stay.

City transport

A complex system of battered public taxis – referred to locally as **motoconchos** – should cover most city transport needs; a one-way ride runs RD$5. **Private taxis** wait at the city parks, though you can call directly for pickup: reliable operators include Camino (☎971-7788), Servi (☎971-6737) and Rosa (☎971-5555). As always, you're best off sticking with an established international firm for **car rental**. Options include Budget, 27 de Febrero (☎566-6666); Honda, Estrella Sadhalá and 27 de Febrero (☎575-6077); Metro, Carretera Jacagua 42 (☎570-5911); and Nelly, Av Salvador E Sadhalá 204 (☎583-6695).

Accommodation

Santiago is pretty well set up for **accommodation**. The *Gran Almirante* is the one five-star hotel in town, but also on the luxurious side is the recently renovated *Centro Plaza*, home to a gymnasium and a sixth-floor restaurant offering huge views over the city. Cheaper options abound: a half-dozen budget hotels are clustered around the corner of **Cucurullo and 30 de Marzo**, while far more basic and less appetizing RD$75 dives can be found around **Parque Valerio** at the far southern end of the downtown rectangle. The hotels on **Calle del Sol** cater mostly to passing businessmen and – with the exception of the *Aloha Sol* – are run-down and overpriced.

Aloha Sol Del Sol 50 ☎583-0090, ⓕ583-0950. Modern hotel with a/c, TV and great hot showers, although the rooms are quite small. Right in the centre of the shopping district and a good alternative for those who want comfortable, Western-style accommodation but can't afford the *Gran Almirante*. ❹

Ámbar Av Estrella Sadhalá Km 2 and Las Colinas ☎575-4811. Reasonably priced hotel with average-sized rooms and modern amenities, inconveniently located 3km northwest of the town centre. ❸

Boston Plaza Valerio (no phone). The cleanest of the extremely basic hotels around Parque Valerio. Expect cold water and few home comforts. ❶

Camp David Carretera Turística Km 12 ☎223-0666 or 626-0587, ⓕ736-7165. Top choice for those wanting to stay out of the city centre, this one time Trujillo mountain home is now a hotel and restaurant that's popular with wealthy Dominicans. The nearly forty rooms are large and comfortable, and many have balconies with stunning views over the city. A museum on site houses many of the former dictator's cars including, eerily, the one in which he was assassinated. ④

Centro Plaza Mella 54 ☎581-7000, ⓕ582-4566, ⓔhcentroplaza@codetel.net.do. Large Western-style hotel, in an ideal central location, with huge, comfortable rooms and all the amenities you could wish for including a gym, an excellent restaurant and a stunning honeymoon suite. Regular special offers make it even more attractive. ④

Colonial Cucurullo and 30 de Marzo ☎247-3122, ⓕ582-0811. Great little budget hotel with friendly service, clean rooms, a/c and TV. ②

Don José Colón 42 ☎581-7480. Large building with a small restaurant and good clean budget-priced rooms in a useful central location. Rooms with private bathrooms and a/c are a bit more. ①–②

Dorado Cucurullo 88 ☎582-7563. Good-value cheapie with fan and hot water. Not quite as nice as *Colonial*, but comfortable enough. ①

Gran Almirante Estrella Sadhalá and Calle 10 ☎580-1992, ⓕ241-1492, ⓦwww.hodelpa.com. Elegant luxury hotel in a wealthy northeastern suburb with tennis courts, swimming pool, three restaurants, a casino and a happening disco. If you've got the money, this is the place. ⑤

Matún Las Carreras 1 ☎581-3107, ⓕ581-8415. Recently renovated Trujillo-era hotel, perfect for those who want to enjoy Santiago's nightlife as it's located right by the monument. Other advantages include a/c, cable TV and a casino. ④

Monte Rey Cucurullo 90 ☎582-4558. Unremarkable downtown budget hotel located in a drab concrete building with a small restaurant attached. ①

The City

Most places of interest are **downtown** and within walking distance of one another; in fact, many visitors spend their whole stay in the area bounded by the monument and the main city park. The outer **barrios** hold a couple of attractions worth the effort, though they're spread out enough to make a taxi the easiest way to get to them.

The monument and around

Defining the eastern boundary of downtown is the **Monument a los Héroes de la Restauración** (Mon–Sat 9am–noon & 2–5pm; free), Santiago's most impressive sight. Built by Trujillo in honour of himself, it was quickly rededicated upon his death to the soldiers who lost their lives in the War of Independence with Spain. A statue of Victory personified as a woman tops its seventy-metre pillar, supported by a marble base, her arms extended martially towards the sky. Helped by its position atop a hill, the monument is visible from the entire city, something locals say was originally intended to symbolize the omnipresence of the secret police. It's possible to climb the stairs to the top of the monument to take in the breathtaking **panorama** of Santiago and the surrounding valley and mountains. The inside is given over to a large **mural** by Vela Zanetti, a social-realist influenced by Diego Rivera, who was forced to leave the country after ignoring Trujillo's request that his painting be a direct tribute to the dictator. The mural depicts Dominican peasants, labourers and soldiers winding up the monument's circular stairway in arduous pursuit of liberty; though much of it is covered to prevent further deterioration, you can see portions of it as you clamber to the top.

Just east of the monument the palatial **Gran Teatro del Cibao** (☎583-1150), a rectangle of Italian marble, was built by Balaguer in the 1980s. Its main auditorium seats fifteen thousand and has near-perfect acoustics. Unfortunately, the majority of Santiago residents can't afford the hefty RD$300 ticket price, so the large hall goes mostly unused. There are, though, a couple of opera productions per year, with occasional merengue concerts, chamber music and theatre in the smaller concert hall. Across the street from the theatre the sprawling **Catholic University**, Pontificia Universidad Católica Madre y Maestro or "Pucamaima" as it's best known, caters to the area's wealthy students and is set on an attractive, wooded campus that provides a bit of a respite from crowded downtown. There are two entrances, one on Autopista Duarte and the other on Estrella Sadhalá; with a photo ID you can get a free visitor's pass from the security guard at either entrance, from where you can wander the tree-lined grounds and check out the lively student scene. **Calle del Sol**, which borders the monument to the west, is the city's major shopping district and the heart of downtown activity, lined with department stores, banks and sidewalk stalls selling clothing, household wares and fast food.

Parque Duarte and around

Follow Del Sol north to 30 de Marzo and you'll pass through the heart of the city before arriving at **Parque Duarte**, a bit overcrowded but covered by a tree canopy and lined with horse-and-carriage drivers giving rides to the monument and back; the price is negotiable, but expect to pay around RD$100. At the park's southern end stands the **Catedral de Santiago** (1895), a lavender, concrete building with intricate carvings on its mahogany portals and stained-glass windows by contemporary Dominican artist Rincón Mora. The marble tomb of nineteenth-century dictator Ulises Heureaux is in the sanctuary. Just across the street is the excellent **Museo del Tabaco**, on 16 de Agosto and 30 de Marzo (Tues–Fri 9am–noon & 2–5pm, Sat 9am–noon; free), housed in a old Victorian tobacco warehouse. Exhibits inside cover the history of the crop's use dating back to Taino times, its social and economic impact on the region and quick looks at various farming methods; there's also a mock cigar room in which you can see how tobacco is processed and rolled. Meanwhile, north of the park on Monción are two of downtown's more attractive buildings, the **Centro de Recreo** – an ornate mansion that looks more like a mosque, built a century ago and today a private social club – and the **Palacio Consistorial** (Tues–Fri 10am–noon & 2–5.30pm, Sat & Sun 10am–2pm; free), a renovated gingerbread that was once city hall but now houses a small museum documenting Santiago's history, mostly through photographs. Around the corner on Calle del Sol and Monción sits the nondescript **Centro de la Cultura**, home of the highly regarded School of Fine Arts and with regular opera, theatre and chamber music productions in its auditorium.

Three blocks south of the park **La Habanera Tabaclera**, 16 de Agosto and San Luis (Mon–Fri 8.30am–4.30pm; free), is the oldest working Dominican cigar factory and one of the few in the city that offers tours, though free samples are not included. You do get to witness cigar rollers at work, one pressing the filler into shape and a second applying the wrap; other employees pull apart huge mounds of dried leaves fresh from the field or affix the brand label and box the finished product.

In the opposite direction, a few blocks northwest of the park, the fascinating **Museo Folklòrico de Tomas Morel**, Restauración 174 (Mon–Fri 9am–1pm & 3–6pm; free; ☎582-6787), is somewhat misleadingly pitched as a house of horrors. The dilapidated condition of the exterior does nothing to alter this expectation, but inside you'll find a remarkable collection of papier-mâché Carnival masks, alongside various Taino artefacts, and a faded sixteenth-century painting of the Virgin Mary. Hidden among the scattered exhibits are the Republic's first telephone, first television and even the first wood saw. There's also an accordion that once belonged to Nico Lora, often thought of as the father of merengue. The masks, though, are the main focus, with an array of spectacularly baroque and evil-looking demons from La Vega, the simpler but no less malevolent *Cimarrón diablos* of Cabral, and several masks from politically oriented San Cristóbal – including one with a skin of American flags and nuclear missiles in place of bull horns. The original proprietor was a local poet and folklorist but, following his death in 1992, his nephew took over. If it's not too busy he'll wander around with you giving you an interesting commentary in Spanish. The museum is also something of a hangout for local artists and intellectuals.

Also close by – and taking up most of the western end of downtown – is the enormous outdoor **Mercado Hospidaye**, the city's largest agricultural market and a fascinating place to wander around although the attraction may not be that obvious at first. The roads leading in are lined with huge bins full of beans, corn, bananas, tobacco, oregano, garlic and cassava but these do little to capture the real atmosphere inside which has an almost timeless, mystic feel to it. Within the market, at the corner of 16 de Agosto and Espaillat, the local **botánica** sells portraits of *Santería* saints and potions whipped up on the spot for every conceivable malady, while in hidden back rooms it's possible to get your **tarot cards** read for a small fee.

The outer barrios

Santiago's **outer barrios** are an uneven mix of heavy industry and residential neighbourhoods; with the exception of wealthy **Los Jardines** (home of the *Gran Almirante* hotel), they should be explored exclusively during the day. The first place to head is the cigar factory of **Aurora Tabaclera**, home of the Aurorais brand, south of the monument in barrio Villa Progresa on the corner of Jimenez 2 and Villa Progresa (9.30am–5pm, closed Sun; free; ✆241-1111). After a look at the process of hand rolling, you're escorted to a lux smoking room, where they've got Presidente on tap, to receive a free cigar.

Another factory that offers tours – though service is less attentive – is the **Bermúdez rum plant**, Libertad and Armando Bermúdez (Mon–Fri 9am–noon & 2–4pm; free), in Pueblo Nuevo northwest of downtown. They don't get as many visitors as the Brugal plant in Puerto Plata (see p.199), so you're likely to get a private tour of the processing, bottling and packing operations, perhaps followed by a complimentary *Cuba libre*. From the plant it's just a short walk west to a far more enticing attraction, **Estadio Cibao** on Avenida Imbert and Domingo Bermúdez, Santiago's professional baseball stadium. Winter games last from mid-November through early February and it's best to book an RD$50–150 ticket in advance as the bigger games can sell out. Check local newspapers for schedules, or to see if one of the **travelling carnivals** that regularly set up shop here in the off-season is in town. The only other potential attraction nearby, the **Mercado Central** on Armando Bermúdez and 6 de Diciembre, is less compelling. The large market, housed in a gutted auditorium, is where locals come to buy produce, household wares and clothes; you won't find any souvenirs but it's a good opportunity to look behind the scenes at local commerce. From here you can round off a tour of the neighbourhood by heading a block west to the **municipal cemetery**, 27 de Febrero and 6 de Diciembre (daily 8.30am–5.30pm), a maze of garish marble statuary and small syncretist altars that hold statuettes of the deceased alongside tools of their trade.

Ten kilometres northwest of town and accessible only by car are the ruins of **Jacagua** – sixteenth-century Santiago – worth a visit if you don't have the time to visit the more extensive ones at La Vega Vieja. You're free to wander the large private plantation that holds the numerous scattered stone foundations and crumbling walls, many of them pockmarked by weeds, though it's difficult to get any real sense of the town's layout from what's left. Conceived as a gold-mining outpost, old Santiago quickly transformed into an agricultural hub before being swallowed in a catastrophic earthquake in the late sixteenth century, after which the city was moved to its present location. If you'd like to see what's left, take Estrella Sadhalá west until you reach the "Plazanutty" sign at the Carretera Jacagua, where you'll go north. A left turn at the fork in the road will lead you 2km to the ruins.

Eating

As befits such a big city, you'll have no problem finding plenty to **eat**, whether it's at fine dining establishments, low-key *comedores* or American fast-food chains. Most of the top spots are clustered in the wealthy barrio **Los Jardines**, near the *Gran Almirante*, but good, moderately priced options also abound near the monument and Catholic University. A bit north of town, up the Carretera Turística, is *Cemi*, an incredibly atmospheric restaurant well worth the drive out (see below for review). If you need to stock up on **groceries**, try the Supermercado Nacional, at 27 de Febrero and Estrella Sadhalá.

El Café Texas and Calle 5, Los Jardines ☏ 587-4247. Swanky, white-linen restaurant specializing in sea bass, rack of lamb and porterhouse steaks, and with an extensive wine list.

Cafetería Norte Cucurullo and 30 de Marzo. Typical, family-run cafeteria with goat stew, fish and *pollo al carbón*. Best for lunch, when the food hasn't been sitting for too long under the heat lamps.

Camp David Carretera Turística Km 12 ☏ 223-0666. Former Trujillo mountain home, now converted into a gourmet restaurant and hostelry (see p.242), that offers a long list of choice seafood dishes and steaks. Look for the turnoff on the Carretera Turística, then drive up a winding road for 2km.

Cemi E Leon Jiménez. Downtown version of the infamous thatched hut on the Carretera Turística (see p.248). Same menu and same excellent pseudo Taino food dished out in a cosy courtyard atmosphere that equals the original, with friendly service that, if anything, is more attentive.

La Chiminea 27 de Febrero and Maimòn. Family-oriented outdoor restaurant with picnic tables and a playground for kids. Santiago's best pizzas, plus *criolla* steaks and *pollo al carbón*.

Cristobal *Gran Almirante Hotel*, Estrella Sadhalá and Calle 10. Pricey Castilian restaurant with wonderfully cooked *chillo*, octopus, paella and *lambí*.

Daiquí Loco JP Duarte and Oueste. Festive outdoor bar with the best grilled sandwiches and burritos in town, some for as little as RD\$10. Frozen daiquiris are also a speciality. Definitely the place to watch the world go by.

El Encuentro Argentina and Las Carreras. Popular outdoor hangout near the monument that serves up tacos and other Mexican fast food.

Maroma Metropolitana, behind Mr Movie. Growing in popularity, this restaurant serves out pricey international cuisine in a smart and relaxed setting. The Italian dishes are superb and there's a great choice of wine to complement them.

Mezzaluna 27 de Febrero 77. An outstanding, formal Italian dining room locally renowned for its wide variety of perfectly cooked fresh pastas and the grilled calamari entree.

Olé JP Duarte and Independencia. Creole restaurant serving Dominican staples and American-style pizzas in a thatch-sheltered terrace just off a small park. Also has a take-out window.

Panchito Restauración and JP Duarte. Neon-lit, Dominican, fast-food joint with good fried chicken and RD\$5 coffees. Great breakfasts.

Pez Dorado Del Sol at Parque Altagracia. High-end *cómida criolla* in a fairly formal environment. Highlights include *pollo a la diana*, grilled octopus, garlic shrimp and sea bass. Also some excellent Chinese offerings.

Puerto del Sol Del Sol at the monument. *Cómida criolla*, fast food and very cold beer. Good for people-watching too.

Rancho Luna Carretera Turística Km 7 ☏ 736-7176. Top-quality steakhouse and piano bar situated on the hill below *Camp David*, with excellent service, a huge wine list and great views over the city.

Las Tapas *Gran Almirante Hotel*, Estrella Sadhalá and Calle 10. A casual tapas bar in the hotel courtyard, with a variety of good Spanish seafood appetizers, including pickled octopus, garlic shrimp and salted cod.

Drinking and nightlife

Santiago **nightlife** is rowdy, diverse and seemingly non-stop; most clubs are completely empty until midnight and don't close until dawn. Several cavernous discos offer a steady stream of top **live music**, there are plenty of enjoyable neighbourhood watering holes, especially beneath the monument where things get particularly lively, and a slew of joints that are frequented almost exclusively by the relatively wealthy university crowd. Most clubs and bars are within a reasonable distance of one another in downtown, making it easy to hit two or three in a night, if you're so inclined. For something slightly more cultural, there's Hollywood 7, at Estrella Sadhalá and Argentina, a seven-screen **movie theatre** near the monument and a new multi-screen cinema in the Plaza International shopping mall. The *Gran Almirante* and *Hotel Matún* both hold **casinos** (nightly 4pm–4am).

Alcazar *Gran Almirante Hotel*, Estrella Sadhalá and Calle 10. The best disco in town, featuring a mixture of music but favouring stuff with a Latino feel: it doesn't get hopping until 1am, but stays full until 7am. Dress sharply. RD$50 cover.

Ambis I Autopista Duarte Km 2. Jam-packed dance venue with slick, American-style decor and regular live music. *Ambis II,* next door, is more of a typical, unpretentious Dominican disco, which tends to get used for specific occasions. RD$50 cover, RD$150 for a major live act.

Bar Code Cuba 25. Popular courtyard bar with live Caribbean music. Laid-back and definitely one of *the* places to hang out.

Casa Bader 16 de Agosto 75. More day-life than nightlife and a real Santiago institution. A once men-only haunt but now open to all, this is the oldest bar in town and definitely the place to drink away a Saturday morning. The beer, the coldest in town, is specially cooled by a complex series of different fridges.

Daiqui Loco JP Duarte and Oueste. Outdoor, roadside bar with the best daiquiris in town and a drive-through liquor window.

Dali Café JP Duarte 1. Lively joint with mixed music, plenty of live entertainment and karaoke.

Open-bar nights every Thursday and some Sundays, with a cover charge of RD$100 (men) and RD$50 (Women).

Estación Estrella Sadhalá 67. Twenty-somethings bar with a selection of live music on Mondays. Close to the university and popular with students.

El Fogòn Calle 7 and Estrella Sadhalá. Casual, two-floor outdoor bar popular with Pucamaima students. A half-block north of the Shell station at the campus's main entrance.

Francifol Del Sol at Parque Duarte. A classy, modern-looking pub in a busy downtown area. An excellent place for drinks and conversation.

Metropolis Billar Café Estrella Sadhalá 7. Upmarket billiard hall and lively bar with a strong dress code and an unusually un-masculine atmosphere.

Pops Estrella Sadhalá and 27 de Febrero behind Supermercado Nacional. Popular bar with good mixed drinks, a large aquarium and a DJ spinning a mix of merengue and rock.

Talanca Restauración and Tolentino. Downtown reggae/jazz bar with a great LP collection, plus a courtyard that's shaded by a huge oak tree.

Las Vegas Autopista Navarrete Km 8. Down-home Dominican disco that books a lot of famous live musicians. RD$30 cover, RD$150 for a major act.

Santiago festivals

Santiago is one of the country's prime places to celebrate **Carnival**. Festivities take place every Sunday in February at the monument with throngs of costumed participants wearing colourful papier-mâché demon masks and assaulting each other with inflated sheep bladders; don't wear anything that you feel too precious about. Things culminate on **Independence Day** (February 27), when the entire city comes out for a parade around the monument, accompanied by mobile freak shows, homemade floats and Haitian *gagá* bands. If the local baseball team wins the Latin American Championship (as they did most recently in 1998) the partying lasts for another week. The local **fiesta patronal**, in honour of patron saint Santiago Apostal, is held on July 22 and features dancing, drinking and live music in an outdoor band shell beside the monument.

Listings

Airlines Air Santo Domingo (☎226-8191); American Eagle (☎542-5151); American Airlines (☎226-0664).

Ambulance ☎911 for emergency, or ☎583-4311 for private ambulance.

Banks and currency exchange The four banks at the corner of Calle del Sol and Sánchez offer the best exchange rates in Santiago. Banco Popular, Del Sol and Sánchez (Mon–Fri 8.30am–4.30pm, Sat 9am–noon), has a 24-hour ATM machine, as does Scotia Bank, 30 de Marzo at Parque Duarte (same hours). Another 24-hour ATM machine is at Codetel, JP Duarte and Estrella Sadhalá. There are a number of fairly discreet change-houses on Calle del Sol but avoid the street money-exchangers; they may offer slightly better rates, but they are known to short-change tourists with a sleight-of-hand trick.

Film processing There's a Fotocolor, on Calle del Sol and Mella.

Hospital If you have a medical emergency, head to Centro Médico Cibao, JP Duarte just west of Las Carreras or Clínica Corominas, Restauración 57 ☎580-1171; you can try calling ☎911 or 583-

4311 for other emergencies.

Internet Coffeesport.com, Mella 54, beneath the *Centro Plaza Hotel*. Wizard, Estrella Sadhalá, by the *Metropolis Billar Café*.

Laundry There's a laundromat at Joseph Cleaners, Las Carreras and Sabana Larga (☎583-4850).

Pharmacy Superfarmacia Cristal, Las Carreras and Tolentino, is open 24 hours.

Police Main office is at Sabana Larga and Calle del Sol (☎582-2331).

Post office Main office is at Calle del Sol and San Louis. EPS, Hostos 3 and Bidó (Mon–Fri 9am–5.30pm, Sat 9am–noon; ☎581-1912).

Telephone Codetel, Estrella Sadhalá and JP Duarte (they also have internet access); Televimenca, JP Duarte and Independencia; Tricom, Las Carreras and Cuba and at 27 de Febrero and Estero Hondo.

Travel agents Abby Tours (☎971-7045); Mary Tours (☎587-6111).

Wiring money Western Union on JP Duarte and Independencia (Mon–Sat 9am–noon & 2–5pm).

Around Santiago

In Santiago's immediate vicinity, the urban sprawl quickly peters out into tobacco farmland, and the villages that exist to support this agriculture are not really set up for visitors – or too worth your time, unless you're interested in getting a firsthand look at how **cigar rolling** is done.

La Cumbre, Navarrete and Villa González

Avenida Bartolomé Colón in Santiago becomes the **Carretera Turística** north of Estrella Sadhalá and leads north towards Sosúa. The highway treads through lush, rolling mountains, making for an incredibly scenic, and fairly easy, trek. Nine kilometres along, **LA CUMBRE** is home to the largest system of amber mines in the world, a setting (and inspiration) for the movie *Jurassic Park*. Several roadside souvenir stalls mark its location; to reach the actual mines take the turnoff marked "La Cumbre de Juan Vegas" and continue west 3km. The mines are extremely basic, just deep holes in the ground supported by gerry-rigged wooden frames, with an extensive network of tunnels leading under the mountain from the bottom of the pit. The miners will sell you chunks of amber (though this is technically illegal), some with insects embedded inside them, and for RD$100 they'll even offer to lead you down into one of the pits, armed only with a flashlight and a pick. The tumbledown shacks that line the road provide snacks and drinks to locals and tourists alike.

While on the Carretera Turística, don't miss **Cemi**, a half-kilometre north of La Cumbre (☎204-7010; ◐), a thatch-roofed organic restaurant set above a beautiful ribbon of valley. Decorated with various odd knick-knacks, including old radios, Taino artefacts, bicycles, musical instruments and pigeon coops, *Cemi* emphasizes any Taino cooking traditions that have survived in Dominican cuisine. They also have a hut for rent; included in the price of accommodation is a tour to the amber mines and three meals. Be warned, at the time of writing, they were trying to charge RD$50 for visitors wishing to take photographs.

Well known among cigar lovers are **NAVARRETE** and **VILLA GONZÁLEZ**, abutting tobacco towns just northwest of Santiago along the Carretera Duarte. In addition to wide fields of tobacco along the highway, dotted with thatch huts used to dry the leaves, you'll find a couple of small-scale **cigar factories** open to the public, Pinar del Río Tabaclero and Túbano's, across the highway from one another in Villa González (both Mon–Fri 8am–noon & 2–4pm; free). Both are used to accommodating visitors; you'll get a glimpse at the cigar rollers and then be escorted to the gift shop. A bit further west in Navarrete, another Tabaclera Jacagua factory, on the parque central (Mon–Fri 7am–4pm; free; ☎585-5702), is less geared towards selling cigars to passing tourists and will give you a better sense of the cigar-rolling craft.

Tamboril

Cigar lovers should consider a side-trip to **TAMBORIL**, one of the most famous tobacco and cigar towns in the world located 10km east on the Carretera 14 from Santiago, then 5km north on the fairly bad Carretera Tamboril. The largest operation in town, **Flor Dominicana**, Calle Real (☎580-5139), is rather security-conscious and somewhat averse to visitors, so you might opt for one of the smaller, mom-and-pop cigar producers scattered throughout Tamboril; try **Fábrica Anilo de Oro**, Calle Real 85 (Mon–Fri 7am–4pm; free; ☎580-5808), manufacturers of Abreu and Presidente, or **Tabaclera Jacagua**, Cappelán 13 (Mon–Fri 7am–4pm; free; ☎580-6600). Each offers tours and a free, fresh-rolled cigar at the end.

Higuerito

Widely hyped as a pottery centre, tiny pueblo **HIGUERITO**, 8km south of Santiago just off the Autopista Duarte, comes across as a bit tacky, its many shops filled to the brim with one after another faceless doll. If you want to bring home some pieces of folk art, you're better off with Carnival masks from La Vega (p.252), or visiting the Artisans' Fair in Salcedo during the summer (see p.267). Still, the potters in Higuerito are exceptionally friendly, and you can generally watch them at work in their backyards.

San José de las Matas

The easiest excursion into the mountains from Santiago is **SAN JOSÉ DE LAS MATAS**, a sleepy hill station looking out over the northern Cordillera Central, here packed with palm trees and coffee plantations. In part it's so quiet because the town has the country's highest per capita rate of immigration to the United States; most who stay home are supported by New York relatives. San José is a great starting-off point for several day-hikes and an arduous five-day round-trip trail to Pico Duarte, and is particularly interesting during the

fiesta patronal – held during the first week of August – when hundreds of relatives return from the States for the festivities, and during Christmas, when there's a horseback, candlelit procession at night.

There's little to do within town but take a leisurely walk and admire the views; for one such lookout, take the dirt path behind the post office, on 30 de Marzo, to a **cliff-top park** with a good vantage over the neighbouring mountains. Most points of interest lie a bit outside San José, such as the **Balneario Vidal Pichardo**, 10km north at the confluence of Río Amina and Río Bao. Just as lovely – and accessible by car – is **Los Montones Arriba**, an elevated mountain campo with the most spectacular views in the area; head 5km east on the road to Santiago, then 7km south to Los Montones. A kilometre hike west from Los Montones will take you to another popular **balneario** along a branch of the Río Amina. An even better balneario – La Toma del Río Antonsape – lies 8km further south at **Mata Grande**, the starting point for the Pico Duarte trek (see p.260); to get there, continue 4km south from Los Montones and take a right at the fork in the road.

Practicalities

If you're arriving from Santiago, it will likely either be by guagua (hourly; RD$20) or by car – simply head west on Calle 30 de Marzo, cross the Hermanos Patiño bridge and continue west for 28km. Most visitors choose to make a day-trip of the town, but those looking to **stay the night** will find a couple of simple hotels. *Hotel Restaurant San José,* 30 de Marzo 37 (T578-8566; ❷), is the best, with basic rooms, ceiling fans and hot water. *Hotel Restaurant Los Samenes,* Av Santiago 16 (T578-8316; ❷), is about the same price but without the hot water. The *Los Samenes* has a good little **restaurant** serving typical Dominican platters, and there are several other eating establishments in town that are worth a look, including *Tropicaribe,* Mella 6, an outdoor patio with the standard range of Dominican dishes, and, a bit north on Calle San Juan, *Luna,* which boasts a candlelit terrace and skilful home cooking like *mofongo* along with grilled steaks.

Monción

A scenic but badly deteriorated road leads west 26km from San José to sleepy **MONCIÓN**, a pretty mountain town unremarkable but for its riverside Taino caves and proximity to one of the country's better restaurants. The former of these, the **Cuevas Dorán**, a Taino archeological site set inside a cave system just south of town, are spread out along the Río Los Cácaos; best to pay one of the local kids who hang out along the river during the day to show you around them. If you're going it alone, take a left at the Pueblo Nuevo turnoff from the main road, another left at the *Cafetería Claribel,* and one more left 3km down the road. Inside the caves are hundreds of petroglyphs and pictographs, though nothing you can't find elsewhere in the country. There's precious little else to do in Monción; if you've got the time, take a tour of the **Industria de Casabe Almonte** (Mon–Fri 7am–8pm; free), a cassava bread (see box p.251) factory 1km north of town on the paved road to Cacique. Inside you can spend a few minutes checking out the various elaborate contraptions for scraping, washing and grinding the tubers and the enormous ovens in which they're baked into bread; samples are included.

Cassava bread

Still a staple Dominican food, **cassava bread** dates back to the Tainos. Low in fat and protein but high in carbohydrates, it makes an ideal accompaniment to a fish or meat dish. It's baked from a flour produced by grating, draining and then drying the tube-like roots of the bitter yuca plant. Traces of ancient cassava production have been found right across the Caribbean and it probably owes its success to the fact that the mother plant, yuca, also known as cassava and manioc, grows easily in poor soil and is hardy enough to withstand both drought and hurricane. The roots are ready to harvest after only ten months but remain useful for up to two years, and the bread, once baked, can be stored indefinitely. Resembling a cracker more than traditionally baked bread, it has little taste of its own but it makes a great side-dish with traditional Dominican stews and is delicious served with avocado and salt.

Practicalities

The road from San José is wide enough that you can take a **car** to Monción; otherwise, a taxi can take you there for around RD$250 round-trip. If you're not visiting San José first, the easiest way to get to Monción is via the paved road that leads from Mao – which is the route **guaguas** from Santiago take – twice the length of the San José road, but just as fast and a much smoother ride.

On the face of it Monción hardly justifies more than a day-trip, but you'll find the locals – who are unused to tourists – extremely hospitable, and you may have a hard time fending off requests that you **stay the night** at a new friend's home. There's a new hotel in town, *Las Americas*, Calle Duarte (☎579-0065; ❸), which is a definite step-up from the usual small and dingy rural establishments, with decent-sized, well-decorated rooms and comfortable beds. The finest **eating** option in the region is the *Cacique Restaurant*, in **Cacique**, 8km north of Monción right on Highway 16, the country's pre-eminent restaurant for goat and lamb dishes, all served with the local cassava bread. It's set on a festive outdoor patio and is open daily for lunch; dinner is served on weekends only. If you can't get out to Cacique, settle instead for the *Amigo Café*, on the main drag through Monción, which grills up deliciously spiced chicken and offers an immensely popular Sunday lunch buffet. For something a bit more lively, don't miss *Cerro Bar*, on Duarte, a fun two-storey outdoor disco that pulls in crowds from a dozen surrounding villages.

Mao and Sabaneta

Just 15km north of Monción, and also easily reachable via paved roads from Santiago, the agricultural town of **MAO** serves as a transport centre for area produce. It's rather nondescript, despite the scenic roads that lead to it – passing through lush rice paddies – and you won't find yourself staying for long, but it does exude a certain rustic charm; indeed, horse-driven carts still deliver milk door-to-door from enormous pails. If you need to **stay the night** for some reason, head to the *Hotel/Restaurant Agua Azul*, Monción 36A (☎572-6280, ℉572-7159; ❷), a large complex that has comfortable rooms, hot water and a swimming pool. On Calle Duarte just off the picturesque parque central, you'll find the popular *Gigante Pica Pollo*, serving fried chicken and goat in a large outdoor square.

Some 20km west of Mao, **SABANETA** is more remote and dominated by banana plantations rather than rice paddies. There's little to do here, but if in the area you may as well check out the **Wednesday market** spread out along the town's main road, when campesinos from the surrounding agricultural outposts head into the "big city" to swap their food for clothing and other goods.

The Cordillera Central

The mighty **CORDILLERA CENTRAL**, slicing through the Dominican Republic's heart, was sparsely populated during colonial times by escaped communities of slaves; as the centuries wore on, the ex-slaves were joined by Cibao Valley peasants pushed out of the Vega Real by large landowners. These settlers would clear-cut sections of forest and fence off small agricultural settlements called *conucos*, moving on to another plot once the topsoil had been washed down the side of the hill. This practice carried on into the twentieth century until the national government put a stop to it, setting up three national parks within which farming is illegal, and which now are growing centres of eco-tourism. Most of the old *conucos* are returning to wilderness, though a couple evolved into thriving towns.

For the most part, the mountain roads are horrific, and getting from place to place often requires a convoluted route; the easiest way to travel between **Jarabacoa** and **Constanza**, for example, is to leave the mountains via one paved road and then re-enter them via another. To head deeper into the range you'll need a donkey; blazed trails lead to **Pico Duarte** from five separate points, with stops in secluded alpine valleys Tétero and Bao. On the eastern edge of the valley, the industrial towns of **La Vega** and **Bonao**, both founded by Christopher Columbus, are mid-sized centres of industry with little of interest most of the year, though La Vega's Carnival is the country's best.

La Vega

LA VEGA, just 30km southeast of Santiago, started out as one of Columbus's gold-mining towns, only to be levelled in a sixteenth-century earthquake and rebuilt as a farming community. Aside from the ruins of this old settlement, known as **La Vega Vieja** – well outside town – there's little in today's noisy, concrete city to hold your attention. However, La Vega's **Carnival** celebrations in February are generally acknowledged to be among the most boisterous and authentic in the nation. A twenty-block promenade is set up between the two main parks, along which parade platoons of demons in impressively horrific **masks**, the making of which is somewhat of a local specialty craft. Many city-dwellers who spend their days as hotel clerks, bankers or auto mechanics use much of their free time perfecting mask making; in addition to papier-mâché, they often use materials like bull horns, bone and sharpened dogs' teeth. There's the usual stack of blaring loudspeakers and food and liquor vendors to animate and feed the crowds, which average up to 70,000 each afternoon – many of them watching from rooftops. If you'd like to **purchase a mask**, try *Robert's Restaurant and Car Wash*, on the Carretera La Vega; if they're out of stock, they can direct you to the individual artists; expect to pay at least RD$200, depending upon how elaborate the design is.

If you're in La Vega at any other time, you'll have a hard time scrounging up much to see. Other than a half-dozen pretty wooden Victorians scattered about town, the city is crowded with unappealing box-style buildings. This theme leads all the way up to the fascinating **Catedral de la Concepción de La Vega**, Calle Mella at the parque central, surely the most subversive piece of architecture in the country, and considered something of a national embarrassment by many. Its team of architects envisioned a people's church built in the same concrete-box mode of most urban dwellings, reflective of the bleak poverty of most of its parishioners. The convoluted main structure is divided into a dozen towers with Gothic portals – note the central cross, fabricated from threaded pipes, and the industrial ornamentation of the facade. There are a few out-of-place colonial elements to the building as well, as it was initially intended (then abandoned) as a celebration of the Columbus Centenary, including brick gun turrets on all sides and the priests' quarters in back. Across the parque central past the matching concrete gazebo, you'll find the **Casa de la Cultura**, Calle Independencia (Mon–Fri 9.30am–noon & 2–5pm; free), with rotating art exhibits and a permanent Carnival mask collection.

Santo Cerro and La Vega Vieja

Five kilometres north of La Vega on the Autopista Duarte, a marked turnoff leads to **Santo Cerro** (Holy Hill), site of an important battle between Columbus and the Tainos. Columbus led an inland expedition in 1494 to round up Tainos to give to his men as slaves. A large company of natives from the valley below attacked his troops here, and supposedly the fight was not going well for the Spaniards until Columbus raised a large, wooden cross on the hill; an apparition of the Virgin perched atop it, and the emboldened Europeans slaughtered the enemy. It's hard to imagine a more peaceful spot today, crowned by a beautiful brick church and an unbelievable view of the Vega Real. Within the sanctuary is an imprint purported to be the place where Columbus planted the cross.

Backtrack 100m from the church, and a turnoff west leads down a steep hill lined with crumbling religious statuary. Make a left at the end of the road to reach **La Vega Vieja** (Mon–Sat 9am–noon & 2–5pm; RD$30), the ruins of Columbus's original city, founded in 1494 after the Santo Cerro battle. It went on to become one of the colony's most important mining outposts before the 1562 earthquake. Protected as a national park, the foundations on display – the fortress, a church, portions of the aqueduct and a few stone houses – make up only a tenth of the original city. The **fort** is the most extensive ruin, with several of its walls intact; colonists plundered much more of the stone in the nineteenth century to build the church at Santo Cerro. Five hundred metres east of the main ruins, a partially intact Franciscan **monastery** sits peacefully on a hillside, with most of its outer walls still standing.

Practicalities

Odd for a city of La Vega's size, there are no good in-town **hotels**; most lack even the most basic amenities like a toilet seat, mosquito net or hot water. *San Pedro*, Cáceres 87 (☎573-2844; ●), is the least seedy and cleanest, but is still not especially comfortable. Also tolerable are *Astral*, Cáceres 78 (☎573-3535; ①), and *América*, Cáceres and Carretera La Vega (☎573-2909; ①). You'll fare slightly better with local **restaurants**, notably the second-floor *Salón Dorado* above Engini Car Wash, Cáceres and Restauración, which has a hip decor, a fun crowd and pool tables; specialities include shrimp vinaigrette, London broil and *lambí*. Also good is *Robert's Restaurant and Car Wash*, on the Carretera La Vega across from Caribe Tours, with the city's best breakfasts and passable pizzas later in the day. There's also a few of the major American fast-food chains if you fancy a change. The major **disco**, *Astromundo*, Carretera La Vega and Las Carreras, is set in a funky 1950s building fronted by an enormous polystyrene solar system.

You'll find a 24-hour ATM machine on the parque central, alongside the requisite phone centres and Western Union. The **bus** stations, Caribe Tours (☎573-3488), Metro (☎573-7099) and Vegano Express (☎573-7079), are all on the Carretera La Vega, just off the Autopista Duarte. **Guaguas** to Jarabacoa set off from the corner of 27 de Febrero and Restauración.

Jarabacoa

JARABACOA, a mountain resort peppered with coffee plantations, is popular with wealthy Dominicans for its cool summers. The pine-dominated mountains – dubbed rather inanely "The Dominican Alps" – immediately surrounding the town hold four large waterfalls, several rugged trails fit for day-hikes, three rivers used for white-water rafting and the busiest starting-point for treks of Pico Duarte. The town is also well served by **public transport**: Caribe Tours, at the main crossroads, across from the Esso station, run four buses daily to La Vega, Bonao and Santo Domingo. Guaguas north pick up and drop off at Esso in the centre and those heading south by the Shell station on Constanza road.

Accommodation

With the recent increase in visitor numbers, Jarabacoa's **accommodation** options have improved radically. The best of the bunch is *Gran Jimenoa*, a new development in a pretty riverside setting with its own restaurant, a useful extra as it's too far out of town to walk. For those preferring to be in the centre of the action, another new hotel, *Brisas del Yaque*, offers surprisingly good facilities. In addition to the possibilities listed below, **camping** is an option around Manabao or at Balneario la Confluencia; if you want to get even further away from civilization than this, most farmers will let you camp on their land, provided you ask first.

Anacaona La Confluencia ☎574-2686. Modern, comfortable and tastefully decorated self-catering apartments with a useful full kitchen and hot-water showers. It's a little out of town, close to the baseball field. ④

Brisas del Yaque Luperón ☎574-4490. Clean, modern hotel just off the town centre. The rooms are quite small but come with a/c, TV and a fridge. Best place to stay if you want to be in the action but can be a bit noisy in the mornings. ③

Giselle Carretera Jarabacoa Km 10 ☎574-4433. Roadside cabanas a kilometre east of town, with cold-water showers and a grubby-looking pool.

Shouldn't be your first choice, but workable in case of emergency. ②

Gran Jimenoa Av La Confluencia, Los Corralitos ☎574-6304, ☏574-4345, ✉hotel@granjimenoal .com. A new hotel in a great riverside setting, 2km from the centre. Large rooms with a/c and TV in a three-storey building overlooking a pleasant pool area that even has a hot tub. Some rooms have excellent views over the river. Price includes breakfast. ④

Hogar Mella 34 ☎574-2739. The best budget hotel in town, with private showers, clean rooms and a pleasant courtyard. You can also get a motoconcho guide here to take you on a tour of the waterfalls and balnearios (RD$300). **❷**

Jarabacoa River Resort La Confluencia ☎574-4688. Modern private cabanas with hot water, kitchen, three bedrooms, two baths and swimming pool. Extremely comfortable but self-catering and probably better suited to a group of up to six people or a family. **❺**

Pinar Dorado Road to Constanza Km 1 ☎574-2820, ☏574-2237, ✉pinardorado@codetel.net.do. Pleasant hotel, owned by the Baiguate group, with TV, a/c, hot water, private balconies, restaurant and bar. More comfortable than *Rancho Baiguate* and an ideal base for some of the group's excursions. Recently renovated, it now offers a good-value meal option as well. **❹**

Rancho Baiguate Road to Constanza Km 5 ☎574-6890, ☏574-4940, ✉rancho.baiguate@codetel.net.do. This sprawling ranch offers seventeen pretty basic rooms, plus a football pitch, basketball court, ping-pong table, swimming pool, horse ranch, and fishing pond. No hotel service at night, but a perfect place if you're looking for peace and quiet. A good option if you want to join in some of the adventure excursions. Price includes three buffet meals. **❻**

The Town and around

Jarabacoa's tiny grid runs right alongside the Río Yaque del Norte; most of the action in town is centred on its major crossroads, a few blocks north of the small parque central, where you'll also find the banks and a small tourist office. The junction of Río Yaque del Norte and Río Jimenoa is a popular spot for swimming and holds a small bar and a densely wooded park, **Balneario La Confluencia**, which gets a bit crowded on weekends. Equally popular but less appealing, **Balneario La Poza** is another river spot at the northern end of town, marred by rubbish on the banks and rum advertisements painted on its boulders; to get there take Libertad north across the small bridge and follow the dirt path at Factoria Yaque down to the river.

The real attractions, however, are the four local **waterfalls** (*saltos*), not too far off from the centre of town, though enough of a trek that you'll want either your own transport or a ride on a motoconcho (RD$50–100 one-way). Most popular is the crashing **Lower Salto Jimenoa** (daily 8.30am–7pm; RD$5), which boasts a deep pool good for swimming, staffed by a lifeguard. It's 3km east of town off the Carretera Jarabacoa, and accessible on foot via a rocky suspension bridge. On your way back, you may wish to check out **Flordom**, also on the Carretera Jarabacoa, 500m east of town (Mon–Sat 9am–5pm), one of the DR's largest flower farms, full of roses, orchids and the like.

Salto Baiguate, 1km south of town on the road to Constanza (daily 8.30am–7pm; free), is, at 60m high, a bit taller than the first falls, plus it has a large cave and a swimming hole at its base. If you're up for a hike, head 2km north along the river from here to the **La Joya coffee factory**, Camino Real (Mon–Fri 9.30am–4pm; free; ☎574-6354; reservations necessary), which offers forty-minute tours that take you through all the complex stages of planting and processing. The coffee bushes – which are native to Ethiopia – require several years of growth before they're ready for harvesting. Once this is done, the beans are separated in three stages according to quality, husked, fermented in wet storage tanks, heated in drying machines, graded for size, tasted for quality and roasted in wood furnaces.

The steepest Jarabacoa waterfall by far is the **Higher Salto Jimenoa**, or **Salto Jimenoa Uno**, as it's often called. This isn't so easy to find but if you head out on the road to Constanza for 7km, you'll pass through a small pueblo before coming to a few shacks on the right, one a small *comedor*. Almost directly opposite these is a jeep-size driveway that quickly deteriorates into a narrow and steep footpath. Continue down to the bottom and scramble over some huge slabs to the pool at the waterfall's base. It's a pretty awesome sight as the water drops 75m from a hidden lake above and thunders into a huge pool at its base. The spray creates delightful rainbow patterns on the rocky walls and it's easy to see why this was chosen as a setting for a scene in *Jurassic Park*. It's certainly worth the effort of getting here and you'll probably have the place to yourself. Beyond this point, the **road to Constanza** deteriorates rapidly, only navigable with a 4WD – though there is some beautiful mountain scenery along the way and it's well worth a tour if your vehicle will allow it.

The final local waterfall is west of Jarabacoa on the **road to Manabao**, a highway that terminates at La Ciénega, which is the most popular setting-off point for Pico Duarte treks (see p.260). Two kilometres west of town you'll see a marked turnoff for **El Mogote** – best of the local day-hikes – a tall mountain with a trail that can be done in three hours round-trip. At its base **Centro Salesiano**, a Salesian monastery where many of the Spanish monks have taken a vow of silence – though the administrator is happy to talk to visitors – supports itself by running a pasta factory. It's another 5km further to **Balneario La Guázaras**, small rapids and a pool great for swimming, with a shaded outdoor bar looking out over the mountains. A hiking trail sets off a kilometre south to the waterfall, **Salto La Guázaras**, a 62-metre cascade that gets few visitors. Back on the highway, it's just 1km to **La Cortina**, yet another balneario – this one set on the edge of a cliff, with a cemented swimming pool and a bar. It's also the setting-off point for a four-hour hiking trail called **Los Dajaos**, which ploughs south through the mountains towards Constanza before looping back to the highway and the tiny pueblo of Manabao.

Eating

Long before Jarabacoa became a centre for adventure-sports tourism, it was the favoured summer retreat of Santo Domingo and Santiago's upper classes. Though most foreign visitors come to Jarabacoa by the busload on day-trips from their beach hotel, those staying the night will find plenty of **restaurants** to choose from, most of them catering to these Dominican weekenders. For **breakfast** head to *Cafetería el Trebol,* an outdoor establishment on the corner of Independencia and Sánchez, next to the parque central. Self-caterers can pick up **groceries** at Supermercado Jarabacoa on Independencia just west of the main crossroad.

Don Luis Colón and Duarte at parque central. Good mid-range restaurant facing the park, with steak, seafood and the usual Dominican staples.

Galeria El Parque Pizzeria Duarte at parque central. Inexpensive and fun outdoor spot for pizza, especially popular with families.

El Mogote Libertad and Piña. Unpretentious 1950s diner atmosphere with RD$30 daily Dominican specials that are a bit greasy but quite tasty nonetheless.

La Parrilla Independencia. A top-notch grill-house serving some great *criolla* dishes including guinea fowl in wine plus the usual goat and fish. Especially popular on weekends.

El Rancho Main crossroads at town entrance. Another part of the Baiguate empire, this excellent high-end restaurant serves pizza plus specialities like baked chicken stuffed with banana, garlic soup, crepes, seafood and steaks. Nice ambience, too; the walls are littered with art by top Dominican painters.

Drinking and nightlife

You'd be mad to miss the **nightly baseball games** at the field on Calle La Confluencia, just west of the crossroads. In addition to the spirited play on the field, there's a bar in the dugout and the outfield abuts an outdoor pool hall – all in all, a great way to spend an evening relaxing and getting to know some locals. For those looking to dance there are three **discos**: *Antillas*, a circular, two-storey building at the main crossroads playing popular merengue and

The Río Yaque del Norte, a beautifully blue, fast-flowing, mountain stream that rises up in the very heart of the Cordillera Central mountain range, plays host to a number of different white-water adventures. The lower sections are used by several **rafting** operators and offer some exciting drops up to grade IV. The nearby Jimenoa and Yasica rivers offer even more severe challenges but these are only accessible to experienced kayakers. Many of Jarabacoa's rivers and waterfalls can also be enjoyed firsthand by taking a **canyoning** trip with one of the local tour operators. Accompanied by an experienced guide, you'll make your way downstream using a combination of swimming, jumping, walking and rappelling. Previous experience isn't necessary and it's a breath-taking way to see some unspoiled countryside. Other local outdoor options include **hiking**, **biking** and **horseback riding**.

Franz's Aventuras del Caribe Hato Viejo 21 ℡574-2669 ℻574-2669, 🌐www .hispaniola.com/whitewater. Top of the bunch when it comes to white-water adrenaline rushes, Franz's stick to what they know best, rivers. Basic rafting trips on the Yaque del Norte start from as little as US$55 (US$65 with food and drink), and they also offer kayaking, from beginners' courses to expert descents of local rivers (from US$65/day), and canyoning down some of the local cascades (US$65). Longer trips are available and they'll even do early-morning pickups from the hotels along the north coast for an extra US$20.

Get Wet ℡586 1170, ✉get.wet@codetel.net.do. The north coast arm of Rancho Baiguate with the same portfolio of tours and adventures in the Jarabacoa area. Most of the package-trip excursions from the north coast book through here.

Iguana Mama ℡571-0908, ℻471-0734, 🌐www.iguanamama.com. Although actually based in Cabarete, on the north coast, Iguana Mama offers many excursions in the Cordillera Central, including Pico Duarte and multi-day mountain bike odysseys across the range. The best of all the island's adventure specialists with impeccable ethics. If you're staying on the north coast, it makes sense to talk to them in Cabarete; if not then check out the website.

Rancho Baiguate Road to Constanza Km 5 ℡574-6890, ℻574-4940, 🌐www .ranchobaiguate.com.do. One of the island's biggest tour operators, with most of their clients coming on excursions from the all-inclusives on the north coast. As well as US$40 culture tours to a cassava bread factory in Hatillo, a coffee factory, the house of a local painter and a flower farm, on bikes, they also run adventure tours, including white-water rafting (RD$775) and canyoning (RD$775). Other excursions include paragliding, mountain trekking, mountain biking, jeep safaris and horseback riding. Longer trips include a guided hike to Pico Duarte and jeep trips up the Constanza–San José de Ocóa road.

Rancho Jarabacoa Road to Sabaneta Km 2 ℡574-4815. Less expensive option than Baiguate for horseback riding in pueblo Sabaneta, 2km north of Jarabacoa – just RD$200 for a day-long excursion.

bachata hits and decorated in the rustic, wood-slat decor of most rural Dominican dance halls; *Plaza Central,* just off the parque central on the corner of Sánchez and Colón, with a pool hall to boot; and *Galaxia,* a pool hall and disco above *Don Luis* restaurant.

Listings

Bank There is a Banco del Progreso, Banco Popular and Baninter at the main crossroads, all of which have ATMs.

Film processing Fotosol is at the main crossroads.
Internet Digimax, 16 Agosto 16 (℡574-7047).

There's also an internet café above Banco Progreso at the main crossroads.

Medical Clínica Cesar Terrero, at the main cross-roads (℡574-4397).

Pharmacy Independencia, Independencia 44 (Mon–Sat 8.00am–12.30pm & 2.00–7.30pm; ℡574-4264).

Police Station is at the main crossroads (℡574-2540).

Post office Better than the extremely slow post office is private EPS, Herrera 1 and Independencia (Mon–Fri 9am–noon & 2–5pm; ℡574-4415).

Telephone Codetel, near the main crossroads; Televimenca, Independencia 43; Tricom, Sánchez and Libertad.

Travel agent Mayra, Independencia 82 (℡574-2640).

Wiring money Western Union, Independencia 43 (Mon–Sat 9am–noon & 2–5pm).

Parques Nacionales Bermúdez y Ramírez

Two national parks protect much of the mountains, cloud forests and pines present in the Cordillera Central, **BERMÚDEZ** and **RAMÍREZ**, each encompassing over seven hundred square kilometres that really need to be explored on an organized trek up **Pico Duarte**, the tallest mountain in the Caribbean. At the very least, you'll need to check in with a ranger and be accompanied by some sort of guide for whatever trip you take into the parks.

Once in, you'll see no small array of **flora**, though the endemic Creole Pine tends to proliferate, with reforested Caribbean Pines in places where there was once agriculture, and scattered palm trees at the fringes. You'll also note many orchids and bromeliads, along with Spanish moss and parasites known as The Count of Pines, their branches winding up the trunks of other trees and slowly strangulating them. There aren't many large **animals** in the mountains – persistent rumours of wild pigs aside – but you'll notice a number of lizards and even Coqui frogs near the summit of Duarte; the relatively rare tarantula or non-poisonous snake is also known to make an occasional appearance. There are plenty of birds, too, especially Hispaniolan parrots, hummingbirds and woodpeckers; near the mountaintop is a raucous population of white-tailed crows.

There's also some **agriculture** in the small valleys along the southern half of Ramírez, though the traditional slash-and-burn farming has been banned. The people here are exceptionally nice; you won't be able to pass a single home without being invited inside for a cup of coffee. If you talk to them for a bit, they may bend your ear about some curious local legends. Many peasants will tell you that small bands of Tainos are still holed up in the deepest mountains waiting for the Spaniards to depart, and that the trails are haunted by **ciguapas**, mythical blue-skinned women with their feet on backwards who seduce young men at night and lure them to their deaths at the bottoms of streams.

Pico Duarte

Five strenuous treks lead up to 3087-metre **Pico Duarte**, which towers over the centre of the mountain range alongside its sister peak La Pelona ("Baldy"; before 1930 they were known as Pelona Grande and Pelona Chica). The lack of fresh water on the mountain has left it uninhabited through the centuries – though Tainos once lived in the nearby Tétero Valley – and it was ascended for the first time only in 1944. Today, though, it's done as a matter of course.

Treks can be made any time of the year, but most people choose to ascend **between November and March**, when there's less chance of heavy rain. Regardless, you should never attempt the hike without a long waterproof coat

△ Holy Week procession

with a hood, winter clothing (at night the temperature can reach freezing), a sleeping bag and good hiking boots. Whichever of the trails you choose, you are required to register in the park office at the head of the trail. Here, you'll need to pay the RD$100 **park entrance** as well as hiring at least one **guide** for every five people (RD$100/day plus meals). It's also a good idea to rent at least one **mule** (RD$125/day); the chances are that the guide will insist upon it, to carry water and food as well as to get you down safely if things go wrong. You'll also need to purchase enough food for yourself and the guide, plus an extra day and a half in case of emergency. Stock up on water as well, and bring purification tablets for any river water you might drink. There are several very basic cabins with wood-burning stoves in which to sleep along the routes, but a couple of the treks will require tent camping for one night (it may be possible to rent these locally but it's best to bring your own or talk to one of the local tour operators on p.257). On any of the five trails below, you'll spend the night before or after your Duarte ascent at the nearby La Compartición cabins.

Climbing to the very top of the Caribbean's highest mountain holds definite cachet, and the view from the treeless peak is magnificent (though even here you can't quite escape from it all – Duarte's face is sculpted onto one of the rocks). If you've come this far, think seriously about extending your trek to include the **Tétero Valley** – a broad savannah with roaring mountain rivers, wild horses and Taino petroglyphs. This can be done by adding a two-day loop into the La Ciénega trek or by following one of the trails that crosses the valley on the approach to the peak. Unless you're a seasoned trekker, you'll do well to stick to the La Ciénega route (see below); you might also consider two **tour operators** who operate trips up this trail: Iguana Mama, in Cabarete (T571-0908, F571-0734, Wwww.iguanamama.com; US$350), who also run extensions to the Tétero Valley or Mata Grande; or Rancho Baiguate, in Jarabacoa (T574-6890, F574-4940, Wwww.ranchobaiguate.com.do), who do cheaper tours with fewer amenities; they'll also quote you a price for a custom tour along any of the other trails.

La Ciénega trail

The most popular trip up the mountain starts from the tiny pueblo of La Ciénega, 25km southwest of Jarabacoa, where you'll need to register for the 46-kilometre round-trip at the office by the park's entrance on the far side of the village. The best bet is to arrive in the afternoon, sort out the formalities and then camp down in the village with a view to starting out early the next morning. The first leg is little more than a comfortable four-kilometre riverside stroll to a bridge across the river at **Los Tablones**. Once over the river, however, the climbing starts for real and you'll gain over 2000m in the next 14km, mostly on a badly eroded track that wends its way through some wonderfully wild woodland. Regular stops at official picnic sights allow you to get your breath back and to peep out through the canopy for a glimpse of the totally pristine wilderness that surrounds you. You'll spend the night in a ramshackle cabin at **La Compartición** and then scramble up the last 5km at around 4.30am to be on the bare rocky summit for sunrise. It's quite a stirring sight to watch the sun creep over the horizon, casting a bright-red hue on the banks of cloud beneath your feet. You'll then backtrack to collect your belongings at the cabin and start the long descent back down to the village.

Mata Grande trail

Allow five days for this ninety-kilometre round-trip trek with elevation going from 850m to 3087m. To get there from San José de las Matas go 5km east on the road to Santiago, take the marked turnoff at the town of Pedegral and head 15km south to the park station at pueblo **Mata Grande**, where you can register and hire a guide and mules; taxis to the park station from San José cost RD$100. The first day of the trip is 20km past abandoned farming towns and sweeping views of Santiago and the Vega Real to the cabin at **Río La Guácara**. A good spot to stop and unpack lunch is 8km south of Mata Grande at the Arroyo Las Lagunas cabin, where you should also load up on water. The second day follows the cloud forest of the Río Bao 12km to the gorgeous **Bao Valley**, a stunning, elevated plain bereft of trees with high grass and wild horses, a large cabin and a view of La Pelona. On the third day, 10km total, you'll ascend La Pelona, then join up with the Sabaneta trail (see below) to hit the top of Pico Duarte.

Sabaneta trail

This trail was supposedly blazed by local messiah **Liborio**, who ducked the American Marines for several years in these mountains (see p.286). You'll need six days to do this 96-kilometre round-trip journey, in which elevation goes from 600m to 3087m. This trek is much harder than La Ciénega and Mata Grande, and you'll encounter few fellow travellers along the way. To get there from San Juan de la Maguana, take the paved road north from the city's Rotunda Anacaona for 20km to the enormous dam, **Presa Sabaneta**. A few hundred metres in front of the dam you'll find a car park and the park station, where you can secure a guide and mules, and camp for the night before setting off. The first day is not particularly long but quite steep, 12km to the cabin at **Alto de la Rosa**, a 1600-metre peak. Along the way you'll pass abandoned banana plantations and farms, many of which were blasted hard by Hurricane Georges. The second day is a slow 22-kilometre slog through dense vegetation to the **Macutico** cabin in the 2200-metre high Río Blanco Valley, where you can stock up on water. The third day is the toughest, climbing Pico Barraco before joining up with the Mata Grande trail at the top of La Pelona and continuing on to Pico Duarte.

Las Lagunas trail

Another strenuous six-day trek, this round-trip of 108 km is even more difficult than the Sabaneta trail. To get there from San Juan de la Maguana, take the Carretera Sánchez east and make a left at the signposted Cruce de las Yayas 9km north to Padre Las Casas. At the town's main crossroad take a left and 100m further on you'll find the **Las Lagunas** park station, where you can hire a guide and mules. They don't get much traffic on this route, so you may have to offer the park officer RD$100 extra to get permission to use the trail. The first day goes through palm and deciduous forest dotted with lagoons and small subsistence farms. Convenient markers along the way are riverside El Limón 3km on; pastel El Botoncillo 2km later; Las Cañitas (a military outpost with camping and a hilltop panorama) 2km further; and **El Tétero** – a traditional cattle-raising campo where you should camp for the night 3km further still. The second day takes you 4km north past numerous farming shacks before joining up with the Constanza trail at Sabana Andres; from here it's another 4km of small farming campos and 6km of dense, unpopulated pine forest to the top of 2100-metre Alto del Valle, then 4km almost straight down to 1500-metre-high **Tétero Valley**. The peaceful valley holds a pine forest adorned with thick cobwebs of Spanish moss, a large cabin, dozens of wild horses, two freezing-cold rivers and – at its eastern end – a number of Taino petroglyphs which archeologists believe denoted an island-wide peace treaty between *caciques*; ask at the park station for directions to these ancient markings. From here it's 5km to El Cruce and up the La Ciénega road to Pico Duarte.

Los Corralitos trail

At 86km and six days round-trip, it's not the longest but is easily the steepest and toughest of the Pico Duarte trails, and for this reason rarely used. From Constanza take a taxi 8km west to **Los Corralitos**, where you can acquire a guide and mules. If you'd like, you can drive another 8km to the cabin at Los Cayetanos, which will cut three hours off your travel time. From here it's three hours past sadly deforested mountainside to the confluence of the rivers Grande and Yaquesillo – the border of Parque Nacional Ramírez – and another 7km through a small valley and over several hills to the **Los Rodríguez** cabin, where two park employees are stationed. The second day is sixteen extremely steep kilometres to the **Tétero Valley** (see above). Four kilometres along the way, the path intersects with the Las Lagunas trail at Sabana Andres; you'll reach the valley and its park cabin 14km further on. The third day goes 5km to El Cruce and then up to Pico Duarte.

Bonao

BONAO's economy is supported single-handedly by the nearby Falconbridge ferronickel mine, an imposing industrial complex a kilometre south of town. Like most mining towns, it's pretty depressing – bleak, concrete and crowded with thousands of zigzagging, dustcloud-raising motorcycles – and holds nothing of particular interest, aside from a few pretty mock-gingerbread houses in barrio Gringo at its northern end.

You may as well just head out to **Falconbridge**, your first glimpse of which will be two enormous smokestacks spewing black gusts into the air beside sky-scraping piles of sand. With its high-tech machinery, omnipresent security staff and fascist-looking falcon head logo emblazoned on everything from the front gate to the shuttle buses, the place is nearly a caricature of evil from a James Bond film. You'll have to cut through some red tape to get to walk through the facility, but it's a rare opportunity to glimpse an industrial operation of such scale. Book at least a week in advance, if interested, with Falconbridge Public Relations (Mon–Fri 9am–noon & 2–5pm; free; ☎682-6041 ext 2311, ℗686-0095); tours are supposed to be limited to geology students, but the staff will usually accommodate anyone with sincere interest. It's surprisingly thrilling to see the giant conveyor belts sifting through the rubble and sand for nickel – though the guides are more eager to show off their reforestation project, which attempts to slowly rejuvenate the landscape that they've mined.

Piñon trees

The **piñon trees** that line the winding rural roads just west of Bonao – as well as many other roads across the country – are thought by many to have magical properties; local *brujos* use their wood for staffs with which to heal the sick. This belief stems in part from a strange physical characteristic: around the time of Good Friday the piñon leaves and bark turn red, which locals claim is in emulation of the Crucifixion. The trees do have some remarkable regenerative properties, too; stick one of the branches in the ground and allow it to take root – within a year the branch becomes another full-grown tree.

More idyllic are the piñon-covered mountains that border Bonao, best experienced by taking a scenic road southwest to the **Boca de Blanco** reservoir and dam a couple of hours outside town. A few kilometres on, turn east at the riverside village **Los Quemados** – which has a couple of places to stop for lunch – and you'll find yourself amid some terrific mountain scenery, including views of two separate waterfalls. The reservoir itself, 15km further on the main road, is a perfect place for an afternoon picnic and a swim, and you're allowed to walk atop the dam.

Practicalities

Few travellers choose Bonao for an **overnight stay**. If circumstances dictate, there are a few tolerable places, starting with *Plaza Nouel*, 12 de Julio and Duarte (no phone; ❷), with a/c, cable TV and an inexpensive restaurant. The street noise can be irksome, though, and you can avoid it by driving 2km west of town along the Boca de Blanco road *to Rancho Wendy* (no phone; ❶), just outside the village of Los Quemados. The no-frills rooms here are at least clean, and there's a swimming pool and several horses for riding into the nearby hills. For a modern hotel with all the amenities, head 4km north on the Autopista Duarte to *Jacaranda*, in the roadside Jacaranda shopping complex (☎525-5097; ❸). There are also two good restaurants on the Autopista Duarte, both named *Restaurant Típico Bonao* and both under the same management. The one at the city entrance gets more locals – and it's a bit of a hangout for Falconbridge engineers – a thatch-roof hut with high-end *criolla* cuisine, including excellent soups, lobster and garlic shrimp.

Constanza

CONSTANZA is a drop-dead gorgeous, circular valley set deep in the mountains at an altitude of 1300m. Populated and farmed since the Taino era, it was created millennia ago by a meteor; as you first pass over the lip of the crater you'll be stunned by the fertile, flat valley – irrigated by thousands of sprinklers and hemmed in on all sides by jagged peaks. Constanza had virtually no contact with the outside world until the end of the nineteenth century, when a decent dirt road was finally blazed to it; later development occurred when Trujillo trucked in two hundred Japanese families in the 1950s, to introduce their farming methods to the valley. All manner of non-tropical crops are grown on the farms today – strawberries, raspberries, apples, garlic and roses; less tantalizing is the military base in town, a permanent presence since Castro attempted a Communist take-over here in 1959.

The town itself, taking up the western quarter of the valley, is mostly residential and fairly compact – as such you can make a go-round of it fairly quickly, though there's not much to see. The hub of activity is the **farmer's market** just north of Calle Luperón – the main thoroughfare – where truckloads of goods are loaded up and shipped to Santo Domingo. At the south end of town sits the decaying **Nueva Suiza**, an abandoned Trujillo manor that was used for a time as a resort spa but is now fenced off and boarded up, alongside a large greenhouse where you can buy orchids, hyacinths, roses and other flowers (roses can also be purchased from roadside shacks along the Carretera Constanza for RD\$15 apiece). Just a few metres further along the road look for the row of run-down shacks called **Colonia Japonesa**, the original Japanese settlement. Most of the colonists who prospered have moved into the

Hiking in Constanza

As you'd expect amongst such dazzling scenery, the Constanza valley boasts a few of the DR's finest hiking trails. One three-hour trip sets off from the *Cabañas de las Montañas* hotel in Colonia Kennedy, which is just east of the main town. From the hotel, take the dirt road north until you reach a white house at the top of the hill, starting point of a trail that leads into the thick of the alpine forest. You can also set off 5km east of Constanza via the Carretera Constanza to the adjoining valley of **Tireo Arriba**, which holds a smaller farming pueblo worth exploring for a look at the local way of life. If you have your own transport, keep going 8km further east to pueblo **La Parma** – just before you reach the road to Jarabacoa – for a hike along the **Río Arroyazo**. Ask locals to direct you to the riverside walking path, from which it's a 45-minute hike to an unspoiled wilderness balneario, with small cascades along the river giving way to a large pool partially enclosed by boulders.

town centre, though a few still call these shacks home and frequent the Japanese Social Club across the street. If you stay the night in Constanza, head to the eastern lip of the valley crater via the highway and check out the unbelievable **sunset**.

A ragged dirt road leads 10km south from Colonia Japonesa to Constanza's major sight, **Aguas Blancas**, a torrential, 150-metre waterfall in three sections with a large pool at the base. The scenery alone is worth the somewhat difficult trek out – towering 2000-metre mountains veined with cavernous valley ribbons, half of it virgin pine forest and half terraced agriculture. Some of the farms are perched on mountaintops so inaccessible that you'll wonder how the building materials ever got there; look also for the many cattle that graze precariously along zigzagging paths worn into the steep mountainside.

Practicalities

To arrive in Constanza via **public transport**, catch an RD$50 guagua at the petrol station at Bonao's town entrance on the Autopista Duarte. From Jarabacoa, you can catch an RD$60 guagua at 9am at the Esso station, but expect a pretty rocky ride. **By car**, the easiest route is the paved road that begins 6km north of Bonao on the Autopista Duarte; it's in good condition (and features great views) but it's also steep and has a few tricky turns. With a 4WD you can instead arrive via Jarabacoa or San José de Ocóa, though these are extremely tough, slow-moving trips and should be done for adventure rather than convenience.

Constanza's two best **hotels** stand beside one another east of town at the end of the marked turnoff to Colonia Kennedy. *Cabañas de las Montaña* (℡539-3268; ⑤) has spacious modern villas with full kitchens and all the amenities, set on the lip of the valley and surrounded by thousands of wildflowers. The staff organize tours across the valley, including half-day hikes into the mountains behind the hotel and a trip to the cascades at La Parma. Next door is *Altocerro* (℡530-6192 or 6181, ℻530-6193, ⓔcmatis@codetel.net.do; ②–④), less expensive but also quite good, a small hotel with some private villas and camping facilities. They offer horseback excursions, bike rental and weekend outdoor barbecues for guests. **Budget hotels** are all within the town itself and aren't especially comfortable. *Reyes Rodríguez*, Gratereaux 39 (no phone; ①), is cheapest and does boast hot water, as does *Mi Casa* (℡539-2764; ②), on Luperón and Sánchez.

Wherever you **eat** in Constanza, you're likely to get a good sampling of the local produce, usually plucked from the fields the same day. The restaurants in the *Altocerro* and *Cabañas de las Montaña* hotels are both popular eating options, as is *La Montaña*, Ureña 40 at Parque Anacaona, which has a pleasant atmosphere in which to enjoy treats like roasted guinea hen, or just a simple breakfast of croissants. The elevator music can grate at *Lorenzo's*, Luperón 83, but the food is impeccable, including steak smothered in onions, and guinea hen al vino, a delicious "special chicken and rice" dish and *coco con leche* for dessert. For authentic staple Dominican food try *JL Comedor*, by the baseball field, which serves up huge portions for less than RD$50 a shot.

South of Constanza: Reserva Científica Valle Nuevo

The gutted, sky-high road that leads south from Constanza to San José de Ocóa – considered by Dominicans as the worst of the country's many poor roads – offers an adventure, however hazardous, you're not likely to soon forget. Do not attempt this unless you have an excellent 4WD and are a very experienced mountain driver – at a couple of points so much of the road has been washed away that you'll have to aim the wheels between a gaping crevice in the centre. Allow five hours and be sure to bring two spare tyres, winter clothing and emergency supplies. The road runs through a national forest preserve known as **Reserva Científica Valle Nuevo**, a steep alpine wilderness with views that extend clear across a large chunk of the Cordillera Central, and for much of the trip you'll be skirting the edge of a cliff far above the clouds. You'll have to make a stop (and pay an RD$20 bribe) at the small military fort at **Alta Bandera**, 30km south of Constanza, where you'll also see a concrete pyramid built by Trujillo to mark the exact centre of the island.

The Vega Real

East of Santiago, the **VEGA REAL**, an unbroken expanse of farmland demarcated by a triangle of Cibao farming towns, is responsible for a phenomenal amount of produce and tobacco, but it's not exactly high on any travel itinerary, lacking any real compelling sights or activities. If you feel like getting lost for a few days, though, you'll likely find its cities more pleasant than those on the over-industrialized Autopista Duarte. **Moca** is an easy enough jaunt from Santiago that you can do as a day-trip, but **San Francisco de Macorís** requires a bit more effort; from the latter you can make the splendid mountain hike into the Cordillera Septentrional at **Quita Espuela**. **Cotuí** features the best scenery, though, flanked by rice paddies, river-veined savannahs, and the Cordillera Oriental; just outside town you'll find the Presa Hatillo dam's artificial lake, arguably the prettiest spot in the valley.

Moca

MOCA, a sizeable farming depot 16km east of Santiago, is set amid some of the most fertile land in the valley. It's better known, though, for two episodes from Dominican history – as the birthplace of the 1842 **Moca Constitution**, which set democratic standards for government that have rarely been adhered to, and as the site of nineteenth-century despot **Ulises Heureaux's assassination**. There's nothing here to commemorate the former, but the latter event is celebrated in downtown Moca at a small park on Calle Vasquez, where you'll find the **Monument to the Tyrant Killers**, a small Deco sculpture honouring assassins José Contreras and José Inocencio, erected right on the spot where Heureaux was shot. Across the street from the park, above Espinal Car Wash, a **miniature locomotive** has been placed to honour the old railroad that brought initial prosperity to Moca, while the rest of downtown is crowded with storefront businesses, warehouses and restaurants.

Nicer than anything in the workaday downtown district, the nineteenth-century **Iglesia de Corazón de Jesús**, corner of Sánchez and Corazón de Jesús a bit east of central Moca, sports a neo-Plateresque facade and a prominent clock tower, and is fronted by a plaza good for people-watching. The interior is spacious, full of light and dominated by an impressive pipe organ. Four blocks north of the church is Moca's jail: a truly depressing place with small windows crowded by inmates all trying to get a small taste of fresh air. Also in the neighbourhood, just east of the church, the much advertised **Moca Zoo**, Sánchez at Isla Gasolina (9am–noon & 2–6pm; RD$5), is best avoided, featuring as it does a rather miserable array of unexotic exhibits – chickens, hamsters, turtles and a lone crocodile in a cement pit. From the church you can also drive northwest down Avenida Duarte to the local cigar factory, **Tabaclera Anónima**, Av Duarte Km 2 across the street from the police station (Mon–Fri 7am–4pm; free; ☎582-3151), a relatively small cigar maker similar to those in Tamboril (see p.249). If you've got the time and your own transport, you can alternately head up the **Moca–Sabaneta road** that extends north from the city into the Cordillera Septentrional. It leads past high views of the valley up to **Puente Grande**, a pretty covered bridge that was once part of the local railway system.

Practicalities

Moca **hotels** cater to passing business people and are centred around busy Avenida Duarte, Moca's main road. The best hotel in town is *Oasis*, Cordova 121 (☎578-5594; ❸), which has 22 comfortable rooms featuring a/c, TV and telephones and is a lot closer to Western standards than the budget options gathered around Avenida Duarte. *Don Carbuccia*, Duarte 127 (☎578-9385; ❶), is the best of this budget lot, with a/c, TV and hot-water bath, but what you get is still a bit musty and cramped, and you should ask for a room in back to avoid the street noise. For a more serene location, head north of the city to *Escapade*, Carretera Moca/Sabaneta Km 9 (no phone; ❷), with spare, clean rooms set in the Cordillera Septentrional and surrounded by forest, though these are used more often as *cabañas turísticas*.

D'Gala, at the corner of Alfonseco and Frey Vasquez, is an excellent local **restaurant** that features seafood, steaks and *criolla* dishes; attached is a large dance floor popular on weekends. For cheaper food head to *Paco Pizza*, Independencia and Alfonseco, which serves pizza and *pollo al carbón* on a lively outdoor patio. Better than the places in town is *Mirador La Cumbre,* 9km north of town on Highway 21 (the road to Sabaneta de Yásica), which has great panoramic views in addition to top-notch food, including filet mignon, crepes, *pollo al carbón* and creole shrimp.

Salcedo

A tiny town midway between Moca and San Francisco, **SALCEDO** is the hometown of the **Mirabal sisters**, martyred victims of Trujillo. The house they grew up in, the **Museo Hermanas Mirabal**, 2km east of Salcedo's centre (daily 9am–5pm; RD$5), was the setting for much of Julia Alvarez's best-selling novel *In the Time of the Butterflies*, but its tacky period furnishings and cordoned-off bath towels stencilled with the sisters' names hold little to engage those not already steeped in Mirabal lore. (For a review of Julia Alvarez's *In the Time of the Butterflies*, see Contexts, p.363).

Back in town, just north of the **parque central**, you'll find the baseball complex of the **Kansas City Royals**, worth a visit during the summer when daily games are scheduled. Also held in the summer is the **Feria Artesanal**, during which hundreds of people from surrounding campos sell local handicrafts, including pottery, intricately woven straw bags and wooden religious icons; look also for the *gajumba* in the centre of the parque central – a musical instrument created by bending a tree over until its top almost touches the ground, tying it with a string of catgut and playing this string with a bow. The exact date of the fair varies; call the Centro de Arte y Cultura Popular in Santo Domingo for more information (see p.79). If you want to **stay the night** in Salcedo, *Lina* (no phone; ❶) is a very basic, run-down hostelry, 1km west of town on Highway 132, while *Druneo,* a popular restaurant and dance spot near the park, serves excellent RD$50 **meals**.

San Francisco de Macorís

The farming city of **SAN FRANCISCO DE MACORÍS**, 200,000 strong in the heart of the Vega Real, owes its prosperity to the **cocoa industry** – the business behind what few major sights are in town. Chocolate is not the only money-making product here; in recent years, San Francisco has served as a laundering point for **cocaine** profits, a far cry from its slightly more benign tobacco-producing days in the nineteenth century. The compact downtown, manageable enough to make the city feel more like a small town, holds most of the major office buildings, restaurants and discos – the latter of which supply San Francisco with some of the DR's best nightlife.

The large **Mercado Modelo**, downtown on Sánchez and Castillo, is worth checking out, an enormous produce and cocoa depot where peasants from the surrounding countryside come with pack animals to sell their goods during the day. There's not much else in the way of entertainment: a small water park, **Plaza Acuatica**, Moca road Km 1 (daily 9.30am–5pm; RD$10), offers some relief, though it's little more than a large swimming pool with a diving board, two slides and a bar, or you can check out a **baseball game** in the winter at the surprisingly modern stadium just east of town on Highway 122 (check at the parque central for posted schedules).

Loma Quita Espuela

More diverting than these scant city sights is a day-trip up to the **Scientific Reserve Loma Quita Espuela**, a virgin rainforest preserve set on the side of a tall Cordillera Septentrional mountain, 15km north of town on Calle Castillo. Two interpretative **trails**, hiked in the company of well-informed local guides, highlight the significance of the flora and fauna of the forest, and the views over the Cibao from the observation tower on the summit of the Quita Espuela are stunning. It's also possible to bathe in the clear waters of the river that runs through the reserve and then sample delicious Dominican food, produced by local people. Longer hikes of two days or more can be arranged by request. It's best to book a guide at least a week in advance and, if you don't speak Spanish, this is best done by fax. (RD$20 entrance and RD$200 for a guide for groups up to twenty people; ℡588-4156, 🄵588-6008, 🄴flqe @codetel.net.do)

Practicalities

San Francisco has an efficient system of RD$3 city **guaguas**, and RD$30 private **taxis** are plentiful as well. Caribe Tours and Metro both drop you off a bit east of the town centre, from where you can catch a quick guagua into town. Despite its rather large size and population, San Francisco doesn't offer too much in the way of either **hotels** or **restaurants**. If you need to stay, head straight to the *Hotel 2000*, Salcedo 100 (℡588-0817, 🄵588-4757; ❷), great value considering the a/c, cable TV and hot water but the rooms are tiny and a little claustrophobic. For dinner there's *Ambar*, Salcedo 100, great Chinese dishes and almost anything you can think of with spaghetti, or *El Rancho del Mofongo y la Parrilla*, Avenida Los Reales, a good Dominican restaurant that doubles as a disco at night. There are plenty of other discos in town, too, that get more than their fair share of big-name **merengue** acts; hand-painted advertisements are posted throughout the city to keep you up to date with who's playing and where.

Cotuí

Tucked away in the farthest southeastern reaches of the Vega Real, **COTUÍ** is the archetypal cow town – friendly and laid-back, full of rice-processing factories and produce-laden trucks. The few visitors who make it here come for the beautiful surrounding countryside, especially **Presa Hatillo**, the largest dam in the Caribbean, and its peaceful reservoir that sits amidst layers of rolling hills. To get there take Calle Sánchez 3km from the parque central to the police station, turn left and continue 9km. There's a hiking trail that leads along the edge of the lake, or you can go instead to **Cotuí Piscina** (daily 9.30am–5.30pm; RD$25), an Olympic-sized swimming pool at the entrance to the dam, fed by lake water and with a small restaurant/bar on the premises.

Rancho del Lago, Av de la Presa Km 3 (℡324-5853, 🄵696-0045; ❹), an attractive, French-run **hotel** near the reservoir, can put you up in comfortable rooms for the night. Most have sensational views across the valley. The hotel restaurant serves a variety of Continental-style dishes, including lake bass in white wine sauce, sauteed shrimp, onion soup and T-bone steaks. More budget-oriented accommodations are available in town, though the quality is generally poor; the best of the bunch is *Santorini*, Calle Colón (no phone; ❶), which also has a good restaurant. *El Meson*, Calle Sánchez a half-kilometre east of the parque central, is a patio **restaurant** that serves the usual Dominican dishes and pizza. Back around the parque central, you'll find your other needs taken care of; it's where **guaguas** come in and depart, and most town businesses are right around it.

Cotuí to Monte Plata

From Cotuí, **Highway 23** heads southeast to Monte Plata (see p.125) through a remote sugar-producing region within the Cordillera Oriental, with just the lure of rural Dominican (actually more Haitian, thanks to the number of field workers who have migrated here from the west) life to egg you on. The road is **paved** for 20km, but then gives way to bumpy dirt road after Los Peralejos. Five kilometres further on, *batey* country starts in earnest, from Cruce de la Jagua east to **Sabana Grande**, and you'll see plenty of Haitian workers slashing their ways into the sugar cane with machetes or carting the day's work back to the shack-filled *batey* with oxen-powered carts. South of Sabana Grande, the road heads to Monte Plata, a scenic enough trip – as is much of the hilly area south and east of Cotuí – but probably nothing to go out of the way for.

THE CIBAO | Travel details

Travel details

The cities along the Autopista Duarte are serviced by a dizzying array of **bus companies**: Espinal, Terrabus, Transporte del Cibao all ply the highway between Santiago and Santo Domingo, with Vegano Express doing express runs between La Vega and the capital. Caribe Tours and Metro do this run along with a number of others. With either of them you can travel to Puerto Plata, or into Cibao heartland towns like San Francisco de Macorís, Salcedo, Cotuí and Moca, before heading all the way north to the Samaná Peninsula. Caribe Tours, Metro and Terrabus also have comprehensive, free printed schedules available in their terminals. For smaller towns you'll find guaguas more efficient, especially in the mountains, where Caribe Tours' run to Jarabacoa is the only existing route. The guaguas range in quality from relatively pleasant, air-conditioned minibuses to battered vans in which you'll be packed in with other passengers like a sardine. Travel times for them vary and so cannot be given exactly; the ones below are ballpark estimates.

Buses

Bonao to: La Vega (33 daily; 45min); Puerto Plata (4 daily; 3hr 30min); Santiago (33 daily; 1hr 20min); Santo Domingo (32 daily; 1hr).
Castillo to: Nagua (4 daily; 25min); Samaná (2 daily; 1hr 30min); San Francisco de Macorís (5 daily; 50min); Sánchez (2 daily; 1hr); Santo Domingo (4 daily; 4hr 20min).
Cotuí to: Maimón (3 daily; 1hr); Pimentel (3 daily; 40min); Santo Domingo (3 daily; 2hr).
Jarabacoa to: La Vega (4 daily; 1hr); Santo Domingo (4 daily; 2hr 45min).
La Vega to: Bonao (40 daily; 45min); Jarabacoa (4 daily; 1hr); Moca (3 daily; 35min); Puerto Plata (3 daily; 3hr 10min); Salcedo (4 daily; 1hr); San

Francisco de Macorís (8 daily; 1hr 25min); Santiago (35 daily; 35min); Santo Domingo (59 daily; 1hr 45min); Villa Tapia (4 daily; 40min).
Maimón to: Cotuí (3 daily; 1hr); Pimentel (3 daily; 1hr 40min); Santo Domingo (3 daily; 1hr).
Moca to: Puerto Plata (3 daily; 2hr 40min); Santiago (3 daily; 35min); Santo Domingo (3 daily; 2hr 20min); La Vega (3 daily; 30min).
Pimentel to: Cotuí (3 daily; 40min); Maimón (3 daily; 1hr 40min); Santo Domingo (3 daily; 2hr 40min).
Salcedo to: La Vega (4 daily; 1hr 5min); Nagua (2 daily; 1hr 40min); San Francisco de Macorís (4 daily; 20min); Santo Domingo (4 daily; 2hr 50min); Villa Tapia (4 daily; 20min).
San Francisco de Macorís to: Castillo (4 daily;

269

45min); La Vega (11 daily; 1hr 25min); Nagua (10 daily; 1hr 20min); Salcedo (4 daily; 20min); Samaná (6 daily; 2hr 30min); Sánchez (6 daily; 2hr); Santo Domingo (16 daily; 3hr 10min); Villa Tapia (4 daily; 40min).

Santiago to: Bonao (30 daily; 1hr 20min); Dajabón (2 daily; 5hr); La Vega (35 daily; 35min); Loma de Cabrera (2 daily; 3hr 45min); Los Indios de Chacuey (2 daily; 4hr 15min); Manzanillo (2 daily; 4hr 20min); Moca (3 daily; 35min); Monte Cristi (4 daily; 4hr); Puerto Plata (10 daily; 2hr 10min); Santo Domingo (40 daily; 2hr 20min); Sosúa (10 daily; 3hr).

Villa Tapia to: La Vega (4 daily; 40min); Salcedo (4 daily; 20min); San Francisco de Macorís (4 daily; 40min); Santo Domingo (4 daily; 2hr 20min).

Guaguas

Bonao to: Constanza (8 daily; 1hr); La Vega (frequent; 45min); Piedra Blanca (frequent; 15min); Santiago (frequent; 1hr 35min); Santo Domingo (frequent; 1hr).

Constanza to: Bonao (8 daily; 1hr); Jarabacoa (daily; 2hr 45min); San José de Ocóa (2 weekly; 5hr).

Cotuí to: Maimón (7 daily; 1hr); Piedra Blanca (7 daily; 1hr 15min); Pimentel (4 daily; 40min); Sabana Grande (daily; 2hr); San Francisco de Macorís (4 daily; 1hr 20min).

Jarabacoa to: Constanza (daily; 2hr 45min); La Vega (12 daily; 1hr); Manabao (10 daily; 40min).

La Vega to: Bonao (frequent; 45min); Jarabacoa (12 daily; 1hr); Salcedo (6 daily; 1hr); Santiago (frequent; 35min); Santo Domingo (frequent; 1hr 45min); Villa Tapia (6 daily; 40min).

Manabao to: Jarabacoa (10 daily; 40min).

Moca to: Sabaneta de Yásica (2 daily; 2hr 15min); Salcedo (frequent; 25min); San Francisco de Macorís (frequent; 45min); Santiago (frequent; 40min).

Monción to: Cacique (11 daily; 15min); Mao (11 daily; 45min); Navarrete (11 daily; 1hr 25min); Santiago (11 daily; 2hr).

Navarrete to: Imbert (frequent; 1hr); Mao (11 daily; 40min); Monción (11 daily; 1hr 25min); Monte Cristi (12 daily; 3hr 20min); Puerto Plata (frequent; 1hr 30min); Santiago (frequent; 40min).

Piedra Blanca to: Bonao (frequent; 15min); Cotuí (7 daily; 1hr 15min); La Vega (frequent; 1hr); Maimón (7 daily; 15min); Santiago (frequent; 1hr 50min); Santo Domingo (frequent; 45min).

Salcedo to: La Vega (6 daily; 1hr); Moca (frequent; 25min); San Francisco de Macorís (frequent; 20min); Santiago (frequent; 1hr 10min); Villa Tapia (6 daily; 20min).

San Francisco de Macorís to: Cotuí (4 daily; 1hr 20min); Moca (frequent; 45min); Nagua (8 daily; 1hr 20min); Pimentel (8 daily; 35min); Salcedo (frequent; 20min); Santiago (frequent; 1hr 30min).

San José de las Matas to: Santiago (15 daily; 1hr 15min).

Santiago to: Bonao (frequent; 1hr 35min); La Cumbre (9 daily; 40min); La Vega (frequent; 35min); Mao (11 daily; 1hr 15min); Moca (frequent; 40min); Monción (11 daily; 2hr); Monte Cristi (12 daily; 4hr); Navarrete (frequent; 40min); Salcedo (frequent; 1hr 10min); San Francisco de Macorís (frequent; 1hr 30min); San José de las Matas (15 daily; 1hr 15min); Santo Domingo (frequent; 2hr 20min).

Flights

Santiago to: La Romana (daily; 50min); Punta Cana (daily; 30min); Santo Domingo (daily; 20min).

The Haitian border

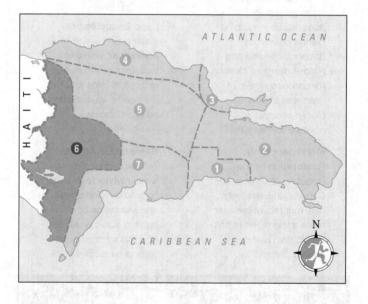

CHAPTER 6

Highlights

✳ **Fort Liberté** Abandoned but intact fort lying in ruins along the Bay of Dauphin, and a chance to see rural Haitian life up close. See p.277

✳ **The Haitian Market at Dajabón** Hundreds of Haitians cross the "Friendship Bridge" twice weekly for this outdoor bazaar, swapping French cosmetics, Babancourt rums and pirated designer clothing for produce, sacks of grain and enormous blocks of sawdust-covered ice. See p.277

✳ **Monument to the Restoration of the Republic** Near Loma de Cabrera, this relatively new monument feels far more ancient and atmospheric than perhaps it should. See p.280

✳ **The Carretera Internacional** Truly the road less travelled, this rough, remote mountain dirt track is the border for over 25km – and allows you to see Dominican and Haitian life in the remote Cordillera Central campos. See p.281

✳ **Lago Enriquillo** Salt-water lake the size of Manhattan, with alligators, tens of thousands of tropical birds and the rhinoceros-iguana-infested Isla Cabritos. See p.288

✳ **Bahía de las Águilas** Ten kilometres of spectacular white-sand beach backed by kilometres and kilometres of uninhabited scrub brush territory that's home to millions of birds. See p.293

6

The Haitian border

The Dominican Republic shares a snaking, 190-kilometre (far longer if every crook and switchback were measured) border with its western neighbour, **Haiti**; liberally sprinkled on both sides are poor, remote outposts, where little goes on but the crossing back and forth of locals, looking to tout their wares in makeshift markets. Most of this traffic, in truth, heads east; in fact, nearly every Dominican town alongside the border has a Haitian market and many of them have a long history of Haitian influence and inhabitance, as these communities overflowed with newly freed settlers after the Haitian revolution. The DR has set up military stations all along the line to try to stem illegal immigration, but it remains absurdly porous; still, as a visitor, you legally cannot cross over to Haiti in a rental car, and will have to rely on public transport such as motoconchos or the like, available near the handful of crossings.

It should come as no surprise that migration is in one direction – the DR's economy has long been far more stable than Haiti's. Even so, the rocky **Haitian border** remains the least developed part of the Dominican Republic. While a few inland roads connect the major border towns with bigger cities like Santiago and Barahona, the majority of it is harder to reach. Parts of three separate mountain ranges cut through the region, in effect cutting it off not only from the rest of the country but from itself: if you're into driving the length of it, you'll need either a motorcycle or a reliable 4WD to traverse the winding, often rutty road. Few visitors do such a trip, though it has become somewhat of a rite of passage for many expats. Even if you're not here long enough to take in the whole of it (for which you should allow a minimum of four days), it's worthwhile to make a few surgical strikes; not only is the mountainous landscape, often interspersed with stretches of rainforest, quite spectacular – and easily visible from border highways, especially the **Carretera Internacional**, where the road *is* the border – but the chance to encounter the area's Haitian and African culture, or even to dart into Haiti itself, should greatly help to contextualize your visit.

Of the border's natural highlights, the most popular is **Lago Enriquillo**, in the south, home to a wildlife sanctuary and, at the lake's centre, **Isla Cabritos**, a desert island literally teeming with iguanas. The lake is flanked by two sets of mountains, the **Sierra de Neiba** to the north and the **Sierra Bahoruco** to the south, neither of which holds too much in the way of sights or great hikes, though both are plenty scenic for a drive through.

Those who want to see how African culture has been transplanted here should try to visit one of the region's many **religious festivals**, among them

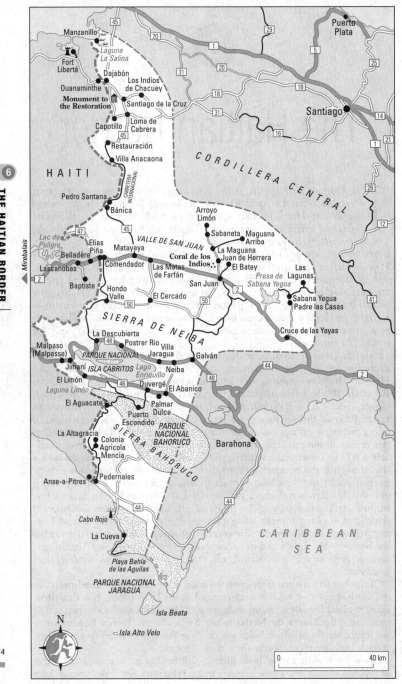

the annual procession to the cave of St Francis in **Bánica**; the Semana Santa festivities in **Elias Piña**, also a major border crossing; and the various fiestas at **San Juan de la Maguana**, a major urban outpost a bit east of the line, but with strong historic ties to Haiti. More religious history can be explored in the mountains north of San Juan, where pueblo **Maguana Arriba** holds a syncretic sect that worships a twentieth-century local faith healer; not far away are two **Taino corrals**, stone circles that once served as the religious and political centres of large pre-Columbian cities.

Of course exotic Haiti is always within arm's reach and constitutes a legitimate attraction in itself; the Haitians have their own language, **Kreyol**, a mixture of West African tongues with French, but most along the border also speak a bit of Spanish, making communication slightly easier. The two official crossings are at **Dajabón** and **Jimaní**, but if you're just interested in a day-trip the soldiers at Elias Piña and **Pedernales** will let you pass for a few hours. Other than experiencing a bit of rural Haitian life, the only prime sight close to the border is run-down **Fort Liberté**, in the far north.

Some history

Until the American invasion of 1916, the border was little more than an official fiction, even though the island had been divided by that time for more than two hundred years. Boundaries were long established at the north and south coasts but the rugged interior was up for grabs, populated mostly by **cimarrones**, escaped slaves who set up scattered farming outposts. When the US took over both halves of the island, it handed over a portion of land populated mostly by Dominicans in the Sierra Bahoruco to Haiti, gave a chunk of the Cordillera Central inhabited mostly by Haitians to the DR, and then blazed a series of dirt roads down the border's length to try to create a meaningful division. When the Americans left, the head of their newly created National Police, **Rafael Trujillo**, wrested control of the government and began the slaughter of all Haitians living on the Dominican side of the line (see box below), in order for the division to become even sharper – he also rechristened numerous Haitian border towns with appropriately patriotic names like Restauración, Pedro Santana, and Villa Anacaona. Relations between the two sides have remained rather chilly since, in part because of the continued abuse of migrant Haitian cane cutters who come, either by force or choice, to work on Dominican sugar plantations.

Operación Perejil

On the night of October 3, 1937, under Trujillo's orders, dozens of secret police dressed as peasants lay in ambush just outside Bánica, where a religious procession was en route to a local cave. The police separated out the Haitians from the Dominicans by inducing them to say the word *perejil* ("parsley"), which native Kreyol-speakers tend not to be able to properly enunciate, lisping the letter "r". The captives were then sent to "deportation" centres, where they were processed (so that it seemed they had been deported), and subsequently taken out at night in small groups and hacked to death with machetes; their bodies were fed to the sharks in the Bahía de Manzanillo. In the following days between 20,000 and 25,000 Haitians were similarly slaughtered all along the border, one of many in a long line of the leader's monstrous acts.

Though navigating the border region has improved in recent years, it can still be quite difficult in places; at points the roads seem nearly impassable, and as stated above, you'll need a good 4WD or motorcycle for some sections if you're going it alone. The northern end is the easier one with good paved roads south from Monte Cristi through Dajabón and on to Restauración and also east from Loma de Cabrera into the mountains. As far as public transport goes, Caribe Tours run **bus routes** from Santiago to Manzanillo, Dajabón and Loma de Cabrera, while numerous **guaguas** and minibus companies go to all of the major towns south of the Cordillera Central. Minivans go daily from Monte Cristi to Restauración, and from Pedro Santana to Elias Piña, but are hard to find elsewhere: one twice-weekly guagua traverses the route from Restauración to Pedro Santana, none goes south of Elias Piña.

Manzanillo (Pepillo Salcedo)

Approaching from the north coast, sleepy **MANZANILLO**, also known as **Pepillo Salcedo** – a legacy of Operación Perejil (see box p.275), when Trujillo renamed most of the border towns – is the first border town you'll hit, set at the base of the Bahía de Manzanillo on the eastern mouth of the Río Massacre. A former shipping point for United Fruit, whose enormous complex sits decaying next to the port, Manzanillo had its prosperity snuffed out in the 1930s, when that company abandoned the DR and Trujillo shut down the port, preferring to steer all shipping to the docks at Santo Domingo, which he owned. Today the small industrial port repairs cargo vessels, and there's a marina that attracts a number of North American sailors just east of town. At the time of writing, there were rumours that a large French corporation were showing interest in what's left of the old complex.

The town **beach** at the end of Calle Sánchez – which extends north and south from the parque central – is nothing special, just a strip of grey sand abutted by a row of concrete bunkers. At the western edge of town the Río Massacre runs right along the border, on the opposite side of which you can spot a small colonial **French fortification**. Haitian and Dominican traders will likely be on boats crossing back and forth to swap clothing and gym shoes for food.

Over on the east end of town, the port road leads past the **United Fruit complex**, with a number of old warehouses and some disused railroad cars in which dock workers store equipment, on to desolate **Laguna La Salina**, a sandy lagoon that is sanctuary to thousands of tropical marsh birds, including more than a thousand flamingos. The lagoon actually constitutes the southern tip of Parque Nacional Monte Cristi (see p.230), but is most easily accessible from Manzanillo. The road all but disappears at the sand, where a barely visible turnoff to the right takes you to the shore of the lagoon. The bay also has 27 sunken ships in its waters, many of them Spanish galleons from colonial days. Unfortunately the dive centre at El Castillo was closed at the time of writing but it would be worth inquiring at hotels in Monte Cristi, Manzanillo or with Northern Coast Diving in Sosúa for any changes to the situation. Further north, the lovely beach at **Playa Luna** is also part of the national park, but you'll need to hire a boat from the town beach or marina to take you there.

Practicalities

Aside from the recreational sailors who pass through, few travellers spend the night in Manzanillo and **accommodation** options are limited. *Puerto Cristal Cabañas* (☎579-9488 or 248-6896; ②), reached by turning right off the road to Laguna La Salina, is pretty run-down but about as good as it gets. **Seafood** is the local speciality; try *Puerto Cristal*, on the marina, serving fresh oceanic entrees for around RD$100. Restaurants worth searching out in town include the *Marlin,* at the parque central on the corner of Sánchez and Duarte, and also the *Coral Bay Café and Restaurant* on Duarte. Both specialize in seafood and are more used to locals than tourists – so expect loud music and Dominican-style service. Note that at 10pm every night, a brief **blackout** occurs in Manzanillo as the town's power supply is switched from the national power company to a nearby station funded by the local government.

Dajabón

DAJABÓN, 20km due south of Manzanillo, is the biggest of the border towns, not surprisingly holding the largest formal crossing and the best of the region's Haitian markets. The Spanish had a fort here from the mid-sixteenth century, but it was little more than a collection of small farms until 1794, when Touissant L'Ouverture slaughtered most of the locals and resettled the spot with Haitians (the river that flows along the border here has been called the Massacre ever since). Dajabón is now firmly Dominican, but hundreds of Haitians pour into town on **market days**, which are held within the eight square blocks bordering the bridge on Mondays and Fridays from 9am to 4pm. Best to get there early, as the action winds down over the course of the day. Freelance Dominican entrepreneurs come from as far as Santo Domingo – buying bulk quantities of grain and produce from Dominican farmers, swapping them to the Haitians for clothing and household goods and then selling the Haitian wares to individual clothing and department stores in the major cities; many of the "designer" labels that you'll find on the streets of Santo Domingo are actually Haitian counterfeits. The Haitians pour across the **"Friendship Bridge"** at the western end of town – the women balancing huge bushels crammed with gym shoes on their heads while the men lift hyperbolically loaded-down wheelbarrows – and claim small patches of pavement for their impromptu shops.

Into Haiti

Dajabón is the most trafficked overland entry into Haiti, partially because it is within striking distance of **Fort Liberté** – 20km to the northwest and the most interesting Haitian sight along the border. One of the oldest and best preserved French forts in the New World, it lies in ruins along the **Bay of Dauphin**, a perfectly round body of deep-blue water 100m west of the town of Fort Liberté, with a bottleneck opening to the Atlantic visible in the distance. Called Fort Dauphin under French rule, it was constructed to defend the strategic bay and large French fleet that the waters harboured. The eastern wall is in rubble at several points, but the bulk of the fortress is intact, its armoury now inhabited by stray goats, and with several passageways leading through the chambers of the large, central building. You can still see the plaza's irrigation system that fed fresh water into a central fountain; the two large holes in the ground nearby led to the prison. The western wall is intact as well, with a narrow, corral walkway from which to peer at the spectacular bay views; on the water you'll see wooden fishing boats with home-made sails. The village of Fort Liberté merits only a quick look; check out the market, with stalls hawking produce, live chickens, fried johnnycakes and various household wares.

In order to get there, you'll have to pass through the Haitian town of **Ouanaminthe**, just across from Dajabón, and referred to by Dominicans as **Juana Méndez**. It's a dusty, concrete desert town crowded with people and with no tourist sights as such, but drinking in the bustling, motorcycle-buzzing atmosphere is fascinating enough to stave off boredom for an hour or so.

Practicalities

Crossing into Haiti at Dajabón isn't cheap: you'll pay a US$10 departure tax (US dollars only) to the Dominicans, then stop off at the Haitian outpost on the other side and pay US$10 in Haitian *gourdes* – available at lousy rates from the **money changers** on the bridge – and perhaps another "informal" US$5 payment to the man who processes your visa. Upon return to Dajabón, you'll have to pay US$10 more, and the *buscone* who helps speed up the immigration process will want around RD$100 as well. Throw in RD$200 for a **motor-cycle driver** and your total comes to US$50. It's probably best to bring a supply of US dollars with you as you may have problems finding reasonable exchange rates in Dajabón itself. You're not allowed to drive a rental car into Haiti, and the bridge in Dajabón isn't wide enough for vehicular traffic in any event. The border is open daily 8am–6pm; if you're late getting back, you can usually convince the border guards to hold your passport for the night so that you can spend the night in Dajabón. In case of emergency, head to the unmarked restaurant at Ouanaminthe's central square, which has a couple of very **basic rooms** for rent (❶).

Don't continue into Haiti without stopping off at Haitian immigration first; police regularly check foreigners for papers. Once your passport is stamped, head onto the small field outside immigration, where you're likely to find a motorcycle driver willing to take you to Fort; if you can't find one there, keep going down the path until you reach Ouanaminthe's parque central, which is just around the bend.

Back on the Dominican side, *Juan Calvo*, Henríquez 46 (☎579-8285; ❶), is Dajabón's best **hotel** by far, with clean, modern rooms, private bath, TV and fan. Even cheaper is *Altagracia*, Calle Ureña (❶), quite basic accommodation and with shared bath. Just north of the town gates is *Hotel Bonanza,* Av Martin Jhofferman 5-A (☎579-8548; ❷), which has clean and relatively cheerful rooms behind a small *comedor*. The *Juan Calvo*'s **restaurant** is also the best bet for food, though there are a few Dominican *comedores* scattered around the town centre. Around the town gate, you'll find Banco de Reservas and Scotiabank along with Codetel, Televimenca, Western Union and the informal guagua station. Caribe Tours is nearby at Beller 30. If you're instead continuing **south by car**, you'll need to take a left at the town's second military installation.

Santiago de la Cruz

Santiago de la Cruz, 10km south of Dajabón, stands at one of the border's main crossroads, but the only thing in town worth noting is its **petrol station**,

△ Taino petroglyphs

La Gasolina, which is also a pickup point for Caribe Tours. When one of the frequent fuel shortages hits Port-au-Prince, a hundred or more Haitians queue up with several containers to drag back across the border and sell.

Five kilometres east of Santiago de la Cruz along Highway 18, **LOS INDIOS DE CHACUEY** offers a worthwhile detour – though it's more a scattering of small farms than a town – thanks to its Taino archeological site. The **Plaza Indigena de Chacuey**, an enormous circle of boulders around a central slab that was once used for religious ceremonies, helps to mark what was one of the largest indigenous settlements before Columbus. Today local kids have made a baseball field out of it, and it was long scoured by freelance treasure seekers who sold hundreds of its artefacts to private collectors around the world. Happily, the government has now protected the place, and it's illegal to pick up even a pebble. From the circle's northwestern edge, a small dirt path leads to the highway and the Río Chacuey; follow the river south for a hundred metres to get a glimpse of boulders with dozens of **ancient petroglyphs** hammered into them. You'll see not only the trademark Taino faces, but also full human figures, snakes, lizards and more abstract symbols. Note also the fan-like leaves of the *guanillo* plants that dominate the riverbanks, used during pre-Columbian times as roofing.

Loma de Cabrera

The beautiful, pine-dominated Cordillera Central begins as you approach **LOMA DE CABRERA**, 20km south of Dajabón and a mellow frontier town named for Restoration General José Cabrera. What there is of a town, more a ribbon of dusty shacks, lines the main road from the north for approximately 1km and then splits at a congested junction, where the road south to Restauración bears right. The only thing of interest within the town itself is the **Haitian market** held on Tuesday mornings. Just east of town, though, you'll find a well-known **balneario** on Calle María Trinidad Sánchez, a pleasant enough place to visit, though it's crowded on weekends. The grounds surrounding it are rubbish-strewn, but the balneario itself has clean mountain water and is set beneath a picturesque cascade.

A few kilometres west of Loma de Cabrera is the **Monument to the Restoration of the Republic** (daily 9am–6pm; free), a stylish twentieth-century tribute to the renewal of Dominican independence, set on the spot where General Cabrera crossed over the border with his rebel troops and began the war against the occupying Spaniards. Designed by Dominican architect Rafael Calventi and completed in 1983, the complex – a series of broad steps rising up to a large building that holds several sculptures, all of it fashioned from Italian marble – has the feel more of abandoned ruins than contemporary civic monument, acknowledged and accented by Calventi through the use of a field of mock pillars scattered along the expansive marble steps, cleanly sliced off at various points to suggest an ancient city gone to rubble. On the elevated central plaza are two structures shaped in the form of stylized axe-heads, the larger of which holds six social-realist murals depicting the conflict. Rising up from a hole in the building's floor is Ranico Matos's *The Flame of Liberty*, a brilliantly contrived sculpture that imparts the hypnotic motion of flame through spiralled steel. Behind the monument a small path leads to a hill marked with a Dominican flag; walk up for terrific views of the Haitian countryside.

Practicalities

Accommodation is basic in Loma de Cabrera, the best option being the *Yobel Yami Hotel* on Calle Duarte across from the police station (no phone; ➊), with clean rooms and private baths. Cheaper still is *El Dormitorio*, Calle Blanc and Duarte (no phone; ➊), a somewhat grungy men-only hostel. The best **places to eat** are *Comedor Restaurant Franseq*, which occupies a second-floor balcony just north of town on the highway and doles out heaping portions of whatever dish the cook has made that night for RD$35, and *Cafeteria Negrito* right next to Caribe Tours. Codetel and Western Union are back on Calle Duarte near the parque central. *Disco Yanill*, the town's top **nightspot**, is just south of the centre, on the road out to Restauración.

Restauración to Bánica

The paved border Highway 45 continues south, climbing steeply and offering some superb views, before dropping slightly into **Restauración**, an outpost with a military fort and a fairly humdrum municipal market. It's the point of departure for **guaguas** down the border to **Pedro Santana**, which run only on Monday and Friday mornings. If in town with your own transport, take the rough dirt turnoff just north of town and head 12km to the **Río Limpio**, a pleasant mountain river. If not, you'll have to content yourself with visiting the local version of the **Monument to the Restoration**, a mock nuclear missile beside the church built in the 1960s and meant to symbolize Dominican determination in the face of supposed Haitian encroachment. There's a couple of basic **accommodation** options in town, the best being *Hotel Comedor San José* (no phone; ➊), opposite the market, which has reasonable rooms and private showers and also serves good but basic Dominican **food**. The other, *San Martín* (no phone; ➊), behind the market, offers fairly dark and dingy rooms, with mosquito nets and a shared bath, in the basement of an immaculately decorated and clean Dominican house.

The Carretera Internacional

The paved border highway heads south another 14km to pueblo Villa Anacaona, where an unpaved, winding mountain road takes over. This difficult stretch, known as the **Carretera Internacional**, was blazed by the Americans in the 1910s when they handed over a good chunk of the Cordillera Central to the Dominicans. Since then, so much of it has been beaten down by traffic that the tyre-gouging, jagged rock beneath it has been exposed, making for a very rocky ride. To add to it, pockets of thick mud form along the highway during heavy rains – you're best off avoiding this road altogether after a severe thunderstorm.

There's a **roadblock** just past Villa Anacaona's clapboard church, which is used to extract unofficial RD$20 "tolls" – drive on unless the soldier manning it stands in front of your car, in which case you'll have to either pay him or act ignorant until he lets you by. If you pass during the morning, you'll see another Haitian market just around the bend – set within stalls that are sheltered from the sun by billowing, brightly coloured cloth canopies.

Beyond the roadblock, the Dominican side is sparsely populated, but you'll see a number of Haitian villages during the trip, the entire length of which should take about 3.5 hours. Two kilometres south of the roadblock you'll come to a crossroads; veer slightly left to continue down the border road. Note the **drawings** on many of the Haitian mud huts along the way. The snakes represent Damballa, one of the most powerful, remote Voodoo deities, and his wife Aida. A rainbow is symbolic of Legba, gatekeeper of the spirit world, and the many vines and trees are shamanic poles that the gods slide down to interact with humans. Along the same ethereal lines, many locals will also tell you that the Carretera Internacional is haunted by wailing *bien-bienes*, the ghosts of dead *cimarrones* who escaped slavery by hiding out here during the colonial era.

Meanwhile, the landscape grows increasingly arid to the south, and the Haitian inhabitants more impoverished; there's a four-kilometre stretch near the end where dozens of small children will chase your slow-moving vehicle for up to a kilometre or more, yelling for you to give them pesos. Eventually you'll arrive at the wide, blue **Río Artibonite**, which marks the highway's southern boundary and is great for a quick dip after the tough journey. From here it's another kilometre or so down Highway 45 to Pedro Santana, an eminently missable town.

Bánica

Four kilometres south of Pedro Santana along a graded road, **BÁNICA** is the oldest European settlement in this area, founded back in 1504. Its **church** is nearly that old, built in 1514, and today it's one of the loveliest colonial relics outside Santo Domingo. Restored in 1993, the original red brickwork is visible in the interior, though much of the facade is submerged under whitewash plaster. The small plaza beside the church holds an eighteenth-century sundial identical to the one in Santo Domingo's Zona Colonial. The church is the ceremonial starting point for the yearly **fiesta patronal**, held in honour of St Francis of Assisi on October 3. Locals then make a candlelit pilgrimage up a steep hill on the northern edge of town to a nearby cave, where they believe St Francis was born, to the eternal consternation of the town's North American Catholic priest. There's nowhere to stay or eat in town; if you're around on a Thursday or Sunday, you can hit the local **Haitian market** for decent fruits and vegetables.

Elias Piña and inland

The dusty border road leads another 30km south through arid farmland dotted with windmills, a recent innovation used to power local wells. It ends at the military outpost Matayaya, from where the Carretera Sánchez leads west to **ELIAS PIÑA**, the most informal of the border crossings. The town has minimal facilities, and most activity buzzes around its pretty, circular **parque central**; just east of the park is a gutted **Trujillo mansion**, 27 de Febrero, a two-storey faux-colonial manor modelled on the residence of Ponce de León in San Rafael de Yuma (see p.137). **Market days** are Mondays and Fridays, when Haitians ply their wares in a hundred or more tarp-roofed vending stalls that sprawl from the parque central to the border checkpoint. Elias Piña also has a very good Haitian-style Semana Santa celebration worth looking out for during the Christian Holy Week.

Of late, Elias Piña's border crossing is rumoured to be a transhipment point for Colombian **cocaine** – which is flown into Haiti, driven to the DR and thence flown to North America; if true, this business is kept tightly under wraps, and you'll find little evidence of it within town.

Into Haiti

The closest Haitian town to the border, sleepy **Belladére**, isn't too much to look at, but you will have to check in immediately with the police here if you've crossed from Elias Piña. The station is beside the town gate – explain that you want to visit for a few hours (some of the guards speak a bit of English or Spanish) and you should have no problem getting permission.

The prettiest spot in this part of Haiti is the enormous dam at **Lac de Peligre**, a large artificial lake with clean water, popular with locals as a place to swim, but it's a pretty long jaunt – 21km west from Belladére to Mirebalais, then another 7km north to the dam. If this seems too gruelling you can opt for **Baptiste**, a tiny hill station with few facilities, but set amid coffee plantations and patches of preserved cloud forest; from Belladére, head 5km west to Lascahobas, then another 5km south.

The only reason you'd want to **stay the night** on the Haitian side are the Saturday night Voodoo ceremonies held by a *houngan* (priest) who lives 5km west of the border on the road to Belladére; he'll give you permission to attend a service if you ask him a few hours in advance, but he speaks only Kreyol, so you'll need an interpreter. Conveniently, there's a small, extremely basic hotel, the *Paradis* (no phone; ❶), right across the street from the *hounfort* (temple) where his ceremonies are held.

Practicalities

Elias Piña is the cheapest place from which to cross for the day into Haiti. The military officers at the small fort on the western edge of town will give you permission, but will expect an RD$100 tip when you return; pass them another RD$100 and they'll sometimes let you (illegally) drive your car in for the day. Beyond the fort is a two-hundred-metre *territoria de nadie* (no-man's-land), though the lack of Haitian military presence here means that only Dominicans are allowed into it; there is no Haitian outpost and so you won't have to deal with Haitian officials at all here. If you just want a quick peek, you'll be able to walk into Haiti for a few hundred metres and check out some of the remote huts scattered around the landscape. If you'd like to head further inland, stand at the edge of the *territoria de nadie* and wait for a Haitian motorcycle taxi, which will charge you around RD$200 for a ride into Belladére and back.

The **hotels** in Elias Piña are geared towards the Haitian traders who stay the night before market days. As a result, they're pretty unappealing – and completely booked on Sunday and Thursday nights – so consider staying at *Rancho Bar Sussy* (☎527-0017, ⓕ527-0019; ❷), a combination hotel/restaurant/dance hall that features rooms with a/c, cable TV and private cold-water bath, located 3km east of town on the highway to Las Matas de Farfán. The plethora of mosquitoes makes malaria a potential problem here as well within the town limits – if spending the night, don't sleep without a generous layer of bug spray and a mosquito net. All of the in-town hotels are of similar quality, but *Francia* (❶), which is right on the parque central, has good mosquito nets and friendly owners. *La Fuente*, 27 de Febrero just east of the park, is the best **restaurant** in town, with a good selection of Dominican staples – though the seafood is best avoided – and a small dance floor that lights up at night. *Ambiente de la 27*, on 27 de Febrero at the parque central, is the major **nightspot**, fun but astoundingly loud. Also around the park is Tricom, in the *Heladería Bon* ice-cream shop, and there's a small **cinema** beside it showing second-run American fare at 8pm nightly (RD$20). Guaguas load up at the small park on 27 de Febrero at the boundary between Comendador and Elias Piña.

Las Matas de Farfán

Founded in 1780, laid-back **LAS MATAS DE FARFÁN**, 20km east of Elias Piña, was named for an eighteenth-century Azua merchant who would stop here for the night on his way to the border, to sleep beneath an enormous tamarind tree by the side of the local river. Still standing, the gnarled tree – identifiable by the Rotario Club sign that hangs from one of its branches – is on Calle Sánchez a half-block south of Independencia, though the river view is now blocked by a concrete playground.

At Las Matas's heart is its singular **parque central**, generally acknowledged to be the most beautiful in the nation, with a lovely gazebo standing in the middle of a densely wooded area – if it weren't for the gazebo you'd swear it was a square patch of untouched, old-growth forest. Twenty years ago it was even better, with enormous oaks at each corner, their branches engineered to sweep over the park and provide it with a solid roof of leaves, but the oaks succumbed to disease and had to be destroyed. Every Sunday at 8pm the local symphonic band plays under the gazebo as the whole town comes out to watch. Wednesday and Saturday are **market days**, when hundreds of campesinos from the surrounding countryside come into town to sell their produce along Calle Independencia.

Practicalities

Las Matas has better **hotels** than you'll find in most border towns, though you still shouldn't expect hot water or a/c. *Independencia*, Calle Independencia (☎527-5439; ❶), is the best of the bunch, with clean basic rooms and private bath. *Kalen*, Calle O Martínez and Independencia (☎527-7439; ❷), is also decent, and *El Cibaeño*, Calle O Martínez and Cruz (no phone; ❶), is even cheaper but with shared bath. For **meals** you shouldn't expect too much. *Gloria's*, on the southeast corner, has a nice outdoor courtyard and a menu of standard Dominican dishes, along with fresh pastries and coconut sweets. If you're more in the mood for fast food, you can make do with *D'Nosotros Pizzeria* with sidewalk seating on Calle St Lucia, where you can enjoy soft-shell tacos (though just mediocre pizza). Afterwards cross the street for an ice cream at the *Heladeria Bon*. *El Bar de Hugo,* on Independencia right by the park, is the most popular nightspot, though there are several spread throughout town. For dancing you'll need to go to *Las Colinas*, a typical outdoor rural dance hall set in a cockfighting arena 2km east of town.

Codetel is on Calle Independencia across the street from the park. To **move on** from Las Matas, pick up guaguas at the corner of St Lucia and 19 de Marzo.

San Juan de la Maguana and around

Further inland, 28km east from the border, **SAN JUAN DE LA MAGUANA**, a major hub of agricultural transport for the surrounding valley, begins a stretch of ugly concrete cities that extends east all the way to the capital.

Founded at the outset of Spanish colonization, the original town was destroyed in the *devastaciones* of 1605, only to be occupied by the *cimarrones*, who were joined by settlers from the Canary Islands in the 1690s. San Juan was known as a wide-open town best avoided by outsiders until the American occupation; the clear shot across the valley from Haiti also made it easy pickings for several invasions.

Today the influence of both Haitians and *cimarrones* is most evident in the colourful **religious festivals** held throughout the year, including a giant Altagracia procession on January 21; the fiesta patronal for San Juan from June 15 to 24, which features a full week of big-name live bands playing in the parque central; Semana Santa (Holy Week), when you'll see processions with large Haitian-style *gagá* bands and the crowning of a city queen; and Espíritu Santo, seven weeks after Semana Santa, the most fascinating ritual. Festivities for the latter begin in the small town El Batey, 18km northeast of San Juan, with a day-long procession in which a porcelain statuette draped in a white cape is carried to the big city. Along the way, many marchers become possessed by the Holy Spirit, Liborio and various Taino ghosts; these "horses" – as the possessed are known – behave in all sorts of ways: collapsing to the ground in a trance-like state, speaking in tongues, or prancing about like coquettish young girls. The statue is paraded door to door around San Juan on Sunday, the Pentecost, and the partying continues for the next day's return to El Batey.

Unless you happen to be driving through from Santo Domingo to the border or vice versa, there are few reasons to stop off the rest of the year, though a quick wander round does give you a sense of Dominican city life far from the tourist traffic. The downtown area surrounding the parque central is busy enough, with street vendors selling everything from pots and pans to religious icons, and repairmen fixing bicycles and clocks. The north town gate, **Rotunda Anacaona**, is a homage to Taino queen Anacaona; a statue of her stands in the centre of the traffic circle, which is itself surrounded by monumental murals depicting Taino life.

Practicalities

San Juan is a big town, but it's still pretty far off the tourist trail; most of its **hotels** are either *cabañas turísticas* or geared towards passing businesspeople. Of the latter, *Areito*, Capotillo and Mella (T557-2045, F557-2772; ❸), is the best, with well-kept rooms, attentive service, a/c, hot water and cable TV. The cheaper *San Rafael*, Calle Duarte and Independencia (T557-2087; ❷), has no hot water or a/c, but does feature rooms with sweeping balcony views of downtown.

For **food** you're best off heading to *Rincón Mexicano* on 27 de Febrero 28 and Capotillo, which has good soft-shell tacos, fajitas, enchiladas and other Mexican favourites. **Nightlife** takes place in the various outdoor clubs strung out along the east side of town, although *Tupinamba Disco* on the south side of the parque central is also extremely popular.

There's also a number of useful facilities in town, including several phone centres, a Western Union on 15 de Agosto and Anacaona and a 24-hour **cash machine**, Anacaona near Independencia. The town's **pharmacy**, Superfarmacia Inmacula, at Independencia and 27 de Febrero, also has a much wider selection of drugs than you'll find in the surrounding pueblos. San Juan is additionally the terminus for many **bus routes** that head west from Santo Domingo. The Caribe Tours and Tengerengue terminals are on Calle Independencia at the town's east gate, while Transport del Valle maintains a station at Duarte 40 near

Independencia (☎557-6219); **guaguas** can be caught on Independencia at the parque central. It's possible to use a taxi to get to some of the more out-of-the-way sites around San Juan; try Maguana Taxi (☎557-6500).

North of San Juan

The mountainous area **north of San Juan** was long inhabited by escaped slaves who established *cimarrón* settlements throughout the Hispaniola mountains. Their religious traditions have been transformed over the last century by the veneration of **Liborio**, who is still considered a living messiah by many here (see box below); if you're interested in the religion, it's worth checking out the local holy sites.

From San Juan a paved road leads 6km north to the **Coral de los Indios**, one of the largest Taino sites on the island and scene of an infamous Spanish massacre. Folk tradition has it that this location was once the capital of a native leader named Caonabo and the Xaragua *cacique* that he ruled at the time of Columbus. Caonabo was tricked into captivity by the Spaniards in 1495, who presented him with a set of arm-and-leg chains which they told him were a form of ceremonial jewellery. When Caonabo put the chains on to honour the Spaniards, they promptly threw him into prison, shipping him off to Spain in 1496. He died of self-imposed starvation en route. His wife Anacaona ruled the Xaraguas after his imprisonment, briefly unifying the Taino *caciques* under her banner. Her efforts to negotiate peace with the Spanish were for naught, however, as a Spanish delegation soon arrived alongside two hundred troops, burning down the settlement and executing her.

All that's left of Caonabo's city can be found in a large field set off by a stone circle, which is visible from the highway and marked by a sign on your left. Since these corrals were originally used to play a game similar to soccer, it seems appropriate that it's now used as a baseball field by locals. Some of the tour

---

The Liborista Massacre

At the beginning of the nineteenth century, a charismatic faith healer named **Liborio** established a self-reliant commune in the mountains north of San Juan de la Maguana that attracted thousands of followers. Local peasants considered him a reincarnation of Jesus and worshipped him as such, though detractors maintained that he planned to march on Santo Domingo and set up a Voodoo theocracy with himself as high priest. He was branded a bandit by the American army during their occupation of the 1910s and 1920s; seeing his populist commune as a threat to their rule, they put a bounty on his head and sent out regular patrols to hunt him down. For six years he evaded capture by hiding out in the heart of the Cordillera Central with a handful of followers. When he was finally caught and murdered by American troops in 1922, rumours quickly spread through San Juan and Las Matas that Liborio had risen from the dead, and the soldiers had to dig up his corpse, drag it through the streets of San Juan in a truck and display it in the parque central to prove otherwise.

The movement he founded, though, continued, with several local *brujos* claiming to have had direct spiritual contact with Liborio. In the early 1960s a group called **Palma Sola**, run by two peasant priests known as The Twins, set up a 1200-member utopian Liborista commune in the fields just west of Las Matas, by all accounts peaceful but deemed subversive enough by the government that on December 11, 1962, the military dropped napalm on them from airplanes – burning six hundred people to death and sending the rest scattering back to their villages. The fields outside Las Matas bear no marker to indicate that the commune members died here, but the Liboristas still dwell in the mountains around San Juan.

Hurricane Georges and the San Juan riverbeds

The summer of 1998 saw one of the most devastating hurricanes in decades, **Hurricane Georges**, hit the Dominican Republic in hard fashion, sweeping through the centre of Hispaniola and taking with it the lives of thousands, not to mention the destruction wreaked in terms of lost housing, business and natural resources. Most of the Dominican fatalities from the natural disaster occurred in the area north of San Juan, when the storm sent floodwaters roaring through riverbeds that had been dry for decades due to deforestation, and where hundreds of campesinos had set up homesteads.

companies ambitiously bill it as "The Dominican Stonehenge", but you'll enjoy it more if your expectations don't reach quite that high. The boulder-lined ring, 750m in diameter, has a ceremonial stone slab in the centre, adorned with a chiselled face – like the ruins at Chacuey (see p.280). From the circle a small stone path laid by the Xaraguas leads to a riverside spring, which is believed to hold a Taino deity. On January 21 a religious festival is held at the centre of the corral in honour of the Virgin of Altagracia, who equates locally with Queen Anacaona.

From the corral, the highway begins to deteriorate as it climbs north into the Cordillera Central on its way to Sabaneta. Eight kilometres on, along a strikingly beautiful ribbon of verdant valley, is the town of La Maguana, from where a rough dirt road turns off from the main highway and leads to pueblo **Maguana Arriba**, the spiritual centre of Liborio's cult. A small thatch-roofed chapel 2km along the dirt road – and directly across from the small national police station – stands on the spot where he was born, and holds a large altar with icons of various saints, an oil painting of Liborio, a venerated photograph of his mutilated corpse and an unassuming rock which is considered to be a "magic stone". It's an enlightening place to discover the brand of *Vodú* practised in the Dominican campos, though the pleasure is watered down somewhat by the local priestess' habit of announcing to newcomers that they have cancer – in order to scare them into making a big donation. From the chapel, the dirt road leads 1km further east to **La Aguita**, a sacred spring that's recently been turned into a concrete religious centre, and is said to be inhabited by Caonabo and his wife Anacaona. Dominicans from across the country come here to bathe – and to become possessed by the spirit of Anacaona. You're likely to see locals carting off gallon jugs of the spring's water for use in healing ceremonies.

Four kilometres further north, the road ends at Sabaneta, an isolated hamlet set beside a large dam called the **Presa Sabaneta**, and the start of an arduous **trek to Pico Duarte** detailed on p.261. The national park office is just east of the dam; there you'll have to pay an RD$40 entrance fee and hire a local guide and perhaps a mule. If you're not setting off on the trek, the main attraction here is the picturesque reservoir, which feeds into the scenic Río San Juan and is dotted with fishing boats. If up for a hike you can either wander along the reservoir's shore, or head 2km north to the **Seboruco Caves**, a set of caverns adorned with religious altars and icons. The pictographs dotted on the walls of these caves are completely different from those made by the Tainos. They come from a tribe of Arawaks that lived on this island millennia ago, and a 5000-year-old body has been retrieved from the caves that is now under study at the university in San Juan de la Maguana. These people, known to us as the Ignati, were hunter-gatherer nomads and fishers who apparently practised cannibalism. To see what little is left of their culture, you'll have to pay a park ranger RD$200; what you'll see are scattered geometric shapes carved here and there into the rock face.

From San Juan the highway leads east through arid landscape and a series of nondescript pueblos all the way to Azua. There's little worth seeing aside from a few attractive spots along **Lago Sabana Yegua**, and you'll need a 4WD to visit these. If you're up for swimming you should try **Loma del Yaque**, a popular mountain swimming hole where the Río Yaque del Sur pours into the lake's northwestern tip; to get there, look for the marked turnoff at pueblo Guanito. An alternative is a look at the rather large dam, **Presa Sabana Yegua**, which is just off the highway 7km east of Guanito and offers nice shots of the lake from above. Those who are up for a hike should instead go to the mountain village of **Padre Las Casas,** the starting point for another, little-used trail to Pico Duarte. The turnoff to it is at Cruce de las Yayas, 13km east of the dam; from there it's another 15km north. The day-hike options here include heading north through the mountains to Las Lagunas, which is also where you'll find the national park office; or west along the Río Las Cuevas to the shore of the lake.

Sierra Neiba

The most beautiful stretch of the border road is the gutted gravel track that leads through the **Sierra Neiba** from Elias Piña to La Descubierta, navigable only by 4WD or motorcycle, though it takes an experienced driver. The steep, winding trip is best done by heading south from Las Matas de Farfán to El Cercado and then west to Hondo Valle, rather than heading straight down the borderline – the road that leads directly to Hondo Valle from Elias Piña is often impassable due to rockslides. Past Hondo Valle you'll make an initial steep ascent, including a few sharp, tricky turns into a lush expanse of virgin rainforest, unfortunately followed by deforestation as you descend the mountain range. After approximately three hours you'll come to the tiny pueblo **Sabana Real**, the first true settlement along the road, where a turnoff leads across the border and dozens of Haitian farmers sell produce to Dominicans. The plentiful *mata de campana* flowers grown throughout the village, shaped like upturned bells with red and yellow streaks, are a potent hallucinogen inherited from the Tainos – who drank a tea made from the flower in an effort to communicate with the gods. Residents are said to use it in their own religious ceremonies, and there's undoubtedly some recreational consumption as well. That doesn't mean you should try it – possession of the flower is punishable by a one-year jail term, and the campesinos are secretive about its use. An hour further south, a steep descent begins, with views of Lago Enriquillo and the desert far below, before arriving at the highway 1km east of La Descubierta.

Lago Enriquillo and around

Habitat for tens of thousands of tropical birds and protected as Parque Nacional Isla Cabritos, **Lago Enriquillo** is an enormous salt-water lake 42km long and slightly larger than the island of Manhattan. At the southern base of the Sierra Neiba, the lake sits at the lowest point in the Caribbean, a full 46m below sea level. If you're not content with circling the lake and seeing it from land (see "East from La Descubierta" p.289), you can get on the water with one of the **boat tours** that depart from the park entrance 4km east of **La Descubierta**, near the lake's northwestern tip. Boats leave daily at 7.30am, 8.30am and 1pm. You'll be taken to an enormous bird sanctuary filled with flamingos and hundreds of other tropical birds, which collectively form an unforgettable multicoloured spectacle; also a hit are the American crocodiles that inhabit this part of the lake, though you should take one of the morning tours if you want to see them – guides get into the water and steer them past the boat for a closer view. From there it's on to the arid, iguana-infested **Isla Cabritos** in the lake's centre, a sandy island covered with cactus where the half-tame rhinoceros iguanas crowd around you in the hope of being fed. The two-and-a-half-hour trip varies in price depending on the size of the party, ranging anywhere from RD$100 to RD$1000.

La Descubierta

LA DESCUBIERTA itself is a rather sleepy desert outpost that contains a small, somewhat inexplicable oasis – an **oak forest** fed by a cold sulphur spring, both of them bordering the concrete parque central and the Carretera Enriquillo that leads east from here to Barahona. There are a couple of short walking paths through the forest, both of which lead to **Las Barias**, the sulphur spring, which is a popular place for locals to swim thanks to its alleged medicinal properties. Another minor local attraction is **Cueva de las Caritas**, a nearby cave that holds dozens of chiselled Taino faces. You'll find its entrance along the Carretera Enriquillo, 6km east of town and quite close to the Lago Enriquillo boat tour entrance; from there you'll have to clamber up a steep escarpment, which offers spectacular views of the lake from on high along with its several dozen pictographs.

La Descubierta is accessible via **guagua** from Santo Domingo and Barahona. The minibuses drop off and load up at the corner of 27 de Febrero and Cua Vicini, near the parque central. There are several adequate and affordable **hotels** to choose from, including *Padre Billini*, Billini 26 (☎696-0327; ❶), and *Hotel del Lago*, Mella and Billini (☎224-9525; ❷), but don't count on much activity at night. The town's only **restaurant**, *Brahaman's*, Deligne 1 at the parque central, is only tolerable. They feature roast chicken with rice and beans for lunch, and chicken with mangú for dinner; both cost RD$20.

East from La Descubierta

A lot of Dominicans make an afternoon of **circling Lago Enriquillo**, though it's hard to understand why; the area is barren limestone desert, and most of the towns along the Carretera Enriquillo are rather bleak. Of course if you're interested in seeing the lake and you're not travelling along the border roads, you'll likely see this stretch, coming from Barahona or other cities east. At the very least, you'll have beautiful lake views on the stretch between La Descubierta and **Villa Jaragua**, a collection of clapboard desert huts with little in the way of facilities. A few kilometres east of there is **Neiba**, a slightly more substantive outpost where the townsfolk sell exceedingly sour grapes, the main local crop, along the highway. There's little else of note here aside from **Las Marias**, a cold sulphur spring 2km east of town, not to be confused with another smaller and dirtier balneario another 1km down the road. Neiba's parque central is a pit stop for guaguas, so it's conceivable you could get stuck here for the night, in which case head to *Hotel Restaurant Babey*, Perdomo and Mella at the parque central (☎527-3353; ❶), which has its own generator, flush-it-yourself-with-a-bucket-of-water toilets and serviceable food in a downstairs dining room. Ten kilometres further east, **Galván** is yet another desert town, this one with even less to offer – a petrol station, a pool hall and little else. If you're circling the lake, though, you'll instead turn south at Neiba onto the Circunvalación, a fifteen-kilometre highway that leads to nondescript pueblo **El Abanico**, from where it's 30km west on Highway 46 through the desert to Jimaní.

Jimaní

An unappealing, concrete desert town just south of La Descubierta, **JIMANÍ** merits a stop only if you're passing through anyway on a bus across the border to Port-au-Prince. Its large **Haitian market**, just beyond the Dominican border outpost on a stretch of *territoria de nadie* known as Mal Paso for its unforgiving terrain, displays an enormous selection of practical goods, including fake name-brand trainers and a large selection of clothing, housewares and Wilson tennis balls (which are manufactured in Haiti). If, for some reason, you need to stay the night here, there is one comfortable **hotel**, the *JV*, 19 de Marzo 14 (no phone; ❷), just off the parque central one block north of 27 de Febrero. You can get classic Dominican staples like rice-and-beans, shredded chicken and mondongo at the *Marassa Restaurant/Car Wash*, which is located just outside town on the road to La Descubierta, or head 4km further south along the same road to the *Parador Turístico El Cabriteño*, a small complex surrounding a popular local river balneario in the village of Boca de Cadrón. Within Jimaní, **guaguas** pick up and drop off at the corner of 27 de Febrero and 19 de Marzo.

About 20km east of Jimaní, on Highway 46, you can glimpse **Laguna Limón**, the largest freshwater lake in the country, not as spectacular as Lago Enriquillo but with a sizeable population of birdlife, including several dozen flamingos.

Into Haiti

Jimaní is one of two **formal border crossings** where you can get your passport stamped; the other is in Dajabón (see p.277). You'll have to pay a US$10 Dominican departure tax (American dollars only), a US$10 Haitian entry tax and a US$10 Dominican entry tax upon your return. Immigration is open daily from 8am to 6pm; if you're late you'll have to either beg the Dominican police to let you pass anyway, or spend the night in Haiti – which you don't want to do, since there are no nearby hotels. The Haitian side is just as desolate as the Dominican, but you can pick up a motorcycle driver at Mal Paso (RD$200) who will take you to the enormous **Etang Saumatre**, a salt-water lake that once connected Lago Enriquillo to the Bay of Port-au-Prince. Like Lago Enriquillo, it's a home for American crocodiles and thousands of tropical birds; there are no organized boat tours to get you on the water, but your driver will be able to take you to a spot along the shore where the birds congregate. Regardless, the lake itself is quite striking, its dark-blue depths surrounded by pale limestone cliffs.

Sierra Bahoruco

The longest of the tough border roads – but easier to manage than the Sierra de Neiba stretch – is the gravel track that begins at **Duvergé**, 30km east from Jimaní on Highway 46, and continues straight through the tall **Sierra Bahoruco**, protected by the government as Parque Nacional Bahoruco, to Pedernales at the country's southwest edge. Though this area was the stronghold of large bands of *cimarrones,* there's nothing left today of their many colonial-era encampments. The mountain range contains a variety of ecosystems, including a vast stretch of pine forest that rivals the Cordillera Central in scope, large swaths of virgin rainforest and thirsty limestone desert in the foothills.

The ascent from Duvergé to **Puerto Escondido**, a village of mountaintop shacks 14km along the way, is easily the bleakest stretch of country, parched mountainside bereft of vegetation, but as the road veers sharply west from here the ecology gradually transforms into rainforest mixed with ferns and pine. After 25km you'll reach **El Aguacate**, a small military outpost on the border. From here the road leads steeply upward to Loma del Torro, the mountain range's highest point at 2368m, and primary-growth rainforest – dotted with orchids and wild strawberries – begins, with clouds passing below the road and several spots with spectacular views of Lago Enriquillo. Five kilometres south of Aguacate is the **potato market**. Very much worth a stop, the market is held daily in a series of tents in the middle of the wilderness where locals from both sides of the border swap Haitian potatoes – grown here in abundance – for clothing and Haitian *gourdes*. It's a good slice-of-life spot, with many of the locals playing poker beneath the central tent and cooking beans over a campfire, while their mules graze nearby. Another 24km south the road begins to head steeply downward at the farming community of Mencia; from there, it's an unexciting 20km further to Pedernales.

Pedernales and around

A pleasant fishing village with a good city beach, **PEDERNALES** is the end of the line for the long border, not much in itself but within striking distance

Enriquillo

The legacy of the Taino bandit and revolutionary **Enriquillo** transcends the colourful details of his life. The orphan of a slain Taino noble, he was educated at the Monasterio San Francisco that now lies in ruins in Santo Domingo, then sent to work under the colonial *repartimiento* system that apportioned Taino slaves to Spanish landholders. In 1519 he escaped, soon gathering a large band of Tainos, allying himself with the *cimarrones* and conducting guerrilla warfare on Spanish settlements from his base just south of the lake now named for him. The Spaniards sent out several parties to capture him, but his hit-and-run tactics – in league with the harsh, mountainous landscape – kept him and his men out of their reach for over a decade. In 1530 the Spaniards relented and a peace treaty was signed; Enriquillo settled with his men around Lago Enriquillo. Free from military threat, they succumbed instead to smallpox, which was introduced to the DR by the Europeans, and many of his men were wiped out over the ensuing decade.

In 1882, author and politician **Manuel Jesús de Galván** turned the bandit chief into the nation's premier cultural icon with his novel *Enriquillo*. An outspoken opponent of African-influenced culture, Galván sought to bring the countryside's African identity more in line with the European mentality of the wealthy classes in Santo Domingo, negotiating the country's annexation to Spain and publishing several diatribes against African religious practices and African-influenced merengue music. In Enriquillo he found an appropriately heroic non-African figure with whom Dominicans could identify. The novel implicitly denies the Spanish-African heritage of the mulatto majority, attributing any presence to holdovers from the Haitian invasion (Dominican mulattos are still referred to as *Indio*). The book instantly became required reading in the schools and succeeded in changing the country's perception of itself, leading to a denial of the African influence on Dominican culture that is just in the process of being re-examined today.

of two enormous national parks. **Playa Pedernales** is the logical spot to head to within town, its uncrowded sands offering a good view of the Jaragua peninsula to the east. The village is also an important border crossing, and it's here that many migrant Haitian workers cross over to be picked up by sugar-plantation agents and shipped to the *bateyes* that dot the Dominican country-side. The **Haitian market** is held on Monday and Friday in the stretch of *territoria de nadie* just beyond the Dominican border outpost, featuring the usual assortment of fake designer labels and housewares.

Into Haiti

The **border crossing** at the western end of Avenida 27 de Febrero is pretty informal (there's no immigration post) and depends upon the whim of the border guards. Usually they'll let you cross for the day if you give them RD$100, but sometimes they'll only let you cross for a few minutes; at best, you'll need to get back before 4pm, though, if you don't want to spend the night in Haiti. Things are informal on the Haitian side as well, allowing you to visit **Anse-a-Pitres**, the village on the Haitian side of the line, during the day; if you do cross for the day, check in upon arrival with the Haitian police station at the village's main square.

In many ways, Anse-a-Pitres is Pedernales's twin, a sleepy, isolated fishing ham-let interesting primarily for its slice of rural Haitian culture, with pipe-smoking

---

Isla Beata and Alto Velo

Pedernales is the best place to find fishing boats willing to take you out on a day excursion to one of the two remote islands that are protected as a part of Parque Nacional Jaragua, **Isla Beata** and the smaller **Alto Velo**. These islands are rarely vis-ited, and for the real inconvenience of getting out there you'll be more than repaid by the pristine natural beauty and some terrific archeological sites on the southern side of Beata. Ask the boat captain to stop off at Beata first. The terrain there is scrub-brush desert, with scattered rock outcroppings covered in guano; the island is big and remote enough that it would take days to explore it entirely. On the south coast of Beata there are also a series of Taino caves where you'll find a plethora of rock art that has yet to be defaced by graffiti – as is unfortunately the case in many other parts of the island. Alto Velo is extremely high, rocky, and surrounded by deep blue waters. It juts high above the waterline like a tremendous stone sailboat – which is said to be the origin of its name ("velo" meaning "veil" and used locally as slang to refer to a boat's sail). Recently scientists have discovered the world's smallest reptile on Velo's shores, the **Dwarf Gecko**, some 1.6 centimetres across – approxi-mately the size of a Dominican 1-peso coin.

A trip to Beata and/or Alto Velo is definitely a bit of an adventure – and strictly for the strong of stomach as the ride is extremely rocky – though the trip to Beata is a slightly easier trip; most of the boats here are rather small twelve- to fifteen-foot fish-ing vessels. The trip takes three to five hours, hugging the coast until you reach its tip and then crossing the channel to one of the two islands. As a result, you should make the trip in a raincoat and waterproof gear if at all possible. Also plan for a full day to book your boat captain, and be sure to help him roll an oil drum to the Pedernales petrol station and pay for him to fill it up (around RD$1200). Ask first at the *Caribe Sur* hotel in Pedernales; if they can't help try the national park station in Oviedo (see p.307). The water gets choppier as the day goes on, so plan on depart-ing at the crack of dawn. You'll also need an RD$50 visitor's permit from the Jaragua park office in Oviedo.

old women promenading beneath umbrellas, women washing laundry in the Río Pedernales and fishermen trawling their boats onto the beach at dusk with the day's catch. As with Pedernales, the beach is pleasant and populated mostly by small children, with a few rickety boats trawling the reef. If you want to be alone, you can pay a motorcycle driver to take you a bit further east to a more isolated stretch of Haitian beach.

Cabo Rojo and Bahía de las Águilas

Back on the Dominican side, Pedernales is in close proximity to the beaches that lie along the western coast of **Parque Nacional Jaragua**'s flint-shaped peninsula, accessible via a well-marked turnoff 12km east of town. Much is made of the wonders of **Cabo Rojo**, the first beach you'll hit heading south into the park, but for all its popularity it's no more than a thin ribbon of grey sand, populated by a number of pelicans and with the hulk of a bauxite plant looming over it to the north. From Cabo Rojo the road devolves into dirt past a series of meagre Haitian beach shacks to the tiny seaside cave settlement known as **Las Cuevas**. It's something of a Dominican tradition to spend a day lying on the beach here, and the cave-dwelling villagers will cook a fresh fish meal for you for RD$30 if you ask, but the setting is less than ideal: the caves are graffiti-strewn and the sand punctuated by enormous mounds of rubbish.

South from Las Cuevas the road radically worsens, with several steep, loose gravel climbs, but it's well worth the drive out to **Bahía de las Águilas**, on the other side of the cape known as Cabo Falso, and facing the remote islands Alto Velo and Isla Beata (see box p.292). You'll hit ten kilometres of virtually uninhabited sand skirting deep-blue surf, backed by a vast plain of prickly scrub brush that serves as a habitat to tens of thousands of migratory birds. For now the place is absolutely pristine, and at most you'll see one or two local 4WDs and perhaps a couple of tents set up along the sand. This may change in a few years, though: the Mejía government has plans to turn this area into another all-inclusive complex.

Parque Nacional Bahoruco

If you don't have a 4WD, the best approach to the rugged, mostly unexplored pine and cloud forest-covered expanses of **Parque Nacional Bahoruco** is the paved road that heads straight into the mountains 12km east of Pedernales (the same road that heads south to Cabo Rojo). After a short initial climb you'll be privy to some of the most sweeping views in the country, with open shots of Pedernales, the entire Parque Nacional Jaragua and the ocean beyond it. The fires scattered about in the mountains higher up are the result of Haitian entrepreneurs who surreptitiously cut some of the trees and turn them into charcoal to sell across the border. The government has recently built a **viewing platform** called Hoyo de Pelempito at the park ranger station 35km north of the highway (which is also where the paved road ends), but to reach the park's most stunning sight, a 250-metre deep canyon covered with virgin pine and inhabited by a wide variety of birdlife, you'll have to ask the park rangers for directions along a dirt road and past a couple of misty, abandoned limestone mines.

Practicalities

You can get to Pedernales via the **guaguas** that ply the route from Barahona, some of which carry on all the way to Santo Domingo. They pick up and drop off at the Shell station at Pedernales's entrance, which holds the only unleaded petrol until Barahona; if you're driving, it's best to fill up here before you go. If you've made it this far, you're likely to be at least **staying the night**. Besides camping down at Bahía de las Águilas, options include *Caribe Sur*, Calle Duarte at the town beach (☎524-0106; ❸–❹), a solid hotel with comfortable rooms, small apartments with up to three bedrooms and kitchenette, and modest private cabanas, all featuring hot water, a/c, TV and access to the hotel's swimming pool. Cheaper is *Carolina*, Deligne 11 and Duarte (☎524-0181; ❷), more basic but still with private bath and adequate rooms. Happily, there are two terrific **restaurants** in town. *Caribe Sur's* restaurant/bar has all manner of fresh seafood; highly recommended is the *sopa de pescado*, which comes with a full fresh fish and broth. *Mary Federal Restaurant*, on 16 de Agosto and Calle 2, has grilled fish, lobster and *lambí* for around RD$80; the unmarked *comedor* across the street becomes an outdoor dance spot in the evening. The town's most popular nightspot, though, is *Bery Disco* on the parque central.

Travel details

Due to the poor quality of the roads along the border, no bus company does the entire border from Dajabón to Pedernales, but you can get from Dajabón to Restauración on a guagua, with twice-weekly connections to Pedro Santana further south. **Caribe Tours** is the only major bus company that operates in this region: it has one route that covers Manzanillo, Dajabón and Santiago de la Cruz from Santiago, and a second route that goes from San Juan de la Maguana to Santo Domingo. Also going from San Juan to the capital are Tengerengue and Transport del Valle; they're best if you're not heading all the way to Santo Domingo because they make additional stops in Baní and San Cristóbal. The southern half of the border is also serviced by various **guagua** routes, which range in quality from fairly comfortable, air-conditioned minivans to battered vans where you're crammed in with other passengers like sardines in a can. Journey times given for guaguas are rough estimates.

Buses

Dajabón to: Guayacanes (4 daily; 2hr 20min); Guayubín (4 daily; 1hr 30min); La Vega (4 daily; 5hr 45min); Monte Cristi (4 daily; 35min); Santiago (4 daily; 4hr 25min); Santo Domingo (4 daily; 6hr 50min); Villa Vasquez (4 daily; 1hr 5min).
Loma de Cabrera to: Los Indios de Chacuey (2 daily; 30min); Mao (2 daily; 2hr); Santiago (2 daily; 3hr 45min); Santo Domingo (2 daily; 6hr 15min).
Los Indios de Chacuey to: Loma de Cabrera (2 daily; 30min); Mao (2 daily; 2hr 30min); Santiago (2 daily; 4hr 15min); Santo Domingo (2 daily; 6hr 45min).
Manzanillo to: Guayubín (2 daily; 1hr 10min); Santiago (2 daily; 4hr 20min); Santo Domingo (2 daily; 6hr 40min).
San Juan de la Maguana to: Azua (13 daily; 1hr 10min); Baní (12 daily; 2hr); San Cristóbal (12 daily; 2hr 50min); Santo Domingo (13 daily; 3hr 10min).

Guaguas

Bánica to: Elias Piña (4 daily; 2hr 15min); Pedro Santana (4 daily; 20min).
Dajabón to: Batey Isabel (15 daily; 25min); Loma de Cabrera (12 daily; 40min); Manzanillo (14 daily; 30min); Monte Cristi (12 daily; 1hr 10min); Sabaneta (8 daily; 1hr 40min); Santiago de la Cruz (12 daily; 20min).
Duvergé to: Azua (12 daily; 2hr); Baní (12 daily; 2hr 50min); Barahona (18 daily; 1hr); Cabral (18 daily; 40min); Jimaní (18 daily; 1hr); Santo Domingo (12 daily; 4hr 30min).
Elias Piña to: Azua (12 daily; 2hr 20min); Baní (12 daily; 3hr 10min); Bánica (2 daily; 50min); Las Matas de Farfán (18 daily; 30min); Pedro Santana (2 daily; 1hr 5min); San Juan de la Maguana (18 daily; 1hr); Santo Domingo (12 daily; 5hr).
Galván to: Azua (12 daily; 1hr 25min); Baní (12 daily; 2hr 15min); Barahona (12 daily; 45min); La

Descubierta (12 daily; 1hr 5min); Neiba (12 daily; 10min); Santo Domingo (12 daily; 5hr).

Jimaní to: Azua (12 daily; 3hr); Baní (12 daily; 3hr 50min); Barahona (18 daily; 2hr); Cabral (18 daily; 1hr 40min); Duvergé (18 daily; 1hr); La Descubierta (15 daily; 15min); Santo Domingo (12 daily; 5hr 30min).

La Descubierta to: Azua (12 daily; 2hr 30min); Baní (12 daily; 3hr 20min); Barahona (25 daily; 1hr 50min); Galván (12 daily; 1hr 5min); Jimaní (15 daily; 15min); Neiba (12 daily; 1hr); Santo Domingo (12 daily; 5hr).

Los Indios de Chacuey to: Sabaneta (7 daily; 40min); Santiago de la Cruz (7 daily; 20min).

Loma de Cabrera to: Dajabón (12 daily; 40min); Restauración (4 daily; 40min); Sabaneta (7 daily; 1hr 15min); Santiago de la Cruz (12 daily; 20min).

Las Matas de Farfán to: Azua (12 daily; 1hr 50min); Baní (12 daily; 2hr 40min); El Cercado (6 daily; 25min); Elias Piña (18 daily; 30min); San Juan de la Maguana (18 daily; 30min); Santo Domingo (12 daily; 4hr 20min).

Manzanillo to: Dajabón (14 daily; 30min); Monte Cristi (11 daily; 40min).

Neiba to: Azua (12 daily; 1hr 35min); Baní (12 daily; 2hr 25min); Barahona (12 daily; 1hr); Galván (12 daily; 10min); La Descubierta (12 daily; 1hr); Santo Domingo (12 daily; 5hr 10min).

Pedernales to: Azua (8 daily; 4hr); Baní (8 daily; 4hr 50min); Barahona (15 daily; 2hr 30min); Enriquillo (15 daily; 1hr 35min); Los Patos (15 daily; 1hr 40min); Oviedo (15 daily; 1hr); Paraiso (15 daily; 1hr 50min); San Rafael (15 daily; 2hr); Santo Domingo (8 daily; 6hr 15min).

Pedro Santana to: Bánica (4 daily; 20min); Elias Piña (2 daily; 1hr 5min); Restauración (2 weekly; 5hr).

Restauración to: Loma de Cabrera (4 daily; 40min); Pedro Santana (2 weekly; 5hr).

San Juan de la Maguana to: Azua (15 daily; 1hr 20min); Baní (12 daily; 2hr 10min); Elias Piña (18 daily; 1hr); Las Matas de Farfán (18 daily; 30min); Presa de Sabaneta (8 daily; 1hr); Santo Domingo (12 daily; 4hr).

Santiago de la Cruz to: Dajabón (12 daily; 20min); Loma de Cabrera (12 daily; 20min); Los Indios de Chacuey (7 daily; 20min); Sabaneta (7 daily; 1hr).

Barahona and the

southwest

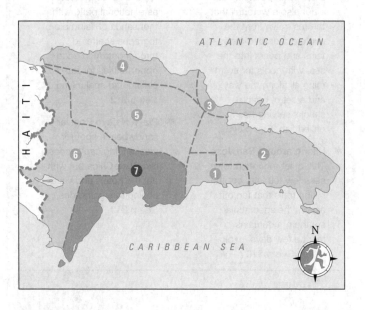

CHAPTER 7

Highlights

* **Carnival Cimarrón** A traditional Carnival celebration during Semana Santa in the town of Cabral, a tradition that harks back to the groups of free Africans that roamed these remote parts during the colonial era. See p.304

* **San Rafael** A beautiful beach with pounding surf – but also a waterfall that thrums down from the rainforest-draped mountains and pours into the sea, with pools for swimming all along the way and a set of beach shacks serving fresh grilled fish. See p.306

* **Hiking around San José** This quiet mountain town sees few tourists, but the hiking trails that fan out across the spectacular southern mountains merit a few days' exploration. See p.310

* **Las Salinas** Set amid rolling sand dunes, this small fishing village holds one of the island's most beautiful beaches – wonderfully uncorrupted by mass tourism but with a fine resort used mostly by wealthy Dominican weekenders. See p.311

* **El Pomier caves** A set of remote caves protected as a national park, with thousands of Taino pictographs scattered throughout. Also good opportunities for rappelling and spelunking. See p.312

* **Playa Najayo** Popular sandy beach spot for weekending *capitaleños*, like Boca Chica but without the hotels and vacationing foreign hordes. See p.313

Barahona and the southwest

The coast west of Santo Domingo curves along the Caribbean with no obvious dynamic core or natural tourist base. Its nominal centre is the city of **Barahona**, an old sugar-processing capital that has seen better days, thanks to the sporadic operations of its mill; inland from Barahona, and from the whole coast really, vast tracts of sugar cane take over, comprising the largely unimpressive **southwest** of the Dominican Republic. This area was once the focus of Trujillo's personal sugar empire, now better known as one of the country's poorest regions as a result of its over-dependence on the crop, its economy collapsing when sugar prices took a nosedive back in the 1960s.

The bigger towns – Barahona, **Azua**, **Baní** and **San Cristóbal** – have tried to emulate the success of the Dominican Republic's other major sugar zone, the southeast, by courting all-inclusive hotel developers to the many **superb beaches** that run from San Cristóbal all the way to the border, but these efforts have thus far been plagued by bad luck. Though the government has built a small international airport just outside Barahona for charter planes to shuttle patrons to the planned all-inclusives, environmentalists are lobbying hard in the Congress to stop any development of **Parque Nacional Jaragua**'s beachfront, west of Barahona, which is the main target for businesses. For now, this means that the coastline is almost completely undeveloped, quite an attraction in itself for independent travellers who don't mind roughing it a bit in terms of facilities and conveniences.

Though Barahona in and of itself is nothing special, west of the city a series of inviting rural fishing villages are sandwiched between the Caribbean Sea and the southern peaks of the **Sierra Bahoruco**, the island's second largest range, covered with rainforest and boasting steep slopes that drop off abruptly at the coast. **Paraiso** – a pleasant town with a long sandy beach – is one of the prime spots along this stretch, while **San Rafael** and **Los Patos** both have rainforest waterfalls tumbling down from the mountains, forming freshwater pools before draining into the sea. At the flint-shaped peninsula taken up by Parque Nacional Jaragua, the far southwestern part of the country, the mountains retreat a bit, and lush greenery evaporates into stark desert.

The area east of Barahona also devolves into arid semi-desert, punctuated by large, industrial cities of interest only for their own nearby beaches. North of

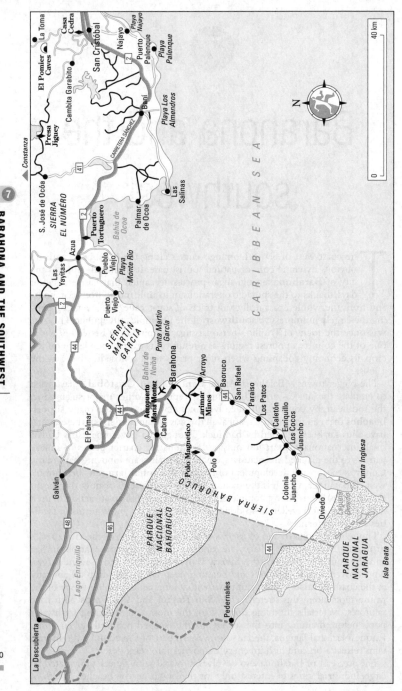

San Cristóbal – one of these cities – the caves of **El Pomier** hold some excellent Taino rock art. There are mountains here as well, including the southern foothills of the Cordillera Central to the north, draped with deciduous greenery; and the pretty, rolling hills of the El Número Mountains that separate Azua from Baní, providing a natural barrier that frustrated persistent Haitian attempts to occupy the Dominican Republic in the nineteenth century. The Dominicans were repeatedly able to quash the invasions in El Número's narrow mountain passes, and today the only Haitian influence lies in the meagre *bateyes* north of Barahona where thousands of Haitian cane cutters live.

The **Carretera Sánchez** that stretches west from Santo Domingo to Azua, where it becomes Highway 44 and continues all the way to the border, is well paved and fairly easy to navigate, though west of Barahona you should watch out for some tricky turns atop high cliffs. Be prepared also for the highway to end abruptly at the major towns, only recommencing at the other side. Off the main highway you'll usually have to make do with rough dirt roads, though paved avenues lead from the Carretera to San José de Ocóa, Cabral, Las Salinas and Palenque.

Barahona and around

Barahona city isn't an especially pleasant place, but it does have a number of hotels, and so many travellers use it as a base to explore the magnificent coastline that runs west of the city all the way to **Parque Nacional Jaragua**. Most memorable of the many beaches along this stretch are the balnearios at **San Rafael** and **Los Patos**, long popular with locals but undiscovered by the outside world. There is one small luxury hotel in these parts, but otherwise you'll have to make do with some pretty basic establishments run by local families. Meanwhile, **north of Barahona** there are thousands upon thousands of square acres dedicated to sugar-cane cultivation; this area is mostly inhabited by Haitian cane cutters, but you will find a few Dominican villages here and there, notably **Cabral**, located next to a pretty, freshwater lagoon that you can visit on boat tours.

Barahona

Founded by Haitian General Toussant L'Ouverture in 1802 as an alternate port to Santo Domingo and once the informal capital of Trujillo's multimillion-dollar sugar industry, **BARAHONA** has fallen on hard times due to the low price of sugar globally and the transition in the US from sugar to corn syrup in all manner of sweetened products. Evidence of this downturn abounds in the uncared-for roads rutted to the point of near-impassability. In truth, Barahona is of use mostly as a base camp: the hotels are more plentiful and a bit better than the few along the coast west of the city, and it's close enough to make day-trips easy along the coast or even to Lago Enriquillo.

Arrival

You're not likely to make much use of it, but **Aeropuerto Internacional María Montéz**, on the Carretera Cabral 1km north of town (☎524-7000), has incoming flights on Caribair (☎542-6688 or 547-2767, Ⓦwww.caribintair .com), with daily connections to Santo Domingo and Port-au-Prince. Most visitors instead arrive **via guagua or car**; coastal Highway 44 connects the city with Azua, Baní and Santo Domingo to the east before continuing west all the way to the border, and a well-marked turnoff 11km east of town leads northwest to San Juan de la Maguana, Las Matas de Farfán and Elias Piña. Once you arrive, you'll find a Codetel and a Banco Popular with 24-hour ATM machine at the parque central.

Accommodation

Most **accommodations** are within a couple of blocks of the wide-open seaside Malecón (also known as Avenida Enriquillo), four blocks south of the parque central. The best accommodation in town is the *Gran Hotel Barahona*, Mota 5 (☎524-3442 or 2415; ❷–❸), with comfortable rooms that have a/c, TV, phone and hot water. *Caribe*, Malecón (☎524-4111, Ⓕ524-4115; ❸), is shabbier but boasts similar amenities, while *Guarocuya*, Malecón 50 (☎524-4121; ❸), is the only hotel in town with a view of the beach, though the water is lukewarm at best and the restaurant should be avoided. *Los Hijos de Dindo*, 30 de Mayo 39 (no phone; ❶), and *Cacique*, behind the Parque Infantil at the Malecón (☎524-4620; ❶), are the cleanest rock-bottom options, with private cold-water baths.

The Town

There's not terribly much to see in Barahona, though it is a decent-sized town, certainly the largest along this stretch of land. Begin with the **Malecón**, also

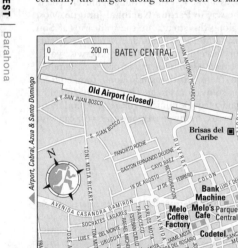

known as Avenida Enriquillo, which gets crowded with food shacks and partying locals at night; its major landmark is a **Parque Infantil** (children's park)
on Calle Uruguay with a slide in the shape of the solar system. West from the
park, past a series of beach shacks, is a modest stretch of beach bordered by
mangroves along the *Hotel Guarocuya*. The town's top public beach, though, lies
at the opposite end of the boardwalk beyond **Ingenio Barahona**, the country's largest sugar mill, though saddled with debt and only sporadically func-
tioning. From there follow the gutted mud track along the water for a half-
kilometre to the peninsula at Barahona's far eastern end, which is ringed by
pristine white sand and backed by palms. Away from the water, there's one
business operation open for visitors – though tours are strictly informal – the
Melo coffee factory, Anacaona 10 (8am–5pm, closed Sun), where coffee
produced in the Cordillera Central and Sierra de Bahoruco is brought for processing and export. Ask the owner at *Melo's Café* next door for permission to
see the facilities.

Eating, drinking and nightlife

There are a couple of exceptional **restaurants** in town. *Melo's Café*, Anacaona
12 (☎524-5437), is the best of the lot, an unpretentious little diner with delicious American breakfasts (try the French toast) and fruit shakes, and nightly
dinner specials at 7pm for RD$45; don't miss the goat dish with bananas, plan-
tains and avocados. On the far eastern end of the Malecón is more formal dining at *Brisas del Caribe* (☎524-2794), a seafood restaurant with impeccable
service and a slew of great menu offerings, including *camarones al ajillo, mero esti-
lo bari, langosta a la plancha* and *carite al limón*. It's also the only place on the island
where you're likely to be served a large Presidente bottle in a champagne ice
bucket. There is also, of course, the expected array of fast-food vendors in the
parque central and along the Malecón.

Barahona is perhaps better known for its popular and somewhat seedy **discos**, the pre-eminent ones being *Lotus* on the northwest corner of the parque
central, a large, darkish dance floor and bar that attracts a mix of local couples
and passing merchant marines trying to pick up local women. Also on the park
are smaller *Legends*, Mota and 30 de Mayo, and *La Campina*, an outdoor beer
hall where patrons sit at tables and look out at the park. The east end of the
Malecón is another major centre for nightlife, most of it gathered around the
unremarkable restaurant *Gazebo de las Flores*, including a fun terrace hangout
called *Los Robles Super Fria* and a line of liquor shacks that feature a few tables
and dancing to boom box merengue.

North of Barahona

Fifteen kilometres northwest of Barahona, the small town of **CABRAL** sits on
the eastern edge of the Parque Nacional Bahoruco, though you'll still have to
go some ways before entering the park (p.293). Cabral itself is home to the
serene **Laguna Cabral** (also known as Laguna Rincón), a lovely patch of
water that's habitat for numerous birds, including Orilla, Criolla and Florida
ducks, flamingos, ibises and herons. You can arrive either by two-hour boat tour
from the park station at the north end of town (RD$50 entrance fee, RD$500
for a boat plus RD$200 for a guide), or independently by heading north on
the paved road that skirts the lagoon to the east to a pueblo called El Peñon,
from where a dirt road leads west of town to the lagoon. Unfortunately, you

Haitian bateyes

For most of the twentieth century, **sugar** was the crop around which the Dominican economy revolved. Though tourism recently replaced it as the top source of foreign currency, sugar plantations still exist all along the southern half of the island, their vast expanses of cane harvested by migrant Haitian labourers who live in meagre company barracks known as **bateyes**.

As early as the late nineteenth century, depressed sugar prices made Dominican labour too expensive for the sugar companies, and masses of **migrant workers** were imported from the British Antilles to fill the void. During the Great Depression of the 1930s, even this labour became too expensive, and formal agreements were reached that paid the Haitian government to recruit and export tens of thousands of cane cutters each year. The *batey* workers came from the poorest rural parts of Haiti, encouraged by the opportunity to save US$30–50 over the course of a season – in four or five years that would be enough to build a modest house and work a small subsistence farm back in their home country. Many, however, have come back empty-handed or, worse, never left at all.

The formal agreement has dissolved, and Haitians who cross into the Dominican Republic to work in the sugar fields do so *aba fil* (under the fence). There is an intense amount of **prejudice** against Haitians in the DR, and when they arrive they are generally captured by one of the numerous local border patrols, herded into sugar company buses and trucked to a *batey* where security guards prevent them from leaving before the harvest season is finished. Whenever there are too few cane cutters, Dominican police round up Haitians living in other parts of the country and ship them off to the *bateyes* as well.

Batey life involves horribly substandard conditions. Manually cutting cane with machetes is backbreaking work, and the labourers are paid as little as RD$3/ton. They have to work at least fourteen hours a day in order to feed themselves, pay a baroque system of bribes to police officers and company officials and save a few pesos for the return to Haiti. Most *bateyes* have no bathrooms or running water, and workers must walk a kilometre or more for water and sleep five or six to a small room. Every year thousands of Haitians fail to earn enough for the journey home, and are forced to stay in the *batey* during the dead season, when there's little work available. The inhuman conditions have led various international human rights groups to declare the situation tantamount to slavery, but there has been little in the way of reform to date.

---

can't get on the water from there, but you will at least have a good vantage point. Otherwise, the only reason for staying around town is if you've arrived during Semana Santa, when the **Carnival Cimarrón** is held, a week of exuberant celebrations in which participants don devil masks (*diablos cojuelos*) and ornate costumes, and carry bullwhips. You can purchase a mask, if you like, by asking around at the park station at any time of year. Similar traditional Cabral celebrations occur during the fiesta patronal in honour of Señora de los Remedios from September 3 to 9. The closest **hotel** to Cabral (though there's no need to stay here, it's close enough to Barahona for an easy half-day trip) is the *Oasis Hotel* (℡470-4902, ℱ248-4680; ❸), a nice little compound that's usually pretty empty but has decent meals in the downstairs restaurant and comfortable rooms with a/c but no hot water or cable TV.

North on Highway 48, which picks up just past El Peñon, begins some of the densest and most primitive **sugar-cane** farming areas in the country. Along the road you'll see Haitian villages and the ruins of the old railroad that Trujillo built to ship the cane harvested here to the Barahona mill. Though there's little to see, pueblo El Palmar 10km up, with its decaying old warehouses and a large community of Haitian cane workers, is a decent stop-off point. Further on towards **Galván** (see p.289), the terrain becomes more arid and is dominated by white-flowering tuna cacti.

Back south of Cabral, about 10km down the Carretera Polo, the **Polo Magnético** (Magnetic Pole) makes for the stuff of rural legend, a place where the law of gravity is apparently defied. At an upward incline in the highway, marked by a roadside billboard, you can pull off on the right-hand fork and put your car in neutral; it will seem to be slowly pulled up the hill, as will any round object that you place on the pavement. A group of student surveyors from Santo Domingo's Catholic University established that the "pole" is an optical illusion, but most locals reject this conclusion, believing that the miracle results from the presence of magnetically charged ore beneath the road's surface.

West of Barahona

The gorgeous coastline west of Barahona is the region's premier attraction, yet it remains virtually undiscovered by outsiders. Drive the length of it and you'll find innumerable small beach coves tucked between high oceanfront cliffs; the first beaches to head for are **San Rafael**, **Los Patos** and **Paraiso**. Also worth a visit are the **larimar mines** north of Arroyo and the flamingo-inhabited **Laguna Oviedo**.

Quemaito and the larimar mines

Heading south from Barahona along Highway 44, **Playa Saladilla** is just 3km away, a little sand cove protected by a reef, with shallow, calm water for swimming. An equally sheltered but more developed beach is at **Quemaito** 3km further on, home to two small hotels and a beautiful little stretch of sand that gets only moderate traffic. If you're willing to trade simple accommodation for secluded natural beauty and gourmet cuisine, head for the singular *Casablanca* hotel (T & F 471-1230; ❸), set along rambling rural grounds perched on a cliff over the beach. The rooms boast few amenities but are charming nonetheless, with private cold-water bath and fan. What draws people here is the food: the proprietor is a gourmet French chef and retired editor-in-chief of a popular European cooking magazine. Breakfast and dinner are included in the price, and dinner is served according to the French *table d'hôte* tradition, by which guests tell the proprietor what they want for dinner in the morning, she goes to the market, buys everything fresh and then prepares it for them. All guests then sit around a common table for the evening meal. If you prefer a/c to haute cuisine, opt for *Club Hotel El Quemaito* (T 223-0999; ❸ for room, ❹ breakfast and dinner included), a small, modern resort with good facilities and a swimming pool and patio, empty most of the time apart from the owner's six German shepherds. Dinners run around RD$125, and the *colmado* along the highway is a popular local hangout.

From Quemaito the rainforested **Sierra Bahoruco** begins to stand imposingly at the very edge of the shore, dropping off precipitously at the water's edge and leading to some hard-crashing surf along much of the coast. Five kilometres further southwest is the pueblo Arroyo, a tiny town with a dirt road turnoff that leads through the mountains to the local **larimar mines**. You're free to visit the mines, though the road is rough. Take the dirt turnoff at the cockfighting arena and head 8km through lush rainforest and past small mountain campos, then walk up the hill from the road. Keep in mind, though, that the road is quite bad, and you're in danger of losing a tyre if not in a 4WD; it's also possible to ask around in Arroyo for a motoconcho that will take you up for RD$40. The main set of mines are little more than deep holes in the ground supported by wooden frames, nothing much in themselves, but it's fascinating to watch local miners acrobatically clamber up and down them; they'll also sell you raw chunks of the stones if you're interested in a souvenir. A hundred metres down the road, a large river with small cascades makes a good spot to cool off after the dusty journey.

Baoruco

It's another 5km back along Highway 44 to **Baoruco**, a tiny fishing village with a pretty beach and some small resorts. Aside from the hotels, though, it's a sleepy little place, and the only activity you'll find is at the set of seaside liquor shacks set up along the north end of the waterfront. The all-inclusive *Bahoruco Beach Resort* (℡524-1111, Ⓕ524-6060, Ⓔbarcelobahoruco@codetel.net.do; ❹) took ten years to construct but is doing only moderate business for the Barceló chain and may be closed down soon. If it's still up and running when you arrive, it's worth checking out for its 105 excellent rooms with all the amenities, its verdant pool area and private access to the southern end of Playa Baoruco. As usual, the buffet food is uninspiring – but at least it's included free with your room. The other resort in Baoruco is *Casa Bonita* (℡696-0215, Ⓕ223-0548; ❺), set on a hilltop above the town that's visible just north of the highway. Catering mostly to wealthy Dominicans, the hotel has a view of the ocean from up high, along with a swimming pool and an elegant restaurant. Don't expect 24-hour service, though, as most of the hotel staff go home at 8pm; and while rooms are marketed as having all the amenities, there are frequent water outage problems. Breakfast and dinner are included in the price; non-guests can have dinner on the patio for around RD$250.

There's a third alternative three kilometres further west, though you'll have to look sharp to find the entrance from the highway to *Barahona Coral Sol* (℡524-4077, Ⓦwww.coralsolresort.com; ❹), another of the independent resorts that have cropped up along the coast in the past few years. Perched rather precariously on a high cliff above the water, the grounds here are beautiful and walking paths zigzag up and down the steep hillside upon which it's set. The majority of guests are wealthy Dominicans from the capital, and it's therefore crowded only on weekends. The rooms have strong fans, balconies with views of ocean, two bathrooms each and are agreeably private, but the service is non-existent outside of mealtimes.

San Rafael, Paraiso and Los Patos

Five kilometres beyond Baoruco pueblo **San Rafael** holds an enticing beach, if one with a strong, crashing surf, crowded with Dominicans on weekends but only moderately populated the rest of the week. Fortunately, a **waterfall** thrums down the nearby mountains and forms a natural swimming pool at the entrance, with an unobtrusive manmade barrier walling it in so that water slowly pours over the edge into the sea. The area around here is a popular camping spot, complete with public shower and bathroom facilities, and some shacks nearby sell excellent grilled lobster and fresh fish. If you want to get some **hiking** in, climb into the mountains along the river's cascades for a few kilometres. Watch also for the turnoff just west of the beach, with panoramic views atop a high cape. Directly above the beach on a Sierra Bahoruco foothill is the **Villa Miriam**, a private complex (RD$100) with exclusive access to some of the best of the waterfall's cascades – which it has cordoned off and turned into a popular local balneario. There's also a small public balneario here that is not fenced off and that anyone can use for free, with a couple more liquor and food shacks.

PARAISO, another 5km to the west, is the biggest town along this stretch, but still doesn't boast much in the way of facilities. It does have a long strand of superb sandy beach, along which stands the *Hotel Paraiso* (☎243-1080; ❷), a decent enough place to stay for the night, with a/c (RD$350) or fan (RD$250), cable TV, and a local-seafood restaurant. More good Dominican food can be found at *Paola*, Highway 44 at Nouel, with daily specials for RD$75. Guaguas meet at the corner of Arzbispo Nouel and Enriquillo.

A better beach lies yet 5km further west, in **LOS PATOS**, where the ocean is joined again by a river descending from the mountains to form a freshwater swimming pool. The beach, surrounded with dense mangroves, stays pretty active throughout the week, and beach vendors are set up to take care of most visitors' needs. In addition to these, the pueblo has an excellent **restaurant**, *Pula*, on the highway across the street from Iglesia San Miguel, with fresh seafood cooked Italian- and *criolla*-style; choose from the *pescado con coco*, goat roasted in a creole gravy, and grilled lobster. The one **hotel**, *Virginia*, Calle Peatonal (no phone; ❶), is pretty basic with private cold-water bath, mosquito net and no toilet seats.

Enriquillo and Los Cocos

The beachfront remains uninterrupted for 11km beyond Los Patos; feel free to stop off along the way at any number of small pueblos such as **Los Blancos**, where beneath a series of high wide cliffs you can have the pebbly beach pretty much to yourself. The first town of any real size is **ENRIQUILLO**, majestically set over a jagged **limestone precipice**. A broad beach stretches to the west, but there are no trees along it and thus little respite from the sun; perched at the edge of a sheer cliff directly above the beach is the most scenic *club gallístico* in the country, with RD$10 cockfights on Saturdays. For seclusion head a few metres east of town and look for the extremely steep dirt road that leads downward to a pebble beach cove. Right on the highway in the centre of town, *Hotel Dayira* (no phone; ❶) is the nicest of the very basic local **accommodation** – and that's not saying much; it has private cold-water baths and a second-floor balcony with partial views of the ocean. *Rosscalta* is the place to go for **dinner**; it's just west of town below the *club gallístico*, and serves fresh seafood cooked in a variety of spicy sauces. If you're headed further west, fill up first at the petrol station in Enriquillo – it's the last chance for petrol until Pedernales, 60km away, and the Pedernales station does not have unleaded.

From Enriquillo the highway follows the coast to **Los Cocos**, a thatch-hut pueblo just 3km on, with coconut trees and a pebble beach. The only activity to hold interest here is checking out the **baseball games** held on the seaside field – many of the kids fashion their gloves from milk cartons or cardboard boxes.

Oviedo

A small desert town with little in the way of facilities, **OVIEDO** is worth a visit strictly as an entryway to **Parque Nacional Jaragua**, particularly the scenic **Laguna Oviedo** that lies at its entrance. To visit the lagoon you'll have to pay an RD$50 admission fee at the national park office (daily 9.30am–4pm) – visible on the south side of the road just before the town (and lagoon) entrance. It is almost impossible to get to, but there is one boat captain in town who does the trip (see below). On the lagoon are 24 islands, some with iguanas, and you can get an entry ticket at the park office for either lagoon tours here or more out-of-the-way excursions on the western end of the Jaragua peninsula (see p.293).

If you just want to wander along the Laguna Oviedo's shore, the entrance is well marked at the east end of town; stop your car and walk left along the fork in the road for the best birdwatching. Along the lagoon's far side are a number of Taino cave sites that have been left relatively undisturbed; to see them – or to organize a boat tour – take the highway west from the park entrance a kilometre to an unmarked yellow gate just past the second "National Park" sign (but still before you reach the town) to Blanco Tours (no phone), a fairly informal operation run by a local Dominican captain who knows the park well. A trip costs RD$800 regardless of how many people you have, and lasts two to five hours, depending on what you want to see. The full trip includes flamingo and bird watching, a trip to visit the iguanas at the lagoon's southwest end, a look at a couple of Taino archeological cave sites and a stop at Cabo San Luis, an island with a small sandy beach at the lagoon's far end. If you'd prefer to hike to the caves – a daunting prospect in this rocky, arid country – you'll have to negotiate a price for one of the national park officers to guide you.

There are no hotels in Oviedo, which is just fine – there's no reason to spend much time here. See pp.291–293 for information on Pedernales, Cabo Rojo and Bahía de las Águilas, all on the western periphery of Parque Nacional Jaragua.

Azua to San Cristóbal

Heading east of Barahona towards the capital, you'll encounter **Azua**, **Baní** and **San Cristóbal**, three industrial towns founded at the outset of Spanish colonization. These days they don't net many visitors, understandable since they're congested and unappealing at first sight, but the nearby beaches make a trip here worth it for those willing to ferret them out. Best of the bunch is the magnificent sandy beach at **Las Salinas** south of Baní, a quiet coastal village surrounded by sand dunes and sporting a top-notch hotel. Near Azua you'll find undeveloped **Playa Monte Río**, which is pebbly in places but does boast one beautiful white-sand cove called **Playa Blanca**; while south of San Cristóbal a paved highway winds through the hills to **Najayo** and **Palenque**, admirable sandy beaches that net heavy crowds of locals on weekends. Away from the sea, the mountain river dotted with cascades just south of **San José de Ocóa** is an equally appealing place for a hike or a swim, as are the popular **La Toma** pools north of San Cristóbal – themselves just three kilometres away from this region's most impressive cultural sight, **El Pomier**, a series of caverns holding thousands of Taino petroglyphs.

Azua

AZUA is one of the very oldest cities in the New World, founded by future conqueror of Cuba Diego Velázquez in 1504, and also the one-time home of Mexico conquistador Hernán Cortes, who served as its mayor in the early sixteenth century. Despite this lofty history, there's nothing left of the original city, which was demolished by a 1751 earthquake; on top of that, Haitian armies occupied Azua a half-dozen different times in the nineteenth century and, despite being repelled in the El Número mountain passes to the east, left the village virtually sacked. Although a celebration is held every March 19 to commemorate one of these battles that resulted in victory over the Haitians, in 1844, the town **Pueblo Viejo** holds no colonial ruins, and **Puerto Viejo** – the old port – is merely an industrial site for the extraction of natural gas.

It's not surprising then that visitors usually just pass right through Azua, meaning they miss out on some excellent beaches, particularly five-kilometre-long **Playa Monte Río**, a few kilometres south of town. To reach the beach, which offers beautiful views of the rolling El Número Mountains, take the turnoff at the Brugal sign, on Azua's eastern edge. There's very little development here at all; rather, the calm waters are lined with fishing boats and a few locally run outdoor restaurants, including *La Rosa*, *Euromar* and *San Miguel*, all of which serve grilled fresh fish with the requisite accompaniments of plantains, rice and beans. A half-kilometre west of these establishments, **Playa Blanca** is even more attractive a spot, a placid turquoise cove with pure-white sand – though unfortunately home to a large number of sand fleas at night.

While you're here you may hear a lot about **Bichi**, a sulphur spring just north of town, famous in the DR for its powers as a laxative (and even believed by some to be a sacred Taino spring), but it's nothing more than a mud pit strewn with trash.

Practicalities

You won't have much need for Azua's few **hotels**, though if you're desperate, the cleanest of the very basic bunch is *Las Flores*, on the Carretera Sánchez at the town's west entrance (no phone; ❶). There are a number of **restaurants** to choose from, but most serve the same line-up of local staples like *la bandera dominicana* and *pollo al carbón*. The best of these is *Francis*, Carretera Sánchez at the eastern end of town, which serves a variety of well-prepared, traditional Dominican dishes, including garlic shrimp and creole red snapper. One quick alternative – and the only one with breakfast – is *Panadería Petra*, 19 de Marzo and Independencia, which offers a variety of serviceable pizzas, sandwiches and baked goods for a few pesos. If you're looking for a bit of nightlife, head to the outdoor dance hall at *Car Wash*, which is a couple of kilometres west of town at the turnoff for San Juan de la Maguana. The phone centre, cash machine and bank are all on 19 de Marzo a block east of the parque central.

San José de Ocóa

Tucked away in the mountains along the Río Ocóa, the mountain hamlet **SAN JOSÉ DE OCÓA**, 27km north of the Carretera Sánchez along Highway 41, attracts weekenders from across the country (though few foreign visitors), mainly in the summer months when temperatures in the valley below can be sweltering. Most are here to visit the river balneario and take advantage of the lovely, sometimes rugged, mountain landscape that surrounds the town, though the fiesta patronal for the Virgin of Altagracia (January 15–21) is also a popular time to visit.

The town itself is easygoing and fairly modest, consisting mostly of clapboard shacks and unremarkable but for its majestic setting, perched atop a high hill with views stretching across the southern Cordillera Central. Just south of town is **El Manantiel**, the local river balneario, a kilometre down a dirt road off the highway, where you'll find several good spots for swimming among the boulders and ice-cold cascades. Plenty of other people – particularly families – opt for the outfits that siphon off fresh water from the river into large swimming pools, such as **Las Jessicas** (daily 8.30am–10pm; RD$10), down a steep incline on the opposite side of the road, where there's a diving board and a water slide. It also turns into a popular dance hall at night.

Better exercise can be had on any number of **hikes** in the surrounding countryside; trails abound, and the easiest option is to simply set off on one of the dirt paths spiralling away from San José into the hills. If you have your own transportation, though, it's worth driving through some small pueblos and beautiful scenery to the **Presa Jaguey**, an extremely remote dam and lake northeast of town. To get there take a right turn at the fork in the road just north of town, and another right 5km further on; it offers an extraordinary vista over Lago Jaguey, a beautiful, little-visited lake set at the base of some very high mountains. Another, more adventurous option is to drive the stunning but extremely bad **San José–Constanza road** (see p.265), leading north of town right into the heart of the Cordillera Central; it's only passable with a good 4WD, spare tyres and emergency supplies.

Practicalities

San José **accommodations** are plentiful but no-frills, including *Sagrato de Jesús*, Cañada and San José (☎558-2432; ❶), and *Pensión San Francisco*, 37 Pimentel (☎558-2741; ❶), niether especially luxurious but perfectly acceptable, with shared cold-water showers and cable TV; *Sagrato* also has a good cafeteria. Alternately, there's plenty of space here for **camping**, though nowhere is it regulated; for security's sake, you should ask permission from a local farmer.

You won't spend much on **food** here, though a couple of local restaurants are quite good. *Baco*, for example, a half-block west of the parque central, serves complete meals like *chivo guisado* (goat stew) or chicken with rice, beans and plantains for RD$30. **Nightlife** consists exclusively of the half-dozen bars spread out along the highway south of town, plus the *Galaxi Disco*, which has live music on weekends. In addition, *La Bella Juliana Car Wash* has a bar and a pool table on its top floor.

To move on, **guaguas** can be picked up on the main road at the south town entrance or at San José's attractive parque central, which also holds a Banco Popular with cash machine, Codetel, Televimenca and Western Union.

Baní

Seventeen kilometres east of the San José turnoff, coastal **BANÍ** has in recent years turned relatively prosperous, thanks to a nearby naval base and the saltpans south of the city, an upswing that has spurred much population growth, if not exactly prettified the place. There are few diversions within town – the

parque central is nice enough for people-watching, and you can stop off at **Botánica Chango** on Duvergé and Carretera Las Calderas for a look at the wares used in the local folk religion. There's also a unique **fiesta patronal** held from June 15 to 24 in honour of San Juan Bautista, with dozens of musicians performing a distinctive Afro-Latin music called Sarandunga, which has heavy rhythmic influences from Senegal but is unique to Baní.

Just outside of town you'll find a number of good **beaches**, including the one most frequented by the locals, **Los Almendros**, 5km south from the parque central on Calle Duarte. It's not as spectacularly scenic perhaps as many of its competitors along the Barahona coast, but is serviceable enough; at the beach entrance you'll find a decent restaurant, *Brisas del Mar*, and the *Costa Brava* outdoor disco, which sometimes gets big-name live acts.

More rural and far more beautiful is quiet **LAS SALINAS**, a small town consisting of little more than a few dozen houses scattered about a white-sand beach, 16km southwest at the end of the Carretera Las Calderas and 2km east of the naval facility at Las Calderas. Sand dunes, saltpans and rolling hills surround the village, which makes for a fine place to do some **windsurfing**. The all-inclusive *Salinas High Wind Center*, Puerto Hermosa 7 (☏310-8141 or 471-9463; ❹), a small resort catering mostly to wealthy Dominicans that has a pool, bar, disco and patio restaurant, serves as an informal windsurfing club on weekends – though you'll have to bring your own equipment. The restaurant has the best food in the area, heavy on seafood; try the house speciality, lobster *criolla* (ask for two big lobsters instead of three little ones), or the *lambí*. It's easily one of the most fun places to stay on the entire island, for the natural beauty, magnificent facilities, and super-hip party scene that pervades on weekend evenings. The downside is that there's no service late at night and you'll have to buy a Codetel card in the town centre in order to make a phone call.

It takes some effort to reach the beach at **Palmar de Ocóa**, just a few kilometres away but only accessible by a winding fifteen-kilometre, newly paved road. The beach disappoints, too, unless you're here to fish: the coarse, grey sand drops off steeply at the water's edge, and plenty of locals can be seen casting their lines from here, but it's certainly not for swimming.

Practicalities

Outside of the **hotel** in Las Salinas, there are not too many places around Baní to bed down; adequate options include the frankly shabby *Caribaní*, San Tomé and Sánchez at the parque central (☏522-5281; ❷), and the somewhat more modest *Alba*, Mella and Billini (☏522-3590; ❶). **Restaurants** are slightly better: *Yarey*, a surprisingly competent pizzeria on the parque central; a home-style Dominican *comedor* by the name of *Mi Estancia* on the corner of Mella and Billini; and a row of grilled-chicken shacks on Duarte a block north of the park. There are plenty of **discos** and **bars**, too. Best are *Costa Brava* at Playa Los Almendros, *D'Cachet Club* on Billini and *El Chapuzón* in Villa Sombrero 3km south of town on the road to Las Salinas, which features live top *bachata* acts like Luis Vargas and Raulin Rodríguez on the 15th and 30th of every month.

Most other necessities can be found around the parque central, including phone centres, Western Union and **guaguas** heading to and from any direction. The town cash machine is on Duarte and Máximo Gómez.

San Cristóbal and around

SAN CRISTÓBAL, Trujillo's hometown, obviously enjoyed its heyday during his rule – being the beneficiary of an enormous cathedral and two palatial presidential residences all paid for courtesy of the government. The cathedral still stands – though there's little reason to visit it – but the mansions are now in ruins, and the cramped, asphalt city qualifies as one of the country's least appealing. That said, it is well situated for exploring some fascinating nearby sights, namely the **La Toma balneario** and **El Pomier caves** to the north, and it is close enough to Santo Domingo – just 30km west of the capital – to make an easy day-trip from there.

El Cerro

The one dubious sight within the city itself is **El Cerro** (The Hill), a 1940s Trujillo mansion perched atop a hill overlooking San Cristóbal and with distant views of the sea. The six-storey, semicircular structure is today an abandoned wreck, looking less like a private residence than a bombed-out office building. During Trujillo's tenure it was decked out with long-pillaged gold and silver plating and mahogany trim. On the old grounds is a field where local kids play baseball; they'll pester you to let them show you inside (where you'll find badly damaged murals by José Vela Zanetti) for a few pesos, but if you don't want their company you can also enter the building by yourself. To get there from the concrete parque central, take Avenida Luperón (the road to Baní) west and turn south at the Isla Gasolina.

North of San Cristóbal

There's far more of interest in the mountains north of San Cristóbal, including **Casa Caoba** (daily 8am–5pm), another, more attractive abandoned Trujillo mansion about 2km north on Constitución, past the 6 de Noviembre highway and then east at the "La Toma" sign; continue for another kilometre. A stylish 1938 building originally built entirely out of mahogany, with clean, stylized angles reminiscent of Frank Lloyd Wright, it was surrounded by manicured Japanese gardens that are now going to weed. Though plans to convert the place into a historical attraction have been hyped for years, only modest renovation has been completed and you'll have to make do with the guard's informal tour (Spanish only; RD$30), which navigates through the various rooms, including a secret chamber through which the dictator's mistress was conducted to his bedroom, and a look at the intricately crafted, stacked woodwork still waiting to be cleaned up.

From the mansion it's due north to El Pomier and the La Toma pools. A bit north of Casa Caoba you'll run into a fork in the road; head right for La Toma, left for El Pomier. **La Toma** (daily 8.30am–7.30pm; RD$5, parking RD$20), lies 9km north of Casa Caoba, consists of a series of large cemented pools supplied with fresh water from the Río Haina, and is unbelievably popular with locals on weekends. There's ample parking at the site, but you can also catch an RD$10 guagua from San Cristóbal's parque central.

Reserva Argueológica El Pomier (daily 9.30am–5pm; RD$50 for park entrance, plus $150 for a guide; bring your own flashlight and wear boots), which lies 10km north of the Casa Caoba fork, protects the most extensive collection of cave pictographs in the Caribbean – some as much as 2000 years old – though this claim to notoriety draws strangely few visitors. There are three major sets of caves, but El Pomier is the only one open to the public (the other two are named Borbón and Santa María). Upon arrival, you'll be assigned a park guide (who speaks Spanish only) who will take you to the first of three enormous, easily accessible chambers, two of which hold a variety of Taino pictographs. In addition to scattered depictions of various birds and animals (which were once used for religious rituals) there are a number of interesting geological formations and one cave filled with thousands of bats. If you want to see the best petroglyphs, though, you're in for a bit of an adventure, including rappelling down some steep cave walls. Domingo Abreu (☎682-1577) runs regular trips to El Pomier from Santo Domingo for individual tourists, and is the best person to contact if you want to go to the spectacular but somewhat inaccessible caves that are off the main tour.

The beaches

San Cristóbal is also quite close to a couple of terrific beaches, with guaguas departing regularly for them from the parque central. **Najayo**, along the Carretera Palenque 14km south of San Cristóbal, has an attractive strip of beige sand; there's also one hotel here (see "Practicalities" below) and several restaurants, the best being *La Criolla* with good fresh seafood. Six kilometres further along the highway and a bit more crowded, **Palenque** was named for a *cimarrón* encampment that survived here until the late eighteenth century. The beach at the town's western end has remarkably calm waters, perfect for lazing about, though you'll be joined by plenty of others, especially on weekends. The entrance is lined with a dozen or so outdoor bar/restaurants to serve the crowds, though the *La Cubanita* chicken shack and *Pizzeria Mi Sitio* back in town are probably better bets. If here for more than a day-trip, during the day you can also check out the baseball camp of the San Diego Padres, which trains recruits year-round; look for the Padres sign on the road between Najayo and Palenque. There's also a decent bit of nightlife here on weekends and especially on Mondays, including live music at *Disco Sonida Anthony* in Palenque town.

Practicalities

The only decent **hotel** in San Cristóbal is basic but clean *Aparta-Hotel Ayala*, Padre Ayala 110 (☎528-3040; ❶–❷). More pleasant are the beachfront accommodations south of the city, *Hotel Najayo Beach Club*, Carretera Najayo (☎471-1134; ❸), with modern facilities, a bar/restaurant and a swimming pool; and *Hotel Playa Palenque* on the Carretera Najayo just before Palenque beach (☎243-2525, ℻243-5000; ❸), which has less appealing rooms, cold-water bath, a pool area and a Tricom booth. **Dining** choices within San Cristóbal are limited: try either *Plaza Carolina*, General Cabral one block south of Constitución, an outdoor pizza and *cómida criolla* spot; or *Pizza y Tacos*, on the corner of Hincado and Constitución, fairly self-explanatory.

Guaguas heading east and west – as well as to La Toma – all take off from the parque central, though transport to El Pomier is via RD\$5 pickup trucks stationed at the north end of the town market on Calle Juanto María and Francisco Peynado. They don't take off until the entire truck fills up, so you may want to travel instead via RD\$20 motoconcho, which can also be picked up at the market.

Travel details

Caribe Tours is the only **bus company** that operates between Santo Domingo and the southwest region, with stops at Azua and Barahona. **Guagua** routes are more extensive, though they range in quality from relatively pleasant, air-conditioned minibuses to battered vans in which you'll be crammed in with other passengers. All travel times for guaguas are ballpark estimates. Caribair runs regularly scheduled **flights** back and forth between Barahona and Santo Domingo.

Buses

Azua to: Barahona (2 daily; 1hr 30min); San Juan de la Maguana (daily; 1hr 30min); Santo Domingo (4 daily; 2hr).

Barahona to: Azua (2 daily; 1hr 30min); Santo Domingo (2 daily; 3hr 30min).

Guaguas

Azua to: Baní (frequent; 50min); Barahona (hourly; 1hr 30min); Cabral (hourly; 1hr 20min); Duvergé (hourly; 2hr); Elias Piña (hourly; 2hr 20min); Jimaní (hourly; 3hr); La Descubierta (hourly; 2hr 30min); Las Matas de Farfán (hourly; 1hr 50min); Oviedo (hourly; 3hr); Paraiso (hourly; 2hr 10min); Pedernales (hourly; 4hr); San Cristóbal (hourly; 1hr 40min); San Juan de la Maguana (hourly; 1hr 30min); Santo Domingo (frequent; 2hr 40min).

Baní to: Azua (frequent; 50min); Barahona (hourly; 2hr 40min); Cabral (hourly; 2hr 10min); Duvergé (hourly; 2hr 50min); Elias Piña (hourly; 3hr 10min); Jimaní (hourly; 3hr 20min); La Descubierta (hourly; 3hr 20min); Las Matas de Farfán (hourly; 2hr 40min); Las Salinas (hourly; 45min); Oviedo (hourly; 3hr 50min); Paraiso (hourly; 3hr); Pedernales (hourly; 4hr 50min); San Cristóbal (frequent; 50min); San José de Ocóa (hourly; 1hr); San Juan de la Maguana (hourly; 2hr 20min); Santo Domingo (frequent; 3hr 5min).

Baoruco to: Azua (hourly; 1hr 50min); Baní (hourly; 2hr 40min); Barahona (frequent; 20min); Enriquillo (frequent; 40min); Los Patos (frequent; 30min); Oviedo (frequent; 1hr 10min); Paraiso (frequent; 20min); Pedernales (frequent; 2hr 10min); San Rafael (frequent; 10min); Santo Domingo (hourly; 4hr 30min).

Barahona to: Azua (hourly; 1hr 30min); Baní (hourly; 2hr 40min); Baoruco (frequent; 20min); Cabral (hourly; 25min); Duvergé (hourly; 1hr); Enriquillo (frequent; 1hr); Jimaní (hourly; 2hr); La Descubierta (hourly 1hr 50min); Los Patos (frequent; 50min); Neiba (hourly; 1hr); Oviedo (frequent; 1hr 30min); Paraiso (frequent; 40min);

Pedernales (frequent; 2hr 30min); San Rafael (frequent; 30min); Santo Domingo (hourly; 5hr 45min).

Cabral to: Azua (hourly; 1hr 20min); Baní (hourly; 2hr 10min); Barahona (hourly; 25min); Duvergé (hourly; 40min); Jimaní (hourly; 1hr 40min); Santo Domingo (hourly; 4hr).

Enriquillo to: Azua (hourly; 2hr 30min); Baní (hourly; 3hr 20min); Baoruco (frequent; 40min); Barahona (frequent; 1hr); Los Patos (frequent; 10min); Oviedo (frequent; 30min); Paraiso (frequent; 20min); Pedernales (frequent; 1hr 30min); San Rafael (frequent; 30min); Santo Domingo (hourly; 5hr 10min).

Las Salinas to: Baní (hourly; 45min).

La Toma to: San Cristóbal (frequent; 30min).

Los Patos to: Azua (hourly; 2hr 20min); Baní (hourly; 3hr 10min); Baoruco (frequent; 30min); Barahona (frequent; 50min); Enriquillo (frequent; 10min); Oviedo (frequent; 40min); Paraiso (frequent; 10min); Pedernales (frequent; 1hr 40min); San Rafael (frequent; 20min); Santo Domingo (hourly; 5hr).

Najayo to: Palenque (frequent; 15min); San Cristóbal (frequent; 45min).

Oviedo to: Azua (hourly; 3hr); Baní (hourly; 3hr 50min); Baoruco (frequent; 1hr 10min); Barahona (frequent; 1hr 30min); Enriquillo (frequent; 30min); Los Patos (frequent; 40min); Paraiso (frequent; 50min); Pedernales (frequent; 1hr); San Rafael (frequent; 1hr); Santo Domingo (hourly; 5hr 40min).

Palenque to: Najayo (frequent; 15 min); San Cristóbal (frequent; 1hr).

Paraiso to: Azua (hourly; 2hr 10min); Baní (hourly; 3hr); Baoruco (frequent; 20min); Barahona (frequent; 40min); Enriquillo (frequent; 20min); Oviedo (frequent; 50min); Los Patos (frequent; 10min); Pedernales (frequent; 1hr 50min); San Rafael (frequent; 10min); Santo Domingo (hourly; 4hr 50min).

San Cristóbal to: Azua (hourly; 1hr 40min); Baní (frequent; 50min); Barahona (hourly; 3hr 10min); La Toma (frequent; 35min); Najayo (frequent; 45min); Palenque (frequent; 1hr); Santo Domingo (frequent; 1hr).

San José de Ocóa to: Baní (hourly; 1hr); San Cristóbal (hourly; 1hr 40min); Santo Domingo (hourly; 2hr 40min).

San Rafael to: Azua (hourly; 2hr); Baní (hourly; 2hr 50min); Baoruco (frequent; 10min); Barahona (frequent; 30min); Enriquillo (frequent; 30min); Los Patos (frequent; 20min); Oviedo (frequent; 1hr); Paraiso (frequent; 10min); Pedernales (frequent; 2hr); Santo Domingo (hourly; 4hr 40min).

Flights

Barahona to: Santo Domingo (daily; 30min).

Contexts

Contexts

A brief history of the Dominican Republic

For one brief moment at the end of the fifteenth century, when Christopher Columbus "discovered" the New World and Spain set up its first colony here, the Dominican Republic took centre stage in world politics, only to be quickly scuttled to the periphery of the Spanish Empire. It has since endured centuries of struggle for independence, having been occupied by France, Haiti, and even Spain again for a time. After winning its freedom, the nation was kept in chaos by competing regional strongmen, an early twentieth-century rule by the United States and then the iron fist of a despot. The last ten years, however, have witnessed the first three consecutive free and fair elections in the nation's history, perhaps a sign of things to come.

Early settlers

Precious little is known about the **Arawaks**, the Dominican Republic's first inhabitants, who migrated to the Caribbean in canoes made from hollowed-out tree trunks. They arrived in four distinct waves from the Orinoco and Amazon river basins in present-day Guyana and Venezuela, beginning around 3000 BC with the **Ciboneys**, hunter-gatherer nomads who lived in caves along the island's rivers and survived by fishing. Around 100 BC the Ciboneys were displaced by the more advanced **Igneri** Arawak culture, who left behind superb ceramics featuring geometric designs. In 600 AD the Igneri were in turn absorbed by the **Tainos**, a late Stone Age culture, although some Igneri may have remained within Taino society in the form of a servant underclass, called the *naborías*. The final Arawak migrants were the warlike **Caribes**, who began moving up the Antilles in 1100 AD and were making regular raiding forays along the eastern coast of Hispaniola when Columbus arrived. In battle they used poison-tipped arrows and were reported to be cannibals. By 1492 – the year of Christopher Columbus's arrival – the Caribes had taken over the Lesser Antilles and were engaged in regular skirmishes with the Tainos of the Greater Antilles, though there was some peaceful contact between the groups as well.

Hispaniola's Tainos were organized into five large **caciques** – a word that signifies both the community and its chief – that controlled big swaths of territory. Though wars broke out between *caciques*, there was a good bit of co-operation too: royal intermarriage was frequent, and all five made pilgrimages to the holy site of **La Aleta** (see p.135). While some Tainos continued to live in caves, most built themselves *bohíos*, stilt-supported, cone-shaped huts thatched with *guanillo* and palm leaves, while the *caciques* lived in large, rectangular great houses made from the same materials.

Much of what we know today about **Taino culture** comes from excavated shards of their beautiful ceramics and the rock art that they left in the many cave systems of the Greater Antilles, though firsthand accounts from the Spanish invaders help greatly to supply some context. The Spaniards reported that the Tainos tied two boards tightly to the heads of their newborn infants, and left the heads bound for the first three years of life, resulting in an artificially flat, narrow forehead. Communal parties were held on feast days – which, as in today's Dominican Republic, occurred with astonishing frequency – where villages would gather to sing narrative **areito** songs, dance to drum-based music and get falling-down drunk. Another major pastime during leisure hours were the **pelota** games (similar to football/soccer) held in large stone circles that can still be seen across the island. After the Taino evening meal, it was considered healthful to head to the nearest river and induce vomiting as a means of cleansing the body.

The Taino **religion** was an agriculturally based faith honouring two major gods and a plethora of lesser deities. Most important were Yocahú – a sort of immanent life principle who was responsible for the growth of crops and animal reproduction – and the evil but incredibly powerful Huracán, who wreaked havoc on Taino society with hurricanes and earthquakes when not properly appeased. The three-pointed stone *cemi* idols that depicted Yocahú were typically placed in the ground in the Tainos' cultivated fields in order to invest the soil with this great deity's life force, and thus enlarge the season's harvest.

The Tainos developed a remarkable system of **agriculture** in which large mounds of mulch were sprinkled with seed, producing enough food for the entire community with very little labour. Staple crops grown in this way included yucca, peanuts, pumpkins and corn. In addition, Tainos fished and hunted rodents, iguanas and manatees – all of which were barbecued, a word that comes from the term they used to describe this cooking form – a diet supplemented with insects, worms and bats. Their **economy** was founded on subsistence barter, and the concept of feudal labour was completely alien, making the Taino ill-prepared for the changes of the late fifteenth century.

The arrival of Columbus

Christopher Columbus was a member of the Genoese sailor and merchant community that came to dominate seafaring trade in Europe in the fifteenth century and, in the service of the Portuguese crown, established fortified trading outposts along the northwestern coast of Africa – eventually creating a maritime link with the Far East. His purpose in crossing the Atlantic was both material and spiritual: he hoped to find an easy **waterway to China and Japan**, where he would sign an exclusive agreement to export Asian goods for gold, and to find the mythical realm of the Christian king **Prester John**, which was believed to lie somewhere in Asia, cut off from the rest of Christianity by the Islamic empire. Portuguese King John II wasn't impressed with Columbus's scheme when it was put to him in 1485; his scientific advisers told him that, while the Earth was indeed round, Columbus had radically underestimated its size. Nor did Spain's **Ferdinand and Isabella** immediately bite; only after they had won the historic surrender of Granada from the Moors in 1492 did they feel confident enough to devote resources to this decidedly risky project.

On the strength of a large royal loan, Columbus outfitted three ships with ninety of the most experienced sailors he could find. He set off from the Canary Islands on September 9, 1492, and spent a troubling month at sea without spotting a shred of land. Then, on October 12, with his crew growing increasingly restless, the ships sighted the tiny Bahamian island that Columbus named **San Salvador**. Seeing nothing there of any value, they hurried on westward to Cuba, which was quickly abandoned in turn when it became clear that it was not Japan. From here the ships headed east to a large island that resembled Spain in shape. Naming it **Hispaniola**, Columbus skirted its northern coast, encountering Tainos adorned with gold jewellery, who told him of a mountain range further south called Cibao, which he optimistically assumed to be Cipango, then the European name for Japan. In an attempt to circle the island from the west, the *Santa María* grounded against a coral reef off the coast of modern-day Haiti on December 25, and had to be abandoned. Taking this as a sign from God, Columbus set up a small fort there, which he named **La Navidad** in honour of the date, left 25 men to guard it and headed back to Spain with his two remaining ships.

Upon returning with a new expedition of 1500 men – mercenaries from the Moorish wars along with a sprinkling of Spanish nobility – in late 1493, Columbus found that La Navidad had been burned to the ground by the Tainos and all of its settlers killed. Only a short distance to the east, a scenic, defensible cape was chosen as the site for the first small colony, **La Isabela**. While still hoping to find the great Asian civilizations nearby, he turned his energies to establishing a trading settlement – modelled on the Portuguese outposts along West Africa – where he hoped to sell cheap European goods to the natives in return for large quantities of **gold**, a new supply of which all European countries were in search of.

Unfortunately for Columbus, gold had no real value for the Tainos, and they proved singularly unwilling to exert much effort mining it. This meant he would have to set up a far more complicated operation to make the colony profitable, with the Tainos enslaved and forced to work the gold mines. But even before Columbus ventured off on his first slave-taking forays into the Cibao, La Isabela's settlers began dying in the hundreds from **malaria and yellow fever**. Panic and dissent swept through the colony, and a petty noble, feeling dishonoured that Columbus had demanded he perform manual labour, took the opportunity to hijack one of the ships with a half-dozen others and headed back to Spain to complain of his treatment. Columbus returned to Spain in early 1496 to defend himself against these charges, leaving his brother Bartolomé in charge of the colony. Bartolomé had even less control over the colonists and a revolt erupted, led by one of Columbus's servants. The rebel colonists abandoned La Isabela, and Bartolomé and the few remaining loyal settlers moved to establish a new outpost at **Santo Domingo**, where there was rumoured to be more gold. Columbus returned in 1498, but the Spanish settlers refused to obey his orders because they considered him a foreigner. Reports of unrest filtered back to the Spanish court, and in 1500 bureaucrat **Francisco Bobadilla** was sent to the new colony to investigate the civil strife. Bobadilla promptly took advantage of the situation by appointing himself the new governor and appeased the rebels by arresting Columbus and sending him back to Spain in chains.

Genocide and gold

Spain's King Fernando replaced Bobadilla in 1501 with **Nicolás de Ovando**, a seasoned administrator of conquered Muslim lands in Andalucia, with instructions to impose order on the unruly colony. Ovando's first act was to deport the rebel leaders to Spain, force their followers to marry their Taino mistresses and then deprive them of their land on the grounds that these marriages ended their Spanish citizenship. Ovando also instigated the monumental construction work that was to turn Santo Domingo into Spain's capital in the New World and – despite Queen Isabela's strong objections – expanded Columbus's system of **repartimiento**, by which Tainos were apportioned to colonists for work in the gold mines. To this end, he waged several campaigns of conquest against the various *caciques*, executing their leaders and herding the rest into the mines. To pacify the Spanish queen, later known as *la reina católica* for her leading role in the Spanish Inquisition, he agreed that the Tainos should be Christianized in exchange for their labour. At this time, the **Catholic Church** was at the height of its power, and was looking towards the New World for expansion opportunities; the Vatican thus decided to turn Santo Domingo into a regional base for Christianity, sending successive waves of missionaries to construct a cathedral, several churches, monasteries and convents from which priests would depart to the American mainland and **proselytize**. For their part the colonists were eager to soften their enslavement of the local population with a veneer of piety, and set up a new system, called **encomienda**, by which the Tainos' souls would ostensibly be saved in return for their slave labour. In reality, though, little religious education took place, and the atrocities against the native population continued unabated; lacking resistance to Old World diseases and subjected to countless acts of random violence, the Taino population quickly dwindled over the next twenty years. By 1514 only 11,000 remained in Spanish control out of a number once estimated at between 500,000 and two million – though a sizeable contingent apparently still lived in remote mountain areas across the island.

To make up for the steep decline in the number of Tainos, the Spaniards embarked in 1505 on their first **slaving expeditions** in the Antilles and along the coast of Central America. Some entrepreneurs set up small forts from which regular forays could be made into the interior, thus laying the foundations for future Spanish colonies, such as Ponce de León in Puerto Rico and Juan de Esquival in Jamaica. Meanwhile, the Columbus family's tireless petitioning of the Spanish court for the return of their rights to the New World at last brought success, and Christopher's son **Diego Columbus** was appointed Ovando's successor in 1509. Diego began by immediately reapportioning most of the enslaved Tainos to himself and a few allies. This caused an uproar among the colonists, and King Fernando was forced to appoint the **Real Audencia**, a royal court of appeals that would check the governor's power; the Audencia did serve to control Diego's abuses, and by the 1520s it had been taken over by corrupt local sugar barons who used it mainly to collect graft. The king also promulgated a series of laws that ordered the colonists to pay the Tainos a fair wage for their labour and give them decent housing, but the decrees were ignored.

Back in Spain, a conquistador-turned-priest named **Bartolomé de las Casas** had been petitioning the court on behalf of the Tainos for several years, with limited success. When, in 1514, Fernando died and Cardinal Cisneros was appointed regent, Las Casas found he had a powerful new ally. One of the cardinal's first acts was to send Las Casas and three Jeronymite priests to Santo Domingo along with a squadron of troops, instructing them to free the Tainos and **resettle** them in several new *caciques*. However, as soon as the Tainos had been moved to their new homes, a smallpox epidemic broke out – brought over by the Europeans – killing all but 3000 of the remaining 11,000 enslaved natives. The Jeronymites took this as a divine signal that the Tainos should never have been freed, and sent the survivors to work in the new sugar mills that were being built around Santo Domingo. Las Casas, though, continued to petition on behalf of the Tainos; in 1515 the cardinal accepted his suggestion that the sugar mills substitute **African slave labour**, which was used successfully in Portugal's West African colonies, setting in motion the African slave trade that was to dominate the New World economy for the next four centuries.

Sugar, slaves and pirates

As the gold economy ground to a halt, sugar swiftly filled the gap as the island's primary source of income. Numerous rural **sugar mills** sprouted up in the 1520s, leading to an exponential increase in the importation of slaves. The mill owners quickly formed a new colonial upper class, and increased Spain's earnings on the island a hundredfold; for this reason, they had little trouble convincing the Crown to appease them with local political power. Instead of appointing the Real Audencia directly, the Spanish kings allowed the plantation owners to choose its members themselves from their ranks. Less wealthy colonists were forced to subsist by hunting the herds of wild livestock that roamed throughout the island, descended from the cattle brought over by Columbus and Ovando. Over time, formal **cattle herding** developed, creating a burgeoning export trade in leather hides.

Meanwhile, the several hundred remaining Tainos banded together behind the banner of a bandit named **Enriquillo** in 1526 and took to raiding the plantations from their base in the Sierra Bahoruco. As a matter of policy they would free any slaves they discovered, who joined the growing bands of **cimarrones** – literally, "wild animals" – escaped African slaves who were colonizing the island's many near-impassable mountain ranges. *Cimarrón* ranks expanded to such an extent that by the 1530s the Spaniards would only travel outside their plantations in large, armed groups.

The Spaniards also began to run into trouble with **piracy** in the 1540s. For most of the sixteenth century, Spain was at war with both the British and the Dutch, and as part of their tactics these nations commissioned **privateers** – royally sanctioned and funded pirates – to infest Caribbean waters, boarding stray Spanish ships and absconding with their cargo, or raiding and torching isolated plantations. In 1541 Spain authorized the construction of Santo Domingo's fortified wall, and decided to restrict sea travel to enormous, well-armed caravans. In another move, one that was to spell the end of Santo Domingo's sugar industry, Havana was chosen as the designated stopping point between Spain and the silver mines of Mexico and Peru. Ships headed for Santo Domingo or Puerto Plata had to break off from the fleet upon arrival in the Caribbean and brave the pirate-choked waters alone, which discouraged most merchants from doing business here. Aside from Santo Domingo, which managed to maintain some legal exports, Dominican ports were forced to rely on **contraband** trade with foreigners, and by the 1550s this was the sole engine of the local economy. Many Dominican colonists felt completely abandoned by their mother country, and Protestantism – brought by the British and Dutch ships alongside their manufactured goods – began to make inroads along the island's north coast.

Colonial decline and French encroachment

The Spanish Empire was conceived by its rulers as a self-contained universe that, through trade with its colonies, would provide itself with everything it needed. Trade with other countries was considered subversive and even heretical, a conduit for new ideas that might taint Spanish culture. After fifty years of futile attempts to force towns along the northern and western coasts of Hispaniola to cease their contraband trade, the Crown decided to wipe them out. In 1605 Governor Antonio de Osorio was ordered to burn the colony's outer towns to the ground and forcibly resettle their residents in the countryside surrounding Santo Domingo. This disastrous action, known ever since as the **devastaciones**, permanently crippled the island's economy. Of the outer colonies' estimated 110,000 head of cattle, fewer than 10,000 were successfully transported across the three intervening mountain ranges, and half the colonists – who were resettled in Bayaguana and Monte Plata just east of the capital – had died from starvation or disease by 1610. Santo Domingo was no longer able to support itself through exports, and Spain was forced to provide a *situado*, a large sum of money presented annually to pay for the island's governance and defence. For the rest of the seventeenth century, colonial Santo Domingo's economy remained in collapse, and colonists, free blacks and slaves alike lived in poverty. This led to a breakdown in the racial hierarchy that still influences **race** relations and attitudes in the country today.

Meanwhile, French and British adventurers took advantage of Spain's sudden retreat into a corner of Hispaniola to colonize the island of **Tortuga**, just off the northwestern coast, in 1629. Despite periodic Spanish raids, the new colony, whose inhabitants survived by pirating, growing tobacco and buccaneering (the hunting of wild livestock on Hispaniola), continued to prosper. In 1640 the **French** kicked the British out and organized the notoriously unruly outpost into an official colony, from which they expanded onto the northern coast of present-day Haiti. The Spanish didn't take kindly to the presence of their new neighbours, and in 1654 **invaded** Tortuga, burning the colony to the ground, slaughtering its inhabitants, and leaving behind a fort manned by 150 soldiers. A year later, though, Santo Domingo itself was beset by an intruder, the **British**, whose virulently anti-Catholic new ruler, Oliver Cromwell, sent out a 10,000-man invasion force in 35 warships. The British set up camp along the Río Haina on April 23, 1655, and attacked two days later, but the Spanish had got wind of their plans in advance and were well prepared; while retreating after heavy losses in their first attempt to storm the city, the invaders were ambushed from the north by 800 Spanish lancers and lost 1500 men. Bruised and embarrassed, they left the island and set sail for less fortified Jamaica, which they successfully captured a month later. Fearing another invasion from the new British base, the Spaniards recalled their 150 troops from Tortuga, and within a decade the French colony, which became known as **St-Domingue**, was once again up and running; by 1725 it was the most prosperous colony in the Caribbean, providing France with a quarter of its wealth.

The French again expanded their outposts to the Hispaniola mainland, and a peace treaty in 1679 saw the beginning of **commercial contact** between the colonies – by this time Spain had loosened its restrictions against foreign contact, and saw co-operation as a means to pull their colony out of a century-long economic slump. Spanish settlers traded livestock for manufactured European goods, and Cibao Valley farmers began growing tobacco for the French market. Despite this outward co-operation, the French encroached further and further into the island, and Spain regularly sent out fifty-man patrols – known as *cincuéntenas* – to attack and destroy new settlements. In the face of continued *cincuéntena* assaults, the French attacked and burned down Santiago in 1690. The Spanish responded by sacking Cap Français – today Cap Haïtien – in 1691, and a combined Spanish and British offensive from Manzanillo completely razed the French colony's north coast in 1694. The whole colony could have been wiped off the island, but – to the astonishment of the Brits – after several days of forced marching the Spanish soldiers complained that their allies had taken all of the booty and disbanded rather than continue south to Port-au-Prince. In 1697 the **Treaty of Ryswyck** was signed, establishing the borders as they are today at the north and south coasts, but leaving open the question of rights to the interior as a large chunk of it continued to be claimed by both countries. Commercial ties recommenced, but disputes continued to break out sporadically, necessitating further treaties in 1731, 1770 and 1777.

The Haitian revolution and occupation

French St-Domingue's unparalleled commercial success relied entirely on the mass importation of African slaves – during the eighteenth century slaves outnumbered Europeans and mulattos by more than ten to one. This unstable situation was made worse by persecution by whites of the growing **mulatto** class. During the early decades of the colony, mulattos were allowed to inherit property and sit in the local legislature, but white planters resented their growing prosperity, and convinced the French crown to promulgate a series of laws that limited their freedoms. As a result, all three ethnic groups were pressing for social upheaval during the 1780s. The mulattos began arming themselves in order to win their rights back. The **white planters** fashioned themselves democrats in the style of Thomas Jefferson, and plotted a revolution in which they would continue the slave system but end the burdensome tax demands of France. Of course the **African slaves** had the most to complain about, being forced to work twenty-hour days of backbreaking labour and subjected to all manner of hideous tortures and abuses; the average lifespan of a St-Domingue plantation slave was two years, and the French had to continually replenish their labour supply with tens of thousands of new Africans annually.

On August 14, 1791, a Voodoo priest named **Boukman** held a secret convocation of hundreds of slaves from plantations across the colony, declared the independence of the new black republic called "**Haiti**" – the Taino word for the island – and sparked a colony-wide revolution in which half of the plantations were burned to the ground within three months. Boukman was killed in the initial fighting, but **Touissant L'Ouverture**, a black slave who had served in the colony's French militia, quickly took over leadership of the revolt, which led to three decades of intense military activity along the Dominican border.

Spain saw the revolt as a perfect opportunity to gain control of the entire island. By promising freedom to all St-Domingue's slaves, they won the allegiance of L'Ouverture and his troops, and soon conquered much of France's inland territory; after the bloody defeat of the British, they seemed set to take over the rest of the island. However, when the French responded by freeing the slaves, Touissant abruptly switched sides and his army forced Spain back to its old borders. In 1800 Napoleon rescinded the emancipation, provoking Touissant into declaring independence, formally setting up a Haitian constitution and government and invading the Spanish colony to protect his eastern flank. A **French invasion** forced him back to St-Domingue again, and in 1801 the Spaniards and French put the final touches on a peace treaty which gave France the western half of the island in exchange for Napoleon's conquered territory in Spain. The French took possession of the Spanish colony in 1802, leading to another invasion in 1805 by Touissant's successor, General **Jean-Jacques Dessalines**, who swept from Dajabón over the Cibao Valley before being rebuffed outside the capital, which was still under the control of the French. Forced to withdraw, the general slaughtered several hundred residents of Santiago and Moca – a **massacre** that's still etched on the national consciousness.

Seeing the French slave colony as a threat to their hard-won freedom, the Haitians continued to have designs on the island's eastern territory, and in 1821 Haitian forces under **President Jean Pierre Boyer**, the country's first elected leader, poured across the border and took control of the whole island. The first act of the 23-year **Haitian occupation** was the **emancipation of slaves**, followed by a promise to provide the newly freed men with farmland. To this end the government enacted a major **land redistribution** in 1822, confiscating church properties, properties in arrears and estates abandoned by owners who had fled prior to the occupation, and handing these over to the peasantry in small plots. They also tried to streamline the traditional system of Dominican property ownership called *terrenos comuneros*, by which several owners had simultaneous rights to the large estates created in the sixteenth century by the Spanish crown. All property owners were required to have their land surveyed and recorded with the government, or risk losing it. Unfortunately, this well-intentioned plan had one glaring flaw: since there had been no need for them in the past, the colony was without a single surveyor. A few were shipped in from other countries, but not nearly enough to map out the entire island within the two years required by the Haitian government. Despite several extensions of the deadline, many white landowners were deprived of their land throughout the 1820s, deepening their resentment of black rule, which was further exacerbated by the demonization of the government from the pulpit by **Catholic priests** outraged at the loss of their property. Even worse, the Haitians managed to alienate their base of support, the mulatto Dominican and black Haitian **peasantry**, by requiring them to grow cash crops for export. Newly freed from slavery, neither was in the mood to take orders, and preferred to sow their small subsistence plots in peace.

In the context of this growing unrest, a number of white intellectuals in Santo Domingo, influenced by South American freedom fighter Simón Bolívar, formed the **Trinitarian movement** in 1838 under the leadership of **Juan Pablo Duarte**, a democrat and merchant whose family business had been ruined by the Haitian reforms. This secret organization aimed to create an independent Dominican state, and to restore all confiscated properties to the Catholic Church. The Trinitarians plotted with Haitian army officers dissatisfied with Boyer's cash crop laws, co-ordinating their movements in a **military coup** in March 1843 that ousted the president from power. Once it was clear that he had gone, the Trinitarians and dissident Haitian officers gathered in

Santo Domingo's Parque Independencia and marched towards the Fortaleza Ozama, the most strategic point in the city. When they arrived at Parque Colón, though, other Haitian troops allied with Haitian coup leader General Charles Hérard fired into the crowd, killing several people and scattering the rest in an attempt to quash the Dominican independence movement. Formal elections were quickly held, but when Dominican separatists won throughout the Spanish half of the island, Hérard marched with his army from town to town and imprisoned the local rebel leaders, forcing Duarte to flee to the island of St Thomas. Hérard then tried to placate the Dominicans by rescinding all land redistribution laws, but the path to independence had been set. Upon learning that a wealthy mahogany exporter named **Buenaventura Báez** was planning a coup for April 1844 that would place the colony under the protection of France, the Trinitarians, under the leadership of Duarte's compatriot Ramón Mella, quickly pre-empted him with a scripted popular uprising on February 27, backed by troops loyal to **Pedro Santana**, a rich cattle rancher from the southeast who commanded a private army of peasants who worked on his estate. After a week of negotiations between the rebels and the government, the Haitians capitulated and handed the eastern half of the island over to the Dominican nationalists without a fight.

Santana and Báez

For the rest of the nineteenth century the new Dominican state would be plagued by incessant internal strife. This was the era of the **caudillos**, strongmen based in every region of the country who commanded large armies of local peasants, and who were usually far more interested in lining their own pockets than running the country. In large part, *caudillo* power was made possible by the constant fear of **Haitian invasions**, which occurred periodically and necessitated large armies to repel them. Once the Haitian army was dealt with, the *caudillo* forces would generally march on Santo Domingo and place their leader in power, a pattern that began at the very outset of Dominican independence. Economic divisions, too, further served to separate the newly independent country. The southern half of the island's economy revolved around cattle ranching and mahogany clear-cutting, with a few **land barons** enriching themselves while the vast majority of people barely survived. Further north in the Cibao Valley, though, a large **middle class** was evolving as farmers supplemented their food earnings with export crops like tobacco and cocoa that increased personal wealth across the board. The lack of popular power made the south increasingly autocratic, while the even distribution of wealth in the north led to a more democratic worldview.

On learning of the surrender of Santo Domingo to the separatists, Haiti's General Hérard assembled a large army in Port-au-Prince and invaded the island's eastern half in March 1844. With no military forces directly under their power, the Trinitarians were forced to name **Pedro Santana**, the most powerful *caudillo*, head of the army; the troops that he mustered from the southeast bogged the Haitians down in the El Número Mountains that separate Azua and Baní, guarding the few mountain passes with guerrilla units, a strategy that he would repeat with success over the next few years. The other half of Hérard's army, under the command of a general named **Jean Louis Pierrot**, invaded from the north and laid siege to Santiago, but when locals convinced him (falsely) that Hérard had been killed in Azua, Pierrot abandoned the campaign, marching his troops to Port-au-Prince so that he might assume command of Haiti. Hérard in turn had to abandon his own campaign, rushing back to stave off a military coup. As the Haitians departed, Santana entered Santo Domingo with his troops and had himself declared president for life. The Trinitarians were all either arrested or exiled, and would never gain power again.

Pierrot won out in the ensuing civil war, and again marched on the Dominican Republic in 1845. Santana again repelled the invaders at the El Número Mountains, this time chasing the defeated army back to the border. The victory was decisive – Haitian troops mutinied when Pierrot proposed another invasion in 1847 – but many of the white economic elite in Santo Domingo, composed mainly of merchants, landowners and priests, were sufficiently scared of Haitian domination that they began pressing for the Dominican Republic to be **annexed** to an outside power. Simultaneous negotiations were conducted through the next two decades with England, France, Spain and the United States.

Santana, meanwhile, focused his attention on personal enrichment, wrecking the **economy** with multiple peso printings (and ensuing hyperinflation); he would buy Cibao Valley crops at an agreed-upon price and then dump hundreds of thousands of pesos on the economy, purposefully causing economic devastation across the country so that he got these goods for a tenth of their worth. The Cibao farmers, who were by this time providing the island with most of its food and selling tobacco to Germany for export, managed to remove the leader in late 1848, but the Haitians invaded again in the following year, and the frightened Dominicans recalled Santana as Commander of the Army. Again he repelled the Haitians at the Sierra El Número, and again his troops occupied the capital and forcibly placed him back in power. This time the general appointed Buenaventura Báez, the Azua *caudillo* whose planned coup in 1844 had been thwarted by the Trinitarians' uprising, to the presidency. Báez was not content to play the role of Santana's puppet, though, and was removed from office and exiled in 1853.

With Báez out of the way for the moment, Santana reverted to his old tricks, repelling another Haitian invasion and perpetuating another mass-peso fraud against Cibao Valley farmers, which ruined both them and the national economy. The Cibao farmers got their revenge when word got out that Santana was planning to sell the **Samaná Peninsula** to the United States; they launched a nationalist propaganda campaign that stirred the peasantry to rise up and oust the government. Buenaventura Báez returned to the country and was named president by popular acclamation; his first act as president was to exile Santana in revenge.

Báez proved no more responsible than Santana; his second act was to print eighteen million pesos and perpetuate his own **fraud** on the relatively wealthy Cibao Valley tobacco farmers, who accepted the bills at the current exchange rate and were ruined when inflation ensued. The farmers subsequently revolted in 1857, gathering a large army and recalling Báez's arch-enemy General Santana to lead it – as it turned out, a fatal mistake. After a year of civil war in which both sides printed millions more pesos, so that the currency was essentially worthless, Báez fled back into exile and Santana marched into Santo Domingo and yet again declared himself president. He then mobilized his troops to suppress his former allies in the Cibao, who were too democratic for his taste, setting up military commanders to rule each of the towns. Once this domestic threat was quelled, he recommenced **negotiations with Spain** for annexation. In addition to protection from Haiti, Santana thought he could perpetuate a fraud on the Spaniards similar to the ones he had put over on the Cibao; when negotiations were concluded and Spain had agreed on an amortization rate for Dominican pesos, Santana printed 33 million more so that Spain would be forced to hand out far more money to him and his friends, to whom he passed the pesos out as gifts.

Spanish annexation and the Restoration

Under the terms of the **Spanish annexation**, finalized and made public in March 1861, General Santana retained military command of the new Spanish province, and was subject only to Spain's regional commander in Puerto Rico. As the year wore on, though, it became obvious that the Spaniards planned to slowly deprive him of all power: his associates were removed from the military, the 33 million pesos he printed were refused for amortization and he was finally deposed in July 1862. The new Spanish authorities managed to alienate the Dominican populace almost as quickly, through **discrimination** against the mulatto majority, who were constantly reminded that they would have been slaves in the neighbouring Spanish colonies of Cuba and Puerto Rico. The Dominicans were further infuriated when the new Spanish archbishop invalidated all **common law marriages** – which constituted 95 percent of all Dominican unions – and declared all children of such marriages to be illegitimate.

Having had their rights gradually eroded for two years, several hundred Dominicans rebelled at Santiago in February 1863, initiating the **War of Restoration**. Spanish soldiers marched on the city and dispersed the rebels quickly, but most fled into the mountains along the border – under the protection of the Haitian government – and engaged in **guerrilla raids** on Spanish targets. In August of the same year, the rebels launched an offensive and took control of the Cibao, burning Santiago to the ground in September in order to supplant the Spanish troops there. The Spaniards lost far more soldiers, though, to tropical disease; by the end of their occupation over 12,000 of their troops were dead from yellow fever. Realizing the futility of the war and not willing to sacrifice thousands more ground forces, the Spaniards began **negotiations** with the rebels, who were themselves in political disarray. Their leader Pepillo Salcedo was deposed in September 1864 by General Gaspar Polanco, who lasted three months before being forced out by General **Pedro Antonio Pimentel**. The Spaniards were unable to gain any concessions from the disorganized rebel force and, knowing that they were losing hundreds of soldiers a day to disease, they unconditionally departed the island in July 1865. Santana had shot himself a month earlier to avoid being tried for treason.

Chaos and caudillos

The overthrow of Dominican rebel leaders during the War of Restoration presaged the most **chaotic period** in Dominican politics by far. By the time the Spaniards departed, the main towns were in ruins, and across the island dozens of *caudillos* were fighting amongst each other for power. Guerrilla general **José María Cabral**, for example, had control over most of Barahona and the south-west during the war, but was in a precarious position because he relied on financial support from Buenaventura Báez's old mahogany-exporting partners in Azua. In Santana's old stomping ground, the southeast, cattle rancher **Caesario Guillermo** had cobbled together a coalition of former *Santanistas* that gave him regional ascendancy, while wealthy Puerto Plata tobacco exporter **Gregorio Luperón** had a firm hold of the north coast. If the **Cibao farmers and merchants** had managed to end their internecine bickering and form a united front, they likely could have won out over these regional power brokers and perhaps brought democracy to the Dominican Republic a century early; instead a stream of squabbles and coups between would-be Cibao *caudillos* drained their democratic movement of all credibility.

Within a month of the nationalist victory, **Cabral** condemned Pimentel as a despot, overthrew him and declared himself "Protector of the Nation". Cabral's supporters, though, were merely using him to get Báez back in office, and by October he was coerced into handing power back to the old *caudillo*. Still enraged at Báez for the fraud he perpetrated on them several years earlier, the wealthy Cibao farmers immediately rose up in arms under the leadership of liberal **Luperón**, forcing Báez to step down in the spring of 1866.

Luperón's various allies immediately fell upon each other once they occupied the capital. General Pimentel staged an unsuccessful military coup in September, which was put down by Cabral – who then installed himself as president. He was able to hang on for a full year, but his secret negotiations for the lease of the Samaná Peninsula to the United States – who didn't yet have control of Guantanamo Bay in Cuba and so were hungry for a strategic Caribbean port – were made public in the fall of 1867, precipitating a new popular revolt that placed Báez back in power in January 1868. Despite his expressions of public outrage at Cabral's negotiations, Báez secretly revived them immediately upon taking office, with the understanding that he personally would be paid a handsome sum of money by the Americans for the prize. Luperón and Cabral understandably saw this as a renewed attack on Dominican sovereignty, and so reunited to wage guerrilla war along the north coast and the western Cibao, but Báez managed to complete a deal with President Ulysses S. Grant in 1869 that sold the entire country to the States for US\$150,000. After two years of heated debate, though, the US Congress rejected the treaty in 1871 – citing the disastrous Spanish occupation as an example of what the US military could expect. Desperate for cash, Báez instead sold Samaná to a coalition of wealthy New York investors who intended to lease it to the US government, which set off an even larger rebellion that pushed him from office in early 1874; the contract was swiftly rescinded.

Cibao General **Ignacio María González** staged his own coup in 1874, and thus wrested control of the government; he quickly enacted a programme of industrialization, democratization and civil liberties, such as freedom of assembly, speech and the press, in a country that was until this time completely agricultural and undemocratic. After a coup attempt in the summer, though, the general was shaken enough to cancel his reforms and declare himself the nation's "Supreme Representative". This betrayal alienated the Cibao farmers, which started yet another revolution in February 1876. A month later, González was on a boat to the Bahamas, and businessman **Ulises Espaillat** had been named the new president by a coalition of Cibao agricultural bigwigs. Espaillat was the first nineteenth-century Dominican leader to make a sustained effort to break from the constant conflict and budget-busting political patronage of the past. In addition to reaffirming the civil liberties that González first initiated, he ended the practice of passing out large bribes to allies, instead paying off some of the burgeoning national debt. Angered at the loss of income, a broad array of *caudillos* banded together under the leadership of the returned González and drove Espaillat from office in December of the same year. Once victorious, the *caudillo* alliance quickly splintered, and troops loyal to Báez brought him back as president. He only managed to stay in control for a year, during which he tried unsuccessfully to revive annexation negotiations with the United States – though the Americans were no longer interested – and perpetrated a customs fraud on the exporters of Santo Domingo. A new rebellion hastily threw out Báez in early 1878. González again took a turn at the presidency in July, but was forced out in September. Southeastern General Caesario Guillermo took control in 1879 and was himself deposed within the year, leaving Luperón – who had long been reticent to take up the reins of power – to assume the presidency in October of the same year.

Luperón and Lilís

Luperón ruled the country from his hometown Puerto Plata, which was enjoying an economic boom at the time due to increased tobacco exports to Germany, with his confidant **General Ulises Heureaux**, known popularly as **Lilís**, acting as his agent in Santo Domingo. In his two years of presidency, Luperón did more for the country than had been achieved in the previous few decades, enacting a **new constitution** that enshrined human rights, setting a two-year presidential term limit, suspending the semi-formal system of bribes, blazing a better road that linked Santo Domingo to the Cibao, finishing a railway that connected Sánchez, Santiago and Puerto Plata and paying off much of the national debt. Luperón was succeeded after his first term by a Catholic priest named **Meriño**, who continued Luperón's policies despite an attempted coup by several *caudillos*. Lilís was then elected in 1882, and the liberal, democratic government the republic had been enjoying was quickly brought to an end.

Lilís allied himself with the southern *caudillos* who were moving from cattle and mahogany to the construction of **sugar mills**, which would become the prime engine of the economy during his rule, reviving the trade that had brought prosperity and expansion centuries before. An influx of Cuban plantation owners, refugees of a revolution in their own country, were granted large tracts of land in the southeast during Lilís' rule, where they constructed a series of mills that brought new prosperity to the region.

Lilís also brought increased stability, crushing a Cibao revolt so harshly in 1886 that it ended the cycle of chronic civil strife for a time. But despite the Dominican Republic's unheard-of prosperity during this era, Lilís brought the government to its knees by borrowing heavily from European and American banks – money that was used to fund the renewed bribe system, pay for a hefty military, help Cuban entrepreneurs set up sugar plantations and line his own pockets. These loans grew so out of control that the dictator was forced to mortgage the nation's customs fees to an American financial firm called the **San Domingo Improvement Company** to forestall military intervention by the West. By the time Lilís was **assassinated** in Moca in 1899 by the Cibao tobacco merchants he had been begging for a loan from, the country's debt was over 35 million pesos, fifteen times the annual budget, and all revenues were administered by an American company that was entitled to take one-third for themselves.

Vásquez and Jimenes

The twentieth century began with the election of two Cibao politicians who promised to end the cycle of *caudillismo*, **Juan Isidro Jimenes** and **Horacio Vásquez**, as president and vice president respectively. This promise went unfulfilled, though, as by 1902 the two had fallen out over the division of patronage to their respective supporters, and the next decade was dominated by their **personal rivalry** and that of their followers. Vásquez gained the support of the Dominican military and deposed Jimenes in a coup in 1903, only to be thrown out the following year by *Jimenista* Alejandro Woss y Gil, who then reneged on a promise to restore Jimenes and established a dictatorship for himself. The betrayed *Jimenistas*, led by Puerto Plata merchant **Carlos Morales**, quickly brought Woss y Gil's government down, but upon taking the capital, Morales betrayed Jimenes as well, aligning himself with the *Horacistas* in an attempt to keep power for himself. A new revolution ensued in 1904, even as Morales negotiated a cut in the national debt with the **United States**, allowing the Americans to administer Dominican customs directly in return. While assuming control of the customs offices, American warships bombed rebel positions, but Morales's cabinet abandoned him anyway, aligning themselves exclusively with *Horacista* vice president **Ramón Cáceres**. The desperate Morales tried to engineer a military coup against his own cabinet in December 1905, but was quickly captured and forced to resign. Cáceres immediately put down the ensuing *Jimenista* revolt, and convinced the United States to cut the debt by a further half. Over the next five years he concentrated on modernizing agriculture and public infrastructure, only to be assassinated in 1910 by the *Jimenistas*.

The American occupation

As the civil war between various permutations of *Jimenistas* and *Horacistas* raged on (and on and on), the United States had become increasingly concerned that this endemic chaos would harm their military interests. Of particular concern were the massive debts that had accrued to European banks and the fact that, since the start of the twentieth century, various European powers had been sending naval warships to Santo Domingo in an effort to intimidate the Dominican government into honouring its financial commitments. The Americans were increasingly active in their defence of the **Monroe Doctrine**, which gave them the self-ordained power to dominate the hemisphere without the interference of Europe, and feared the Germans might use the Dominicans' failure to pay their debts as a pretext to invade and set up a naval base at Samaná. To preclude this they insinuated themselves further and further into the country's governance. When Cáceres was murdered by soldiers loyal to **Desiderio Arias**, a token *Jimenista* in the Cáceres cabinet, thereby launching the bloodiest period of civil war in the nation's history, the Americans sent a **Pacification Committee** to negotiate an end to the strife, nominating neutral Archbishop Alejandro Nouel to be the new president.

No sooner had the archbishop assumed office, though, than Arias began another military coup that occupied the presidential offices. The Americans sent another commission suggesting the election of a *Horacista*, Congressman **José Bordas Valdez**, who was accepted by all parties as a temporary solution until democratic elections could be held. But Bordas quickly manoeuvred to stay in power, aligning with the *Jimenistas* and naming Arias his secretary of defence. When Bordas sold the Cibao railroad in 1913 to *Jimenista* interests, the *Horacistas* revolted, which brought yet another American commission that promised democratic elections in return for peace. Despite their assurances, the **January 1914 elections** were rigged by Bordas, who got a new million-dollar loan and kept the support of the increasingly intrusive Americans by agreeing to the direct US control of public expenditure.

Through his concessions to the Americans, Bordas alienated both Dominican parties, and the *Jimenistas* and *Horacistas* combined in a new revolt to remove him from power. US President Woodrow Wilson responded in June 1914 with the **Wilson Plan**, which gave the Dominicans three months to end hostilities and choose a president, after which time the US Marines would intervene and impose a government upon them. **Jimenes** beat Vásquez by a wide margin in the October elections, and reinstated Arias as secretary of defence. From the start, he came into conflict with the Americans by refusing to recognize the American comptroller – who still controlled public expenditures – and rebuffed US demands that a **national police** be created under direct American command. The US meanwhile **occupied Haiti** in July 1915, with the implicit threat that the Dominican Republic might be next. The pretext came when Arias staged a military coup in April 1916. US Marines were sent into Santo Domingo to "protect the lives of resident foreigners"; by May they had taken control of the capital and were steadily expanding into the rest of the country. When a new government refused American demands in November, President Wilson announced a formal **military occupation**.

From 1916 through 1924 the **US Navy** administered the Dominican Republic from its base in Santo Domingo. While in power, the Americans reorganized the tax system, accounting and administration, built a new system of highways and improved primary education. They also allowed American products to flow into the country without taxation, censored the press, banned firearms and constructed a repressive **National Police Force** with which they battled and tortured various **guerrilla factions** that staged raids on US targets from the mountains. In the east, the highly organized **Gavilleros** bandits, operating in groups of thirty, harassed the invaders for the duration of their stay; opposition was more scattered in the west, with groups like the **Liboristas** aligning with the Haitian opposition and staging raids along the border. Nevertheless, this was an economic boom time for the nation, largely due to the destruction of beet farms in France during World War I, which led to sky-rocketing sugar prices and produced the prosperous era known as the **Dance of Millions**, when old fishing villages like San Pedro and La Romana were transformed into more cosmopolitan port cities – though they were not to stay that way. In 1921 Warren Harding replaced Wilson as US president; having attacked Wilson during the campaign for the continued, in his view immoral, American presence in Hispaniola, Harding demanded a quick withdrawal from the island upon taking office. The Americans' initial demands to keep control of the National Police were refused, and they left in 1924 with only customs still under their control.

The Trujillo era

The most devastating consequence of the US occupation was the formation of a National Police trained in the repressive techniques of an occupying force. The Americans had thought that this would end the power of the *caudillos*, but the new order produced instead a super-*caudillo*, **Rafael Leonidas Trujillo**, who was to maintain totalitarian control over the Dominican Republic for three decades. When the Americans left, Horacio Vásquez became the new Dominican president and appointed Trujillo chief of the National Police in recognition of his loyalty. In 1930, though, with Vásquez desperately ill, Trujillo staged a military coup that forced his former boss from the country. Sham elections were held later that year: Trujillo's police shot several other candidates and broke up all opposition rallies, and the vote was rigged to ensure his success.

Over the next 31 years, Trujillo transformed the entire country into his **personal corporation**, and appointed family members to the highest positions in the government. He operated monopolies in sugar, salt, rice, beef, milk, insurance, cement and cigarettes; he deducted ten percent of all public employees' salaries (which ostensibly went to his political party); operated two large banks; and received a percentage of all prostitution revenues. By the end of his regime, he directly employed sixty percent of the Dominican workforce. To this end he transformed **Santo Domingo** from a mere administrative capital to the centre of the nation's industry, initiating the urban expansion that continues to this day.

Trujillo's regime was one of the most astonishingly intrusive and **oppressive** in Latin American history. All citizens were required to carry identification cards that identified them by number; if they couldn't provide the police with a good reason for why they were walking the streets at a certain time, they were arrested. Real and suspected political opponents were imprisoned, tortured and assassinated by the thousands. But his most horrific accomplishment was the extermination of between 20,000 and 25,000 Haitian peasants who were farming on the Dominican side of the border. The genocide began on the night of October 4, 1937, when hundreds of soldiers ambushed a religious procession to the Cave of San Francisco outside Bánica and killed several hundred Haitians who had crossed the border to worship. For the next two months soldiers singled out and murdered as many Haitians as they could identify living in the Dominican Republic.

As his tenure wore on, Trujillo's megalomania became ever more apparent. An all-encompassing **propaganda** campaign was mounted throughout his reign, with merengues in their thousands about the virtues of his leadership played 24 hours a day on the radio, pictures of him posted over all hospitals, schools and private homes, and pro-Trujillo messages on just about everything, including "For this water we thank Trujillo" atop all public toilets and drinking fountains. Among his many self-appointed titles were "Benefactor of the Fatherland", "*Generalissimo*", "Father of the New Fatherland" and "Protector of the Catholic Faith". Opposition newspapers were shut down, and all publications, school textbooks, radio programmes and television stations did little more than sing his praises day and night. To top it all off, Santo Domingo was renamed Ciudad Trujillo and today's Pico Duarte was called Pico Trujillo.

Trujillo also styled himself to be a major player on the international scene, if one with little to no consistency, professing admiration for Hitler while at the same time accepting thousands of German-Jewish refugees during World War II; taking a strong anti-Communist stance during the Cold War; murdering exiled Dominican scholars who spoke out against his regime in the United States; and even attempting the assassination of Venezuelan President Rómulo Betancourt in 1959. For most of his rule, Trujillo was actively supported by the **United States** because of his professed anti-Communism. President Franklin D. Roosevelt's classic line describing American policy in Latin America during the Cold War was made in reference to Trujillo: "He may be an SOB, but he's *our* SOB." In the late 1950s, though, Cuba's Fidel Castro took an interest in overthrowing the dictator, and concerns about a possible Communist takeover prompted the CIA to train a group of Dominican dissidents, who **assassinated** Trujillo in a dramatic car chase on the highway between Santo Domingo and San Cristóbal on May 30, 1961.

Fledgling democracy and American intervention

Upon Trujillo's death, Vice President **Joaquín Balaguer** rose to power under the tutelage of the Trujillo family, who had responded to the dictator's murder with multiple arrests, tortures and murders of political opponents real and imagined. A series of new opposition political parties were formed despite this repression, most notably writer **Juan Bosch**'s Partido Revolucionario Dominicano (PRD), which banded together with reform-minded military officers and threw the entire Trujillo family out of the country in 1961 – but not before the Trujillos absconded with over US$100 million of government money. The following year, Balaguer was forced into exile as well, thanks to a nationwide strike that paralyzed the country for three months. **Democratic elections** were held in December of 1962, which were won in a landslide by Bosch. The PRD set out to re-establish **civil liberties**, ending the system of identification cards and lending funds to new, independent newspapers and radio stations. Bosch had few friends in the military, however (he had mistakenly been labelled a Communist), and in September 1963 he was deposed by a military junta. This military council was extremely unpopular, and for the next two years the opposition parties of Bosch and Balaguer joined forces with a minority of the military officers. On April 24, 1965, the PRD's communications director, **José Francisco Peña Gómez**, announced over the radio that the revolution had begun, and tens of thousands of people took to the streets in the capital. The **popular uprising** took control of the entire city and was preparing to launch a strike on the San Isidro Air Force Base east of the city – the military's last stronghold – when US President **Lyndon Johnson**, under the mistaken belief that the uprising was a Communist takeover that would create "another Cuba", sent 45,000 troops into the capital on April 28 and installed a temporary military junta composed of officers from San Isidro; the possibility of a more democratic, peaceful regime was therefore thwarted by American paranoia. A new election was called for June 1966, with Balaguer and Bosch the main candidates, but Balaguer's troops, a holdover from the Trujillo forces, assassinated and intimidated hundreds of PRD supporters and placed Bosch under house arrest. As a result, Balaguer won the election by a slim margin, and was installed as president for the next twelve years.

The Balaguer era

Balaguer began his regime in 1966 by founding a secret police unit called **La Banda**, which carried out the assassination of hundreds of his political enemies under the auspices of an "anti-Communist" campaign, and clamped down on newspaper and television stations that were critical of him. He did, however, continue the programme of **industrialization** begun under Trujillo, this time funded by foreign investment. Much of the government's budget was provided by assistance from USAID, the IMF and the World Bank; a sugar quota was established with the United States that insulated the sugar mills somewhat from world price fluctuations; and plans to turn the country into a centre for tourism were developed. Political opposition was restricted to PRD members, many of whom were in exile in the United States, including Bosch in New York City, who felt that the PRD had moved too far to the right and so formed a new party, the **Partido de la Liberación Dominicana** (PLD), leaving **Peña Gómez** to assume command of the PRD. By cultivating the endorsement of the rural peasants and urban poor throughout the 1970s, Peña Gómez became something of a national hero, though for a long while he was prevented from running for public office by La Banda's terrorist activities.

Despite Balaguer's violence against the citizenry and the widespread **corruption** of his government, he enjoyed US political and financial support until the election of **Jimmy Carter** in 1976. Under US pressure, La Banda was disbanded and elections were held in May 1978. On PRD presidential candidate **Antonio Guzmán's** resounding victory, Balaguer's troops turned off all electricity throughout the country, stormed the election centre, beat the polling officers and burned many of the ballot boxes, declaring themselves the victors the next day. Carter refused to recognize the election, and pressured the Organization of American States to follow suit. When it was clear that no further economic aid was coming and that the sugar quota was about to be suspended, Balaguer gave up and stood down in favour of Guzmán.

Guzmán fired Balaguer's cronies in the military and reinstated freedom of the press, but he also set about transforming himself into a new *caudillo*. His children, relatives and friends took all the country's key posts and millions of pesos were printed, wrecking the economy, so that he could hire hundreds of PRD members to newly created government jobs. Despite this attempt to buy them off, the PRD leadership denounced him for betraying the party's ideals, and nominated **Salvador Jorge Blanco** for the next presidential election in 1982. Guzmán tried to convince the military to have Blanco assassinated before the election, but they would have none of it. When Blanco defeated Balaguer in the election and took office in May 1982, Guzmán became increasingly depressed, and in July he committed suicide. Faced with the economic crisis created by his predecessor, Blanco was forced to negotiate an austerity package with the **International Monetary Fund** that cut salaries, raised prices and put restrictions on imports. So that he wouldn't be associated with these unpopular moves, Blanco initiated a propaganda campaign against the IMF even as he was negotiating a deal with them. This proved to be a fatal blunder, for when he implemented the Fund's reforms in April 1984, a massive three-day riot broke out in the capital that was quelled only after the army had killed dozens of protesters. Once implemented, though, the reforms worked, stimulating agriculture, strengthening the peso and creating growth. The unpopularity of the package nevertheless carried serious political consequences, and Balaguer forced Blanco out of office in the election of 1986.

Balaguer's first priority was the **persecution of Blanco** so that he would never challenge for the presidency again. For an entire year, Balaguer staged weekly television broadcasts in which he denounced Blanco's administration as thoroughly corrupt and tore apart the former president's reputation. Blanco remained silent under the weight of these attacks and before long public opinion was firmly against him. He was finally arrested and imprisoned in April 1987, upon which he had a heart attack and was released for medical treatment in the United States. Though he was tried in absentia, found guilty and sentenced to 25 years, in the early 1990s he returned to the country and appealed the decision – the case was dropped by Balaguer in exchange for a promise to never enter politics again.

On the economic front, Balaguer dedicated himself to the total **reversal of the IMF austerity plan**. He set the official rate of exchange between pesos and US dollars at a ridiculously high rate, forbade public transactions in foreign currency and forced all businesses and tourists to convert their hard currency at the government's Central Bank at the artificial exchange rate. He also printed millions of new pesos without backing, leading to high inflation and an economic recession. In 1989 Balaguer exacerbated his problems by refusing to pay back the country's debts to foreign banks. Credit was cut off and exports – including medicine, electricity and oil – were shut down, creating the worst economic crisis of the century. Regardless, Balaguer managed to edge Bosch and Peña Gómez out in the **election of 1990**, though each got approximately a third of the vote, through a fraud that took thousands of Peña Gómez's rural supporters off the rolls, and a virulent campaign that depicted Bosch as a corrupt Communist and Peña Gómez as a Voodoo priest.

Recession and power blackouts dominated the next four years, though Balaguer heaped hundreds of millions of dollars on extravagances like El Faro (see p.89) and the Gran Teatro del Cibao (see p.243). His popularity had waned to such an extent by the **election of 1994** that his only hope was a systematic, nationwide vote fraud. The same tired faces reappeared for this presidential contest: 84-year-old Balaguer, 82-year-old Bosch and 74-year-old Peña Gómez. Of these, only Peña Gómez generated much enthusiasm from his traditional constituency, and all the polls had him ahead by a wide margin. But in his usual fashion Balaguer managed to destroy tens of thousands of his opponents' votes after a count that took three months to complete. Election monitors led by former US President Carter documented hundreds of irregularities by Balaguer supporters, and to quell another **nationwide strike**, Balaguer agreed to reduce his new term to two years.

The Dominican Republic today

Peña Gómez was the only one of the three latter-day *caudillos* to take part in the 1996 election: Balaguer didn't run as part of his 1994 deal, and Bosch decided to make way for his young protégé **Leonel Fernández**, who edged Peña Gómez by a few thousand votes. The **rapid growth in tourism** and the end of Balaguer's restrictions on hard currency helped pull the country out of its decade-long recession, and Fernández's administration will be remembered for giving the Dominican Republic the fastest-growing economy in the entire hemisphere for four straight years, though little actual legislation changed with the turnover in power thanks to a strong majority for Balaguer's party, the PRSC, in both houses of Congress.

The 1998 **local and congressional campaigns** were the most free in the nation's history, with no restrictions on campaigns and rallies and with independent monitors to verify a lack of corruption in the vote count. Peña Gómez ran for mayor of Santo Domingo, but died of cancer a month before the vote. As a result, a tremendous wave of nostalgic fervour for the man who had championed the poor swept the country, and his party, the PRD, took a **majority in Congress**. In 2000 the PRD built on this momentum when **Hipólito Mejia** was named the nation's president, succeeding Fernández. Unfortunately for the PRD, though, it's unlikely that they'll maintain this position of power, as Mejia's governance has been less than superb and the once-strong Dominican economy took a nosedive shortly upon his taking office. While the **slowing economy** in the United States – and resulting drops in tourism revenue – are partially to blame for this recent state of affairs, much of the responsibility must be laid squarely at Mejia's doorstep. His first act upon entering office was to hire tens of thousands of his political supporters to non-essential new government jobs, and he abandoned the Fernández administration's focus on industrialization in favour of an ill-conceived plan to make the Dominican Republic a major agricultural exporter. As a result, it's hard to find anyone on the Dominican street these days who has anything good to say about their current president, and it looks virtually certain that the PLD will regain the presidency in 2004, despite an ongoing attempt – torn straight from the political playbook of dictator Balaguer – by Mejia's administration to paint Fernández as corrupt.

Regardless of which party gains power, they'll have serious problems to contend with. Despite the recent economic growth, glaring **social inequities** remain entrenched – and the jobs being created often don't pay enough to pull workers above the poverty line. The good news is that the **sugar monoculture** that existed for most of the twentieth century is slowly being replaced by a more diversified economy based on tourism, agriculture and industrial piece work, the last a result of the **industrial free zones** that have been instituted across the island. These sectors cover land set aside for the construction of factories where the minimum wage is suspended and companies don't have to pay taxes to the Dominican government, not in actuality great for most workers, although the zones have made for a marked increase in wage labour for **women**.

All-inclusive tourism constitutes an even bigger chunk of the economy but, as with the free zones, wages are low and hours long. Another downside is that government officials often seem unconcerned about the **environmental damage** that many resorts cause, including the cutting of coastal mangroves and the destruction of wildlife habitat.

Money also comes from the hard currency poured into the economy by the million-strong **Dominican-American immigrant community** in New York City, which sends more than a billion dollars annually to relatives back home. Another influence from abroad is drugs: the island of Hispaniola has become a favoured transit point for the **Colombian cocaine cartels**, who ship about a third of their product into Haiti, drive it across the border and then fly it from here to the United States.

A more thorny issue, perhaps, is the Dominican Republic's ongoing rocky relationship with its neighbour, **Haiti**. Thousands of Haitians pour over the border to work in the DR, and many are subjected to all manner of prejudice and abuses, especially the *braceros* who are herded into *bateyes* to cut sugar cane. Paranoia on both sides keeps things rather cold, and while Mejia and Haitian President Jean-Bertrand Aristide have attempted to build bridges, antagonism remains. Much of the distaste for Haitians comes from a peculiar brand of **racism**, in which the African portion of Dominican heritage has been long denied. Ultimately, despite current financial crisis and past disappointments, there's a feeling today in the Dominican Republic of **guarded optimism**. Though things have grown worse for the average Dominican in the past two years, there's a sense that the political and economic gains of the past six years are irreversible – and that the Dominican people, for the first time in their history, are finally in control of their own destiny.

Environment and wildlife

The Dominican Republic is on the most ecologically diverse island in the Caribbean, one that features more than six thousand indigenous flowering plants, a vast array of birdlife and ecosystems ranging from arid desert and tropical rainforest to dense mangrove swamps and towering, pine-covered mountain ranges. Much of this flora and fauna is found nowhere else, and nearly all is fairly easy to see – the country is relatively small and plenty of tours are organized around the goal of getting close to nature.

Specific highlights include: the **humpback whale nursing and mating grounds** in the Bahía de Samaná and within the Silver Banks Marine Sanctuary just north of the Samaná Peninsula; the mammoth **mangrove swamps** of Parque Nacional Los Haitises along the southern end of the Bahía de Samaná; the tall **pine forests** – interspersed with ribbons of deciduous cloud forest – and wilderness hiking trails of the sky-high Cordillera Central mountains; the thousands of flamingos and other tropical birds present around the Dominican Republic's many **lagoons**, especially Lago Enriquillo, where you'll also find American crocodiles and rhinoceros iguanas; the arid **desert** plains of both the southwestern and northwestern sections of the country, and their diverse collection of cacti; the **virgin rainforest** in sections of the Sierra Neiba and Bahoruco mountain ranges in the southwest; the many large **cave systems** carved from porous limestone rock throughout the country; and the intact **coral reefs** along the far northwest coast, inhabited by brilliantly coloured fish.

Geography and climate

The four **mountain ranges** that bisect the entire island allow for a series of fairly isolated ecosystems, each with their individual flora and fauna. The **trade winds** bring a lot of rain to the windward (northeastern) half of the mountains, which themselves cast vast rain shadows over the leeward (southwestern) ends. As a result the northern and eastern ends of the mountain ranges tend to be more densely vegetated, with lots of tropical rainforest, cloud forest and pine forest, while the southern and western sides are often semi-arid.

The **Cordillera Septentrional** along the country's north separates off a valley ribbon along the coastline from the larger Cibao Valley, and is itself dominated by a mix of tropical rainforest and evergreen forest. Stretching from Monte Cristi to Nagua, where after a brief trough it continues on as the Cordillera Samaná on the Samaná Peninsula, along its northern side it gets a tremendous amount of precipitation, before dropping precipitously down into the Cibao along its southern ridge.

The fertile **Cibao Valley** has four separate ecological regions, including the humid agricultural plains of Haiti's **Plaine du Nord**, which once provided France with much of its colonial wealth; the desert region of the **Yaque river basin**, which begins on the Haitian side of the border and extends through Monte Cristi towards Santiago; the broad and phenomenally fertile savannah known as the **Vega Real** that stretches east of the Cordillera Central within

△ A river runs through the mountains near Jarabacoa

the triangle of Santiago, La Vega and San Francisco de Macorís; and the often impassable stretches of swamp and wetland within the enormous **Yuna river basin**, which borders the Bahía de Samaná from the southwest.

By far the most massive of the island's mountain ranges – indeed the biggest in the entire Caribbean – is the **Cordillera Central**, which takes up a third of the island's mass, including a broad section of the DR's centre, before continuing through Haiti as the **Massif Central** and then ploughing underwater to Cuba and Honduras. These are extremely steep, craggy mountains that climb to a height of more than three thousand metres and are often covered with pine forests, some of them still virgin. They also serve as the DR's primary water source, with a dozen different **rivers** spiralling outward from the range to fertilize the valleys that surround them; these rivers have also been dammed in recent decades to provide the energy-poor nation with hydroelectricity. Interspersed throughout are several small alpine valleys which have been cultivated to varying degrees, on a large scale in the circular **Constanza Valley**, and by subsistence farmers in the smaller Tétero and Bao valleys that you'll find further west. After a brief trough along today's Autopista Duarte, the mountains continue into the nation's southeast as the **Cordillera Oriental**, though here they're somewhat smaller, more humid and dominated by palm forest. South of the Cordillera Oriental is the **Santo Domingo Valley**, which encompasses not only the capital but the vast sugar-growing region to the east and the arid territory that stretches west of it.

South of the Cordillera Central lies the **San Juan Valley**, which stretches into Haiti as the Plaine Centrale, shielded from most of the rain by the mountains just north of it and thus semi-arid. It's traditionally been used for cattle grazing, but does boast some irrigated agriculture. The northern face of the **Sierra Neiba** that borders the San Juan Valley to the south manages to soak up a good bit of precipitation, though, and along the Haitian border where it's least developed boasts the most extensive virgin rainforest left on the island. This is the end of the line for most of the rain, though; along its leeward slopes the range is parched limestone terrain, and the **Neiba Valley** that lies further south is flat, unrelenting desert, the least hospitable climate on the island, until you near the city of Barahona where the Río Yaque del Sur fertilizes land used for sugar-cane plantations.

The **Sierra Bahoruco** that lies south of the Neiba Valley is the second largest of the island's ranges, stretching west through Haiti where it's known as the **Massif du Sud**, and encompasses the most diverse mix of mountain environments of the ranges. Along the eastern half, where the semiprecious stone larimar is mined, you'll find that rainforest predominates, while further west is an enormous pine forest and, beyond that, a mixture of deciduous forest and rainforest along the northern half and semi-arid, deforested farmland along the southern half. South of these mountains is the scrub- and cactus-dominated desert of the **Jaragua Peninsula**, which is seasonal home to hundreds of migratory bird species, and has some of the island's best beaches.

As with the rest of the Caribbean, temperatures don't vary much over the course of the year, though **rainy season** runs from May through mid-November. Not all heavy rains are concentrated into these months, though; you can often get two weeks of unbroken sunshine in the summer and torrential downpours in January. **Hurricane season** (July through mid-October) is a more serious concern, as a major one blasts the island every decade or so. In 1998 Hurricane Georges did extensive damage to the year's crops, wreaked havoc on buildings along the southern coast and swept away several small villages in the southwestern part of the country.

Flora

Long-term **deforestation** from both commercial timbering and slash-and-burn subsistence agriculture has taken its toll on the once extensive forests of the Dominican Republic, but several reforestation projects in various parts of the Cordillera Central are beginning to repair some of the damage. If you're willing to head a bit off the beaten path, you'll still be able to find a wide variety of forest types within the DR, a small handful of them intact virgin ecosystems. The mountain ranges still contain vast square kilometres of pine forest, along with scattered cloud forests, a few stretches of rainforest and dry forest mixing deciduous with ferns, palms and pines. At lower altitudes you'll find everything from mangrove swamps and wetlands to grassy, cultivated savannahs, arid deserts and vast tracts of irrigated land denuded of its original vegetation and given over entirely to sugar cane.

Trees and shrubs

The DR is home to a wide array of **trees**, many of them endemic. Of special import to the local economy have been the precious woods that have been logged for centuries, particularly the **Hispaniolan mahogany**, which can still be seen in parts of the Cordillera Central, Sierra Bahoruco and Parque Nacional del Este. **Calabash** was used for gourds first by the Tainos and later by colonial *cimarrones* and today's rural farmers, while the **piñon**, known to the outside world as Mother-of-Cocoa, takes on enormous significance both practical and religious. Known for its miraculous ability to grow back from a single branch, it is used by farmers for fencing off their land and for an easily replenished source of firewood. Meanwhile, it holds mystical significance for devotees of Dominican *Vodú*, in part because it "bleeds" red sap during the weeks leading up to Semana Santa. The sap is also a powerful poison used in local folk medicines, and branches of the tree are used as staffs by rural faith healers.

The dominant tree in the pine forests, meanwhile, is the **Creolean pine**, another endemic species. Cedars, copeys, myrtle, laurel, cherry, wild sumac, juniper, walnut and cashew trees also proliferate in the mountains, whereas the deserts are dominated by a profusion of acacias, copeys, gumbo-limbos, frangipanis, mesquite, lignum vitae, poisonwood and sage. The deserts are also home to several variety of cacti, some of them quite beautiful – particularly the **prickly pear cactus**, known locally as "Tuna", bearing beautiful white flowers and a fruit that's consumed raw by denizens of the Dominican Republic's southwest.

Of the sixty different types of palm tree spread across the island – most densely along the Samaná Peninsula – the graceful **Hispaniolan royal palm** is one of only a few thought to be indigenous; climbing to twenty metres or more in height, its leaves are used for rural roofing, the trunk for walls and the nuts for feeding livestock. The tightly bunched leaves of the **Hispaniolan hat palm** convey the illusion of a dark-green, frazzled wig high atop their fifteen-metre or higher trunks, and are found most plentifully around Punta Cana. The classic **coconut palm** can also be found there as well, and along the beaches of Samaná; every part of their fruit is used for something or other, be it food or floor mats. On other parts of the Dominican coast you'll see lots of **sea grape**, a small gnarled tree with fan-shaped leaves, named for the extremely sour fruit that hangs from its branches; or the swamp-dwelling **gri gri** that are remark-ably resistant to tropical storms and hurricanes, and can be found along the island's lagoons and mangrove estuaries. Even more prevalent are **red man-groves**, though you'll also find **button mangroves** in the Bahía de Manzanillo and **white mangroves** in Parque Nacional Los Haitises. All the mangroves are central to the health of coastal ecosystems, affording protection from hurricane surges and providing a protected nursery for an array of sea creatures and birds.

Flowers

Flower farming and export is becoming a major business in the DR, largely because of the wide array of beautiful **tropical flowers** that are endemic here, including four hundred different types of **orchid**, over half of which grow in the Sierra Bahoruco. Also throughout the island in abundance are **heliconias** and **bromeliads**, while **bougainvillea** is to be found along the coast west of Barahona, **hortensias** in the area surrounding Bonao, **frangipani** in the arid regions and **roses** in the flower farms of Constanza.

Fauna

Though likely not as diverse as the vegetation on the island, thanks in part to the number of species that have gone **extinct** since humans have settled on Hispaniola, the animal kingdom in the Dominican Republic still has a colour-ful and vital presence, if often confined to habitats that are, out of necessity, cordoned off for preservation and run by the national government.

Marine life

Much of the **coral reef** – astonishingly complex ecosystems that support diverse marine life, from various algae to tiny crabs and eels, not to mention to brilliantly coloured coral itself – that once ringed the entire island of Hispan-iola has been destroyed by pollution, development and the careless practice of some subsistence fishers, who make a habit of dropping anchor over the reef when they fish. The only place where you'll find a substantial stretch of intact reef – with an accompanying spectacular array of colourful sea life – is along the northern coast **west of Luperón**. Here in the reefs live a broad array of tropical fish, anemones, sponges and the like. Smaller, but quite beautiful, sec-tions of the original reef survive at the eastern tip of the Samaná Peninsula, around Islas Saona and Catalina in the Parque Nacional del Este and at some points surrounding Parque Nacional Jaragua. Forty kilometres further out from the island's north coast, the rocky shelf that supports the island gives way abruptly to the 9000-metre **Brownson Trough**, one of the deepest underwa-ter pits in the world, and entirely unexplored. Along the edge of the trough north of the Samaná Peninsula sits another, largely unspoiled reef, protected by the Dominican government as the **Silver Banks Marine Sanctuary**, which also serves as feeding ground for large schools of dolphin and big fish, and win-ter mating ground for thousands of humpback whales.

The **whales** are the single most spectacular marine animal inhabiting the sur-rounding waters, and if you're not up for a week-long boat excursion to Silver Banks, you'll find plenty of day-trip boats to take you out to see them in the

Bahía de Samaná. Other marine mammal life close to Dominican shores includes the highly endangered **manatee**, a famously gentle relative of the seal that ancient mariners may have mistaken for mermaids. More commercial species include **big fish** like marlin, swordfish, sea bass, snapper, mackerel, tuna, kingfish, and **crustaceans** such as spiny lobsters, shrimp, crabs and sea urchins – the latter are shipped off en masse to Japan's restaurants.

Amphibians, reptiles and insects

Large **reptiles** are among the DR's most spectacular wildlife species, especially the **American crocodiles**, which grow up to nearly 5m in length and inhabit Lago Enriquillo, Parque Nacional Monte Cristi and Laguna Gri-Gri, as well as the salt-water Etang Saumatre just across the border in Haiti. Also evident in Lago Enriquillo, the northwest and the southwest are **rhinoceros iguanas**, which grow to 2m in length – at Isla Cabritos in Lago Enriquillo they are tame enough to feed, and have begun to prefer sweet cakes over the cactus flower that was once their native food. A variety of smaller **lizards** inhabit virtually every corner of the island, including the **world's smallest reptile**, *Sphaerodactylus ariasae*, a miniature gecko recently discovered on Alto Velo in the nation's southwest that stretches a mere 1.6 centimetres in length.

The tens of thousands of enormous **sea turtles** that laid their eggs on Hispaniolan shores during the time of Columbus are mostly a thing of the past, but some can still be found in the islands called Los Siete Hermanos outside Monte Cristi, along Playa Limón, just east of Miches, and in Parques Nacionales Jaragua and del Este, along with Isla Tortuga off the northern coast of Haiti. Unfortunately, local hunting threatens to drive them to total extinction; turtle meat is used in soups, intact shells can fetch a high price and bits of shells are sometimes used as protective covers for roosters' claws in cockfights. The largest of the sea turtles is the appropriately named **leatherback**, which bears a thick, tough hide in place of a hard shell. Other species that inhabit the island are the **hawksbill**, extremely rare because its shell fetches such a high price on the black market; the stocky, small-headed **loggerhead**; and the vegetarian **green turtles** that lay their eggs en masse along the shores of Los Siete Hermanos. Tiny freshwater **slider turtles** can be found in the Laguna Cabral just north of Barahona. Further inland, the island is home to a number of small **tree frogs**, including – in a small zone of the Cordillera Central right around Pico Duarte – the astonishingly loud **coqui frogs** that were once thought only to live on Puerto Rico.

Insect life is abundant throughout the DR but numbers and diversity reach their peak in the mangrove estuaries and lagoons, particularly Parque Nacional Los Haitises. The arid country west of Barahona, though, is the best place for **butterflies**, and lepidopterists come to study the many varieties of swallowtail, monarch and flambeaus. Elsewhere, insect life makes itself known mainly through the variety of bites and sores incurred: **mosquitoes** are particular pests, and can sometimes spread malaria and dengue fever, while **sand fleas** are a major problem along some of the island's beaches, particularly Punta Rucia, Playa Limón and Playa Monte Río.

Birds

Some three hundred **bird** species make the DR their year-round home, with two hundred more, including a wide variety of North American songbirds, coming here for winter. The southwest is of special interest, with four large lagoons, two offshore islands, the Jaragua peninsula and the Sierra Bahoruco holding a near limitless spectrum of birdlife.

The DR's many **lagoons and mangrove estuaries** have the widest variety of birdlife on offer, inhabited not only by thousands of **flamingos**, the most ostentatiously beautiful of the lagoon birds, but also herons, egrets, wood storks, ibises, roseate spoonbills, cuckoos, black-cowled orioles and village weavers, the last an African import. The **freshwater lagoons** are also inhabited by eleven varieties of duck, alongside rails, jacanas and grebes, while the **mangrove coasts** add a number of seafaring birds, especially the entertaining brown pelicans, cormorants, boobies, frigate birds, cave swallows and gulls. Predatory birds in these areas include the occasional osprey and peregrine falcon.

In the **mountains** you'll find some of the most interesting native birds, including the endemic **Hispaniolan woodpecker** and the **yellow-bellied sapsucker**, both woodpeckers that are menaces to local trees – and thus despised by farmers – along with narrow-billed todies, red-tailed hawks, white-necked crows, thrushes, tanagers and siskins. The rare **Hispaniolan parakeet**, known locally as the *perico*, dwells in the Cordillera Central and sections of the Neiba and Sierra Bahoruco, while the endemic **Hispaniolan emerald hummingbird** – which you'll often see along the Pico Duarte hiking trails – is still widespread in the Cordillera Central and is occasionally found elsewhere on the island. Many mountain-dwelling birds have recently been placed at risk due to changes in coffee-growing practices. As much of the original tree canopy of the mountain ranges was destroyed over the last century, migratory songbirds adapted by nesting in the **shade overstories** that were traditionally used by coffee growers. The increasing popularity of espresso beans has caused farmers to do away with shade cultivation in favour of an open-air method that produces a stronger coffee, destroying an important bird habitat. Happily, many of the **co-operative coffee plantations** that have recently sprung up around Jarabacoa stick to the old shade method, but species numbers are still plummeting.

Along the **open country** you'll find an enormous range of birds, though the most commonly espied are the **cattle egrets** that pick parasites off local herds and gather at dusk by the hundreds at a few select sites. Also evident across the island are the large **turkey vultures** that you'll see circling the countryside from high above; you may also catch a glimpse of the island's various warblers, honeycreepers, grackles, palmchats and terns. The yellow-black **bobolinks** can be found seasonally in the western Cibao's rice fields, while caves, ruins and dense woodlands across the country are home to numerous **Stygian owls** and **barn owls**. The **predatory birds** that dominate the flatlands are the endemic Ridgway's hawk and the small, lizard-eating falcon known as the American kestrel. Today the **Hispaniolan parrot**, locally known as the *cotica* and considered the national bird, is quite rare, its plumage all emerald but for a small spot of white on the forehead.

Land mammals

There are few **land mammals** in the Dominican Republic aside from pack animals and the dogs and rats brought over early on by the European colonists and still common denizens of city streets. Aside from a dozen different species of **bat**, which can be seen in the island's many caves, the only ones native to the island are highly endangered, and your only real hope of seeing them is at Santo Domingo's zoo. Of these, the **solenodon** is a primitive nocturnal anteater with a comically long snout, the only insect-eating mammal native to the Caribbean, while the **hutia** is a one-foot-long, tree-climbing herbivore. Both also live in small numbers in Parques Nacionales del Este and Los Haitises.

Threats and restrictions

Much of this natural beauty is **under threat** from the ongoing effects of deforestation and development. The Dominican government has been working hard to protect what remains of its wilderness by creating a series of **national parks and scientific reserves**, but their limited resources mean that upkeep of these areas is often less than ideal. It is imperative for paying visitors to be responsible and endeavour to support the vital educational programmes that seek to preserve these remnants.

It should be stressed that not only is it extremely irresponsible, it is also **illegal** to buy, even as souvenirs, most items that involve the use of wild animals or flowers in their production. This applies specifically to tortoise-shell, black coral, various species of butterfly, products made from crocodile skin and turtle shells. Trade in living animals, including tortoises, iguanas and parrots (often sold as nestlings), is also illegal. Mahogany once proliferated in Dominican forests, but is now endangered. While the cutting of mahogany is restricted in the country today, the sale of mahogany products is still technically legal, though that shouldn't serve as encouragement to buy it.

Merengue, bachata and Dominican music

On its home turf, the Dominican Republic, **merengue** is ubiquitous. It pours out of passing cars, thrums from boom boxes, and blares from every store-front. And in the countless rural taverns and high-tech dance clubs that dot the island, merengue is the main item on every menu.

No wonder then that merengue's explosion onto the New York scene in the 1980s and ensuing dissemination across the globe is a source of intense pride for all Dominicans. The music is so closely identified with the local character that, for them, to love merengue is to love the island itself and the people who inhabit it. The 1970s icon **Johnny Ventura** has now returned home to become a major political figure with presidential ambitions. And multi-platinum Latin superstar **Juan Luís Guerra**'s conquest of the world, topping even the sales of crooner Julio Iglesias, is an unparalleled national success story.

Certainly not all have caught the fever, and public perception of merengue often involves the vision of Vegas-style performers lip-synching on a Spanish-language cable network. Let that not be your lasting vision, however; this ever-evolving musical style is just now coming into its own.

Roll call

As with all Afro-Caribbean genres, merengue is easily identified by its omnipresent **beat pattern**. When compared to salsa or calypso, the merengue pattern seems aggressively unsyncopated, its souped-up military rat-a-tat landing squarely on 1 and 3. But one of several interlocking patterns rattles through the rhythm section over this signature on-the-beat thump the way a city seethes around its neatly numbered grid.

The **instrumentation** is a blend of traditional rural orchestration with con-temporary electronics and muscly, salsa-influenced horn sections. **Saxophones** and **trumpets** are always present in contemporary bands, with a trombone occasionally added. The main purpose of the horns is to rip off a series of crisp, pyrotechnic riffs. The **bass** never strays far from thumbing out the underlying groove. The **piano** underlines the harmony with arpeggios and syncopated chord movement and is often electric. And that quintessential old-time instru-ment, the **accordion**, is still utilized in a few modern bands.

The **percussion section** is the backbone. The **congas** slap out a series of African beats that provide the primary fire and groove. The **tambora** is a two-headed lap drum that is anchored by a hand at one end and rapped with a stick at the other. Often a **bass drum** is used, an innovation that began as Dominican performers incorporated disco elements into their repertoire dur-ing the 1970s in order to stave off bankruptcy in the face of the Bee Gees. And always beneath its more ostentatious neighbours is the incessant scrape of the **güira** – traditionally fashioned from a kitchen utensil – a cultural inheritance of the Tainos who inhabited the island before Columbus, its tireless hoarse rasping like that of a dying man begging to be remembered.

Let us not forget those who skim the cream off this rich cross-cultural blend, getting most of the credit and all of the wanton glances – the **singers**. The most traditional merengue voice is a reedy, nasal style that occasionally manages to be haunting amid the up-tempos. Guerra is the principal exponent today. But the more richly sonorous Latin tradition is evident as well, most notably in the work of Ventura, the Dominican answer to Elvis. Choruses tend to come in threes, engaging in extended call-and-response sections with the lead, which is swapped among them when there is no superstar. Meanwhile, they engage in virtuostic floor shows, dancing in split-second formations like the Temptations on speed and maintaining an impossibly fast hand-jive. Bandleaders engage in the proceedings to varying degrees. Ventura's hip-swivelling histrionics are on a par with the legendary James Brown, while trumpet great Wilfrido Vargas maintains a dignified distance from his chorus's erotic foreplay.

Double and triple entendres involving sexuality and politics are standard procedure in the **lyrics**, while direct polemics are eschewed in favour of irony. "Dominicans have a wry sense of humor," says Guerra. "Irony works better than heavy messages and it's more fun!" In his writing, a first-rate poetry emerges using surrealistic images culled from campesino life. More often, though, merengue is the language of escapism, and its lyrics seek to banish the exhausting outside world.

The immaculate conception

There are many stories regarding the **origins of merengue**, most of them patently apocryphal. One tale dates its inception to the Dominican Revolution against Haiti in the early nineteenth century. A soldier named Tomas Torres abandoned his post during a critical battle that the Dominicans later won, and the first merengue song was composed by the victors to mock poor Tomas's glaringly unpatriotic survival instinct.

The main purpose of this fabrication is to shield Dominican society from the unsavoury fact that it was probably transported from Haiti and owes a debt to the traditions of Africa as well as Europe – an acknowledgement most Dominicans couldn't bear to make. Nevertheless, a musical form called **mereng** with an alarmingly similar rhythmic structure developed in Haiti (then St-Domingue) during the eighteenth century among the landed mulatto classes. Until the colony's last years, Europeans and Africans were allowed to intermarry, permitting some of African heritage to attain a level of power and wealth, even while others were subjected to the worst plantation slavery system of them all. The Europeans brought with them an abiding love of contra dance – the primary ballroom genre throughout the colonial Caribbean. Mereng was a "danza" form infused with African rhythm, and is, by the way, still current in Haiti, in a slower and more lilting form.

Meanwhile, the European settlers of Santo Domingo were from an early date subject to chastisement by their priesthood for excessive fervour while dancing. Merengue first infiltrated the country through the pueblos, via Haitian invaders and former French gentry fleeing the machete after the revolution across the border, from whence it made its way to elite urban ballrooms. There it encountered entrenched resistance from prominent literary figures, largely on the basis of its "African-ness". Victims of the latest dance craze were likened to virgins who had soiled their good names. From that point, any bumpkin musician who happened to innocently offer a merengue during a high society dance set could expect to have a revolver pointed at him.

Utterly taboo in the ballrooms, merengue was left to the auspices of rural Dominican folk. Partly because it was easy to dance, party because the lyrics were irreverent and lewd, it completely took over amid the vast agricultural stretches of the Cibao Valley in particular. The Cibao's central city Santiago became the focal point for *merengue típico cibaeño*, still considered the definitive form.

One final touch was needed to achieve the classic form, and it came, oddly enough, via Germany. The country was an important business partner for the Dominican Republic during the latter half of the century, buying a great deal of the tobacco grown in the Cibao plantations. Many German exporters made a side business out of selling accordions, which quickly made inroads into the merengue ensemble, replacing the older string instruments. This generated huge concern for the survival of traditional merengue, partly because the first accordions in the country played only in one major key, rendering them inflexible and banishing all minor-key merengues to the dustbin of memory for a time.

Latin exodus

Merengue was finally completely adopted as the national Dominican music by all segments of society during the **isolationist regime of Trujillo** in the mid-twentieth century. Trujillo used it to emphasize his peasant roots and gain popularity with the masses, and a number of major stars emerged from the era, including ballroom king **Luis Kalaff** and saxophonist **Tavito Vásquez**, often called the Dominican Charlie Parker. A top-notch big-band group would follow Trujillo around on campaign stops, and state radio stations blasted favourite tunes between edicts. The entrenched antipathy of the urban elite began to melt as **El Jefe** started to frequent their salons, a pistol in his pocket and a song in his heart, causing a stately ballroom merengue to re-emerge.

For this and other offences, Trujillo was eventually assassinated. But once merengue was removed from the closet, there was no stopping it. The end of Trujillo's isolationist policies sparked a wave of migration to the major cities of North America, where Dominicans joined Puerto Ricans, Cubans and others in the vast urban barrios that served as cultural cauldrons from which modern Latin music fomented. Back home, Johnny Ventura was busy marketing his music to compete with the North American imports. Ventura was the first of the *merengueros* to fashion for himself a **pop icon status** similar to the ones being generated up north, using large-scale advertising, trademark floor shows and a sound more closely aligned with that of the American record industry. The end result for merengue was a sharp, stuttering momentum that the old style only hinted at.

The migration continued on an even more massive scale in the 1980s due to a major recession. The increased Dominican presence in New York and Miami meant a much higher profile for the music. The resultant explosion onto the world music scene is still being felt, even as the impingement of outside influences on this previously insular style has forever transformed it.

Wilfrido Vargas was the top star of this golden era, pushing the music into uncharted harmonic and rhythmic territory. Vargas has always been an interesting mix of culture and commerce, and his band had started out playing bossa novas and rock 'n' roll because he thought it was the best way to make a buck. For a time he even featured disco covers, though it apparently caused him a certain degree of embarrassment. When it became financially viable for him to focus solely on merengue, he was much more open to outside elements than artists of the past, incorporating forms such as salsa, compa, zouk, reggae, and recently even house music and rap into his own native idiom. His experiments initially met with a certain amount of resisitance from the purists, but his expansion of the vocabulary is now considered orthodoxy. Other big stars have followed suit, notably singing great **Cuco Valoy**, whose passion is Cuban music and calypso given a political slant.

Bachata blitzkrieg

The explosion of outside influences on traditional Dominican music gave rise to the towering figure of the 1990s, **Juan Luís Guerra** and his band, **4:40**. Weaned on a mixture of traditional merengue and Western pop influences such as the Beatles and Manhattan Transfer, Guerra has contributed a vast amount to the music, injecting South African choruses and Zairian guitar work, slowing it down to a more lyrical level, infusing it with rich vocal harmonies and writing some of the most beautiful song lyrics ever conceived. "I studied literature in Santo Domingo," he says, "and the lyrics reflect my enthusiasm for poets like Neruda and Vallejo." Many of the songs, such as *Let's Hope it Rains Coffee in the Fields*, betray an affinity with magical realism: "[That] comes from an anonymous poem I found when I went to the city of Santiago de los Caballeros. It's probably the work of a campesino – a peasant – and it was such a beautiful metaphor, I had to develop it."

This sentiment conveys the spirit and the conflict behind Guerra's phenomenally popular sound. For even as he incorporates an ever-widening menagerie of world music influences ("You look in Juan Luís' bag," says one collaborator, "and you see West African tapes, South African tapes, Indian music – he's listening to a whole different thing"), it is his urgent life's work to produce a populist music to which the people back home can relate. "I certainly write for a home audience. [At one point] we decided to shift back toward our roots – toward merengue. We felt in a way we were playing a music that seemed elite, and we wanted to play a music that appealed to everyone at home, a music that seemed more natural and intuitive." The high poetry of his lyrics focuses on Dominican images and issues, such as the *Cost of Living*, addressing long-term economic stagnation, and *Guavaberry*, an indigenous fruit that causes the skin to itch upon contact, and the outside musical colours he inserts function strictly in the service of Dominican music.

Guerra really blew the lid off the Latin music charts when he turned to a disreputable Dominican fusion of Cuban bolero and ranchero called **bachata**. Long popular with the Dominican underclasses, *bachata* began as a twangy rural guitar form performed by campesinos during outdoor parties, and was transported to the bars and brothels of the desperately poor outer barrios around Santo Domingo during the mass urban migrations of the 1970s and 1980s. In part because of its social context, *bachata* – like its predecessor, merengue – was at first looked down upon with extreme distaste by Dominican society, and it was impossible to even purchase a *bachata* record in a mainstream music store. This allowed a handful of enterprising bottom-feeders like record producer Radhames Aracena and his **Radio Guarachita** a near-monopoly on the production and sales of *bachata* stars like **Leonardo Paniagua**, **Melida Rodríguez** and legendary guitarist and singer **Luis Segura** – whose records were hawked informally from outdoor stalls alongside fried snacks and split coconuts. The signature hit of this era was Segura's *Pena*, a typically doleful look at the pain of unrequited love that sold somewhere around 200,000 copies in 1983 – even though *bachata* was still banned from the record stores.

Guerra's upper middle-class background is not that of the usual *bachatero*, but he was smart enough to see through the negative stereotypes associated locally with the music and turn out an entire album of *bachatas* on his legendary *Bachata Rosa*, giving them a slick, commercial production along with his trademark lyrics and vocals. The album went platinum across Latin America and was at the tops of the Latin charts in North America and Europe, instantly making him the biggest name in Dominican music and completely transforming the perception of *bachata* back in the home country. Many of the original *bachateros* resent Guerra's sudden co-opting of their musical form, but his success has resulted in new-found respect and fame for them as well. Segura and Paniagua – both now in their sixties – today sell more albums than they did in their youth and are in demand for concerts worldwide, while a new generation of *bachata* stars has arisen – pre-eminent of whom are **Luis Vargas** and **Raulín Rodriguez** – who haven't had to face the old social barriers.

Merengue mañana

Bachata's place in the Dominican musical landscape has been permanently enshrined; listen to Dominican radio today and you'll hear at least one *bachata* tune for every two merengues. Most bands today stick to one or the other, but a growing movement of young musicians like **Antony Santos** and **Teodoro Reyes** has fused the two into a new form – **bachatarengue** – which speeds up *bachata*'s twangy guitar arpeggios and places them within merengue's up-tempo thump. The end result is a bit of a surprise – though the African roots of the two separate forms are not always obvious at first glance, *bachatarengue* sounds very much like Congolese soukous, an unintentional connecting of the fragmented strands of African music that survived in the Caribbean for 500 years, bringing it back full-circle to its origin.

Another movement that has started to catch on – particularly in the Dominican barrios of New York and Boston – is **Dominican Roots**, a more

Discography

Compilations

• *Grandes Soneros: 100% Dominicanos* (Camaleón, US).
Rare recordings of the Dominican Republic's great stars in the field of Cuban *son* – an absolute must for any Latin music lover's collection. Includes cuts from little-known but top-notch soneros who frequent the dark, dicey *son* clubs of Santo Domingo, like Santiago Cerón, Cuco Valoy, Manolé and Los Hijos del Rey.

• *Merengue: Dominican Music and Dominican Identity* (Temple University, US).
A collection of rare historic recordings by scholar Paul Austerlitz, including rural fiestas patronales, stately c.1900 salon merengue and special emphasis on the role of women throughout the history of Dominican music.

• *The Rough Guide to Merengue and Bachata* (Nascente, UK).
A truly excellent collection (if we do say so ourselves) that gives a particularly good look at the *bachatarengue* taking over the airwaves in the Dominican Republic today, as well as classic *bachatas* from Luis Segura and Luis Melo and old-style accordion merengues from Samuelito Almonte y Su Conjunto Típico.

Artists

Xiomara Fortuna
This woman is a true national treasure, though she's gotten more recognition in Europe and North America than back in her home country. This is changing, though, and her latest hits have been scaling the charts back home.

• *Kumbajei* (Circular Moves).
Heavily influenced by contemporary West African pop, this album is filled with iconoclastic renderings of various traditional Dominican rhythms – which in her hands are utterly transformed into a new pop style. She's also backed up by the best musicians of the Dominican Roots movement, including Tony Vicioso and Willian Alemán.

Fulanito
By far the best of the merenhouse bands, and with a huge international following across Latin America.

• *El Hombre Mas Famosa de la Tierra* (Cutting Records).
Well, humble they're not – as the album cover proves – but they do a terrific job of tearing accordion merengue into the twenty-first century, with heavily sampled accordion, tambora and güira behind rapid-fire rap lines and heavy-handed hip-hop production.

Juan Luís Guerra
Juan Luís Guerra and his band 4:40 have cut a swath through the field of Latin American popular music with their brand of magical realist merengue fused with discreetly erotic lyrics and mildly critical socio-political themes. Although the basis of the band's music is salsa and merengue, Guerra and his band also draw on South African choral music, Congolese guitar and Western pop for a blend of energy and romance that sweeps all before it.

• *Bachata Rosa* (Karen, US).
The revival of the old-time *bachata* and top-selling Dominican album of all time. Available everywhere and utterly sublime.

• *Los Grandes Exitos* (Karen, US).
This recently released greatest hits album is the best introduction to Guerra's extensive oeuvre, though it inexplicably excludes a couple of essential hits from *Fogarate*.

continued overleaf

Los Hermanos Rosario

The Rosario brothers have led one of the most popular merengue bands on the island and abroad for over fifteen years.

• *Y Es Fácil!* (Karen, US).
Los Hermanos Rosario best represent the exuberant excesses of merengue since the 1980s, and this is the album for which they won a Latin Grammy, a high-octane, cardiac-arresting thrill ride through hit after hit. Also probably the most garish album cover in recording history – these guys did not get where they are today on their good looks.

New York Band

Dominican trombone legend Franklin Rivers' first and most popular band features a lineup of the top Dominican horn players of the era.

• *Los Años Dorado* (Karen, US).
New York Band was one of the best bands to come out of the 1980s international explosion. Includes their big hit *Colé*, which was banned in the Dominican Republic for its supposed obscenity (*colé* can mean either "dance" or "shag", and the censors were pretty sure they meant "shag").

Boni Raposo y La Ventiuno División

• *Illuminando el Tesoro Escondido* (Chivita).
A huge hit with the Dominican community in New York and rapidly spreading to Europe and Latin America, this is a breakthrough album for Raposo and his band – and the highest-quality recording of traditional *Vodú* drum-and-chorus music that you'll find anywhere. *La Ventiuno División* is a reference to the 21classes of spirits in Dominican Voodoo.

Luis Segura

The great star of pre-Guerra *bachata*, with a soulful, reedy voice that's truly timeless.

• *El Disco de Oro* (Kubaney).
Two-CD tribute that contains all of his classic hits, which span over twenty years of recording. The seminal song *Pena Por Ti* is deemed so important by the compilation's producers that it's included twice – once on each disc.

Francisco Ulloa

The greatest of the merengue accordionists, he will permanently end your associations between the instrument and Lawrence Welk. On some cuts he also incorporates the marimbula, a descendant of the African thumb piano, a wooden box with strips of metal attached that when plucked give off a deep, reverberating thrum.

---

conscious attempt to pay tribute to the African aspects of Dominican culture by a set of young musicians who grew up with the traditional *Vodú* music of the campos and outer barrios of Santo Domingo, then immigrated to the cities of the United States. Once in the States, many of these kids were shocked to find themselves considered "black" by their new society – which in turn sparked a renewed interest in the long-buried African influence on their home country. The grandfather of Dominican Roots music is **Luis Díaz**, whose 1970s ensemble Convite was part rock band and part ethnomusicological enterprise; they scoured the countryside learning about and recording the music that was played in villages across the island, then translated this folk music into a new rock-based idiom. But while Díaz' music attracted a sizeable cult following for twenty years, it wasn't until the mid-1990s that a slew of **emerging musicians** like Willian Alemán,

- *!Merengue!* (Globe Style,UK).
Never has the accordion sounded like this. His most famous recording, featuring frantic arpeggios from accordion and saxophone, free-sounding triple-time bass and a driving throb from the tambora. Wild music from a man who must have more than the natural complement of fingers to bring it off.

- *!Ultramerengue!* (Globe Style, UK).
Features merenguized renditions of lesser-known Dominican traditional music like the mangulina, plena, canto de hacha and pambiche. The latter is a bastardization of "Palm Beach" and was originally created as a more jerky merengue that matched the arrhythmic dance movements of American soldiers stationed here in the 1920s and 1930s.

Cuco Valoy
Although Cuco Valoy – "El Brujo" as he is known with good reason – is from the Dominican Republic, he is as likely to perform *bachata* or Cuban-style *son* as merengue. He's equally virtuostic in all three styles.

- *Salsa con Coco* (Discolor, US).
This collection of some of the man's greatest hits is well worth getting, not least because it contains perhaps his most famous song, *Juliana*, and the typically loopy *La Muerte de Don Marcos*.

Wilfrido Vargas
The legendary merengue innovator and dignified elder statesman who brought the influence of a dozen different world musical forms into the family, along with an expansion of the harmonic vocabulary comparable to the achievement of Charlie Parker.

- *Abusadura* (Karen, US).
One of his most striking and popular recordings, with influences across world music and merengue versions of a couple of classic *bachata*s.

Johnny Ventura
The Dominican Elvis did a lot to update the music, and was the first merenguero to fashion for himself an image as a pop icon. The old-timer has recently gone into politics and become Mayor of Santo Domingo as a means of escaping the Chuck Berry RV Show & State Fair tour circuit.

- *Guataco* (Kubaney, US).
A classic Ventura album with many of his hits. Great singing with an old-time saxophone sound (sort of an accordion impression with arpeggios and mile-wide, furious vibrato), even as the influence of disco begins to creep in.

Boni Raposo, Edis Sánchez and Tony Vicioso began setting up their own roots-based ensembles. The music that they've created varies wildly – from Raposo's straight-ahead *Vodú* drum-and-chorus lines to Sánchez's psychedelicizing of Dominican *gagá* music and Vicioso's massive ensembles combining rara, palos drums and electronics – but in all of their groups you can hear the traditional rumba, calypso and merengue beats of the Caribbean, grooving just as hard as in mainstream Latin music but with a defiantly populist Voodoo slant. Taking this trend a step further is singer **Xiomara Fortuna**, who is the first Dominican musician to ride this movement to the top of the World Music charts in the West. Like other Dominican Roots artists, Fortuna co-opts the lesser-known beats of the countryside like *pri-pri*, *mangulina* and *salves* – but combines them with a more forward-looking production akin to contemporary West African pop.

Other emerging artists have instead been focusing on North America hip-hop, although most of the **merenhouse rap** at the top of the charts these days has yet to approach the best of either genre. This development is predictably decried in more traditional circles, but the history of merengue is an account of similar reinventions and consequent destructions; merengue has always adapted and survived. The genre's regular beat structure is well suited to house music fusions, and many of the dance remixes work extremely well. The result is a slew of merenhouse bands with one ear on the *périco ripao* grooves of their parents and the other on the multi-layered industrial urban noise of young African America. Those who grew up with the music can take comfort that the old forms lie embedded in the new like geological strata. The most prominent merenhouse band, **Fulanito**, for example, pays homage to the history of their music by large-scale sampling of the accordion and other traditional instruments, whispering in the background like a ghost memory.

A version of this essay can also be found in the Rough Guide to World Music, Volume 2: The Americas and Asia

Baseball

The Dominican Republic is responsible for a disproportionate number of today's top baseball players: just to start, Sammy Sosa, Pedro Martínez and Alex Rodríguez are all household names in the United States; among the very best at their positions, they command salaries in excess of ten million dollars a year. It's the result of a century-long Dominican passion for the game that makes North American baseball fanaticism pale in comparison. Dominican boys are exposed to baseball from almost the moment they're born, and playing fields can be found in even the smallest villages. Dominican professional games command huge crowds, and the successes and failures of Dominicans in the major leagues are televised across the country and assiduously reported in the newspapers. The veneration heaped upon these homegrown players can't be overstated; when Sosa arrived back from his MVP season with the Chicago Cubs in 1998, he was greeted by a line of cheering locals for the full 40km from Santo Domingo's airport to his hometown of San Pedro de Macorís.

Baseball, America and sugar

In the late nineteenth century, the **United States** began to export its national pastime to countries around the world, especially those where it had some sort of military presence. The game was thus spread to Cuba, Central America, Mexico, Venezuela and Japan, though it would take slightly longer for the sport to take root in the Dominican Republic. Here its history is inextricably linked to the rise of sugar plantations in the 1860s, when wealthy **Cuban plantation owners** fled a revolution in their own country that freed their slaves and destroyed much of their property. Many resettled in Santo Domingo, where they founded several youth clubs devoted to baseball that weaned local kids away from football (soccer); others headed to the DR's southeast, buying land from the government, forcibly evicting any peasants who happened to live there and establishing sugar mills around tiny fishing hamlets La Romana and San Pedro de Macorís. In the 1880s the Cuban owners began providing minimal baseball equipment to their workers as a cheap diversion to keep up morale.

By the early twentieth century, the game had been adopted to such an extent that several **semi-professional ballclubs** were formed in Santo Domingo, Santiago, San Pedro and La Romana, both to play each other and face teams from Puerto Rico and Cuba in various tournaments. The **American occupation** that lasted from 1916 to 1924 resulted in further inroads, as military administrators saw baseball as a convenient way to insinuate US culture into the country. They provided money to form amateur Dominican clubs and purchase equipment, and organized their troops into teams that regularly played Dominican squads. The Dominicans, though, saw these games as a matter of pride; whenever they defeated a military club, impromptu parties carried on well into the night.

Towards the end of the occupation, **professional baseball** in the country took on the shape and structure that remains today, with two teams in Santo

Domingo – Licey and Escogido – and one each in San Pedro, La Romana and even Santiago, which at the time was an arduous four-day muleback trek for any visiting team. When **Rafael Trujillo** came to power in 1930, though, his son Ramfis – a rabid baseball fan – forced Licey's ownership to sell out to him, and in turn signed some of the best talent in the country to contracts far too lucrative for local box office revenues to support. For the Trujillos this was no problem; they had ownership of all major industries in the country and were rich enough to write off Ramfis' pricey hobby as a public relations expense. But the other teams followed suit in order to keep up – despite the fact that their owners depended far more on baseball earnings for their profits – and a tremendous bidding war ensued for both the best Dominicans as well as the cream of the crop from other Caribbean islands and the American Negro Leagues, the latter of which were unable to break into the major leagues in the States until Jackie Robinson did so, in 1948.

Trujillo and the legendary 1937 season

In 1936, **San Pedro de Macorís** (a city the Trujillos hated for its opposition to their rule) beat Licey in the national championship behind Dominican sluggers **Tetelo Vargas** and **Mateo de la Rosa**, the first great batsmen the island produced. In response to his defeat, Ramfis joined Licey and Escogido together into a Ciudad Trujillo super-team that he hoped would restore the family honour. To counter this San Pedro's scouts flew off to Pittsburgh to sign the top Negro League stars from the **Pittsburgh Crawfords**, which were run by local mobster Gus Greenlee. Despite being arrested upon arrival – on orders from Greenlee – the scouts did, once out of custody, manage to sign the team's three best ballplayers (all three now in the baseball hall of fame): pitcher **Satchel Paige**, slugger **Josh Gibson** and lightning-fast centre fielder **Cool Papa Bell**.

These signings should have made San Pedro de Macorís invincible, but more bad fortune was to befall the scouts. Upon the representatives' return to San Pedro, Trujillo's men threw them in jail, and government troops informed the three players that they would be suiting up instead for Ciudad Trujillo. Paige, Gibson and Bell were joined on that team by several other top Negro Leaguers and infielder **Perucho Cepeda**, father of hall-of-famer Orlando Cepeda, and considered the best Latin player of his day. A third team, Santiago, got into the act, signing Dominican hero **Horacio Martínez** along with Venezuelan shortstop **Luis Aparicio** and Cubans **Luis Tiant** (father of the Boston Red Sox pitching star of the same name) and hall-of-famer **Martín Dihigo**, a versatile pitcher/outfielder who had played in Mexico, Venezuela, Cuba and the US, where he had the Negro League's highest batting average and lowest ERA (the mark by which pitchers are rated) in the same year.

The hard-fought battles between these three teams are still legendary in the Dominican Republic, though for Paige, Gibson and Bell the bizarre antics of the Trujillo family were probably more memorable. After Ciudad dropped the season opener to San Pedro, Paige reported that the team was surrounded by a phalanx of soldiers who fired their automatic weapons into the air while shouting, "The Benefactor doesn't like to lose!" If a fight broke out during a game, the National Police swarmed the field and clobbered the opposing team;

meanwhile, the Americans were routinely jailed the night before a game to ensure they got a good night's rest.

After a gruelling regular season, the **Ciudad Trujillo Dragones** knocked off Santiago and faced defending champion San Pedro in a best-of-seven **championship series**. Taken from their prison cells to Quisqueya Stadium under armed escort, the Dragones were edgy enough that they dropped the first three games. For his part, Paige was firmly convinced that if they didn't come from behind to win the series they'd be going back to the States in pinewood boxes; he spent the entire series popping antacid tablets as he glanced warily from the dugout at the troops who surrounded the field. Fortunately, his theory was never tested: the Dragones took the next four games to win the national championship. A week-long city festival ensued, but the vast amounts of money used to finance the 1937 season bankrupted the other owners and **ended professional Dominican baseball** for ten years, shifting local sentiment to the **amateur national teams** the country put together – using a unit of the Dominican army as Trujillo's personal farm club.

The English

Though professional Dominican baseball went into a tailspin, the sport was attracting a new generation of players and fans in the rural sugar *bateyes*. The most prominent such group was the Cocolos, also known as "**The English**", impoverished immigrants from the British Caribbean who came to the DR at the turn of the century as seasonal cane cutters and settled around San Pedro de Macorís. There was little to alleviate the misery of their squalid living conditions other than benefits from the Improvement Organizations founded in the 1910s by **Marcus Garvey**'s UNIA, which collected money for workers' medical expenses, held social events and created a sports league. This sports league, however, was for **cricket**, the pastime that the Cocolos had brought over from the British Antilles, but during the hype of the 1937 baseball season many were weaned from their native sport and won over to this new Dominican obsession.

At first the English ballplayers were largely ignored in the rest of the DR and excluded from the amateur national teams. **The first wave** of Dominican players to catch the eye of the newly integrated major leagues in the early 1950s came from the talent pool that had worked its way through the army and Trujillo's amateur team, including the Alou brothers, hall-of-famers Ozzie Virgil and Juan Marichal – all of whom were signed by the San Francisco Giants – and Dodger great Manny Mota. But when a team from **Batey Consuelo** north of San Pedro whipped the military team several years in a row in the 1950s, players from the *bateyes* began to gain far more prominence, being recruited for the national team and falling under the watchful eye of American scouts. The first Cocolo to break through to the big leagues was slugger **Rico Carty** in the 1960s; shortly thereafter the majors would be swamped with the sons of San Pedro, including Pedro Guerrero, George Bell, Juan Samuel, Tony Fernández, Alfredo Griffin, Manny Lee, Julio Franco, Joaquín Andujar, José Offerman, Mariano Duncan, Sammy Sosa and on and on.

From the Dominican leagues to the major leagues

Today, an astounding ten percent of the players in the US major and minor leagues comes from the Dominican Republic, more, in fact, than the rest of Latin America put together. Of those professional players, an equally astounding number hail from around the city of San Pedro, known in baseball circles, in fact, as "the city of shortstops". This pipeline of talent has been honed into a **well-oiled business**; the downside of all the success – as much wealth and fame as it may bring both to individual players and to the country as a whole – is that Dominican baseball is no longer operating nearly as independently as it once did.

The old **Dominican professional league** alignment still largely exists: two Santo Domingo teams and one each from Santiago, La Romana and San Pedro face off against each other in a regular **winter season** that features a blend of Dominican stars from the majors, up-and-coming young local talent and American minor leaguers looking to sharpen their game, often coached by retired stars like Santiago's Tony Peña. The champion of the winter season goes on to face off teams from Venezuela, Puerto Rico and Cuba in the Latin American championship.

Professional teams in the Dominican Republic, however, all enter into formal agreements with **North American clubs** and act as little more than a developmental team for the parent club. Meanwhile, fewer and fewer of the **best Dominican players** are willing to endanger multimillion-dollar careers by playing back home, and they're strongly discouraged from doing so by their major league club, for fear of injuries. The entire country is scoured by **scouts** from professional teams in the United States, Canada and even Japan; most kids who display some talent are signed and whisked off to a major league camp by the time they're 16 or 17. As a result, many of the top young Dominicans never play professional ball locally.

But while other North American companies that move into the DR and take control of an economic sector are resented here, baseball's major leagues are positively lionized for it. Today every North American club has a complex in the DR where they recruit and train young Dominicans for up to three years before moving the best of the bunch on to their minor league system. Major league scouts have been known to commit a variety of **abuses** in the quest for cheap Dominican talent, including signing underage players, hiding prospects from their families so that they won't be stolen by another team and failing to pay out promised signing bonuses. Some of their jobs are being taken over by unofficial **buscandos**, who track down talented youngsters, sign them to an agreement and then auction them off to the highest bidder for a percentage of the signing bonus. The competitive fever pitch in search of the next Pedro Martínez or Sammy Sosa has climbed so high that the traditional attraction for major league clubs – inexpensive talent that can be bought for less than a third of what it would take to sign a comparable kid in the United States – is very much in danger. Ten years ago, **emerging stars** like New York Yankees second-baseman Alfonso Soriano and Cincinnati Reds minor league pitcher Ricardo Aramboles would have felt lucky to sign a US$3000, three-year development contract with a North American organization, but today they're being signed to minor league contracts in excess of $1 million per year. Meanwhile, less-coveted players as young as 13 and as old as 23 regularly purchase **fake birth certificates** to claim that they're 16 or 17 years old, the optimum legal age to begin training.

Books

Dominican literature is not very well known worldwide, mainly because so little of it is available in translation, but recently there has been a surge in influence by a younger generation of Dominican authors, most residing in the United States and writing in English, rather than Spanish. Led by Julia Alvarez and Junot Diaz, they have begun to find both critical and commercial success. The following books, a selection of the best fiction, history (however limited), and other works, should be readily available in the UK, US and the Dominican Republic. Where a book is published in both the UK and the US, publishers are listed UK first, US second. Out-of-print books are designated by o/p, but should be findable in good secondhand stores. The symbol indicates a highly recommended book.

History

Juan Bosch *The Unfinished Experiment: Democracy in the Dominican Republic* (Praeger). The country's foremost contemporary novelist and a former president banished by American military intervention tells the story of his abbreviated democratic regime.

Bartolomé de Las Casas *The Devastation of the Indies* (Johns Hopkins). A translation of the document that Las Casas, a priest who fought tirelessly for the rights of the Tainos, read to Spain's Fernando and Isabela in an effort to end colonial injustice against Native Americans.

Eric Thomas Chester *Rag-Tags, Scum, Riff-Raff and Commies* (Monthly Review Press). This new account of the American intervention/invasion of 1965 makes use of recently declassified documents to reconstruct the attitudes and reasoning of the Lyndon Johnson White House that led up to the conflict.

★ **Barbara Diederich** *Trujillo: The Death of the Goat* (Waterfront/Little Brown). A history that reads like a spy thriller, reconstructing the intrigues surrounding Trujillo's assassination – including CIA involvement that abruptly ended just as the murder was about to be carried out.

Jonathan Hartlyn *The Struggle for Democratic Politics in the Dominican Republic* (North Carolina). An even-handed case study that tracks the state of Dominican politics through the past century and a half.

Samuel Hazard *Santo Domingo Past & Present with a Glance at Hayti* (Dominican Ministry of Culture). A lively, if sometimes unsavoury in its racist commentary, mid-nineteenth century account of travelling the entire country, written from the perspective of an American bureaucrat trying to push forward US annexation.

Francine Jacobs *The Tainos: The People Who Welcomed Columbus* (Putnam). A good introduction to what we know of the history, culture and daily life of the Tainos, but written before the groundbreaking discoveries in Parque Nacional del Este.

Harry Kelsey *Sir Francis Drake: The Queen's Pirate* (Yale). The best of the dozen Drake biographies in print, depicting the British knight as an amoral privateer skilfully harnessed by Queen Elizabeth I to her own ends. Includes an account of his sacking of Santo Domingo.

★ **Kris E. Lane** *Pillaging the Empire* (Sharpe). A terrific history of piracy in the Caribbean from 1500 through 1750, including lively accounts of the buccaneers who hunted wild animals off Hispaniola's north coast and the pirates who made a lair of the Samaná Bay – among the colourful cast of characters are Jack Banister, Cofresí, Calico Jack Rackham, Sir Francis Drake, Henry Morgan and female pirates Anne Bonney and Mary Read.

Abraham F. Lowenthal *The Dominican Intervention* (Johns Hopkins). A blow-by-blow analysis of the chaotic events that led to American intervention in 1965. The author uses this military action to prove that foreign policies are as controlled by bad analogies (in this case "Another Cuba") and insufficient intelligence as they are by rational strategies.

W.J. Nelson *Almost a Territory* (St Martins). A lucid history of the various nineteenth-century attempts by the United States to annex either the Dominican Republic or the Samaná Peninsula. The colourful cast of characters, including Dominican *caudillos* Buenaventura Báez and Pedro Santana and US President Ulysses S. Grant, keep the book lively.

Thomas O. Ott *The Haitian Revolution* (Tennessee). The best account currently published in English of the slave revolt that created the world's first black republic on the western end of Hispaniola, including Touissant L'Ouverture's occupation of Santo Domingo.

★ **Frank Moya Pons** *The Dominican Republic: A National History* (Hispaniola). Written and translated by the Dominican Republic's foremost historian, this is the definitive history to the country.

A blessing since it first came out in 1995, as before then a good history of the country didn't exist in English.

Eric Paul Roorda *Dictator Next Door: The Good Neighbor Policy and the Trujillo Regime, 1930-1945* (Duke). An essential history of American presidents Herbert Hoover and FDR's failed "Good Neighbor" Policy in Latin America, detailing how Trujillo managed to maintain support in Washington by siding against first the Fascists and later the Communists, despite the blatant horrors of his regime.

★ **Irving Rouse** *The Tainos* (Yale). The definitive work of scholarship on the Tainos, tracing their migration from the Amazon River basin to the Antilles and their eventual extermination at the hands of the Spaniards. This book is a must if you're planning to see some of the Taino sites spread across the DR.

Kirkpatrick Sale *The Conquest of Paradise* (Knopf). This diatribe against the myth and civic veneration surrounding Columbus thankfully corrects a number of misconceptions we have about the man, but the constant, shrill invective sheds less light on the events of the 1490s than it should.

Hugh Thomas *The Slave Trade* (Macmillan/Touchstone). The definitive history of the Atlantic slave trade from its beginnings along Africa's west coast to its death throes in North America and the Caribbean. Includes a detailed account of the slave trade in Santo Domingo, the first place in the New World where Africans were imported.

Howard Wiarda & M.J. Kryzanek *The Dominican Republic: A Caribbean Crucible* (Westview). A history of how American intervention and hegemony in the Dominican Republic has played out over the past two centuries.

Edwin Williamson *The Penguin History of Latin America* (Penguin). This excellent history contains by far the best and most judicious account in print of Columbus's voyages and Santo Domingo's early days.

Fiction and poetry

Julia Alvarez *In the Name of Salomé*; *Homecoming: New and Collected Poems*; *How the Garcia Girls Lost Their Accents*; *In the Time of the Butterflies*; *Yo!* (Plume, Penguin). A leading American writer who grew up in the Dominican Republic, Alvarez's lucid prose, by turns comic and sublime, rewards any time spent with it. *Garcia Girls* and *Yo!* centre on middle-class Dominican immigrants in New York, while *Butterflies* recounts the tale of the Mirabal sisters, who stood up to Trujillo's repression and were assassinated for it. *Salomé*, the latest novel, is a singular work that blends a story of immigration similar to *Garcia Girls* with the tale of a short-lived nineteenth-century revolution inspired by Dominican poet Salomé Ureña.

Ramón Aristy *Over* (Taller). The great Dominican novel of the 1940s, an account of the lives of sugar-cane cutters famous for its lyrical capturing of the rural local dialect.

Juan Bosch *Antología Personal* (Puerto Rico). A compilation of fiction, mostly stories with a magical realist undercurrent. Unfortunately not translated into English, but a treasure trove for Spanish-speakers.

★ Edwidge Danticat *The Farming of Bones* (Abacus/Soho). Best-selling historical novel by a young Haitian-American, set along the Haitian border during the terror of Operación Perejil. The writing is lush and moving, and the events come vividly to life.

★ Junot Diaz *Drown* (Faber and Faber/Putnam). A powerhouse collection of semi-autobiographical short stories set alternately in the Dominican Republic and New York's Dominican neighbourhoods. These stories work together as a coherent whole in a way that few short-fiction collections do, creating a gritty world peopled by painfully true-to-life characters. Highly recommended.

Rita Dove *Selected Poems* (Vintage). This definitive collection from one of the leading living poets of the United States includes "Parsley", a brilliant piece on Trujillo and Operación Perejil.

Peter Furst *Don Quixote in Exile* (Northwestern). An interesting autobiographical novel of a German Jew who fled Europe in the early days of World War II and was forced to reside in the rural Dominican Republic for the next decade. The picaresque, film-noir atmosphere makes for good reading, but conveys no small distaste for the country and its people.

Manuel Jesús de Galván & Robert Graves *The Cross and the Sword* (AMS). Robert Graves' classic English translation of *Enriquillo*, the nineteenth-century novel that transformed Dominican identity.

Viriato Sención *They Forged the Signature of God* (Curbstone). Artful novel tinged with magical realism, taking a swipe at fictionalized versions of dictators Trujillo and Balaguer as it follows the lives of three young seminarians losing their innocence.

Society, politics and culture

Joaquín Balaguer *La Isla al Réves: Haiti y el Destino Dominicano* (o/p). Still available in Santo Domingo and in many American libraries, this is a frighteningly xenophobic account of the "pernicious" influence of both Haitians and blacks on Dominican culture. Doubly unbelievable as it's written by the man who was president for much of the twentieth century.

Michiel Baud *Peasants and Tobacco in the Dominican Republic, 1870–1930* (Tennessee). A detailed and surprisingly engaging account of peasant society in the Cibao Valley during the great Dominican tobacco boom, with a lot of information on the intricacies of the market.

Marcos Breton & José Luis Villegas *Away Games* (University of New Mexico). Follows the life of Oakland A's shortstop Miguel Tejada from his initial signing to a US$2000 contract through his life in the Dominican and minor leagues and up to his entry into the majors and emerging stardom. Not just a rah-rah book, though; it clearly outlines the trials and troubles of the thousands of Dominican prospects that never make it that far.

James Ferguson *Beyond the Lighthouse* (Latin American Bureau). A revealing book on the excesses of the Balaguer regimes. The surreal story of the building of Altos de Chavón proves beyond doubt that truth is stranger than fiction.

Barbara Fischkin *Muddy Cup* (Scribner). This is a remarkably well-written and moving book that tracks a Dominican family for four generations as they make the transition from a tiny Dominican mountain village to the Dominican barrios of New York.

Eugenia Georges *The Making of a Transnational Community: Migration, Development and Cultural Change in the Dominican Republic* (Columbia). Interesting scholarly study of the mass Dominican migration of the past decades, and the economic dependence and cultural interplay of the Dominican communities at home and in New York.

David Howard *Dominican Republic in Focus: A Guide to the People, Politics and Culture* (Latin American Bureau/Interlink). The authoritative book on contemporary Dominican politics, economy and society. This one will greatly enrich your experience of the country.

José Itzigsohn *Developing Poverty* (Pennsylvania State). An analysis of the effects of industrial free zones and the informal economies of the Dominican Republic and Costa Rica on overall economic health and job growth. Presents a well-balanced look at the pros and cons, and though the material is a bit dry, it will give you a good inside look at the inner workings of Dominican work life.

Allan M. Klein *Sugarball: The American Game, the Dominican Dream* (Yale). A fun book-length essay on baseball in the Dominican Republic, analyzing the country's obsession with it, and how it plays into the relation between the DR and the United States.

Peggy Levitt *The Transnational Villagers* (University of California). Based on detailed fieldwork by the author, this is an account of a family of Dominicans from the Dominican campo of Miraflores who split their time between their hometown and the Jamaica Plain neighbourhood of Boston. Challenges the idea that transnationality and cultural assimilation are in conflict, and provides an interesting examination of the challenges the transnational migrants receive to their notions of gender and race in the United States.

Samuel Martínez *Peripheral Migrants: Haitians and Dominican Republic Sugar Plantations* (Tennessee). A scholarly and sobering examination of the mass migration of Haitian labourers to Dominican sugar *bateyes*, with plenty of fascinating description of their dangerous journeys across the border and their living conditions once they arrive.

Heinz Meder *Tales of a Caribbean Isle: The Dominican Republic by and for an Insider* (Ediciones Nuevo Mundo). A hodge-podge of curiosities and trivia about Dominican history and culture, written by a longtime German expat. Shifts between informative tidbits and banalities.

Rob Ruck *The Tropic of Baseball* (Carroll & Graf). A history of baseball in the DR, including eyewitness accounts of sandlot games, profiles of major Dominican stars and a definitive history of the Cocolos of San Pedro de Macorís.

Helen Safa *The Myth of the Male Breadwinner: Women and Industrialization in the Caribbean* (Westview). An interesting analysis of the changing role of women in the DR, Puerto Rico and Cuba, showing how low-wage industrialization, like that in the assembly lines of Dominican industrial free zones, has altered Dominican society.

★ **Michele Wucker** *Why the Cocks Fight: Dominicans, Haitians and the Struggle for Hispaniola* (Hill & Wang). This extremely well-written, thoroughly researched account of the conflict between the Dominican Republic and Haiti is a must-read for those who want to understand the island. The author, a journalist who has long covered the island for various papers and magazines, mixes firsthand accounts of her travels with trenchant observations on history and politics.

Music, art and architecture

Paul Austerlitz *Merengue: Dominican Music and Dominican Identity* (Temple). Engagingly written ode to merengue, including the first complete history of the music and an analysis of what it reflects about Dominican society. Indispensable for understanding Dominican music and culture.

Fatima Bercht & Estrellita Brodsky *Tainos: Pre-Columbian Art and Culture from the Caribbean* (Monacelli). A beautifully presented coffee-table book with photographs of the most impressive Taino relics extant.

★ **Deborah Pacini Hernández** *Bachata: A Social History of*

Dominican Popular Music (Temple). Highly recommended journey into the heart of Dominican *bachata*, including an account of its origins in various pre-existing Caribbean forms, its transmission to the cities via waves of urban migration, and the somewhat informal industry that built up around it before it gained social acceptance with the Dominican middle classes. Also has a great account of the Trujillo family's effect on the music industry during their reign.

Marcio Veloz Maggiolo & Adriano Tejada *500 Años de Historia Monumental* (Bermúdez). Coffee-table book with a thorough cataloguing of colonial relics across the island, a bit of history on each one and beautiful colour photographs.

Eugenio Pérez Montás *Colonial Houses of Santo Domingo* (Museo de las Casas Reales). An engaging bilingual study of the many early sixteenth-century houses extant in Santo Domingo's Zona Colonial, including an analysis of their restoration. Available only in the DR.

Veerle Poupeye *Caribbean Art* (Thames and Hudson). The best source book for information on the visual art of the Caribbean, including a generous section dedicated to contemporary Dominican painting.

Henry Shukman *Travels with my Trombone: A Caribbean Journey* (Crown). A lively account of a freelance musician's wanderings across the Spanish Caribbean, including the Dominican Republic, in various Latin bands.

Suzanne Stratton *Modern and Contemporary Art of the Dominican Republic* (Americas Society and the Spanish Institute). The one good book in English devoted entirely to contemporary Dominican visual art, with thirty colour plates, essays on different strains in Dominican art over the course of the last century and biographies of all of the major figures of the past fifty years.

Religion

Karen McCarthy Brown *Mama Lola: A Vodou Priestess in Brooklyn* (University of California). An anthropologist's account of a Haitian Voodoo priestess who spent several years in the Dominican Republic before migrating to New York City. Contains interesting background on Dominican syncretic spirits.

Martha Ellen Davis *Afro-Dominican Religious Brotherhoods: Structure, Ritual and Music; La otra ciencia: El Vodú dominicano como religión y medicina populares; Voces del Purgatorio: Estudio de la salve dominicana* (University of Illinois; Santo Domingo). Some of the best works by the world's foremost scholar on Dominican folk religion. Only the first is in English, a groundbreaking dissertation on the Dominican *cofradías*, available through Xerox University Microfilms, Ann Arbor MI 48106 (☎734/761-4700).

H. McKennie Goodpasture *Cross and Sword* (Orbis). A history of Roman Catholicism in the New

World from its birth in Santo Domingo's Zona Colonial.

Laennec Hurbon *Voodoo: Search for the Spirit* (Abrams). Of the many books in print on Haitian folk religion, this is the best introduction to the religion that is practised in the sugar-cane fields of the Dominican Republic, a close relative of the syncretic religion of many Dominicans as well.

Jan Lundius *The Great Power of God in San Juan Valley* (Lund). A wonderful, sorely needed study of rural Dominican messiah Liborio and his lasting influence on the religion of peasants in the San Juan Valley. Difficult to get hold of as it's published in Sweden, but worth the effort.

David Martin *Tongues of Fire* (Westview). An analysis of the explosion of Pentecostalism in the Dominican Republic and across Latin America over the past few decades.

★ **Dagoberto Tejeda Ortiz** *Cultura Popular e Identidad Nacional* (Instituto Dominicano de Folklore). A wonderful, two-volume survey of various aspects of Dominican folk religion, with a refreshingly frank explanation of the African as well as Spanish roots of many local festivals and beliefs.

Nature

James Bond *Field Guide to Birds of the West Indies* (HarperCollins/Houghton Mifflin). The classic bird book from which Ian Fleming took the name of his fictional hero.

Ken DuPree *Whales of Samaná* (Samaná). A very informative pamphlet on the humpback whales of the Bahía de Samaná and Silver Banks Sanctuary, widely available in the city of Samaná.

Jurgen Hoppe *Flowering Trees of the Dominican Republic; National Parks of the Dominican Republic* (APEB; Fundación Barceló). Available only in Santo Domingo, these are excellent paperback guides to the flora and fauna of the DR, with beautiful colour photographs.

Eugene Kaplan *A Field Guide to the Coral Reefs of the Caribbean and Florida* (Houghton Mifflin). An excellent and attractive guide to the region's reefs and reef life.

G.W. Lennox & S.A. Seddon *Flowers of the Caribbean; Trees of the Caribbean; Fruits and Vegetables of the Caribbean* (Macmillan UK). Handy pocket-sized books, with glossy, sharp, coloured pictures and a good general introduction to the region's flora.

Renato Pérez & Andreas Schubert *Hacia el Techo del Caribe: Caminatas al Pico Duarte* (Maritima Dominicana). Spanish-language guide to the five Pico Duarte hiking trails, which can be found at the National Parks Office in Santo Domingo (see p.67; call first to make sure they're not out of stock) or at one of the many bookstores along El Conde in the Zona Colonial. One of many put out for the DR's National Parks Department, but this one is especially useful, with lots of practical information, a pull-out topographical map of the Cordillera Central and a guide to flora, fauna and legends of the area.

George & Roberta Poinar *The Amber Forest: Reconstruction of a Vanished World* (Princeton). A wonderful book that analyzes hundreds of animals and plants trapped in Dominican amber in order to reconstruct the tropical jungle that existed here in the time of the dinosaurs.

Food

María Ramírez Carcias *Dominican Cuisine* (Pilon). A handy and comprehensive guide to preparing a vast array of Dominican dishes, from simple staples like rice and beans and *morir soñando* through complicated day-long recipes for *sancocho* and *pescado con coco*.

C

CONTEXTS | Books

Language

Language

Language

T hough most people who work in the tourism industry speak English – often along with German, French or Italian – you'll find that almost everyone you meet outside the resort areas speaks only Spanish. The only places where English is spoken as a first language are parts of the Samaná Peninsula, where a community of nineteenth-century African-American migrants still exists, and in the sugar-cane *bateyes* around San Pedro de Macorís, where many of the older folk came to the Dominican Republic from English-speaking islands like St Thomas and Tortola as migrant sugar-cane cutters.

If you want to get to know Dominicans, then, it makes sense to acquire some Spanish before you arrive. You'll have to learn quite a lot to get to know people, surely, but the basics will make travelling easier and more enjoyable, since you'll be able to ask bus times, get food, rooms, etc. Dominicans are endlessly patient with those struggling to speak their language, and will not only tolerate but appreciate the attempt. Spanish is also one of the easier languages to learn: Berlitz offers excellent Spanish **courses** that you can order over the phone – materials include a dictionary, a verb reference book, several workbooks and cassettes for practising pronunciation – or for the basics you can come armed with the *Rough Guide to Mexican Spanish* **phrasebook** (available in bookstores everywhere or from an online bookstore – head first to Ⓦ www.roughguides.com), which will equip you with an array of practical Spanish snippets necessary for getting around the country. The *Collins Gem Spanish Dictionary* is a comprehensive, pocket-sized **dictionary** that's easy to carry around and quite comprehensive; it's available in most bookstores in the English-speaking world. For a quick introduction to Dominican slang, try the interactive Dominican Spanish phrasebook at Ⓦ www.hispaniola.com.

The rules of **pronunciation** are pretty straightforward and strictly observed. Unless there's an accent, all words ending in l, r and z are stressed on the last syllable, all others on the second last. In the Dominican Republic the final "s" of a word sometimes gets dropped; thus you'll often hear "buena" for "buenas" or "do" for "dos". All vowel sounds are pure and short.

A somewhere between the A sound in "back" and that in "father".

E as in "get".

I as in "police".

O as in "hot".

U as in "rule".

C is soft before E and I, hard otherwise: *cerca* is pronounced "serka".

G works the same way: a guttural H sound (like the *ch* in "loch") before E or I, a hard G elsewhere: *gigante* becomes "higante".

H is always silent.

J is the same sound as guttural G: *jamón* is pronounced "hamón".

LL is pronounced as a Y at the beginning of a word, a soft J elsewhere: *llama* is pronounced "yama", but *ballena* (whale) becomes "bajzhena" instead of "bayena".

N is as in English, unless it has a tilde accent over it, when it becomes NY: *mañana* sounds like "manyana".

QU is pronounced like the English K.

R is rolled, RR doubly so.

V sounds more like B, *vino* becoming "beano".

Z is the same as the soft C: *cerveza* is thus "serbesa".

Spanish words and phrases

Basics

yes, no - sí, no
please, thank you - por favor, gracias
where, when - dónde, cuando
what, how much - qué, cuanto
here, there - aquí, allí
this, that - este, eso
now, later - ahora, más tarde

open, closed - abierto/a, cerrado/a
with, without - con, sin
good, bad - bueno/a, malo/a
big, small - grande, pequeño/a
more, less - más, menos
today, tomorrow - hoy, mañana
yesterday - ayer

Greetings and responses

Hello, goodbye - Hola, adiós
Good morning - Buenos días
Good afternoon/night - Buenas
   tardes/noches
See you later - Hasta luego
Sorry - Lo siento
Excuse me - Con permiso/perdón
How are you? - ¿Como está?
I (don't) understand - (No) Entiendo
What did you say? - ¿Como?
Not at all/you're welcome - De nada
Do you speak English? - ¿Habla inglés?

I don't speak Spanish - No hablo español
My name is . . . - Me llamo . . .
What is your name? - ¿Como se llama
   usted?
I am English - Soy inglés(a)
. . . American - . . . americano/a
. . . Australian - . . . australiano/a
. . . Canadian - . . . canadiense/a
. . . Irish - . . . irlandés(a)
. . . Scottish - . . . escosés(a)
. . . Welsh - . . . galés(a)
. . . New Zealander - . . . neozelandés(a)

Needs – hotels and transport

I want - Quiero
I'd like - Quisiera
Do you know . . . ? - ¿Sabe . . . ?
I don't know - No sé
There is (is there?) - (¿) Hay (?)
Give me . . . - Deme . . .
 (one like that) - (uno así)
Do you have . . . ? - ¿Tiene . . . ?
. . . the time - . . . la hora
. . . a room - . . . un habitación
. . . with two beds - . . . con dos camas
. . . with a double bed - . . . con una cama
   matrimonial
It's for one person - Es para una persona
. . . two persons - . . . dos personas
. . . for one night (one week) - . . . para una
   noche (una semana)
It's fine, how much is it? - ¿Está bien,
   cuánto es?

It's too expensive - Es demasiado caro
Don't you have anything cheaper? - ¿No
   tiene algo más barato?
Can one . . . ? - ¿Se puede . . . ?
. . . camp near here? - ¿ . . . acampar aquí
   (cerca)?
Is there a hotel nearby? - ¿Hay un hotel
   aquí?
How do I get to . . . ? - ¿Por dónde se
   va a . . . ?
Left, right - Izquierda, derecha
Straight on - Derecho, siga
Where is . . . ? - ¿Dónde está . . . ?
. . . the bus station - . . . el estación de
   autobuses?
. . . the nearest bank - . . . el banco más
   cercano?
. . . the post office - . . . el correo?
. . . the toilet - . . . el baño?

Where does the bus to . . . leave from? - ¿De dónde sale el autobus para...?

I'd like a (return) ticket to . . . - Quisiera un tiquete (de ida y vuelta) para . . .

What time does it leave (arrive in . . .)? - ¿A qué hora sale (llega en . . .)?

What is there to eat? - ¿Qué hay para comer?

What's that? - ¿Qué es eso?

What's this called in Spanish? - ¿Como se llama este en español?

Numbers and days

1 - un/uno/una	80 - ochenta
2 - dos	90 - noventa
3 - tres	100 - cien(to)
4 - cuatro	101 - ciento uno
5 - cinco	200 - doscientos
6 - seis	201 - doscientos uno
7 - siete	500 - quinientos
8 - ocho	1000 - mil
9 - nueve	2000 - dos mil
10 - diez	2001 - dos mil uno
11 - once	
12 - doce	first - primero/a
13 - trece	second - segundo/a
14 - catorce	third - tercero/a
15 - quince	
16 - dieciséis	Monday - lunes
20 - veinte	Tuesday - martes
21 - veintiuno	Wednesday - miércoles
30 - treinta	Thursday - jueves
40 - cuarenta	Friday - viernes
50 - cincuenta	Saturday - sábado
60 - sesenta	Sunday - domingo
70 - setenta	

Dominican food and drink terms

Basics

¿Hay?... - Do you have? (Is there…?)

Un menú, por favor - A menu, please

La cuenta, por favor - The bill, please

Quiero... - I would like…

Soy un vegetariano/a - I'm a vegetarian

Sin carne - Without meat

Dos cervezas - Two beers

Salud! - Cheers!

Pan - Bread

Pan de cassava - Cassava bread

Arroz - Rice

Mantequilla - Butter

Queso - Typical white Dominican cheese

Queso frito - Fried cheese

Sal - Salt

Pimienta - Pepper

Cilantro - Coriander

Azúcar - Sugar

Sin azúcar - Without sugar

Huevos - Eggs

Al ajillo - Garlic sauce
La bandera dominicana - Rice and beans, sometimes with bits of chicken
Barbacoa - Barbecued
Al carbón - Grilled
Cómida criolla - Dominican cuisine

Criolla - Tomato-based creole sauce
Frito - Fried
Al horno - Roasted
Al orégano - Oregano and heavy cream sauce

Soups and salads

Crema de habichuelas rojas - Creamed red bean soup
Crema de maiz - Cream of corn soup
Ensalada aguacate - Sliced avocados with oil and vinegar
Ensalada camarones - Shrimp salad
Ensalada campesina - Watercress, tomatoes, oregano and radishes
Ensalada mixta - Mixed salad
Ensalada típica - Shredded cabbage and carrots with oil and vinegar

Ensalada verde - Green salad
Mondongo - Tripe stew
Sancocho - Stew with several kinds of meat, tubers and an array of spices
Sopa de guandules - Pigeon pea soup
Sopa haitiana - Bone marrow soup
Sopa de morros - Black bean and rice soup
Sopa pescado - Fish soup
Sopa de pollo con fideos - Chicken noodle soup
Sopa verdura - Vegetable soup

Meat

Bistec - Beefsteak
Bistec encebollado - Beefsteak with onions
Carne ripiada - Shredded beef
Chicarrones - Fried bits of pork or chicken
Chivo - Goat
Chuletas de puerco - Pork chops
Conejo - Rabbit
Empanadas - Ground beef-filled pastries
Guinea - Guinea hen
Jamón - Ham
Longaniza - Spicy sausage made from pork tripe, ground pork, garlic and oregano

Mofongo - Pork rinds, plantains and garlic
Parrillada - Argentine-style meat platter
Patitas de puerco - Pig's feet
Pollo al carbón - Grilled chicken
Pollo asopao - Chicken and rice served in a rich, creamy sauce
Pollo frito - Fried chicken
Puerco - Pork
Quipes - Cracked wheat fritters with ground beef
Tocino de puerco - Salt pork

Seafood

Atún - Tuna
Calamar - Squid
Camarones - Shrimp
Camarones mariposa - Butterfly shrimp
Cangrejo - Crab
Carite - Kingfish
Chillo - Red snapper

Lambí - Conch
Langosta - Clawless lobster
Mariscos - Seafood
Mero - Sea bass
Pescado con coco - Fish in coconut milk sauce
Pulpo - Octopus

LANGUAGE | Dominican food and drink terms

Fruits and vegetables

Aguacate – Avocado
Chinola – Passion fruit
Fresas – Strawberries
Guineo – Banana
Lechoza – Papaya
Limón – Lemon
Limoncillo – Tiny, lime-like fruits with tasty pulp
Mango – Mango
Naranja, China – Orange
Piña – Pineapple
Tamarindo – Tamarind
Zapote – Egg-shaped fruit with brown skin and sweet red pulp
Batata – Sweet potato
Berenjena – Aubergine/eggplant

Cassava – Yucca
Cebolla – Onion
Habichuelas – Red beans
Maíz – Corn
Mangú – Mashed plantains with onions and oil
Morros – Black peas and rice
Ñame – An indigenous tuber that's a popular alternative to potatoes
Palmito – Heart of palm
Papa – Potato
Papas fritas – French fries
Plátano – Plantain
Tomate – Tomato
Tostones – Double-fried plantains
Yautía – Popular native tuber

Desserts

Arroz con leche – Rice pudding
Dulce con coco – Coconut sweet
Dulce de batata – Sweet potato dessert
Dulce de leche – Milk sweet
Dulce de naranja – Orange marmalade sweet

Flan – Flan/custard
Flan de leche – Milk custard
Flan de maiz – Corn custard
Helado – Ice cream
Pudin de pan – Bread pudding

Drinks

Agua – Water
Agua purificada – Purified water
Batida – Fruit shake with pulp
Café con leche – Coffee with hot milk
Café solo – Black coffee
Cerveza – Beer
Cuba libre – Rum and Coke
Jugo – Juice
Jugo de naranja, jugo de china – Orange juice

Leche – Milk
Limonada – Lemonade
Mama Juana – Bark, leaves, honey, rum and wine
Morir soñando – Orange juice, condensed milk and sugar
Refresco – Juice with sugar
Ron – Rum
Ron ponche – Rum punch
Vino – Wine

Glossary

Below are some useful Dominican terms and phrases not necessarily listed in the above Spanish language section. Many of them have been used throughout the guide, and can commonly be heard in daily parlance in the Dominican Republic.

aba fil – literally "under the fence", a Kreyol term for Haitian migrants who sneak across the border to work in Dominican sugarcane fields.

agua de melao – shallow or without substance.

El Almirante – Christopher Columbus.

apagón – power blackout.

areito – long narrative songs used by the Tainos to depict and celebrate battles and other important events, used by Juan Luís Guerra as the title of a famous album.

bachata – twangy ballad music, with a steadily emphasized offbeat. Once reviled as the low-culture music of dock workers, sailors and peasants, it has now gained widespread acceptance.

bahía – bay.

balneario – loose term for pretty much any Dominican swimming hole.

la bandera dominicana – literally "the Dominican flag", it refers to the national dish of rice and beans.

barbacoa – barbecue, originally meant to indicate a specialized way of smoking meat.

barrio – Dominican neighbourhood.

batata potato.

batey – originally a Taino word that signified a populated, circular stone clearing;

Belie Belcán – patron spirit of the Dominican Republic, both a benevolent protector and a military strongman.

El Benefactor – standard – and now largely ironic – title for former dictator Rafael Leonidas Trujillo.

bien-bienes – the wandering souls of dead cimarrones, who haunt the Haitian border at night, stealing food from peasants' gardens.

botánica – shop where various items related to folk religion can be purchased.

bracero – Haitian cane cutter.

brujo/a – the standard, sometimes derogatory way to refer to a priest or priestess of Vodú dominicana.

buscando – a "finder", or someone who offers himself as a freelance guide for tourists.

cabaña turística – sets of hotel rooms with attached garages and hourly rates, used mainly by local couples as sex stops.

calle – street.

campesino – rural Dominican peasantry.

campo – settlement too small to be considered a pueblo.

canchanchan – buddy or partner.

Caribe – Native American culture prevalent in the southern Caribbean at the time of Columbus's arrival.

carretera – highway.

casa de cambio – small currency exchange shop.

casa de huespedes – also called pensión, a private home with rooms to let to travellers.

caudillo – nineteenth-century strongman who ruled the country by force of arms.

chin – a little bit.

ciguapa – the souls of dead Taino women who escaped the rapacious Spanish settlers by hiding out in the Cordillera Central.

cimarrón – an escaped African slave living in the remote mountain passes of the island's mountain ranges during the colonial era.

ciudad – city.

club gallístico – circular, two-tiered wooden venues for cockfights.

Cocolo – disparaging term referring to the English-speaking, black seasonal sugar labourers who cut Dominican cane around the turn of the twentieth century.

cofradía – Dominican religious brotherhoods that involve the worship of patron African deities syncretized to Catholic saints. Most are called Hermanidad del Congo and worship Kalunda/the Holy Spirit.

colmado – Dominican grocery shack, especially prevalent in the countryside.

comedor – small, family-run restaurant serving local food.

cómida criolla – Dominican cuisine.

congo – pejorative term similar to "hillbilly", referring to Haitians who have just come over the border to work in the bateyes.

Coño! Diablo! – Balls! Devil! Universally used on Dominican streets to indicate anger and frustration.

Cuba libre servicio – popular way to drink in Dominican discos and bars: two Cokes, a bottle of rum and a bucket of ice.

detelengue – tight clothes.

devastaciones – a historical event that took place in 1655, when Spain forcibly removed all settlers from the western half of the island and the north coast in order to prevent contraband trade and the encroachment of Protestantism.

Dominican York – a Dominican who has emigrated to the United States, though increasingly perjorative, referring to flashy Dominican drug dealers from New York.

encomienda – an attempted reform of the Taino slave system by the Spanish crown, according to which Tainos were to be paid a fair wage for their forced labour and educated in Catholicism.

Evangélico – a convert to the burgeoning Pentecostal movement in the Dominican Republic.

fiesta patronal – festival for the patron saint of a town or city.

la frontera – the Haitian border.

gagá – Haitian rara music played on keyless metal instruments during Semana Santa in the bateyes, as well as in poor Dominican areas like Haina, Nigua, Villa Mella and San Juan de la Maguana.

gajumba – outlandish musical instrument created by bending a tree over until its top almost touches the ground, then tying it there with catgut – the string is plucked or played with a bow.

gavilleros – the organized units of bandits from the southeast who fought a guerrilla war against the occupying American army in the 1910s and 1920s.

gomero – Dominican tyre repair shop.

gourde – Haitian unit of currency.

guagua – privately owned vans and minibuses that are the primary form of transportation in the DR.

güira – a metal scraper used in merengue bands.

guloya – style of music played by the Cocolo mummers in San Pedro de Macorís, involving fife-and-drum bands and dancing.

hato – a large, rural Spanish estate used for raising cattle.

hounfort – Voodoo temple.

houngan – male priest of Haitian Voodoo.

iglesia – church.

jevito – teenager or twentysomething who always wears the latest fashion.

jonrón – a baseball home run.

larimar – semiprecious, turquoise stone unique to the Dominican Republic, mined in the Sierra Bahoruco west of Barahona.

Liboristas – members of a cult prevalent around San Juan de la Maguana and Las Matas de Farfán, who believe that a twentieth-century faith healer named Liborio was a reincarnation of Christ.

mafioso – rip-off artist or a thug.

Malecón – boardwalk avenue along the ocean.

mambo – female priest of Haitian Voodoo.

mayimbe – the leader of a group, or the greatest at some skill.

merengue – the fast-paced national dance music, less rhythmically intricate than salsa, with a repetitive thump right on the beat.

merengue périco ripao – old-style acoustic merengue using an instrumentation of accordion, tambora, güira and African thumb piano.

misterio – a most powerful and mysterious deity of Vodú dominicana.

momise – the Dominican mispronunciation of "mummers", dancers who parade around San Pedro de Macorís at Christmas and during the fiesta patronal, performing from door to door in exchange for money and rum.

motoconcho – small-engined motorbikes used for inter-city transport.

pájaro – a popular euphemism, meaning "bird", that is used to refer to gay men.

parque central – the square central parks in every Dominican town that generally serve as the centres of socializing and commerce.

pensión – a private home with rooms to let to travellers.

perestil – the pole at the centre of a Vodú temple, which the gods/saints are said to travel down in order to interact with humans.

peso – the unit of Dominican currency.

público – weather-beaten automobiles used as public transport in the cities and between towns along the north coast.

pueblo – small Dominican town.

repartimiento – system under which Tainos were allotted to Spanish settlers to be used as slaves.

río – river.

sanky panky – practice of some underpaid Dominican resort employees acting as "escorts" to tourists in exchange for money and gifts.

Santera – standard term used to refer to Dominican syncretism, without any of the pejorative associations of Vodú.

Semana Santa – Christian and Voodoo Holy Week.

sierra – mountain range.

son – Cuban form of guitar music which is especially popular in Santo Domingo, and which many Dominicans claim was created here.

Taino – Native Americans who inhabited the Dominican Republic and much of the Caribbean at the time of Columbus's arrival.

tambora – a lap drum that's a standard instrument in merengue bands, held and slapped by a hand at one end while it's drummed with a stick at the other.

todo incluido – all-inclusive.

Trujillismo – a reference to the continuation of Trujillo's despotic methods and self-glorifying policies, used mostly in reference to Balaguer.

velación – a private religious party featuring African musical and spiritual elements, in which guests pay the host pesos and rum in order to attend.

viejo – Haitian cane cutter who has permanently settled in the batey.

Vodú dominicana – Dominican Voodoo, often with a slightly more negative connotation than Santera.

yola – leaky fishing boats used by Dominicans to illegally emigrate to Puerto Rico.

Tainoisms

A number of **Taino words** have made their way into the contemporary Dominican vocabulary, though the meaning has drifted a bit over the centuries. Below is a listing of some of the most prominent.

batey – the public plaza at the centre of every Taino community, today it refers to the meagre rows of shacks where Haitian cane cutters live and work.

bohío – once the circular thatch homes of Taino commoners, it now means a thatch-and-mud hut of a rural Dominican farmer.

buhiti – Taino herbal healer and priest.

cacique – Taino word signifying both a political leader and the tribe which he commanded; sometimes used today to denote a corrupt town boss.

caney – large rectangular great house of the Taino nobles.

canoa – small wooden canoes used to travel rivers.

casava – the bread made from yucca root which served as the major staple in the Taino diet, and is still quite popular locally.

cemi – stone Taino idol with flared nostrils and inward-spiralling eyes that was believed to hold benevolent spirits.

conuco – originally, an environmentally sound method of Taino agriculture (in which multiple crops were grown within mulched large mounds), the word later came to denote the slash-and-burn farming settlement in the wilderness – once the primary method of agriculture for the campesinos.

dujo – intricately carved wooden throne for a cacique, usually made of lignum vitae.

guaragao – red-tailed hawks that once populated the island in abundance.

haiti – the island of Hispaniola.

hamaca – hammock, which was invented by the Tainos.

hupía – the spirits of the recently dead, thought to return at night.

Huracán – the great Taino god of evil, who had to be constantly appeased in order to avoid the destruction of the community. His most visible manifestations were the hurricanes that still plague the Caribbean.

iguana – a lizard (of any type).

maco – a frog.

macuteo – a bride.

maguey – traditional Taino drum.

manatí – manatee.

mao – a cotton neck garment worn by caciques.

nagua – the extremely small, hip-covering cloth worn by married Taino women.

naiboa – the toxic flesh of uncooked yucca roots, used by Tainos as bait for fishing.

nigua – an extremely small insect that buries its eggs inside your flesh, causing nasty lesions.

papaya – the English word for this fruit comes from the Taino language.

tabacú – tobacco.

tiburón – shark.

uiku – Taino liquor, made from corn masticated by teenage girls and then allowed to ferment.

Index

and small print

Index

Map entries are in colour

Twenty Years of Rough Guides

In the summer of 1981, Mark Ellingham, Rough Guides' founder, knocked out the first guide on a typewriter, with a group of friends. Mark had been travelling in Greece after university, and couldn't find a guidebook that really answered his needs. There were heavyweight cultural guides on the one hand – good on museums and classical sites but not on beaches and tavernas – and on the other hand student manuals that were so caught up with how to save money that they lost sight of the country's significance beyond its role as a place for a cool vacation. None of the guides began to address Greece as a country, with its natural and human environment, its politics and its contemporary life.

Having no urgent reason to return home, Mark decided to write his own guide. It was a guide to Greece that tried to combine some erudition and insight with a thoroughly practical approach to travellers' needs. Scrupulously researched listings of places to stay, eat and drink were matched by careful attention to detail on everything from Homer to Greek music, from classical sites to national parks and from nude beaches to monasteries. Back in London, Mark and his friends got their Rough Guide accepted by a farsighted commissioning editor at the publisher Routledge and it came out in 1982.

The Rough Guide to Greece was a student scheme that became a publishing phenomenon. The immediate success of the book – shortlisted for the Thomas Cook award – spawned a series that rapidly covered dozens of countries. The Rough Guides found a ready market among backpackers and budget travellers, but soon acquired a much broader readership that included older and less impecunious visitors. Readers relished the guides' wit and inquisitiveness as much as the enthusiastic, critical approach that acknowledges everyone wants value for money – but not at any price.

Rough Guides soon began supplementing the "rougher" information – the hostel and low-budget listings – with the kind of detail that independent-minded travellers on any budget might expect. These days, the guides – distributed worldwide by the Penguin group – include recommendations spanning the range from shoestring to luxury, and cover more than 200 destinations around the globe. Our growing team of authors, many of whom come to Rough Guides initially as outstandingly good letter-writers telling us about their travels, are spread all over the world, particularly in Europe, the USA and Australia. As well as the travel guides, Rough Guides publishes a series of dictionary phrasebooks covering two dozen major languages, an acclaimed series of music guides running the gamut from Classical to World Music, a series of music CDs in association with World Music Network, and a range of reference books on topics as diverse as the Internet, Pregnancy and Unexplained Phenomena. Visit **www.roughguides.com** to see what's cooking.

Rough Guide credits

Text editor: Stephen Timblin
Series editor: Mark Ellingham
Editorial: Martin Dunford, Jonathan Buckley,
Kate Berens, Ann-Marie Shaw, Helena Smith,
Judith Bamber, Olivia Swift, Ruth Blackmore,
Geoff Howard, Claire Saunders, Gavin
Thomas, Alexander Mark Rogers, Polly
Thomas, Joe Staines, Richard Lim, Duncan
Clark, Peter Buckley, Lucy Ratcliffe, Clifton
Wilkinson, Alison Murchie, Matthew Teller,
Andrew Dickson, Fran Sandham (UK); Andrew
Rosenberg, Stephen Timblin, Yuki Takagaki,
Richard Koss, Hunter Slaton, Julie Feiner (US)
Production: Susanne Hillen, Andy Hilliard,
Link Hall, Helen Prior, Julia Bovis, Michelle
Draycott, Katie Pringle, Zoë Nobes, Rachel
Holmes, Andy Turner, Michelle Bhatia

Cartography: Melissa Baker, Maxine Repath,
Ed Wright, Katie Lloyd-Jones
Cover art direction: Louise Boulton
Picture research: Sharon Martins,
Mark Thomas
Online: Kelly Cross, Anja Mutic-Blessing,
Jennifer Gold, Audra Epstein,
Suzanne Welles, Cree Lawson (US)
Finance: John Fisher, Gary Singh,
Edward Downey, Mark Hall, Tim Bill
Marketing & Publicity: Richard Trillo, Niki
Smith, David Wearn, Chloë Roberts, Demelza
Dallow, Claire Southern (UK); Simon Carloss,
David Wechsler, Megan Kennedy (US)
Administration: Tania Hummel, Julie
Sanderson

Publishing information

This second edition published November
2002 by **Rough Guides Ltd**,
80 Strand, London WC2R 0RL.
Penguin Putnam, Inc., 375 Hudson Street,
NY 10014, USA.
Distributed by the Penguin Group
Penguin Books Ltd,
80 Strand, London WC2R 0RL
Penguin Putnam, Inc.
375 Hudson Street, NY 10014, USA
Penguin Books Australia Ltd,
487 Maroondah Highway, PO Box 257,
Ringwood, Victoria 3134, Australia
Penguin Books Canada Ltd,
10 Alcorn Avenue, Toronto, Ontario,
Canada M4V 1E4
Penguin Books (NZ) Ltd,
182–190 Wairau Road, Auckland 10,
New Zealand
Typeset in Bembo and Helvetica to an
original design by Henry Iles.

Printed in Italy by LegoPrint S.p.A

©Sean Harvey 2002

No part of this book may be reproduced in
any form without permission from the
publisher except for the quotation of brief
passages in reviews.

424pp includes index
A catalogue record for this book is available
from the British Library.

ISBN 1-85828-912-2

The publishers and authors have done their
best to ensure the accuracy and currency of
all the information in **The Rough Guide to
the Dominican Republic**, however, they can
accept no responsibility for any loss, injury or
inconvenience sustained by any traveller as a
result of information or advice contained in
the guide.

Help us update

We've gone to a lot of effort to ensure that
the second edition of **The Rough Guide to
the Dominican Republic** is accurate and up
to date. However, things change – places get
"discovered", opening hours are notoriously
fickle, restaurants and rooms raise prices or
lower standards. If you feel we've got it
wrong or left something out, we'd like to
know, and if you can remember the address,
the price, the time, the phone number, so
much the better.

We'll credit all contributions, and send a
copy of the next edition (or any other Rough

Guide if you prefer) for the best letters.
Everyone who writes to us and isn't already a
subscriber will receive a copy of our full-
colour thrice-yearly newsletter. Please mark
letters: **"Rough Guide Dominican Republic
Update"** and send to: Rough Guides,
80 Strand, London WC2R 0RL, or Rough
Guides, 4th Floor, 345 Hudson St, New York,
NY 10014. Or send an email to
mail@roughguides.com

Have your questions answered and tell
others about your trip at
www.roughguides.atinfopop.com

Acknowledgements

Sean Harvey: Special thanks to Stephen Timblin, who did a tremendous job with the editing and improved the book immensely. Thanks also to Julie Feiner for her totally tubular editing work; Andrew Rosenberg for supervision, plus all the work he did on the first edition of the book, as well as Martin Dunford, Yuki Takagaki, Simon Carloss and Dave Wechsler; Katie Pringle for typesetting; Derek Wilde for proofreading; Maxine Repath and Ed Wright for a splendid job on maps; and Sharon Martins for photo research. Special thanks, too, to Paul Austerlitz, Bob Corbett and his Vultures, Martha Davis, Tim Hall, Felix Polanco, Boni Raposo, Hector Rojas, Rich and the gang at Iguana Mama, Michele Wucker and her Minions, and everyone at the Institute for Dominican Studies at CCNY. Most of all I'm indebted to my wife Tory Dent for her love, strength and support during a time when she was experiencing some unbelievably arduous health crises – I'm in awe of and in love with you.

Tom Hutton: My contribution to this book would not have been possible without the help and support of countless others. Firstly I'd like to thank Andrew Rosenberg for his faith in taking me on and his understanding when needed. My editors, Stephen Timblin and Julie Feiner, have been both encouraging and inspiring, and I feel that my professionalism has grown as a result of working with them – though, truth be told, Julie did not do nearly as much as Stephen. Still, she had a nice voice, and talked with me about my dogs. I take my hat off to Sean Harvey for the thorough job that he did with the first edition; I'm grateful to him for his help with this update and for allowing me to tamper with his excellent work. Out in the DR, I enlisted the help of so many people it would be impossible to list them all. A special mention must go to Patricia, Richard and all the staff at Iguana Mama; these guys really made things happen. Others in Cabarete who I'm eternally indebted to include my old friend Mike Braden, Udo and Brigitte, Get Wet Mike and of course Gerard, Gundula and Claudia, for their exceptional hospitality. Thanks also go to Tim Hall, Angie Wolff, Urs at Sunshine, Kim Beddall, David Buglass and all the wonderful people of the Dominican Republic that I met along the way. In the UK, I received a lot of advice from Sabrina Cambiaso from the DR Tourist Board. Finally, I'd have never completed the research trip without the constant companionship of my partner, Steph; piña coladas never taste as good when you're on your own! And, for keeping me sane during the writing and editing of the guide, I'd like to say a big thanks to two special friends, Honey and India.

The editor would like to thank: Maxine Repath and The Map Studio for their mapmaking expertise; Julia Bovis and Katie Pringle for their seamless production work; Sharon Martins for her creative and colourful photo research; Derek Wilde for his diligent and helpful proofreading; and Andrew Rosenberg for his guidance and support.

Readers' letters

Lastly, thanks to anyone who wrote or emailed or provided help and information, especially those listed below (apologies for any misspellings):

Bart de Bruycker, Emma Lowery, Ronald and Jennifer Welbaum

Photo credits

SMALL PRINT

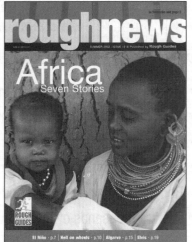

Rough Guides travel

Europe
Algarve
Amsterdam
Andalucia
Austria
Barcelona
Belgium
 & Luxembourg
Berlin
Britain
Brittany
 & Normandy
Bruges & Ghent
Brussels
Budapest
Bulgaria
Copenhagen
Corsica
Costa Brava
Crete
Croatia
Cyprus
Czech & Slovak
 Republics
Devon & Cornwall
Dodecanese
 & East Aegean
Dordogne
 & the Lot
Dublin
Edinburgh
England
Europe
First-Time Europe
Florence
France
French Hotels
 & Restaurants
Germany
Greece
Greek Islands
Holland
Hungary
Ibiza
 & Formentera
Iceland
Ionian Islands
Ireland
Italy
Lake District

Languedoc
 & Roussillon
Lisbon
London
London Mini Guide
London
 Restaurants
Madeira
Madrid
Mallorca
Malta & Gozo
Menorca
Moscow
Norway
Paris
Paris Mini Guide
Poland
Portugal
Prague
Provence & the
 Côte d'Azur
Pyrenees
Romania
Rome
Sardinia
Scandinavia
Scotland
Scottish Highlands
 & Islands
Sicily
Spain
St Petersburg
Sweden
Switzerland
Tenerife & La
 Gomera
Turkey
Tuscany & Umbria
Venice
 & The Veneto
Vienna
Wales

Asia
Bali & Lombok
Bangkok
Beijing
Cambodia
China

First-Time Asia
Goa
Hong Kong
 & Macau
India
Indonesia
Japan
Laos
Malaysia,
 Singapore
 & Brunei
Nepal
Singapore
South India
Southeast Asia
Thailand
Thailand Beaches
 & Islands
Tokyo
Vietnam

Australasia
Australia
Gay & Lesbian
 Australia
Melbourne
New Zealand
Sydney

North America
Alaska
Big Island of
 Hawaii
Boston
California
Canada
Florida
Hawaii
Honolulu
Las Vegas
Los Angeles
Maui
Miami & the
 Florida Keys
Montréal
New England
New Orleans
New York City

New York City
 Mini Guide
New York
 Restaurants
Pacific Northwest
Rocky Mountains
San Francisco
San Francisco
 Restaurants
Seattle
Southwest USA
Toronto
USA
Vancouver
Washington DC
Yosemite

Caribbean & Latin America
Antigua & Barbuda
Argentina
Bahamas
Barbados
Belize
Bolivia
Brazil
Caribbean
Central America
Chile
Costa Rica
Cuba
Dominican
 Republic
Ecuador
Guatemala
Jamaica
Maya World
Mexico
Peru
St Lucia
Trinidad & Tobago

Africa & Middle East
Cape Town
Egypt
Israel & Palestinian
 Territories

Jerusalem
Jordan
Kenya
Morocco
South Africa,
 Lesotho
 & Swaziland
Syria
Tanzania
Tunisia
West Africa
Zanzibar
Zimbabwe

Dictionary Phrase-books
Czech
Dutch
European
 Languages
French
German
Greek
Hungarian
Italian
Polish
Portuguese
Russian
Spanish
Turkish
Hindi & Urdu
Indonesian
Japanese
Mandarin Chinese
Thai
Vietnamese
Mexican Spanish
Egyptian Arabic
Swahili

Maps
Amsterdam
Dublin
London
Paris
San Francisco
Venice

Rough Guides publishes new books every month:

Music

Acoustic Guitar
Blues: 100 Essential CDs
Cello
Clarinet
Classical Music
Classical Music: 100 Essential CDs
Country Music
Country: 100 Essential CDs
Cuban Music
Drum'n'bass
Drums
Electric Guitar & Bass Guitar
Flute
Hip-Hop
House
Irish Music
Jazz
Jazz: 100 Essential CDs
Keyboards & Digital Piano
Latin: 100 Essential CDs
Music USA: a Coast-To-Coast Tour
Opera
Opera: 100 Essential CDs
Piano
Reading Music
Reggae
Reggae: 100 Essential CDs
Rock
Rock: 100 Essential CDs
Saxophone
Soul: 100 Essential CDs
Techno
Trumpet & Trombone
Violin & Viola
World Music: 100 Essential CDs
World Music Vol1
World Music Vol2

Reference

Children's Books, 0–5
Children's Books, 5–11
China Chronicle
Cult Movies
Cult TV
Elvis
England Chronicle
France Chronicle
India Chronicle
The Internet
Internet Radio
James Bond
Liverpool FC
Man Utd
Money Online
Personal Computers
Pregnancy & Birth
Shopping Online
Travel Health
Travel Online
Unexplained Phenomena
Videogaming
Weather
Website Directory
Women Travel

Music CDs

Africa
Afrocuba
Afro-Peru
Ali Hussan Kuban
The Alps
Americana
The Andes
The Appalachians
Arabesque
Asian Underground
Australian Aboriginal Music
Bellydance
Bhangra
Bluegrass
Bollywood
Boogaloo
Brazil
Cajun
Cajun and Zydeco
Calypso and Soca
Cape Verde
Central America
Classic Jazz
Congolese Soukous
Cuba
Cuban Music Story
Cuban Son
Cumbia
Delta Blues
Eastern Europe
English Roots Music
Flamenco
Franco
Gospel
Global Dance
Greece
The Gypsies
Haiti
Hawaii
The Himalayas
Hip Hop
Hungary
India
India and Pakistan
Indian Ocean
Indonesia
Irish Folk
Irish Music
Italy
Jamaica
Japan
Kenya and Tanzania
Klezmer
Louisiana
Lucky Dube
Mali and Guinea
Marrabenta Mozambique
Merengue & Bachata
Mexico
Native American Music
Nigeria and Ghana
North Africa
Nusrat Fateh Ali Khan
Okinawa
Paris Café Music
Portugal
Rai
Reggae
Salsa
Salsa Dance
Samba
Scandinavia
Scottish Folk
Scottish Music
Senegal & The Gambia
Ska
Soul Brothers
South Africa
South African Gospel
South African Jazz
Spain
Sufi Music
Tango
Thailand
Tex-Mex
Wales
West African Music
World Music Vol 1: Africa, Europe and the Middle East
World Music Vol 2: Latin & North America, Caribbean, India, Asia and Pacific
World Roots
Youssou N'Dour & Etoile de Dakar
Zimbabwe

Rough Guides music, reference & CDs

Rough Guide restaurants series

THE ROUGH GUIDE TO
French Hotels
& Restaurants
2002

"THE BEST LONDON RESTAURANT GUIDE."
The Guardian

THE ROUGH GUIDE TO
London Restaurants
2003

Dining out

WHERE TO EAT WELL, FROM DOWNTOWN TO NAPA VALLEY

The Rough Guide to
San Francisco
Restaurants

The Rough Guide to
New York
Restaurants

Annually updated

£7.99–£12.99/US$12.95–US$19.95.